PHARAONIC KING-LISTS, ANNALS and DAY-BOOKS

D1557880

PHARAONIC KING-LISTS, ANNALS and DAY-BOOKS

A Contribution to the Study of the Egyptian Sense of History

DONALD B. REDFORD

SSEA Publication IV

Benben Publications, Mississauga, 1986

DT
83
.R42
1986

General Editor: Loretta M. James

Cover Art: Rosemary Aicher

Copyright © 1986 by Donald B. Redford
All rights reserved. No part of this publication may be reproduced, stored in a retrieval system, or transmitted in any form or by any means, electronic, mechanical, photocopying, recording or otherwise, without the prior written permission of the copyright owner.

CANADIAN CATALOGUING IN PUBLICATION DATA

Redford, Donald B.
Pharaonic king-lists, annals and day-books

(SSEA ; v. 4)
Bibliography: p. 339
Includes index.
ISBN 0-920168-08-6 (bound). - ISBN 0-920168-07-8 (pbk.)

1. Egypt - History - To 332 B.C. - Sources.
2. Egypt - Historiography. 3. Egypt - Kings and rulers. I. Title. II. Series.

DT61.R43 1986 932'.01 C86-093125-0

Published by BENBEN PUBLICATIONS, 1483 Carmen Drive, Mississauga, Ontario, Canada, L5G 3Z2

Printed in Canada by Tri-graphic Printing (Ottawa) Limited

JESUIT - KRAUSS - McCORMICK - LIBRARY
1100 EAST 55th STREET
CHICAGO, ILLINOIS 60615

Contents

List of Plates		vi
Preface		vii
Abbreviations		ix
Introduction		xiii
1.	King-lists and Groups of Kings	1
2.	*Gnwt*	65
3.	Day-books	97
4.	The Egyptian Sense of the Past in the Old and Middle Kingdoms	127
5.	The King-list Tradition in the New Kingdom	165
6.	The King-list Tradition in the Late Period	203
7.	Manetho on the Old to New Kingdoms	231
8.	The Narratives at the End of *Aegyptiaca* II	257
9.	Manetho's *Aegyptiaca* Book III	297
10.	Conclusions	333
Selected Bibliography		339
Indices		343
Subject		
Egyptian		
Demotic		
Greek		
Akkadian		

List of Plates

I Stela of Pahu and Neferkha^{c}u from Thebes (reproduced by courtesy of the Brooklyn Museum).

II Stela of Siptah, Qurneh.

III Assemblage of Ramesside royal statues, Karnak.

IV Thoth, inscribing cartouches and annals (Ramesseum).

Preface

The present work is an outgrowth of a seminar on "Histories and Historians of the Ancient Near East," held in Toronto in 1974, to which the writer contributed a paper on Ancient Egypt. Two seminars at the University of Toronto, "Egyptian Historiography" (1979-1980), and "Egyptian Historical Texts of the Late Period" (1982-1983), assisted further in refining some of the themes here presented. Thanks are due to a number of colleagues: to Dr. A. Kadry and Dr. Aly el-Kholy; to Messrs. Mes-Sugheir, Sayed Abdul Hamid and the other officials of the Egyptian Antiquities Organization for their co-operation in allowing us to study certain unpublished blocks; to Dr. Lanny Bell, director, Chicago House, for permitting us to make hand-copies and to use photographs of royal figures in Theban Tomb 284; to the Egyptian Department of the Brooklyn Museum for permission to publish a photograph of stela 37.1503E, and to the Griffiths Institute for copies of Wilkinson's drawings of the offering table of Paneb, and the University Museum, University of Pennsylvania, for photographs of the scene in Theban Tomb 306. I wish also to thank several assistants who are also my students, for helping in the preparation of the MS: my wife, Susan Redford; Mr. E. Bleiberg, Mr. E. Brock, and Mr. D. Berg.

Finally and especially I wish to thank Mrs. Loretta James, editor of the present work, by whose idefatigable efforts and meticulous work the enormous task was accomplished of seeing the MS through the minutiae of the editing process to final publication.

This book has been published with the help of a grant from the Canadian Federation for the Humanities, using funds provided by the Social Sciences and Humanities Research Council of Canada.

IN MEMORIAM MATRIS

Kathleen B. Redford

Abbreviations

Acta Or.: *Acta Orientalia*
AEO: Sir A. H. Gardiner, *Ancient Egyptian Onomastica* (3 vols.), Oxford, 1947
AfPap: *Archiv für Papyrologie*
AfO: *Archiv für Orientforschung*
AJA: *American Journal of Archaeology*
AJSL: *American Journal of Semitic Languages and Literatures*
AKL: *The Assyrian King-list*
ANET^2: J. B. Pritchard (ed.), *Ancient Near Eastern Texts Relating to the Old Testament* (2nd edition), Princeton, 1955
Arch. Or.: *Archiv Orientalni*
ASAE *Annales du service des antiquités de l'Egypte*
AWMainz: *Akademie der Wissenschaften, Mainz*
AWWien: *Akademie der Wissenschaften, Wien*
BA: *The Biblical Archaeologist*
BABA: *Beiträge zur Aegyptischen Bauforschung und Altertumskunde*
BASOR: *Bulletin of the American Schools of Oriental Research*
BD: *Book of the Dead*
BES: *Bulletin of the Egyptological Seminar of New York*
Bib. Or.: *Bibliotheca Orientalis*
BIE: *Bulletin de l'institut d'Egypte*
BIFAO: *Bulletin de l'institut d'archéologie orientale*
BM: *British Museum*
BMMA: *Bulletin of the Metropolitan Museum of Art, New York*
BSEG: *Bulletin de la société d'égyptologie de Genève*
BSFE: *Bulletin de la société française d'Egyptologie*
CAH: *Cambridge Ancient History*
CBQ: *Catholic Biblical Quarterly*
CCG: *Cairo, catalogue génerale*
CdE: *Chronique d'Egypte*
CQ: *Classical Quarterly*
CRAIBL: *Comptes rendus de l'académie des inscriptions et belles lettres*
CT: Coffin Texts
Dendera: E. Chassinat, F. Daumas, *Le temple de Dendara* (8 vols.), Cairo, 1934-
DN: Divine name
EA: J. A. Knudtzon, *Die El-Amarna Tafeln*, Leipzig, 1907-15
Edfu: E. Chassinat, *Le temple d'Edfou* (14 vols.), Cairo, 1892-1934
EES: Egypt Exploration Society
FIFAO: *Fouilles de l'institut français d'archéologie orientale*
Gardiner, *Grammar*^{3}: Sir A. H. Gardiner, *Egyptian Grammar* (3rd edition), Oxford, 1957
Gauthier, *Dictionnaire géographique / DG*: H. Gauthier, *Dictionnaire des noms géographiques ...* (7 vols.), Cairo, 1925-31
Gauthier, *LdR*: H. Gauthier, *Le livre des rois d'Egypte* (5 vols.), Cairo, 1907-17

GGA: *Göttingische gelehrte Anzeigen*
GM: *Göttinger Miszellen*
GT: W. B. Emery, *Great Tombs of the First Dynasty* (3 vols.), Cairo and London, 1949-58
Helck, *Manetho*: W. Helck, *Untersuchungen zu Manetho und des ägyptischen Königslisten*, Berlin, 1956
HO: *Handbuch der Orientalistik. Aegyptologie* 2 *Literature*, B. Spuler (ed.), Leiden, 1952
Hieroglyphis Texts ... B.M.: *Hieroglyphic Texts from Egyptian Stelae, etc., in the British Museum* (10 vols.), London, 1912-82.
HTR: *Harvard Theological Review*
IFAO: *Institut français d'archéologie orientale*
JA: *Journal asiatique*
JASO: *Journal of the American Oriental Society*
JARCE: *Journal of the American Research Center Egypt*
JCS: *Journal of Cuneiform Studies*
JdE: *Journal d'entrée*
JdS: *Journal des savants*
JEA: *Journal of Egyptian Archaeology*
JESHO: *Journal of the Economic and Social History of the Orient*
JNES: *Journal of Near Eastern Studies*
JSSEA: *Journal of the Society for the Study of Egyptian Antiquities*
Kitchen, *RI*: K. A. Kitchen, *Ramesside Inscriptions*, Oxford, 1968-
Kitchen, *Third Intermediate Period*: K. A. Kitchen, *The Third Intermediate Period in Egypt*, Warminster, 1973
LCL: *Loeb Classical Library*
LdÄ: *Lexikon der Ägyptologie* (4 vols.), Wiesbaden, 1972-82
LD: R. Lepsius, *Denkmaeler aus Aegypten und Nubien* (12 vols.), Berlin, 1849-59
L.E.: Lower Egypt
L.P.H.: Life, Prosperity and Health
MAS: *Münchner Aegyptologische Studien*
MB: Middle Bronze Age
MDAIK: *Mitteilungen des deutschen Istitutes für ägyptische Altertumskunde*
MIFAO: *Memoires de l'institut francais d'archéologie orientale*
MIOF: *Mitteilungen des Instituts für Orientforschung*
MMA: *Metropolitan Museum of Art*
MS(S): Manuscript(s)
MVAG: *Mitteilungen der vorderasiatische-ägyptischen Gesellschaft*
Naville, *Todtenbuch*: E. Naville, *Das aegyptische Todtenbuch der XVIII. bis XX. Dynastie ...*, Berlin, 1886
NGWG: *Nachrichten der königliche Gesellschaft der Wissenschaften zu Göttingen*
OCD: *Oxford Classical Dictionary*, N. G. L. Hammond, H. H. Scullard (eds.), London, 1970
O.K.: Old Kingdom
OLZ: *Orientalistischen Literaturzeitung*

OMRO: *Oudheidkundige Mededelingen uit het Rijksmuseum van Oudheden te Leiden*
Om. Am.: Onomasticon Amenemope
Or. Am.: *Oriens Antiquus*
P.: Papyrus
Petrie, *RT*: W. M. F. Petrie, *The Royal Tombs of the First Dynasty* (2 vols.), London, 1900-01
P-M: B. Porter, R. Moss, (2nd edition by J. Malek), *Topographical Bibliography of Ancient Egyptian Hieroglyphic Texts, Reliefs and Paintings* (7 vols.), Oxford, 1927-
PSBA: *Proceedings of the Society of Biblical Archaeology*
PT: Pyramid Texts
PWK: Pauly-Wissowa-Kroll, *Real-Encyclopädie der klassischen Altertumswissenschaft*, Stuttgart, 1893-
Ranke, *PN*: H. Ranke, *Die ägyptischen Personennamen* (2 vols.), Glückstadt, 1935-52
RB: *Revue Biblique*
RdE: *Revue d'Egyptologie*
REA: *Revue des études anciennes*
RHR: *Revue de l'histoire des religions*
RIDA: *Revue internationale des droits de l'antiquité*
ROM: Royal Ontario Musuem
RSO: *Revista degli studi orientali*
RT: *Recueil de travaux relatifs à la philologie et l'archéologie égyptiennes et assyriennes*
rt.: *recto*
SAK: *Studien zur Altägyptischen Kultur*
SAWWien: *Sitzungsberichte der Akademie der Wissenschaften, Wien*
Sauneron, *Esna*: S. Sauneron, *Le temple d'Esna* (5 vols.), Cairo, 1959-69
SBAW: *Sitzungsberichte der bayerischen Akademie der Wissenschaften*
Sethe, *Lesestücke*: K. Sethe, *Aegyptische Lesestücke*, Leipzig, 1928
SSEA Newsletter: *Newletter of the Society for the Study of Egyptian Antiquities*
TAPA: *Transactions of the American Philosophical Association*
TC: Turin Canon
TLZ: *Theologische Literaturzeitung*
U.E.: Upper Egypt
UF: *Ugarit-Forschungen*
Urk.: *Urkunden des ägyptischen Altertums*, Leipzig, 1903-
vs.: *verso*
VT: *Vetus Testamentum*
Waddell, *Manetho*: W. G. Waddell, *Manetho*, London, 1940
Wb.: A. Erman, H. Grapow, *Wörterbuch der Aegyptischen Sprache* (5 vols., with references), Leipzig and Berlin, 1926-55
Wildung, *Die Rolle*: D. Wildung, *Die Rolle ägyptischer Könige im Bewusstsein ihrer Nachwelt*, Berlin, 1968
WO: *Welt des Orient*
WZKM: *Wiener Zeitschrift für die Kunde des Morgenlandes*
ZÄS: *Zeitschrift für ägyptische Sprache*

ZDMG: *Zeitschrift der deutschen morgenländischen Gesellschaft*
ZDPV: *Zeitschrift des deutschen Palästina-Vereins*
ZPE: *Zeitschrift für Papyrologie und Epigraphik*

Introduction

Some time ago the writer delivered an address on Ancient Egypt in the context of a symposium on Near Eastern historiography.[1] It would not perhaps have been immediately apparent from the title of the symposium "Histories and Historians of the Ancient Near East" that the genitive involved is an attributive, and not an objective, one. The object of our inquiry was not people who write histories of the ancient Near East and the histories they write, but ancients who write "histories" of the Near East and the "histories" they wrote. The distinction has some importance in defining the scope of the investigation; for what a modern would call an "historical document," and use after critical examination in the history he was writing, is different from a piece of ancient history-writing, and this it seems is true even before defining history. But if then one's subject matter is the ancient piece of history-writing and the man who wrote it (whom we might dub "historian," though it is doubtful whether he would have used the appellative), a prior understanding of what is meant by "history-writing" is imperative. If the ancient Egyptians themselves had had a term for it, the task might have been simpler; but their language lacked such a word,[2] a fact which itself is of considerable significance.

One who works in a rather narrow discipline, comparatively recently distinguished from the other fields, is always tempted to bring to his work a technical terminology fashioned elsewhere.[3] As his task forces him on to increasingly restricted paths, out of touch with his fellows, this terminology inevitably undergoes distortion, so that, when he re-emerges to consort with his colleague once again, both may have difficulty in understanding each other, like two deaf men shouting at each other in different dialects. Something like this may have happened in Egyptology. We have blurred the distinction between "historical document" and "history-writing," and have construed them both as encompassing any writings having to do with the Egyptian past which are grist for the *modern* historian's mill. Thus

[1]"Histories and Historians of the Ancient Near East," held at University College, University of Toronto; November, 1974.

[2]On *ḫprt*, see H. Goedicke, *The Protocol of Neferyt* (Baltimore, 1977) 64, n. *j*.

[3]The best example of this wide spread failing is from the field of syntax. In the study of Egyptian it has often been the case that a terminology originally devised for Indo-European languages has been transplanted into Egyptian, with misleading results.

records, stelae, journals, biographies, annals and even letters are classed under the rubric "historical texts" in one famous compendium. This shoddy classification could be defended by resorting to a loose definition of history which would make it "any writing having to do with a culture's past."[4] But this will not do. To extend the definition and loosen its meaning to the extent that correspondence and business documents are put on the same footing as a serious attempt to record and find a rational pattern in past events, is to make a mockery of attempts at classification, and to render meaningful comparison between cultures impossible.

"History-writing," as the term seems generally to be used and understood today, means the telling of events involving or affecting human beings (not necessarily though usually in narrative form), which took place prior to the time of composition, the chief aim of which is to explain those events for the benefit, predilection and satisfaction of, contemporaries, and not for the enhancement of the writer's personal reputation. The form will be without artifice or metaphor, that is it will not be drama, epic poetry, cult prescription or the like. The historian is attempting to interpret past events in that he either shows his readers how he (the reader) is personally affected and/or related to said events; or invites the reader vicariously to share and experience those events. And the reader can only share and experience those events if they are described and interpreted for him.

On this definition little of the vast quantity of written documents left behind by the ancient Egyptians qualifies as "history-writing." Of course much of the intent and thrust of our modern historical writing will in antiquity have been transmuted into the expression of myth.[5] But myth is still not history-writing in a modern sense. There is no document prior to the 4th Century B.C. (and even that time refer-

[4]Cf. J. J. M. Roberts, in *CBQ* 38 (1976) 3, n. 15: "historiography I would define as a literary phenomenon involving the recording and analysis, explicit or *implicit*, of past events. As such it would include a number of literary genres — king-lists, chronicles, annals, epics, royal apologies etc." The problem is that countries other than those of the ancient Near East, like Greece, Rome, or European states from the Middle Ages to the present, also had these genres in their repertoire; but *in addition* they had a genre called "history-writing" which is largely absent in the Near East. The difference may be a minor one, but to me historiography is not a "literary phenomenon," but a *bona fide* genre. All countries ancient or modern, display an awareness of the past which always, somewhere in their literature, crystalizes in a philosophical sense of the past; but not all could boast historiography as a genre.

[5]See L. Kákosy, *Selected Papers 1956-1973* (*Studia Aegyptiaca* VII; Budapest, 1981) 93ff; for the allegation that history and cosmology are combined in Egyptian myths, see S. Morenz, *Die Heraufkunft des transzendenten Gottes in Aegypten* (Leipzig, 1964) 10.

ence may be too early) whose single purpose is to explain a segment of the Egyptian past to the writer's contemporaries; and even before that century those parts of a document which could be termed "historiographical" on the above definition are embedded in texts of a different genre. Thus I think we may call Thutmose III's retrospective at the beginning of the Karnak "annals" a piece of history-writing; but it is found among extended excerpts from the palace journal and a treasury document. Hatshepsut's "state of the union" address in the Speos Artemidos, with its frequent references to the past, is a similar work but it is in the form of a speech.[6] Ramesses III writes a bit of history on the anarchic end of the 19th Dynasty;[7] but it is tucked away in an inventory of his benefactions to the gods. Osorkon is writing what might be called a history of his tenure of office; but it is worked into an *apologia pro vita sua*, interwoven with a list of his good deeds for Amun.[8] Ankhtify and Khnumhotpe, Ahmose si-Abina and Ineni, wrote "history" about themselves and their ancestors, but the form their texts take is that of the biographical statement.[9] To ferret out these "lapses into history-writing" and examine them critically is a valid and worthwhile endeavour, but it presupposes a detailed form- and source-critical analysis of a great range of documents the majority of which will not be found to be covered by the definition. Moreover such an investigation has other ramifications involving such side issues as scribes and the scribal art, the role of oral tradition, use of written text, libraries, etc. In the course of the investigation it will be found that the Egyptians talked about and made use of the past in forms of writing and oral declaration much different from what we would class as "history."

The search for a form of Egyptian composition (during pharaonic times) to which we could apply the term "historiography" has thus come to an abrupt end: we cannot find one.[10] Rather, we find our inquiry suddenly deflected into an exercise concerned more with what might be called "the form, transmission and use of national traditions." Here the road divides. One branch leads into a study of

[6] Below, p. 261f.
[7] Below, p. 267ff.
[8] Cf. below, p. 272ff.
[9] Cf. J. G. Griffiths, *The Origins of Osiris and His Cult* (Leiden, 1980) 5.
[10] It may be that the educated Egyptian could have shared the Graeco-Roman view that history was "a rational, intelligible continuity, an integrated nexus or concatination, operating in a unified world, capable of investigation and illumination by historical method" (E. Dinkler, in R. C. Denton [ed.], *The Idea of History in the Ancient Near East* [New Haven, 1955] 172), but his own history was not so chequered that he was moved to write about it. On the absence of a chronicle tradition in Ancient Egypt, see J. Van Seters, *Orientalia* 50 (1981) 176.

mythology since, as pointed out above, this is one form the national tradition takes in the thoroughly Egyptian way of interpreting the past. The other leads into an analysis of records and record keeping, for putting into writing the events of the *immediate* past was the traditional way of demonstrating the thoroughly Egyptian tenet of the *continuum* of history.[11]

Once the historian's task in Egyptology is defined as examining the Egyptians' use of the past, instead of chasing after the will-o'-the-wisp of history-writing in a classical sense, the door will be open to a legitimate examination of records in general. But the examination *must* proceed along the lines of a rigorous methodology. There is in Egyptology today more than ever before a need for a form-critical evaluation of texts we use as historical sources.[12] We are often content to bring to the discussion, whether philological or historical, terms forged to meet the requirements and canons of another discipline; and the result is always the forcing of either the evidence or the nomenclature. In the field of historical source criticism we have first to ask what genre terms did the Egyptians themselves apply to their own texts, which we are pleased to lump under the one rubric of "historical."[13] Names for genres will not always appear; often a pattern will be all that one can isolate. But somewhere these patterns ought to be capable of being matched up with verbal descriptions, or social situations which will reveal their *Sitz im Leben*. Since as Buss has observed. "all genres are abstractions ... and ... virtually all human experiences involve a combination of categories,"[14] we should expect combinations and hybrids as well as "pure" genres; but this does not release us from the obligation to isolate the latter first.

That the Egyptians developed no distinct historiographical genres should not be taken to mean that the ancient community along the

[11]Cf. G. Goossen, *Sacra Pagina* I, 247f.

[12]Cf. D. B. Redford, in K. Weeks, (ed.), *Egyptology and the Social Sciences* (Cairo, 1979) 14ff.

[13]Cf. the apt remarks of J. Cansina concerning the oral genres of Africa in F. Gilbert, S. R. Graubard (eds.), *Historical Studies Today* (New York, 1972) 424.

[14]M. J. Buss, in J. H. Hayes (ed.), *Old Testament Form Criticism* (San Antonio, 1974) 53.

Nile had no regard for, nor consciousness of, its past.[15] It had, in fact, a strong sense of its own past, if not a developed idea of history.[16] This view characterized the past with reference to a number of hallowed, overarching abstractions, which may be described as follows.

1. Changelessness and Cycle

The divine will had already been expressed in ordered creation,[17] and social or political evolution towards higher forms was therefore unnecessary. There was, however, the possibility or even likelihood that the divine will would, from time to time, be frustrated by the powers of chaos. A cycle could be envisaged: (a) retrogression of the state through the ruler's failure to do the right; (b) disorder and misery in the community; (c) divine punishment of the malefactors; (d) divine appointment of a righteous king who would restore *Maꜥat*. A broader cyclic rhythm was also conceivable: texts speak of "the beginning of eternity, the onset of everlastingness,"[18] and destruction of the cosmos with the implicit new beginning is also alluded to. Contemplation of cyclic history involved withal problems related to theodicy.

[15]H. Frankfort avers (*Ancient Egyptian Religion* [New York, 1948] 50) that the Egyptians "could not be deeply interested in historical detail" (cf. also H. Brunner, *Saeculum* 21 [1970] 151); but it is a fact that the majority of the evidence he trots forth, and which clearly has affected his judgement, is of cultic or propogandistic nature. If an Amenophis III is at pains to stress his divine birth, who cares if he copies an earlier text *verbatim*? If a Pepy II is trying to overawe illiterate peasants, or even semi-literate priests, who cares if he plagiarizes from an earlier king? Lacking imaginative draftsmen, he probably found it easier to copy! But I am very sure that the sober *gnwt* of these kings' reigns, composed by and to be used by scribes, would have paid careful attention to historical detail.

[16]Cf. the judgement of P. Schubert, in *The Idea of History in the Ancient Near East*, 338. In fact, the Egyptians' view of the past probably came very close to what R. G. Collingwood called "the common-sense theory of [history]" in which "the essential things ... are memory and authority": *The Idea of History* (Oxford, 1946) 234ff. The form their few examples of historical writing took was that of simple narrative: cf. M. Mandelbaum, *The Anatomy of Historical Knowledge* (Baltimore and London, 1977) 25f; cf. also Kákosy, *Selected Papers*, 93ff.

[17]"Being" and "non-being" in Egyptian ontology is sometimes put down as the difference between differentiation and non-differentiation of entities: see H. Te Velde, *Studia Aegyptiaca* III (Budapest, 1977) 161. In fact, as many texts make plain, the concept of "being" derives from a wholly tactile base: earth and its forms constitute "being," while anything in the Nun (watery abyss) belongs within the realm of "non-being," undifferentiated though it may be.

[18]J. Assmann, *Zeit und Ewigkeit im alten Aegypten* Heidelberg, 1975.

2. Permanence and Continuity

That names and events should "abide" forever in written and oral record was not only a wish but a confident expectation. In a sense the divine creation would go on uninterrupted forever, viewed from the a-historical vantage point of myth as the two-tiered generation sequence Osiris-Horus. But when his thinking was divorced from a cultic context the Egyptian could and did, look at his country's past as a succession of reigns, a sequence of occupancies of the "office" of king.[19] Collectively they are the *nsyw*,[20] the *bityw*,[21] less often the *nsyw-bityw*,[22] occasionally *ityw*, "sovereigns,"[23] very rarely *isyw*, "ancient kings,"[24] or "old timers";[25] when the reference is to all power-wielders of yore, whether kings or commoners, the terms are *tpyw-ꜥ*, *imyw-ḥꜣt*, or *ḏrtyw*,[26] or *pꜣwtyw*.[27] Most often these ancestral kings are lumped together in a negative construction, denying that an event of an accomplishment which distinguished the speaker's lifetime had ever occurred in theirs. But a man might refer to "the kings in whose times I lived,"[28] and group them according to "houses," or the cities from which they had come. Not often is judgement passed on the moral quality or on the success of their reigns; they are the royal ancestors, the successors of the sun-god, and it is the office they hold that is most important.

3. Longevity

The test of value was, in part, how long a man had lived, or a family survived. Length of years became almost a cliché, both for the individual and for society. Not often did the feeling for time enveigle the keeper of annals into altering figures of past periods of time, but it did influence the concept: good conditions, and curiously bad as well, are said to last "many years." When the historified gods are assigned reigns, their divinity requires fantastic spans be assigned them; and when the pensive speaker contemplates the future it stretches away into tens of thousands of years.

[19]Cf. Merikare 116-118; also the term *pẖr-nsw*, "royal successor," *Edfu* VII, 57, 59 etc.; *Wb*. I, 547.
[20]*Wb*. II, 329; H. Goedicke, *Die Stellung des Königs im alten Reich* (Wiesbaden, 1960) 17ff.
[21]*Wb*. I, 435.
[22]*Edfu* VII, 4:4.
[23]*Edfu* VII, 5:6.
[24]J. Leclant, *Montouemhât, quatrième prophète d'Amon et prince de la ville* (Cairo, 1961) 68 (10).
[25]*Hꜣyw*: *Urk*. I, 85:5-6; 107:10-11; *JEA* 63 (1977) pl. 23:1.
[26]*Wb*. II, 457:5; P. Tresson, in *Mélanges Maspero* I, 2 (Cairo, 1934) 820 (5, 8).
[27]*Edfu* III, 14.
[28]M. Dewachter, *BIFAO* 71 (1972) pl. 20, p. 89.

4. Order

While perhaps not espousing wholly the notion that "bigger is better," the Egyptians did place a premium on concrete achievements of practical value. These presupposed an all-embracing order in society, nature and the divine world, the antithesis of which was stultifying chaos. Change meant only the restoration of order in place of chaos which had triumphed temporarily.

5. Divine Precedent

Surpassing the accomplishments of the ancestors was an accepted and legitimate activity which involved differences in degree, not of essence; but in no case did an action lack a precedent "in the time of God," or "at the moment of creation" (*sp tpy*).[29] Good and worthy actions, then, simply reproduced the divine patterns at the dawn of time.

6. Divine Prehistory

Myths as represented in the cult are not history. Their meaning has nothing to do with their having occurred in the past, but rather with their present significance. Commemoration and mimetic repetition of these myths, viz. the archetypal acts of the god in the cult,[30] are also in themselves not "historical," nor connected with any concept of history.[31] Horus's championing of his father, the upliftings of Shu, the murder of Osiris — these are all primordial events, timeless and ever-present; and neither king nor priest who re-enacts them can be said to fulfil an historic role, or to be commemorating "history." There is indeed commemoration of "history" in the cult, but it is akin to what one recent historian has felicitously called "civic religion,"[32]

[29]On *rk Rᶜ/ntr*, see C. Desroches-Noblecourt, *Le petit temple d'Abou Simbel* I (Cairo, 1968) 147f, n. 64; B. Couroyer, *RB* 67 (1960) 42ff; on *sp tpy*, see H. Altenmüller, *WO* 10 (1979), 116; D. Meeks, *Année lexicographique* III (Paris, 1982) 248; Brunner, *Saeculum* 21, 158; cf. F. Daumas, *Les moyens d'expression du grec et de l'égyptien* (Cairo, 1952) 119 (την ἀρχήν).

[30]On the relationship between myth and ritual, see E, Blumenthal, *OLZ* 73 (1978) 535f, and the literature there cited.

[31]A good deal of fuzzy thinking and unnecessary confusion has been introduced by blurring the line between myth and history: cf. E. Hornung, *MDIAK* 15 (1957) 120ff. For the writer myth is an event the protagonists in which are the gods who act on a divine level, and which is always of immediate significance to the present community by virtue of cultic mimesis (cf. E. Brunner-Traut, *Gelebte Mythen* [Darmstadt, 1981] 1ff). History is never so treated.

[32]N. Bellah, in J. C. Brauer (ed.), *Religion and the American Revolution*, Philadelphia, 1976; the term derives ultimately from Rousseau.

and is markedly different from the cult of the gods. The commemoration of the military successes of a Thutmose III or a Ramesses III in the "feasts of victory" are recollections and celebrations of historic events. The gods are not in essence deceased kings of blessed memory; and one senses a real difference between "the time of king N" and "the time of God X."

Nevertheless, outside the cult, the urge to see a continuum from the beginning of things to the present led, on one plane of thinking to an extension of the time frame to the realm of the gods, and ultimately to a synthesis of the human past with the divine present. The gods were turned into kings: they had reigned and passed on. Their reigns had far surpassed the puny spans of mortals, however, and their deeds had similarly been gargantuan; and the contrast between the two in such documents as the Turin Canon is marked. Nevertheless an Osiris had reigned a finite period, as had a Khufu, and this period could be placed in a temporal sequence of reigns: the gods were *ipso facto* historified.[33]

This strong inclination to view myth as part of history, in fact the history of the gods, on the same plane as the history of man, and different from it not in essence but degree, is not the temptation of the priestly celebrant, but the scribal intellectual. A priest repeating parts of the Osiris myth in the ritual is no more commemorating history than a bishop celebrating mass is studying the history of Palestine in the 1st Century! The scribe, however, is a collector of facts, a maker of lists; he lists commodities, foreign captives, taxes, creatures on earth and in heaven, laws, receipts and disbursements — and when he comes to the past, he lists kings and their deeds. He must see all time as a dominant unit, and no living thing — *not even a god* — is outside it. Chronicle, which Croce has labelled "dead history ... past history,"[34] knows no distinction between men and gods.

7. Divine Causation

The gods infuenced the course of history in several ways, but none all-encompassing. They could show favour to mankind and appoint "their son" to the kingship. Through bad judgement or negligence, they could even bring disaster on their earthly flock and thereby warrant human censure. In all they were bound by the contractual

[33]On the historification of the realm of the gods, see U. Luft, *Beiträge zur Historisierung der Götterwelt und der Mythenschreibung*, Budapest, 1978. Griffiths (*Osiris and His Cult*, 23) speaks of the "stamp of human experience crassly applied to the world of the gods." Cf. also Kákosy, *Selected Papers* 99ff.

[34]B. Croce, *History, its Theory and Practice* (tr. D. Ainslee; New York, 1921) 17.

relationship with their devotees, whereby in return for faithful temple service and offering, they granted divine favour to the community and strength, victory and wealth to their royal son, the Pharaoh.

To say that "history, like the drama and the novel, grew out of mythology, a primitive form of apprehension and expression in which ... the line between fact and fiction is left undrawn"[35] is grotesque and wholly misleading. In Egypt, as *mutatis mutandis* in all early "hydraulic" civilizations, the view of the past is conditioned, as is the mythology of the community, by geography, climate, type of economy, and the political structure. There is of course an interaction through time between history and mythology, but one does not stem from the other. Both answer different needs of the community, the one the need for the saving presence of god *now*, the other the need to know one's roots.

The present book attempts to analyse a type of text (or scene) rather common in ancient Egypt, and certainly germane to any historical study, viz. groupings of kings in name or representation, which are loosely classed as "king-lists," in an effort to study the genesis and development of the king-list tradition. Two ancilliary genres, annals and day-books, are similarly subjected to analysis. The investigation of these three types of text constitutes the point of departure for a diachronic examination of the sense of history which manifests itself in the king-list tradition over the three millennia of ancient Egyptian history. Chapter 4 marshals the evidence for the Old and Middle Kingdoms, and attempts to discover when and how the king-list came into being. Chapter 5 examines the vicissitudes of the king-list during the New Kingdom (18th and 19th Dynasties), and the changes in their attitude to their past wrought on the Egyptians by their experience of empire. In chapter 6 Manetho, his background and sources, and the format of his work are scrutinized, while chapters 7 and 9 look closely at the state of the king-list as reflected in the three books of the *Aegyptiaca*. Chapter 8 is devoted to an analysis of the Harmais legend, the historical pericopes of the New Kingdom, and the plot-motif of invasion from the north.

[35] A. J. Toynbee, in H. Meyerhoff (ed.), *The Philosophy of History in Our Time* (New York, 1959) 115.

1

King-Lists and Groups of Kings

In this chapter we shall proceed to deal empirically with groupings of kings' names or representations of kings with an eye to the formal characteristics of each group. Form criticism of the document shall take precedence over the historical problems which might arise from it. Comments on the contents of a king-list tradition and historical reliability will await the second chapter. As a general rule of thumb collocation of three or more kings or royal figures constitutes a "group" and pairs of names have been ignored (although occasionally alluded to in the notes). The order is not strictly chronological, the longer and better known groupings taking precedence.

1. True King-lists[1]

Under this heading should be placed all groupings of kings, their representations and/or names which set out (a) to arrange the names in correct historical sequence, (b) to give for each name the length of reign, (c) to note conscientiously any gaps in (a) or (b). Thus the document enables its users to identify rulers of antiquity and to place them in correct chronological sequence, and to tell exactly how long, as well as how long ago, they had reigned.[2] Given this definition of a king-list, the Egyptologist must admit that for Pharaonic times he can

[1]See J. von Beckerath, in *LdÄ* III (1980) 534f.

[2]The general intent of most ancient Near Eastern king-lists: D. B. Redford, *History and Chronology of the Eighteenth Dynasty of Egypt: Seven Studies* (Toronto, 1967) 185ff; A. Malamat, in *Speiser Festschrift* (New Haven, 1968) 163ff; A. K. Grayson, in *Lišān Mitḫurti, Festschrift W. F. von Soden* (Neukirchen-Vluyn, 1969) 105ff.

produce but one exemplar, viz. the Turin Canon of kings,[3] although it is quite clear that this is only the sole survivor of a long line of similar lists which must have been copied over many centuries.[4]

Written in the 19th Dynasty during the reign of Ramesses II (cf. *rt.* viii, x + 5-6), the papyrus now 1.7m long,[5] comprises on the *recto* an indeterminate number of pages of a tax list (probably of an original 20),[6] now hopelessly fragmentary. The height of the papyrus, viz. 41cm, proves it to have been of the normal dimensions of chancery documents of the New Kingdom.[7] The papyrus became tattered some time after the tax scribe wrote on it, and there is no telling how much later the unknown scrivener of kings' names used the *verso*; but we may venture to guess that it was sometime subsequent to the height of Ramesses II's reign, and probably as late as Merneptah or Sety II.[8]

On the *recto* of the papyrus is a list of personal names and names of institutions, along with what appears to be the tax assessment of each. The fragments that remain suggest a geographical distribution: the first section (columns i and ii) mention the "Lake of Sobek" (the Fayum?),[9] *Ihrᶜ*, *Rmn*, and *I-wr*, northern locations abounding in fish. Lines iii, 19-22, with reference to "the dues of the staffs[10] [of temples (?)]", "[from] Elephantine [to ...]," "every town in the southern part

[3]See among others, E. Drioton, J. Vandier, *L'Egypte*[4], (Paris, 1962) 159; E. Otto, *HO* I, 2 (1952) 142; J. von Beckerath, *Untersuchungen zur politischen Geschichte der zweiten Zwischenszeit in Aegypten* (Glückstadt, 1965) 20ff; W. K. Simpson, in W. K. Simpson, W. Hallo (eds.), *The Ancient Near East: A History* (New York, 1971) 193; J. Malek, *JEA* 68 (1982) 93ff; J. von Beckerath, *SAK* 11 (1984) 39ff.

[4]Whether the *Vorlage* of TC contained fuller entries for each king, including his two cartouches and the calendrics of his accession and death (cf. M. Eaton-Krauss, *JSSEA* 12 [1982] 18) must remain a moot point; but on the evidence of practice elsewhere in the ancient Near East, I would say no.

[5]G. Farina, *Il papiro dei Re restaurato* (Rome, 1938) 15.

[6]*Medinet Habu* III (Chicago, 1934) pl. 150:548.

[7]J. Černý, *Paper and Books in Ancient Egypt* (London, 1947) 16; cf. the height of similar taxation documents: P. Amiens (Sir A. H. Gardiner, *Ramesside Administrative Documents* [London, 1948] vi), P. Gurob (*ibid.*, ix), Turin Strike Papyrus (*ibid.*, xiv), Turin Indictment Papyrus (*ibid.*, xxii).

[8]Farina, *Papiro dei Re*, 13; G. Möller, *Hieratische Paläographie* II (Osnabruck, 1927) 10f.

[9]Gauthier, *Dictionnaire géographique* V, 127.

[10]*S³w n smdt:* cf. A. H. Gardiner, *Late Egyptian Miscellanies* (Brussels, 1937) 28, 3; P. Chester Beatty V, *rt.* 6, 2ff; 8,1-5.

[11]*AEO* I, 82*ff.

(i.e. Upper Egypt)" undoubtedly constitute a heading introducing the tax-bearing principalities and officials of Upper Egypt. Column iv, x + 5 refers to something "of Kush," and vi, 11, 15-18 to the "Medjay," the police units of Upper Egypt.[11] In viii, x + 7 is "the break-down of the quota *(ḥtr)*[12] of the Southern and Northern Oasis." Broadly speaking, then it seems that the scribe organized his material into sections corresponding to 1. Lower Egypt, 2. Upper Egypt, 3. the land route to Asia,[13] and 4. the oases of the western desert.[14] The word for "tax" is sometimes *ḥtr* which means "estimated tax, (annual) levy,"[15] sometimes *bꜣkw*, "products of labour," or *šꜣyt*, "dues." Although these technical terms might put one in mind of the royal treasury at Memphis as the appropriate repository for such a document, levies were most often raised for the benefit of specific temples and their provisioning throughout the year.[16] One cannot rule out the possibility, therefore, that the present papyrus was drawn up in a temple and deposited in a temple archive. Does the papyrus contain the estimated taxes due the temple of Amun in a specific year (cf. iv, 12), perhaps some time during the 20th Dynasty?

As the beginning of the papyrus on the *verso*, which would have contained an introductory statement including the name of the piece and perhaps the scribe's name, is now lost, we are ignorant as to

[12] D. B. Redford, in J. W. Wevers, D. B. Redford (eds.), *Studies in the Ancient Palestinian World* (Toronto, 1972) 144ff; R. A. Caminos, *A Tale of Woe* (Oxford, 1977) 54, n. 4-6.

[13] Cf. the predominance of "wells" *(ẖnmt)* on the land route to Gaza: Kitchen, *RI* I, 7-8; on *ẖnmt*, "well, basin," see *Wb.* III, 382; *AEO* I, 7*; Gardiner, *The Wilbour Papyrus* II (Oxford, 1952) 30f.

[14] On the administration of the oases in Ramesside times, see the present author in *JSSEA* 7 (1977) 2ff.

[15] See the present writer in *Studies in the Ancient Palestinian World*, 151.

[16] *Ibid.*, 145f; cf. also for a discussion of the terms for tax, W. Helck, in *LdÄ* I (1972) 3ff; for additional treatment of the *recto*, *idem*, *Materialien zur Wirtschaftgeschichte des neuen Reiches* III (Wiesbaden, 1963) 468ff; J. Janssen, *SAK* 3 (1975) 173ff.

what term the Egyptians applied to this genre of writing.[17] Nor do the circumstances of discovery help in ascertaining who wrote the king-list, for whom, and where it was kept. The papyrus was discovered by Drovetti in 1822 in the Theban necropolis, and its peregrinations from that moment until its definitive publication by Farina[18] and later by Gardiner[19] have often been told.[20] Too much need not be made of the Theban provenience. If any single city can be said to have shaped the king-list tradition reflected by TC, it is Memphis;[21] but the unity of the tradition during Ramesside times

[17]In other types of groupings (see below, *passim*) the terms used most often denote the content of the grouping rather than its form: *itw*, "fathers" (A. H. Gardiner, N. de G. Davies, *The Tomb of Amenemhet* [London, 1915] pl. 7; Sethe, *Lesestücke*, 66:15-16), "[her] fathers and her mother[s]" (Osiris Heka Djet, Karnak [own copy]: P-M II^2, 206(15), "the fathers and the mothers (i.e. the ancestors?) in Djeme" (M. Doresse, *RdE* 25 [1973] 124; cf. also J-P. Corteggiani, in *Hommages à Serge Sauneron* [Cario, 1979] 127, 129), *nsyw bityw*, "the kings of Upper and Lower Egypt" (*Urk.* IV, 608:6; Chester Beatty IX, *rt.* 7, 11; E. Meyer, *Aegyptische Chronologie* [Berlin, 1904] pl. 1), *twt nw itw.i bityw*, "the statues of my fathers the kings of Lower Egypt" (P. Barguet, *Le Temple d'Amon-rê à Karnak* [Paris, 1962] 124; *LD* III, 162-3); *rnw nw itw*, "the names of the fathers" (*Urk.* IV, 607:8), *nsyw*, "the kings" (Abydos, Inscription Dédicataire, 25); *nbw nḥḥ*, "the Lords of Eternity" (*LD* III, 2d, 173), *nbw imntt*, "the Lords of the West" (*LD* III, 2a). In the ritual for Amenophis I the "multitudinous clan" (*t*^{3} *mhwt* ^{c}*š*^{3}*t*) is used after the names of Amenophis, Ahmes Nofretari and princess Sat-Amun as an implied reference to a host of unnamed royalty on whose behalf the celebrant declares himself pure (V. Golenischef, *Papyrus hiératiques* [*CCG* 83; Cairo, 1927] v, 5); but whether this refers to the line of ancestral kings, or to the family of the early 18th Dynasty, is unclear. *Sḫwy*, "collection, list" suggests itself as an appropriate term, but this is most often used of lists of things in which sequence is not an important consideration: cf. A. De Buck, *Egyptian Readingbook* (Lieden, 1963) 64:4; R. A. Caminos, *The Chronicle of Prince Osorkon* (Rome, 1958) 136; *Urk.* IV, 690:15, 780:4; Great Harris x, 1; lxvii, 1. If the piece were intended for didactic purposes (cf. below, n. 22) one wonders whether it began with *ḥ*^{3}*t*-^{c} *m sb*^{3}*yt mtrw rnw nsyw bityw* or the like (cf. On. Am. I, 1ff [*AEO* III, pl. 7] Amenemope I, 1-4 [see U. Luft, *ZÄS* 99 (1973) 115]); on *ḥ*^{3}*t*-^{c} *m sb*^{3}*yt*, see C. Kuentz, in *Griffith Studies* (London, 1932) 101; on *sb*^{3}*yt* and *mtr* see A. Volten, in *Studi in Memoria di Ippolito Rosellini* II (Pisa, 1955) 274; cf. also Farina, *Papiro dei Re*, 14; B. van de Walle, *Bib. Or.* 17 (1960) 233.

[18]Farina, *Papiro dei Re*, 14.

[19]Sir A. H. Gardiner, *The Royal Canon of Turin*, Oxford, 1959; cf. also J. Lopez, *RdE* 25 (1973) 178, n. 2. The present investigation largely accepts Gardiner's placement of the fragments. On the possibility that the fragments of column i should be elevated considerably, below, p. 11, n. 41. Von Beckerath's suggestion (*ZÄS* 93 [1966] 18f) that fragment 48 + 36 should be placed in column iv, lines 22-26, founders on the proposed collocation of two cartouches in one line (23), which would be unique. The same scholar's placement of fragment 44 (*JNES* 21 [1962] 140ff) seems one line too high. On the very plausible placement of another fragment by Wildung, see below, n. 54.

[20]See Meyer, *Chronologie*, 106ff; H. E. Winlock, *The Rise and Fall of the Middle Kingdom in Thebes* (New York, 1947) 4; G. Maspero, *A History of Egypt* I (London, 1900) 322, n. 1.

[21]Von Beckerath, *Untersuchungen*, 20.

should not be underestimated. It is doubtful whether any of the major "lists" we are going to pass in review represents any rival tradition of essentially different origin.

A text written on the back of an old papyrus, evidently discarded by a fiscal officer, can scarcely qualify as an "official" record. This observation should not, however, prejudice us against a text *a priori*: it deserves a form critical analysis, and assessment of its putative sources. Only when the *Sitz im Leben* of the piece is identified can a perspicacious judgement be cast of its accuracy.[22]

Organization of the Columns of TC

Columns i to v of the king-list on the *verso* contain approximately twenty-five or twenty-six lines each, but as the end approaches the scribe has attempted to squeeze in more material per column, making vi at least twenty-seven, and ix and x at least thirty, lines long. In some cases the formulaic expressions to be discussed below lengthen a line to the point where it must either encroach on the adjacent column, or be divided in half. The scribe does not eschew encroachment (e.g. iv, 15-16, vi, 3, vii, 3), but divides the offending line off from the other column by a curving black line. Indentation, spacing or blank space seem not to have been employed to section the contents. This was done by introductory lines and lines of summation, in no way different in positioning from those of individual entries.

Mode of Designation of the Kings

The Turin Canon scribe or, more likely, one of his predecessors in the succession of copiists, had rationed himself to one cartouche per king. For the early kings one name only could be enclosed, unless outright fabrication was to be indulged in; but from the mid-5th Dynasty the tradition had a choice, usually, between nomen and prenomen. For the first two dynasties it was the Horus name that in the main appeared in the cartouche, and, after the introduction of the cartouche in the 3rd, the name which historically had been thus enclosed. From the introduction of the second cartouche in the 5th Dynasty the following table shows the distribution:

[22]My student, Miss Lynda Green, has tendered the intriguing suggestion that TC was the product of the House of Life, and was intended for didactic purposes. Another avenue of attack, viz. the measuring of TC's contents against contemporary documents, is beyond the scope of the present investigation.

	Prenomen	Nomen	Both (in Cartouche)	Both (Nomen outside Cartouche)
iii,	17			
	23			
	24			
		25		
iv		8		
				9
	10			
		11		
	20			
		21		
	22			
	24			
v,	16-17			
	20			
vi,	1			
	2			
	5			
				6
		7		
	8			
		9		
	10-15			
		16		
	17-18			
			19-20	
				21-22
	23			
			24-25	
		26		
			27	
vii,	1-4			
			5-6(?)	
				7
			8	
		13		
				14-15
	16+			
viii,		1		
	2-8			
	10-27			
ix,	1-9[-]			
				28-30
xi,	only			

It is quite clear that the tradition preferred to record the prenomen of an incumbant king. The prenomen, as the international correspondence of the New Kingdom indicates, was the "official" name of the king, by which he would be alluded to as a holder of the *office* of King of Egypt. It is interesting to note that all of the kings in the extant parts of the papyri to be designated by their nomens alone are otherwise almost wholly unknown, and clearly ephemeral. Since the formulation of the "Great Names," of which the prenomen was one, was the preserve of the lector-priests at the coronation,[23] kings with very short reigns might lack a prenomen, not having had a chance to undergo a coronation. The occasional inclusion of a nomen and prenomen in a single cartouche begins only after the end of the 12th Dynasty, and clearly reflects the practice of what in Manetho is the 13th Dynasty of piling up "dynastic" names within a single cartouche.[24] Of the 8 examples preserved half display the nomen Sobekhotpe (vi, 19, 24, 27, vii, 8). Similarly those examples of a name added after, and outside of, the cartouche begin, with one exception after the close of the 12th Dynasty. Of 9 examples 4 are foreign names, 1 is a military title, and 1 may have been intended to be within the cartouche (vii, 7). It looks as though the individuals accorded this treatment are those who, for whatever reason, had been known before their assumption of the prenomen, by a name which stuck in the tradition. This would be understandable with foreigners or natives who had made a mark for themselves before they came to the throne. It is interesting that the "precision" represented by columns C and D in the chart is confined to columns vi through ix, i.e. Manetho's 13th Dynasty.

The *Ir.n.f m Nsyt* Formula

The basic format of the king-list consists of a line in which the following elements occur: 1. *nsw-bity*, "king of Upper and Lower Egypt"; 2. the cartouche containing the king's name (prenomen when available; otherwise Horus- or *nebty*-name, rarely the personal name); 3. a figure, which can be in tripartite form, i.e. years, months

[23] *Urk.* IV, 261:2-4.

[24] Note the preponderence in column vi, at least, of the names Amenemhet/Ameny and Sehtepibre. Any theory which seeks to explain the theory of kingship under the 13th Dynasty would do well to ponder long the spiritual descent the 13th Dynasty wished to promulgate from the outgoing 12th.

and days, but which sometimes gives only the number of years of the reign.[25] For the kings from Menes to Djoser a fourth element seems also to be present, viz. the length of life, added after the total for the reign.[26] At certain points in the papyrus these elements are incorporated into a fuller format, which constitutes a syntactically complete statement: *nsw-bity* N *ir.n.f m nsyt rnpt* X *ibd* Y *hrw* Z, "king N functioned in the kingship X years, Y months, Z days." The complete list of all preserved examples of this formula is as follows:

1. ii, 11, [*nsw*]*-bity Mny ꜥ.w.s ir.n.f* [*m nsyt* ...], "King Menes, L.P.H. functioned [in the kingship ...]."
2. iii, 5, *nsw-bity*[27] *Ḏsri ir.n.f* [*m nsyt*] *rnpt* 19 *ibd* 1 *ꜥḥꜥw.f m ꜥnḫ* [...], "King Djoser functioned [in the kingship] 19 years, 1 month, his lifetime being [...]."
3. iii, 19, [*nsw-bity Kꜣkꜣy*[28]] *ir.n.f m nsyt* [*rnpt* X], "[King Kakai] functioned in the kingship [X years]."
4. fragment 48 + 36[29] [*nsw-bity* ...] *ir.n.f* [*m nsyt rnpt* X], "[King ...] functioned [in the kingship X years]."
5. v, 20, [*nsw-bity Sḥt*]*p-ib-*[*rꜥ*] *ir.n.f m nsyt* [*rnpt* X], "[King Sehte]pibre functioned in the kingship [X years]."
6. vi, 1, *nsw-bity Mꜣꜥ-ḫrw-rꜥ ir.n.f m nsyt rnpt* 9 *ibd* 3 *hrw* 27, "King Makhrure functioned in the kingship 9 years, 3 months, 27 days."
7. vi, 5, *nsw-bity Ḫw-tꜣwy-rꜥ* [*ir.n.f m*] *nsyt rnpt* 2 *ibd* 3 *hrw* 24, "King Khutowyre [functioned in] the kingship 2 years, 3 months, 24 days."
8. vi, 16, *nsw-bity Rn-snb ir.n.*[*f m nsyt* (?)*ib*]*d* 4, "King Rensoneb function[ed in the kingship (?)] 4 [months]."
9. vii, 3, *nsw-bity Mr-nfr-rꜥ ir.n.f m ns*[*yt*] *rnpt* 23 *ibd* 8 *hrw* 18, "King Merneferre functioned in the king[ship] 23 years, 8 months, 18 days."
10. viii, 4, *nsw-bity Sḥb-rꜥ ir.n.f m nsyt rnpt* 3 *ibd* [...] *hrw* 1, "King Sehebre functioned in the kingship 3 years, [...] months, 1 day."
11. viii, 20, *nsw-bity Sḫm-*[...]*-rꜥ ir.n.*[*f m ns*]*yt* [*rnpt* (?) ...], "King Sekhem[...]re function[ed in the king]ship [... years (?)]."
12. ix, 20, *nsw-bity Šmsw ir.n.*[*f m nsyt* ...], "King Shemsu function[ed in the kingship ...]."

[25]For the Old Kingdom and Herakleopolitan period the practice varies; but beginning with the 12th Dynasty months and days are constantly given.
[26]Meyer, *Chronologie*, 113, 140. For the mythical kings "kingship" and "years of life" (*rnpt.sn m ꜥnḫ*) seem to be equated; C ii, 4.
[27]In red.
[28]The position two places after Userkaf guarantees the identity of the king: but whether *kꜣkꜣy* or *Nfr.ir.kꜣ.rꜥ* was used is a moot point.
[29]Gardiner, *Canon*, pl. 9; the names preserved on the fragment suggest that the context is the Herakleopolitan group (i.e. the bottom of column iv, or the top of column v); see also above, n. 19.

13. ix, 27, *nsw-bity* [...] *ir.n*[*f m nsyt* ...], "King [...] functioned [in the kingship ...]."
14. fragment 163,[30] [*nsw-bity* ...] *ir.n.f m nsyt* [...], "King ...] functioned in the kingship [...]."
15. fragment 40,[31] [*nsw-bity* ...] *s³-Ptḥ ir.n.*[*f m nsyt* ...], "[King ...] son of Ptah functioned [in the kingship ...]."

The formula's sporadic occurrence has been variously interpreted as marking an important break with the preceeding names, and thus marking off "embryonic dynasties," as it were;[32] or as the full form of the formula (whence the more common tabular format was derived) which stood at the head of each column in TC's *Vorlage*, and was copied slavishly by the scribe, even though his columns were longer.[33] The first hypothesis founders on the singular positioning of the formula. Although examples 1, 5 and 7 do, in fact, correspond to the beginning of Manetho's 1st, 12th, and 13th Dynasties respectively, in which tradition was Neferirkare ever identified as the founder of a dynasty (no. 3), not to mention Amenemhet IV (no. 6), or any of the non-entities from no. 9 on? The second hypothesis is likewise baseless.[34] Helck believed he detected a pattern of entries averaging 13 to 16 lines apart, but this is not the case. Between no. 1 and 2 twenty lines intervene, and we can be certain that no example of the formula now lost occurred here.[35] The next certain example, no. 3, is only fourteen lines removed from no. 2. Nos. 5 and 6 are separated by only six lines and nos. 6 and 7 by five! We are, moreover, invited to suppose that the scribe, who up to column vi had been copying his *Vorlage* slavishly, became aware of the correct use of the formula at the top of column vi, only to forget it again in the next few lines! Nos. 7 and 8 are separated by twelve lines, 8 and 9 by fourteen, 9 and 10 by certainly over twenty-five,[36] 10 and 11 by sixteen, and 12 and 13 by only seven.

[30]Gardiner, *Canon*, pl. 4.
[31]*Ibid.*, pl. 9; also below, n. 54.
[32]Meyer, *Chronologie*, 113; W. C. Hayes, *JNES* 12 (1953) 34, 38; I. E. S. Edwards, in *CAH* I² (1965) 24, 30.
[33]Helck, *Manetho*, 83f; von Beckerath, *Untersuchungen*, 23.
[34]It is only fair to say that it was hatched at some considerable time prior to Gardiner's definitive publication, and its author therefore did not have the benefit of Gardiner's placement of fragments.
[35]The placement of the numerals in fragment 30, of column ii makes it quite certain that no *ir.n.f* formula occurred here, and certainly not with Anedjib.
[36]That there was not any occurrence of the formula between 9 and 10 is proved by the fact that no other indentation of column viii is in evidence, except that occasioned by example no. 9; and columns vii and viii are sufficiently close that an indentation would have been inevitable.

The problem is singularly difficult to solve. One is struck, in spite of the naïveté of the theory championed by Meyer, by the fact that certain kings who stood out in the memory of the ancients as well as ourselves were singled out for application of the formula: Menes, Djoser, Wahankh Antef (?), and Ammenemes I, among others. Moreover, at least three of the names which stood at the head of larger groupings (1, 5, 7) receive the formula; for other groups, e.g. the "6th" Dynasty, the Herakleopolitan group, and the "11th" Dynasty, lacunae prevent our being able to tell. Could the answer be that the *ir.n.f m nsyt* formula was of ambivalent significance, denoting importance in a vague sense, or entailing the intent to arrest attention, or even designed to draw attention to an entry which might otherwise be misinterpreted (cf. no. 8)?[37]

Headings and Summations

The text of TC is divided up into sections by headings and lines of summation. The former are less numerous that the latter, which may be partly due to the state of preservation of the papyrus. In both types of entry red ink is nearly always used for the first word. Headings take the following form: "Kings (red) of such and such a place," accompanied sometimes by another qualifying element. Lines of summation show greater variety in construction. They employ the heading as a core, preceding it by "total" (*dmḏ*, in red), and following it by a numeral; the whole is then followed by an indication of how long the group in question ruled, in any of the three following patterns: 1. "... making X years" (*ir n rnpt* X);[38] "they made X years" (*ir.n.sn rnpt* X);[39] 3. "their kingship, their years of life, X years" (*nsyt.sn rnpt.sn* (*m ʿnḫ*) *rnpt* X).[40] The broad groupings which thus emerge from the use of these diacritical lines are as follows:

[37]Example no. 2 suggests that the formula is somehow to be construed as antithetic to, or in contrast with, the king's total length of life.
[38]Cf. v, 18; vi, 3.
[39]Cf. x, 13, 21.
[40]Cf. ii, 4; iv, 16.

1. *Heading*: lost.

Summation: i, 21,[41] *dmḏ* (red) [*nsywt* X *rn*]*pt.*⸢*sn*⸣[...], "total [X kings;] their [ye]ars [...]."

Group distinguished: Ptah and the Great Ennead.

2. *Heading*: i, 22, *dmḏ* (black) [*nsywt*] 9 [*n psḏt nḏst*?], "total of 9 [kings of the Lesser Ennead?]."

Group distinguished: Horus and the Lesser Ennead.

3. *Heading*: lost.

Summation: ii, 4,[42] [*dmḏ ꜣḫw*(?)] X + 10 *nsyt.sn rnpt.sn m ꜥnḫ rnpt* [...], "[Total spirits(?)] X + 10; their kingship, their years of life [...] years."

Group distinguished: the *ꜣḫw*.

4. *Summation*: ii, 9[43] [*dmḏ rnpt*(?)] *nfryt-r Šmsw-Ḥr rnpt* 13, 200 + X, "[total of their years(?)] down to the Followers of Horus, 13, 200 + X years."

Group distinguished: part of the group of mythical kings.

5. *Summation*: ii, 10,[44] [*dmḏ* ...(?) *nfryt-r*(?)] *nsw-bity Mni ꜥ.w.s.* [...], "[total ...(?) down to (?)] King Menes, L.P.H. [...]."

Group distinguished: the mythical kings.

[41]There is nothing inherent in the contexts of this column, nor on the *verso* (Gardiner, *Canon*, pl. 8, viii) that would militate in favour of placing the fragments of column i so low down. In fact all the rest of the columns are fairly well preserved at their tops. Fragment 12 is probably the sum total of the years of the Lesser Ennead, and is therefore rightly placed at the bottom of column i (in spite of Gardiner, *ibid.*, note to i, 24). The rest of the cluster of fragments should probably be elevated by some five or six lines. This would make Gardiner's present line 22 into line 16, and leave nine lines lost at the bottom of the column. Since line "22" (=16) records a King Horus, we are probably to reconstruct the rest of the column to record the remaining eight members of the Lesser Ennead; (their presence in Manetho is assured by the Syncellus version). This would leave the last — 25th — line of the column for a total.

[42]Helck (*Manetho*, 6) claims three dynasties of demigods are mentioned here, and believes they are to be equated with the dynasty of 9 which Syncellus gives. But the latter's 9 (Orus to Zeus) are clearly to be equated with the section of the Canon beginning at the bottom of fragment 12 with "Horus," and comprising the Lesser Ennead. Moreover the Armenian version of Eusebius does not give "9 heroes" following Horus, as Helck's table (*ibid.*, 8) would indicate. Only an unspecified dynasty of "heroes" is mentioned, with a total of 1,255 years. Whether Helck's suggestion (*ibid.*, 6) that we have here the "Souls" (*bꜣw*) of Pe, Nekhen and Heliopolis is to be accepted is a moot point, though the idea is attractive. The question arises with respect to the first four lines of column ii, which, if any, are lines of summation? Line 1 does not appear to be, but line 2 poses a problem. For, apart from the four lines in question, *nsyt* occurs only in iv, 16 in the grand total of all kings from Menes to the end of the 6th Dynasty, and again in the ubiquitous type of heading *ir.n.f m nsyt*. On the other hand, if fragment 3 is rightly placed, neither lines 2 or 3 begin with the expected *dmḏ*, "total." On balance it seems preferable to construe the first 3 lines at least as separate entries, with line 4 as a possible summation.

[43]It is possible that ii, 8 is also a line of summation.

[44]Cf. S. Morenz, *ZÄS* 99 (1972) xii; on the other hand, this line could easily be the introduction to what follows, in which case we ought to restore "[Kings who followed] the king of Upper and Lower Egypt, Menes ...."

6. *Summation*: iii, 26-27(?), *dmḏ* (red) *nsywt š3c-*[*m*] *Mni r-mn* [*Wnis* X *rnpt.sn* ...], "total of kings beginning with Menes down to [Unas, X; their years ...]."

Group distinguished: Manetho's 1st to 5th Dynasties.

7. *Summation*: iv, 14-15, [*dmḏ*] *nsywt* [*nfrty-r*(?) ... X *rnpt.sn*] 181 [*ibd*] 6 *hrw* 3 ⌜*wsf* 6⌝ *dmḏ* (red) [....], "[Total] of kings [down to(?) ... X; their years] 181, 6 [months], 3 days; ⌜*wsf*[45] 6⌝; total [....]."

Group distinguished: Manetho's 6th Dynasty.

8. *Summation*: iv, 15-17, [*dmḏ*(?)] *nsyw* [*š3c m*] *Mni nsyt.sn rnpt.sn wsf.*[*sn*(?) ...] ⌜9⌝*hrw* 15 *wsf rnpt* 6 *dmḏ* [*nsyw* X *rn*]*pt* 955, *hrw* 10, "[Total] of kings [beginning with] Menes, their kingship, their years, [*their*(?)] *wsf* [...], ⌜9⌝ [months], 15 ⌜days⌝, *wsf* : 6 years. Total [of kings, X]; 955 [ye]ars, 10 days."

Group distinguished: Manetho's 1st to 6th Dynasties.

9. *Summation*: v, 10, *dmḏ* (red) *nsyw* 18 [*rnpt.sn* ...], "Total of kings: 18; [their years ...]."

Group distinguished: Manetho's 9th and 10th Dynasties.

10. *Heading*: v, 11, *nsyw* (red) [....], "kings of [....]."

Summation: v, 18, [*dmḏ*] *nsyw* ⌜6⌝ *ir n rnp*[*t* ...] ⌜*wsf*⌝ (?) 7[46] *dmḏ* 143; "[Total] of kings, 6; making [...] years; [*wsf*] (?) 7; total, 143."

Group distinguished: Manetho's 11th Dynasty.

11. *Heading*: v, 19, [*nsyw*] *ẖnw Iṯ-t3wy*, "[Kings] of the Residence Itj-towy."

Summation: vi, 3, *dmḏ* (red) *nsyw n ẖnw* [*It-t3wy*] 8 *ir n rnpt* 213 *ibd* 1 *hrw* 17; "total of kings of the Residence [Itj-towy], 8; making 213 years, 1 month, 17 days."

Group distinguished: Manetho's 12th Dynasty.

12. *Heading*: vi, 4, [*nsyw*] (red) [... *ḥr*]*-s3* ⌜*Iṯ*⌝-[*t3wy*][47] *Sḥ*] *tp-ib-rc c.w.s.* "⌜kings⌝ [... fol]lowing [Itj-towy (?) of Seh]etepibre, L.P.H."

Summation: x, 12-13, [*dmḏ nsyw* ...] *ir. n. sn rnpt* [....], "[Total of kings ...]; they made [....] years."

Group distinguished: Manetho's 13th and 14th Dynasty.[48]

13. *Heading*(?): x, 14(?), lost.

Summation: x, 21, *ns*[*yw ḥḳ3w-*]*ḫ3swt* 6 *ir.n.sn rnpt* 100 + X, "Ki[ngs, Hyk]sos, 6; they made 100 + X years."

[45]See below p. 14ff.

[46]H. E. Winlock, W. C. Hayes, *JEA* 26 (1940) 118, n. 2.

[47]This, it seems to me, is the most plausible restoration of IV, 4: see Gardiner, *Canon*, 16.

[48]There is no evidence at all that a summation occurred at the bottom of column vii (so von Beckerath, *Untersuchungen*, 23ff. On the possibility that the group of names from ix, 14 to x, 11 comprises a separate group (though perhaps not distinguished by the TC scribe, see D. B. Redford, *Orientalia* 39 (1970) 20ff; also below, p. 199ff.

Group distinguished: Manetho's 15th Dynasty.

14. *Summation*(?):[49] x(?), 30(?), [*dmḏ*] *nsyw* [....], "[Total of] kings of [....]."

Group distinguished: uncertain.

15. *Summation*: xi, 15, [*dmḏ*] *nsyw* 5[50] [....], "[Total] of kings, 5 [....]."

Group distinguished: a group of Theban(?) kings, contemporary with the Hyksos.[51]

16. *Heading*: fragment 4,[52] *nsyw* (red) [....], "Kings of [....]."

Group distinguished: uncertain.

Compared with the later "Manethonian" divisions of the king-list tradition, the groupings of TC may be listed as follows:

TC	*Manetho*
Great Ennead	"Gods"
Lesser Ennead	"Demigods"
Divine spirits	"Heroes"
[The House of] Menes	Dyn. 1-5
[The kings of *Ḏdi-swwt*]	Dyn. 6-8
The kings of [Herakleopolis]	Dyn. 9-10
The kings of [Thebes]	Dyn. 11
The kings of Itj-towy	Dyn. 12
The kings who followed the [House] of Sehtepibre	Dyn. 13-14
The Hyksos	Dyn. 15
[?]	Dyn. 16(?)
[?]	Dyn. 17(?)

Two observations are in order. First, it seems reasonably certain, even though several key passages are lost in lacunae, that the principal criterion in dividing up the names was change of residence. Second, to all intents and purposes the tradition of number and sequence of Middle Kingdom dynasties reflected in Manetho, is present in the same form in TC a millennium earlier. The Manethonian divisions of the dynasties of the Old Kingdom and the First Intermediate Period, however, are not yet part of the tradition in Ramesside times, and are therefore a later development.

[49]Otherwise we should expect red.

[50]Von Beckerath (*Untersuchungen*, 25) argues that, through scribal error, a "10" has fallen out, and that the resultant "15" kings comprise x, 30 to xi, 14.

[51]Winlock (*Rise and Fall*, 104) assumed this to be the 16th Dynasty.

[52]Gardiner, *Canon*, pl. 9.

These attempts to subdivide the list[53] betray the presence of information available to the ancient scribe outside the bounds of the king-list tradition itself. The view reflected therein is, however pretentious the word might sound, an historical one. King had not succeeded king in endless and boring succession; but families and cities had risen and fallen. Occasionally additional, purely historical data is supplied by the scribe in the form of epitheta added to the name. For example, beside the entry for Huny (iii, 8) is the partly preserved phrase "[...] the builder and ... (*pꜣ ḳd sšm*) which Wildung has ingeniously reconstructed as a reference to the death of Imhotpe;[54] and Neferka (iv, 9) is qualified as "the child." In some cases, as noted above, a *Beinamen* is added after the cartouche (cf. vi, 6, 21, 22; vii, 14; ix, 28-30), while in others the parentage is given (iv, 15, 25; fragment 40).

The *Wsf*-entries

A hieroglyphic group, usually read *wsf*,[55] is sometimes found at the end of a notation of numerals. The first three examples, viz. in nos. 7, 8 and 10 above, appear in lines of summation, and are followed by a second *dmḏ*, "total," in which *wsf*-figure is included in the number. The primary use of *wsf*, however, was in a line giving the name and length of reign of an individual king, as four other occurrences demonstrate:

1. vi, 6, "King Sekhemkare A[menemhat Sonbef ... X] years, [X months, X days]; *wsf*: 6 years."
2. viii, 12, "King Awetibre [X years, X months, X days]; *wsf*: 18 days."
3. viii, 14, "King Nebsenre [X years], 5 [months], 20 days; *wsf*: [ ].
4. xi, 8, "King Seuserenre, 12 years; *wsf*: [...] ⸢days⸣."

The group is now almost universally understood as an indication of a gap or lacuna in the source from which the Turin scribe copied his text.[56] There are, however, difficulties with this view. If the group does mean "missing," or "lacuna," or the like, what in fact was missing? The numeral, which in all cases follows it immediately? If

[53]Cf. H. Ranke, *CdE* 6 (1931) 279ff.
[54]D. Wildung, *Imhotep und Amenhotep* (Munich and Berlin, 1977) 30ff; cf. Meyer, *Chronologie*, 115. In the New Kingdom the tradition of original invention of stone masonry attached itself to Djoser: cf. the epithet "he who inaugurated stone(work)": G. Jequier, *Deux pyramides du moyen empire* (Cairo, 1938) 14; S. Schott, *Bemerkungen zum ägyptischen Pyramidenkulte* (Cairo, 1950) 246, n. 313.
[55]*Ḏfꜣ* by H. Goedicke, in *JEA* 42 (1956) 51.
[56]Helck, *Manetho*, 14; Goedicke, *JEA* 42, 52; von Beckerath, *Untersuchungen*, 33; W. C. Hayes, in *CAH* I^2 (1961) ch. 6, 12.

so, how did the scribe know the precise number which was missing? Is it the name of the king, which would have followed in the succeeding line, that is missing?[57] If so, is it not a surprising coincidence that in all seven cases it was the name that was broken away in the *Vorlage*, never the length of reign? In fact in the entire papyrus there is no formula to cover precisely such an instance, viz. that of a king's name whose length of reign was obscured by a lacuna! Clearly the meaning of this hieroglyphic group in the Turin scribe's usage, and even its reading, deserves a closer look.

Example 10 under "Headings and Summations" notes seven years designated by this hieroglyphic group. If this were a resumption in the summation line of an instance entered after the notation for one of the six kings of the dynasty, it could only be postulated in the first two lines, the last four being complete and showing no case of the formula. But scholars are unanimous in following Winlock's explanation of the seven years as the anarchic period between Se^{c}ankhkare and Amenemhet I, i.e. the end of the dynasty during which Nebtowire Montuhotpe III ruled.[58] The latters's name is not found in the list; but his brief reign, on this hypothesis, is duly entered as seven years. It is not a case of a scribe apprising us of a lacuna in the text he was copying: the memory of the last Montuhotpe of the dynasty had been anathematized and his name suppressed. In all probability the term read *wsf* is to be construed as a technical expression for "suppressed," or "(intentionally) omitted,"[59] and inspite of some scholars' rejection of the idea, may even have denoted to contemporaries a "kingless" (literally "vacant, unoccupied") period.[60] This explanation will, I think satisfy all examples in TC, but whether the word is to be read *wsf* is unclear. *Wsf* means "to be idle,"[61] and in business memoranda means "off the job (of a workman)."[62] Conceivably we could have a derived noun *wsf*, "(state of) being off the job," i.e. a period with no king. But a base *ḏfꜣ* is

[57]So von Beckerath, *Untersuchungen*, 33.
[58]*Idem*, *ZÄS* 92 (1965) 8 (with references).
[59]So *idem*, *ZÄS* 84 (1959), 84; *idem*, *JNES* 21, 145.
[60]See L. Borchardt. *Die Annalen und die zeitliche Festlegung d. alten Reiches* (Berlin, 1917) 44, n. 1; Sir A. H. Gardiner, *Egypt of the Pharaohs* (Oxford, 1961) 124, 442. The ancient Near Eastern cultures *could* and *did* conceive of "kingless periods": cf. the ἀβασιλευτα ἐτη of Ptolemy (F. Schmidke, *Der Aufbau der babylonischen Chronologie* [*Orbis Antiques* 7; Munster, 1952] 41).
[61]*Wb*. I, 357:2-11; W. Helck, *Altägyptische Aktenkunde des 3. und 2. Jahrtausends v. Chr.* (Munich and Berlin, 1974) 98ff.
[62]Cf. Sir A. H. Gardiner, J. Černý, *Hieratic Ostraca* (Oxford, 1957) pl. 83-84; D. Valbelle, *BIFAO* 77 (1977) 132; D. Meeks, *Année lexicographique* II (Paris, 1981) 105.

also a possible reading of this group, and one might compare *ḏfy*, "to sink down out of sight," which is used in the the Litany of Re and in Amenemope as a term for annihilation.[63] A derivation from this latter root might come close to the nuance of "suppression" more closely than *wsf*.[64]

The Addition of *ʿnḫ wḏꜣ snb*

The benedictory formula is added only rarely to the cartouches contained in the TC. The complete list of preserved occurrences is as follows: 1. Thoth (i, 18), 2. Menes (ii, 10, 11), 3. Huny (iii, 8), 4. Amenemhet I (vi, 4), 5. Heribre (viii, 13), 6. Ia[ ]re (viii, 23). One might expect the formula to be used with the names of outstanding kings, and nos. 2 through 4 seem to meet such a requirement. But nos. 5 and 6 are nonentities, and even Thoth has no priority of place in the Ennead. The occurrences in columns i, ii, and iii seem consistently placed about 20 to 24 lines apart. If iv, 5 (Pepy II) and v, 4(?) were glossed by the formula, we should have reasonably consistent spacing through the first six columns. Could the formula originally have been attached only to those names heading columns in a *Vorlage* of narrower dimensions?

One naturally craves an explanation derived from the format of the present document; but the real reason may well be extraneous. Nos. 2 through 4 were the subject of narrative, and others may well have been also. Could the formula have clung to these names through the recollection of its constant use in literature?

Every indication is that TC is not a *de novo* composition, but was copied from some older MS. Evidence will be presented below[65] that the ancestral MS, either the immediate *Vorlage* or another, one or two removes from TC, was the product of the 19th Dynasty at least in the precise form TC reflects. But its ultimate sources were more ancient. Suffice it for the moment to point to the remarkable accuracy, when checked against contemporary monuments, with which the composition and length of rule of the 12th Dynasty is

[63]Cf. the Litany of Re, 153; Amenemope 9, 4.

[64]Why scholars have so emphatically rejected the idea that the Egyptians could conceive of an interregnum, I do not understand. Certainly Hatshepsut's Speos Artemidos inscription, as well as the historical pericope of the Great Harris papyrus, shows that anathematized rule, without divine sanction was imaginable in ancient Egypt, however undesirable: this is surely tantamount to the idea of a period without a (legitimate) king; cf. the present writer, *History and Chronology*, 188ff.

[65]Cf. chap. 5, p. 197ff.

transmitted in TC.[66] Moreover, from the 11th Dynasty on the division into dynasties TC displays remained unchanged, and had therefore early achieved canonicity. From the 12th Dynasty on it becomes *de rigueur* to define the length of a king's reign down to the number of months and days; before that point the practice is rare enough to be conspicuous. While columns vi through viii give the semblance of precision in recording, ix and x (with the exception of the Hyksos) strike one as the product of wild fantasy: few if any of these names are believable, in their present form. Working back from the 12th Dynasty, one has defended the record of TC for the 11th Dynasty,[67] but we have no means of telling what the sources were for the Herakleopolitan kings. Columns iii and iv are very fragmentary, but the sequence of names seems largely accurate when checked against the monuments. This statement must be qualified, however: there are more strange entries and omissions here than in the Middle Kingdom section, and one at once suspects inaccuracy and error resulting from inferior source material. One may mention the garbled names in iii, 2 and 7, the curious uniformity in lengths of reign in the early 4th Dynasty,[68] the acceptance in the tradition of the sons of Khufu filling out the 4th Dynasty,[69] and the omission of some 10 names at the end of the Old Kingdom.[70] Clearly the tradition was hard put to it to ascertain the identity, or even the number, of kings of the 3rd Dynasty; and the 4th seems already to be suffering from folkloristic distortion. The section which in Manetho became the 1st and 2nd Dynasties (viz. ii, 11 to iii, 5 [including Djoser]), differs in a number of respects from what follows. First, as Helck has shown,[71] a substantial number of the curious names here can be explained only by presupposing the misreading of a hieratic *Vorlage*; and it is a good guess that the ultimate source of this part of the papyrus lies in a hieratic original. Second, only here among the human kings prior to the Middle Kingdom (with the exception of v, 10-13) are reigns broken down into years, months and days. Third, only here among the human kings is a length of life added after the reign. Any theory which attempts to explain the

[66]Cf. W. J. Murnane, *Ancient Egyptian Coregencies* (Chicago, 1977) 26ff; Eaton-Krauss, *JSSEA* 12, 17ff.

[67]Hayes, in *CAH* I^2 (1962) ch. 6, 11f (with references).

[68]Huny 24, Sneferu 24, Khufu 23 + X(?). Could the figures here rest on rough generation estimates? There certainly are discrepancies between TC and contemporary mounuments at this point: cf. W. S. Smith, in *CAH* I^2 (1962) ch. 14, 9ff.

[69]See below, p. 25.

[70]Von Beckerath, *JNES* 21, 140ff.

[71]Helck, *Manetho*, 9ff.

evolution of the king-list tradition in Egypt will have to do justice to the varying degress of accuracy with which these sections of the tradition have been transmitted.

II
Cultic Assemblages of Deceased Kings
(Royal: Abydene Tradition)

The term "king-list" is often, misleadingly, applied to those groupings of royal names or images which occur in temple contexts.[72] While reasonably complete, and in chronological order, the purpose of these lists was not "historical," but rather cultic.

1. The Abydos List of Sety I[73]

This assemblage of names is found in the mortuary temple of Sety I at Abydos, on the west wall of the passage ("the Gallery of the Lists") leading from the 2nd Hypostyle Hall to the "Butcher's Hall." On the left stands Sety I in the blue crown and *šndyt*-kilt, censor in one hand, gesticulating with the other towards the scene on the right. Before him stands Prince Ramesses in side-lock, wearing a fine pleated skirt from which the stole of a lector ascends over his left shoulder. He is holding up an open papyrus to read from, and the accompanying column of text identifies the performance as "the 'Jubilant Summons' (*ḥknw*) by the hereditary prince and eldest legitimate king's son, whom he loves, Ramesses, justified." Six columns of text above his head gives the king's utterance: "spoken by King Menmare (Sety I): 'I bring the god to his food offering,

[72]Cf. Drioton, Vandier, *L'Egypte*[4], 159; in general H. R. Hall, *The Ancient History of the Near East*[11] (London, 1950), 11f; Gardiner, *Egypt of the Pharaohs*, 50. In the following discussion we have generally avoided groupings which depend entirely on the veneration of a family dyad (e.g. some of the repetitive scenes depicting Amenophis I and Ahmes Nofretari), or on the connexion of a specific king with a certain place (e.g. the juxtaposition of Sneferu and Amenemhet III at Sinai: Sir A. H. Gardiner, T. E. Peet, J. Černý, *The Inscriptions of Sinai*[2] [Oxford, 1952] pl. 47, nos. 124-5). Sequences of kings' names in private titles have also been avoided unless the arrangement shows an appreciation of chronological order.

[73]For bibliography see P-M VI, 25 (nos. 229-230 on plan, p. 22); Drioton, Vandier *L'Egypte*[4], 159; also A. Wiedemann, *Aegyptische Geschichte* (Gottha, 1884), 75f; Hall, *Ancient History*, 12; A. Scharff, in A. Moortgat, A. Scharff, *Aegypten und Vorderasien im Altertum* (Munich, 1950) 28; Gardiner, *Egypt of the Pharaohs*, 48ff; Simpson, *The Ancient Near East: A History*, 194; R. David, *Religious Ritual at Abydos*[2] (Warminster, 1982) 195ff.

(viz.) the bestowal of offerings for the kings of Upper and Lower Egypt. Hail to thee, Ptah-Sokar, South-of-His-Wall! Come that I may perform for thee the choice things that Horus performed for his father Osiris.'"

To the right of the royal pair are three registers of cartouches facing left, in columns, and across the top of the whole runs an explanatory caption: "the performance of the *ḥtp-di-nsw* to Ptah-Sokar-Osiris, Lord of the Secret Place who resides in the Mansion of Menmare (i.e. the Abydos Temple), even the bestowal of offerings on the kings of Upper and Lower Egypt, by the King of Upper and Lower Egypt, Lord of the Two Lands, Menmare, son of Re, Sety-Merenptah: a thousand of bread, a thousand of beer, etc." The uppermost and the middle registers are occupied by 76 kings' names in vertical cartouches, 38 to a register, and before each is the phrase *n nsw*, "to King ...." This phrase is thus the syntactic continuation of the formula "a thousand bread, etc." and the whole finds its completion in the columns of the third register (each lined up directly under the upper columns), which read "through the bestowal of" Sety I. The latter's prenomen, preceded by *nsw* and determined by seated king in white crown, alternates throughout the bottom register with the nomen preceded by *s³ Rᶜ*, and determined by king in red crown. The complete formula, then, which presumably Ramesses is reading from his papyrus, runs as follows: "a thousand of bread, a thousand of beer etc. to king so-and-so, through the bestowal of King ... (Sety I)."

The organization of the cartouches is straightforward and by and large accurate historically:[74] the top register begins at the left hand side with Menes, and the middle register ends on the far right with Menmare, i.e. Sety I, the reigning king. There are, however, omissions of whole blocks of names which are recorded in TC, and one significant addition of a group of kings absent from the Turin papyrus. After Pepy II a sequence of eighteen names intervenes which is not found in the Canon; while the eighteen Herakleopolitan kings and the first four kings of 11th Dynasty, faithfully copied in the Canon, are omitted at Abydos. Similarly all the names of the "Second Intermediate Period," beginning with Sobeknefrure and concluding with Kamose, have been ignored by the complier of the Abydos list: Ahmose follows Amenemhet IV directly. The other omissions, viz. of Hatshepsut and the "Amarna Pharaohs," are comprehensible on the basis of independent historical information.

[74]Scharff, *Aegypten und Vorderasien*, 28; Hall, *Ancient History*, 12.

The reasons for these aberrations are not always clear.[75] Most of the omissions being of kings who did not rule over the whole land, or who were for political reasons suppressed in tradition, one wonders whether we are dealing with a more or less conscious anathematization as an immediate factor in the creation of this particular sequence of names. On the other hand, while disfavour in the tradition may very well lurk somewhere in the background, the present assemblage may owe its shape to a mechanical cause, viz. the presence or absence of a royal name in the offering list tradition. Thus the strong cultic connection between the Memphite royal house of the Old Kingdom and the Abydos list is duly reflected in the orderly progression from Menes to the fifty-sixth name; even the later scions, to us ephemeral names only, are entered, since they, being in the legitimate line of the Memphite succession, were as much honoured in the offering ritual at Abydos as their predecessors. It was only with the disastrous wars and political divisions of the 9th and 10th Dynasties, and the consequent rupture in the life and traditions of Memphis and Abydos, that royal names ceased automatically to be entered in the lists.[76] A similar hiatus could reasonably be argued for 13th through 17th Dynasties.

On the other hand, there remains the very real possibility that the Abydos list's dimensions were dictated simply by *wall space*: the kings following the 12th Dynasty were ephemeral, by anyone's standard, and were therefore expendable.

2. The Abydos List of Ramesses II[77]

The scene in which this list was found (before its removal to the British Museum) occupied the west wall of chamber II, immediately east of the first octostyle hall, in the temple of Ramesses II at Abydos. Like the "list" of Sety I, described above, the format of which it copies, the Ramesses II exemplar shows the king officiating

[75]Gardiner, *Egypt of the Pharaohs*, 50.
[76]Whether the number "18" has any significance is hard to determine. Does Abydos reflect an anathematization of the Herakleopolitan regime (Manetho's 9th and 10th Dynasties), resulting in a compensatory insertion of 18 names from the end of the preceding Memphite rule? On the signifcance of the number "9" in the king-list tradition, see below, p. 235f. The omission of the Herakleopolitans and the early 11th Dynasty has been put down to the fact that they failed to rule all Egypt: von Beckerath, *JNES* 21, 141, 145. It should also be noted that for the period in question Abydos lay on the border between the two rival states.
[77]For bibliography see P-M VI, 35(27), to which add T. G. H. James, *Hieroglyphic Texts ... B.M.*, pt. 9 (London, 1970) pl. 8, p. 13f.

at an offering ritual on one side (the right), facing four deities, three seated gods and one standing goddess, on the other (the left). Between the royal celebrant and objects of his worship were placed twenty-six columns, divided by three horizontal lines into four registers, of which only three in part survive today. The three upper registers contained a total of 78 cartouches of king's names, duplicating exactly, with the addition of the two cartouches of Ramesses II at the end, the list of Sety I. The inclusion of *n nsw-bity*, "to the king of Upper and Lower Egypt" before each cartouche, indicates the presence originally of an offering formula identical to that in the earlier list. The bottom register completes the formula, as did Sety, with the recurring *m dd s³ Rᶜ-ms-sw Mry-imn* (alternating variant *nsw-bity Wsr-m³ᶜt-rᶜ Stp.n.Rᶜ*), "through the bestowal of the son of Re, Ramesses Maiamun."

III
Cultic Assemblages of Deceased Kings (Private: Memphite Tradition)

1. Saqqara "List" of the Chief Lector Tjuloy[78]

This grouping comprises 58 vertically arranged cartouches in two registers of 29 each, in a relief from a tomb chapel or funerary kiosk[79] of "the festival director of all the gods, construction manager of all the monuments of the king, the king's-scribe and chief lector-priest, Tjuloy, deceased." The owner is shown on the left of the scene, with his book-roll in hand, gesticulating *iwn-mwt.f* fashion towards the figure of Osiris who is standing on the far right. Between the two figures stands the "grid" of cartouches. Two columns of text, one at each extremity of the cartouche registers, identify the ceremony as "[the performance of the *ḥtp-di-nsw*[80] for the ki]ngs of Upper and

[78]CG 34516: P-M III², 192; J. Malek, *JSSEA* 12 (1982) 21, n. 1, 2; position of tomb unknown, but undoubtedly south of the Unas causeway. For Tjuloy himself, who flourished under Ramesses II, see H. Kees, *Das Priestertum im ägyptischen Staat* (Leiden, 1953) 110. There is a statue of him in Cairo (no. 1105), and he is also mentioned on a stela of his brother, the chief of builders Paser: James, *Hieroglyphic Texts ... B.M.*, pt. 9, pl. 24; at Khatana-Qantir he is called "king's-messenger [to foreign lands], he who fortells what is to come": L. Habachi, *ASAE* 52 (1954) 498, pl. 27.
[79]A. Mariette, *Revue archéologique* 10 (1864) 169.
[80]Or possibly *w³ḥ-ḫt*, "bestowal of offerings"; for Wildung's restoration, see his *Die Rolle*, 34.

Lower Egypt and for Osiris, through the agency of King Usermare Setepenre, son of Re, Ramesses Maiamun." The next column goes on to specify the private purpose of the act: "that they may allow the receipt of offerings which go forth from their presence daily, for the *ku* of ... Tjuloy." The cartouches are preceded by the word *nsw*, "king," determined by seated kings wearing alternately the white and red crowns; the determinatives to the word in the two columns at the extremities of the upper register are the white crown, of the lower the red.

Above the king-list is the fragmentary continuation of the "grid" with enough preserved to show that originally there were two rows of columns recording the forms of Osiris (and Sokar ?) in various cult centres. On the left the traces show that Tjuloy was again figured, above the representation of himself gesticulating to the ancestral cartouches, presumably addressing the multitude of divine names. The whole constituted an invocation offering to Osiris, (Sokar ?) and the royal ancestors; and the collocation of the groups is strongly reminiscent of the arrangement of the "Hall of Kings" in the Abydos temple of Sety.[81]

Tjuloy's relief is clearly modelled on the type of contemporary royal scene exemplified in the "lists" of Sety I and Ramesses II at Abydos; but its composition is irregular and somewhat erratic. Starting with Ramesses II, Tjuloy worked back to Ahmose, expeller of the Hyksos, omitting of course Hatshepsut and the Amarna pharaohs as was customary in the 19th and 20th Dynasties. At this point he inserted Nebhepetre Montuhotpe I of the 11th Dynasty. As will be suggested below (p. 35 and n. 126), this grouping was probably occasioned, not only by the fact that both Nebhepetre and Ahmose had accomplished a similar feat, viz. the union of the Two Lands, but also by the dominance of the first Montuhotpe in the *Theban* offering tradition. The two are juxtaposed in those "abbreviated lists" of Theban tradition which give the kings of the 18th and 19th Dynasties, and then one or two selected pharaohs from the millennium and a half of antecedent history (see below, p. 45ff).

[81]On the other side of the wall, which must have been an internal one, Tjuloy is shown facing right, adoring Re-Harakhty on a throne, while on the right (facing left) is "the king's-scribe, overseer of the harim of the king's-wife, Nakht." To the right of this scene is a hymn to Osiris. Tjuloy's title on the lintel above, "chief *sm*-priest of the dais on the south," suggests at least the first jubilee of Ramesses II as a *terminus post quem* for the tomb.

Tjuloy's list, in its final form, does not pretend to such brevity, but the contemporary practice, as reflected in Theban private lists, has influenced its composition. Having interpolated Nebhepetre at just this point, the scribe was obliged either to terminate his group after the fashion of the "abbreviated" variety of grouping, or run the risk of omitting the important 12th Dynasty. What he in fact did was to preclude such an omission by suspending his retrograde order and adopting from Nebhepetre to Sobekneferu the correct historical sequence. He then reverted to the retrograde order with which he had commenced. But the number of columns, 58, which had been allotted in the prior lay-out, were too few; already 22 had been used. Drastic cuts would have to be made if the list were to reach back to Menes. Cuts were made largely on the basis of whether a king was known by a contemporary mortuary cult and a place in the local Memphite *nis ḥknw*. Thus the ephemeral kings of the 6th Dynasty who had followed Pepy II were not represented in the local ancestral offering cult; and the entire 8th Dynasty (nos. 39 to 58 in the Abydos list, virtually one-quarter of the entire group) were omitted, as well as the obscure Userkare, Nebka and Semempses. Even with these cuts, however, five additional omissions would have had to be made in order to include Menes. Such tampering the scribe was apparently not prepared to tolerate, and the list ends with Merbiapa.

As an historical source Tjuloy's relief is decidedly less trustworthy than the Abydene groupings, or TC. The lack of forethought in laying out a grid with too little space, and the singular change of order and format at the beginning of what in Manetho was to be the 18th Dynasty, both suggest that expediency rather than independent historical information was responsible for the omissions. No weight at all, therefore, is to be placed on the fact that the list begins with the sixth king of the 1st Dynasty,[82] or that some names do not appear. What was uppermost in Tjuloy's mind was the desire to show himself, in respectful imitation of his sovereign, officiating at the offering to the deceased royal ancestors; and while it is not quite correct to imply that any royal ancestors would fill the requirements

[82]Edwards, in *CAH* I^2 (1965) ch. 11, 10f, 23; E. Naville, *RT* 24 (1902) 118; Ranke, *CdE* 6, 282, n. 3.

of this type of scene, absolute historical accuracy did not have priority.[83]

2. The Giza Drawing Board[84]

In 1904 in a Giza mastaba of 5th Dynasty date the fragments of a scribe's writing palette were unearthed. On one side approximately 51 vertical columns had been drawn in ink, each delineated with a single line, except the line between columns 1 and 2, and 9 and 10, which was triple. Two broader columns are to be seen at the extreme left end, marked off into panels. The first 9 columns had been left blank, but beginning in the 10th eleven separate texts had been written in the columns, each being repeated with no variation in 4 columns (except for the last text which is repeated in only 3). The first text is a list of six cartouches reading, from the top: Neferirkare, Sahure, Khafre, Djedefre, ⸢Tety⸣, and Bedjau. The remaining texts, which appear to be lists of deities (beginning with Sokar) and towns, suggest that the general context is that of a mortuary temple. One is tempted to see in the list the roster of deceased royal ancestors and gods worshipped in a particular temple, and the towns and estates belonging thereto.[85] As the board clearly dates to the 5th Dynasty, and since the name that heads the list is that of Neferirkare, one wonders whether it comes specifically from his mortuary establishment. The prominence of Sokar at the head of the list of gods presages the patronage this deity exercised over the rite of offering to the royal ancestors at Memphis.

[83]To maintain that the difference between Abydos and Tjuloy is that the latter is "less elaborate" (von Beckerath, *JNES* 21, 144) is not quite true; Tjuloy is more complex, and combines different formats, which make it, if anything, *more* elaborate than Abydos. Its composition may exhibit less care, but that is another matter. That Tjuloy's list is an excerpting of blocks of names, sloppily done, with omissons, from a papyrus in the TC tradition, but written in pages of 16 lines each (cf. Malek, *JSSEA* 12, 21, n. 1, 2), is most ingenious, but does not inspire confidence. One is left to wonder what sort of lector-priest Tjuloy was, if he could not copy a king-list correctly, regardless of whether he was able to interpret the names. The point that must be stressed is that we are dealing here with the offering list in the Theban tradition, not a king-list; and entries or omissions depend on whether the name occurs in the ancestral offering cult of the region.

[84]Cairo 37734: G. A. Reisner, *ZÄS* 48 (1910) 113ff; further bibliography in P-M III^2, 52.

[85]The four-fold repetition of each column is puzzling. In the light of the common cultic practice of saying a spell four times, could our text have been intended for recitation?

3. The Wady Hammamat "List"[86]

In the Wady Hammamat, near a stela dated to year 4(?) of a Sobekhotpe of the 13th Dynasty, a crude graffito of a private individual incorporates a row of five, vertically arranged cartouches, preceded by "king of Upper and Lower Egypt, given life for ever." The five kings thus honoured are Khufu, Redjedef, Khafre, Hordjedef and Bauefre. Though in actual fact the last two were only princes and had never reigned, this late Middle Kingdom text attests the rising interest in the 4th Dynasty which characterizes the 12th Dynasty (see further below), and which blew up the personalities of "Khufu and his sons" to heroic proportions, ultimately inflating (in TC and Manetho) the number of kings in the 4th Dynasty.[87]

4. The Elephantine "List"[88]

On a large rock to the northwest of the museum building on Elephantine island occur the names and titles of 5 kings: Unas, Pepy I, Pepy II, Wahankh Antef and Amenemhet I. With the exception of Pepy I, each king is represented by the motif of the "universal presence," viz. cartouche and sundry appelative adjuncts enclosed with *pt* and *tꜣ* signs, vertically separated by *wꜣs* pillars. That the individual units were added at different times was argued on stylistic grounds by Petrie, though possibly the Old Kingdom entries belong to a single occasion.

5. The Abusir "List"[89]

From the village of Abusir, presumably from a private tomb in the neighbourhood, came this fragment of relief, now in the Berlin Museum. A row of at least 5 seated kings are shown facing left, each with an identifying cartouche before his face, with *nsw*, "king." The

[86]E. Drioton, *BSFE* 16 (1954) 41ff; cf. also C. M. Zivie, *Giza au deuxième millénaire* (Cairo, 1976) 34f.
[87]To insist, simply on the basis of the cartouches that Hordjedef and Bauefre must have reigned, however briefly (so Drioton, Vandier, *L'Egypte*[4], *Supplement*, 641f), is to introduce the kind of mechanical reasoning all too common in Egyptology. Suffice it to say that there is not the slightest evidence from contemporary sources for such a contention; cf. N. Kanawati, *The Egyptian Administration in the Old Kingdom* (Warminster, 1977) 76.
[88]W. M. F. Petrie, *A Season in Egypt* (London, 1888) pl. 12 (nos. 308-12); P-M V, 226.
[89]*LD* II, 152d; *Aegyptische Inschriften aus den Staatlichen Museen zu Berlin* II (Berlin, 1924) 201 (1116).

first cartouche is larger than the rest, and positioned more in front of the king, which suggests that he was the first in the row. This first cartouche is hacked, but the next three can be read as *Ḏd.f-rꜥ*, *Mn-kꜣw-rꜥ*, and *Ḥr-*[*ḏd.f*]. The fifth and last preserved cartouche shows the sun-disc at the top, but *nfr* and *kꜣ* which some have claimed to see beneath it, are very doubtful. Since those of the group which can be identified are kings of the 4th Dynasty, it seems most likely that the first cartouche should be restored either Khufu or Khafre, and the last Bauefre (as in the Wady Hammamat graffito [above]). Whether there were additional rows of kings in the pristine relief, one hesitates to say; at any rate, the context is undoubtedly that of an offering performed by the tomb owner, and is clearly Ramesside in date.

6. List of Kings and Illustrious Ancestors[90]

Two blocks from a private tomb at Saqqara yield what may be a grouping of royal figures. Three registers are in evidence, in which all figures face right. The uppermost shows traces of 13 seated kings, each holding the crook and flail; but as the relief has clearly lost an undetermined amount on the right, the original total may have been significantly higher. The figures are crowded together — in all cases the toes slightly overlap the throne in front — so that there is no space for intervening columns of hieroglyphs. The cartouches must have been carved above the king's heads, and are now lost. It is impossible, therefore, even to hazard a guess as to the identity of the kings. The other two registers, and an intervening band of text, commemorates a selection, by no means complete or in chronological order, of illustrious viziers, lectors, high-priests of Re and Ptah, to name but some. A number can be identified, and some seem to have been "literary" figures. One wonders, then, whether the unifying theme of the piece is the desire to revere "wisemen of the past." If this is the case a number of kings come to mind (e.g. Atothis, Sneferu, Djoser, Amenemhet I, etc.), but chronology or historical sequence would play no role.

[90]P-M III^{2}, 571f; W. K. Simpson, *The Literature of Ancient Egypt* (New Haven, 1973) pl. 6; H. G. Fischer, *Varia* (*MMA Egyptian Studies* I; New York, 1976) fig. 3 (facing p. 63).

7. The "List" from the Tomb of Mahu[91]

A fragment of limestone relief from the tomb of Mahu at Saqqara shows a line of kings facing right towards a figure of Re-Harakhte and a human form wearing a double crown, who may be Atum. A third figure is evidenced only by the presence of his ankh. Each king is kneeling, holding a crook in his lowered right hand, while the left is raised in adoration. The headdress is the *nms*, and a heart pendant hangs on each chest. Cartouches in front of the face identify the figures. While only three kings are completely preserved, the edge of the cartouche of a fourth proves that we have little reason for saying how many kings were originally depicted. The first three are, however, identified as Djeser-nub(?), Tety and Userkaf. If the Tety named is identified with the (Djoser)-Tety who appears in some "lists" among the 3rd Dynasty kings,[92] then the three named are those who have their pyramids in close proximity to each other at Saqqara; and this may well supply us with the *raison d'être* of the list. They are those kings whose cult seats are in North Saqqara.

Summary

It is clear from the collocation of the 18th Dynasty names with Nebhepetre, in the Tjuloy "list" that the Ramesside age had witnessed the incursion of a Theban tradition into the Memphite region. Nevertheless, as the Abusir and Mahu "lists" make plain, a local tradition remained strong; and this grouped kings according to geographic clustering. A "Giza" and a "North Saqqara" group can be distinguished, and this practice will have to be taken into account when the later division of the king-list into dynasties is investigated.

IV
Cultic Assemblages of Deceased Kings
(Royal: Theban Tradition)

1. The Sequence of 11th Dynasty Kings at Tod[93]

The French excavations at Tod in 1935-36 produced two blocks *inter alia*, apparently the jambs of a gate which belonged originally to

[91]P-M III^2, 556.

[92]TC iii, 6; Abydos i, 17; Saqqara i, 13; cf. also below.

[93]J. Vandier, *BIFAO* 36 (1936) 101ff, with plate; L. Habachi, *MDAIK* 19 (1963) 46, fig. 22; W. Barta, *Das Selbstzeugnis eines altägyptischen Künstlers* (Berlin, 1970) 23ff.

a shrine of the time of Montuhotpe I.[94] On the right a king in kilt and double crown offers jars to a hawk-headed deity who must be Montu. The identification of the king is lost, but most scholars now agree that it is Nebhepetre Montuhotpe. Behind him, on the left, is Hathor in the horned-disc headdress, and behind her in turn a row of 3 kings, about half the height of the figure of Montuhotpe. Each is striding to the right and profers a conical loaf. The costume and mode of identification of the trio is identical: each wears a *nms*-headcloth and a *šndyt*-kilt, and are identified by a Horus-name in *serekh* and a cartouche above their heads. The scene is bordered by the familiar device of a *pt*-sign, supported on both sides by elongated *w*^{3}*s*-sceptres.

Two decades of scholarly discussion have established beyond question that the three kings are the three predecessors of Nebhepetre Montuhotpe I, [Nakht-nebtepnefer] Antef III, ⸢Wahankh⸣ Antef II, and Seher-towy Antef I. Their function differs from that of the other groups examined heretofore, in that they are not here the objects of worship or the recipients of offerings, but the co-celebrants of the offering ritual along with their illustrious descendent. It is not without significance that the line is extended back only to Antef I: it was apparently this member of the family that was formally construed by his immediate family as having begun the rebellion against Herakleopolis by arrogating unto himself a royal titulary. But the clan to which he belonged, as a family of nomarchs, extended back beyond his time, and the founder of the house is apparently named in TC.[95] But Montuhotpe I had but lately come into the kingship over a re-united country, and his own legitimacy as king needed to be stressed.

2. The List of Middle Kingdom Kings on an Amulet[96]

On a plaque, probably of Second Intermediate Period date, occur the names of the 12th Dynasty kings from Amenemhet I to Amenemhet III inclusive. The plaque is divided into six squares, and the kings are identified by their prenomina.

[94] D. Arnold, *MDAIK* 31 (1975) 177, abb. 1, 178, abb. 2 (2116); with Arnold's further conclusions about the reason for the relief's presence (p. 178f) I cannot agree, as will appear below.

[95] TC clearly added a name before that of Seher-towy Antef I (v, 12), presumably that of Monuthotpe the Elder.

[96] W. M. F. Petrie, *Historical Scarabs: A Series of Drawings from the Principal Collections* (London, 1889) 9-10; for further literature and discussion, see Murnane, *Ancient Egyptian Coregencies*, 221.

3. List of Middle Kingdom Kings from the Third Pylon, Karnak[97]

One of the buildings standing before the Amun temple and demolished by Amenophis III to make room for his third pylon, displayed an offering list of ancestral kings. Three names are preserved, viz. Nebhepetre, Seᶜankhkare, and the "god's-father" Senwosret. The text therefore seems to have incorporated Manetho's 11th Dynasty, and the name of the father of Amenemhet I,[98] which suggests that the inspiration for drawing up the list came from the 12th Dynasty. How many names from the "House of Sehtepibre" were included is not known; but as the style of the block points to Amenophis I (who clearly recopied an older text),[99] the entire dynasty may have been present.[100]

4. The Karnak List of Thutmose III[101] (see Chart)

The tiny chamber in which this "list" was inscribed stood, until it was taken in 1843 to the Louvre, in the south-western corner of the complex known as *Mn-ḫpr-rᶜ ³ḫ-mnw*, the festival hall erected by Thutmose III east of the main temple at Karnak. Unlike the later "lists" at Abydos, the royal ancestors are here pictured in the form of seated statues with their identification in columns placed above their heads. The scene ranges over three walls of the room, as shown in the accompanying figure, and involves four registers of kings, facing on each side-wall representations of Thutmose III (one for the two upper, and one for the two lower registers). As might be expected, all four representations of Thutmose III show him "performing the *ḥtp-di-nsw* for the kings of Upper and Lower Egypt."[102] The number of statues in the registers on the left wall (A in the figure) and on the right (B in the figure) yield each from top to bottom 5-5-4-5, the reduction of the third row being necessitated by the increased size of

97H. Chevrier, *ASAE* 38 (1938) 601; L. Habachi, *ASAE* 55 (1958) 185 ff, pl. 4; Barta, *Selbstzeugnis*, 27f.
98Habachi, *ASAE* 55, 185ff, pl. 4; G. Posener, *Littérature et politique dans l'Egypte de la XIIᵉ dynastie* (Paris, 1956) 50f; W. C. Hayes, in *CAH* I^2 (1962) ch. 20, 34 and n. 7.
99Chevrier, *ASAE* 38, 601; for a summary of the Amenophis I material from Karnak, see G. Björkman, *Kings at Karnak* (Uppsala, 1971) 58ff; F-J. Schmitz, *Amenophis I* (Hildesheim. 1978) 71ff.
100See further below, p. 171.
101For bibliography see P-M II^2, 112(342); Drioton, Vandier, *L'Egypte*^{4}, 159; Barguet, *Temple*, pl. 28, p. 167. n. 2; D. Wildung, *GM* 9 (1974), 42ff; *idem*, *MDAIK* 25 (1969) 214ff.
102*Urk*. IV, 608:5.

THE KARNAK CHAMBER OF ANCESTORS

	1	2	3	4	5	6	7	8	8	7	6	5	4	3	2	1
NSW-BITY		X				X	X				X				X	
NTR NFR	X	X	X	X	X	X		X	X	X		X	X	X		X
NB 3WT-IB		X														
NB IRT HT		X				X	X								X	
NB T3WY						X					X					
HR																
TURIN CANON										11/4	6/10 or 8/18	6/5 or 6/19		6/25	6/27	
DYNASTY	6	4	5 →	5 →	5	?	?	16	13?	16?	13	13	13?	13	13	13
NSW-BITY						X		X	X		X		X		X	
NTR NFR						X	X			X		X		X		X
NB 3WT-IB																
NB IRT HT					IRY-P^cT	X			X		X		X		X	
NB T3WY						X	X	X		X						
HR	X	X	X	X												
TURIN CANON										7/1			11/8	7/8	7/6	
DYNASTY	?	11 ←	11 ←	11 ←	11	6 →	6 →	6	13?	13	?	?	16?	13	13	?
NSW-BITY		X		X		X	X		X		X	X		X		
NTR NFR			X		X	X		X		X			X		X	
NB 3WT-IB																
NB IRT HT		X		X		X	X		X		X	X		X		
NB T3WY			X		X	X		X		X			X		X	
HR																
TURIN CANON									11/2			6/5 or 6/19	7/4		11/1-2?	
DYNASTY		12	12	?	?	12 →	12	11?	16?	?	?	13	13	16	16	
NSW-BITY		X		X		X					X	X		X	X	
NTR NFR	X		X		X	X	X	X	X	X		X	X	X	X	
NB 3WT-IB																
NB IRT HT	X		X	X	X	X	X	X	X	X	X	X		X	X	
NB T3WY		X				X	X	X	X	X		X	X	X	X	
HR																
TURIN CANON												11/9	11/5			
DYNASTY	12	17 ←	17	5 OR 15	16	11	8	?	?	?	?	16	16	?	?	

the offering pile: while the back wall shows 6 figures in each register, 3 facing right, and 3 left. Thus the list is bifurcated into two groups which are divided vertically down the middle of the back wall: 31 on the left (A-B) face left, and 31 on the right (C-D) face right. All the kings are shown wearing the *nms* and *šndyt*, and the bull's tail.

While the arrangement of the seated kings is not entirely without logic, the orderly progression along chronological lines which is evidenced in the Abydene lists, is conspicuously absent.[103] Even if the order were chronological, there would be enormous, and inexplicable, gaps, totally different from the intentional lacunae at Abydos; the Karnak group does not in fact give the impression of having aimed at completeness. The reason for this is not entirely clear and explanations vary. Wiedemann[104] and Lacau[105] suggest that the kings included were those who had reigned at Thebes, or at least left traces of their building activity in the temple. Von Beckerath[106] speaks of selection of kings who were known at Karnak. Maspero,[107] on the other hand, put forward a rather more specific hypothesis: the late French scholar maintained that the scene contained only those kings whose statues were present in the temple of Amun in the time of Thutmose III. Wildung[108] accepted and elaborated upon Maspero's thesis, suggesting that in his renovations Thutmose III had had to remove several score of royal statues which had been set up by his pre-18th Dynasty predecessors, and that these had passed, via an inventory of removed pieces, into the present list.

While the theory championed by Maspero and Wildung is attractive, the type of scene in which the reigning monarch offers to his deceased forebears is much too common in art and literary

[103]Cf. Meyer, *Chronologie*, 103: "völlig räthselhaft"; Simpson, *The Ancient Near East: a History*, 194.
[104]Wiedemann, *Geschichte*, 77f.
[105]P. Lacau, *BIFAO* 30 (1930) 885.
[106]Von Beckerath, *Untersuchungen*, 26f.
[107]G. Maspero, *ASAE* 2 (1901) 281; 3 (1902) 189; *idem*, *Etudes de mythologie* 7 (Paris, 1913) 263.
[108]Wildung, *Die Rolle*, 60ff; *idem*, *GM* 9, 46ff; cf. Arnold, *MDAIK* 31, 178f.

reference to arrest attention in this one case.[109] There is no need to invoke a general clean-up operation Thutmose III may have carried out at Karnak to explain this "list." The dedicatory text in the south corridor of the Akh-menu[110] has application both to the chamber of ancestors and to rooms VII through XII, which opened off said corridor and constituted store-rooms for the ancestral offering rites.[111] The chamber, however, does not open onto the corridor, but into the pillared hall. Just as hall III and corridor IA face the barque rooms XXXVI - XXXVIII directly across the pillared hall, and thereby constituted an access route for the barque processional, so the chamber of ancestors faced corridors XXXIX and XL across the same hall, and it was by this route that the procession of royal statues came.[112] The chamber was therefore the focal point of the processional, and simply provided the locus for the age-old rite of offering to the ancestors. This the dedication plainly says.[113] The four-fold royal command applies specifically to the decoration and purpose of the chamber: "to inscribe the names of the fathers [i.e. the cartouches], to set down their offering portions [scil. the offering list], to fashion their images in all their likenesses(?) [scil. the representations of the statues], and to offer to them great, divine oblations [scil. the rites the chamber was intended for]."

As for the specific royal names, other lists used in the rite of offering to the ancestors at Karnak make it plain that there was a constant awareness of all those kings whose names were connected with two types of event of importance to the Amun priesthood: 1. construction activity, or dedications for Amun at Thebes (*mnw*),[114] 2.

[109] See below, p. 45. The offering to the royal ancestors in a cultic context is an old rite: cf., from the Middle Kingdom, the passage in the hymns to Senwosret III, "How euphoric are [thy (i.e. the reigning king's)] fa[thers] who were aforetime, now that thou hast enlarged their offering portions!" Sethe, *Lesestücke*, 66:15-16; similar statements *apud* Ramesses II: *ZÄS* 96 (1969), pl. 5:7-8. Sporadic Old Kingdom references make it plain that such offerings were current during that period as part of the cult of deceased ancestors: cf. Palermo stone, *verso*, s.v. Neferirkare, year 9 or 10; P. Posener-Kriéger, J-L. de Cenival, *Hieratic Papyri in the British Museum* V Series *The Abusir Papyri* (London, 1968) pl. 4-5 (offerings to the royal statues). In general on the royal ancestors see H. Frankfort, *Kingship and the Gods* (Chicago, 1948) 89ff.
[110] *Urk.* IV, 606-7.
[111] P-M II^2, plan XIII, 2.
[112] P-M II^2, plan XII (see p. 123[432]).
[113] *Urk.* IV, 607:8-11; cf. H. H. Nelson, *JNES* 8 (1949) 314.
[114] S. Tawfik, *MDAIK* 27 (1971) 227ff.

coronation (presumably at Karnak).[115] Whether a list of such monarchs was kept, or whether their identity was ensured by oral tradition, I do not know. At any rate, at any given moment a list could be complied simply by consulting ancient offering lists[116] or standing inscriptions within the temple of Amun.

There is a certain order and logic in Thutmose III's treatment of his royal ancestors' memories. Though, as noted above, the order of kings is erratic, a broadly coherent scheme does emerge. In the A-B section the four rows are headed from top to bottom by Neferkare (Pepy II),[117] [Antef?], Amenemhet I and Senwosret I. The rationale in placing the last two at the head of their rows seems clear: Amenemhet I founded the dynasty, and Senwosret I built the *Ipt-swwt* temple. The identity of the king at the head of row 2 is in doubt; but reason would be sufficient if he were Seher-towy or Wahankh. Pepy II, the long-lived monarch, may have had much to do with Thebes, although we know of no special importance Thutmose III attached to this king's work. Again, in the titulary[118] with which each statue is glossed some pattern occasionally manifests itself. For example, the first statue in each row in the B section displays all four major titles (see Chart p. 30); in row 3 of A *nsw-bity nb irt-ẖt* alternate with *nṯr nfr nb t*^{3}*wy*, while in row 4 of A *nṯr nfr nb irt-ẖt* occurs in every other position. In the A-B section most of register 1 and the rear of 2 is devoted to selected kings of the 4th, 5th, and 6th Dynasties, most of 3 and the front of 4 to the 12th; while the remainder of 4 contains what in Manetho would become the 17th. Again, awareness of correct sequence is often in evidence. If we proceed in B, row 2, from left to right and then go to the head of A, row 2, we achieve a complete sequence for the 6th Dynasty: Tety, Pepy I, Merenre, Pepy II. A similar sequence might be possible for the 11th Dynasty, but we should have to read from the back to the front of A, row 2, then drop to B, row 4, first position (Nebhepetre). The 12th Dynasty also has some integrity in the list.

[115] Cf. Chester Beatty IX, *rt.* 8:1 (see below, p. 37f) where the standard list of New Kingdom kings is qualified as "those kings of Upper and Lower Egypt who made monuments for Amun-re, Lord of Karnak, and for Amun, Lord of Luxor, in Karnak." Cf. also *rt.* 12, 8ff, where the same list is followed by "and all the kings of Upper and Lower Egypt, that they may receive the white crown and elevate the red crown, on those heads they are fixed, and on whose brows they appear ...."

[116] Some connexion with the offering cult is implied by *Urk.* IV, 607:11-12.

[117] Unless this be an 18th Dynasty form of the 3rd Dynasty *Nb-k*^{3} (J. Černý, *MDAIK* 16 [1958] 25ff), with an intrusive *rꜥ*.

[118] The four major titles, viz. *nsw-bity*, *nṯr nfr*, *nb irt ẖt*, and *nb t*^{3}*wy*, are precisely what one would expect in statue texts. This militates in favour of imagining a hall of real statues in the round as the *Vorlage* of the present assemblage.

The sequence, as much as is preserved, is in order: Row 3 Amenemhet I, Amenemhet II, ?, ?, Amenemhet IV, Sobeknefrure. Senwosret I, removed to row 4 for the reasons given above, would fill out one position; but for the three kings between Amenemhet II and Amenemhet IV we have but two places. Nevertheless, the 6th, 11th and 12th Dynasties seem reasonably complete. In the light of the known proclivity of the kings of the 12th Dynasty to honour their forebears with statues, it may not be wide of the mark to imagine a part of the ambulatory in the Middle Kingdom temple devoted to *ex voto* statues of the 6th and 11th Dynasties, continued by those of the 12th, set up in chronological order.

The opposing sections, C-D, contains members of Manetho's 13th and 14th Dynasties exclusively. Thutmose's immediate ancestors, from Ahmose on, who do not figure here, were given much more prominent positions. For them Thutmose constructed two rows of shrines[119] running west-east along the southern and northern lateral walls of the peristyle court of the Amun temple, behind the sixth pylon, and included a naos shrine for his own statues among them. The whole installation is described as [120] "naos shrines of stone with doors of true cedar, so that the statues of [My Majesty] may proceed to it[121] together with the statues of my fathers, the kings of Lower Egypt." Thus the special place in tradition given to the kings from Ahmose on, which is strongly attested in the 19th Dynasty, was already the conscious intent of the third of the Thutmosids.

5. The Min-reliefs of the Ramesseum[122]

On the western face of the north wing of the second pylon at the Ramesseum two groups of statues of deceased royal ancestors are depicted in conjunction with the Min-festival of Ramesses II. The larger of the two scenes depicts 14 statuettes (c. 30-40cm in height,

[119] *Kry*, "naos shrine,": *Wb*. V, 107f, specifically a repository for a cult image: *AEO* I, 67* (*twt m ẖnw kry.f*); Amenemope ii, 18; iii, 3. It is often used of the sun-god's shrine: cf. A. H. Gardiner, *Late Egyptian Stories* (Brussels, 1932) 40:15; CT II, 113h; R. A. Caminos, *Literary Fragments in the Hieratic Script* (Oxford, 1956) 44; i.e. the cabin of the solar boat: P. Berlin 3050, V, 7, S. Sauneron, *BIFAO* 53 [1953] 69 and 87). See B. Menu, *RdE* 21 (1969) 193f.

[120] *Urk*. IV, 168f; Barguet, *Temple*, 124.

[121] Antecedent unclear.

[122] *LD* III, pl. 162-3; J. Champollion, *Monuments de l'Egypte et de la Nubie* II (Paris, 1845) pl. 149-50; H. Gauthier, *Les Fêtes du dieu Min* (Cairo, 1931) 61f, 204ff; Ranke, *CdE* 6, 283f; H. Jacobsohn, *Die dogmatische Stellung des Königs in der Theologie der alten Aegypter* (Glückstadt, 1939) 29ff; C. J. Bleeker, *Die Geburt eines Gottes* (Leiden, 1956) 69ff.

to judge by the size of the adjacent human figures), identically clad in *nms*-cloth and short kilt, with a long staff in one hand and an *ʿnḫ*-sign in the other. The images are carried on the shoulders of stolist priests, divided into two unequal registers of 5 and 9 persons respectively, the whole party being led by a gesturing chief lector-priest. Immediately to the right 2 birds are being released, and someone enjoins the 4 sons of Horus to hasten to the four points of the compass to announce that the king has been crowned.[123] Appropriately enough, the royal ancestors, through whom in part the king's legitimacy is derived, are witnesses at this re-affirmation of kingship. The number "14" was presumably chosen to make the ancestral line conform in size to the number of *ku*'s (personifications of the life-force) both the king and sun-god are supposed to have had.[124]

The order of the 14 kings (all identified by prenomen cartouches placed before them) is impeccable. The line begins with the first member of the bottom register, who is the reigning king, Ramesses II, and continues with Sety I, Ramesses I, Horemheb, Amenophis III, Thutmose IV, Amenophis II, Thutmose III, Thutmose II, (upper register) Thutmose I, Amenophis I, Ahmose, Montuhotpe I, and Menes. The gaps in what would be Manetho's 18th Dynasty are to be expected: the Amarna pharaohs[125] and Hatshepsut had been deprived of status and stricken from the king-list tradition. To fill out the number 14 two additional kings, Montuhotpe I from Manetho's 11th Dynasty, and Menes from Manetho's 1st Dynasty were selected, probably because both they and Ahmose had accomplished a like feat, viz. the union of the country after a period of political dissolution.[126]

A smaller group of kings is depicted on the same face of the pylon further to the right. Just beyond the scene of the fertility rite known

[123]See Frankfort, *Kingship and the Gods*, 189f. On the essential nature of the Min-festival as a harvest rite, see H. W. Fairman, in S. H. Hooke (ed.), *Myth, Ritual and Kingship* (Oxford, 1958) 85.

[124]Frankfort, *Kingship and the Gods*, 74f; Jacobsohn, *Die dogmatische Stellung*, 32.

[125]See the present writer in *JNES* 25 (1966) 123.

[126]*Idem*, *History and Chronology*, 38, n. 48. The ubiquity of Montuhotpe I in Theban tomb groupings may also be accounted for by that king's importance in the Theban necropolis, thanks to the presence there of his tomb. Of old the region was called *int Nb-ḥpt-rʿ*: cf. J. Černý, *A Community of Workmen at Thebes in the Ramesside Period* (Cairo, 1973) 94. To speak of Menes (and Montuhotpe) as "Symbolfigur," and to assume an awareness of two historical "phases" (Old and Middle Kingdoms) already in Ramesside times (cf. Ranke, *CdE* 6, 281f; Morenz, *ZÄS* 99, xii) is, I think, wrong-headed. Where in Ramesside times is there ever allusion to an historical phase of which Montuhotpe was the inaugurator or representative? Even TC does not accord him such an honour.

as the "Cutting of the Sheaf" (a harvest rite, appropriate to Min, god of fertility), a row of royal statues is shown, resting on the ground beside the "White Bull." Only 6 statues are now preserved, but the original number must have been 8 or 9.[127] Reading from the front of the line one can reconstruct the group as follows: [Ramesses II, Sety I], ⌜Ramesses I⌝, Horemheb, Amenophis III, Thutmose IV, Amenophis II, Thutmose III. Costume and accoutrements are the same as before, save that Thutmose III now wears the blue crown.

The texts are redolent of Ramesses II's kingship. In the first of the above vignettes the lector-priest in front of the upper line of kings enjoins his colleagues to release the birds to proclaim Horus's coronation: the kings in attendance, then, are witnesses to the act. At the cutting of the sheaf the lector intones, in part, to the god "mayest thou allow him (the king) to live. May he adore thee, and thou be pleased with him. For he is that unique one whose office and titulary thou didst proclaim for him." Again the royal ancestors are witnesses.

6. The Min-reliefs of Medinet Habu[128]

In the scenes depicting the celebration of the Min-festival on the north and east walls of the second court of Ramesses III's mortuary temple at Medinet Habu, two groups of royal ancestral statues are shown, in much the same context as in the corresponding Ramesseum reliefs. At the rite of releasing the birds, seven stolist priests in two registers carry statuettes of seven kings upon their shoulders, led on by a chief lector-priest. The 3 statuettes in the lower register are identified by cartouche as belonging to Ramesses III, Sethnakht (his father), and Sety II (from front to rear), while those in the upper register show, beginning at the front, Ramesses III, Sethnakht, Ramesses II and Merenptah. All wear *nms*-cloths and *šndyt*-aprons and carry stave and *ʿnḫ*-sign, except for Ramesses III who is shown both times in the blue crown. Above the lower register is a line of text identifying the group as "the statues of the kings of Upper and Lower Egypt who are before this august god Min-kamutef ...."[129] The text above the entire scene puts us in the same cultic context as the offering to the ancestors in Sety I's temple at

[127]If Ramesses II were figured twice (for nomen and prenomen)? The corresponding scene at Medinet Habu (see below) shows a row of 9 statues.
[128]H. H. Nelson, *Medinet Habu* IV *Festival Scenes of Ramesses III* (Chicago, 1940) pl. 203, 205, 207, 213. See also the literature cited above in n. 122.
[129]Gauthier, *Fêtes*, 204f.

Abydos: 'Elevation of Offerings'[130] at the laudatory invocation[131] for this god; similar performance for the living *ku* of the king and the kings of Upper and Lower Egypt."

Beyond, (i.e. to the right of) the scene showing the cutting of the sheaf, a row of 9 royal statues is shown standing on the ground, exactly as at the Ramesseum. They are accoutred exactly as they were before, with the same exception. From the front the following names are present: Ramesses III, Sethnakht, Sety II, Merenptah, Ramesses II, Sety I, Ramesses I, Horemheb, and Amenophis III.

The order of the first group, that of the 7, is in disarray, but the group of 9 does show the expected chronological order. The particular historical view Ramesses III took of the "Time of Troubles" which preceded his father's brief reign, has led him to suppress the names of Amenmesse, Siptah and Tawosret;[132] and Amenophis III begins the series presumably because, with the traditional omissions and the prior requirement of the number "9,"[133] his was the ninth position in retrograde order from the reigning king. Thus the historical sequence of New Kingdom monarchs had by no means been lost to memory, or otherwise distorted, by the time the 20th Dynasty appeared. The first group (of 7) does, on the other hand, attest a tradition that Ramesses III fostered boldly and never attempts to conceal, viz. that he enjoyed the direct inspiration of, and stood as the direct successor to, Ramesses II in the completion of that monarch's work.

7. The List of Kings in the Daily Liturgy for Amenophis I.[134]

The ceremony referred to in the "Gallery of the Lists" at Abydos (see above, II, 1) and at the Min-festival at Medinet Habu (above,

[130] *F³t ẖt*, *Wb*. I, 573:11.

[131] *Nis ḥknw*: the same recitation is performed by Prince Ramesses before the Abydos list of Sety I: see above, p. 18. For the expression see also below, n. 135.

[132] Cf. The similar suppression of these names on the sphinxes at Nebesheh: W. M. F. Petrie, *Nebesheh and Defenneh* (London, 1888) pl. 10(a-c).

[133] For "9" as a "desirable" number of kings in the ancestral family of the reigning monarch, see below, p. 235f.

[134] For the Chester Beatty MS, see A. H. Gardiner, *Hieratic Papyri in the British Museum* III Series *Chester Beatty Gift* I (London, 1935) 78ff; II, pl. 50ff; for the Cairo and Turin MSS, see the literature cited by Gardiner, *ibid.*, I, 79, n. 1, 2. See also Fairman, in *Myth, Ritual and Kingship*, 100ff.

II, 6), viz. "the laudatory invocation" (*nis ḥknw*),[135] presupposes an order of service used in the offering ritual wherein the recipients of the offerings are summoned. That this order of service was in the form of a written liturgy upon papyrus is proven in the case of the "Gallery of the Lists" by the figure of Prince Ramesses actually reading from a papyrus roll. As suggested earlier, we are presumably to construe the repetition of the offering formula, with a new king's name substituted each time; i.e. the accompanying king-list itself, as the substance of the text the young prince is reading. We are fortunate to have just such an order of service, complete with name list of ancestral offerings recipients, in the daily liturgy used in the mortuary cult of Amenophis I. All the exemplars of the text date from the Ramesside period.

The list of kings occurs twice, once in the spell for placing the lamp (*tkꜣ*) before the god's shrine,[136] and once in the recitation to accompany the "Elevation of offerings."[137] The first passage specifies that a lamp be given for three forms of Amun worshipped at Thebes, to Amaunet his consort, the god Montu of neighbouring Armant, to the Ennead, and even to the portable shrine; then follows "to the *ku* of King Usermare Setepenre (Ramesses II)" and the list of royal ancestors comprising 14 names.[138] The second passage is found in a recurrent refrain, sung by the lector: "Come, O servants! Elevate the offerings meant for the 'Presence!' Elevate offerings for ..." followed by the name of the recipient. The first recipients are Amun and Amunre, followed by Amunre-Kamutef, the Ennead of Karnak, the deceased Amenophis I, and, in the final repetition of the formula, Ramesses II and the same fourteen ancestors. Presumably the same list was invoked on the sixth day of the month also, at the

[135] *Nis*, literally "to call, summon," is especially common of summoning the deceased spirit in the form of his *bꜣ* to the offering: cf. *Wb.* II, 204:13-14; J. Leclant, *Enquêtes sur les sacerdoces et les sanctuaires égyptiens à l'epoque dite 'éthiopienne'* (Cairo, 1954) 8, n. 1; Elephantine stela 1080; Louvre A. 66: R. Anthes, in *Festschrift Berlin Museum* (Berlin, 1974) 42; for the "laudatory invocation" in the context of the temple cult, cf. *Dendera* VII, 144, 169, 188; VIII, 81, 115 etc. (chief lector-priest presiding); also *ẖrw ḥr nis ḥnwt n nbw ẖrt-nṯr*, "audibly enunciating the due (mortuary) services for the Lords of the Necropolis," Nauri, 16 (=Kitchen *RI* I, 48:10-11). *Ḥknw* is the term for "(royal) acclamation" used of the formal laudation of the king (Gauthier, *Fêtes* 92; J-C. Goyon, *Confirmation du pouvoir royal au nouvel an* [Cairo, 1972] 110, n. 242, and the literature there cited), or of the ancestral kings: cf. "offering thanks for gods and (former) kings; giving a great exultation by all the plebs": P. Lacau, H. Chevrier, *Une chapelle d'Hatshepsout à Karnak* (Cairo, 1979) 328. The *ḥknw* was intended to "bring the god to his food": Cairo 42214, c, 1.

[136] Chester Beatty IX, *rt.* 7, 11-8, 1.

[137] *Ibid.*, *rt.* 12, 8ff.

[138] For the reason for 14, see above, p. 35.

presentation of the bouquet of Amun.[139] We thus have a context which would provide a remarkably appropriate *Sitz im Leben* for both Abydos "lists" and the list in the Karnak "Chambre des ancêtres."

The list in the present liturgy recalls the sequence of names in the Ramesseum: Ramesses II, Sety I, Ramesses I, Horemheb, Amenophis III, Thutmose IV, Amenophis II, Thutmose III.[140] Thutmose II, Thutmose I, Amenophis I, Ahmose, Kamose, Senwosret I, Montuhotpe I. Unlike the Ramesseum, the liturgy names Senwosret I in place of Menes, and Kamose, the short-lived brother of Ahmose, has been added. That Senwosret I should find a place in such a list, although he was not the founder of a house, is not surprising: of all Middle Kingdom kings he contributed most to the building and decoration of the temple of Amun, and was ever after remembered for it.[141] The inclusion of Kamose foreshadows what will become apparent later, namely, that in Ramesside times the "family" of New Kingdom ancestors was often traced back beyond Ahmose into what the later tradition rather confusingly combined into a 17th Dynasty.

8. The Turin Litany[142]

An exemplar of the text of the *nis ḥknw*, probably dating to the reign of Ramesses II, is contained in a fragmentary papyrus in Turin. Inserted into a list of invocations to the gods, in which the preserved portions mention forms of Osiris, Horus and Anubis, is a list of kings, princes and princesses. The sequence is as follows: Thutmose II, Thutmose I, Amenophis I, Ahmose, Kheperkare Senwosret I, Ahmes Nofretari, Tiy, Nofretari, and four daughters of Ramesses II. Presumably, on a page not preserved, the official list of the seven kings from Thutmose III to Ramesses II was given. The whole well reflects, as does the offering liturgy of Amenophis I (above), and the later Ptolemaic abbreviated texts (see below, sec. X), the practice of offering to the royal ancestors current in state temples from the 18th Dynasty. Variations in lists of queens and offspring were undoubtedly related to which particular temple and town the specific order of service was drawn up for.

[139]Gardiner, *Hieratic Papyri* I, 97; cf. G. R. Hughes, *MDIAK* 16 (1958) 159.
[140]Omitted by mistake in 7, 12.
[141]See especially P. Barguet, *BIFAO* 52 (1952) 152ff; *idem*, *Temple*, 153ff; Wildung, *MDAIK* 25, 212ff.
[142]W. Pleyte, R. Rossi, *Papyrus de Turin* (Leiden, 1869) pl. 12.

V
Lists of Royal Names in Cartouches (Private: Theban Tradition)

1. The List of Cairo Ostracon 25.646[143]

A Theban ostracon, dated palaeographically to the second half of the 19th Dynasty, contains a list of kings without introduction or any other explicative statement. The list on the *recto* is as follows: Usermare Setepenre, Neb[pehty]re, Djeserkare, ᶜOkheperkare, ᶜOkheperenre, Menkheper[re], ᶜOkheprure, Menkheprure, Nebmare, Djeserkheprure Setepenre, Menpehtetre, Menmare. Thus the sequence incorporates the expected 19th Dynasty tradition from Ahmose to Ramesses II (placed first, it seems, to indicate that he is the reigning king). The *verso* contains two cartouches, side by side, the prenomen of Horemheb and Montuhotpe I. The inclusion of the latter is, as we have seen, entirely in keeping with the practice of the 19th Dynasty.

Sauneron suggested that the purpose of the ostracon was basically didactic, the text being composed by or for a student scribe.[144] In view of the probable provenience of the object in the Theban necropolis, it is more likely that we have here a scribe's copy intended to guide the artist or sculptor in labelling the royal figures in the type of private scene (see below) in which the tomb owner worships the royal ancestors.

2. The Row of Cartouches in Horemheb's Tomb[145]

Thutmose III, in *nms* crowned by *atef* and holding the crook and flail in obvious impersonation of Osiris, sits facing left in a kiosk with offering table. Above him three columns of text read "Osiris Khentiamentiu, the Great God, Lord of Abydos." These are continued to the left by four columns of text facing in the opposite direction and reading "may he give all life, permanence and dominion, all health and all happiness to the *ku* of King Menkheperre given life like Re every day." The disposition of these

[143]J. Černý, *Ostraca hiératiques*, (*CCG*; Cairo, 1930-35) pl. 64, p. 48; S. Sauneron, *CdE* 26 (1951) 46ff; further discussion and bibliography in A. K. Phillips, *Orientalia* 46 (1977) 116ff.

[144]Sauneron, *CdE* 26, 47.

[145]P-M I^2, 155(11); Murnane, *Ancient Egyptian Coregencies*, 208; C. Seeber, *Untersuchungen zur Darstellungen des Totengerichts im alten Aegypten* (Berlin, 1976) 133.

texts might suggest that the seated figure is Osiris; but the kiosk, offering table and costume suggest at least an amalgam of the king and god, and the role of each in a single representation.[146]

Before the kiosk are three registers: in the uppermost are 4 upright cartouches, facing left (Thutmose III, Amenophis II, Thutmose IV, and Amenophis III, reading outwards); in the middle the 4 Children of Horus, and below 3 seated gods before an offering table and labelled "the Great Ennead which is in the Necropolis."

All these are witnesses of the scene being enacted on the left. Thoth on the left with palette, and Maᶜat on the right stand watching a kneeling Horus adjust a balance in which the heart is being weighed against the feather. Seventeen columns of text above the scene constitute an adoration (*rdit iꜣw*) of Osiris Khentiamentiu (with proskynesis), at the outset of which Horemheb has occasion to mention his service for Amenophis III, "his son" Thutmose IV, and "his son" Amenophis II (prenomen with nomen). He then proceeds with an apocopated protestation that he is guiltless, which begins "I never contravened anything they said ... (i.e. the aforementioned kings)."

Thus the historical fact of his impeccable service to three monarchs is pressed into service in making his case for his acquittal before the tribunal; and the three kings in question are present as witnesses and as magistrates through their cartouches which, spatially, enjoy equal position with the Ennead and the Children of Horus. But the line of kings (in proper chronological order, it should be mentioned) is pushed back one generation earlier by the inclusion of Thutmose III, under whom Horemheb had never served. Moreover he is given an enhanced position over the other three. This might possibly be an early example of the image of Thutmose III transformed into a sort of dynastic ancestor, which his memory sometimes enjoyed from the end of the 18th Dynasty onwards. On the other hand it is just possible that he is mentioned simply because Horemheb had been born during his reign.[147]

[146]On the king represented as Osiris, see the present author, *A Study of the Biblical Joseph Story* (Leiden, 1970) 222ff; cf. in general, A. Radwan, *Die Darstellungen des regierenden Königs und seiner Familienangehöngen in den Provatgräbern der 18. Dyn.*, Berlin and Munich, 1969.

[147]See B. M. Bryan, *The Reign of Tuthmosis IV* (PhD dissertation, Yale University, 1980), 32f.

3. The Libation Vase of Nefer-ᶜabet[148]

This cultic object from Deir el-Medina arranges the double cartouche of Amenophis I, the single cartouche of Ahmes Nofretari and the single cartouche of Meryet-amun in a horizontal row all facing right. A column of text on the extreme right qualifies the group as "beloved of [Amun], Lord of Karnak, the great god," and beneath are the name and titles of Nefer-ᶜabet. The object belongs in the category of *ex votos* dedicated to Amenophis I and Ahmes Nofretari, expanded in the commemoration by one or two additional members of the family.[149]

4. The Medinet Habu Lintel[150]

A lintel from Medinet Habu displays the cartouches of Amenophis I, Ramesses II, and Thutmose IV. Of undoubted Ramesside date, the object reflects not only the customary veneration of Amenophis I, the great patron the the "Place of Truth," but also the importance of Thutmose IV in the veneration of the royal ancestors, an importance also indicated by other objects of the period.

5. Deir el Medina 50081[151]

A fragment of limestone with part of an offering text from Deir el-Medina displays successively the double cartouches of Amenophis I, followed by those of Ahmes Nofretari, and Sety I (Menmare). The piece is a reflection of the private veneration of the divine patrons of the necropolis, coupled with the name of the reigning king.

6. Theban Graffiti nos. 753-6[152]

A graffito from western Thebes, associated with a private name, lists four cartouches: Ramesses II, Merenptah, and Sety II (nomen and prenomen). Presumably the scribe responsible had served under all three.

[148]R. Moss, *JEA* 35 (1949) 134, fig. 1.

[149]See below, p. 52.

[150]JdE 59895: P-M II^2, 776.

[151]M. Tosi, A. Roccati, *Stele e altre epigrafi di Deir el Medina n. 50001 - n. 50262* (Turin, 1972) 297, 119f. Cf. no. 50090 (*ibid.*, 301), where Sety I and his vizier officiate before the same couple.

[152]W. Spiegelberg, *Aegyptische und andere Graffiti aus der thebanischen Nekropolis* (Heidelberg, 1921) 61.

7. Offering Table of Qenhirkhopshef, Scribe in the Place of Truth[153]

This rectangular cultic object, destined for food offerings and libations, is carved with a *ḥtp-di-nsw* formula incorporating some 34 cartouches in two rows which go completely around the perimeter. The inner row constitutes the rectangular border of the table, and begins on either side of the run-off spout with parallel formulae: on the right "an offering which the king gives (to) King User[ma]re Setepenre ...," and on the left "an offering which the king gives (to) King Ramesses Maiamun ...." The rest of the border contains 10 cartouches, all vertical, arranged around left and right sides of the bottom. Those on the right and bottom face in towards the table; those on the left side face out.[154] The sequence beginning on the right after User[ma]re Setepenre is as follows: Amenhotpe [I?], Thutmose III,[155] Thutmose II, Thutmose IV, Horemheb, Ramesses I and Sety I. The remaining three names are on the left, and from the top are Nebhepetre, Thutmose I and Amenophis III. On either side of the spout is a queen's cartouche, Ahmes Nofretari on the left, and Ahhotpe on the right. Outside the border is an outer row of 20 cartouches facing towards the owner whose figure appears at the lower right corner (when seen from above). In sequence these are: Usermare Setepenre, Ram[esses] Maiamun, Senakhtenre, Seqenenre, Wadj-kheperre, Nebhepetre, Ahmose, Ahhotpe, Ahmes Nofretari, ᶜOkheperkare (Thutmose I), Menkheperre (Thutmose III), ᶜOkheperenre (Thutmose II), Djeserkare (Amenophis I), ᶜOkheprure (Amenophis II), Nebmare (Amenophis III), Horemheb, Ramesses I and Menmare Sety-merneptah. The group thus comprises all the kings of 18th and 19th Dynasties, down to the reigning Ramesses II, with the expected omissions and the customary inclusion of a Middle Kingdom worthy to accompany Ahmose; but now the line of the 18th Dynasty has been traced back to its ostensible founder, Senakhtenre Taᶜo of the 17th Dynasty. Moreover two queens have been added. Ahhotpe presumably the first of the name and wife of Seqenenre Taᶜo II, and Ahmes Nofretari the wife of Ahmose. The order is somewhat erratic but was partly occasioned by the curious desire of the scribe who laid out the text (Qen himself perhaps) to list all the Thutmosids together in one sequence, and all the

[153]Now in Marseilles, no. 204; bibliography in P-M I^2, 743; also von Beckerath, *Untersuchungen*, 293(3).
[154]Unless otherwise noted, all are identified by prenomen.
[155]At this point a blank seems to have been left, perhaps for Thutmose I.

Amenophids in another.[156]

8. Offering Table of Paneb and His Son ᶜOpehty[157]

This offering table from Deir el-Medina invokes in its *ḥtp-di-nsw* formula Amun-rᶜ of *Ṯḥn-nfr* and Meret-seger. Several depictions of the latter, along with stylized offerings, adorn the top; on the "back" on the left Ahmes Nofretari, followed by ᶜOpehty, "deputy [ ] in the Place of Truth," offers to Meret-seger, while on the right Amenophis I, followed by Paneb "Foreman of the gang in the Place of Truth," offers to Amun-re. Above Ahmes Nofretari's head appears the cartouche of Ramesses II. On top of the object appear 11 royal names, 10 in cartouches, 5 to the left of the bisecting columns of the offering formula, and 5 to the right. The prenomen of Sety II is split by the text, *Wsr-ḫprw* being on the right, and *mry-Imn* on the left. The cartouches on the right are in three columns: 1. Nebhepetre, Kheperkare, 2. Thutmose III, Amenophis II(?),[158] 3. Thutmose IV. On the left again the arrangement is in three columns: 1. Amenophis III, Horemheb, 2. Ramesses I, Sety I, 3. Merneptah.

Thus there are 14 royal names alluded to here, a figure which ought to recall the number of kings at the Min-festival.[159] The inspiration, viz. the 14 *ku*s of the king, is probably the same in both cases. Of equal interest is the observation that the sequence is unbroken from Thutmose III to Sety II, under whom the object was undoubtedly carved, save for the expected omissions of the Amarna pharaohs. That Thutmose III should have been the point of departure recalls the prominence Thutmose III enjoyed, during the New Kingdom, as a dynastic forefather.[160] If one consideration was the placing of Thutmose III at the head of the list, another was the desire to revere Amenophis I and Ahmes Nofretari, a natural focus for the piety of a foreman of the gang. This left two positions open, if the number 14 were to be achieved, and these significantly were allotted to two "founding fathers," Montuhotpe I who had founded the earliest and major cult centre on the *west* of Thebes, and Senwosret I who held a similar distinction on the *east* side, having founded the Amun temple called *Ipt-swwt*.

[156]The reigning king in ancient Egypt was usually referred to by epithets or circumlocutions, deceased kings by their prenomena. It is interesting, therefore, to see evidence of the continued significance to the ancients of their kings' personal names.

[157]P-M I^2, 743f. I wish to thank the Griffith Institute and Miss Helen Murray for copies of Wilkinson's drawings of this piece.

[158]*ᶜ3-ḫpr-rᶜ*.

[159]Above, p. 35.

[160]See below, p. 52.

9. The List of Cartouches in Theban Tomb 306[161]

This tomb, belonging to one Irdjanen, a doorman in the estate of Amun, displays on the hither right hand wall of the transverse room a group of 14 cartouches divided into two rows. The group comprises the following: Ahmes Nofretari, Seqenenre Taᶜo, Amenophis I, Ahmose, ?, Queen Tamer[ ], [queen], Queen Nebt-towy, Senwosret I, Queen Ahmose, Kamose, Queen Sentsonbu, In[ ], [ ]. We thus have an uninterrupted sequence of kings from Seqenenre Taᶜo to Amenophis I, an assortment of queens from the same period, and, as in Paneb's offering table, Senwosret I and (probably after Ahmose) Nebhepetre. Once again the inspiration derives from the cult of the deified Amenophis I, and honours the two "founding fathers" of the Middle Kingdom. It is interesting to note that no Thutmosid kings are mentioned.

VI
Cultic Assemblages of Deceased Kings (Private: Theban Tradition)

The motif in art of offering to, or worshiping, the royal ancestors, made fashionable by New Kingdom royalty, appears not infrequently in private tombs, or on private stelae beginning in the 18th Dynasty, and becoming common in the 19th. (While showing the king in private tomb scenes was apparently an inspiration of the Middle Kingdom, royalty is seldom seen in private reliefs before the New Kingdom.)[162] Tombs of the 18th Dynasty, at least from the reign of Hatshepsut, take delight in publicizing their owners' relationship to the crown, and to that end the reigning king and his family are often shown.[163] But the worship of the royal ancestors by the deceased, employing the same scene types as were current in royal art, is conspicuous by its absence before Ramesside times.

The scene of offering to the royal ancestors is no different in concept or lay-out from the scene showing a son offering to his parents, or a tomb owner to his family and contemporaries. In the larger groupings the figures are seated and must be construed as

[161]P-M I^2, 384(5). I am grateful to Dr Lanny Bell, in whose concession this tomb lies, for allowing me to examine the scene, and to the University Museum for photographs of it.
[162]Cf. A. H. Gardiner, N. de G. Davies, *The Tomb of Antefoker* (London, 1929) pl. 16.
[163]Cf. Radwan, *Die Darstellungen des regierended Königs*.

statues as in the Chamber of Ancestors. Occasionally the figures are shown standing. There follows a tabulated list of such scenes from the Theban necropolis, both on stelae and in tombs.

1. B. M. Stela 347 (690).

Reference: *Hieroglyphic Texts ... B.M.* VI (London, 1922) pl. 30.

Owner: no name preserved.

Date: Late 18th Dynasty?

Scene: 4 kings, standing ("Osiride" with back pillars), in two pairs facing each other over offering table; all figures in *sd*-costume. Inner pair (left in white crown, right in double) identified by two sets of double cartouches as Amenophis I; rear figure on right (in red), identified by single cartouche as Nebhepetre; rear figure on left (in white) has no cartouche.

Text: none preserved.

2. Turin Stela 1455.

Reference: *Regio museo di Torino*: A. Rabretti, F. Rossi, V. Lanzzone, *Antichita egizie* (Turin, 1882) 121f; P-M I², 734.

Owner: Sen-nefer.

Date: Ramesside.

Scene: (above) 4 royal figures, seated, in two pairs, face in towards a central lotus flower; (left to right) Thutmose III, Thutmose I, Ahmes Nofretari and Amenophis I; (below) owner on left adoring, Amenophis II, Sapair (both seated on right).

Text: no designation of ceremony.

3. Theban Tomb 153.*[164]

Reference: P-M I², 262(1).

Owner: name lost.

Date: possibly Sety I.

Scene: (right back wall of transverse hall) 3 standing royal figures facing right; identified by cartouches as (right to left) [Ahmes] Nofretari, Amenophis I, Thutmose III; owner on right censing.

Text: no designation of ceremony.

4. Theban Tomb 19.*

Reference: M. Foucart, *Le tombeau d'Amonmos* (*MIFAO* 57; Cairo, 1935) pl. 11-12; P-M I², 33(4).

Owner: Amenmose, First Prophet of Amenhotpe of the Forecourt.

Date: Sety I.

Scene: owner in kilt and stole with censor before offering table, followed by smaller figure; to the right are two rows of seated royal figures, facing left (backed on to a sacred lake), the upper register

[164] Asterisk indicates author's collation of text.

with 6 kings and 2 queens, the lower with 6 kings. Identities: [ ] (queen), Ahmes Nofretari, Nebhepetre, Ahmose, Amenophis I, Thutmose I, Thutmose II, Thutmose III, (second row) Amenophis II, Thutmose IV, Amenophis III, Horemheb, Ramesses I, Sety I.

Text: no preserved offering text.

5. Deir el-Medina, Tomb 7.*

Reference: P-M I^2, 15-16(3).

Owner: Ramose, scribe in the Place of Truth.

Date: mid-Ramesses II; in office year 5 through 38 (J. Černý, *A Community of Workmen at Thebes in the Ramesside Period* [Cairo, 1973] 321ff); with vizier Paser on rear wall (W. Helck, *Zur Verwaltung des mittleren und neuen Reichs* [Leiden, 1958] 449, who omits the reference to this tomb).

Scene: left reveal of door, small top register (c. 40-50 cm. tall): owner facing in adores 4 seated royal figures facing out, viz. Amenophis I, Ahmes Nofretari, Horemheb, and Thutmose IV.

Text: no preserved offering text.

6. Deir el-Medina Stela 79.

Reference: B. Bruyère, *Fouilles de Deir el-Médineh (1935-40)* (*FIFAO* 20; Cairo, 1952) pl. 12, p. 68; P-M I^2, p. 696; A. K. Phillips, *Orientalia* 46 (1977) 120.

Owner: Ramose, scribe in the Place of Truth.

Date: same as 5.

Scene: (below) owner (right) adores cartouches of Ramesses II; (above) 3 seated kings, facing right: [Ramesses II(?)], Horemheb, and Sety I.

Text: no preserved offering text.

7. Deir el-Medina Stela 88.

Reference: Bruyère, *Fouilles de Deir el-Médineh*, pl. 36, p. 67.

Owner: Ramose, scribe in the Place of Truth.

Date: same as 5.

Scene: owner on right, kneeling, adores Hathor cow on left; above cow 3 cartouches: Ramesses II, Thutmose IV, Horemheb; before cow statuette and cartouche of Thutmose IV.

Text: *šsp bw nfr Ḥt-ḥr nbt nht rsyt m-drt sš m*^{3c} *R*^{c}*-msi*.

8. Theban Tomb 10.*

Reference: P-M I^2, 21(6).

Owner: Penbuy, servant in the Place of Truth.

Date: early to middle, reign of Ramesses II.

Scene: (left wall of inner shrine, middle register) Penbuy with censor followed by his brother, faces in towards 5 seated royal figures facing left: Amenophis I, [Ahmes Nofretari], [lost], Ramesses [I?], Horemheb.

Text: *wdn ẖt nbt nfrt w*^{c}*bt n k*^{3}*.tn*.

9. Theban Tomb 10.*

Reference: same as 8.

Owner: Kasa, servant in the Place of Truth.

Date: same as 8.

Scene: (right wall of inner shrine, middle register) Kasa followed by his son offer to 3 seated royal figures, facing right: Sety I, Ramesses I and Horemheb.

Text: *irt ḥtp-di-nsw ... n k³.tn r nbw r nḥḥ.*

10. Theban Tomb 51.*

Reference: N. de G. Davies, *Two Ramesside Tombs at Thebes* (New York, 1927) pl. 5; P-M I², 97(9).

Owner: Userhat, First Prophet of Thutmose I.

Date: Sety I.

Scene: owner, with relatives, offers to Thutmose I seated under a canopy in long gown and blue crown, with queen Ahmes behind him dressed as the West.

Text: none.

11. Theban Tomb 31.*

Reference: N. de G. Davies, *Seven Private Tombs at Qurneh* (London, 1948) pl. 15, 18; P-M I², 47.

Owner: Khonsu, First Prophet of Thutmose III.

Date: Ramesses II.

Scene: owner offers bouquet to Montuhotpe I; elsewhere Thutmose III, in blue crown and gown, is drawn in boat.

Text: none.

12. Theban Tomb 2.*

Reference: now Berlin Museum 1625 - *Aegyptische Inschriften* II (Berlin, 1924) 190ff; P-M I², 7(10).

Owner: Khaᶜ-bekhner, servant in the Place of Truth.

Date: Ramesses II.

Scene: owner, facing left, depicted twice behind two offering tables, in front of two rows of seated royal figures, facing right; top row: Amenophis I, Ahmes Nofretari, Seqenenre Taᶜo, Ahhotpe (sic), 9 queens, and Sapair; bottom row: Nebhepetre Montuhotpe, Ahmose, Sekhentenre (sic), Kamose, 5 princes, 4 queens.

Text: *wdn ḫt nbt nfrt wᶜbt* etc. ... *n k³.tn n nbw r nḥḥ.*

13. Theban Tomb C.7.

Reference: J. Champollion, *Notices descriptives* (Geneva, 1973) i, 517-18; P-M I², 459.

Owner: Hormose, chief keeper of the treasury in the king's mansion on the west of Thebes.

Date: Ramesses II.

Scene: 9 royal figures, facing right: Thutmose I, II, III, Amenophis II, Thutmose IV, Amenophis III, Horus.

Text: none preserved.

14. Theban Tomb 284.*
Reference: P-M I², 366(2-3).
Owner: Pahemneter, scribe of the offerings of all the gods.
Date: Ramesside.
Scene: deceased adores two rows of standing royal figures, facing left; upper row: 5 queens, a prince, a commoner, 6 princes, 3 princesses; lower row: 1 queen, 3 kings, 7 queens, 2 princes, 7 princesses. Kings and queens have cartouches, but in no case can they be read with certainty.
Text: none preserved.
15. Cairo stela 34029.
Reference: P. Lacau, *Stèles de la nouvel empire* I (*CCG*; Cairo, 1901), I, pl. 22.
Owner: Amenomope.
Date: Ramesside.
Scene: in the upper register Amenophis I, Ahmes Nofretari and Sat-Amun seated, facing right (king in blue crown, ladies in modius) towards Ahmes Sapair facing left across offering table.
Text: none.
16. British Museum stela 355 (297).
Reference: *Hieroglyphic Texts ... B.M.* VI, pl. 33.
Owner: Amenmen, servant.
Date: Ramesside.
Scene: upper register: owner adores Osirian triad; lower register: owner facing left adores Amenophis I, Ahmes Nofretari (black skin) and Satkamose.
Text: none.
17. Cairo stela 34037.
Reference: Lacau, *Stèles* I, pl. 24; P-M II², 800.
Owner: Smentawi, deputy priest.
Date: Ramesside.
Scene: upper register: left of offering table, facing right Ahmose seated in blue crown, embraced from behind by Ahmes Nofretari in feathers; right of offering table, facing left Amenophis I in *nms*, embraced from behind by Ahmes Nofretari; lower register: owner adoring.
Text: *rdit i³w* hymn; also *wdn ḫt nbt nfrt wʿbt* etc.
18. Dier el-Medina relief (Cario JdE 41469).
Reference: B. Bruyère, *Meretseger à Deir el-Médineh* (Cairo, 1929-30), fig. 109.
Owner: ?
Date: Ramesside.
Scene: owner, right, censing towards 4 standing figures, facing right: Snofru, Amenophis I, Ahmes Nofretari and Meret-seger.
Text: none.

19. Deir el-Medina stela 45a.
Reference: Bruyère, *Fouilles de Deir el-Médineh*, fig 164, p. 89f.
Owner: ?
Date: Ramesside.
Scene: the ends of two registers of seated royal figures are in evidence. Upper register: x + 1 (name gone), x + 2 Ahmes Nofretari, x + 3 Ahhotpe, x + 4 Si-Amun; lower register: 2 figures of queens, both cartouches gone.
Text: none preserved.

20. Theban Tomb 277.*
Reference: J. Vandier d'Abbadie, *Deux tombes ramessides à Gournet-Mourrai* (*MIFAO* 87; Cairo, 1934) pl. 6, 14; P-M I^2, 353ff.
Owner: Amenemone, god's-father of the Mansion of Amenophis III.
Date: Ramesside.
Scene: statues of Amenophis III and Tiy in procession; owner censes and libates to Montuhotpe I and Queen Neferys.
Text: none.

21. Cairo stela 34034.
Reference: Lacau, *Stèles*, pl. 23.
Owner: name lost.
Date: Ramesside.
Scene: upper register: owner on right, censing to Amun, Amenophis I and Ahmes Nofretari; lower register: owner, right, before offering table and Thutmose III seated, left.
Text: none.

22. Stela of Rom-Roy in the Rijksmuseum, Leiden.
Reference: P-M II^2, 807; G. Lefebvre. *Inscriptions concernants les grands prêtres d'Amon Romê-Roy et Amenhotep* (Paris, 1929) 42f.
Owner: Rom-Roy, high-priest of Amun.
Date: Sety II.
Scene: owner, with a keeper of the treasury of Amun and his wife, adores two rows of figures: upper, Osiris, Isis, Re-Harmakhis, Mut; lower, Amenophis I, Ahmes Nofretari, Ahhotpe.
Text: none.

23. Theban Tomb 359.*
Reference: P-M I^2, 422 [4]; to which add D. Wildung, *Imhotep und Amenhotep* (Munich and Berlin, 1977), 283f.
Owner: Anhur-kha^{c}u, foreman of the gang in the Place of Truth.
Date: Ramesses IV.
Scene: owner, with wife, censes before two rows of seated royal figures, facing right; upper row, Amenophis I, Ahmose, 3 queens, Si-Amun (sic), 4 queens, Sapair; lower row, [Ahmes Nofretari], Ramesses I, Montuhotpe I, Amenhotpe, Seqenenre, [ ], Ramesses IV, [ ], Thutmose I, Amenophis son of Hapu.

Text: *irt snṯr n nbw nḥḥ wrw nw ḏt.*

24. Theban Tomb 65.*

Reference: P-M I², 130[4].

Owner: Imiseba, chief of the altar, chief of the temple scribes of the temple of Amun.

Date: Ramesses IX.

Scene: king right, facing left and censing towards the barque of Amun behind which are 12 standing kings, arranged in registers of 1, 1, 5 and 5. Top register, Ramesses III (so Champollion, but our collation suggested a blank cartouche); second register, Ramesses IV; third register, Sety II, Thutmose I, Thutmose III, Amenophis II(?), Ramesses VI; bottom register, Ahmose, [Kam]ose, Se[qenen]re, [ ], [ ].

Text: *irt snṯr n Imn-rʿ nsw-nṯrw.*

25. Abydos stela of Mer-su-iotef.

Reference: A. Mariette, *Abydos* II (Paris, 1880) pl. 52(left); A. Radwan, *MDAIK* 31 (1975) 103, fig.7.

Owner: priest of Seth-nakht, Mer-su-iotef.

Date: Ramesses III.

Scene: upper register: Ramesses III (right), libates and offers incense to the Osirian triad, seated; lower register: the owner, right, adores across an offering table the seated Seth-nakht (in *nms*) and his wife Teye.

Text: no designation of ceremony.

26. Stela of Pahu and Neferkhau, now in the Brooklyn Museum (see pl. I).

Reference: P-M I², 799.

Owner: sculptor Pahu, carver Neferkhau.

Date: late Ramesside.

Scene: vignette: Pahu (right) adores the Abydene triad, followed Ahmes Nofretari, Ahmose (blue crown), and Amenophis I (*nms*), all kneeling.

Text: *ḥtp-di-nsw.*

The context of these scenes is that of offering or worship, the former predominating. The scene is usually constructed so as to show the owner making a food offering, reciting a *ḥtp-di-nsw*, or censing before the assembled kings. Sometimes he wears the leopard skin of the *Iwn-mwt.f* priest, occasionally a stole. The offering fomulae which are used, viz. *wdn ḫt nbt nfrt wʿbt*, and *irt snṯr*, are the same as are employed in the offerings to the gods; and the offering tables, censors, vessels and bouquets are indistinguishable from those used by the deities. In not a few examples gods and royal figures are shown being worshipped in the same scene in essentially the same way.[165] The royal ancestors are, of course, divine and on a par with the gods; both are "Lords of Eternity," and receive equal veneration at the festival which probably provides the *raison d'être* for most of the tomb scenes, viz. the Feast of the Valley.[166]

The reason for the inclusion of specific royal figures varies. In some cases the king-list tradition dictates order and inclusion; in others it is the composition of the family of Amenophis I. Paneb's list has four foci: the two "founding fathers" of Theban shrines, Amenophis I (the patron of the owner's mode and place of employment), and Thutmose III, the "father of the fathers" of Theban kings. In yet others the criterion is a more personal one, viz. the attachment of the owner by birth or employment to the cults of specific kings (see further below). When the king-list tradition is being served, the text rarely mentions the precursors of Ahmose: the latter was clearly stamped for all time as marking a new beginning by his expulsion of the Hyksos. When Amenophis I and his immediate family are uppermost in the owner's mind, the list will rarely mention the Thutmosids. In most cases selection of specific royal individuals was superceded in importance by the need to cater to *numerical* predilections. Groups numbering 3, 9, and 14 are very common, and suggest that the owners were using the triad, Ennead and the standard number of royal *ku*s as archetypes. It would be dangerous, then, to rely heavily upon the omission of a name from such lists in historical theorizing.

Lack of sequence and order becomes more noticeable in no. 24, *temp.* Ramesses IX. In this respect it partakes of the general selectivity and spottiness of other 20th Dynasty groupings,[167] as opposed to earlier ones, no. 23 also, though partly derived and inspired by no. 12, shows a startling "mix" of royal persons, with curious omissions and the inclusion of a commoner (Amenophis son of Hapu).

The connexion of these lists with the cult of the deified Amenophis I is clear. The vast majority of private individuals we

[165]Cf. nos. 7, 13, 18, 22; Tossi, Roccati, *Stele*, 50029 (Amenophis I with Ptah), 50031 (Amenophis I with Hathor, Osiris, and Re-Harakhte), 50032 (Amenophis I with Amun, Montu; Ahmes Nofretari with Ra^{c}<et>); 50033 (Amenophis I with Meretseger and the ithyphallic Amun).

[166]S. Schott, *Das schöne Fest vom Wüstentale*, (Wisebaden, 1953) 8ff and *passim*; cf. the epithet of "Amenophis of the Forecourt" in Amenmose's tomb: "who sees his father Amonrasonther, in his beautiful Feast of the Valley," M. Foucart, *MIFAO* 57 (1935) pl. 6. Note that in the Feast of the Valley, Amun is considered to be "the first (*tpy*) of the kings": Kitchen, *RI* II 636:5. 637:5.

[167]Cf. no. 23, the altar of Ramesses IX (below, p. 58f) and the Min-reliefs from Medinet Habu: above, p. 36f).

have listed, whose tombs display royal groupings, were employed in the necropolis, the "Place of Truth," as scribes, servants, foremen, or priests; and it was here that Amenophis I and Ahmes Nofretari were especially revered as patrons.[168] The influence of the Amenophis cult produced basically two types of assemblage: 1. a list in which, although Amenophis I and Ahmes Nofretari may be given prominence, the sequence of kings is orderly and includes (a) the beginning of Manetho's 18th Dynasty, and (b) the reigning king;[169] and 2. a list in which Amenophis I and Ahmes Nofretari and their immediate relatives take precedence, and any attempt at sequence or completeness seems to be ignored.[170]

All the royal and private assemblages we have passed in review in the preceding pages show the royal statues accoutred in a variety of crowns and costumes. There is a strong likelihood that what the sculptors are trying to represent in each case is a specific cult statue kept in a mortuary temple in the neighbourhood of the necropolis. This is demonstrable in the case of Amenophis I. Two distinct forms of Amenophis can be distinguished, one "of the town," shown wearing the *ibs* occasionally surmounted by *atef* and ram's horns,[171] the other "the Image of Amun" in blue crown.[172] Of course there were other cult forms of this king,[173] including "Amenophis of the Garden,"[174] "... of the Forecourt,"[175] "... who rows upon the deep,"[176] "... of Khenty,"[177] but these are less easy to identify iconographically.

[168]J. Černý, *BIFAO* 27 (1927) 159ff; *idem*, *REA* 2 (1930) 200ff; *idem*, *A Community of Workmen*, 29f; R. A. Caminos, *Late Egyptian Miscellanies* (London, 1954) 175; A. J. Sadek, *GM* 36 (1979) 51ff. On scenes such as we have reviewed, see also B. Schmitz, *CdE* 106 (1978) 211f.

[169]Cf. nos. 4, 13, and the offering tables of Qenhirkhopshef and Paneb.

[170]Nos. 5, 8, 12, 15-19, 21-23.

[171]Černý, *BIFAO* 27, 165f. For *ibs*, see *Urk.* IV, 1277:20, G. Jequier, *MIFAO* 47 (1920) 8; M. Gitton, and others, *Kêmi* 19 (1969) 309; K. Mysliwiec, *Le portrait royal dans les bas-reliefs de nouvel empire* (Warsaw, 1976) 20ff.

[172]For *pꜣ ḥꜣty*, see E. Otto, *Topographie des thebanischen Gaues* (Berlin, 1952) 58; Černý, *BIFAO* 27, 168, n. 1; F-J. Schmitz, *GM* 27 (1978) 51ff.

[173]Černý, *BIFAO* 27, 162ff; Otto, *Topographie*, 58ff. Locations of the shrines in question are not always easy to identify: presumably the shrine *Mn-st*, (P. Derchain, *Kêmi* 19 [1969] 18) shared jointly by the cults of Amenophis and Ahmes Nofretari, housed one of the forms referred to above (P-M II^2, 422f; Otto, *Topographie*, 57), possibly "Amenophis of the Garden," (Černý, *BIFAO* 27, 164; but K. Sethe, *GGA* 1902, 31); for discussion and literature, see Schmitz, *Amenophis I*, 105ff.

[174]*Ibid.*, 116f.

[175]*Ibid.*, 117f; the temple is pictured in the tomb of Amenmose (Foucart, *MIFAO* 57, pl. 28); Sethe long ago showed that, as in the case of the other forms, the epithet qualifies the king's name and not *pr*: *GGA* (1902) 30. This is the longest-lived of the cult forms of Amenophis I, still operative in the 22nd Dynasty: Cairo 42232.

[176]Theban tomb 134: P-M I^2, 249f; *LD* III *Text*, 282.

[177]Otto, *Topographie*, 59.

Presumably the members of the family of Amenophis I found a place in the lists because they were represented in Amenophis's shrines by cult statuary.[178] Thutmose I,[179] Thutmose III,[180] and Thutmose IV most often wear the blue crown in the assemblages examined above. In Thutmose III's case this must be the cult image of his mortuary temple.[181] Thutmose II, although shown wearing the blue crown only once (Amenmose's tomb, above, no. 4), most certainly possessed a cult image provided with this head-gear.[182] That the Ramessides seem to have favoured the *nms* may be an indication of the cult headdress in fashion under the 19th and 20th Dynasties.

In the light, however, of the relatively small number of examples, such a conclusion in every case may be misleading. Other motives for the choice of a specific item of apparel, other than the remembered appearance of a particular cult statue, may have dictated the choice of representation. For example, the three kings in the badly preserved scene in Pahemneter's tomb (above, no. 14) wear, in the order they occur, the white crown, the *ibs*, and the red crown.[183] It would seem that the variation of the headdress here is an attempt to convey the notion of the plurality of crowns a cult image might wear, just as in more elaborate examples of the script *twt*, "statue(s),"

[178]On the family in general, see Schmitz, *Amenophis I*, 38ff, and the literature there cited.
[179]But cf. Tosi, Roccati, *Stele*, 262 (50002), in *nms*.
[180]Cf. also W. M. F. Petrie, *Illahun, Kahun and Gurob* (London, 1891) pl. 24; Tosi, Roccti, *Stele*, 263 (no. 50004); P. A. A. Boeser, *Beschreibung der Aegyptischen Sammlung des niederländischen Reichsmuseums der Altertümer in Leiden* III *Stelen* (The Hague, 1913) pl. 7, no. 8 (with Amenophis II, also in blue crown).
[181]Cf. Foucart, *MIFAO* 57, pl. 13; In the few relief fragments from his mortuary temple, Thutmose III wears the *nms* (H. Ricke, *Der Totentempel Thutmoses' III: Baugeschichtliche Untersuchung* [Cairo, 1939] pl. 9), but these are not representations of cult images.
[182]Cf. B. Bruyère, *Deir el-Médineh, Année 1926* (*FIFAO* 3; Cairo, 1926) p. 43, fig. 23; pl. 5, 6, 7.
[183]Theban tomb 284 (P-M I^2, 366[2-3]). I should like to thank Dr. Lanny Bell, director of the Drah abbu'l Nagga expedition of the University Museum, University of Pennsylvania, in whose concession this tomb lies, for allowing me to examine this relief. The red paint of the cartouches and their yellow background have greatly deteriorated, making any reading very doubtful. I can do nothing with the first cartouche, but the other two seem to show *rʿ* at the top. In addition, the second shows what may be a *nb* at the bottom, and an oblong sign in the middle (*Nb-pḥtt-rʿ*?).

or *ḫntyw*, "images," might be determined by three figures with different crowns.[184]

27. The "List" of Cairo 38189[185]

On a bronze statuette of Harpokrates of Ptolemaic date, purchased in Luxor, there occur the cartouches of four royal figures of the late Second Intermediate Period. The "Good God Sewadjenre, deceased," and "the Good God Neferkare, deceased" are written on the front of the base, while "Binepu" and "Ahmose" (without accompanying epithets) are found on the sides. The general concensus nowadays[186] appears to be that Sewadjenre and Neferkare are, respectively, Nebereraw I and II, who reigned shortly before the family of Senakhtenre Taᶜo took over the rule of Thebes; while Binepu and Ahmose are princes (probably brothers) who belonged to the Taᶜo clan. What connexion Harpokrates and the unknown dedicator of the statuette had with these remote figures is quite unknown: had accidental discovery brought to light traces of their burials in Drah abbu'l Nagga north? At any rate, this singular collocation of names does attest the liveliness and accuracy of a Theban offering tradition 1500 years after the bearers of the names had lived.

28. The "List" of Cairo 22200[187]

A very crude stela of Ptolemaic date in the Cairo museum similarly commemorates, long after their death, the names of five royal figures of the New Kingdom. The scene shows two pairs of seated figures facing each other and separated by a tree. They are identified as Horemheb (in blue crown) and Sety I (in *atef*) on the left, and Thutmose IV (in blue crown) and a queen (in feathers) curiously

[184]Cf. Posener-Kriéger, de Cenival, *The Abusir Papyri*, pl. 4-5 (determinative of *twwt*, showing three seated statues, wearing white cown, red crown and *nms*); also the determinative of *ḫnty* in the building inscription of Ramesses II in the first court at Luxor (east side), above the line of personified mine-lands (P-M II^2, 307[26]): seated king in double crown, standing king in double crown, standing Osiride figure in white crown. For conscious attempts to vary the headdress of the king, even in trial pieces, see B. E. J. Petersen, *Zeichnungen aus einen Totenstadt* (Stockholm, 1973) pl. 12; cf. also the variety of crowns of the kings' statuettes supporting the Abydene Osiris emblem: H. E. Winlock, *Bas-reliefs from the Temple of Ramesses I at Abydos* (New York, 1973) pl. I, and p. 20.

[185]G. Daressy, *Statues de divinités* (*CCG*; Cairo, 1905-6) 55f; G. Legrain, *Répertoire généalogique et onomastique de musée du Caire* (Geneva, 1908) no. 21; von Beckerath, *Untersuchungen*, 289(6), with the literature there cited.

[186]For discussion, *ibid.*, 183f.

[187]A. Kamal, *Stèles ptolèmaïques et romaines* (*CCG*; Cairo, 1905) no. 22200.

identified by the name "Amunhotpe" (sic!). In both cases the rear figure is embracing his partner. Beneath this scene in the accompanying horizontal text, the prenomen of Ramesses IV appears. What brings this motley group together is difficult to say. All of these individuals, save Ramesses IV, are honoured by Ramose in his Deir el-Medina tomb (no. 7: above, no. 5), and it may be that the present stela simply derives from the dedicant having visited and become familiar with Ramose's tomb.

Most of the reliefs and documents we have examined up to this point presuppose a ritual of offering to the statues of bye-gone kings, assembled together in one spot.[188] Occasionally a chance find will produce a collection of such statues in an archaeological setting. Thus at Elephantine, a favoured cult seat of the 11th Dynasty, fragments of a group of statues were discovered representing a number of 11th Dynasty kings.[189] At Memphis statues of Khafre, Menkaure, Neuserre, Menkauhor and another (uninscribed) were recovered from a chamber west of the sacred lake.[190] At Tanis the founders of the town in the 11th Century B.C. had arranged in line a number of colossal staues of kings of the Middle Kingdom and 19th Dynasty, brought from elsewhere to the site.[191] Similar groupings of statues at Thebes may be evidenced by the Karnak cachette.[192]

Although the reason for the grouping of statues was cultic, one senses that the Egyptians were awed by a long and uninterrupted historical sequence which was thus manifest in concrete form, and exhibited pride in the proof it afforded of the permanence of their family, society and state.[193] When similar groupings of non-royal ancestors became fashionable in the First Millennium B.C., the size of the group was an enviable mark of distinction: if one's ancestral line was insufficiently long, one took steps to lengthen it, artificially if necessary.

[188]The practice of arranging in chronological sequence a group of ancestral images is mentioned by classical authors, and is well attested in the First Millennium B.C. in the context of private genealogies: cf. the present writer, *Biblical Joseph Story*, 5ff.

[189]L. Habachi, *Archaeology* 9 (1956) 8ff; *idem*, *ASAE* 55, 167ff.

[190]P-M III^2, 221.

[191]P-M IV, 18f. The row includes statues of Amenemhet I, Senwosret I, Senwosret II, Mermesha, and Khaneferre, as well as a number of queens and princesses. That an offering ceremony was specifically envisaged by the arrangement is not clear, though the intent seems certainly to have been commemorative.

[192]G. Legrain, *Statues et statuettes des rois et des particuliers* (*CCG*; Cairo, 1906-25), *passim*.

[193]This seems to have been the attitude of the priests of Amun when they showed the statues of their high-priests to Herodotus: ii, 143.

VII
Late New Kingdom "Lists" (Royal: Theban Tradition)

Examples of assemblages of kings, such as we have examined above, begin to fail us as the New Kingdom draws to a close. This is probably not to be put down solely to the chance of preservation: the Ramessides were in process of discrediting themselves and, in areas where royal sponsorship counted, the ancestral offering tradition may temporarily have fallen under a cloud.

1. Qurneh Temple "List" (pl. II)

Flanking the central door in the colonnade of Sety I's temple at Qurneh are two small, balancing stelae.[194] The one on the left has been badly battered, but the one on the right is intact. The vignette at the top shows a king in blue crown on the right (facing left), and officiating before four standing figures. The two cartouches seen above him at present yield the prenomen and nomen of Siptah, but these are clearly re-cut over those of earlier kings, possibly Sety II and Amenmesse. On the left the four standing figures are 1. Amunrasonther, proferring the sword; 2. Ahmes Nofretari in tall feathers; 3. Sety I in *nms* with crook over shoulder and sword; 4. Ramesses II in blue crown, similarly accoutred. The composition of the group thus reflects simply the divine and deified dwellers in the Qurneh temple and its environs; Ramesses I, who also was honoured in the temple, may be the single king pictured in the stela on the left of the door.

2. Unpublished Karnak "List" (pl. III)

A few metres west of the chapel of Osiris Neb-onkh[195] at Karnak lies a fractured sandstone block, slightly less than a metre in length, among the blocks that fringe the southern edge of the "musée en pleine air." The relief shows (statues of?) at least four royal figures, the last remaining evidenced only by his staff, facing left towards a kiosk. All are standing, holding long staves in their right hands, and wear *nms*-headdresses from which sashes hang down behind. Over

[194]P-M II², 409(14-15); R. A. Caminos, in O. Firchow (ed.), *Aegyptologische Studien* (Berlin, 1955) 17ff; L. Habachi, *MDAIK* 34 (1978) 60.
[195]P-M II², plan VI, at D.

each is a sun-disc with two uraei from which dangle *ʿnḫ*-signs, while before each disc is a single cartouche, followed by *di ʿnḫ*, identifying the figure beneath. Only the cartouches of the second and third figures are preserved, and they have undergone modification. The final form achieved by the cartouche of the third figure is clearly *Nb-m³ʿt-rʿ mry-Imn*, i.e. Ramesses VI, a fact which suggests we are confronted by yet another of the usurpations he perpetrated against his immediate predecessors.[196] The original reading of this cartouche shows a *stp.*[*n*][197] at the bottom, and therefore cannot be the prenomen, of Ramesses V. Ramesses IV, however, incorporated *stp.n Imn* in his prenomen, and this clearly is the original form of the name here; we should, then, read an original [*Ḥḳ³-m³ʿt*]*-rʿ Stp.*[*n*]*-Imn.*[198] The disposition of signs in the cartouche attached to the second figure suggests that the original reading was *Rʿ-ms-s(w) ḥḳ³ m³ʿt*, again Ramesses VI. This was subsequently changed to another Ramesside nomen, but which one I cannot say. It seems clear, however, that the author of this assemblage of statues was Ramesses IV (unless he usurped a group previously carved, with cartouches left blank), and that one figure was allotted to each cartouche, with the sequence repeated at least once.

2. The Memphite Altars of Ramesses IX[199]

Two altars, in all probability from Memphis, and now in the Louvre and the Marseilles Egyptian museum, bear the titularies of four kings on their sides. The dedicant, Ramesses IX, undoubtedly intended thereby to involve three of his predecessors in the offerings to be presented, and thereto inscribed the names and titles of Ramesses II, Ramesses III, and Ramesses VIII (? *it.i Imn*)[200] along with his own. The commemoration of these particular predecessors has some bearing on the *Thronwirren* of the first half of the 20th Dynasty; but it also points up the importance both Ramesses II and III had attained by the close of the 11th Century B.C. as *Stammväter*

[196]For Ramesses VI's animosity towards Ramesses IV and V, and the family relationships of this part of the clan, see K. C. Seele, in *Aegyptologische Studien*, 296ff; C. F. Nims, *Bib. Or.* 14 (1957) 137; J. Černý, *JEA* 44 (1958) 31ff; K. C. Seele, *JNES* 19 (1960) 184ff; J. Monnet, *BIFAO* 63 (1965), 209ff; W. J. Murnane, *JARCE* 9 (1971-2) 121ff; E. F. Wente, *JNES* 32 (1973) 223ff.

[197]The *n*, save for the ends, is now obliterated by *nb*.

[198]The presence of an *s* on the upper right hand side may suggest an attempt on the part of Ramesses V to modify the cartouche to accomodate his own prenomen.

[199]J. von Beckerath, *ZÄS* 97 (1971) 9ff, where the earlier literature is cited.

[200]Von Beckerath (*ibid.*, 10) believes this to be Ramesses IX's father.

of the Ramesside house. Eight centuries later the *Aegyptiaca* of Manetho is, as we shall see, much indebted to these kings for the historical material which informs the Sebennytic priest's history.[201]

VIII
Kings Mentioned in Private Titularies and Related Texts

The example of the tomb of Horemheb (above, p. 40ff) introduces us to a type of "list" which is occasionally seen in biographical texts which give the title of the tomb owner. The common mortuary inscription, used in tombs and stelae alike, which records for the edification of viewers the various posts held by a man during his career, along with his name and sometimes a representation of him, were apparently referred to by the ancients under the general term *i*^{3}*wt*, "offices."[202] The same term seems to have been used for the expanded biographical text, an offshoot of the title list, which attempted to "flesh out" the bald list by adding to it a narrative section.[203] In the narrative biographical text, though not always in the title list, the description of the man's career is often chronological: he describes his offices in the sequence in which he held them, often by blatantly resorting to the pattern "my first office was ...," "my second office was ...," and so forth.

A tendency to adopt a chronological sequence is also in evidence for the title list when the titles involve the names of deceased kings. Already in the Old Kingdom this preference is in evidence in that sort of list of epithets which adopts the recurrent pattern "honoured under (revered before, or the like) ..." followed by the king's name.[204] In lists of mortuary functions in several pyramid temples

[201]Below, p. 253ff.

[202]See H. Fischer, *Dendera in the Third Millennium B.C.* (Locust Valley, N.Y., 1968) 145, 180; R. W. Smith, D. B. Redford *The Akhenaten Temple Project* I *Initial Discoveries* (Warminster, 1977) 111ff.

[203]The major ways in which a biographical text differs from a title list are: (a) its first person narrative form, and (b) the presence of *ḏd*, "who days" (H. Fischer, *Inscriptions from the Coptite Nome* [Rome, 1964] 16, n. 1), or *ḏd.f*, "he says," which introduces it. The biographical text was thus understood as an oral declaration on the part of the deceased: cf. *Urk*, I, 88:6-7.

[204]Cf. the stela of Mertityotes (*Urk.* I, 16-17), the false door of Ptahshepses (*ibid.*, 51ff; cf. T. G. H. James, *Hieroglyphic Texts ... B.M.* I^2 [London, 1961] pl. 17), listing no less than seven kings under whom he had served; or Sabu (*Urk.* I, 81ff).

the kings' names will also be in correct sequence.[205] In the New Kingdom any sequence which is historically correct seems to depend on whether the titles were themselves connected with a royal mortuary cult. Thus Mose, a mortuary priest of Thutmose I, Taᶜo and Kamose, arranges the names of these kings in this order,[206] and general Si-ese, who was steward of the mortuary estates of Ahmose, Thutmose III and IV, does not hesitate to invert the order of the latter two.[207] Sennefer and Amunhotpe, on the other hand, attached to the mortuary cult of Amenophis I, correctly arrange the names of Amenophis I, Ahmes Nofretari, Queen Ahmes, and Thutmose I in their titles.[208] Ahmose Panekhbit presents an ordered list of the five royal names from Ahmose to Thutmose III, and in his other biographical statements never confuses them.[209] A similarly flawless sequence of six royal names is to be found in the titulary of the unnamed owner of a funerary cone in Berlin, who must have ended his career early in the reign of Thutmose III.[210] He apparently held some priestly function in the cults of Ahmose, Amenophis I, Thutmose I, Thutmose II, Hatshepsut and Thutmose III, all of whom are named, and in the order given. The identity of the kings and the inclusion of Hatshepsut suggests a royal mortuary cult, probably connected with the temple at Deir el-Bahri. On the other hand, Dedia, who under Sety I was authorized to do reconstruction work in the mortuary temple of Nebhepetre, Ahmose, Ahmes Nofretari, and Thutmose III, does not display the cartouches of these kings in order.[211]

[205]Cf. Sekhemkare (*LD* II, pl. 41a), listing Khafre, Menkaure, Shepseskaf, Userkaf and Sahure; Tjauty and Idu (*LD* II, 113g, 114g; *Kêmi* 6 [1938] 87, 111; *Urk.* I, 257), listing Pepy I, Merenre, and Pepy II; Neferbauptah (*LD* II, pl. 55), listing Khufu, Sahure, Neferirkare, and Ne-userre; Netjery-pu-nysu (H. Gauthier, *ASAE* 25 [1925], 180), listing Djedefre, Khafre, Menkaure, Shepseskaf, Userkaf and Sahure; cf. also P. Kaplony, *Monumenta Aegyptiaca* (Geneva, 1968) pls. 2, 11, 18; p. 20ff, no. 9 (Den, Miebis, Semerkhet, Qaᶜa; cf. P-M III^2, 402); L. Borchardt, *Statuen und Statuetten von Privatleute* I (*CCG*; Berlin, 1911), pl. 1:1 (no. 1; Hotep-sekhemwy, Ra-neb and Nyneter), W. S. Smith, *A History of Egyptian Sculpture and Painting in the Old Kingdom* (New York, 1946) 15; H. Fischer, *Artibus Asiae* 24 (1961) 46, n. 6; cf. also the personified estates (N. de G. Davies, F. Ll. Griffith, *The Mastaba of Ptahhetep and Akhethetep at Saqqara* II (London, 1900) pl. 16 [Isesi, Menkauhor and Sahure]); normally, however, lists of personified estates are organized along different lines (cf. H. K. Jacquet-Gordon, *Les noms des domaines funéraires sous l'ancien empire égyptien* [Cairo, 1962], *passim*); cf. the disarray in R. F. E. Paget, A. A. Pirie, *The Tomb of Ptahhotep* (London, 1898) pl. 23; *LD* II, 59a.

[206]Cairo 34030: P. Lacau, *Stèles du nouvel empire* (*CCG*; Cairo, 1901) pl. 22.

[207]Cairo 13460; see on this individual, H. De Meulenaere, *CdE* 46 (1971) 223ff.

[208]For titles and bibliography, see W. Helck, *Zur Verwaltung des mittleren und neuen Reiches* (Leiden, 1958) 466, 526.

[209]*Urk.* IV, 34ff.

[210]Berlin 8755: *Aegyptische Inschriften, Berlin* II, 303.

[211]Louvre C. 50: D. A. Lowle, *Oriens Antiquus* 15 (1976) pl. 1-2; cf. also Mose, a priest of the mortuary cults of Thutmose I, Taᶜo and Kamose, given in that order: Legrain, *Répertoire onomastique*, no. 1.

Often, it would appear, the kings honoured by an individual are a simple reflection of the tomb or stela owner's life and occupation. Ramose, the scribe in the Place of Truth, is the best example of this.[212] Ramose was probably born under Horemheb, and, on reaching maturity, became scribe of the House of Menkheprure.[213] Early in his career he was also "document scribe (var. letter scribe) of the Crown Prince (*iry-pꜥt*)," possibly Sety I or Ramesses II.[214] In year 5 of Ramesses II he received his most important appointment, viz. "scribe in the Place of Truth."[215] Now, the choice of kings he includes in his inscriptions is fully explained by this brief *curriculum vitae*.[216] Horemheb is included because he was born under him,[217] Thutmose IV because he functioned in his mortuary priesthood,[218] Sety I probably because his early appointments were at his behest, Ramesses II probably because he had been his secretary before his accession, certainly because his most important promotion came early in his reign, and Amenophis I and Ahmes Nofretari because they were the patrons of the Place of Truth. Similarly, in Userhat's tomb the owner pictures Thutmose I simply because he was high-priest of his cult.[219] Khonsu reveres Thutmose III because he was *his* high-priest,[220] and Amenemone offers to Amenophis III and Tiy because he was god's-father in his temple.[221] Wennofer reveres Ramesses II under the guise of Osiris because at one and the same time he was a faithful servant of both the god and the king.[222] In a similar vein Thutmose IV intercedes with Osiris on behalf of his two

[212]For a sketch of Ramose's career see Černý, *A Community of Workmen*, 317ff.
[213]*Ibid.*, 317.
[214]*Ibid.*, 318, notes 1 and 2 for references. Černý (*ibid.*, 317) connects the title with the mortuary priesthood of Amenophis son of Hapu, but he fails to convince. "Letter Scribe" entails a service to the living, and would be most unusual in a mortuary context.
[215]*Ibid.*
[216]The monuments in question are: Deir el-Medina stela no. 79: B. Bruyère, *Fouilles de Deir el-Médineh (1935-40)* (*FIFAO* 20; Cairo, 1952) pl. 12, p. 68 (owner, adoring cartouches of Ramesses II; above 3 mummiform kings, Ramesses II, Horemheb, Sety I); Deir el-Medina stela no. 88: *ibid.*, pl. 36, p. 67 (owner kneeling, and adoring Hathor-cow above whose back are the cartouches of Ramesses II, Thutmose IV, and Horemheb); Statue Louvre E 16346: P-M I^2, 697 (cartouches of Thutmose IV and Horemheb on left shoulder, Thutmose IV and Ramesses II on right shoulder); Deir el-Medina tomb no. 7 (owner adoring Amenophis I, Ahmes Nofretari, Horemheb and Thutmose IV: see above, p. 47).
[217]Certainly not because Horemheb's reign is considered to mark the beginning of a new dynasty; *pace* Phillips, *Orientalia* 46, 116ff.
[218]For Thutmose IV honoured with Amenophis I and Ramesses II see lintel Cairo JdE 59895 (above, p. 42).
[219]N. de G. Davies, *Two Ramesside Tombs at Thebes* (New York, 1927) pl. 5.
[220]*Idem*, *Seven Private Tombs at Kurneh* (London, 1948) pl. 15.
[221]P-M I^2, 354 (2, 3).
[222]G. A. Gaballa, in J. Ruffle (ed.), *Glimpses of Ancient Egypt* (Warminster, 1979) 47.

faithful men, Neferhat and Tjuna.[223] On his stela Yuf of Edfu[224] reveres Queen Sobekemsaf, Queen Ahhotpe, Queen Ahmes and Thutmose I, and in the biographical statement tells us why: he had restored the tomb chapel of the first, and had been taken into the service of the the other two queens. Thutmose I was presumably added as husband of Ahmes, and Ahmose perhaps because Yuf was born during his reign.

The wholesale revival of Old Kingdom royal mortuary cults in the Late Period gives us several examples of priests who functioned in the cults of kings long since deceased; but inspite of a general awareness of the periods in which specific kings had lived, there is no striving after chronological order.[225]

IX
Sequences of Kings' Names in Genealogies

Although the purpose of a genealogy is different from that of a list of kings, occasionally a sequence of royal names is found in the pedigree of a high dignitary. The body of texts providing such examples dates almost exclusively from the First Millennium B.C., that is the post-New Kingdom period.[226] It would be pleasant to report that, in a period where order and identity of kings are still imperfectly known, the royal component in family trees is substantial. Unfortunately it is not. When a Libyan or Saite genealogy encounters a royal name in the particular line it is tracing, it either stops or shifts to a collateral branch of the family.[227] One major exception to this pattern is the genealogy of Psenhor, who lived late

[223]Cairo 34022, 34023.
[224]*Urk*. IV, 29ff; Legrain, *Repertoire onomastique*, no. 36.
[225]Cf. Berlin 14765: A. Erman, *ZÄS* 38 (1900) 114ff; Wildung, *Imhotpe und Amenhotep*, 33ff; (Netjery-khet, Djoser, Djoser-atet, cult images of Amasis, Imhotep, Atet). The context might suggest that the revival of these 3rd Dynasty kings' mortuary cults had something to do with a cult installation of Amasis. Cf. E. Chassinat, *RT* 21 (1899) 69, where a priest of the cult images of Nectanebo is also priest of Men and Atet; also Serapeum stela 291 (E. Chassinat *RT* 22 [1900] 173) where a priest of the time of Darius also serves the cults of Khufu, Khafre and Redjedef; cf. also *LD* III, 276; in general, also W. Spiegelberg, *OLZ* 5 (1902) 44f; Morenz, *ZÄS* 99, xiii; E. Otto, *MDIAK* 15 (1957) 193ff.
[226]There is no implication here that genealogical information was not carefully kept, nor family trees sometimes set forth, in earlier times. But it is simply a fact that extended genealogies on private stelae and in statue inscriptions become usual only in the aftermath of the decline of the 20th Dynasty: Redford, *Biblical Joseph Story*, 5ff.
[227]Examples are legion: cf. Cairo 41035 (Takelot), 42189 (Osorkon), 42211 (Harsiese, Takelot), 42221e (Sheshonk), 42229 (Osorkon), Berlin 19717 (Sheshonk), 20136 (Takelot), *MDIAK* 12 (1943) 33f (Takelot), *ASAE* 55 (1957), 27 (Takelot), *JEA* 43 (1957) pl. 1 (Takelot), J. E. Quibell, *Ramesseum* (London, 1898) pl. 25:3 (Harsiese), pl. 27:7 (Takelot), pl. 27:8 (Osorkon) and so forth.

in the 22nd Dynasty. He was at pains to show that his branch of the clan had enjoyed an enviable longevity in its tenure of the priestly office in the temple of Arsaphes at Herakleopolis; and to that end he lists 16 generations of his male ancestors.[228] His great-great-great grandfather had been Prince Namlot, younger son of King Osorkon II; and at that point Psenhor's ancestry coalesces with the royal line of the 22nd Dynasty, traced back through its first king Sheshonk I to a remote Libyan ancestor, six generations further back. Undoubtedly, as the context is cultic, the information for this genealogy, as for all others in the First Millennium B.C., ultimately derived from statue inscriptions set up in temples, as well as the priestly "annals" which recorded mainly initiations into office.[229]

Of a slightly different nature are the royal names with which the genealogy of the Memphite priests is glossed.[230] In this relief 60 standing statues of high-priests of Memphis are represented in four registers, all facing right towards the large figure (now lost) of a king who was probably Sheshonk IV. Before each statue is a formula text giving the name and titles of the priest, followed by "in the time of king so-and-so." The words "son of ..." at the end of the identification lead on to the next statue. The sequence thus purports to be unbroken from father to son over sixty generations extending from the supreme pontif who held office under Montuhotpe I down to the incumbant who was a contemporary of Sheshonk IV. The last 15 priests (the first in the retrograde order) are otherwise attested, and the order seems to be correct;[231] but for the earlier names the sequence, date and, in some cases, the identity of the priests, are in question.[232]

Although with respect to the specific information it profers the Memphite genealogy may be unreliable, it was inspired by prototypes which could in theory have conveyed accurate information. Not only were temple records and journals faithfully kept by archivist scribes, but it was customary for priests to carve statue inscriptions of themselves to be placed in the temples for receipt of offerings and for posterity to admire. On such statues one usually incised beside the name, titles and genealogy of the owner, the cartouches of the

[228]For bibliography, see Kitchen, *Third Intermediate Period*, 105, n. 105.
[229]The Karnak "annals" are the significant evidence (G. Legrain, *RT* 22 [1900] 51ff), but these are probably only extracts from the day-book of the temple.
[230]L. Borchardt, *SBAW* (1932) 618ff; *idem*, *Die Mittel zur zeitlichen Festlegung von Punkten der ägyptischen Geschichte*, (Cairo, 1935) 96ff, and pl. 2.
[231]*Ibid.*, 101ff.
[232]E.g. between the priest contemporary with Amenemope of the 21st Dynasty (11th Century B.C.) and the contemporary of Ramesses II (13th Century B.C.) only one name intervenes!

contemporary king whom the priest had served, and at whose behest the monument had been set up. It is a great assemblage of this sort of memorial statue, probably a common sight in the great shrines during the First Millennium B.C., that the Memphite genealogy is trying to represent, both graphically and by its inscriptions.

X
Miscellaneous Examples

1. Dendera Assemblage[233]

In an upper register on the wall of the ambulatory flanking the inner shrine at the temple of Dendera is an offering scene showing the king and queen before gods and deceased royalty. The royal couple (cartouches blank) on the right, face left towards the following group of seated figures, each in its shrine: 3 bull-headed deities; 3 kings in the white crown; 3 kings in the red crown; 2 royal mothers; 2 king's-wives; 2 royal children (with sidelock). The accompanying text reads in part: "I come to you, O ye mighty powers and great kings, pre-eminent in Egypt! Your offering table is provided with all good things, I adore your *ku*s ...." None of the figures is further identified: the cartouches of the kings are filled with *nsw* or *bity*, depending on the crown worn.

While the ritual depicted was probably no longer performed, it is an acknowledgment, if only a perfunctory nod in the general direction, of the traditional offering to the ancestors. As such it bears comparison to ...

2. The Osirian "Book of Hours"[234]

Here, amid the invocations to a host of "Osirian" deities, we find also listed "the kings of Upper Egypt and the kings of Lower Egypt, in White Fort; the kings' consorts in White Fort, the kings' mothers in White Fort, the kings' children in White Fort." The content is strikingly similar to the Dendera assemblage, and probably reflects the only reality underlying the relief scene: the royal ancestors are invoked *en bloc* by the lector-priest in the daily offering liturgy.

[233] *Dendera* II, p. 54f, pl. XCVIII.
[234] R. O. Faulkner, *Ancient Egyptian Book of Hours* (Oxford, 1958) 18(25:13ff.).

2

Gwnt[1]

That the Ancient Egyptians from remote antiquity had faithfully kept annalistic records, was a commonplace in the works of classical writers. In fact, in the broad range of ancient Near Eastern peoples, the Egyptians were singled out as the most painstaking chroniclers of all nations. Herodotus more than once registers his admiration for their gifts in this connexion. In ii.77.1 he states "the Egyptians who live in the cultivated parts of the country, by their practice of keeping records of the past, have made themselves much the best historians of any nation of which I have had experience."[2] Later, in ii.100.1 he relates how "the priests read to me from a written record the names of 330 monarchs ...."[3] Both Theophrastus and Hecataeus of Abdera cite "records" (ἀναγράφαι) concerning Egyptian kings as sources for their information.[4] Tacitus, in recounting the details of Germanicus's visit to Egypt, has occasion to refer to the hieroglyphic records at Karnak;[5] while Tatian alludes to the "precise chronological annals" the Egyptians possessed, and from which Ptolemy of Mendes extracted material for his history.[6] Syncellus speaks of an "old chronography" which he believed to have been used as source by Manetho;[7] and the same writer refers to "Egyptian records and lists" (Ἀιγυπτιακοῖς

[1]See the author in *Studien zu Sprache und Religion Aegyptens* (Göttingen, 1984) 327ff.
[2]A. de Selincourt (tr.), *Herodotus: The Histories* (Harmondsworth, 1954) 131; on the passage in question, see W. W. How, J. Wells, *A Commentary on Herodotus*[2] (Oxford, 1928) 205; A. B. Lloyd, *Herodotus, Book II: Introduction* (Leiden, 1975) *ad loc.*
[3]De Selincourt, *Herodotus*, 138. Similar records, sounding suspiciously like king-lists, are mentioned in Diodorus i.44.
[4]Theophrastus *De lapidibus*, 24; Diodorus i.31.7, 43.6, 44.4, 46.7-8, 63.1, 69.7, 81.4, 96.2; J. Krall, *SAWWien* 96 (1880) 243f.
[5]*Annals* ii.67.
[6]*Oratio adversus Graecos*, 38.
[7]Waddell, *Manetho*, 226.

ὑπομνήμασι και ὀνόμασι) used by Eratosthenes to compile his Theban dynasty.[8] Josephus cites Manetho as admitting his sources to have been, in part, "sacred tablets" (δέλτων ἱερῶν),[9] a possible awareness of the role extant stelae played in the composition of Manetho's history. Later he shows himself aware of Manetho's dependence on written records and oral tradition.[10] Syncellus too records Manetho's dependence on temple stelae: "he (Manetho) wrote from stelae in the Seriadic land, inscribed, he says, in sacred language and holy characters by Thoth ...."[11]

Although most of these classical authors are attempting to bolster their own claim to authenticity by alluding to such sources, the terms

[8]*Ibid.*, 213. Later (*ibid.*, 225) Syncellus specifies the sacred scribes of Diospolis (Thebes) as Eratosthenes' source, a late reminiscence of the dominance of Thebes in the king-list tradition (see above, p. 29ff; below, p. 151).

[9]*Contra Apionem* i.14.73; "sacred books" (*ἱερων γραμμάτων*) in i.26.228.

[10]i.15.104-5; cf. also i,31.287.

[11]Waddell, *Manetho*, 208. Thoth was generally acknowledged as "master of the hieroglyphic script (*nb mdw-ntr*: *Wb*. II, 181:6)," and its creator (cf. the term for the script *drf n Ḏḥwty*, "Thoth's script": Berlin 7316): cf. S. Schott, *ZAS* 99 (1972) 20ff. *Sš n mdw-nṯr* (*Urk*. II, 197, 213) and its variant *sš n pr-ᶜnḫ* (*Urk*. II, 154) are the standard terms in the Late Period for the formal hieroglyphic (as opposed to the Demotic) script: A. H. Gardiner, *JEA* 24 (1938) 172. According to Plato (*Phaedra* 274) Thoth invented writing and presented it to Amun who was somewhat critical: cf. E. Iverson, in J. R. Harris (ed.), *The Legacy of Egypt*[2] (Oxford, 1971) 172; *idem*, in *Textes et langages de l'Egypte pharaonique* I *L'Ecriture* (Cairo, 1972) 68. As divine scribe of the gods, he is "the one who puts words into writing" (*rdi mdw <m> drf*: C. Robichon, A. Varille, *Rapport des fouilles à Karnak nord* III [Cairo 1951] 107). Thoth was also supposed to be responsible for the different languages of mankind: cf. J. Černý, *JEA* 34 (1948) 121; S. Sauneron, *BIFAO* 60 (1960) 31ff. Besides being the author of the script and the language, certain specific texts were supposed to have come from Thoth's pen (cf. the "Books of Thoth": G. Worrell, *Orientalia* 4 [1935] 31; for the *Corpus Hermeticum* see Iversen, in *The Legacy of Egypt*[2], 176): a creation account ("copy which Thoth made ... it is called 'the Formula of the Holy Places of the First Primaeval One'": *Edfu* VI, 181; A. Barucq, *BIFAO* 64 [1966] 130, laws in general (H. Gauthier, H. Sottas, *Décret Trilingue en l'honneur Ptolemée IV* [Cairo, 1925] *h*., 2; *d*., 2);temple instructions (Ptolemy II "made his regulations in this temple ... in accordance with what was found in Thoth's script": *Urk*. II, 38:14-16), the "litany" to Min-Amun ("all that exists gathered in one place in the writing of Thoth, for Amun," Kitchen, *RI* II, 627), temple procedure in general: (*Reliefs and Inscriptions at Karnak* III *The Bubastite Portal* (Chicago, 1954) pl. 18 1. 32); the standard offering list (".... god's offerings of Amun-re, conforming to [*ḫft*] the writing which Thoth made in the House of the God's-book": H. H. Nelson, *JNES* 8 [1949] 220, fig. 18, lines 9:10 [cf. S. Schott, *ZÄS* 90 (1963) 103ff]), mortuary ritual ("may they perform for you rites conforming to [*ḫft*] this writing which Thoth placed in the House of the God's-book": A. M. Blackman, *The Rock Tombs of Meir* II [London, 1915] pl. 6), a decree for Osiris ("Thoth sanctifies it as follows in writing": H. Junker, *Das Götterdekret über das Abaton* [Vienna, 1913] 7). Of course the *gnwt*, the *imyt-pr*, the official titulary and the writing on the *išd*-tree are usually ascribed to Thoth: H. H. Nelson, *The Great Hypostyle Hall at Karnak* I (Chicago, 1981) pl. 96 ("in the writing of my own fingers"); A-P. Zivie, *Hermopolis et le nome de l'ibis* (Cairo, 1975) 231; in general, A-A. Saleh, *BIFAO* 68 (1969) 15ff.

used by them do find some correspondence in ancient Egyptian parlance. Thus the "tablets" and "stelae" recall the *wḏ*, "monumental text," *ʿḥʿ* "standing inscription," and the *ʿnw*, "tablet," of the hieroglyphic terminology.[12] The "lists" sound like king-lists. What of "chronographies," and "records," or in other words annals? The Egyptian word which is usually rendered "annals" is *gnt*,[13] singular, which is far more common in the plural, *gnwt*.[14] Its fundamental meaning is rather difficult to determine, but the following cognates help to set the parameters of its reference:[15] *gnw*, "twig, branch, piece of a tree";[16] *gnn*, "aromatic wood";[17] *gnw*, (a kind of bird);[18] *gnw*, (a kind of pool);[19] *gnwty*, "wood carver";[20] It would seem best to posulate the existence of an otherwise unattested (or perhaps obsolete?) root *gn* (or *gni*), "to cut, inscribe," whence we might derive "cut or detached piece of wood," i.e. a branch, a prepared wooden tablet (*gnt*), and a *nisbe* from the latter, inscriber of a piece of wood. One arrives, in fact, at a form strikingly similar to the wooden and ivory "labels" of Protodynastic times.[21]

Nevertheless we are chagrined to find scarcely any examples of either the verb *gn* or the derived noun *gnt/gnwt* in the Old Kingdom, and none which would clinch the identification with the labels. Whether the title *imy-r gnwty*(?), known from the earliest dynasties into the 6th,[22] has anything to do with the inscribing of such official records of the past is a moot point. Nevertheless, form and implied content of the *gnwt*, as will be seen from the examples marshalled below, correspond so well to the tablets of the Archaic Period that the identity of the two can scarcely be doubted.

There follow a number of occurrences, with the contexts apertaining thereto, of the word in question, from the earliest attestation down to Roman times. By the Ptolemaic period the use of

[12]The author hopes to treat each of these terms in a subsequent work on oral *versus* scribal tradition in the historiography of ancient Egypt.
[13]*Wb.* V, 173:5.
[14]*Ibid.*, 173:6ff.
[15]Cf. Helck, *Manetho*, 3; *idem*, in *LdÄ* I, (Wiesbaden, 1972) 278f.
[16]Admonitions, 4:14 (parallel to *nhwt*, "trees").
[17]*Wb.* V, 173:6ff.
[18]C. Gaillard, *Kêmi* 2 (1929) 19ff; B. van de Walle, *La Chapelle funéraire de Néferirtenef* (Brussels, 1978) 46.
[19]*Wb.* V, 174:7.
[20]*AEO* I, 66*f; J. A. Wilson, in *JNES* 6 (1947) 233f.
[21]E. Drioton, J. Vandier, *L'Egypte*[4] (Paris, 1962) 136; Sir A. H. Gardiner, *Egypt of the Pharaohs* (Oxford, 1961) 62; W. Kaiser, *ZÄS* 86 (1961) 53f. For *gni*, "to carve," whence *gnwt*, see D. Meeks, *RdE* 26 (1974) 64, n. 6.
[22]Cf. W. Helck, *Untersuchungen zu den Beamtentiteln des ägyptischen alten Reiches* (Glückstadt, 1954) 75.

gnwt had become so stereotyped and banal that not all examples are here deemed necessary to the eliciting of meaning or the establishing of a case, and some are therefore omitted.

I
Old and Middle Kingdom Examples

1. PT 1160 (Pepy I, Pepy II). *wdi.f gnt.f ḫr rmṯ mrwt.f ḫr nṯrw*, "he sets his annals[23] among men, love of him among the gods."
2. PT 2085 (Pepy II). *gn P mm.sn m gn wr sḫpy r imy-wrt*, "Pepy is recorded among them as a great recorded one who has been rapt away to the West."

These two examples, the only ones known to me from the Old Kingdom, find their time reference at the moment of the king's passing from life to death. At his decease and transfiguration he is duly enrolled and recorded in the list of monarchs, and the record of his reign formally deposited in the archives among men.
3. CT II, 147d-f. "(I have come as your fourth, O ye imperishable ones), *irw gnwt n Ḫpr wn-ḥr n št³w swwt*, who make the annals for Khopry, and are vigilant over the mysteries of the cult seats."
4. P. Lacau, H. Chevrier, *Une chapelle de Sésostris Ier à Karnak* (Cairo, 1965) 191. *s³.i Snwsrt n ẖt.i smn.i gnt.k m nsw-bity*, "O my bodily son Senwosret! I establish your record as king of Upper and Lower Egypt." (Amun to the king).
5. *Ibid.*, (1969) pl. 39. *smn.n.i gnt.k m ir ḥḥ n sdw*, "I establish your record as a celebrator of a myriad of *sd*-festivals." (Amun to the king).
6. F. Bisson de la Roque, *FIFAO* VIII (1930) pl. 8. *ḏd-mdw di.n.i ʿnḫ w³s nb ḫr.i smn.i gnwt.k m sdw ʿš³ wrt*, "Utterance:[24] 'I establish your annals with[25] very many *sd*-festivals.'" (Senwosret III).
7. *Ibid.*, pl. 10. *ḏd-mdw di.n.i n.k ʿnḫ w³s nb ḫr.i smn.i gnwt.k m sdw ʿš³ wrt*, "Utterance: 'I grant you all life and prosperity from me; I establish your annals with very many *sd*-festivals.'" (Amenemhet-Sobekhotpe II).[26]

[23]Cf. K. Sethe, *Ubersetzung und Kommentar zu den altägyptischen Pyramiden Texten* V (Glückstadt and Hamburg, n.d.) 48; L. Kákosy, *Selected Papers, 1956-73* (*Studia Aegyptiaca* VII; Budapest, 1981) 31.
[24]By whom is not clear; perhaps Amun or Montu.
[25]I.e. the predicted reign will comprise so many years that numerous jubilees (beginning traditionally in the 30th year) will be celebrated.
[26]J. von Beckerath, *Untersuchungen zur politischen Geschichte der zweiten Zwischenzeit in Aegyptens* (Gückstadt, 1965) 237.

Examples 4 and 5 show that, already in the Middle Kingdom, *gnwt* is an element used in both literature and iconography, in the context of the jubilee and the re-affirmation of kingship in general. To promise many *gnwt* marked by many *sd*-festivals is tantamount to promising a long reign. In both the gate of Senwosret III and that of Sobekhotpe II which was copied from it, jubilee symbolism is evident: the text in which *gnwt* occurs is in a column between two vertical year-branches, which in the New Kingdom are to become exceedingly common in scenes in which *gnwt* are promised.

It is not without significance that this most popular scene appears first in the 12th Dynasty. The promise of years, jubilees and *gnwt* is tantamount to an assurance of legitimacy, at a period of Egypt's history when to establish one's right to rule was of paramount importance. The "gods-on-earth" of the Old Kingdom needed no such assurance: they already knew of whom they were the seed!

II
New Kingdom Relief Scenes

1. Thoth in Principal Role

Most numerous are scenes in which a major god (Amun or Atum) confers the symbols of kingship, while Thoth inscribes the record of the act on a branch or tablet.

8. *LD* III, pl. 59 (Kummeh). *ḏd-mdw in Ḏḥwty wr nb Ḫmnw s³t Ḫnm ḥry nst.f M³ʿt.k³-rʿ mryt.f smn.i gnwt.* [*ṯ* ...], "Utterance by great Thoth, Lord of Hermopolis: 'daughter of Khnum, upon his throne, Makare whom he loves! I establish [your] annals ....'" Caption to a scene in which Thoth writes with his pen on a year-branch held by Khnum.

9. *Urk*. IV, 288:11-12 (Karnak, eighth pylon; Thoth speaks). *smn.i gnwt nt s³t.i M³ʿt-k³-rʿ*[27] *tpt ḥḥ m sd ʿš³ wrt*, "I establish the annals of my daughter, Makare, as the first of very many *sd*-festivals." Caption to a scene in which Thoth writes on a year-branch inside which the following text is placed: "the Lord of Hermopolis writes for you your years like Atum, your kingship is the kingship of Horus."

10. P. Lacau, H. Chevrier, *Une chapelle d'Hatshepsout à Karnak* II (Cairo, 1979) pl. 11, no. 186 (Karnak, Red Chapel). *ḏd-mdw in Ḏḥwty nb Ḫmnw nb mdw-nṯr n Imn nb nswt-t³wy smn.(i) gnwt nt s³t.k* [*M³ʿt-k³-rʿ*] *m irt ḥḥw m sdw ʿš³ wrt ḫʿ.t(i) m nsw-bity*, "Utterance by

[27]Changed by Thutmose III to *ʿ³-ḫpr-n-rʿ*.

Thoth, Lord of Hermopolis, master of the hieroglyphs, to Amun, Lord of Karnak: 'I establish the annals of thy daughter, [Makare], she that is to perform very many myriads of *sd*-festivals, now that she has appeared as king of Upper and Lower Egypt.'" Text accompanying a scene in which Amun (in kiosk) and *Wrt-ḥḳ*^{3}*w* affix the accoutrements of Hatshepsut.

11. *Ibid.*, pl. 14, no. 52 (Karnak, Red Chapel). *ḏd-mdw in nb Ḫmnw s*^{3}*t.(i) M*^{3c}*t-K*^{3}*-r*^{c} *smn.(i) s*^{c}*ḥ.t m nsw-bity gnwt.ṯ m ḥḥw nw rnpwt*, "Utterance by the Lord of Hermopolis: 'O my daughter Makare! I establish thy rank as king of Upper and Lower Egypt, and thine annals by the millions of years.'" Text accompanying Thoth who writes on a year-branch, while Amun embraces Hatshepsut and Amaunet watches.

12. *Ibid.*, pl. 14, no. 149 (Karnak, Red Chapel); scene balancing no. 11, with variant. *gnwt.<ṯ> ḥr išd šps*, "... <thine> annals being upon the blessed *išd*-tree."

13. H. H. Nelson, *The Great Hypostyle Hall at Karnak* I *The Wall Reliefs* (Chicago, 1981) pl. 49 (Karnak, south wall of hypostyle). *ḏd-mdw in nb Ḫmnw sš.i n.k ḥfnw m ḥbw-sd smn.i gnwt.k m Ḥr-k*^{3}*-nḫt Mry-m*^{3c}*t*, "Utterance by the Lord of Hermopolis: 'I write for thee myriads of *sd*-festivals, I establish thine annals in (the Horus name) *Horus-mighty-bull: Beloved-of Ma*^{c}*at*," Text accompanying Thoth writing on two year-branches before Amun, who affixes Ramesses II's crown; Seshat is also present.

14. *Ibid.*, pl. 52 (Karnak hypostyle; Thoth speaks). *mk <wi> ḥr irt mi wḏ.n it.k nb nṯrw smn.n.i gnwt.k m ḥḥ rnpwt ḥfnw m sd di.i* ^{c}*ḥ*^{c}*.k r mitt ḥrt*, "behold, <I> am acting in accordance with what thy father, the Lord of the Gods, has ordained. I have established thine annals in millions of years and hundreds of thousands of *sd*-festivals; I make thy lifetime approximate that of the Heavens." Text accompanying Thoth who writes on a year-branch in which is the Horus-name and double cartouche, before a kiosk in which the kneeling king receives the sceptre from Amun. (see pl. IV)

15. P-M II^{2}, 437 (Ramesseum; pl. 4; Thoth speaks). *sš.i n.k* ^{c}*ḥ*^{c} *n R*^{c} *rnpwt Ḥr m nsw irrt Itn ḥr wbn gnwt.k r-mitt rn.k mn mi imy pt*, "I write for thee the lifetime of Re and the years of Horus as king of what the sun-disc creates when it shines, thine annals likewise, thy name abiding like him who is in Heaven!" Text accompanying Thoth who is inscribing the king's name, while the king kneels in a kiosk before Amun.

16. *Medinet Habu* V, pl. 313 (east wall of first hypostyle; Thoth speaks). *smn.i gnwt.k mitt R*^{c} *ḏt sp-sn*, "I establish thine annals after the manner of Re, for ever and aye!" Text before Thoth who, with Horus, introduces the king to Amun and Mut.

17. *Medinet Habu* VI, pl. 368 (second court, column in south colonnade; Thoth speaks). *sš.i n.k ḥb-sd n Rᶜ rnpwt nt Itm di.i nḫbt.k mitt ḥrt gnwt.k mi imy.s*, "I write for thee the jubilee of Re, the years of Atum; I make thy titulary as the likeness of Heaven, thine annals like (those of) him that is in it." (Thoth writes on a year-branch loaded with pavillions, while the king offers to Amunre-Kamutef and Amaunet.

18. J. Champollion, *Monuments de l'Egypte et de la Nubie* II (Paris, 1845) pl. 138 (Edfu; Thoth writes on a palette, while Hathor suckles the divine child). *nḫb.i gnwt*, "I entitle the annals."

19. H. Junker, E. Winter, *Das Geburtshaus des Tempels der Isis in Philä* (Vienna, 1965) 376 (Philae mammisi; Thoth speaks). [*spḫr.i*] *gnwt n sꜣ Ist m ḥḥ n ḥbw-sd*, "[I copy out] the annals for the son of Isis in millions of *sd*-festivals." Thoth writes on a notched frond while Khnum fashions the child.

2. Thoth Alone.

In a closely related type of scene, with similar purport, Thoth is found, not as an ancilliary figure, but as the sole functionary.

20. *LD* III, 55b (Semneh; Thoth speaks). *ir.i rn.k m Ḏḥwty-ms smn.i gnwt nfrwt m ᶜnḫ wꜣs nb m ir ḥḥ m ḥb-sd*, "I make thy name 'Thutmose'; I establish thine annals in all life and prosperity, as one who shall perform millions of *sd*-festivals." Text accompanying a scene in which both Thoth and the king write with pens on three tablets(?), while the king holds a year-branch.

21. P. Barguet, *Le temple d'Amon-rê à Karnak* (Cairo, 1962) 207 (Karnak, room xlii). [*Ḏḥwty*] *nb* [*Ḫmnw*] *smn gnwt.k*, "[Thoth], Lord of [Hermopolis] establishes thine annals." Part of caption text of Thoth and Seshat, squatting and writing on their tablets before Thutmose III.

22. Karnak, room xlii (j: own copy). [*Mn-ḫpr-ᶜ*] *smn.n.(i) gn*[*wt.k*] *m ᶜnḫ ḏd wꜣs nb*, "[O Menkheperre!] I establish [thine] annals in life, endurance and prosperity!" Text above Thoth who profers to the king a tray on which are three year-branches.

23. Temple of Sety I, Abydos, storeroom B, east wall (own copy). *ḏd-mdw* [*in Ḏḥwty*] *smn.i n.k gnwt.k* ⸢ ... ⸣ *mi Rᶜ*, "Utterance [by Thoth]: 'I establish for thee thine annals ... like Re.'" Text accompanying a painting of the kneeling Thoth, writing on two branches, the whole being a decorative panel on one of the chests depicted on the wall.[28]

[28]See P-M VI, plan on p. 22. These painted scenes are not noted here, and I must thank the late Mme. Bulbul Meguid who saw them when they were clearer, and who kindly shared her copies with me. No. 9 I saw with my own eyes; no. 10 has faded beyond recall.

24. Temple of Sety I, Abydos, storeroom B, east wall. *ḏd-mdw in* ⌜*Ḏḥwty*⌝ *smn.i n.k gnwt.k m sšw ḫr-ḥ³t.k ᶜnḫ.*[*ti*], "Utterance by ⌜Thoth⌝: 'I establish for thee thine annals in writing, in thy presence – may [you] live!'" Context identical to that of no. 9.
25. Temple of Sety I, Abydos, storeroom C, east wall. *ḏd-mdw in Ḏḥwty smn.i* <*n*>*.k gnwt.k m sšw mi Rᶜ ir ḫr-ḥ³t* [... ·], "Utterance by Thoth: 'I establish <for> thee thine annals in writing, as (was done for) Re, I do it(?) in [thy] presence [...]'" Context identical to that of no. 9.
26. Abydos (A. Mariette, *Abydos* I [Paris, 1869] 30c). *Ḏḥwty nb mdw-nṯr nḫb.i n.k gnwt m wḥm*, "I Thoth, master of hieroglyphs, entitle thee to additional annals."
27. *Belegstellen* to *Wb.* V, 173:13 (Luxor forecourt). *smn.i gnwt.k nt ḥḥ m rnpwt*, "I establish thine annals of millions of years."
28. G. Legrain, *RT* 22 (1900) 126 (Temple of Osiris, Ruler of Eternity, facade). *ḏd-mdw smn.i gnt m sd*, "Utterance: 'I establish the record with a *sd*-festival.'" Text accompanying Thoth who holds out two year-branches to the Divine Worshipper Amenirdis.
29. O. Firchow, *Thebanische Tempelinschriften aus Griechisch-Römischer Zeit* (Berlin, 1957) 83 (Bab el-Amara). *nḫb.i n.tn ᶜḥᶜ r nsyt nt Rᶜ spḫr.i n.tn gnwt n Itm*, "I entitle you to a lifetime as king as long as the kingship of Re, I copy out for you the annals of Atum." Text accompanying Thoth who holds three year-branches within which are the cartouches and *serekh* of Ptolemy III.
30. *Ibid.*, 23 (Bab el-Abd). *šsp.n gnwt m-ᶜ Š³yt ³m.n rnpwt ḫr wḏ Rnnt*, "we receive the annals from Shayet, we take years at the behest of Renenut." Response of Ptolemy III and his queen to Thoth who writes on a year-branch.
31. E. Chassinat, *Le Mammisi d'Edfou*, (Cairo, 1908) pl. 37 (rear right corner pillar). *spḫr.i gnwt n psḏt*, "I copy out the annals of the Ennead." Words of Thoth who writes on a year-branch which he profers to the child Horus.
32. *Ibid.*, pl. 32 (rear left corner pillar). *nḫb.i gnwt n nṯrw spḫr.i sd.k m ḥḥ*, "I draw up the annals of the gods, I copy out thy *sd*-festivals by the millions." Words of Thoth, in the same context as no. 31.
33. *Belegstellen* to *Wb.* V, 173:10 (Philae). *ḏbᶜw.i ḥr nḫb gnwt.k*, "my fingers draw up thine annals." Thoth to the royal child.
34. *Edfu* III, 120. *rnpwt.tn m ḥḥ ḥr ḥḥ gnwt.tn m ḥfnw*, "your years number millions upon millions, your annals hundreds of thousands." Thoth to the royal couple.
35. *Edfu* III, 190. *spḫr.i gnwt.k r ḥntyw rnpwt*, "I copy out thine annals to aeons of years." Thoth to the king.
36. *Edfu* VI, 335. *nḫb.i gnwt.k m ḏbᶜw.i ḏs.i mi ir.n.i n Ist*, "I draw up thine annals with my own fingers, as I did for Isis." Thoth to the king (cf. *ibid.*, III, 92).

3. Khonsu or a form of Horus in the Principal Role.

In some texts from Karnak and Edfu Thoth's place is sometimes taken by Khonsu or Horus.[29]

37. Nelson, *The Great Hypostyle Hall* I, pl. 198 (Karnak, north wall of hypostyle). *smn.i gnwt.k m ḥḥ rnpwt nsyt.k mi Ḥr*, "I establish thine annals in millions of years, thy kingship like (that of) Horus." Horus purifies the king in company with Thoth.

38. Firchow, *Tempelinschriften*, 69. *nẖb.i n.k rnpwt nsyt n ḥḥ ḥr nst Rʿ ḏt spẖr.i gnwt.k r ʿḥʿ n Rʿ rnpwt.k* [...] *ḏt*, "I entitle thee to a million years of kingship upon the throne of Re for ever, I copy out thine annals, as many as the lifetime of Re, thy years [...] for ever!" Words spoken by Khonsu to the king, while writing.

39. *Ibid.*, 70. *spẖr.i gnwt.k m ḥḥ n sdw ḥfnw ḏbʿw m rnpwt*, "I copy out thine annals with millions of *sd*-festivals, and hundreds and tens of thousands of years." Khonsu speaks to Ptolemy III.

40. *Ibid.*, 83. *nẖb.i n.tn ʿḥʿ r nsyt nt Rʿ spẖr.i n.tn gnwt n Itm hꜣw.tn pw hꜣw pt ḥr sḥnwt.s*, "I entitle you to a lifetime approaching the kingship of Re, I copy out for you the annals of Atum; your timespan is the timespan of Heaven upon its supports." Khonsu, writing, speaks to the royal couple.[30]

41. *Ibid.*, 12. *spẖr.i gnwt.k r ʿḥʿ* [...], "I copy out thine annals approaching the lifetime [of Re(?) ...]." Harpare to the king.

42. *Edfu* I, 63. *nẖb.i n.k rnpwt rnpwt m ḥḥ ḥr nst Rʿ ḏt .... di.n.i n.k šn(t) nb n Itn t ḏr.f m imyt-pr.k spẖr.i gnwt.k r ʿḥʿ n Rʿ nsyt.k ḥnty ḏt*, "I entitle thee to prosperous years by the millions, on the throne of Re for ever .... I grant thee all that the sun-disc encircles, the entire earth being thy bequest. I copy out thine annals approaching the lifetime of Re, thy kingship (to) the span of eternity." Khonsu to the king.

43. *Edfu* I, 378. *spẖr.i gnwt.k r ʿḥʿ n Rʿ ḥnty ḏt*, "I copy out thine annals approaching the lifetime of Re, the span of eternity." Khonsu-Thoth to the king at the ceremony of elevating *maʿat*.

4. A Goddess in the Principal Role.

Less frequently a goddess connected with the art of writing replaces Thoth and his congeners in this type of scene.

44. Champollion, *Monuments* IV, pl. 342 (Luxor). *ḏd-mdw in Sfẖt-ʿbwy nbt sš ḫntt pr mḏꜣt-nṯr smn.i* [*gn*]*wt.k m ḥḥ m sdw*, "Utterance

[29]For the similarity of Khonsu and Horus in the Late Period at Karnak, see D. B. Redford, *JSSEA* 9 (1979) 33ff.

[30]Cf. similarly *Edfu* I, 26.

by Sefkhet-abwy, mistress of writing, foremost of the House of the God's-book: 'I establish thine annals with millions of *sd*-festivals.'" Text accompanying Sefkhet-abwy, sitting with pen in hand.

45. Kitchen, *RI* II, 630:15 (Luxor forecourt, back pillar of colossus). *ḏd-mdw in Sfḫt-ꜥbwy nbt sš ḥnwt pr-mḏꜣt smn.i gnwt.k n ḥḥ n rnpwt*, "Utterance by Sefkhet-abwy, mistress of writing, lady of the House of Books: 'I establish thine annals to millions of years.'"

46. *Medinet Habu* V, pl. 295 (terrace behind second court). *ḏd-mdw in Sšꜣt wrt ḥnwt pr-mḏꜣt sš.i n.k ḥbw-sd m ḥfnw rnpwt mi šꜥ n wḏb smn.i gnwt.k ḥr ḥwt.k sps ḏt*, "Utterance by Seshat the great, lady of the House of Books: 'I write for thee *sd*-festivals in hundreds of thousands of years like the sand of the seashore! I establish thine annals upon thy noble temple for ever.'" Words of Seshat who writes on a year-branch, while the king receives the sceptres from the triad of Atum, Ius-aas and Nebethotpet in kiosk.

47. W. Helck, *ZÄS* 82 (1957) 135 (Khonsu temple). *smn.i gnwt.k m ḥḥ m rnpwt ḫꜥ.ti ḥr st Ḥr*, "I establish thine annals in millions of years, now that thou hast appeared upon the Horus-throne." Words of Seshat, who is in the act of writing.

48. G. Legrain, *ASAE* 3 (1902) 58 (Ptah temple, text of Taharqa). *smn.n.i gnwt.k m sdw ḫꜥ.ti ḥr st Ḥr m nsw-bity sšm.k ꜥnḫw nb mi Rꜥ ḏt*, "I establish thine annals with *sd*-festivals, now that thou hast appeared upon the Horus-throne as king of Upper and Lower Egypt, that thou mayest lead all the living like Re for ever."

49. *Edfu* I, 291. *spḫr.i gnwt.k m ḥḥ n sdw*, "I copy out thine annals in millions of *sd*-festivals." Seshat to the king in the scene of the *išd*-tree.

50. *Edfu* VI, 337. *mk ḏbꜥw.i ḥr nḫb gnwt.k m sš m ḏbꜥw.i* (sic) *ḏs.i in Rꜥ ḏd.f m rꜣ.f*, "behold, my fingers draw up thine annals in writing, even my own fingers; Re it is that said it with his mouth." Text accompanying Seshat who, with scribe's equipment, writes on a year-branch, while Nekhbit and Edjo bear the white and red crowns respectively.

51. *Edfu* I, 259. *spḫr.i gnwt.k r sd n Tꜣ-tnn*, "I copy out thine annals approaching the jubilee(s) of Ta-tenen." Hathor to the king at the rite of wine-offering.

52. P-M VI, 77 (246; Dendera, west exterior wall, top register). *nḫb.i n.ṯ gnwt m ḥḥ rnpwt*, "I draw up for thee annals in the millions of years." Thoth and Seshat write on year-branches before the seated Hathor.

53. P-M VI, 97 (57-58; Dendera roof, east Osiris room). *ḏd-mdw in Sšꜣt nbt sš ... ḥnwt pr-mḏꜣt ... spḫr.i n.k gnwt m ḥḥ n rnpwt m wḏt n.k it.k ...*, "Utterance by Seshat, mistress of writing ... lady of the House of the Book ...: 'I copy out for thee annals by the millions of years, as thy father ordained for thee ....'" Hekau, Seshat and Thoth, in a procession of 18 gods, facing Harsiese, Isis and Osiris, profer notched year-branches; Seshat and Thoth are writing on theirs.

5. The Presiding God or Celebrant Speaks.

Occasionally, instead of the divine secretary, it is the presiding deity or the priest that authorizes the granting of annals.

54. *Urk.* IV, 281:16. [*smn.i gn*]*wt.ṯ m nsw*, "[I establish] thine [an]nals as king." Amun speaks to Hatshepsut.

55. H. Brunner, *Die südlichen Räume des Tempels von Luxor* (Mainz, 1977) pl. 97 (Luxor, columned antechamber). *di.n.i n.k rnpwt.k ꜥḥꜥ n Rꜥ gnwt nḥḥ ḥr st Ḥr*, "I grant that thy years (be as) the lifetime of Re, with eternal annals upon the Horus-throne." Amun to Amenophis III.

56. *Ibid.*, pl. 63. *ib.i m ṯḥḥwt mꜣ.i nfrw.k smn.i n.k gnwt.k m ḥḥ m rnpwt*, "my heart exults at seeing thy beauty! I establish thine annals for thee by millions of years." Amun to Amenophis III.

57. P-M II², 324 (141; Luxor ambulatory). *smn.n.f n.f rnpwt nḥḥ di.f ḥryt.f m tꜣw ḥnmmt ẖr ṯbty.fy smn.n.f gnwt.f m ḥḥ n sdw*, "he (Amun) has established for him eternal years, he has put the terror of him among the lands, the sun-folk being beneath his feet; he has established his annals with millions of *sd*-festivals." *Iwn.mwt.f* priest to the Ennead.

58. *Karnak* 5 (1975) fig. 7 (Karnak, tenth pylon; east colossus base). *di.k n.f ꜥnḫ ḏd wꜣs nb ḏt n ḥkꜣ nḏm-ib ẖkrw ḫꜥw Rꜥ m tp.f smn.k gnwt.f m ḥḥ n rnpwt*, "mayest thou grant him all life, stability and dominion eternally, as joyful ruler, with the accoutrements and diadems of Re upon his head; mayest thou establish his annals in millions of years!" *Iwn-mwt.f* speaks to Amun-re.

59. Karnak, south wall of hypostyle (above, no. 13). ... *di.n.i n.k ḥkꜣt iꜣt.i nst.i smn.(i) gnwt.k m ḥḥ n rnpwt*, "... I give thee the scepter of my office, and my throne; I establish thine annals by millions of years." Amun speaks to the king who kneels before him; Thoth and Seshat are also present.

60. P-M II², 414 (73; Qurneh temple, room xv). *ḏd-mdw in Rꜥ-ḥr-ꜣḫty ḥry-ib ḥwt-nṯr ꜣḫ-Swtḫ-mr.n-Ptḥ m pr Imn ḥr* [*imntt Wꜣst*] *smn.i gnwt.k n ḥḥ m rnpwt ntk sꜣ.i*, "Utterance by Reharakhty, resident in the temple 'Effective-is-Sety-Merenptah in the House of Amun on [the West of Thebes]': 'Let me affix thine annals to millions of years; thou art my son.'" Sety kneels before Reharakhty while Ius-aas crowns him.

61. P-M VI, 5 (38: Sety's temple at Abydos, outer colonnade). [*ḏd-mdw*] *in Rꜥ-ḥr-ꜣḫty nb pt* [*di.n.i n.*]*k ḥkꜣ ꜣms Ptḥ* [*Ḏḥwty*] *ḥr smnt gnwt.k*, "[Utterance] by Reharakhty, Lord of Heaven: '[I grant] thee

the crook and flail of Ptah, [while Thoth] establishes thine annals.'" Reharakhty speaks to Ramesses, while Ptah writes the king's name on the *išd*-tree, and Thoth writes on three year-branches.
62. Legrain *RT* 22, 132 (Temple of Osiris, Ruler of Eternity, third room, east wall). *ḏd-mdw in Itm nb tꜣwy Iwnw sꜣ.i mry.i Tkrt smn.i gnwt.k m tꜣ r* [...] *snn.i m iwꜥ n Šw*, "Utterance by Atum, Lord of the Two Lands, the Heliopolitan: 'O my beloved son, Takelot! I establish thine annals in the land [...] thou being my likeness, heir of Shu!'" Atum speaks to Takelot III who squats in the *išd*-tree.
63. P-M VI, 189 [77]; *temp.* Ptolemy VII (Kom Ombo, inner hypostyle). *spẖr.i gnwt.k m ḥḥ rnpwt*, "I copy out thine annals in millions of years" (Harweris to the king, proferring two fronds with *sd*-signs).
64. P-M VI, 130; M. E. A. Ibrahim, *The Chapel of the Throne of Re at Edfu* (Brussels, 1975) pl. 19, scene 11[119] (Edfu, chapel IX). *spẖr.i gnwt.k m ḥḥ n sdw*, "I copy out thine annals in millions of *sd*-festivals" (Horus to king; parallel to *nsyt.k*, *rnpwt*).

III
References in Passages Accompanying Reliefs

Often, in examples such as those above, *gnwt* is implicit in the scene itself, and specific reference to it is left to the accompanying text.
65. *Urk.* IV, 276:11-12. *spẖr.n* [*it.s*] *Imn rn.*[*s*] *wr ḥr i*[*šd*] *šps* ⸢*smn.f*⸣ (?) *gnwt.s n ḥḥ*, "[her father] Amun copies [her] official name upon the august *i*[*šd*]-tree, he established [her] annals by the millions."
66. *Urk.* IV, 358:15. *smn.n it.s Imn rn.s wr Mꜣꜥt-kꜣ-rꜥ ḥr išd gnwt.s m ḥḥ nw rnpwt smꜣ m ꜥnḫ ḏd wꜣs*, "her father Amun established her official name Makare on the *išd*-tree, and her annals in millions of years, united with life, stability and prosperity."
67. *Urk.* IV, 383:12-13. [*s*]*mn rn.s wr mi pt smnḫ gnwt ḳnn.s ḥr wꜥrt* (sic) *nt tpt-ḏw*, "her (Hatshepsut's) official name was established like Heaven, the annals of her brave deeds published upon the desert-tract of 'Her-Who-Is-Upon-The-Mountain'" (i.e. the Speos Artemidos).
68. Lacau, Chevrier, *Chapelle d'Hatshepsout*, 141f, pl. 54 (Red chapel of Hatshepsut). A goddess *ḥr smnt rnpwt.i m wꜣḏt rnpwt ḥr ḫtt gnwt.i m sd*, "establishes my years as 'Flourishing-one-of-years,' and carves my annals in the *sd*-pavillion."
69. *Urk.*, IV, 166. *wḏ n.k nsyt.f smn ḫꜥw.k ḥr st Ḥr smn gnwt.k m nsw-bity*, "his kingship was ordained for thee, thy crowns were affixed

upon the Horus-throne, thine annals were established as king of Upper and Lower Egypt." The courtiers laud Thutmose III.

70. Brunner, *Die südlichen Raume*, pl. 92 (Luxor antechamber). *smn gnwt.f m pr it.f Imn*, "his (the king's) annals are established in the house of his father Amun."

71. *Urk.* IV, 1780:19 (tomb of Ramose). *di.f n.k ḥḥ n rnpwt gnwt.k <m> sdw*, "may he grant thee millions of years of thine annals (with) *sd*-festivals!" Ramose intones a benedictory hymn to Amenophis III.

72. Helck, *ZÄS* 82, 136 (Luxor architrave). *Ḏḥwty ḥr smn<t> gnwt.k*, "Thoth establishes thine annals."

73. G. Lefebvre, *ASAE* 51 (1951) pl. facing p. 176, 1. 24 (Sety I). *di.f n.i nḥḥ m nsyt Rꜥ swꜣḥ.f rnpwt.i m ḥḥ nn ḥsb.f šꜣy.i nn ḫꜥmw.f nsyt.i mitt gnwt.f*, "he granted me eternity in the kingship of Re, he increased my years by the millions without reckoning my fate which did not encroach upon my kingship nor my (sic) annals"(?).

74. Helck, *ZÄS* 82, 125 (Aksheh temple) [*smn*?] *rnpwt gnwt.f ḥfnw ḥr išd šps di ꜥnḫ ḏt* "the years of his annals [are established] by the hundreds of thousands upon the precious *išd*-tree, given life for ever." Caption to a scene in which Ramesses II kneels before a god in a coronation ceremony.

75. Mariette, *Abydos*, pl. 52, 6 (Sety's temple at Abydos, south wall, corridor 'Y'). *diw rn.k ḫnty ḫꜣbs gnwt.k m ḥḥ*, "thy name is placed foremost in the starry sky, thine annals are in the millions!" Part of Thoth's long speech adulating the deceased Sety.

76. *Ibid.*, pl. 50-51, 23-4 (Sety's Abydos temple, north wall corridor 'Y'). *ꜥšmw bsw tp iꜣwt.sn imyw wiꜣw kriw wꜥ nb im.sn ḥr skꜣ mnḫw.k r ꜣḫt r ḥrt n imyw itn.f r dwꜣt n Wsir smn.sn gnwt.k mi pt m ḥḥ n rnpwt*, "the images of the hallowed ones upon their standards, or in the sacred barques of the shrines, each one of them exalts thine excellence to the Horizon, to Heaven, to those who are in his disc, to the Underworld, to Osiris! They establish thine annals like (those of) Heaven, in millions of years!" Sefkhet-abwy speaks to Sety in an encomium like that of no. 75.

77. Kitchen, *RI* II, 659:2. *wnn m ḥḳꜣ ꜥnḫw i<w> ḥm.i ḥr smnt gnwt.k*, "O thou who art ruler of the living! My Majesty is establishing thine annals ...." Ptah speaks to Ramesses II.

78. Kitchen, *RI* II, 884::3. *ḏd.i ḫr.k ḥr.k n.i sḏm.k n.i pꜣ sr n Inbw-ḥḏ nsyt.k m ḥḥ n ḥḥ gnwt.k ḏt nḥḥ*, "I speak unto thee; pay heed to me and mayest thou hearken unto me, O thou prince of Memphis! Thy kingship is (reckoned) in millions upon millions (of years), and thine annals are for ever and aye!" Khamwese addresses Ptah.

79. Helck, *ZÄS* 82, 129. [... *rnpwt*] *n nsyt.f r-mn gnwt.f* [...], "[... the years] of his kingship (Re's?) as many as his annals [...]."

79a. Karnak block: musée en pleine air (unpublished). *smn.n.i gnwt.k m ḥḥ* [...] ⌜*m*⌝ *irr.k ḥḥ wḥm.k ḥḥ* [...], "I establish thine annals by the millions [...] as thou accomplishest millions and continuest with millions."
80. Gardiner, *JEA* 41 (1955) pl. 7 (P. Turin 1882, *rt.* i.5-7). *sp tpy n mdt n(t) nṯr pn r ḥn sꜣ.f mry.f r dit wn.f <m> ḥkꜣ* [ ] ... *ḥbw-sd ḳnw i.ir.f ḥr tp tꜣ ḥsbw mn ḥr rn* {*n*} *wr n ḥm.f* ꜥ.*w.s.* ꜥ*ḥ*ꜥ*w.f wnw ḫ*ꜥ*w ḥr wṯs* [*ḫ*ꜥ*w*(?) ... *n*]*ṯrw sṯn.f st spḫrw ḥr gni.f mnšw.f m nḫbw.f mntf Ḥr ḥry-tp* <*n*> *srḫ*, "the first occasion of the speech of this god in order officially to regulate (for) his beloved son, and to make him ruler [ ] ... the many jubilees he would(?) perform upon earth, being reckoned and established in the Great Name of His Majesty, L.P.H., and his lifetime (viz.) he who had appeared in glory, wearing [the diadems ... the g]ods whom he exalted(?) — they are recorded in his annals, his cartouches being provided with his titulary: he is Horus who is upon his *serekh*."
81. J. Yoyotte, *BIFAO* 61 (1962) 116 (geographical procession, Memphis, Kom Ombo and Opet). *i.n nb tꜣwy ḫr.k Ptḥ in.n.f n.k Gnwt m tꜣ-s st.k nfr m Km-wr in kꜣ.k sḫpr gnwt m kꜣt.k*, "The Lord of the Two Lands comes unto thee, O Ptah, bringing thee Genut from Lake-land, thy fair seat in the Great-Black! It is thy *ku* that creates annals through thine activity!"
82. *Belegstellen* to *Wb.* V, 173:10 (Philae). *nḫb gnwt.f m ḫt nn mst.f*, "whose annals were intituled in the womb before he was born."
83. J. D. C. Lieblein, *Que mon nom fleurisse* (Leipzig, 1895) 47, 12-13. *gnwt ... ḫr išd šps m 'Iwnw m sšw n Ḏḥwty ḏs.f*, "the annals ... which are under the august *išd*-tree in Heliopolis in the writing of Thoth himself."
84. S. Schott, *NGWG* (1964) line 24. *di.f n.i nḥḥ m nsyt R*ꜥ *swꜣḥ.n.f rnpwt.i m ḥḥ nn ḥsb.f šꜣy.i nn ḫ*ꜥ*mw n nsyt.i mitt gnwt.f*, "may he grant me an eternity in the kingship of Re, may he set my years in millions, without the reckoning of my fated span, nor shortening my kingship, like his annals!"
85. Kitchen, *RI* VI, 4:14-5:1. Ramesses IV is *mn gnwt twt mi Ḥr ḥr srḫ*, "(endowed with) abiding annals, fair like Horus upon the *serekh*."
86. *Edfu* VI, 94. *Ḏḥwty wr ḥr smn(t) gnwt.f m ḥḥ n sdw ḥfnw m rnpwt*, "Great Thoth establishes his (the king's) annals with millions of *sd*-festivals and hundreds of thousands of years."
87. *Edfu* VI, 189. *wnn Sšꜣt smn mnw.k pḏ šs m ḥwwt.k n mꜣw sp tpy n smn(t) gnwt.k*, "Seshat establishes thy monuments and stretches the cord over thy mansions anew — the first act of recording thine annals."
88. *Dendera* VI, 109. *s*ꜥ*šꜣ* ꜥ*ḥ*ꜥ*.f sḏd nswt.f mtnw.s m ꜣw nḥḥ spḫr n.f gnwt.f m ḥḥ n ḥbw-sd ḥfnw m rnpwt*, "his (the king's) lifetime is

extended, his kingship established — it is registered for the length of eternity! — his annals are copied out for him in millions of jubilees and hundreds of thousands of years!"

89. *Belegstellen* to *Wb.* V 173:6 (Philae). *ḳd.n.f gnwt n s^{3}.f Wsir*, "he (Khnum-Ptah) fashioned annals for his son Osiris."

90. A-P. Zivie, *Hermopolis et le nome de l'ibis* I (Cairo, 1975) 163f (P. Louvre 3079.iv.1-3). *B^{c}ḥ ẖr wḏt.k Ḏḥwty wp rḥ.wy <ḥr> smn<t> gnwt.k*, "Bah is at thy disposal, Thoth establishes thine annals." To Osiris.

IV
Gate Inscriptions

The inscribing of columns of text mentioning *gnwt* on the jambs of monumental gates, known from the Middle Kingdom (see above, nos. 4-7), is also well represented in the New Kingdom. Here Thoth and Seshat play the part of the sovereign's dutiful scribes, positioned at the aperture through which he may either appear, or send forth his edicts and decisions which are immediately put into writing.

91. P-M VI, 4(65, 69, 70, 71; cf. E. Brunner-Traut, in J. Assmann and others (eds.), *Fragen an die altägyptischen Literatur* [Wiesbaden, 1977] 143, abb. 1). *ḏd-mdw in Ḏḥwty nb mdw-nṯr sš.i n.k ḥbw-sd mi R^{c} gnwt.k mi itn m pt*, "Utterance by Thoth, master of the hieroglyphs: 'I write for thee jubilees like Re, annals like (those of) the sun-disc in Heaven.'" Thoth squats with his palette, writing on a year-branch.

92. P-M VI, 16 (152; Sety's temple at Abydos, second hypostyle). *ḏd-mdw in Sš^{3}t wrt nbt sšw di.n.(i) n.k rnpwt m ḥḥ ḥbw.k mi Iwnw ... gnwt.k r ^{c}ḥ^{c} n pt*, "Utterance by great Seshat, lady of writing: 'I grant thee years by the myriad, thy jubilees being like (those of) the Heliopolitan ... thine annals approaching the lifespan of Heaven!'" Seshat kneels, writing on a year-branch.

93. P-M VI, 23 (204b; Sety's temple at Abydos, second hypostyle). *ḏd-mdw in Ḏḥwty nb Ḫmnw ḫnty Ḥsrt ... smn.i gnwt.k mi pt*, "Utterance by Thoth, Lord of Hermopolis, pre-eminent in Hesret ...: 'I establish thine annals like (those of) Heaven.'" Thoth and Seshat squat, writing.

94. P-M II^{2}, 432 (1, h-i; Ramesseum, first pylon, west face). *ḏd-mdw di.n.i n.k ^{c}nḫ w^{3}s nb ḫr.i smn.n.i gnwt.k m sdw ḫ^{c}.ti ḥr st Ḥr.*, "Utterance: 'I give thee all life and prosperity from me, I establish thine annals with *sd*-festivals, since thou hast appeared upon the Horus-throne.'"

95. *Medinet Habu* V, pl. 251 (first pylon, west jambs of gate). *ḏd-mdw in Imn-r^{c} nb nswt-t^{3}wy di.n.i n.k ^{c}nḫ ḏd w^{3}s nb ḫr.i smn.(i) gnwt.k* *m sdw ḫ*ᶜ*.ti ḥr st Ḥr*, "Utterance by Amun-re, Lord of Karnak: 'I grant thee all life, stabilility and prosperity from me in the *sd*-(pavillion?), thou having appeared upon the Horus throne.'" Thoth and Seshat, on either side of the gate, with the hypostaseis of "Seeing" and "Hearing," write texts within two tall year-branches, extending up the sides of the gate.

96. P-M II², 194 (2, a-b; temple of Osiris, Lord of Provisions, Karnak). [*smn.i*] *gnwt*[*.ṯ* ... *ḫ*ᶜ]*.ti ḥr* [*st*] *Tfnwt*, "[I establish thine] annals [...], thou [having appeared] upon [the throne] of Tefnut."

V
Epithets of Divinities

As most of the examples already cited indicate, *gnwt* seem inseparably linked with the *sd*-festival. The connexion is further stressed by the epithets of certain gods and goddesses.

97. *Urk.* IV, 1756:3; (Turin Ptah-statue). Amenophis III is *mry Ptḥ nb m*ȝᶜ*t nṯr* ᶜȝ *nb sd ḥry-ib sḥ n gnwt*, "beloved of Ptah, lord of Truth, the great god, lord of the jubilee-pavillion who resides in the chamber of annals."

98. L. Habachi, *ZÄS* 97 (1971) pl. 6c (Louvre Nephthys-statue). *Nbt-ḥwt ḫntt sd ḥryt-ib sḥ n gnwt*, "Nephthys, pre-eminent in the jubilee-pavillion, who resides in the chamber of annals."

99. L. Habachi, G. Haeny, *Untersuchungen im Totentempel Amenophis III* (Wiesbaden, 1981) 121, abb. 18 (Medinet Habu statue of Seshat, now lost). *nṯr nfr Nb-m*ȝᶜ*t-r*ᶜ *mry Sš*ȝ*t ḫntt ḥwt*(?) *nb sd ḥryt-ib sḥ n gnwt*, "the Good God, Nebmare, beloved of Seshat, pre-eminent in the mansion(?), mistress of the jubilee, who resides in the chamber of annals."

100. T. G. H. James, *Hieroglyphic Texts ... B.M.*, pt. 9 (London, 1970) pl. 3:2 (no. 91), Amenophis II is *mry M*ȝᶜ*t nbt sd ḥryt-ib sḥ n gnwt*, "beloved of Maᶜat, mistress of the jubilee-pavillion, who resides in the chamber of annals."

This most numerous category of occurrences consistently links *gnwt* with the symbolism of divine kingship. The verbs used all denote authorized inscription: "to establish" (*smn*, the verb used of officially "publishing" and inscription),[31] "to entitle" (*nḫb*, from *nḫbt*,

[31]Cf. *Urk.* IV, 199, 336, 338f, 684, 1004; H. Grapow, *Studien zu den Annalen Tuthmosis des Dritten und zu ihnen verwandten historischen Berichten des neuen Reiches* (Berlin, 1949) 7, n. 3.

"official titulary"),[32] "to copy out" (*spẖr*),[33] "to publish" (*smnḫ*)[34] or "to engrave" (*ḫti*).[35] The adverbial adjuncts time and again refer to authorized and divinely-sanctioned kingship: "as king" (no. 54), "as king of Upper and Lower Egypt" (nos. 10, 11, 69), "on the Horus-throne" (nos. 47, 48, 55, 69). The context is redolent of coronation imagery (cf. nos. 10, 11, 14, 15, 27, 50, 74,). It is obvious that the association in most contexts of the *gnwt* with millions of years and *sd*-festivals is tantamount to the promise of a long reign.

The tenor of the iconography is consistent with the import of the texts. The element which had the longest currency is the year-branch, almost always the notched variety. The oldest arrangement is a column of text bordered on either side by vertical year-branches (cf. nos. 6, 7, 94, 95). By the early 18th Dynasty (cf. nos. 8, 9) a more dramatic representation has come into vogue, showing a god holding the branch while either he or another god writes upon it with a pen. The writer is usually Thoth, attested in the earliest examples from the reign of Hatshepsut, either performing the act alone, standing or sitting, or with a major god conferring blessing, kingship and the like. In later texts and reliefs occasionally Horus or Khonsu may act as a substitute for Thoth. A goddess, usually Seshat or Sefkhet-abwy, is also fairly common in this role.[36] The functions here performed by the Thoth and Seshat type of deity have mainly to do with scribal activities vis-à-vis the gods; and one motif stresses the fact by showing these divine secretaries squatting in front of the gate of the god, inscribing the *fiats* which resound therein. Amun authorizes the inscribing of the *gnwt* (cf. no. 14), and he can also do the writing (nos. 54, 57, 65, 66). Occasionally it is Ptah (no. 77),

[32] *Wb.* II, 307:10-15; also "to register" (items in a list: cf. Amenemope i.17), in the case of a king's name possibly to enter it in a king-list.

[33] *Wb.* IV, 106:11ff, almost synonymous with *sš*, "to write"; but also in the Late Period, to sketch pictures on walls (*ibid.*, 107:3-6); early, "to make copies": H. Goedicke, *Königliche Dokumente aus dem alten Reiches* (Wiesbaden, 1967), Koptos R, 5-6; cf. also abb. 28; *hence* "to send information," W. Spiegelberg, *ZÄS* 64 (1929) 76f; see also R. A. Caminos. *Late Egyptian Miscellanies* (London, 1954) 248; to "take down dictation", On. Am. i, 2 (=*AEO* III, pl. VII); Kitchen, *RI* VI, 22-23.

[34] *Wb.* IV, 136:13; R. O. Faulkner, *A Concise Dictionary of Middle Egyptian* (Oxford, 1962) 228.

[35] *Wb.* III, 347-8.

[36] On *Sš3t* as a sort of Egyptian Klio, see D. Abou-Ghazi, *Das Altertum* 15 (1969), 195ff; G. A. Wainwright, *JEA* 26 (1940) 30ff; on her epithet "lady of writings in the House of Life," see Gardiner, *JEA* 24, 174; "Pre-eminent in the Mansion of Writings," Sauneron, *Esna* II, 11. Other goddesses by attraction share in her work, e.g. Nephthys: C. de Wit, *Les inscriptions du temple d'Opet à Karnak* (Brussels, 1958) 21, 144. Cf. also C. J. Bleeker, in F. F. Bruce, E. G. Rupp (eds.), *Holy Book and Holy Tradition* (London, 1968) 26.

Atum (no. 62), Harweris (no. 63), Horus (no. 64) or Re (nos. 50, 60, 61) that authorizes or writes, while once (no. 76) it is all the gods. It is also appropriate that the *iwn-mwt.f* request annals from the major gods (nos. 57, 58). The process of euhemerization results in the crediting of the gods themselves with *gnwt* (Osiris: nos. 89, 90; Isis, no. 36; Ptah, no. 78; Tatenen, no. 51; Re, nos. 79, 84; Atum, nos. 17, 29, 62; of the Ennead, no. 31; of the gods, no. 32); and to stress the longevity of the king the *gnwt* of Re (nos. 15-17, 23, 38, 40-42, 43, 55, 79) or of Heaven (nos. 14, 17, 40, 92, 93) may be compared. As early as the reign of Hatshepsut (cf. nos. 12, 65, 66, 74) the annals are linked with the *išd*-tree (nos. 49, 66, 74, 83), that eternal plant in Heliopolis on whose leaves the name of the reigning king is emblazoned,[37] or said to be inscribed within the *sd*-pavillion (nos. 68, 97, 98).

The inscribing or authorizing of annals at the outset of the reign (cf. nos. 10, 60), or even before the future monarch had been born (cf. no. 82), may call into question whether they were actually construed by the ancients as "records" or "annals." Reference to such concrete objects as the *išd*-tree or the *sd*-pavillion conjures up a cultic context, in which the *gnwt* may simply have degenerated into an item of cult paraphernalia required by a stereotyped ceremony. On the other hand, one cannot entirely exclude the possibility that a formal display of the record of the reign to date formed a part of the jubilee proceedings.

[37]Cf. Nelson, *The Great Hypostyle Hall*, pl. 137, 192. For discussion see Helck, *ZÄS* 82 (1957) 131ff; L. Limme, *Orientalia Lovaniensia Periodica* 6/7 (1975-76) 373, n. 1; J. Bergman, *Ich bin Isis* (Uppsala, 1968) 234ff; Sir A. H. Gardiner, *JEA* 39 (1953) 18, *dd*; D. Müller, *OLZ* 67 (1972) 121f. On the antiquity of the practice of writing on leaves, see W. Helck, *Altägyptische Aktenkunde des 3. und 2. Jahrtauseds v. Chr.* (Munich and Berlin, 1974) 2f. The *išd*-tree is early connected with the fight between the solar cat and the serpent in Heliopolis: see CT IV, 282; R. O. Faulkner, *The Ancient Egyptian Coffin Texts* I (Warminster, 1973) 261f. The writing of the king's name on a leaf of the tree is known at least as early as Senwosret I (cf. *BIFAO* 73 [1973] pl. 22); later, by extension, the *res gestae* were also considered to have been written on the tree: Kitchen, *RI* II, 215:4, 218:4. It was probably rationalized and mythologized as an act originally performed for Re himself in the *ḥwt-nbw*: Gardiner, *JEA* 32 (1946), 50 (g). In the Late Period the associations of the tree with Osiris are many: cf. Junker, *Götterdekret*, 50f, 68 and *passim*; in general, J. Leclant, *Recherches sur les monuments thébains de la XXVe dynastie dite éthiopienne* (Cairo, 1965) 275ff.

VI
Gnwt as Written Reference Works

The text and reliefs which we have passed in review above constitute a widely-attested but stereotyped and much restricted context. The word herein investigated also occurs in literary passages which are similarly restricted, but of different purport.

101. *Urk.* IV, 86:3. *n m³³.tw m gnwt nt ḏrtyw ḏr šmsw-Ḥr*, "it (i.e. the far-flung conquests and fame of Thutmose I) could not be seen in the annals of the predecessors since the Followers of Horus."[38]

102. *Urk.* IV 500 (Hatshepsut). *srwt ḏdwt r.s n ḫpr mitt ḏr rk nṯr ḏr gnwt nt imyw-ḥ³t*, "as for that which was predicted and said of her, the like had never happened since the time of God, since the annals of those who were aforetime."

103. Lacau, Chevrier, *Chapelle d'Hatshepsout* I, 137. *n sḏm.tw grt ḏr rk t³ pn ḥnty wbn m Nwn n ḫpr mitt n nsyw bityw ḥ³t-ᶜ ḥr ḫt tpt n sḏm.tw m sft nt mdt ḥnty rmṯ nṯrw n p³ ḫpr ḏr rk rmṯ n p³ sḏm ḏr rk nṯr nn m gnwt imyw-ḥ³t*, "it had indeed not been heard of since the primordial time of this land, the period of him who shone forth in the Nun; it did not happen to the kings of Upper and Lower Egypt beginning with the first generation, nor had it been heard in narrative discourse(?)[39] during the time of men or gods; it had not occured during the time of mankind, nor been heard of since the time of God; it was not in the annals of those who were aforetime."

104. Kitchen, *RI* II, 275:9 (Abu Simbel marriage stela of Ramesses II). *bw sḏm.f ḏr nṯrw gnwt št³ m pr-mḏ³t m h³w Rᶜ r-mn ḥm.k*, "it had not been heard of since the gods, (in) the secret annals in the House of Books, from the time of Re down to your majesty."

105. Kitchen, *RI* IV, 4:11-12 (Merneptah). *pḥ.sn ḏww n wḥ³t šᶜd.w {n} w n T³-iḥw mty.ḫr.tw ḏr nsyw ḥr gnwt kt-ḫt h³w nn rḫ.tw* [...], "they (the Libyans) reached the mountains of the Oasis, they cut off the district of Farafra; thorough search was made,[40] since the (period of the) kings of Upper Egypt, in the annals of earlier times, but they were unable to [...]."

106. *Ibid.* IV, 6:15. *bw ptr.f ḥr gnwt bityw ist wn t³ pn n Kmt m-ᶜ.sn m ᶜḥᶜ i³dt m rk nsyw*, "it (the battle) had not been attested in the annals of the kings of Lower Egypt, when this land of Egypt was in their charge in constant plague, in the times of the kings of Upper Egypt."

[38]Cf. *sšw n ḏrtyw*: Kitchen, *RI* I, 42:15 (in a similar context).
[39]Lacau, Chevrier, *Chapelle d'Hatshepsout*, 140, n. *t*.
[40]Read *mtr.ḫr.sn*; the slightly archaic *sḏm.ḫr.f* — a more contemporary form would have been *ḫr tw ḥr mtr* — conveys a notion of action extended over a period of time.

107. *Ibid.*, VI, 6:14-15 (Ramesses IV). [*iw*].⌜*sn*⌝ *irt smtr gnwt p^{3}wty nsyw n h^3 ḥr ^{c}nḫ r h^{3}w tpyw-^{c} bw ḫpr n.sn nn mitt ḥm.f*, "[they] made a search of the annals from the most ancient kings who had been put down on the 'Life'-book(?),[41] down to the time of the ancestors; (but) nothing like this which happened to His Majesty had happened to them" (concerning the miracle of the king's name being inscribed in a certain mysterious colour on the *išd*-tree).
108. Petrie, *Tanis* II, pl. 9 (Taharqa stela, 8). *rdi.n ḥm.f in.tw n.f gnwt nt tpyw-^{c} ḥr m^3 Ḥ^{c}py ḫpr m h^{3}w.sn n gm.tw mitt iry im*, "His Majesty had brought to him the annals of the ancestors to see what inundations had happened in their time; but nothing like this was found therein."

The examples cited are with one exception, all cast in a negative locution. Something unusual has just happened — an invasion, a battle, a conquest, a miracle, a marriage, a flood — and investigation is made in the *gnwt* to see if a similar event had ever happened in the past; but nothing comparable is ever found. While the device is a rhetorical one, these examples do reveal that a practice was followed of consulting the *gnwt* from time to time, but only in an effort to seek guidance in a time of crisis.

VII
Miscellaneous Examples

109. Amenwahsu (Theban Tomb 111: A. H. Gardiner, *JEA* 24 [1938] 161) is a *sš spẖr gnwt ntrw ntrwt m pr-^{c}nḫ sš mḏ^{3}t-ntr*, "scribe who copies out the annals of the gods and goddesses in the House of Life, scribe of the God's-book."
110. Kha^{c}emope (son of Amenwahsu: W. Spiegelberg, *Aegyptische Grabsteine und Denksteine aus süddeutschen Sammlungen* I [Strasbourg, 1902] pl. 18, no. 32) is *sš mḏ^{3}t-ntr n nb t^{3}wy spẖr gnwt ntrw nbw m pr-^{c}nḫ*, "scribe of the God's-book of the Lord of the Two Lands, who copies out the annals of all the gods in the House of Life."
111. Anastasi I, i, 7 (A. H. Gardiner, *Egyptian Hieratic Texts* I, 1 [Hildesheim, 1964] 6*, 6.) the scribe is one who *wh^c itnw gnwt mi ir*

[41] *Wb.* I, 204:17.

st, "can decipher the difficult passages[42] of the annals like him that composed them."

112. Kitchen, *RI* VI, 10:16. Ramesses IV is "intelligent like Thoth, *sw ꜥḳ m gnwt mi ir st mꜣ n.f sšyt pr-ꜥnḫ*, "he is familiar with the annals like him that composed them, one who looks for himself through the writings of the House of Life."[43]

113. L. Borchardt, *Statuen und Statuetten von Königen und Privatleute* I (*CCG*; Berlin, 1911) 50 (no. 457). *wꜥ iḳr nfr bit n smn gnwt n nb tꜣwy Wsr-ḥꜣt*, "a uniquely competent person, with a good character for establishing the annals of the Lord of the Two Lands, Userhat."

114. W. Erichsen, *Eine neue demotische Erzählung* (Mainz, 1956) iii, 8, 9, 14. *knyt n sẖ*, "a written ... (?)," parallel to a *mḏꜣt n ḏmꜥ*, "a book-roll," and a *sꜣw n snsn*, "a prophylactic for breathing," all made by a scribe in the embalming house of Psammetichus I, for inclusion with the mummy.[44]

None of the contexts in which *gnwt* are mentioned offer much assistance in our attempt to discover what the objects actually were, what they looked like, or where they were kept. That they purported to be records of some kind, arranged by regnal years, seems fairly clear in the vast majority of examples cited. Moreover, the occasional qualifying phrase or clause, or candid comment, would suggest that an edition of the *gnwt*, remarkably similar to those of the Old Kingdom and probably running through later reigns, did in fact exist in the New Kingdom. Thus the *gnwt* are difficult to read and therefore probably involve archaic forms and syntax (cf. nos. 111, 112). By implication they encompass records of accession and coronation (nos. 47, 48, 55, 94 etc.), *sd*-festivals (no. 80 and *passim*), and temple foundation (cf. nos. 80, 87). Notices of inundations, battles and miracles can be expected in the *gnwt* of one's predecessors. In short, the content is precisely the same as that of the yearly "rectangles" we encounter in the Protodynastic labels and the Palermo and Cairo fragments.

[42]For *itnw* see *Wb.* I, 146:1-3. The root meaning approximates "difficulty, problem," occasioned by wording or writing which defies easy interpretation: cf. D. Meeks, *Année lexicographique* I (Paris, 1980) 50. It does *not* designate any genre of text, such as "mysterious writings," or the like, *pace* E. A. E. Reymond, *From Ancient Egyptian Hermetic Writings* (Vienna, 1977) 114.

[43]Gardiner, *JEA* 24, 161.

[44]W. Erichsen (*Eine neue demotische Erzahlungen* [Mainz, 1956] 72) renders "Schriftrollen" and does not hestitate to connect the word with *gnwt*.

The Origins of the *Gnwt* in the Old Kingdom

Although we lack the originals of the early annals, the Protodynastic tablets being merely adaptations of the archetype for the purposes of clerical notation, it is possible to make a good estimate of their form and evolution. At the outset, as the genre came to birth, the scribe clearly was motivated by ambivalent directives: was he to *record* major events, or to *name* the years in which he wrote? For the early reigns at least commemoration and identification can be seen in tension in the purposes of the recorder. But shortly the archivist's instincts took hold, and it became desirable to record all the events deemed important by the administration, though this made a mockery of the *prima facie* need to name a year for the purposes of identification only. To accomodate the annalist's intent, the format sometimes adopted a series of horizontal registers, usually divided off by lines.[45] The placement, number and orientation of royal designations vacillates in the reigns of Narmer[46] and Aha,[47] but by the reign of Djer had gravitated to the left hand side of the upper register, facing right, viewing as it were the "events" on the right which for the most part face in the opposite direction.[48] The *serekh* conveys the royal name most frequently, the *nb.ty* name occuring more sporadically; but by the close of the dynasty *nsw-bity* can also be found. The *rnpt*-sign is introduced in the reign of Edjo[49] as a long, bracketing device on the right of the rectangle, and this is construed to be in a bound construction with the events immediately to the left. Beginning under Den[50] a strict horizontal format restricts itself to the "event" section on the right side of the rectangle, enclosed by the *rnpt*-sign and a straight, vertical divider; on the left, outside this box so delineated, the *serekh* floats free in a vertical format, in association with variable elements. Under Semempses and

[45]Cf. Petrie, *RT*, II (London, 1901) pl. 10, 2; 11, 2; W. B. Emery, *Archaic Egypt* (Harmondsworth, 1961) 50, fig. 10.

[46]Petrie, *RT* II, pl. 1, 4 (*serekh* on right, facing right, at the head of the text).

[47]Petrie, *RT* II, pl. 3, 2 (*serekh* left, rest of text on right, facing left); pl. 3, 4 (*serekh* left, all glyphs facing right).

[48]Petrie, *RT* II, pl. 5, 1; J. E. Quibell, *Excavations at Saqqara, 1912-14* (Cairo, 1923) pl. 11, 2-3; W. B. Emery, *The Tomb of Hemaka* (Cairo, 1938) pl. 17, 18A.

[49]*GT* II (London, 1954) 102, fig. 105; pl. 35; Sir A. H. Gardiner, *JEA* 44 (1958) 38ff. It would seem reasonable to conclude that the connexion between the year-branch and the *gnwt* was early established through this scribal practice. In later iconography the branch came to be notched simply because many *gnwt* were referred to.

[50]Petrie, *RT* I, pl. 15, 12, 16, 25 and *passim*; II, pl. 7, 11 (presumably from the "event" box, with the vertical on the right being the *rnpt*.)

Qa-a, while the basic division into a right side (events) and a left side (royal name and variables) remains, even the former has surrendered to a vertical format.[51]

The kinds of events memorialized in these tablets include cultic acts,[52] progresses,[53] taxation,[54] sculpting,[55] construction,[56] and battles,[57] in short content identical in every way save one with that of the Palermo stone and the Cairo fragments. The missing information on the tablets involves the variable element: the tablets contain clerical notations not present on the annals fragments, while the latter include inundation heights absent from the labels.

The explanation lies in the different functions fulfilled by the archetypal *gnwt* and the derived labels. The single piece of information of most concern to the king's bureaucracy in a "hydraulic" society was the record of the annual flood;[58] and the royal *gnwt* therefore record these data. The latter, however, were of no use to the official of the treasury, charged with dating by means of a label the contents of a bale, jar or room. Hence the position in the format occupied, in the case of the prototypical *gnwt*, by the Nile datum, was used by the clerk for his notation; and since in the earliest format the Nile height was placed in the *bottom* register of the earliest horizontal arrangement, this is also where the earliest clerical

[51]Petrie, *RT* I, pl. 17, 26-28; II, pl. 8, 1-5. This format might have been introduced slightly earlier (Adj-ib?): cf. *GT* I (Cairo, 1949) pl. 45A, no. 74, p. 115. (Although tomb X bears sealings of Den, the style of architecture is later: *ibid.*, 107).

[52]Petrie, *RT* II, pl. 3, 6; 10, 2 (reg. 2); 11, 1; Emery, *Archaic Egypt*, 50, fig. 10 (reg. 2); *idem*, *Hemaka*, pl. 17 (reg. 2); Petrie, *RT* I, pl. 4, 12; 15, 16 (*sd*); 16, 25 (Min?); 17, 27-28 (*ḫ*ᶜ*-nsw-bity*);Petrie, *RT* II, pl. 8, 5 (*ḫ*ᶜ*-nsw-bity*).

[53]Petrie, *RT* II, pl. 10, 2 (reg. 1); Emery, *Archaic Egypt*, 50, fig. 10 (reg. 1); Quibell, *Excavation*, pl. 11, 2-3 (reg. 1, 3); Petrie, *RT* I, pl. 17, 26 (*šms Ḥr*); II, pl. 8, 1-3 (6th occurrence of *šms Ḥr*).

[54]Petrie, *RT* II, pl. 3, 4; Quibell, *Excavation*, pl. 11, 2-3 (reg. 3); Emery, *Hemaka*, pl. 17 (reg. 1); Petrie, *RT* I, pl. 15, 16, 18(?).

[55]Petrie, *RT* II, pl. 3, 4 (*ms wt Ḥr*), 10, 2 (reg. 1: *ms wt*), 11, 1 (*ms inpw*); Emery, *Hemaka*, pl. 17 (reg. 1, 2); *GT* II, 102, fig. 105 (*ms ḏḥwty ...?*); Petrie, *RT* I, pl. 14, 12 (*ms Ḏḥwty*).

[56]Petrie, *RT* II, pl. 10, 2 (reg. 1: *ᶜḥᶜ ḥwt-Nit*); Quibell, *Excavation*, pl. 11, 2-3 (reg. 1, 2); *GT* II, 102, fig. 105; possibly Petrie, *RT* I, pl. 13, 5.

[57]Petrie, *RT* II, pl. 10, 2 (reg. 3: for the hoe read *b³*); Emery, *Archaic Egypt*, 50, fig. 10 (reg. 1); Petrie, *RT* II, pl. 11, 1; *GT* II, 102, fig. 105; Petrie, *RT* I, pl. 15, 16, 18.

[58]K. A. Wittfogel, *Oriental Despotism* (New Haven, 1957) 50ff; K. W. Butzer, *Early Hydraulic Civilization in Egypt* (Chicago, 1976) 28, 41ff and *passim*.

notices are placed in the labels.[59]

Though our contemporary sources fail for the 2nd Dynasty, we may safely surmise that the *gnwt* at the beginning of the reign of Hotep-sekhemwy had evolved the following format: 1. a large enclosing *rnpt*-sign on the right, bracketing on the left, 2. (a) a notice of the Following of Horus, followed by (b) sundry other events (usually cultic?); then, beyond another vertical line on the left, 3. the designation of the king, probably in the form in which we see it in the inscriptions on the vessels from the Step-pyramid,[60] and 4. the height of the Nile, either on the extreme left, or (more likely) in a horizontal band running beneath the king's name.

For the subsequent development of the form we are obliged to rely in the main on the 5th Dynasty publication represented by the Palermo stone and the Cairo fragments. On the basis of this evidence it may be stated that, by the reign of Ny-nuter at the latest, while the Following of Horus still takes precedence in 2.(a), it now alternates with years designated by *ḫᶜ-(nsw)-bity*;[61] and an amplification of the Following of Horus, indicating the ordinal position of that occurrence in a series for the reign, is inserted beneath it.[62] Between registers 4 and 5 of the *obverse* of the Palermo stone a most interesting change has taken place. While in vernacular parlance the phoneme represented by the *rnpt*-sign may still have been construed in a bound construction with the designation of the number of the *ṯnwt*, the graphic format of the *gnwt* has now given precedence to a number of non-recurring, unique events. These are

[59]With the passage of time during the 1st Dynasty, as we have seen, the notice of the commodity in the case of labels tended to gravitate to the *left*, leaving the "event" box on the right. The information in the clerical notice could thus be easily separated out, and upon occasion could *alone* occupy a rectangular label: with *serekh*, cf. Quibell, *Excavation*, pl. 11, 5 *GT* II, pl. 35 (no. 394); Petrie, *RT* II, pl. 3, 1; 5, 1-2, 4; 12, 3; Petrie, *RT* I, pl. 13, 2-3; with official's name, cf. Emery, *Hemaka*, pl. 18B; R. Macrammallah, *Fouilles à Saqqara* (Cario, 1940) p. 16, fig. 17 (A-D), pl. 48; Petrie, *RT* II, pl. 2, 3, 9-18; 12, 1, 4; *GT* I, p. 115, fig. 65; *GT* II, 104f, figs. 107-125.

[60]Cf. P. Lacau, J-P. Lauer, *La pyramide à degres* I (Cairo, 1959), nos. 50, 52, 57, 61-66 and *passim*.

[61]Cf. P. Kaplony, *MDAIK* 20 (1965) 1; on *šms-Ḥr* see L. Borchardt, *Die Mittel zur zeitlichen Festlegung von Punkten der ägyptischen Geschichte* (Cairo, 1935) 32, n. 1; H. Kees, *Ancient Egypt: A Cultural Topography* (London, 1961), 102f.

[62]Cf. Palermo stone *obv.* 4, *passim*: for the full formula and the adjuncts to the royal designations, all of which probably occurred in the original *gnwt*, see P. Posener-Kriéger, J-L. de Cenival, *Hieratic Papyri in the British Museum* V Series *The Abusir Papyri* (London, 1968) pl. 1 and *passim*; P. Posener-Kriéger, *Les archives du temple funéraire de Néferirkarê-Kakaï* I (Cairo, 1976) 3ff; II 483ff. It is very difficult to say whether, in the case of Palermo stone *obverse* 4 and 5 *all* the information contained in the "event" box of the archetype has been reproduced; but I suspect that in fact it has.

placed, in columns immediately after the *rnpt*, the *ṯnwt*-notice being reserved for the bottom of the last column. Thus *rnpt* and *ṯnwt* enclose, at either end, the contents of the year.[63] The final stage in the evolution vouchsafed to us is represented by the reverse of the Palermo stone and Cairo fragments G and H,[64] comprising the reigns of Shepseskaf and the first three kings of the 5th Dynasty. Now position 2. (a) is occupied by the perfunctory and slightly archaic coronation ceremonies and *ḫ^{c}-nsw-bity* (if these are in fact ever performed); while 2. (b), expanded beyond expected proportions, comprises benefactions labelled by the broad formula *ir.n.f m mnw.f.* Bringing up the rear (2. [c]) are notices of campaigns and foreign expeditions, and *ṯnwt* records.[65]

Over the six centuries or so attested by the sources we have been following, not only did the format evolve, but the content as well. The Following of Horus, so common during the first two dynasties (26 examples) virtually ceases after Palermo *obverse* 5.[66] The celebration of festivals, important enough to account for 17 notices to the middle of the 2nd Dynasty, ceases thereafter to captivate the archivist, and for the remainder of the preserved material only 4 references are extant. 21 of the 30 odd entries having to do with the fashioning of cult images fall in the first two dynasties, and although the practice retained sufficient importance to ensure its continued recording, most of the notices from the 4th Dynasty on refer to royal statues. In addition, from Djedef-re, *wpt-r* is also included.[67] While the construction of buildings continues to be recorded fairly regularly, the archaic *ḥ^{3}* is given up before the close of the Protodynastic Period;[68] and from the 3rd Dynasty ship-building assumes an importance it had not enjoyed before. From Ny-nuter's reign at the latest the biennial numbering is carefully noted, but the recurrence of certain feasts (like the Running of the Apis) continues faithfully to be entered. The archivist does not fail to record occasional expeditions and military campaigns, though from Snofru on he reveals a new interest, viz. the amount of booty brought back or goods acquired.

A major introduction, probably under Khufu,[69] is the heading *ir.n.f*

[63]On the Cairo fragments the reigns of Snofru and Khufu seem to be similarly organized: *Urk.* I, 235f, 237.
[64]*Urk.* I, 240ff.
[65]*Urk.* I, 240:4-5; 245:3; 246:3-5; under Snofru these were still "floating": 236f.
[66]One (archaic?) example under Khufu: *Urk.* I, 238:16.
[67]*Urk.* I, 238:13.
[68]*Wb.* III, 8:4.
[69]*Urk.* I, 238:7.

m mnw.f, "he made it as his monument ...," to quote the standard translation. Under this is subsumed the grants of offerings, fields and personnel made to the gods, records of which assume a preponderant importance from Khufu on, the fashioning of images and the construction of temples. Clearly a new source of information is being employed by the recording scribe.[70]

While we lack sources for the remainder of the Old Kingdom, examples 1 and 2 above leave little doubt that until the close of the 6th Dynasty *gnwt* continued to be compiled little different from those drawn up under Neferirkare.

The Evolution of *Gnwt* from the Close of the Old Kingdom

Darkness closes in with the termination of the Memphite monarchy at the end of the 8th Dynasty; and although Merikare's father makes much of the records of the ancestors, he is probably talking more about Wisdom literature than annals. Numerous questions suggest themselves, but answers are scarcely to be expected. Had the *gnwt* retained the rectangular format with year-branch on the right? How far back had they been written on papyrus? How many (if any) "publications" of *gnwt* had been made over the course of the Old Kingdom, assuming that the practice attested by the Palermo stone had become a fad? With respect to this last question the evidence suggests that, sometime after Djoser but before the 5th Dynasty, the *gnwt* from Menes to Djoser had achieved some kind of published form in which (a) some of the names are already garbled, (b) lengths of life are included for each reign, and (c) the salient events for each reign are noted.[71]

From the Middle Kingdom the examples of the term used in the word study above become almost our sole source. Examples under II through V and VI mention *gnwt* only peripherally, the first in the cultic context of the legitimation of kingship, the second as a rhetorical device emphasizing the uniqueness of an event. So common is the first that one wonders whether the *gnwt* had entered the vocabulary of the cult and was now, by extension, applied to mythological records. The linking of *gnwt* with the "Followers of

[70]On the expression see in general S. Tawfik, *MDAIK* 27 (1971) 227ff; D. Meeks, in *Hommages à Serge Sauneron* I (Cairo, 1979) 230.
[71]See above, p. 8 on TC; p. 136, n. 36 on the Giza Drawing Board; below, p. 212f on the Manethonian tradition.

Horus" (no. 101), the "time of God" (nos. 102, 103, Re (no. 104), Osiris (no. 89), and "gods and goddesses" (nos. 109, 110) might suggest this. One additional consideration which supports this postulated cultic extension of the term is the place where the *gnwt* are said to be kept. They are in the *sd*-pavillion (no. 95), on or under the *išd*-tree in Heliopolis (nos. 65, 83), or in a special chamber named for them with a god who presides over the jubilee (nos. 97-100). Elsewhere they are in the "House of Books" (no. 104), a term which at least in the New Kingdom refers to a repository for essentially religious literature, or in the "House of Life" (nos. 110, 112), an institution with similarly strong cultic overtones.[72] When the king has occasion to seek guidance from the records of antiquity, a need which we might consider would entail the consultation of annals, he in fact is found to be perusing mythological texts. Thus in the great Abydos stela of Neferhotpe[73] the court enjoins the king: "'let Your Majesty proceed to the Houses of Books in order that Your Majesty may see all the hieroglyphic texts';[74] so His Majesty proceeded to the House of Books, and His Majesty opened the books together with his companions." The king then decides to fashion a new cult image for the god. Similarly Ramesses II in preparation for construction work at Luxor "... sought out the Chamber of Writings, he opened the records of the House of Life and apprised himself of the hidden things of heaven, and all the secrets of earth. He discovered that Thebes, the 'Eye of Re,' had been a 'Mound' which had come into being formerly, at the time when this land was [formed(?) and] when Amun-re was king, shining in the heavens, when he divided their circuit looking for a place where he could alight."[75] Ramesses IV, in anticipation of various beneficent acts, says

[72]Cf. the title of the steward and festival-leader Nebsumenu: "pupil of His Majesty, king's-scribe of the God's-book in the *pr-ᶜnḫ*": Kitchen, *RI* III, 183:10. For *pr-ᶜnḫ* see especially Gardiner, *JEA* 24, 157ff; A. Volten, *Demotische Traumdeutung* (Copenhagen, 1942) 17ff; P. Derchain, *Le Papyrus Salt 825* (Brussels, 1965) 19ff; J-C. Goyon, *Confirmation du pouvoir royal au nouvel an* (Cairo, 1972) 104f, n. 207. The elusive nature of this institution (part scriptorium, part academy, part library, part cult-centre), together with the curious inability of anyone to localize it in space, in relation to any known standing temple, makes one strongly suspect that *pr-ᶜnḫ* is an abstraction, a cult organization rather than a physical building.

[73]Lines 6-7: M. Pieper, *Die grosse Inschrift des Königs Neferhotep in Abydos* (MVAG 32, 2 [1929]); W. Helck, *Historisch-biographische Texte aus der 2. Zwischenzeit und neue Texte der 18. Dynastie* (Wiesbaden, 1975) 22.

[74]*Mdw-ntr nbw.*

[75]Kitchen, *RI* II, 346; D. B. Redford, *JEA* 57 (1971) 113; M. Abdul Razik, *JEA* 60 (1974) 142ff.

"then in my heart I pondered on my father, my lord ⸢in⸣ [the ...][76] of Thoth, which is in the House of Life. I left none of them at all unexamined, in order to seek out both great and small among the gods and goddesses. [I] found [...] as(?) a complete Ennead, and all thy forms. How difficult is their wording! Now those days of which they speak happened before Nut had become pregnant with thy beauty, when ⸢gods⸣ were living like men, animals, birds and water creatures likewise."[77] In a similar vein Imhotpe, in response to Djoser's request to investigate the causes of a famine, repairs to the House of Life and opens the "Souls of Re" which inform him about Elephantine and its god.[78]

The question arises as to whether we today possess any text which the ancients would have called "the *gnwt* of a god." The answer probably is, yes we do. Although couched in the narrative style of a Märchen rather than the terse tabulary form of the Old Kingdom annals, stories of the gods abound in which the "historical" events of their "reigns" are recounted.

Such "historicization" of deity[79] arises out of a particular view of myth which is at once sophisticated and secondary to its primary use. Although we know next to nothing about the myths which circulated in Egypt in preliterate times before the 1st Dynasty,[80] we can be sure that their prime purpose was to hypostasize the natural powers at work in the world, and to describe their interaction in human terms relating to the human community. Historic phenomena such as the pharaonic kingship and evolving temple ritual, elicited myth to underpin and "potentize" new forms, or (more often) created new myths as archetypal hypostases for ritual acts and relationships.[81] Such a relationship between a phenomenon and an underlying myth has a certain ineffable and direct quality about it, which is not, and need not be, scrutinized dispassionately for interest's sake alone. The myths, however, progressively assume the dimensions of material for a corpus, knowledge of which may be useful for other purposes than

[76]Possibly the name of a book, or a generic term for writings: G. Posener, *De la divinité de pharaon* (Paris, 1960) 72. A "book of Thoth" is mentioned in *BD* 68, 9-10: cf. P. Boylan, *Thoth, the Hermes of Egypt* (London, 1922) 94. On "books of Thoth" in their Hermetic guise, see above n. 11, also A. A. Barb, in *The Legacy of Egypt*^{2}, 146f; J. G. Griffiths, *Plutarch's De Iside et Osiride* (Cambridge, 1970) 519f.

[77]Kitchen, *RI* VI, 22.

[78]J. Vandier, *La famine dans l'Egypte ancienne* (Cairo, 1936) 132ff; on the b^3w R^c, see Gardiner, *JEA* 24, 166, 168; E. A. E. Reymond, *CdE* 47 (1972) 124; also below, p. 215, n. 52.

[79]In general see U. Luft, *Beiträge zur Historisierung der Götterwelt und der Mythenschreibung* (*Studia Aegyptiaca* IV; Budapest, 1978).

[80]Some attempt to specify them in R. Anthes, *JNES* 18 (1959) 179.

[81]E. Otto, *Das Verhältnis von Rite und Mythos in Aegypten* (Heidelberg, 1958) 100ff.

that for which they were originally created. One such use involves the power inherent in the *knowledge* of myths, their details and *dramatis personnae*. Here we hover on the periphery of magic. A speaker in a religious text will claim knowledge of an intellectual sort of a specific mythological event in the past which explains a present situation. Thus in CT spell 154[82] the speaker claims to know how there came about the reduction of the monthly festival, and how the harpoon, the *snwt*-staves and the priest with side-lock originated. Though in a body of texts concerned with identification and cultic ritual, the allusion to the myth which follows at this point is couched in narrative form,[83] and tells of the fight between Re and the *Imy-whm.f* serpent.[84] Far from belonging to the timeless world of cosmogonic or fertility myths, Re's battle with the snake is a single occurrence located in past time; it could be treated as *ḫprt*, "that which has happened," i.e. history.[85]

These myths, recounted in the spells labelled "Knowing the Manifestations of ...," are well on their way to becoming "events" of the time of the gods which, in spite of their use here to empower an individual magically, can be coupled with others to form embryonic annals. A further stage is reached when such "historic events" from the time of the gods are used to gloss texts which in their original form were now felt to need such explanation. Thus in CT spell 335[86] allusion is made from time to time to the twin Souls of Osiris, to Re as a cat, the splitting of the *išd*-tree and the day of making war. In each case a gloss has been added to the original text, giving "historical" information by way of aetiological explanation. The spell itself still entails the power that knowledge can bring (cf. the rubric at the end); but the glosses evince an interest in the byegone events almost for their own sake.

The bringing of the gods into relationship with each other in the great cycles, a process datable to the early Old Kingdom, abetted their translation out of the timeless relationship with a single community into a pseudo-historic framework of successive reigns. One of the chief agents was the earthly phenomenon of kingship. On the mundane level divine king had succeeded divine king; similarly, on the heavenly god had succeeded god. The inspiration was the earthly phenomenon of regimes in sequence, a prospect charged with

[82]CT II, 266ff; K. Sethe, *ZÄS* 57 (1922) 1ff; Faulkner, *Coffin Texts* I, 132f. Similar are the spells for "Knowing the Souls of Pe" (CT II, 326ff), and "Knowing the Souls of Nekhen" (CT II, 349ff).
[83]Cf. the use of such constructions ạs *N pw ḥr mdt*, *N pw ḏd.n.f*, *sḏm.in.f*, *ᶜḥᶜ.n.f ḥr sḏm*, etc.
[84]On *Imy-whm.f*, see J. F. Borghoutts, *JEA* 59 (1973) 114ff.
[85]See H. Goedicke, *The Protocols of Neferty* (Baltimore, 1977) 64.
[86]CT IV, 184ff; Faulkner, *Coffin Texts* I, 262ff, and the literature cited in note 1.

transitoriness. The influence of this phenomenon was wholly different from that of the passing of the god-king, which had called forth rites of passage whose archetype, the Osiris myth, partook of that timeless quality we normally associate with myth. But now, on this slightly more sophisticated level the gods are not timeless archetypes alone, though their deeds may be archetypal; they are simply "primordial kings." The process had already begun by the time the Pyramid Texts were inscribed. Conceivable was a time "when[87] Re was chief of the Two Enneads, and the chief of the plebs was Nefertum" (PT 483b). By the First Intermediate Period the "reigns" of the gods have surfaced in the collective consciousness of the nation.[88] "In the time of ...," the formulaic way of referring to a reign,[89] is found in the Old Kingdom, but only as a reference to earlier historic kings.[90] From the Middle Kingdom on, however, it is applied equally to the historified gods.[91]

The mind and intent that induced the collection of events from the times of the gods into corpus form can at once be labelled "scholarly." The original purpose of aetiology or archetypal act is now laid aside; to a greater degree curiosity in identifying events, and putting them in sequence predominates. The immediacy of the relationship between rite and myth is unknown here; the scribe is motivated by the archivist's dispassionate aim to be complete.

By the New Kingdom several cycles of myths had begun to take shape around the gods of the Great Ennead. The "Book of the Cow of Heaven"[92] collects a great deal of material from the time of Re, and although the intent is in part aetiological, the narrative sets the incidents carefully in sequence. The El-Arish naos[93] text yields, in a style approximating a chronicle, an account of the "reigns" of Shu and Geb. Here the thematic material is not noticeably aetiological, and approaches in nature the categories of information known from Old Kingdom annals: building accounts, military campaigns, death of the old king, accession of the new, inventory texts, etc. There are, of course, some bizarre scenes like the rape of Tefnut and the stinging of Geb which would have found no place in a set of royal annals. No

[87] *Sk*: E. Edel, *Altägyptische Grammatik* (Rome, 1964) § 1031.
[88] E. Otto, *WO* 3 (1966) 171f.
[89] *Wb*. II, 457 (*m rk*); II, 477 (*m* h^{3}*w*).
[90] *Urk*. I, 37, 51, 85, 107, 131 etc.; Posener-Kriéger, de Cenival, *The Abusir Papyri*, pl. 19; Goedicke, *Königliche Dokumente*, Koptos I, col. 2.
[91] Admon. 1, 7; Prisse 6, 5; London 581, 3; see also below, p. 161, n. 165.
[92] C. Maystre, *BIFAO* 40 (1941) 53ff; G. Roeder, *Urkunden zur Religion d. alten Aegypten* (Jena, 1923) 142ff; A. Piankoff, *The Shrines of Tutankhamen* (New York, 1955) 27ff. E. Hornung, *Der ägyptische Mythos von der Himmelskuh*, Göttingen, 1982; and the present writier's forthcoming review in *Religious Studies Review*.
[93] G. Goyon, *Kêmi* 6 (1936) 1ff.

complete cycle dealing with the generation of Osiris has come down to us, alhough one must have existed.[94]

The latter portions of the Osiris myth, viz. those in which Horus is the chief protagonist, display two foci of interest around which tales tend to cluster: the tribulations of baby Horus and his mother in the northern marshes, and the battle between the grown Horus and Seth. The former attracted to itself a wide variety of myths, usually concerned with Horus's rescue from snake bite or the like, and put to use as magic spells.[95] The latter early achieved a set order of events, and presented a partially closed "canon" which did not permit much variation or new creation.

All this material, and more besides, from the "reigns" of the gods of the Lesser Enneads and of the later demigods, would, we submit, have been classified under the broad category of *gnwt*. By Manetho's time one can conceive of this material ordered and organized along the lines of a narrative chronicle, very much like the text from the naos of El-Arish.

If by extension *gnwt* could encompass mythological texts which in the eyes of the ancients constituted records of the past, there is some indication that it came also to be extended loosely to hieroglyphic inscriptions with a vaguely chronicling intent. The wording of example 46, cited above, suggests that it is the inscriptions on the walls of Medinet Habu that Seshat claims to be writing. Example 79 might be similarly construed: at least the *gnwt* are said to be *in* the House of Amun. Example 67 provides the strongest evidence. "She-who-is-Upon-the-Mountain" is fairly certainly to be identified with the lioness Pakhet, to whom the shrine was dedicated.[96] and the "desert tract" is simply an allusion to the east bank where the Speos Artemidos is located, and by extension to the Speos itself. The "publication," then, of the "annals of her brave deeds" becomes a reference to the cutting of the very inscription wherein the passage is found.[97] *Gnwt ḳnn.s*, "annals of her mighty (deeds)" would, in fact,

[94]Cf. "King Osiris and his Vizier" (P. Chester Beatty V, *vs.* 1, 1-2); Plutarch's account presupposes some sort of written *Vorlage*, though it may be derived from some such account as Manetho (cf. the allusion to the "List of Kings" [11, 355C], and the "genealogies of the kings" [38, 366C]).

[95]Partly collected into a compendium: cf. the Leiden and Metternich stelae: A. Klasens, *A Magical Statue Base* (Leiden, 1952) *passim*. The setting fostered the creation of new myths of similar import, however, which did not always enjoy inclusion in such collections: cf. the narratives of P. Geneva MAH 15274, *rt.* iv, 5ff, and P. Jumilhac.

[96]Gardiner, *JEA* 32, 46, n. 3.

[97]This is a superior construction to the one espoused by Gardiner (*ibid.*, 46): "... the annals of her supremacy over the region of Her-that-is-Upon-the-Mountain." What special significance had the east bank of nome 15 that her "supremacy" over it should be stressed? *Ḥr wʿrt* obviously is better construed with *smnḫ* than with *ḳnn.s*.

be a fitting description of the Speos Artemidos text, concerned as it is with recording the major events and accomplishments of the queen's reign, albeit not by year.[98]

That in the New Kingdom (or for that matter in the Middle) a true annalistic *Gattung* called *gnwt* existed, seems doubtful on the examples marshalled above. In section III the *gnwt* said to have been consulted inevitably belong to the past, and the remote past, at that; reference to the contemporary compilation of *gnwt*, viz. yearly annals, is lacking. Those who attempt to read the *gnwt* to which in their day they have access, find them very difficult to understand (nos. 111, 112), suggesting that the language and/or orthography is archaic.[99] The statue inscription of Userhat (no. 113) might indicate a living genre; but his high-flown rhetoric might point to nothing more than the cultic extension of the term elicited above.

The conclusions to the preceding discussion may be summarized as follows: 1. *gnwt* came into use in the early Old Kingdom as a term for the yearly record of the king's government, probably kept on papyrus from a very early date. 2. By the close of the Old Kingdom the *gnwt* were tending more and more to become a list of benefactions. 3. By the Middle Kingdom the annalistic needs which originally had called forth the genre were probably largely being fulfilled by other types of documents; and *gnwt* seem to have been adopting pious and cultic overtones. 4. Already in the Middle Kingdom it is used in a stereotyped scene, much more common in the New Kingdom, to affirm the king's legitimacy and longevity. 5. An ill-defined, though infrequent, extension of the term in the New Kingdom leads to its being applied to texts with a vague intent to record for posterity. 6. By the same period it has come to refer to mythological texts which purport to record the primordial times of the gods.

[98]Several scholars have opined that the so-called "annals" of Thutmose III at Karnak are to be classed as *gnwt*: cf. H. Grapow, *Sprachliche und schriftliche Formung ägyptischer Texte*, (Glückstadt and New York, 1936) 60, n. 26; E. Otto, *HO* I, 2 (1952) 143; but see Grapow, *Studien*, 5. The text itself, however, from the standpoint of form, is called a *wḏ*, "formal hieroglyphic inscription" (*Urk*. IV, 647:6; 734:15), and its sources are variously listed as the "journal of the king's house" (*Urk*. IV, 693:11), " a leather roll in the temple of Amun" (*Urk*. IV, 661:2,5), and an unspecified record in the treasury (*Urk*. IV, 694:7-8). There remains the possibility, however, that in the looser usage of the New Kingdom, these Karnak records of campaigns could have been called *gnwt*.

[99]Cf. the boast of the typical New Kingdom polymath: "there was no sign at all of which I did not know the working; shapes which had no[t been drawn(?)] ... old, worn writings, I [was knowledgable] about them": *Urk*. IV, 1082:2-5; "every wiseman is one who can understand what the early ancestors said": *ibid*., 1084:8; "I was inducted into the God's-book, and saw the 'Tools of Thoth'; I was prepared in their secrets, and opened up all their difficult passages": *ibid*., 1820:12-14.

3

Day-books

References to *gnwt* become at an early date so highly stereotyped that one may reasonably conclude that the form, at least as originally conceived, had become obsolete in Egyptian archival usage by the Middle Kingdom. Whether their place was taken by any other type of document signalizing the major events of a year we do not know; but certainly at an early date the central government and its institutions had developed a genre of daily record for the practical requirement of day to day business.

The Egyptian term denoting such a "journal" varies over the two millennia of its occurrence. In what must be its pristine form it appears as *hrwyt*, "day-(book),"[1] derived fairly certainly from *hrw*, "day";[2] but in the New Kingdom and later *hrwyt* turns up as *h^{3}yw*,[3] *h^{3}ry*, or *h(^{3})r*, or is rendered by a circumlocution such as *^{c}r(t) h^{3}w*, "roll of days." Examples, however, are infrequent, even though the genre denoted must have been very common. Those known to the author are set forth below in chronological order.

1. P. Berlin 10012.[4] *ḥ^{3}ty-^{c} imy-r ḥwt-ntr Nb-k^{3}w-r^{c} ḏd n ẖry-ḥb ḥry-tp Ppy-ḥtp ḏd rḫ.k r-ntt ḫpr prt Spdt m ^{3}bd* 4 *prt sw* 16 *iḫ ḥr im* [*n*] *wnwt*

[1] *Wb.* II, 500:26; see also D. Meeks, *Année lexicographique* I (Paris, 1980) 231; D. B. Redford, in *LdÄ*, s.v. *Tagebuch*, (forthcoming).

[2] J. Černý, *JEA* 31 (1945) 32, n. *a*; H. Grapow, *Studien zu den Annalen Thutmosis des Dritten und zu ihnen verwandten historischen Berichten des neuen Reiches* (Berlin, 1949) 51.

[3] *Wb.* II, 476:2.

[4] Sethe, *Lesestücke*, 96f, no. 32b; see J. Černý, in S. Donadoni (ed.), *Le fonti indiretti della storia egiziana*, (Rome, 1963) 35. Cf. also P. Berlin 10044 from Illahun: U. Kaplony-Heckel, *Aegyptische Handschriften* I (Wiesbaden, 1971) no. 34, p. 20f. The vast majority of the fragments described in this work are clearly from day-books, but as they are in such a fragmentary state, they have not been included in the discussion below where the Kahun material is treated; see below, n. 21.

ḥwt-ntr ... ḥnʿ rdit ir.t(w) tꜣ šʿt ḥr hryt nt ḥwt-ntr, "the count and superintendent of the temple Nebkaure speaks to the chief lector-priest Pepy-hotpe thus: ‘know you that the Going-Forth of Sothis takes place in the fourth month of *proyet*, day 16. Bring this to the attention of the temple staff ... and have this letter entered in the day-book of the temple.’"

2. *Urk.* IV, 693:8-14. (the specific quantities of food-stuffs with which Thutmose III’s coastal garrison ports were stocked) *ʿšꜣ st r ḫt nbt r rḫ mšʿ n ḥm.f nn m iw-ms iw.sn mn ḥr hrwyt pr-nsw ʿ.w.s. tm.tw rdit rḫt.sn ḥr wḏ pn r tm sʿšꜣ mdwt r irt ẖrwt.sn ḥr tꜣ st iry s[t im]*, "were more numerous than anything, beyond the comprehension of His Majesty’s army, and that is no wild statement. They are set down on the day-book of the king’s house, L.P.H. That a tally of them was not put in this inscription was so as not to lengthen the text,[5] in order to accommodate them in the place [where] th[ey] ought to be recorded."[6]

This entry accompanies the text recording the 7th Campaign, and the victualing of the garrison posts which it explicates is here mentioned for the first time. If the writer’s intent was to excuse himself from repeating the description, or at least the list of provisions, on each subsequent campaign, he proved to be inconsistent; for at least six additional passages were to come describing the same practice, and upon occasion listing the specific food-stuffs. But in all probability the scribe’s parenthetic remark has reference only to the amounts of the provisions.

Thutmose’s annals contain two additional passages naming reference texts:

2a. *Urk.* IV, 694:7-8. (regarding the harvest of Syria and the amounts of incense, oil, wine, fruit etc.) *iw.tw r šnt st r pr-ḥḏ mi ip bꜣkw n Nḥ[s]*, "It (the specific tally) may be looked up in the treasury, even as the reckoning of the labour of the Southland."

Again this reference occurs during the account of the 7th

[5]Literally "make words numerous."

[6]The last phrase sounds tautologous. Literally it can be rendered "to make their requirements in the place where they are made," and could refer to the day-book entries. On the other hand, *st* might be a concrete, locative, reference to the harbours themselves, and the phrase be linked to *iw.sn mn ḥr hrwyt ....* In that case the explication of their absence in the present text would be parenthetic, and the main passage would translate "they are set down upon the day-book of the king’s house ... in order to make their requirements in the place where they are made." Would this mean that their being recorded in the king’s archives is to govern and regulate the practice of stocking the garrison posts in the future? The same meaning could be arrived at if *st* referred to the king’s house, i.e. the place which authorized the stocking and whence most of the goods would be sent out.

Campaign. One wonders whether it applies to the harvest garnered on that campaign alone, or whether it explains the absence of specific amounts of grain throughout the rest of the annals. The *prima facie* probability is that both passages have reference only to the 7th Campaign, and indicate that it was a much bigger enterprise than would otherwise appear.[7]

2b. *Urk.* IV, 661-662:5. *ir<t>.n nbt ḥm.f r dmi pn r ẖrw pf ẖsy ḥnꜥ mšꜥ.f ẖsy smnw m hrw m rn.f m rn n nꜥt* ⸢*m*⸣ *rn*[*w*(?)] *nw imy-r mn*[*fyt*(?) ....[8] *iw.s*] *n smn ḥr ꜥrt nt dḥr m ḥwt-nṯr nt* [*Imn*] *m hrw pn*, "Everything His Majesty did against this town (viz. Megiddo) and against this vile chief and his vile army, recorded by specific day, by name of expedition, ⸢by⸣ name[s] of the inf[antry(?)] commander [....] they [are] recorded on a leather roll in the temple of Amun unto this day."

Interposed as it is between the description of the investment of Megiddo and the final surrender of the town, this passage would seem to be an allusion to a record of minor expeditions undertaken during the 7-months seige of the town.[9]

3. *Urk.* IV, 2156:6; J-M. Kruchten, *Le Décret d'Horemheb* (Brussels, 1981) 154f. (Edict of Horemheb). *di.n.i tp-rd m ḥr.sn hpw m hrwyt.*[*sn*(?)], "I set the instructions in front of them (the new judges he had appointed), the laws in [their] day-books."

4. J. Černý, *JEA* 31 (1945) pl. 8, i, 1ff. *ḥꜣt-sp* 3, *ꜣbd* 4 *ꜣẖt*, *sw* 5, *ẖr ḥm n* (Ramesses V's titulary); *hrw pn irt hꜣry n ꜣẖt.s in ꜥnẖ(t) n niwt N m-bꜣḥ ḳnbt n* (14 names occur at this point), "Regnal year 3, fourth month of *akhet*, day 5, under the Majesty of (Ramesses V); on this day (occurred) the making of the dated declaration regarding her property by citoyenne N in the presence of the (following) court ...."

5. *Ibid.* (*verso*). The identifying docket marks the document as the *ꜥwty hꜣry i.*[*ir.N*] *n ꜣẖt.s*, "the roll of the dated declaration which [N made] regarding her property."

In spite of the variation in orthography, it would be difficult to separate the term *hꜣry* in origin from *hrwyt.* In column vi, 9 of the same papyrus as nos. 4 and 5 the document is referred to as *nꜣ sšw i.ir N*, "the writings which N made."

6. P. Berlin 10496[10] (docket on *verso*). *tꜣ hꜣyw nt tꜣ ꜥḥꜥ(t)*, "the day-book(?) of the tomb(?)."

[7]The reference to the "labour of the Southland" is peculiar, as that particular amount of income is detailed for this very campaign (*Urk.* IV, 695-6). The comparison, however, probably has to do only with the location of the data as stored: figures both for the harvest and the labour of the Southland are to be found in treasury records.

[8]Nearly 2 metres are lost at this point.

[9]*Urk.* IV, 1234:18-19.

[10]A. Erman, *SBAW*, 1910, 333.

7. Amenemope xxi, 9ff. *m-ir ir n.k h^{3}rw n ^{c}ḏ^{3} st štmw ^{c3} n mwt st ^{c}nḫyw ^{c3} n sḏf^{3}-tr st n smtr n wḥmw*, "do not make false journal entries, for that is a serious capital offence. They (involve) serious oaths of allegiance(?),[11] and are destined for criminal investigation."[12]

8. Wenamun ii, 8-9: *iw.f dit in.tw ^{c}rt h^{3}w n^{3}y.f itw iw.f dit ^{c}š.tw.s m-b^{c}ḥ.i iw.w gm ḫ^{3} n dbn n ḥḏ nty nb r t^{3}yf ^{c}r(t)*, "he had the 'roll of days' of his fathers brought, and he had it read before me; and there was found thousands of *deben* of all types of money in his roll (*scil.* the payment made by Egypt in exchange for timber)."

9. *LD* III, 255 (Annals of the priests of Karnak).[13] *ḥ^{3}t-sp* 11 *ḫr ḥm n* (titulary of Takelot II) *ii in w^{c}b ^{c}ḳ n pr Imn* ... *Ḥr-s^{3}-* [*Ist*] ... *r-ḏd ink w^{c}b ^{c}ḳ n Ipt-swt ink s^{3} ḥmw-ntr ^{c3}w n Imn ḥr mwt.i* ... *iw it n itw.i n it-ntr ḥry-sšt^{3} n p^{3}wty-t^{3}wy šsp t^{3}y.i h^{3}w*, "Regnal year 11 under the Majesty of (Takelot II) there came the priest with right of access of the House of Amun ... Harsi[ese ...] saying: 'I am a priest with right of access at Karnak, I am the son of great prophets of Amun on my mother's (side?) ... the father of my fathers belonging(?) to the (rank of?) god's-father and master of the mysteries of the Primaeval One of the Two Lands. My dated declarations (?) have been received ....'"

Though doubtful, it is within the realm of possibility that *h^{3}w* here is the same word we have been ferreting out, in its meaning of official declaration, validated by a date (cf. nos. 4, 5, 7, 10). In Harsiese's case it almost has the force of "credentials."

10. Serapeum Stela no. 87 (M. Malinine, G. Posener, J. Vercoutter, *Catalogue des stèles du Sérapéum de Memphis* [Paris, 1968] pl. 25). *Ḥp-iw* owner of the stela, and *imy-r h*(?) *n p^{3} nṯr*, "overseer of the ...(?) of the god." The reading of the abnormal hieratic here must be viewed with caution. But if we are dealing with the same word as in no. 9, it is interesting to note that it belongs to a god (i.e. the temple), in this case presumably Apis. One would then be put in mind of no. 1 above. On the other hand, it seems rather more likely that the sign should be read *wsḫt*, "court," and the owner construed as a domestic functionary of the temple.

11. P. Louvre 3228, 8.[14] *bn iw.i rḫ st^{3} t^{3} hr nty r-ḥry*, "I shall be unable to rescind the dated declaration which is above."

This formula, which recurs in varying patterns in several abnormal

[11]On *sḏf^{3} tryt*, see now D. Lorton, *The Juridical Terminology of International Relations in Egyptian Texts through Dyn. XVIII* (Baltimore, 1974) 132.
[12]Literally "investigation of the reporter."
[13]See Gauthier, *LdR* III, 352, (V); also *Wb.* II, 470:6. A somewhat doubtful example.
[14]M. Malinine, *Choix de textes juridiques* (Paris, 1953) 48, n. 20.

hieratic and demotic business documents, is a formal renunciation by a litigant who has just made a declaration, dated and carrying legal force.[15] That a document *per se* is envisaged is proven by the alternation with *hr* of such variants as *sẖ*, "writing"[16] and *md̠*, "document."[17]

The examples cited above, though few in number, make it certain that *hrwyt* (and its variants) denotes a document which records an event or series of events by dates. The fact that the word "day" is the base from which the term (undoubtedly a *nisbe*-formation) is derived, underscores the overriding importance of the calendric notation: the *hrwyt* has meaning only because it is provided with specific dates. In the case of the later New Kingdom extension of the term into legal jargon, it is the date that validates or gives legal force to the document.[18] The importance of the *hrwyt* in the life of the community is thus practical and of an immediate nature.

The institutions whose functioning involves the keeping of a day-book can be identified by the syntactic adjuncts: the temple (nos. 1, 2b), the king's house (no. 2), the necropolis (no. 6), the ancestral archives (no. 8), and, in the case of the related passages, the treasury (no. 2a.). At first sight it might seem strange that magistrates in a court of law are advised to peruse so practical and prosaic a document as a diary (cf. no. 3); but a moment's reflection will reveal the answer. The term *hrwyt*, originally perhaps denoting a single entry in a document dated by a calendric notation, must by extension have come to mean a book made up of such dated entries. By the 19th Dynasty the word had also developed a specialized meaning denoting a dated record of a legal act or declaration (cf. nos. 4, 5, 7, 9, 10). Archives of such legal records would have been kept by each *ḳnbt*, and would have been available to magistrates in quest of legal

[15]F. Ll. Griffith, *JEA* 12 (1926) 218, n. 3; Černý, *JEA* 31, 32, n. *a*.
[16]Malinine, *Textes*, 60, 74.
[17]*Ibid.*, 13, n. 16.
[18]Cf. the overriding importance of the date of enactment in the text of a modern parliamentary statute.

precedent.[19] But ordinary day-books, as will shortly appear, contained *inter alia* decrees and directives with legal force; and all such journals would have provided precedents of importance to the courts. Thus under the rubric *hrwyt* of Horemheb's decree are subsumed both ordinary day-books, and collections of dated copies of deeds, wills, transcripts etc., all being quasi-juridical in extent.[20]

Something of the range of content of this genre of text is conveyed by the examples we have ranged in review. A day-book could contain copies of official correspondence (no. 1), the itemized list and specific amounts of food-stuffs and other commodities doled out to the army (no. 2), or received in payment (no. 8) by an institution; it might contain official directives or edicts (the "laws" *hpw*, of no. 3), the daily "acts" of the necropolis (no. 6), or the dated depositions of litigants (nos. 4, 5, 7, 9, 10). In the similar references to source

[19]Good examples of the kind of raw material which would have gone into a journal to be laid before a judge are provided by the contents of those ostraca which contain the transcripts of *ḳnbt* hearings. Of special interest, because it cites a precedent, is J. Černý, Sir A. H. Gardiner, *Hieratic Ostraca* (Oxford, 1957) pl. 46, no. 2; cf. M. Théodoridès, *RIDA* 16 (1969) 129ff. After the transcript of the trial of a woman accused of theft, and the statement of the composition of the court, the scribe adds a note of admonishment for the benefit of the vizier for whom the copy was intended: "Now with respect to the crime of this town, viz. the theft of the tool that was in it, and further (its being) in the possession of the widow, (this) is to inform my lord of the procedure in this regard, to wit: the citoyenne Tanodjmehemsi formerly stole a vessel of 1 1/2 *deben* (which) was here in the town in the time of the vizier Neferronpet ... and the vizier had the scribe Hatiay come and he had her taken down to the harbour (*scil.* for punishment). My lord shall have *this* woman (viz. the accused in the present trial) punished for taking the tool and also the vase, so that no other woman like her will do the same thing again." The dated depositions in criminal cases may also have fallen under this same rubric, at least in the vernacular. Officially, however, such transcripts were named more after the contents, and examples usually are identified as *ʿwty ḏdt.n N*, "scroll of N's statement": cf. P. Ambras, II, 2, 10 and *passim* (T. E. Peet, *The Great Tomb Robberies of the Twentieth Egyptian Dynasty* [Oxford, 1930] II, pl. 38); A. H. Gardiner, *The Inscription of Mes* (Leipzig, 1905) 12, n. 2; Černý, *JEA* 31, 40, n. *a*.

[20]It is interesting that the passage in the decree identifies the contents of the *hrwyt* as *hpw*, "laws," and joins them with *tp-rd*, "instructions." The latter is what the king or a knowledgable person gives in a situation of teaching or remonstrance (cf. the present writer in *JEA* 57 [1971] 115, n. *i*). *Hpw* has slightly broader application than "law" alone, containing like Hebrew *mišpat* a nuance of custom or accepted procedure (cf. C. F. Nims, *JNES* 7 [1948] 243. Nims' judgement that in pre-Demotic texts "the meaning 'custom' seems infrequent" stems from a misreading of the differing sources of his documents, the Demotic texts being mainly business documents wherein "customs" is an expected meaning, while the hierogl-hieratic texts are for the most part governmental promulgations where "edicts" are most often in the writer's consciousness). Yet *hp* can also mean written edicts of a particular king, issued on a specific occasion, and comparable to our "statutory law" of the "imperative" variety (if we modify somewhat Sir Edward Coke's definition of "statute"). Consequently we can find occasional passages in which *hpw* are paralleled by *wḏw*, "edicts": cf. Anastasi I, 9, 2; G. A. Reisner, *ZÄS* 69 [1933] pl. 8, 1. x+8.

material, given by Thutmose III (nos. 2a, 2b), the treasury is said to possess a similar document listing the harvest of Syria, both in grain and the produce of gardens, orchards and vineyards (2a); while the temple of Amun could boast a leather roll detailing the military excursions of part of the Megiddo campaign. Specifically the latter displayed the following (probable) format: 1. the date (presumably in regnal years, month and day), 2. the number of the expedition, 3. name(?) of the military commander, [4. booty(?)].[21] While the leather roll is a rather special document, it is probably excerpted, or derives ultimately, from a day-book of the sort referred to in no. 2.

Quite clearly the day-book of an institution was a heterogeneous collection of dated entries, recording a variety of events which would be of use to that institution in the future. The dependence of the organization of these events on a simple, chronological format shows that the criterion for filing was that of an archive: the *hrwyt* was a diary, and items would be looked up under date.

Once this characteristic is appreciated, it becomes apparent that a fairly sizable group of texts has long been available which the ancients would have classified as *hrwyt*. That the word does not occur in the texts themselves shows merely that *hrwyt* is a popular descriptive term, and had no status as an official denominative. A resumé of the specific contents of each of these documents will give a clearer picture of the intent of the institution in question in keeping such a prosaic record; and an examination of the verbal forms used will provide an assessment of the syntax.

1. The Kahun Day-book[22]

pl. 32 [heading lost]

III, 1 A, pp. 3:4

i-ix - apparently the transcript of a letter from a subordinate to a superior;

[21]See further below, p. 122. At first glance it might seem that this is a reference to the day-book itself, from which the Karnak annals presumably derive, and its distinctive format (so W. Helck, *Die Beziehungen Aegyptens zur Vorderasien im 3. und 2. Jahrtausend v. Chr.*[2] [Wiesbaden, 1971] 122), but there are difficulties with this view. The leather roll, as described in the annals, has important formal differences. In the annals *wdyt* is the word used for "expedition," in the leather roll *nꜥt*; while in the roll individual officers were apparently named no military commander apart from the king is mentioned in the annals. Moreover, it is specifically stated that the roll recorded only activity during the siege of Megiddo.

[22]F. Ll. Griffith, *Hieratic Papyri from Kahun and Gurob* II (London, 1898); (plates numbered in the text above). There are probably other fragments of day-books in this cache, but pls. 32-33 provide the only connected pieces.

x - notation of a total;
xi - date (year 34, ix, 20);
xii - date (year 34, ix, 21);
xiii-xiv - arrival of a treasurer by ship;
xv - arrival of another treasurer by ship;

pl. 33

III, 1 A, *vs.* pp. 1-2
xii - final account for day 22;
xiv - date (ix, 23);
xv - division of the plots which are on the east bank;

pl. 32

III, 1 C
xxxvii - the coming of a retainer;
xxxviii - food given to him;
xxxix - division of the plots which are on the [ ] bank;
xliv - date (year 34, ix, 24);
xlv - [ ] of the corvée (*mnyw*) of this town, placed in the storehouse;
xlvi - date (year 34, ix, 25);
xlvii - the coming of a scribe.

As for the syntax of verbs, the piece is so fragmentary that little can be said. *Spr* in III, 1 A, pp. 3-4, xiii and xv could be the infinitive; but *ii* in the same position in III, 1 C, xxxvii and xlvii seems to be the *sḏm.f*. The non-formulaic part of the text does not concern us.

2. Middle Kingdom Tax Assessor's Day-book[23]

I lines 1-6 - list of the assessor's staff;
II line 7 - date (year 2, ii, 15 to 19);
lines 7-12 - notation of surveying;
III line 13 - date (year 2, ii, 20);
lines 13-14 - notation of the "writing up of the exaction ...";
IV lines 15-22 - notation of the "call-up in the office of the seal-bearer ..." followed by a "list of the scribes of the field who attended the call-up" comprising 6 names;
V line 23 - date (year 2, ii, 21);
lines 24-25 - notation of the "writing up of the exaction ..."

The scribe seems to use the absolute infinitival construction throughout: *šsp* (1), *wrš* (12, 14, 26), *snhy* (15).

[23]P. C. Smither, *JEA* 27 (1941) 74ff.

3. The Semna Dispatches[24]

Letter I, lines i, 1 to ii, 6:
- report of a frontier patrol(?);
- report about natives coming to Semna West for trade in year 3, viii, 7, evening;
- date (year 3, viii, 8, morning), and farewell formula.

(space left)
- 6 Nubians arrive at Semna West for trade on year 3, viii, 8;
- ⌜report of frontier patrol⌝;
- farewell formula.

(space left)

Letter II, lines ii, 7 to iii, 6:
- rubric ("another letter brought to him ...");
- salutation;
- report of frontier patrol on viii, 4, evening;
- questioning of Nubians ...;
- farewell formula.

(space left)

Letter III, lines iii, 7 to iv, 5:
- rubric ("another letter brought to him through the retainer N ...");
- salutation;
- report of two soldiers, on viii, 2, year 3, breakfast time;
- report of patrol on 30, vii, year 3; ...
- farewell formula.

(space left)

Letter IV, lines iv, 6 to iv, 12:
- rubric ("copy of the document brought to him as a dispatch from the fortress of Elephantine");
- salutation;
- report regarding Medjay who came on vii, 27 of year 3 for work;
- interrogation of them concerning the state of the land.

(space left)

Letter V(?), lines v, 1 to v, 7:
- ⌜rubric⌝;[25]
- salutation and date([year 3, viii,] 8, morning);
- [ ];
- farewell formula.

(no space left!)

[24]P. C. Smither, B. Gunn, *JEA* 31 (1945) 3ff.
[25]This must indicate the beginning of a new letter.

Notation, lines v, 8 to v, 13:

- note regarding copy ("copy of this letter was made concerning the letter sent to him regarding the Nub[ians]; (viz.) arrival at the fort 'Powerful is Khakaure deceased' on viii, 7, time of evening; dismissal to the place whence they had come on viii, 8, time of morning. Transcribed in the letter sent to the honorable, the spokesman of Nekhen, N [by(?) ...] the town's district officer N [ ], the chief steward N ...")

As Smither noted[26] this is a note regarding an incident reported in the first letter (i, 7). Thus three additional copies of the excerpt quoted were sent to three high officials in letters to them. The fact that this note, which has to do with the first letter, is so far removed from it, suggests that letters I through V belong together as a group; and it is very likely that what they share in common is that they were received on the same day. It is of interest to note that those dispatches which, inasmuch as they contain both salutation and farewell, seem complete, are called *šᶜt*, while letter IV which lacks a farewell and seems quoted only in part, is labelled *mit n snn*. *Mit* would seem almost to have something of the nuance "excerpt."

Letter VI(?), lines vi, 1 to vi, 7:

- ⌜report of arrival of Nubians and trading⌝;
- salutation;
- rubric (name only);

(space left)

Letter VII, lines vi, 8 to vi, 13:

- rubric ("copy of the writing sent to [....]");
- salutation;
- date (year 3, viii, [ ]);
- report of trading, [year 3, viii], 7.

After the copies of letters received it would be reasonable to expect copies of answers sent back. It is interesting to note that in the only rubric preserved such a written reply is qualified by nothing more specific than the generic *sšw*, "writings."

The dates in the dispatches help, not only in our appreciation of the mechanics and speed of operation of the chancery, but also in pinpointing the locale where the un-named recipient of the correspondence was stationed. Letter I from Semna West reports on events of viii, 7-8; letter III from 'Repelling the Medjay' gives the report of a patrol sent out on vii, 30 which arrived back on viii, 2, i.e. six days earlier than the latest entry in letter I; letter II, apparently

[26]Smither, Gunn, *JEA* 31, 10, n. 3.

from Aken, gives a report of viii, 4, four days earlier than the entries of letter I; letter IV from Elephantine gives a report compiled on vii, 27, eleven days earlier than the entry in letter I. A letter sent out by the recipient (no. 7) reports on events of [viii], 7. It would seem that the present text is the entry for the day-book of the fortress for one particular day, in all probability day 8 or 9, recording letters received and answers sent out. If this is correct, then the places mentioned can be ranged in order depending on their relative distance from the recipient (measured in number of days elapsing since the events reported on): Semna West (1 or 2 days), Aken (4 days), 'Repelling the Medjay' (6 days), Elephantine (11 days). The recipient must, then, have been posted very close to Semna West, perhaps across the river at Kummeh.

4. Day-book of the King's House of Sobekhotpe III(?)[27]

Year 3, [ii, 26] (xv, 1 to xviii, 13):
- list of people;
- withdrawal from the fortress (list of incense and bread);
- offered in temple of Medamud (offering list);
- requisitions to give food to harim and nursery;
- withdrawal from fortress of fruit and wine;
- "benevolences (*inw*) of the Department of the Deep South which are in arrears";
- list of court functionaries receiving provisions on this day;
- account of food for royal household for day 26.

Year 3, ii, 27 (xviii, 14 to xx, 12):
- [damaged section];
- reckoning of the income of farm hands (list of animals, etc.);
- requisition;
- second requisition for people of the nursery;
- list of people of the nursery and their allotment;
- "copy of the document" sent out by the vizier's office;
- final account of provisions.

Year 3, ii, 28 (xx, 13 to xxi, 12):
- two requisitions for food, with list;
- withdrawal from the fortress for offerings;
- account of food for king's household.

Year 3, ii, 29 (xxi, 2 to xxiii, 10):
- two requisitions for food;
- account of food for the king's household.

[27] A. Scharff, *ZÄS* 57 (1922) 51ff.

Year 3, ii, last day (xxiii, 12 to xxiv, 10):

- requisition for food, with list;
- allotments to the officials, king's sisters and people of the nursery;
- account of food for the king's household.

Year 3, iii, 1 (xxiv, 11 to xxvii, 16):

- withdrawal from the fortress, with list of food;
- benevolences of the steward for the queen's house;
- benevolences for the Department of the Deep South, in arrears;
- withdrawal;
- emolument (*fḳꜣw*) of city officials, retainers and citizens;
- requisition for food for queen, king's sisters, brothers and children;
- list of those receiving food on this day;
- the benevolences of this day, with list;
- account of food for this day.

Year 3, iii, 2 (xxvii, 17 to xxviii, 25):

- emolument to the Medjay;
- account of food for this day.

Year 3, iii, 3 (xxix, 1 to xxx, 12):

- reception of the Medjay "in the presence," with list;
- copy of a document sent out by the *iry-ʿt*, with list of Medjay;
- requisition for food for aforesaid Medjay;
- copy of a document sent out by the *iry-ʿt* for various grains to be sent on day 4 by various departments;
- benevolences of the chamberlain;
- final account of the butler, with list of confections;
- account of food of [king's house for this day].

Year 3, iii, 4 (xxx, 13 to xxxiv, 11):

- annalistic account of punitive expedition to neighbouring town;
- ⸢fragmentary list of food-stuffs⸣;
- [ ];
- the benevolences of this day, with list of dignitaries;
- withdrawal from the storehouse, with list of commodities;
- account of food for king's house for year 3, iii, 16 (sic!).

Year 3, iii, 17 (xxxv, 1 to xli, 10):

- requirements for the festival of Montu;
- list of officers introduced to eat in the hall (61 names);
- food given to artisans, etc.;
- arrears of benevolences;
- requisition for food;
- account of food for king's house.

Year 3, ii (sic), 28 (xlii, 1 to xlii, 13):

- withdrawal from the fortress for offerings to Montu in Madu, when the king went there;
- emolument to various officials on this day.

Year 3, ii, 29 (xlii, 3, 1 to xlii, 3, 3):

- final reckoning of arrears to the treasury.

Year 3, iii (sic), 18 (xliii, 1 to xlvi, 21):

- arrears [ ];
- benevolences of various officials;
- arrival of a chief of the Medjay at Thebes;
- copy of a document sent by the district officer of the Department of the Deep South for food for the chief;
- requisition for food;
- list of royal wives, mothers, sisters, children in receipt of food allowance;
- requirements for the feast of Montu;
- list of officers introduced to eat in the hall.

(remainder too fragmentary for translation or placement).

The verbal forms occurring in this text are as follows:

1. participles: *šdy* (xv, 1; 3, 1; xxiv, 12; xxv, 2, 22; xxxiii, 1; xlii, 2, 2); *mꜣʿ* (xviii, 3, 15; xlii, 2, 4); *ḫrp* (xv, 2, 1); *spr* (xxix, 5; 2, 2; xliii, 2, 2); *in* (xviii, 3, 4, 5; xxi, 2:3, 4; xxvii, 2:5, 6, 7; xxix, 2; xxx, 2:3, 4, 5; xxxiv, 3, 4; xliii, 2, 1; liv, 5, 6, 7); *di* (xv, 3:1, 6; xviii, 7, 10, 11; xx, 9, 10; 2, 18; xxi, 2:6, 9, 10; xxiii, 2:16; xxvii, 2:9, 12, 13, 19; xxx, 2:7, 10; xxxiii, 15-18; xxxiv, 6; xl, 1-7; xlii, 2:2; liv, 9, 12); *fꜣy* (xvi, 1; xix, 2:4; xxvi, 10; xliv, 1); *ꜣwy* (xix, 3:15; xxix, 11; 2:9; xliii, 2:4); *wḏḏt* (xliii, 4); *sip* (xix, 3:16; xxxiii, 3; xliii, 2:5); *šsp* (xxix, 2).

2. Relative forms: *it.n N ḥr.s* (xv, 2:6; 2:14; xx, 14; xxi, 2:14; xxii, 13; xxiii, 12; xxvi, 7; xxix, 2:1; xli, 13; xliii, 2:15).

3. *sḏm.f*: (xviii, 3:16, 4; xlii, 2:3; xlvii, 5).

4. passive *sḏm.f*: *ir(w)* (xv, 2:8, 18; xix, 5; 2:3; xx, 18; 2:17; xxi, 2:16; xxii, 18; xxiii, 14; xxvi, 10; xxix, 20; 2:3; xli, 16; xliii, 2:17; 1, 5); *di r tꜣ* (xxx, 2:17, 19); *di m ḥr* (xli, 17; xliii, 2:18); *irḫꜣyt* (xxx, 2:18).

5. absolute infinitive: *wḏꜣ* (xxx, 2:13, 16); *nʿt* (xxx, 2:15); *sḳdwt* (xxx, 2:16); *m ḫd* (xxx, 2:16); *rs* (xxx, 2:20); *r wnm* (xxxvii, 1; xlv, 1); *rdit* (xliii, 4).

6. *ḥnʿ rdit*: (xv, 2:16; xx, 16).

7. Imperative: *imy fꜣ.tw n N* (xv, 2:7, 15; xix, 2:2; xx, 15; 2:14; xxi, 2:15; xxii, 17; xxiii, 13; xxvi, 8; xxix, 2:2; xli, 14; xliii, 2:16; 1, 2); *imy ʿḥʿ.tw* (xxix, 14; xliii, 2:8); *imy inn.tw* (xxix, 2:12).

8. Pseudo-verbal: *stꜣ* (xxxvii, 1; xlv, 1); *mnmn* (xx, 15).

5. The Day-book Excerpt in the Rhind Papyrus[28]

"Year 11, x: one entered Heliopolis.

- i, 23: the Bull of the South(?) gored his way as far as(?) Tjaru.
- Day 20 [+ X]: it was heard tell that Tjaru was entered.

Year 11, i, 'Birth of Seth': sound of thunder was emitted by the Majesty of this god. 'Birth of Isis': the sky rained."

Is is difficult to acquire an appreciation for the syntax of so brief a fragment. But it is somewhat surprising to find, out of six examples of verbs, four cases of *sḏm.f*, and only one clear(?) example (III, 3, *irt*) of the infinitive in absolute use!

6. Louvre Papyrus E 3226[29]

Whether the Louvre account papyrus E 3226 from the reign of Thutmose III is what the ancients would have called a *hrwyt* is difficult to say. Certainly the calendrics are of paramount importance standing, as they do, at the beginning of virtually every line, and thus providing the skeletal framework of the document. But the scribe is concerned with but two activities involving the bakery where the papyrus apparently originated, viz. 1. the receipt of cereals and fruit from various localities, agencies, scribes and transports, and 2. the accounting for confections produced by said institution.[30] Moreover, although this is not a difficulty for assigning the text to the *hrwyt* category, only widely-spaced dates throughout the year are noted. The reason obviously is because only on those days did the activity of interest to the scribe take place: only on the days named were commodities received at the confectionary.[31] The accounting entries,[32] of which there are variants of no great divergence, usually

[28] A. B. Chace, H. P. Manning, L. Bull, *The Rhind Mathematical Papyrus: B. M. 10057 and 10058* (Oberlin, 1927-9) pl. 108 (par. 30, no. 87).

[29] See now M. Megally, *Le papyrus hiératique comptable E 3226 du Louvre* (Cairo, 1971). The beginning of the A-text is lost; B, *rt.* 1 (*ibid.*, pl. LXX) begins, after the date, with *šsp* which reminds one of the *ʿwty n šsp* (below, p. 113, n. 46). B, *vs.* 1 (*ibid.*, pl. LXXIV) begins with *sḫ*^{3} *n*^{3} *n bnryw*, "memorandum concerning the confectioners."

[30] The localities from which the food-stuffs come are: Esna, Thinis, Pamuha, Takayet, Iomitru, Coptos, Nefrusy and Qus; the agencies: the temple, the granary, the great granary, the granary of the <divine> adoratress, and the work-house; scribes are only named, and the transports are mainly cargo vessels identified by skipper.

[31] The ubiquitous *rdit m* with toponym or name of agency, must always be rendered "given from ...," and construed as denoting the origin of the commodities in question.

[32] A *rt.* iii, 5-10; A *rt.* vii, 1-9; A *vs.* vii, 1-7; B *rt.* ix, 1-9+ B *rt.* xiv, 5-10; B *vs.* iv, 1-7; B *vs.* x, 1-9; B *vs.* xvi, 5-10.

run as follows: "Year ..., month ..., day ...; reckoning of the confectioners from year ..., month ..., day ..., down to year ..., month ..., day .... The confectioners who are under the authority of scribe N of the superintendent of the granary N. Remaining with him of the reckoning of year X ... (figure); year X; 2, given him ... (figure); Total ...."

7. The Account Papyrus BM 10056[33]

Of similarly ambiguous category is this text, the ledger of a shipyard at Peru-nefer,[34] dated to the reign of Amenophis II.[35] The *recto* of the papyrus covers five days from i, [12(?)] to i, 17 (sic), the *verso* four days from iii, 28 to iv, 1, as well as v, 14, 17, vii, 4, 8 and 20. Though but a fragment of an undoubtedly much more extensive group of records, enough is preserved to show that for many consecutive days activity of the sort the scribe was concerned with was going on at the shipyard. That activity was almost entirely of one sort, viz. the withdrawal of timber from storage or transports, and its allotment to individual shipwrights for the construction or repair of vessels. Basically there are three types of entries. The first, of which there is but one example (*rt.* 10, 7) begins "specification of the allotments to the craftsmen," and is followed by a series of names and items introduced by *ntt n*, "that which (was given) to N." A little more frequent are the "withdrawal" formulae[36] which record that amounts of various lumber were "withdrawn (*šdyt*) from" the lot which someone had brought, or "the stores (*šmmwt*) at the lake," by some high-ranking officials including, on several occasions, the king's son. Most frequent are those headings which begin "given to ... (*rdit n*)" followed by a dative construction ("to him," "to N," "to the craftsman N"), the source of the lumber handed out ("from the stores,"[37] "from what the district officers brought,"[38] "from the boat of skipper N"[39]), or the purpose of the allotment ("for the boat of

[33]S. R. K. Glanville, *ZÄS* 66 (1930) 105ff; 68 (1932) 7ff.
[34]Apparently a settlement connected with Memphis, possibly its harbour: cf. Helck, *Beziehungen*², 447; see also E. Edel, *ZDPV* 69 (1953) 155; D. B. Redford, *JEA* 51 (1965) 109, n. 2.
[35]On the attribution to Amenophis II, see *ibid.*, 110.
[36]*Rt.* 10, 1, 4; 15, 14; *vs.* 3, 1, 6; 4, 1; 9, 8; 12, 1.
[37]*Rt.* 3, 6.
[38]*Rt.* 4, 10.
[39]*Rt.* 5, 4; 6, 12.

skipper N,"[40] "for boards for the cabin of this boat"[41] etc.).

8. St. Petersburg Papyrus 1116A and B, *verso*[42]

A little more varied are the contents of an account papyrus emanating, it seems, from a granary or storehouse for commodities at Peru-nefer. Again this text is primarily concerned with disbursement, rather than income, and it uses the same participial formations noted above, *rdit n.f*, "given to him," and *šdyt*, "withdrawal." Text A runs from about x, 15 of year 18 of Amenophis II[43] to xi, 10, while Text B encompasses a period from v, 13 to iv, 20 of an unspecified year of the same king. The recipients comprise a mixed group. There are royal craftsmen (pl. 26, 15ff), treasurers (pl. 16, 48-50), messengers of foreign kings (pls. 15, 2; 17, 67-78; 22, 184-190), servants (pl. 19, 132), and the military (pl. 19, 140). Withdrawals are also made for food offerings to the gods: "to Seth in Peru-nefer" (pl. 16, 42), "the statue of the Lord, L.P.H." (pl. 19, 118), to the divine barques of kings (pl. 27, 56), and for festivals of the lunar months (pl. 19, 123, 126). Since Peru-nefer is known to have been a royal residence, and since messengers of foreign kings would scarcely be found at any town other than where the king was staying, there is every reason to believe that around year 18 of his reign Amenophis II and his court were in residence at Peru-nefer. Yet this papyrus does not in any way note the presence, movement or activity of the king, as Boulaq XVIII did. The reason, it would seem, is that P. Petersburg 1116A and B did not constitute a "day-book of the king's house." If it qualified at all for the appelative *hrwyt*, it must have been the **hrwyt nt šnwty*, "day-book of the granary."

9. The Accounts of the Rollin Papyri[44]

Four papyri, Rollin 1882, 1884, 1885, 1889, now in the Bibliothèque Nationale in Paris, come from the second and third

[40] *Rt.* 15, 12.
[41] *Vs.* 4, 11.
[42] V. Golénischeff, *Les papyrus hiératiques ... de l'Hermitage impériale à St. Pétersbourg* (St. Petersburg, 1913) pl. 15-22, 26-28; on the wrong appelation of *verso*, see Černý in *Le fonti indirette della Storia egizianna*, 37, n. 18.
[43] Golénischeff, *Papyrus hiératiques*, l. 15, l. 19.
[44] W. Pleyte, *Les papyrus Rollin de la Bibliothèque Impériale de Paris* (Leiden, 1868), pl. 1-14, 17-20; studied by W. Spiegelberg, in his *Rechnungen aus der Zeit Setis I* (Strassburg, 1896).

years of Sety I (c. 1317-16 B.C.), and have to do with military requisitions and the preparation of food. All but 1882 apparently were written by a scribe connected with the storehouse of the residence and "the hall (*h³yt*)[45] which is under the authority of the major of Memphis (cf. pl. 13, 2)," while 1882 itself originated, it seems, in the king's garrison. The following are the major headings of the papyri, in their probable chronological sequence:[46]

Rollin 1885:

-(pl. 14, 1-5) "regnal year 2, fourth month of *shomu*, day 23, of the King of Upper and Lower Egypt Menmare, L.P.H., son of Re, Sety Merneptah, L.P.H., living for ever and ever, like his father Re, daily! On this day one was in Memphis, in the House of ᶜOkheperkare. Scroll[47] of the receipt of corn from pharaoh's granary in Memphis, for the purpose of making it into rations in the hall ... [under] the charge of the major of Memphis."

(A series of receipts follow, all in the fourth month).

- (pl. 12, 1-2) "regnal year 2, first month of *akhet*, day 2: when one was in Memphis, in the House of ᶜOkheperkare. Specification of the assignments of flour to the bakers ..."

(The assignments extend to days 3 and 4, on each of which the king is noted still to be in Memphis).

[45]This surely cannot be construed as "entry, porch", the prototype of the later propylaea (cf. J. Leclant, *Recherches sur les monuments Thébains de la XXVᵉ dynastie dite 'éthiopienne'* [Cairo, 1965] 202, n. 8; W. Erichsen, *Demotische Glossar* [Copenhagen, 1954] 377; E. Kraeling, *Brooklyn Museum Aramaic Papyri. New Documents of the Fifth Century B.C. from the Jewish Colony at Elephantine* [New Haven, 1953] 240, n. 9; J. Vercoutter, *BIFAO* 49 [1950] 95, n. *o*), the place of judgement (S. Sauneron, *BIFAO* 54 [1954] 122). It must have reference rather to a hall with the purpose of a refectory or kitchen.

[46]Rollin 1889 gives an uninterrupted sequence from iii, 21, clearly of year 2 (cf. pl. 18, 1) to x [29] of the same year (pl. 20, 13). In the entries for this period there is no change of regnal year, and therefore Sety I's accession most probably fell between x, 30 and iii, 21 of the calendar year (*pace* W. Helck, in *Studia Biblica et Orientalia* III [Rome, 1959] 117f, and E. Hornung, *Untersuchungen zur Chronologie und Geschichte des neuen Reiches* [Wiesbaden, 1964] 40). From III, 8 to iv, 30 there is also no change in regnal year (cf. pl. 10), and we may therefore place the accession before iii, 8. From i, 2 to iii, 6 there is no change in year (pl. 12-13), and unless iii, 7 was the date of accession (which seems very unlikely — why did pl. 13, 23 stop at day 6, or pl. 10 begin on day 8?), the accession must have fallen between x, 30 and i, 2. Now the formal introduction on pl. 14 (Rollin 1885) falls on xii, 23, and is moreover the sole entry in any of these texts identifying the type of document. It would not in any way be hazardous, then, to opine that xii, 23 may very well have been the day on which Sety I came to the throne.

[47]*ᶜwty*, usually an official document, register, or the like: *Wb.* I, 173:9-10. But the term denotes the actual form of the writing, (on a roll), rather than its contents: R. A. Caminos, *Late Egyptian Miscellanies* (London, 1954) 93.

- (pl. 13, 1-2) "first month of *akhet*, day 7, when one was on a progress through the northern district.[48] Receipt of the rations of the hall which is under the authority of the mayor of Memphis, in the storehouse of the residence. Receipt this day, in the storehouse of the residence, through the agency of ... N (followed by a figure)."

(This latter formula is repeated for all the receipts on this plate, extended at intervals of 2 to 4 days, down to iii, 6).

- (pl. 10, 1) "third month of *akhet*, day 8: receipt in the storehouse of the residence through the agency of ... N (followed by a quantity of confections)."[49]

(Entries from iii, 8 to iv, 30).

Rollin 1889:

- (pl. 17, 1-4) "regnal year 2, fourth month of *akhet*, day 7, of the King of Upper and Lower Egypt Menmare, L.H.P., son of Re, Sety Merneptah, L.P.H. living for ever and ever, like his father Re every day. On this day one was on progress in the northern district. Specification of the assignments ..."

- (pl. 18, 1) "third month of *akhet*, day 21; given to the bakers in flour ... (followed by a figure).

(This formula is repeated for all the days from iii, 21 to iv, 6 inclusive, omitting iv, 5).[50]

- (pl. 19, 1) "regnal year 2, fourth month of *akhet*, day 7; the day of the withdrawal of corn from the granary in Memphis."

(The entries run from the aforesaid day to X, [29]).[51]

Rollin 1884:

- (pl. 5, 1-2) "first month of *akhet*, day 5: specification of the assignments to the bakers of flour, in order to make ... (a certain type of confection)."

(The entries cover five plates, and run from i, 5 to 25).

Rollin 1882:

- (pl. 1, 1-2) "regnal year 3, first month of *shomu*, day 18,

[48]*ᶜ-mḥty*, most often applied to the north of Egypt: W. Helck, *Zur Verwaltung des mittleren und neuen Reichs* (Leiden, 1958) 13f; but as *ᶜ-rsy*, "the southern district," can at times include Nubia (cf. D. Dunham, J. M. A. Janssen, *Second Cataract Forts* I *Semna, Kumma* [Boston, 1960] pl. 27, 86), *ᶜ-mḥty* might possibly have been extended to include parts of western Asia.

[49]The entries on pl. 10 clearly follow those of pl. 13.

[50]This 15-day period of doling out corn, ending on the sixth, is the object of the reckoning of pl. 17, 1-4, written upon the seventh. The latter day thus marks the end of the fiscal interval, and the succeeding notation of corn withdrawals commences with the same day.

[51]The withdrawals seem regularly to be made at 10-day intervals, though occasional examples of 3, 7, 9 and 13 days occur.

when one was in Heliopolis; the day of [ ] requisitioning the requisitioned wood in the town, (for) the king's garrison ...."

(The entries run for four plates, and encompass a period from ix, 18 to 27).

The verbal forms occurring in these formulae may be tabulated as follows:

1. absolute use of infinitive: *nḥm* (pl. 1, 1); *šsp* (pl. 10, 1; 13, 2, 3; 14, 4); *wḏ* (pl. 13, 12); *šdt* (pl. 19, 1);
2. participle: *rdyt* (pl. 18, 1);
3. circumstantial *iw.f ḥr sḏm*: pl. 1, 1; 12, 1; 13, 1; 14, 3; 17, 3.

10. The Ship's Log of Leiden I, 350, *verso*[52]

I - [...] (X + 1-5);
- departure(?) (X + 6);
- arrival of letter(?) (X + 9);
- punishment of certain people (X + 10);
- receipts(?) (X + 16-21).

II - list of men (1-2);
- receipts of food-stuffs (2-13);
- disbursement of food-stuffs (14-18);
- date (year 52, vi, 26), "in Pi-Ramesses Meryamun." (19);
- disbursement of food-stuffs (20-26);
- receipt of food-stuffs (27-28);
- disbursement of food-stuffs (29);
- receipt of food-stuffs (30-31).

III - departure of letter carrier (1);
- rations for letter carrier (2);
- receipt of food-stuffs (3-4);
- disbursement of food-stuffs (5);
- date (year 52, vi, 27), " in Pi-Ramesses Meryamun; *psḏntyw*";[53]
- receipt of food-stuffs (7-8);
- arrival of officer (9);
- disbursement of food-stuffs (10-12);
- leaving (*ḫ3c*) of certain scribes (13-14);
- disbursement of food-stuff (15-21);
- receipt of food-stuffs (22);

[52] J. J. Janssen, *Two Ancient Egyptian Ship's Logs*, Leiden, 1961.
[53] R. A. Parker, *JNES* 16 (1957) 42f.

- departure to bring an ox (23);
- date (year 52, vi, 28), "in Pi-Ramesses Meryamun" (24);
- disbursement of food-stuff (32-33).

IV
- [....] (1);
- receipt [...] (2);
- disbursement of food-stuff (3);
- list of people of the *sm*-priest (4-9);
- departure of letter carrier (10);
- date (year 52, vi, 30), "in Pi-Ramesses Meryamun" (11);
- disbursement of food-stuff (12-16);
- receipt of tax(?) (17);
- date (year 52, vii, 1), "in Pi-Rammesses Meryamun" (18);
- departure of letter carrier (19);
- receipt of food-stuff (20-21);
- disbursement of food-stuff (22);
- name of man "to be brought," with note as to where he is "found" (23-25);
- *verbatim* statement by a priest (26-28);
- disbursement of food-stuff (29);
- list of people (30-31);
- "departure from Pi-Ramesses Meryamun at time of evening" (32);
- disbursement of food-stuff (33).

V
- [date] (1);
- disbursement of food-stuff (2-10);
- date (year 52, vii, 3), "strong south wind in the sky" (11);
- "departure from Tjedᶜo, docking at ...; the wind strong" (12);
- disbursement of food-stuff (13-21);
- date (year 52, vii, 4), "arrival at Heliopolis at time of evening" (22);
- departure of letter carrier (23);
- disbursement of food-stuff (24 - VI, 10).

The occurrance of the verbal forms employed in the document are as follows:

1. *sḏm.f*: I, X + 11; IV, 24, 27.
2. passive *sḏm.f*: I, X + 13; II, 5.
3. *sḏm.n.f*: IV, 2(?); 26.
4. infinitive: III, I, 13, 14, 23, 26; IV, 10, 19, 32; V, 12, 22, 23.
5. infinitive with *ir.n*: III, 9, 31.
6. *iw.f ḥr sḏm*: III, 13.
7. *iw.f r sḏm*: IV, 23.
8. passive participle: II, 14, 18, 20-25, 29; III, 2, 5, 10, 11, 15, 16, 27-30, 32, 33; IV, 3, 12, 22, 29; V, 2, 10, 13, 21, 24 (all *rdyt*).

It should also be noted that a *ḫr ir ḥr s*ꜣ construction, which might almost be considered "literary," occurs once (III, 13).

11. Day-book of an Official on the Eastern Frontier[54]

Each entry in this unfortunately brief excerpt begins with a date, and goes on to note only arrivals and departures of messengers at a frontier fortress in the eastern Delta. The format is rather rigid, and contains the following elements: 1. verb in the infinitive (*ṯst*, "going up," for departures into Asia, and *spr*, "arrival," and *iit*, "coming," for arrivals from Asia); 2. the name of the messenger, his filiation and/or title and posting; 3. those who accompany him (optional); 4. the number of letters he is carrying and the addressees. Since this text was composed for the benefit of schoolboys learning the secretarial and recording skills of the scribe, there may be some grounds for believing that a true day-book of a frontier official might have looked somewhat different, in content if not in syntax. Be that as it may, the journal of Anastasi III presents us with one kind of notation which must, *mutatis mutandis*, have appeared in the records of a border post.

12. The Ship's Log of Papyrus Turin 2008-2016[55]

I - date ([year 7, v], 17), "two months since the departure from Thebes" (1);[56]
- arrival at Heliopolis (2);
- [.....] (3-4);
- arrival at Memphis (5);

(lines 6 through 12 record, for days 18 through 23, the simple fact that the ship is now at Memphis).
- arrival of a cult object(?) at Memphis in the evening (13-14);
- date ([year 7, v], 24), at Memphis (15-16).

II - date (year 7, v, 25), note of how long since departure from Thebes (1);
- "ninth day at the harbour of Memphis" (2);
- receipt of food-stuff (3-17);

[54]Anastasi III *vs.* vi, 1ff: Sir A. H. Gardiner, *Late Egyptian Miscellanies* (Brussels, 1937) 31f.
[55]Janssen, *Two Ancient Egyptian Ship's Logs*, pl. 3, pp. 58ff.
[56]A similar note concerning the amount of time elapsed since the departure from Thebes, accompanies every date.

- date (year 7, v, [26], at Memphis (18-19);
- date (year 7, v, 28), departure from Memphis (22);
- arrival at "The Pylons of the House of Osiris"; waiting for an official (23);
- departure of another ship (24);
- date ([year 7, v], 29), second day at the "Pylons" (25);
- ⌜waiting for the same official⌝ (26);

III - date (year [7, v], 30), note that this is a festival day (1);
- third day at the "Pylons" (2);
- waiting for 11 men (named) (3-5);
- note that they had been sent off one month, eleven days ago (6);
- date (year 7, vi, 1) (7);
- departure from the "Pylons" (8);
- docking at "The New Land of the Pylons of the House of Osiris" (9);
- departure of officers (10);
- date (year 7, vii, 2), "at this place" (11);
- waiting for the same official as in II, 23 (12);
- date (year 7, vii, 3), (13);
- "in this place"; waiting for the same official (14);
- departure of several officers to look for him (15-17);
- disbursement to them for the trip (18-20);
- note of 5 men who had already gone to look for him (21-23);
- total of men looking for him, 9 (24);
- list of people formerly with him (25-28).

The verbal syntax of this document shows the absolute use of the infinitive abounding, over 30 examples being discernible. Only 2 examples of the participle appear (III, 18-19), and one doubtful case of the *sḏm.f* (III, 21).

13. Necropolis Journal[57]

- [date], distribution of rations (1, 1);
- [date], distribution of rations (1, 2);
- [date], work assignments (1, 3);
- [....], (1, 4);
- [date], arrival of someone in the city (1, 5);
- [date], receipt of workmen's assignments (1, 6);

[57]Sir A. H. Gardiner, *Ramesside Administrative Documents* (Oxford, 1948) 64ff.

- [date], distribution of rations (1, 7);
- [date], distribution of rations (1, 8);
- [...], date, with note concerning the mustering (1, 9);
- [date], dispatch of persons listed for wood (1, 10-11);
- [....],
- [date], dispatch of masons listed (1, 15);
- [....], ...
- date, work assignments, with note of rations (2, 1);
- date, dispatch of masons listed (2, 3);
- date, note of arrival of workers (2, 4);
- date, note regarding the departure of the workers (2, 5);
- date, dispatch of masons listed (2, 6);
- date, note of departure of workers (2, 7);
- date, work assignments (2, 8-9);
- date, return of the masons (2, 10);
- date, dispatch of the staff (*smdt*) listed (2, 11);
- date, completion of the receipt of certain commodities (2, 12);
- date, dispatch of staff for wood (2, 13);
- date, dispatch of workers to the vizier (2, 14).

As in the ships' logs, the absolute use of the infinitive is ubiquitious in the necropolis journal (20 examples, at least). There are 3 examples of *sḏm.f*, of which one is doubtful, one dubious example of *sḏm.n.f*, one example of *i.sḏm.f*, and one *iw.f ḥr sḏm*.

14. The Turin "Strike" Papyrus[55bis]

- list of men (*vs.* 1, 1 to 2, 5);
- date, breakdown of tasks and list (*vs.* 3, 2 to 4, 11);
- date, payments to doctor (*vs.* 5, 3-12);
- legal deposition (*vs.* 5, 13 to 6, 5);
- date, food notation (*vs.* 1a-b);
- date, deposition of doorkeeper (*vs.* 2, 8);
- date, report on strike (*vs.* 3, 1);
- date, distribution of rations (*vs.* 3, 24 to 6, 14);
- date, deposition of official (*vs.* 7, 1-7);
- date, strike report (*rt.* 1, 1 to 4, 16a);
- date, death notice (*rt.* 2, 1);
- date, deposition (*rt.* 3, 20).

Though by nature of its contents this text is more discursive, nevertheless the absolute infinitival use is encountered everywhere, as are *sḏmt.n.f* relative forms introducing transcribed speeches.

15. The Turin Taxation Pypyrus[58]

Once again, as in the case of Rollin 1885, this text introduces the specific denomination "scroll of the receipt of corn,"[59] adding in this case the qualifying phrase "of pharaoh's *khato*-land,[60] in charge of the prophets of ...."[61] Thus one is again obliged to wrestle with the problem as to whether *hrwyt*, "day-book," being an unofficial appelative of the vernacular, might have been applied to the present text. The format is an follows: 1. date (year 12, ii, 16)[62] followed by the titulary of Ramesses XI (1, 1-2); 2. the denominatory phrases identifying the type of document and rendered above (1, 3); 3. the name and titles of Paynehsi, the viceroy of Kush (1, 4-5); 4. the name and title of the writer of the text, the scribe Thutmose, preceded by *irw n*, "done by ..." (1, 6); 5. destination(?) of the grain (1, 7); 6. "specification of the receipts" (1, 8). This last rubric introduces the individual entries, which may be of two kinds: 1. notations of receipts of grain from those obligated to produce a predetermined quota, and the town where it was received; 2. notation of the depositing of said amount of grain with one in charge of the stores back in Thebes. Both types are usually dated to the year, month and day of the reign of Ramesses XI, but the date does not take precedence in the ordering of elements in a given line. The rubric *šsp*, "receipt of ...," and often the agent (Thutmose), the town, and the grain producer, are placed ahead of the date. Whether this order is characteristic of the style peculiar to Thutmose, or to the age in which he lived (as opposed to the reign of Sety I, two hundred years earlier), is a moot point.

16. Day-book of a Memphite Shipyard(?) under the Persians[63]

Slightly beyond the period this book attempts to cover, yet within

[58] *Ibid.*, 36ff.

[59] See above, p. 113f and n. 46.

[60] For this type of land see Caminos, *Miscellanies*, 20; Helck, *Verwaltung*, 129ff; B. Menu, *Le regime juridique des terres et du personnel attaché à la terre dans le papyrus Wilbour* (Lille, 1970) 92ff.

[61] Gardiner, *Ramesside Administrative Documents*, 36, 3.

[62] This is the date of the earliest receipt recorded, not the date the papyrus was finally completed and deposited.

[63] N. Aime-Giron, *Textes araméens d'Egypte* (Cairo, 1931) pl. 2ff, pl. 13ff; likewise beyond the range of our materials are such Demotic examples of day-books as P. Dem. 30618 and 30841. If more evidence survived, it would undoubtedly appear that the ἐφημερίδες of the Ptolemaic court derived directly from the practice of the pharaonic administration.

the scope of the form we have isolated, are the fragments of a journal emanating, like the Petersburg papyri a millennium earlier, from a shipyard at Memphis.[64] The date of the text is some time during the 5th Century B.C., and the political authority is therefore Persian. Each day's entry seems first to be dated by the semitic calendric belonging to the reign of an unspecified Persian king, and then to be equated with the appropriate month and day of the Egyptian calendar.[65] Exactly as was to be expected in day-books from an earlier period, this example from the regime of an occupying power notes movements of workers and officials, work accomplished and yet to be done.

From this examination of concrete examples of day-books it transpires that the *hrwyt* in essence is a record of human events and activity, acts and states of nature, or statements of purpose or intent. The calendrical notations constitute the single most important criterion in ordering the material. And since it is a daily record, such a document does not contain intelligences which could only have been gleaned *post eventum*. Thus the *hrwyt* commonly notes astronomical or meteorological conditions, the arrival and departure of officers and messengers on official business, and receipts and disbursements of commodities with which the institution in question is concerned. It can also record verbal declarations, or contain copies of official correspondence. In connexion with receipts and disbursements, lists of people are not uncommon. Of course the type of activity noted is peculiar to the group, office or institution involved. A ship's *hrwyt* might note the vessel's own movements or the state of the weather, a necropolis *hrwyt* the work to be assigned, a government officer's the work accomplished, or the *hrwyt* of the king's house the monarch's movements and activities. Finally, the term seems to have been vernacular in origin. When we are allowed to glimpse the official title of a document of this type, an appelative is used which is derived from the specific contents rather than the

[64] *Ibid.*, pl. 2, 11 and pl. 3, 10b, *vs.* 3.
[65] For the double-dating system in Aramaic documents of the Persian period, see S. H. Horn, L. H. Wood, *JNES* 13 (1954) 1ff.

format (e.g. "scroll of corn receipts ...").[66]

Syntactically, as one might expect of the literary style of a diary, the writers have constant recourse to the "absolute" use of the infinitive,[67] a predilection which stamps the form clearly as literary in origin, and sets it off markedly from a form derived from an oral *Vorlage*.[68] But it would be a mistake to use the occurrence of this infinitival construction as a mechanical criterion, since our syntactic analysis shows other verbal forms and expressions (especially formulae involving participles) to occur as well, albeit less frequently.

It is significant, both for the investigation of the word *hrwyt* as well as for pointing out the aberrations of modern scholarship, that no example known at present displays the form **hrwyt nt ꜥḥꜣ*, or **hrwyt nt mšꜥ*, although it was some such form, I take it, German scholars had in mind when they began speaking of a "Kriegstagebuch" which lay behind Thutmose III's Karnak annals.[69] No passage in the Karnak annals that the present writer is aware of speaks of a "war-diary." The account of the 7th Campaign refers the reader to the "day-book of the king's house" for the specific quantities of food with which the garrisons were stocked (above, p. 98); an adjacent passage, related to the same campaign refers to an unspecified record in the treasury for the tally of the Syrian harvest (above, p. 98f); and at the point in the account of the 1st Campaign where the siege of Megiddo ought to have been set forth in detail, the writer states that "everything His Majesty did against" Megiddo and the king of Kadesh was recorded on a leather roll and deposited in the Temple of Amun. Of the three documents the last is the only one with specifically

[66]The "day-book" is, of course, a type of accounting document common to many cultures and many centuries. Our Egyptian examples sound markedly like the day-book of Trimalchio's estate, wherein acquisitions of livestock, wheat, slaves and money were duly noted along with such events as the crucifixion of a slave or the destruction of a house by fire: Petronius *Satyricon*, 53. The *hrwyt nt pr-nsw* sounds remarkably like the *commentarii principis* of the Roman empire: A. H. McDonald, N. G. L. Hammond, H. H. Scullard (eds.), *Oxford Classical Dictionary*[2] (Oxford, 1970) 273.

[67]Gardiner, *Grammar*[3], § 306.

[68]The use of the infinitive has sometimes been utilized as a criterion of "Annalenstil" (Helck, *Beziehungen*[2], 120; Grapow, *Studien*, 48ff), but it is no more characteristic of day-books or annals than ony other "official" document of an administrative institution. If the style in which infinitives abound is to be labelled at all, it ought clearly to be linked to the practice of abbreviation and laconism inherent in the *written* style of secretaries in a chancery.

[69]The word has become a commonplace in Egyptological parlance: cf. A. Alt, *Kleine Schriften zur Geschichte des Volkes Israel* I (Munich, 1959) 97ff; M. Noth, *ZDPV* 61 (1938) 50, n. 4; *idem*, *ZDPV* 66 (1943) 156ff; Grapow, *Studien*, 50; E. Otto, in *HO* I, 2 (1952) 143; W. Helck, *Die Einfluss der Militärführer in der 18. ägyptischen Dynastie* (Leipzig, 1939) 14; R. O. Faulkner, *JEA* 28 (1942) 2.

military overtones; but the material of the roll and the place where it was kept suggest a unique situation. The victory at Megiddo had been an event of such singular importance, and Amun's part in it so paramount, that a special document had been written up and piously laid before the god.

Nor does Tjaneny's autobiographical statement lend any support at all to the hypothesis of a special "war-diary." Tjaneny declares that "it was I that set down the victories he (the king) achieved over every foreign land, committed to writing in accordance with what happened."[70] Frequently this passage has been taken to mean that Tjaneny kept the war-diary of the army,[71] but at least one scholar has had the perspicacity to see that this is not necessarily the case.[72] Moreover Tjaneny's use of the verb *smn*, "to set down," (as well as the high flown *nḫtw*, "victories") suggest that his scribal task was a more formal one. *Smn* is a more emphatic word than *sš*, and is used frequently of inscribing the *gnwt* by the gods,[73] and of providing a fixed, authoritative version (often inscribed)[74] of texts or laws.[75] Thutmose III uses it several times with respect to the inscribing of texts on the walls of the Karnak temple,[76] and of the inscribing of the annals themselves.[77] It seems plausible, and indeed in the light of the argument presented, highly likely, that Tjaneny is referring to the inscribing of the present "annals" themselves in year 42, for which (rightly or wrongly) he takes the credit.

If there is no independent evidence for a war journal, and if the leather roll is a special document, are we justified in postulating the existence of any kind of journal behind the inscribed war annals of Thutmose III at Karnak, or the stelae of Amenophis II? The answer, on the basis of the results of form criticism, is of course in the affirmative. The "absolute" use of the infinitive, the general laconism of the style, the preference for unintroduced prepositional phases, the attraction of simple tabulation — all this smacks of the style of the

[70] *Urk.* IV, 1004:9-10.
[71] J. H. Breasted, *Ancient Records of Egypt* II (Chicago, 1906) § 392; Grapow, *Sprachliche und schriftliche Formung ägyptischer Texte* (Glückstadt and New York, 1936) 22f; Helck, *Mitilärführer*, 14; *idem*, *Beziehungen*², 122.
[72] A. R. Schulman, *Military Rank, Title and Organization in the Egyptian New Kingdom* (Berlin, 1964) 65: "this sounds as if he did this for the entire army, but it could also be interpreted as keeping a war journal for his company."
[73] See above, p. 80; also Grapow, *Studien*, 7, n. 3.
[74] Cf. *Urk.* IV, 336:6, 338:15, 339:11.
[75] *Wb.* II, 488:13.
[76] The Hall of Ancestors: *Urk.* IV, 607.
[77] *Urk.* IV, 684:9-10, 734:13-15.

day-books we have earlier passed in review.[78] Now the only day-book mentioned in the annals is the day-book of the king's house. And a moment's reflection will suffice to show that broadly speaking the content of the Karnak annals, after the literary re-working of the 1st Campaign has been excised, is precisely that of those examples of day-books which we have earlier seen to have originated in the court of the king. Boulaq 18, and even the Rollin papyri, are both primarily concerned with the receipt and disbursement of commodities. The Karnak annals are concerned with the same activities, save that it is now the receipt of booty (*ḥ³ḳ*) and benevolences (*inw*),[79] appropriate enough in military contexts, and the disbursement of sustenance to the inmates of barracks. Boulaq 18 and the Rollin papyri, as well as the Rhind fragment, also record the whereabouts of the king, his movements from place to place, and upon occasion his activity (which in the well known example of Boulaq 18, xxx, 2:13-20[80] is of a military nature); they are not concerned with the activity of anyone outside the purview of the court. Precisely the same concern informs the Karnak annals. The king's whereabouts, his movements from town to town, and his activity (of necessity in this context almost purely military) are the only interests of the recorder: collateral expeditions of detachments sent off on their own, or activity in the Sudan is of no concern, because the scribe keeping the journal stayed with the king. In short, the day-book from which the Karnak annals were drawn is simply the day-book of the king's house. As in the case of Boulaq 18, a journal of the same category, the king's house is located wherever the king and his entourage happen to be; and when the king was on campaign, the "king's house" was tantamount to the general staff of the army. The recording scribe accompanied the king and, as at home, recorded those three basic types of information any day-book was concerned with: receipts, disbursements and the activity of the king.

Hence there is no reason whatsoever in the Karnak annals to separate records of military activity from the list of booty and benevolences, and to postulate "zwei Gruppen von Unterlagen" viz.

[78]Grapow, *Sprachliche und schriftliche Formung*, 22f. The second part of the Karnak annals beginning with the 5th Campaign, and inscribed on the north wall of the chamber west of the shrine (A. J. Spalinger, *JARCE* 14 [1977] 41ff), displays this style in unadulterated form; the first part (1st Campaign, with notices of years 40 and 24) on the north wall of the ambulatory, is heavily worked in literary fashion, but the underlying *hrwyt*-style shows through frequently.

[79]On the exclusively royal aspect of *inw*, see in particular E. Bleiberg, *The Egyptian Concept of Empire in the New Kingdom* (PhD dissertation, University of Toronto, 1984).

[80]Grapow, *Studien*, 51f.

"Tributlisten und die Kriegstagbücher."[81] Both types of record occur in the same day-book genre, as the examples cited above plainly prove.

Whether the day-book was used as a source for toponyms, the recorded stopping places of the army being extracted and transmuted into a formal list of "conquered" cities,[82] is a moot point. But the evidence, together with *a priori* considerations, does not favour such an hypothesis. One is obliged at the outset to admit that Thutmose III's topographical list[83] has been somewhat artificially rearranged, no matter what its sources were; for Kadesh and Megiddo (nos. 1 and 2) were not the first towns on the Egyptian army's route of march! They were, however, the leading protagonists in the 1st Campaign, but that introduces a wholly different factor into the discussion, viz. political posture vis-à-vis Egypt. But even if one were to contend that in some of its individual sections the topographical list does in fact reflect an orderly progression of sites, about one day's march apart, one would be hard put to it to prove that this section reflects a simple extraction of places from a day-book.

In the first place, the progression of sites, when plotted on a map, produces such a curiously meandering line at times that one might easily be led to the further supposition that the field commander of the Egyptian army was drunk. In the second place, in the one known route march recorded in the day-book and thence reflected in the annals, viz. that from the Egyptian frontier to Megiddo on the 1st Campaign,[84] the corresponding section in the topographical list (nos. 57 to 71) does not agree at all! Sile and Gaza, which certainly did figure in the day-book account,[85] are nowhere to be seen in this section of the list, while Aruna occurs[86] not here but earlier as no. 27! On the other hand this part of the list contains places the Egyptians never saw on the 1st Campaign, e.g. the Negeb (no. 57). One can only conclude that a simple combing of the day-book for toponyms was not the method used in compiling the topographical list.

This is not the place to extend the discussion into the structure and origin of ancient Egyptian toponym lists. But it may not be amiss to suggest an alternative which the author, intuitively up to

[81] *Ibid.*, 50, quoting Noth, *ZDPV* 66, 156ff.
[82] Cf. Alt, *Kleine Schriften*, I, 101, n. 3; Noth, *ZDPV* 61, 54.
[83] See J. Simons, *Handbook for the Study of Topographical Lists Relating to Western Asia* (Leiden, 1937), *ad loc.*
[84] See Noth, *ZDPV* 61, 26ff; Edel, *ZDPV* 69, 154; Helck, *Beziehungen*^{2}, 122ff.
[85] *Urk.* IV, 647:12 and 648:11 respectively. The style is clearly that of the day-book.
[86] *Urk.* IV, 652:14; again the language is that of the day-book.

this point in time, has always favoured. Routes of travel across western Asia and northeast Africa had been established and known from time immemorial. Since the early Old Kingdom Egyptian messengers had been frequenting the towns and cities of the Levant both by ship and on foot; and by the 15th Century B.C. the roads and stopping places of Palestine and Syria, and even Mesopotamia, must have been very well known. Papyrus Anastasi I proves that an intimate knowledge of the best routes and the cities scattered along them was considered a *sine qua non* in the education of an Egyptian military scribe and courier;[87] while the Old Babylonian itinerary to the Euphrates[88] strongly suggests such routes were committed to writing. It seems at least a possibility worth looking into that, underlying the topographical list of Thutmose III is a series of written itineraries of western Asia, known to and used by Egyptian couriers of the day, and kept in the government archives.[89]

[87]Cf. 20, 7ff. This is an itinerary along the coast (in reverse order, i.e. applicable to a homeward journey) from Byblos to Shechem.
[88]A. Goetze, *JCS* 7 (1953) 51ff.
[89]See in particular the present author in *JSSEA* 12 (1982) 55ff, for an extended discussion of the topographical lists and their relationship to the day-book.

4

The Egyptian Sense of the Past in the Old and Middle Kingdoms

In a passage in his first book[1] Diodorus characterizes the 52 immediate successors of Menes as having accomplished nothing noteworthy; they are therefore passed over in silence. The "52" kings are in all probability Manetho's 1st through 6th Dynasties, the group singled out already in TC as a unit. It is probably the same Old Kingdom group, ending with Nitocris, whom Herodotus mentions as having left nothing to commemorate their reigns.[2] This testimony of the alleged silence of the Old Kingdom kings is curious in the light of the wealth of information about these worthies vouchsafed to us by pharaonic folk traditions, later hieroglyphic records, Herodotan stories, and Manethonian "one-liners," to name but a few repositories of factual data. Certainly, the writer of Westcar, Sisine and the General, and Neferty, as well as Akhtoy III, Thutmose III, Ramesses II and Manetho, not to mention Herodotus and Diodorus themselves, had access to *some* kind of sources purporting to be from the Old Kingdom. How, then, did the notion arise that the 52 successors of Menes had left no memorials?

As it stands, the tradition in Herodotus and Diodorus is an accurate reflection of the obvious fact that the kings of the 1st to 6th Dynasties did not practice the publication of their deeds (military, constructional or beneficential) or praises of themselves in the form

[1]Diodorus i.45.

[2]Herodotus ii.101. Herodotus has introduced some ambiguity by the inherent implication that it is the "330" kings (ii.100) that were undistinguished. Actually the "330" must refer to the sum total of kings the priests had on their role down to the time of writing. The fact that in ii.102 "Moeris" is supposed to be the last of this undistinguished group proves that the "330" cannot be the antecedent.

of permanent texts placed for all to see.[3] The so-called "historical stela" did not put in an appearance until the 11th Dynasty[4] and when first seen is a simple offshoot of that type of private biographical text which had its origins among the royal bureaucrats of the later Old Kingdom; the Theban Antefs were, after all, only glorified nomarchs at the outset.[5] The Old Kingdom monarchs could, and did, erect or carve monuments of permanence throughout their domain, but with very practical ends in view: to publish specific decrees for the

[3]The terms for the various kinds of "published texts" (i.e. those on public view) will concern us in a later publication. Here a few general remarks will suffice. The generic term for published text seems to be *wḏ*, applied both to standing stelae and inscriptions on architectural surfaces. (The former could also be called by the more specific term *ʿḥʿ*, "standing stela"). The bombastic, and often partly poetic, record of a king's military victory or his mighty acts was called a *wḏ n nḫtw*, "triumph inscription"; while the common laudatory hymn to the king, in which the cartouches recur at regular intervals (poorly dubbed "rhetorical stela" by some) was called by the Egyptians a *ḥst*, "song." A stela with offering list or ordinances was a *wḏ r ḥn*, "stela to regulate," followed by the name of the temple or institution to which it was issued; while a boundary stela would be a *wḏ ḥr tꜣš*, "stela (placed) on the border of ...." A text engraved on a more precious substance, or overlaid or inlaid with silver or gold, would be an *ʿnw*, "tablet."

[4]The situation under Herakleopolitan rule is difficult to ascertain through lack of evidence. Merikare mentions "monuments" (*mnw*), but these may be only traditional memorials dedicated to a god (cf. S. Tawfik, *MDAIK* 27 [1971] 227ff; G. Vittmann, *WZKM* 69 [1977] 21ff: cf. 63 (A. Volten, *Zwei altägyptische politische Schriften* [Copenhagen, 1945] 33; M. Lichtheim, *Ancient Egyptian Literature* I [Berkeley, 1973] 102), "make [many] monuments for god, for it means the perpetuating of the name of him who does it"; cf. lines 65-67, "prosper the libation stone, increase food offerings, add to the daily menu, for it is beneficial for him that does it. Implant your monuments in keeping with your affluence: a single day bestows for eternity, and one hour may ensure for the Hereafter. God knows about him who does things for him." It would seem likely, *a priori*, that Herakleopolis conceived of itself as being very much a successor to Memphis in carrying on an Old Kingdom tradition.

[5]The earliest of these royal texts are the tablet stelae which come from the tomb of Antef Wah-ankh (of which Winlock thought there were originally many more, all located in the great open court: see *JNES* 2 [1943] 258): Cairo 20512,, New York 13.182.3: *ibid.*, pl. 36; J. J. Clère, J. Vandier, *Textes de la première période intermédiaire et de la XIe dynastie* (Brussels, 1948) 9ff; W. Schenkel, *Memphis, Herakleopolis, Theben* (Wiesbaden, 1965) 96ff; Lichtheim, *Literature*, I, 94ff. The great stela (Cairo 20512) is very much in the private mortuary tradition of provincial magnates, with its biographical section, its address to the living, and its charming scene showing the king with his dogs. Clearly the family of the Antefs, but lately arrived at the kingly office, are inadvertently showing their relatively humble origins! By contrast, the Herakleopolitans, at least to judge from Merikare's father's words, entertained a more traditional view of kingship (above, n. 4), albeit somewhat tainted by the notion of its function within the governmental bureaucracy: cf. p. 144f.

reference of specific parties.[6] to provide apotropaic protection against foreign attacks,[7] and to decorate the insides of their mortuary temples with deeds appropriate to kings.[8] Events which in the New Kingdom might find their way into stelae on public view, still to be seen hundreds of years later, were in the Old Kingdom preserved in the royal archives in the form of administrative documents (O.K. ᶜ), or annalistic documents (*gnwt*). Small wonder, then, that information concerning the Old Kingdom pharaohs should have descended to later generations via the route of the folk-tale or oral tradition: there were no "historical" stelae of a Khufu or a Pepy for Herodotus to see! The essential difference between the Old Kingdom and later times, as far as use and purpose of the stela form of text was concerned, was transmuted into a folk tradition with aetiological intent: Old Kingdom kings had left no records because they had done nothing worth setting on record.[9]

[6]Cf. Koptos B (H. Goedicke, *Königliche Dokumente aus dem alten Reich* (Wiesbaden, 1967) abb. 8, 46-48; cf. *idem*, *JARCE* 3 [1964] 37); "the King of Upper and Lower Egypt Neferkare ... has ordained that a text of this decree be published, set upon a stela of sandstone (*wḏ n inr rwḏ*) and placed at the gate of Min of Koptos, so that the functionaries of this nome may see it ..."; sim. Koptos R (Goedicke, *Königliche Dokumente*, abb. 28, 5-7): "... so that the sons of the sons may see it."

[7]This is the intent of the monumental stela with the motif of the king slaying the foreign foe which turns up in Sinai and related scenes from Nubia: cf. for the former, Sir A. H. Gardiner, T. E. Peet, J. Černý, *The Inscriptions of Sinai*^{2} (London, 1952, 1955) *passim*; for the latter, A. J. Arkell, *JEA* 36 (1950) 27ff; *idem*, *A History of the Sudan* (London, 1959) 39f, fig. 5; W. B. Emery, *Archaic Egypt* (Harmondsworth, 1961) 59f, fig. 22; *Urk.* I, 110. For the significance of this type of scene, see G. Posener, *Littérature et politique dans l'Egypte de la XIIe dynastie* (Paris, 1956) 104; H. Schäfer, *WZKM* 54 (1957) 168ff; H. Kees, *Ancient Egypt: A Cultural Topography* (London, 1961) 40; P. Derchain, *Bib. Or.* 18 (1961) 47ff; S. Moscati, *Historical Art in the Ancient Near East* (Rome, 1963) 78ff; cf. also below, nos. 24 to 26.

[8]See E. Otto, *WO* III, 3 (1966) 162; Moscati, *Historical Art*, 80; for Sahure, see L. Borchardt, *Das Grabdenkmal des Königs Sa-hu-reᶜ* II (Leipzig, 1913) pl. 3, 12 (Syrian expedition); *ibid.*, pl. 1 (Libyan expedition). For Unas, see S. Hassan, *ZÄS* 80 (1955) 137, fig. 1 (transport of stone); *ibid.*, 139, fig. 2 (warfare); E. Drioton, *BIE* 25 (1942-43) 45, fig. 3 (famine); W. S. Smith, *Interconnections in the Ancient Near East* (New Haven and London, 1965) fig. 179 (harvesting); for Pepy II: G. Jequier, *Le monument funéraire de Pepy II* II (Cairo, 1939) pl. 8, 36 (head smiting); cf. pl. 13-14.

[9]This is a far better explanation than the assumption that Herodotus, having heard information about only 14 pre-Saite kings, reasoned that all the rest had been ciphers! Cf. R. Drews, *The Greek Accounts of Eastern History* (Cambridge, Mass., 1973) 171, n. 33.

The Historic Consciousness in Embryo

Precisely why the Old Kingdom kings felt no constraint to propogandize on their own behalf is difficult to say; but it may have had something to do with the concept of the Egyptian state and the figure of the king around whom it was built. The naked use of brute force by some sixteen generations of pre- and proto-literate chieftains,[10] to bring unity to the Nile Valley, resulted in the creation around 2650 B.C. of an absolute theocracy centred upon the city of Memphis, where a god ruled as king over mankind. The chieftain had become a supreme divinity upon earth, an ideal, not a particular person. But the absolute divinity which attached itself to the monarch was not a natural concomitant of political power, but rather a reflex of the institutions's success from the 3rd Dynasty on; for the identity of king and transcendent god does not appear in the consciousness of the nation during the Protodynastic Period.[11] It was a distinction that had to be striven for and won by dint of effort. The final pacification of the country under Khasekhemwy, the aggrandizement of the throne's landed property, the spectacular success of a workable bureaucracy, the repeated victories over neighbouring peoples, the appearance of tens of thousands of foreign workers in the country, the increase of food production through irrigation and the gigantic funerary memorials of the king — all these

[10]The attempts to trace back such fundamental concepts as Osiris, his myth and cycle of gods to the 1st Dynasty, usually end in frustration for all. Not only does the 1st Dynasty yield no evidence, but also what little information we can glean betokens a far different aura surrounding the person of the king. The personal names of the kings indicate belicosity, (cf. J. Krall, *SAWWein* 95 [1879] 137), rather than the personification of benevolence and fertility: cf. *Nʿr-mr*, "the raging *nʿr*-fish," P. Kaplony, *Orientalia* 34 (1965) 142; *Ḥr-ʿḥꜣ*, "Horus fights," *Sḫty*, "the Ensnarer," *idem*, *Orientalia Suecana* 7 (1959) 58ff; *Wꜣḏy*, "Cobra-like," B. Grdseloff, *ASAE* 44 (1944) 282ff; *Dn*, "the Cutter," E. S. Meltzer, *JNES* 31 (1972) 338f; *Ḳꜣ-ʿ*, "with uplifted arm (i.e. ready to strike)." The earliest royal symbols — bull, lion, falcon, etc. — indicate the victory of a *warlike*, perhaps partly nomadic, culture (E. Otto, *WO* I, 6 [1952] 443); falcon, lion, or bull cults of the Delta stem from *historical* insinuations of royal hypostaseis, thanks to the victory of Narmer and Menes (H. Stock, *WO* I, 3 [1948] 137f). For the union of the king with Osiris a slightly later date is indicated, no earlier in its earliest stages than the 2nd Dynasty: Otto, *WO* I, 6, 452; H. Kees, *Totenglauben und Jenseitsvorstellungen der alten Aegypten*^{2} (Berlin, 1956) 153f; S. Schott, *Mythe und Mythenbildung im alten Aegypten* (Berlin, 1945) 57, 65; W. Helck, *Arch. Or.* 20 (1952) 84. The royal names of 2nd Dynasty kings indicate a changing theoretical base in the theology of kingship: H. Goedicke, *Unity and Diversity* (Baltimore, 1975) 213f and n 48.

[11]See S. Morenz, *Die Heraufkunft des Transzendenten Gottes in Aegypten* (Leipzig, 1964); also the comments of J. Zandee, *TLZ* 91 (1966) 261ff; H. Brunner, *GGA* 231 (1979) 3.

were signal accomplishments in a record unblemished by a reverse! What further proof did anyone need that the king of Upper and Lower Egypt was on a level far above mankind? Was he not truly a god, the "greatest god,"[12] older than the eldest etc., in fact one of that sort of numina the people had worshipped from of old, now come to earth and proven to be greater than all his brothers the gods? While it may be true for most of Egyptian history to say that the Egyptian king in his being and role is no (true) deity, but distinct and subordinate to the pantheon,[13] this does not articulate correctly the concept and intent of the monarch and his coterie during the high Pyramid Age. At that period the intensity of the averrals that pharaoh is in every aspect a god, and the insistence at times on his being endowed with more and distinctive attributes than his fellow gods, suggests that someone was trying to enhance and aggrandize the king's cultic and societal role at the expense of the non-royal cultic establishment. Out of the solemn pomp and grandeur of his court and the dignity of his transfiguration at death there crystalized an archetypal rationalization of the new phenomenon of kingship.[14] The earth, nature, and with it Egyptian society had come from the creator's hand in a perfect condition, and had passed by inheritence though a chain of cosmic gods to the king, the "perfect god," their descendent. As the antithesis to this perfect order malevolent disorder lurked beyond the fringe, ever present, ever threatening.[15] It took many forms: natural forces, dirty foreigners, unseen spirits, full-fledged gods. Creation itself, the act of "the First Occasion" in Egyptian parlance, had involved the defeat of disorder,[16] but it reared its head once again at the death of a king; and the elaborate web of mortuary rites had as a general object to nullify the activity of the forces of chaos. At death the king passed triumphantly to his eternal abode, the monumental mortuary complex, his "(cult)-seat," and became virtually the personification of that "seat" in the epithet "seat

[12]Wildung, *Die Rolle*, 112; cf. PT 619a: J. G. Griffiths, *The Origins of Osiris and His Cult* (Leiden, 1980) 37.

[13]E. Hornung, *Der Eine und die Vielen* (Darmstadt, 1973) 131f.

[14]R. Anthes, *JNES* 18 (1959) 169f; cf. K. Sethe, *Urgeschichte und älteste Religion der Aegypter* (Leipzig, 1930) sec. 94f; Kees, *Der Götterglaube im alten Aegypten*[2] (Berlin, 1956) 112ff; *idem*, *Totenglauben*[2], 133ff; Helck, *Arch. Or.* 20, 81f; Sir A. H. Gardiner, *JEA* 46 (1960) 104. Though an application of the Lévi-Strauss method (cf. C. Lévi-Strauss, *Journal of American Folklore* 68 [1955] 428ff) to the Osiris myth opens up refeshingly new vistas, I cannot see that it is necessarily relevant to the problem of the origin of the myth.

[15]E. Hornung, *ZÄS* 81 (1956) 28f; other literature cited by D. Müller, in *OLZ* 67 (1972) 122, n. 4.

[16]S. Morenz, *Aegyptische Religion* (Stuttgart, 1960) 175.

of the celebrant" (*st-ir*).[17] Horus, his son, became king in his stead.

This simple myth is involved innumerable times in the Old Kingdom corpus of mortuary literature known as the Pyramid Texts, to rationalize the pharaonic monarchy. It is applied as an archetype to every reign, and succeeds in masking the individuality of the Old Kingdom kings. Moreover the myth is imbued with the concept fundamental to Egyptian society. viz. *maʿat*, sometimes rendered "truth, justice," but corresponding more to our "order, rightness, normalcy."[18] It is at one and the same time a cosmic and a social force,[19] since in the Egyptian view the universe was a unity, and Egyptian society was simply part of the divinely ordained nature of things. And inasmuch as Egyptian society and kingship conformed to *maʿat* and was a creation of god, it was the best thing that could be devised, and should not be changed. Change in the nature of things could only be for the worse. It would produce uncertainty, chaos, lawlessness, pain and suffering, and anyone advocating it was thus an evil person. The idea of revolution would have seemed to the Egyptians completely abhorrent.[20]

The only concept of betterment in the body social or the body politic was one of restoration. The king could only better the lot of his people by bringing back the normative condition of *maʿat*; and this could only be done if the country had retrogressed from the pristine state of *maʿat* ordained by heaven. But in this there is no notion of progress.

Thus the myth of Egyptian kingship and the concept of *maʿat* at all periods of Egyptian history, but especially during the Old Kingdom when they were new and vibrant, provided an explanation for the Egyptian of his past and of his place in the society which had emerged in that past.[21] But they did so by creating patterns of

[17]Cf. the excellent article by K. P. Kuhlman, *SAK* 2 (1975) 135ff. I would take *st* in the very common Old Kingdom usage of "(cult)-seat" (cf. *Wb.* IV, 2f; J. G. Griffiths, *Plutarch's De Iside et Osiride* [Cambridge, 1970] 258; cf. the frequent use of *st* from the end of the 4th Dynasty in the names of pyramid complexes: J. Bennett, *JEA* 52 [1966] 175f), and *ir* as in *iri ḫt*: *Wb.* I, 124:9. For other suggested derivations, see Griffiths, *Osiris and His Cult*, 87ff; *idem*, in *LdÄ* IV (1982) 623ff; and the discussion of W. Barta, in *MDAIK* 34 (1978) 9ff; for the most recent defence of his position by W. Westendorf, see *GM* 48 (1981) 55ff.

[18]On *maʿat* and the concept of kingship, see Otto, *WO* III, 3, 164ff; H. Frankfort, *Ancient Egyptian Religion* (New York, 1948) 53ff.

[19]P. Derchain, *BIFAO* 58 (1959) 78.

[20]"It is little wonder that in this perfectly constituted land, deficiencies should seem due to backsliding": C. Bradford Welles, in R. Denton (ed.), *The Idea of History in the Ancient Near East* (New Haven, 1955) 154.

[21]H. Junker, *Pyramidenzeit* (Zurich, 1949) 46ff.

general application.[22] There is little to suggest, at least on the evidence available at present from the Old Kingdom, that a need was felt to give a more particular explanation of any specific event or set of events in the immediate or remote past.[23]

It is nonetheless true that at certain times in the course of the eight centuries during which the Old Kingdom held sway, Egypt seems overtaken by a self-consciousness about its own present achievements, sometimes coupled with a perfunctory nod to the past.

As the time of "Dynasty 0" approaches and the incarnate Horus in the white crown makes his appearance on the stage in the Nile Valley, there appears a number of artistic works which point to an urge to signal the uniqueness of events rather than an aesthetic need to decorate.[24] These events are commemorated by such objects and *ipso facto* recorded; they are not however narrated, and it is doubtful whether we can ever speak of "narrative" in Egyptian art. It has been claimed that such motifs as the king smiting the sprawling enemy are timeless,[25] and in fact elaborate ideograms. But it is the *specific* nature of the scene rather than its recurrence as a motif, that provides the element of novelty and importance. At the outset of the 1st Dynasty the head-smashing scenes of Narmer and Den, for example, are not simply to be taken to mean: Horus, under the aegis of the gods and numina, dompts the filthy beduin, thus restoring law and order and a state of equilibrium to the land. Such a meaning is, of course, implicit;[26] but of far greater importance is the fact that it is the *specific* bedu of "Harpoon Lake" (?) that Narmer is defeating, and the *specific* victory in "the first occasion (not the second, third, or all lumped together) of smiting the East" that the Den tablet signals. The head-smashing motif is being used to commemorate historic events.[27] The series of palettes from the period of the union of the country under Narmer and Aha reflects a feeling of its own importance and historical significance which was rising in the

[22]Cf. A. B. Lloyd, *Herodotus, Book II: Introduction* (Leiden, 1975) 96: "since all historical study involves general and particular, attempting to place particular phenomena against a background of general principle or law, there is always a tension between the two, and *this tension is resolved in Egypt overwhelmingly in favour of the latter*" (italics in the original).

[23]The feeling of timeless continuity one senses during the Old Kingdom is well expressed in the continuum of government: "lo, their offices are like those of [their] fathers," *Urk.* I, 85:11.

[24]Cf. T. Burton-Brown, *Third Millennium Diffusion* (Oxford, 1970) 23.

[25]H. A. Groenewegen-Frankfort, *Arrest and Movement* (London, 1951) 21.

[26]Posener, *Littérature et politique*, 104; Kees, *Ancient Egypt*, 40.

[27]Cf. H. Frankfort, *Kingship and the Gods* (Chicago, 1948) 7ff; G. A. Gaballa, *Narrative in Egyptian Art* (Mainz, 1976) 17.

collective consciousness of the new state.[28] It may even be, as one scholar has dared to postulate, that these commemorative objects were put on display at Hierakonpolis for subsequent generations.[29] Certainly such memorials were still available for examination fourteen centuries later on the eve of the Amarna period.[30] The palette soon became obsolete as a means of recording for posterity, and during the 1st Dynasty we find the urge to commemorate dramatically being overshadowed by the dispassionate desire to record. The exigencies of the new nation state demanded that the past be retained in precise form for purposes of comparison: not only Nile levels, census and tax data from former times had to be retained, but political and military events as well. The upshot was the phenomenon known as the "annals" (*gnwt*), employing the full-fledged script.[31]

A second occasion on which Egypt suddenly became conscious of the course along which it was proceding was the reign of Djoser, the "great divide" as it were, between the turbulence and uncertainty of the Protodynastic age and the centralized theocracy of the 3rd and 4th Dynasties. Presumably in the preparation of the Saqqara plateau for his tomb, Djoser was obliged to remove earlier mortuary installations, and choose to preserve their contents in his own. But this act was more than a passing whim to display his piety: the entire mortuary complex which arose on the heights overlooking Memphis was a retrospective acknowledgment of the pharaonic monarchy, and a chart for the future. In one complex Djoser united in space the disparate elements of the Upper and Lower Egyptian kingships, and in time all the generations of the ancestors who had gone before.[32]

A heightened consciousness of the past, and a desire to "edit" it, is evidenced from the reign of Neferirkare. The biographical statements of this king's officials, along with his entry in TC, strongly

[28]Of the three basic needs which called forth the earliest script, viz. the need to keep accounts, the need to identify, and the need to commemorate, needs felt only by the centralized service of the king, new phenomena both, the treatment of palette and macehead surfaces exemplifies the last quite clearly.

[29]J. A. Wilson, *JNES* 14 (1955) 235.

[30]B. V. Bothmer, *JARCE* 8 (1969-70) 5ff.

[31]See above, p. 86ff; also R. T. Ridley, *Acta Antiqua* 27 (1979) 39ff.

[32]That the Djoser complex was such a focus in the evolution of Egyptian kingship emerges strongly from an examination of the whole: cf. H. Ricke, S. Schott, *BABA* V (1950); H. Bonnett, *JNES* 12 (1953) 257ff; E. Drioton, J. Vandier, *L'Egypte*[4] (Paris, 1962) 184f; on the texts from the hypogea beneath the pyramid, see W. Helck, *ZÄS* 106 (1979) 120ff.

suggest that he proved to be a memorable figure.[33] It was probably in this reign, it will be remembered, that the Giza drawing board was written;[34] and undoubtedly to him should we ascribe the Palermo stone, or its original.[35] This "edition" of the early annals was to pass into the mainstream of Egyptian historical tradition to manifest itself ultimately in TC, and was to be used again as the basis for Manetho's 1st and 2nd Dynasties (see below, p. 212ff). We have seen in the case of TC (above, p. 88ff), and shall see later in the case of Manetho (below, p. 213), that reliance upon the *gnwt* seems to come to an end with the reign of Djoser. Should it be assumed that the "edition" of Neferirkare stopped at that point? And why should it? He obviously possessed, in fact, annalistic material in even fuller form for the 3rd and 4th Dynasties. Conceivably on a bifacial monument like the Palermo stone, the 1st to mid-3rd Dynasties might cover one face entirely (although the Palermo stone reaches Sneferu's reign at least on one side). But was the fixing of a terminus due to a simple "mechanical" mistake, like reading a single side of a bifacial stela? It seems much more likely to the present writer that, with the coming of the "high Old Kingdom" under Djoser, the recording of annals changed in format and material (papyrus in place of wood?), and perhaps in means of filing as well; and that it is this "hiatus" as it were which is reflected in the fact that the 1st and 2nd Dynasties

[33]Neferirkare stands out in texts from his time as one monarch the mask of myth does not entirely conceal. He appears to have been, or perhaps better, intended to appear, a friendly, rather human king. Two biographical texts reveal that he suffered favoured officials, as a mark of his favour, to kiss his foot rather than kiss the ground as was customary (cf. *Urk.* I, 41:14-15; 53:2-3); and the famous biography of Wash-ptah indicates a commendable solicitude for a fatally-sick friend (*Urk.* I, 42f), even though the setting up of the inscription was by express royal wish. A similar concern for Rawer, whose foot was injured through the accidental slip of the king's *ꜣms*-scepter, is evidenced in his biographical inscription which, in like fashion, was authorized by the king (*Urk.* I, 232). The account of Khufu-[ ], who was issued a carrying-chair when he was sick (H. Goedicke, *JEA* 45 [1959] pl. 2) may also be from his reign; style and orthography would suit admirably. It should be noted also that it was in the reign of this king that the first standardized system of ranking titles was introduced: K. Baer, *Rank and Title in the Old Kingdom* (Chicago, 1960) 296. It is moot whether any significance is to be attached to the fact that in formal dedicatory inscriptions the tag "beloved of god X" is first used during the reign of Neferirkare: P. Kaplony, *MDAIK* 20 (1965) 33f. For Neferirkare's modifications in the realm of official titulary, see S. Schott, *Zur Krönungstitulatur der Pyramidenzeit* (Göttingen, 1956) 74ff.

[34]See above, p. 24f.

[35]Drioton, Vandier, *L'Egypte*[4], it is a moot question as to whether the present copy derives from the 25th Dynasty: cf. W. Helck, *Geschichte des alten Aegypten* (Leiden, 1968) 28, n. 2.

constituted a closed corpus.[36]

Another break in the historical tradition of the Old Kingdom, and certainly recognized as such by the time of the creation of the king-list in the 12th Dynasty, was the reign of Unas.[37] Many considerations point to a cultural break about this time: the discontinuance of the building of sun-temples, the apparent change in the ranking system,[38] the appearance of the Pyramid Texts, the curious scenes in the Unas causeway,[39] etc. It is impossible at this distance in time to say what the events were; but it may be significant that the period from Asosi on knows a marked tendency to expand and elaborate the biographical statements in tombs.

It must be admitted, however, for most of the remainder of the Old Kingdom, the ascendency of the mythical concepts which rationalized kingship and the state effectually dampened an historical attitude towards the past. The publication of the royal annals in the 5th Dynasty, represented by the Palermo stone,[40] demonstrates this. The *gnwt* of the Protodynastic Period, and even those of the reign of Sneferu, are concerned with particular events of immediate importance: the destruction of an (enemy) city, the building of a temple, the celebration of a feast. By the time of the 5th Dynasty, however, such events are deemed transitory and ephemeral, and not worthy of much attention. The *gnwt* now concentrate on one kind of activity indulged in by the god-king: grants and benefactions to the gods, acts which characterize in true fashion a "Horus," and properly show forth his piety. From being simple records of outstanding events, the *gnwt* have now developed into quasi-religious memorials which tend to conceal the individuality of reign behind the mask of the mythical prototype.

The largest body of texts we have from the Old Kingdom, viz. the aforementioned Pyramid Texts, consistently refer to a mythological past, and not an historical one. Thus the reigning king, a Unas or a Pepy I, is "himself a Heliopolitan, born in Heliopolis" (not when his predecessor Asosi or Tety was king, but) "when Re was the chief of

[36]Note that, as the Giza drawing board shows, by Neferirkare's reign the misinterpretation of the hieratic writing of early royal names was a fact: cf. Bedjau for Khasekhemwy.

[37]Ricke, Schott, *BABA* V, 149; J. Spiegel, *Orientalia* 26 (1957) 150ff; N. Kanawati, *The Egyptian Administration in the Old Kingdom* (Warminster, 1977) 76.

[38]Baer, *Rank and Title*, 297.

[39]See above, p. 129, n. 8.

[40]Drioton, Vandier, *L'Egypte*[4], 156f; Helck, *Manetho*, *passim*; W. Kaiser, *ZÄS* 91 (1964) 86ff; J-L. de Cenival, *BSFE* 44 (1965) 13ff; also above, p. 88.

the Two Enneads, and Nefertum was chief of mankind."[41] He is not the offspring of his human predecessor, but "the heir of his father Geb."[42] The royal ancestors may occasionally be referred to, but it is always under the rubric of such collectives as "lords of the *ku*s,"[43] the "gods who were aforetime," or "the gods who went to their *ku*s."[44] Succession to the throne is hinted at, but then only vaguely in texts from the end of the Old Kingdom: "N has acted as successor to the king, and his service is with his earthly survivors; they shall perform his festivals."[45]

Similarly in the private sector the "unhistorical" eye of a mythopoeic society presented the past as a never-changing continuum. One might speak of a man's "fathers," "lords" or "his *ku*s" with reference to his ancestors who will assist him in the next life.[46] or to "those fathers of his who were aforetime, who are buried in the necropolis";[47] one might even *picture* the forebears, male and distaff lines, in groups of couples or single figures.[48] But the ancestral line remained an undifferentiated, though known, bloc of names: nothing had changed. All one craved was length of years[49] and the approbation of the community. "I am one of you!" cried the eager farer into the Beyond to his surviving priestly colleagues;[50] "see! he is a true revered one!" say the courtiers of an estimed associate.[51] A sense of community pervades the entire Old Kingdom, and historical change was alien to people's thinking.

For the Egyptians of the Old Kingdom — and in a certain sense they set a pattern for posterity — human activity could be subsumed

[41]PT 483a-b; for discussion see R. Anthes, *ZÄS* 80 (1955) 81ff; *idem*, *JNES* 18, 176f.
[42]PT 483c; father Atum: PT 395b.
[43]PT 598a, 906e; U. Schweitzer, *Das Wesen des Ka* (Berlin, 1956) 44ff. For *ku* with respect to the living king, see H. Goedicke, *Die Stellung des Königs im alten Reich* (Wiesbaden, 1960) 37ff.
[44]PT 514; L. Kákosy, *Selected Papers 1956-73* (*Studia Aegyptiaca* VII; Budapest, 1981) 37.
[45]PT 1942b-c; emended slightly from the Neith text: R. O. Faulkner, *The Ancient Egyptian Pyramid Texts* III (Oxford, 1969) 41. Succession of rulers was, however, present in the national consciousness in the thriving offering list tradition, and this began remarkably early: cf. the Old Kingdom examples from the 1st Dynasty on, listed above, p. 60, n. 205 (to which add Cairo 936).
[46]*Urk.* I, 189; R. F. E. Paget, A. A. Pirie, *The Tomb of Ptahhetep* (London, 1898) pl. 39; *Urk.* I, 217; J. A. Wilson, *JNES* 13 (1954) pl. 18A, 5.
[47]L. Borchardt, *Denkmäler des alten Reiches* II (Cairo, 1964) 113; H. Fischer, *CdE* 43 (1968) 310f.
[48]H. Junker, *Giza* IX (Wien, 1950) pl. 16a; 114ff, abb. 48: three couples followed by two single males; anepigraphic
[49]H. Fischer, *ZÄS* 105 (1978) 50f.
[50]W. Helck, *ZÄS* 104 (1977) 89ff.
[51]Wilson, *JNES* 13, pl. 18A, 7.

under only three time-headings: 1. "to-day, under king N (*min ḫr N*)," 2. "in the time of (a) king NN, (b) the ancestors, (c) those who were aforetime, (d) early predecessors (*m rk NN/tpyw-ᶜ/ imyw-ḥ³t/ ḏr.tyw*),"[52] 3. "in the time of Re (*m rk Rᶜ*)." "To-day under ..." referred to the present, or at least the reign of the present king, under whom the speaker lived and held office;[53] Thus the mythologizing of kingship in a two generation sequence, Osiris-Horus, is mirrored in the workaday world in this simple dichotomy of time now and time remembered. No text suggests that events or situations designated by phrase no. 1 differed in any way from those designated by phrase no. 2 (a): historical development or evolution was foreign to this Old Kingdom mentality. Patterns 2 (b), (c) and (d), and 3 are, however, usually used of a (remote) time when things were generally different from what they are at present.[54] But they are different only in that an event or a situation which that remote period had witnessed, had never been repeated *until now.* The cliché is employed almost wholly by private individuals; no real change in the body politic is denoted in this way.

Nevertheless the Old Kingdom Egyptian could and did look to events which had taken place in the past. No ancient state had set up so complex a machinery for recording data as had the pharaonic in its hierarchical bureaucracy; and the Egyptian was able with comparative ease to discover what an ancestor or predecessor in office had done. But it was perhaps this very ease of reference that stifled any spontaneous interest in the past; aetiology and iconatrophy always flourish in a community in imperfect systems of written records; and these primitive forms of inquiry are often the stimulus for the development of an historical sense.

One phenomenon, awareness of which the creation of a graphic system of recording did sharpen, was the sequence of "time units" in the past. The year, treated as a formal unit of measure, is probably pre-historic; with the creation of the pharaonic state the reign came to constitute a larger time span. All reigns may have been presented formally as patterned on a pure and wholly acceptable archetype; but

[52]Cf. *Wb.* II, 457.

[53]Shepsesptah (*Urk.* I, 51:12, 15) uses *m rk* of Menkaure under whom he was born, of Shepseskaf under whom he grew up, but thereafter uses *n*, "attached to," followed by the king's name. Azy, who must be writing under Pepy I (cf. *BIFAO* 37 [1937] 115ff) uses *m rk* of the now defunct Izezy, Unas and Tety: E. Edel, *ZÄS* 79 (1954) 13; cf. also *Urk.* I, 249:18; 253:18 (*m rk Tty*); but 254:2 (*ḫr Ppy*); contrast 250f.

[54]For *m rk Rᶜ*, see W. Helck, in S. Donadoni (ed.), *Le fonti indiretti della storia egiziana* (Rome, 1963) 60, n. 2; C. Desroches-Noblecourt, *Le petit temple d'Abou Simbel* (Cairo, 1969) 147f, n. 64.

the consciousness of the *sequence* of such a string of identical units is in itself an interpretive approach, however rudimentary, to *our* concept of history. That society was supposed to have remained unchanged since its formulation, in an unbroken chain of repetitions of the "time of the god," is most certainly a proposition of an historical nature. It is significant that the earliest awareness of sequence of reigns[55] is found in lists of mortuary priesthoods:[56] it is the offering cult, and specifically the cult of the ancestors, that made men look to the past.

The following table gives a selection of passages from Old Kingdom texts in which the speaker has occasion to allude to persons or events in the past and the putative source of these data.

Reference	*InformationRemembered*	*PutativeText*	*Date*	*Source*
1. Abusir Papyri (pl. 19)	"... of the time of Kakai" (dates from Isosi/Unas)	festival book (*md̠^{3}t*)	Dyn. 5	temple
2. *Urk.* I, 131	Treasurer Bawerded's trip to Pwenet "in the time of Sahure"	official text (work-order?)	Dyn. 5	royal

[55]Cf. above, p. 94, n. 89; the closest approach to the idea of "reign" is the term *h^{3}w*: cf. *Urk.* I, 85:5-6, "lo, the like had never been done to any high-priest of Ptah in [any of the] former reigns"; *Urk.* I, 107:10-11, "never in the past, in any of the former reigns (determinative: seated king in double crown) had the *Ibh^{3}t*-Elephantine run been made by a single warship"; cf. also Koptos I, col. 2 (Goedicke, *Königliche Dokumente*, abb. 18); Naville, *Todtenbuch* II, 99 (*m h^{3}w Mn-k^{3}w-r^c*); T. E. Peet, *The Rhind Mathematical Papyrus* (London, 1923), title (*m h^{3}w [Ny-]m^{3c}t-[r^c]*); A. Mariette, *Karnak* (Leipzig, 1875) pl. 40 (the *^{c}t w^{c}bt* of the high-priests of Amun, made *r h^{3}w H̱pr-k^3-r^c*); N. de G. Davies, A. H. Gardiner, *The Tomb of Antefoker* (London, 1920) pl. 37, 29 (a tomb *n h^{3}w H̱pr-k^3-r^c*); cf. *ibid.*, pl. 35, 3; U. Luft, *ZÄS* 99 (1973) 111 (a medical text found *n h^{3}w ḥm Nsw-bity Ḥsp.ty*; cf. E. A. W. Budge, *Facsimilies of Egyptian Hieratic Papyri in the British Museum* [London, 1910] pl. 42, pl. 41:9-11 [*m h^{3}w Mn-k^{3}w-r^c*]); Kitchen *RI* IV, 11:3-4 (*h^{3}w.i nfr{w}*, Merneptah of himself); *Dendera* VI, 173 (*m h^{3}w n nsw H̱wfw*); F. Ll. Griffith, *Two Hieroglyphic Papyri from Tanis* (London,1889) pl. 14 ([*m h^{3}w(?)*] *nsw H̱w[fw]*); the *ky h^{3}w* of Harris I, 75, 4 would correspond nicely to the reign of Siptah; J. Lopez, *Ostraca hieratici* (*Catalogo del museo egizio di Torino*; Milan, 1978) no. 57037, *rt.* 1 (a tomb [?] *iry r h^{3}w* Ramesses II); A. H. Gardiner, *The Inscription of Mes* (Leipzig, 1905), 54 (S 14: *m h^{3}w p^3 ẖrw n ^{3}ẖt-itn*); M. Malinine, G. Posener, J. Vercoutter, *Catalogue des Stèles du Sérapéum de Memphis* (Paris, 1968) pl. 8, no. 22 1.4-5 (*ḥ^{3}t-sp* 28 *r h^{3}w* Sheshonk III); Kitchen *RI* II, 870:4 (*d̠r h^{3}w* [king N] *r š^{3c} r p^3 nb*; J. Karkowski, *Faras* V *The Pharaonic Inscriptions from Faras* (Warsaw, 1979) pl. XLI, no. 291 (temple built of brick *m h^{3}w iswt*). Perhaps a slightly later development, is the "time of the ancestors": Kitchen *RI* IV, 3, 7-9; "in the reigns of the former ones": P. Tresson in *Mélanges Maspero* I (Cairo, 1934) 817ff (lines 4-5); "since the reigns of those who existed earlier": *Urk.* IV, 1681:18-19; "since (former) reigns": *JEA* 63 (1977) pl. 23, 1, line 6 x. *M rk* (see above) is largely synonymous with *m h^{3}w*, but has broader application, and might correspond to the entire period of one's existence on earth.

[56]See above, p. 60, n. 205.

3. Coptos C	"former kings"	exemption decrees (royal archives)	Pepy II	royal
4. Coptos I	"former kings"	same	Dyn. 8	royal
5. Ipuwer 6, 5-9	[official documents]	"writings, work-orders (*wpwt*)," of the "sacred keep" and its "offices."	Dyn. 8	royal
6. *Urk.* I, 37	offerings to Persen "... in the time of Sahure."	[endowment text]	Dyn. 5	private
7. *Urk.* I, 43:5	examples of royal favour extended to courtiers (*ḏr p^{3}t t^3*)	[mortuarytexts, oral tradition]	Dyn. 5	private
8. *Urk.* I, 51:12, 15	earlier career of Shepsesptah	[personal memory]	Dyn.5	private
9. *Urk.* I, 84	examples of royal favour extended to courtiers ("by any sovereign")	[mortuary texts, oral tradition]	Dyn.6	private
10. *Urk.* I, 85:5-6	examples of royal favour extended to high-priests of Ptah (*ḥr h^{3}w nsyw nb*)	[mortuary texts, oral tradition]	Dyn. 6	private
11. *Urk.* I, 254:10	excellence of livestock production	[mortuary texts, oral tradition]	Dyn.6	private
12. *Urk.*I, 189	"fathers," "*ku*s"	mortuary texts	Dyn. 6	private
13. *Urk.* I, 267	"... as the ancestors who lived aforetime said."	[proverbs, oral tradition]	Dyn. 6	private
14. *Urk.* I, 270	"... as accrued to(?) the fathers therein, the ancestors .... when they came into this office of *sḏ^{3}wty-bity*"	[mortuary texts, official records]	Dyn. 6	private
15. *Urk.* I,107	Other expeditions which had reached *Ibh^{3}t*" in the time of any other king."	[work-orders? graffiti?]	Dyn. 6	private
16. Vandier, *Mo-^{c}alla*, 186	Bringing the council from Thinis; not done before by "other nomarchs who had been in this nome."	[nome archives mortuary texts]	Dyn. 7	private
17. Akhmim, no. 9	"[other nomarchs(?)] of this nome in the tax ass-essment (*ip-ḫt*) of the Residence (i.e. grain tax)"	[nome archives, mortuary texts]	Dyn. 6	private

18. Vandier, *Mo^calla* 220f	Famine relief, not equalled "by former rulers," or "by any general of this nome" (sim. "fathers").	[nome archives, mortuary texts]	Dyn.7	private
19. *Ibid.*, 185	Supassing what the (ancestors had done).	[mortuary texts]	Dyn. 7	private

The putative sources of this information about the Old Kingdom past fall basically under three heads: 1. official records (both those of the central authority and those of the nomes), 2. mortuary records (both those basic to the on-going cult, and mastaba texts open to view) and 3. oral tradition. Of these the last plays a role we cannot yet exactly define (although to judge from number 13 above aphoristic material was part of the tradition already in the Old Kingdom).[57] The first may have provided the most accurate source material, but its presence is less frequently implied than the second, mortuary records. Iy-kaw, Qar, the nomarchs of Meir, or Ankhtify were able to speak of their "fathers" as much by reference to their names preserved in cultic contexts, as by consulting the official archives. The names of the ancestors, invoked in chronological order in the offering liturgy, constituted the rudiments of a genealogical table; and when translated into the realms of royal ancestry, the basis of a king-list.

It is to Saqqara, Giza and Abusir that we should look for the list tradition that finally entered the hands of the Itj-towy scribes. "The Fathers," "the *ku*s" and the "Lords of the *ku*s" are often encountered in mortuary contexts during the Old Kingdom as a collective reference to the line of royal ancestors;[58] and "offerings to the (royal) statues" were regulary presented at festivals in the pyramid temples.[59] While such "cultic assemblages" of royal ancestors are not in themselves historical, in the modern sense, they do presuppose a particular view of the past, and sometimes make that view explicit.

[57]Cf. Merikare 34: "... those who know that he knows cannot attack him, and [misfor]tune can [not] happen in his time. Ma^cat comes to him 'in pure form,' after the manner of speaking of the ancestors." The final parenthetic remark seems to characterize the aphorism as cast in the quaintly archaic form in which old proverbs were generally thought to be couched. For *^ctḫ.ti*, cf. A. H. Gardiner, *JEA* 1 (1914) 25, n. 9; also R. O. Faulkner, in W. K. Simpson (ed.), *The Literature of Ancient Egypt* (New Haven, 1973) 182.

[58]Cf. *Urk.* I, 189; 270:15; Cairo CG 1652 (Borchardt, *Denkmäler* II, 113); A. Kamal, *ASAE* 10 (1910) 121; PT 598a; Sethe, *Lesestücke*, 72, 73:10f, 74:18ff.

[59]Cf. P. Posener-Kriéger, J-L. de Cénival, *Hieratic Papyri in the British Museum.* V Series *The Abusir Papyri* (London, 1968) pl. 4-5. The determinative (three statues, with white, red and *nms*-crowns) may indicate that a variety of images was intended; but whether they are all of Neferirkare, or of several ancestral kings, is not clear.

Unfortunately for the Old Kingdom few examples of cultic lists of royal names have come down to us; but the continuum in life and tradition down to the close of the 6th Dynasty, as well as the general concern for maintaining ancestral offering cults, makes it certain that at the major cult centres of Memphis and Abydos offering lists were kept up naming byegone kings in chronological order. It is interesting to note that in the "list" of the Giza drawing-board[60] the columns with the six royal names are immediately followed by a list of deities, the first of whom is Sokar. Already in the Old Kingdom the offering to the royal ancestors was coming under the aegis of this Memphite deity; and in the drawing-board we can see a distant prototype of the Sokarian corridor in Sety's Abydos temple.[61]

There is some indication that official inscripturation of a king's name at the moment of his accession may have constituted, over a period of years, the rudiments of a king-list. The Pyramid Texts speak of the king's name written on "the ledger of the two great gods in Qebehu," but what precisely this "ledger" (^{c}) consists of is not made clear.[62] The mythological archetype is instructive, as it may reflect ancient earthly usage. The *Book of the Defeat of Seth* describes Horus's accession in this way: "he ruled the land in the kingship of Tatenen; great *Isdn* put it in writing, Seshat drew up the *imyt-pr*, and Horus succeeded (^{c}*ḥ*^{c}), the *mks* in his hand, his father's *imyt-pr* in his possession."[63] Three documents are mentioned: a formal inscripturation, a property transfer, and a *mks* (perhaps the "enabling" act).[64] Preservation in the archives of such documentation, used cultically at the coronation, would constitute the rudiments of a list.

Of course the Old Kingdom chancery maintained, probably until the end of its existence under the ephemeral successors of Pepy II, the practice of recording yearly events in a series of "annals" (*gnwt*). Even if these had degenerated, as suggested above, into a medium for recording a king's piety towards the gods, and nothing more, still here was the type of written record out of which a formal king-list could have been distilled with ease, simply by extracting names and totalling the number of year rectangles.

[60] See above, p. 28.
[61] On the Abydos "list" see above, p. 18; for the "kings of Upper and Lower Egypt" in the invocations of the cult of Ptah-Sokar-Osiris in the Late Period, see R. O. Faulkner, *An Ancient Egyptian Book of Hours* (Oxford, 1958) 6, 7; 13, 22; 25, 12.
[62] PT 467a-c: "Osiris has commanded that N appear as the vicar of Horus. Those four Souls who are in Heliopolis have written it in the ledger of the two great gods in Qebehu." Cf. Griffiths, *Osiris and His Cult*, 181; on ^{c}, with its nuance of incontestable title, see H. Goedicke, *JNES* 15 (1956) 30; P. Posener-Kriéger, *Les archives du temple funéraire de Néferirkarê-Kakaï* II (Cairo, 1976) 479.
[63] P. Louvre 3129, C, 8; S. Schott, *Urk.* VI, 11.
[64] Cf. K. Myslewiec, *BIFAO* 78 (1978) 171ff.

The two types of document the existence of which has just been postulated, viz. name lists connected with the offering cult, and embryonic king-lists, point to different institutions as their places of origin and development. Offering lists are by their very nature connected with temples. For the Old Kingdom such chronological lists of kings who are to receive offerings must be assumed to have existed 1. in the scattered pyramid temples from Meidum to Abu Roash, 2. in the temple of Ptah at Memphis and 3. in the Osiris temple at Abydos.[65] The prototype of the king-list will have been confined to the record office (*pr-mḏ*^{3}*t*)[66] in Memphis.

Although it could be argued that the civil strife which attended the outgoing Old Kingdom (specifically Manetho's 8th Dynasty) dislocated the peaceful continuum of the urban centres of Egypt, the evidence suggests otherwise. The Abydene offering list of royal names continues without a significant break down to the last known king who ruled from Memphis, viz. *Ḏmd-ib-t*^{3}*wy Nfr-ir-k*^{3}*-r*^{c} (II).[67] A hiatus occurs in the list at that point, not because the temple ceased to operate, but because the priests refused to countenance the legitimacy of Meryibtowy Akhtoy I.[68] The list was not, in fact, continued until the reunion of the country under Nebhepetre conferred legitimacy on the Theban line.

[65]The Abydene role in the cult of the ancestors remained strong in Egyptian memory; the site was the "excellent seat since the time of Osiris, which Horus established for his father": BM 581 (Sethe, *Lesestücke*, 80, 12-13). The practice of keeping a "running" list of royal ancestors to whom offerings are due seems to be attested, for the New Kingdom at least, in the Abydene Dedicatory Inscription of Ramesses II, line 25 (H. Gauthier, *La grande inscription dédicatoire d'Abydos* [Cairo, 1925] 4): "he (Ramesses II) bestowed on him (his father, Sety I) offerings provided with food-stuffs, through his titutlary (which was) among (those of the former) kings." The practice reflected is undoubtedly that of the offering to the royal ancestors, specified by name and formally entered in the list, which the Abydene exemplars attest. Already in the Middle Kingdom we hear echoes of such a list at Abydos in allusions to "the offering table of the 'Noble Ones' (*s*^{c}*ḥw*)" (Cairo 20040), and to "the fathers, the progenitors (*ḳm*^{3}*w*), and the 'Noble ones' (*s*^{c}*ḥw*) of the First Occasion" Cairo 20099). That the Abydene tradition is essentially different from the one nurtured in the royal Memphite residence is doubtful: throughout the Old Kingdom, Abydos remained closely associated with the ruling house: H. Fischer, *Dendera in the Third Millennium B.C.* (Locust Valley, N. Y., 1968) 67ff.

[66]W. Helck, *Untersuchungen zu den Beamtentiteln des ägyptischen alten Reiches* (Glückstadt, 1954) 71.

[67]W. C. Hayes, *JEA* 32 (1946) 2ff.

[68]Kamal, *ASAE* 10, 185; G. Michaelides, *BIFAO* 64 (1966) 121ff.

The Past Forgotten and Remembered: the Paradox of the 9th-10th Dynasties

Whatever in fact happened in the generation immediately following the death of Pepy II, the effect was initially to produce bewilderment and then a skepticism on the part of Egyptians towards the traditions they had revered in the past. Tombs, even those of royalty, had been pillaged,[69] and even the structures themselves had been torn apart to provide good building stone.[70] "When those who authorized construction had become gods, their offering tables fell into desuetude, as though (they had been merely) 'weary ones' who died on the river bank ... (i.e. the poor)."[71] The reaction of the poet is no surprise: "the gods who lived aforetime, who rest in their pyramids, and whose mummies and spirits are likewise buried in their pyramids – shrines were built (for them), but their cult-seats do not exist. See, what has happened to them! I have heard the orations of

[69]Ipuwer vii, 2ff: cf. Faulkner, in *The Literature of Ancient Egypt*, 219; Lichtheim, *Literature* I, 155f. The questioning of the traditional date in the First Intermediate Period, in favour of the Second intermediate, by J. Van Seters, though eloquently argued (cf. *JEA* 50 [1964] 13ff; *The Hyksos: a New Investigation* [New Haven, 1966] 103ff) has failed to convince most scholars. (Cf. G. Fecht, *Der Vorwurf an Gott in den "Manworten des Ipuwer"* [Heidelberg, 1972] 10ff, 185f, who argues for a First Intermediate Period origin, with a redaction in the 13th Dynasty). Sadly, the view that Ipuwer is "a work of the late Middle Kingdom and of purely literary inspiration" which has "no bearing whatever on the long past First Intermediate Period" has achieved some currency, if only because of the forcefulness with which this view has been presented (Lichtheim, *Literature* I, 149f; cf. Goedicke, *Unity and Diversity*, 212, no. 19. In fact Ipuwer is *not* a literary piece, but an exemplar of oral formulaic composition (as the mnemonic devices clearly show: D. B. Redford, K. A. Grayson *Papyrus and Tablet* [Englewood Cliffs, 1973] 32), of a type well known in the Ancient Near East (cf. R. C. Culley, *VT* 13 [1963] 113ff; *idem*, *Oral Formulaic Language in the Biblical Psalms* [Toronto, 1968], *passim*). As the misplaced and garbled pericope in Amenemhet indicates (Ipuwer vi, 10f = Amenemhet iii, 2) the formulaic material on which Ipuwer draws was already popular at the beginning of the 12th Dynasty; and by the middle of that dynasty the topos had become so overworked and hackneyed that Khakheperreseneb specifically bemoans the fact: G. E. Kadish, *JEA* 59 (1973) 77ff. Clearly this genre of oral composition had a long history, and most appropriately its early evolution can be confidently placed in the First Intermediate Period. well before the Middle Kingdom. That its origin is to be sought in the social distress and bewilderment which attended the collapse of the Old Kingdom can scarcely be doubted; although that is not the same as reading history into it! That it shares with other topoi of loyalist, mortuary and didactic intent certain locutions (e.g. the *tm/nb* phrase) peculiar to the "description of chaos" theme, is noteworthy (cf. F. Junge, in J. Assmann and others, *Fragen an die altägyptische Literatur* (Wiesbaden, 1977) 275ff); but in Ipuwer it is culpable neglect at the *political* level that has caused the chaos.

[70]Merikare 78-9: "do not destroy another man's monuments, cut your own stone from the quarry; do not build your tomb out of dismantled (structures)."

[71]Lebensmüde, 62-4; H. Goedicke, *The Report about the Dispute of a Man with his Ba* (Baltimore, 1970) 127.

Imhotpe and Hordedef, whose tales are told so often. Look at their cult-seats! Their walls are broken down, and their cult-seats are not, as though they had never existed!"[72] Under these circumstances it would have been difficult to take the past seriously.

But if one trend of the times was to treat the past with contempt, a reactionary tendency was to revere it more than ever before. Merikare's father sets the pious tone towards the traditions which have come down from antiquity: "imitate your father, your ancestors ... look, their words remain in writing; open that you may read ...."[73] Later he proceeds to give an example of this traditional wisdom,[74] and in passing alludes to the paedagogical practice of having schoolboys chant the ancient writings.[75] In the uncertainty of the age this interest in the words of the fathers sometimes manifested itself in a compulsive and anxious search for *prophecies* of the ancestors, enunciated long ago, concerning the present troubles. Merikare's father finds grim satisfaction in the fact that the ancestors' prediction has come true: "generation shall make trouble for generation, just as the ancestors prophesied concerning it: 'Egypt shall have fighting (even) in the necropolis.'"[76] Later he advises Merikare to refrain from a certain course of action because of a prophecy: "do not be mean with the southern district (the Thebaid), for you know the prophecy of the Residence concerning it."[77] The accuracy of the ancient prophecy was rapidly becoming a cliché: "as for those wise scribes from the period which came after the gods, they who

[72]BM 10060, *rt.* vi, 6ff. I have no hesitation in placing the Harper Song of Harris 500 in the 11th Dynasty (cf. D. Wildung, *Imhotpe und Amenhotep* [Munich and Berlin, 1977] 23), even though recent studies have tended to discount such an historical placement: cf. H. Goedicke in *Fragen an die altägyptishen Literatur* 185ff; and the important article by Assmann himself, *ibid.*, 55ff; (M. V. Fox's date in the Amarna Period [*Orientalia* 46 (1977) 400ff] is difficult to support, and meets an obstacle in the name "Antef"). The rotund harper, singing for his deceased lord in a mortuary context, is already a stereotype in the Middle Kingdom: cf. T. E. Peet, *The Cemeteries of Abydos* II (London, 1914) pl. 23, 5; and a note of despair can already be detected in his delivery: cf. Leiden V, 95 (W. Ward, *JEA* 63 [1977] pl. 9; cf. the slight note of hedonism and the exhortation to cease weeping in some Old Kingdom harpers' songs: H. Altenmüller, *SAK* 6 [1978] 17). I see no difficulty in the span of seven centuries or more which would separate the text copied in Harris 500 from the next examples of the genre in post-Amarna times: the revival in interest in the past evidenced from Amenophis III's reign (below, p. 187ff) would be quite sufficient to explain the resurrection of a form from remote antiquity. On the motif in general see C. M. Zivie, *Giza au deuxième millénaire* (Cairo, 1976) 36f.

[73]Merikare 35-6.

[74]*Ibid.*, 109-10.

[75]*Ibid.*, 51.

[76]*Ibid.*, 68-70.

[77]*Ibid.*, 71.

prophesied what would come to pass — and it did! — their names abide for ever!"[78] The prophetic genre became even a vehicle for political propoganda, as Neferty shows.[79] The assiduous inscripturation of the words of the ancestors which the Herakleopolitan Period seems to have inaugurated,[80] must be viewed in the light of this great weight the distressed Intermediate Period attached to the lore of the wisemen of old. Written editions of the great corpora of proverbial wisdom were prepared, and attached, rightly or wrongly,[81] to legendary wisemen of the Old Kingdom.[82] A similar ascription of particularly efficacious spells to the searches of great men of the past was about to be made explicit in mortuary

[78]Chester Beatty IV, *vs.* 2:5ff.

[79]Neferty protests (v, f: W. Helck, *Die Prophezeiung des Nfr.tj* [Wiesbaden, 1970] 22) "I will say that which is before mine eyes; I never prophesy what has not yet come"; but this is a rhetorical device to impress upon us the concreteness and the veracity of the vision. Neferty *describes* what he *sees*: it is as though these future events — they must be, as Neferty lives under Sneferu! — were happening right now before his very eyes. Admittedly *sr* contains a nuance of enunciation rather than cogitation (which would have been conveyed by *k*^{3}*i*, "to think"), but the basic meaning remains one of *prediction* (*pace* H. Goedicke, *The Protocol of Neferyt* [Baltimore, 1977] 81); cf. the unequivocal meaning of *sr* in Chester Beatty IV, *vs.* 2, 6 (above, n. 45), or of *proclamation* before the event (cf. its use in the advance anouncement of jubilees: E. Hornung, E. Staehelin, *Studien zum Sedfest* (*Aegyptiaca Helvetica* I; Geneva, 1974) 56, 89, n. 32).

[80]J. Yoyotte, *Histoire universelle* I (Paris, 1956) 166; H. Brunner, and others, *HO* 2 (1952) 15f.

[81]The editorial concern about *locating* ancient texts of anonymous authorship in time and place, is widespread in the ancient world: cf. M. Smith, in *Entretiens sur l'antiquité classique* XVIII (Geneva, 1972) 198.

[82]Lichtheim, *Literature* I, 7, 62; A. Polaček, in *Akten des XIII. Internationalen Papyrologenkongresses* (Munich, 1974) 339f. I can see no difficulty in postulating an early oral stage in the transmission of aphoristic material, deemed unworthy of inscripturation during the high Old Kingdom. One thing is certain, however, from the early Middle Kingdom on the proverb, though by definition residing in the realm of oral tradition, became a *literary* form, checked and transmitted mainly if not wholly in written form. Anastasi I, 11, 1ff is an illuminating passage: "you speak to me about a saying of Hordedef, (but) you do not know whether it is good or bad (i.e. correctly or sloppily copied?). Which paragraph (*ḥwt*) comes before it, which [comes after] it?" In other words there was a *canonical* order to the works of the wisemen of the past, which a skilled scribe would follow assiduously; and that that canonical order implied a written, rather than oral, tradition is clearly indicated by the fictional setting for the enunciation of Kagemni's wisdom: (Sethe, *Lesestücke*, 43) "the vizier (Kagemni) had his children summoned, after he had completed 'The Condition of Man' (the name of his book) ... and in closing he said to them: 'as for anything which is in writing on this scroll, hearken to it just as I have said it. Do not embellish (*sni ḥ*^{3}*w ḥr*) what has been authorized.' Then they took it to heart, and read it in accordance with what was in writing." Thus the author *wrote* it first on papyrus, *then* he presented it to his intended readers, and enjoined them to treat it as a *canonical text*.

literature;[83] and even Thoth himself was being commonly credited with the authorship of any widely-used cultic text of antiquity.[84]

The Provincial Pride of Family of the 11th Dynasty

We know little of how the rite of the offering to the ancestors fared during the early Intermediate Period. The Abydene list preserves the 8th Dynasty intact,[85] but thereafter a gap occurs, suggesting that with the seizure of power by Herakleopolis and the concomitant civil war, the priests were unable or refused to countenance any ruler. Herakleopolis and its traditions during its heyday are scarcely known to us, though there is some evidence that the kings of this house attempted to don a Memphite guise.[86] Whether the Sokarian offering to the ancestors was preserved in a Herakleopolitan milieu is not known, though the presence of 18 names in TC suggests that it was. What happened in the Memphite region is even less certain, though there are signs of a continuity of life and tradition.[87] The statement by the father of Merikare is least

[83]E.g. Hordedef: Naville, *Todtenbuch*, 137A, 23; II, 99; 137, 37-39 (Ani); E. A. W. Budge, *The Hieroglyphic Transcript of the Papyrus of Ani* (New York, 1960) 440f; *idem*, *Egyptian Hieratic Papyri*, pl. 41, 9-11; Luft, *ZÄS* 99, 111; Wildung, *Die Rolle*, 219; C. J. Bleeker, in F. F. Bruce, E. G. Rupp (eds.), *Holy Book and Holy Tradition* (London, 1968) 28; in general on the motif of finding ancient literature in antiquity, see W. Speyer, *Bücherfunde in der Glaubenswerbung der Antike*, Göttingen, 1970.

[84]S. Schott, *ZÄS* 90 (1963) 103; C. J. Bleeker, *Hathor and Thoth* (Leiden, 1973) 141f; the wise lector-priests of old were also becoming the subjects of popular folklore: Wildung, *Imhotep und Amenhotep*, 17f; H. Goedicke, *JEA* 41 (1955) 31ff.

[85]Hayes, *JEA* 32, 2ff; W. S. Smith, in *CAH* I^2 (1962) ch. 14, 56ff.

[86]For the presence of the Memphite rites of Sokar at Herakleopolis see A. Moret, *Sarcophages de l'époque Bubastite et l'époque Saite* (*CCG*; Cairo, 1913) 16 (41001); on the aetiological attempt to localize Osirian rites there, see CT IV, 87ff; H. Kees, *ZÄS* 65 (1930) 65ff; A. Rusch, *WZKM* 54 (1957) 161ff; R. T. Rundle-Clarke, *Myth and Symbol in Ancient Egypt* (London, 1959) 78, 136ff; for the royal Hathor cult at Herakleopolis, see J-C. Goyon, *RdE* 20 (1968) 93, n. 44; *idem*, *Confirmation du pouvoir royal au nouvel an* (Cairo, 1972) 101, n. 177bis.

[87]Old Kingdom toponyms continue (cf. *Ḫnw inw*, of Cairo 1336), and personal names are still compounded with the names of the Old Kingdom kings: H. Junker, *ZÄS* 63 (1928) 57f; Cairo 57014, 57209; J. E. Quibell, *Saqqara (1906-1907)* (Cairo, 1908) pl. 8:1, 2; 10(1); D. Dunham, *Naga ed-Deir Stelae of the First Intermediate Period* (Boston and London, 1937), 111, nos. 43-45; for mortuary titles compounded with the names of Pepy I and II, see Fischer, *Dendera*, 131. Service in the royal cult centres in the great necropolis at Saqqara continued sporadically: cf. the titles of 10th Dynasty tomb owners: P-M III^2, 538f.

equivocal:[88] with respect to the thriving population of the region of *Ḏdi-swwt*, apparently by extension a designation of Memphis and its environs, he states "a civil service has been there since the time of the Residence." The latter expression most probably designates that period, from Menes to Neferirkare II when Memphis was the residence of the king. Here, then, is *prima facie* evidence for the continuity of tradition amid stable conditions in Memphis;[89] and there need be no doubt that the offering list tradition emerged from the Time of Troubles unscathed.

The Theban contribution to the king-list tradition begins in this period, but its provincial origins are painfully evident in the beginning. The early 11th Dynasty kings are simply barons of the township, self-important but nonetheless boastful *ndsw* who, like Trimalchio, inevitably give themselves away. For them their world is Thebes,[90] and even after their conquest of the north they continued to reside there. Their tombs are provincial, rock-cut grottos, built on a pretentious scale, with a ludicrous pyramid at one end to link them with the pharaonic tradition.[91] On his stela Wah-ankh Antef II sits like a commoner, with his dogs, and like a commoner boasts that he had done what the ancestors had not, had not expropriated anybody, and so on.[92] And the "Musical Stela," in which he asks the divine denizens of the sky to remind Hathor of his devotion to her, though touching and original, is not the sort of text normally authored by a royal personage.[93] These earliest royal stelae of the Intermediate Period are in the tradition of biographical statements, *ergo* of non-royal origin, and even the descendents of the form in the 12th Dynasty continue to show forth, here and there, traces of their genesis.[94] Royal speeches, a favourite form of pharaonic

[88]Merikare, 102.

[89]It is *a priori* unlikely that the speaker is dissimulating, as it would have been more to the enhancement of his own reputation to claim to have *restored* stable conditions.

[90]Cf. the importance of Montu, who is said to have united the Two Lands for his son, Montuhotpe I: Turin 1447/49.

[91]H. E. Winlock, *The Rise and Fall of the Middle Kingdom in Thebes* (New York, 1947) 11ff; D. Arnold, *MDAIK* 30 (1974) 155ff; *idem*, *Gräber des alten und mittleren Reiches in el-Tarif* I (Cairo, 1976), *passim*.

[92]Clère, Vandier, *Textes*, 10f.

[93]Winlock, *JNES* 2, pl. 36; Clère, Vandier, *Textes*, 9f; see Lichtheim, *Literature* I, 94ff, for references and new translation.

[94]Cf. the expression *iri m ḫpš.f*, "one who acquires by means of his strong arm," a common epithet of the *nouveaux riches* of the period (for literature see Fischer, *Dendera*, 142, n. 626), and also applied later to Senwosret I: Sinuhe B52. The phrase, or at least the meaning it conveys, lived long: cf. Herodotus's reading of a text in a relief from Asia Minor attributed to Sesostris: "by the strength of my shoulders I won this land," ii.109.

communication during the Middle Kingdom, are essentially biographical statements, translated from a mortuary context into the realm of the living; and even though in his choice of subject matter a Senwosret I or a Senwosret III is every inch a king, the bombast and braggadocia of the local baron still manifests itself.[95]

The early 11th Dynasty, prior to its victory over the North, was already conscious of constituting a succession of progressive princes, and their liegemen often betray their awareness of having served under an on-going series of kings.[96] Wah-ankh Antef II added his own name to the "list" of Old Kingdom kings at Elephantine,[97] and Nakhtnebtepnefer Antef III piously acknowledges his obligation to the ancestors by refurbishing the delapidated shrine of Heḳa-ib at Elephantine and restoring its cult.[98] With the union of the country once again, under Montuhotpe I, increased consciousness of family surfaced in the formal and public honouring of the king's immediate forefathers. Montuhotpe delighted in grouping himself in statuary or wall reliefs with his father, grandfather, or great-grandfather,[99] albeit

[95]Senwosret I was an inveterate and earnest speech-maker, most of his addresses being delivered at "royal sittings" (*ḥmst-nsw*): cf. his address at the inauguration of construction work at Heliopolis, A. De Buck, *Studia Aegyptiaca* I (Rome, 1938) 48ff; the unfortunately almost completely destroyed text and scene on the outer wall of the rooms south of the Karnak sanctuary, P-M II^2, 107 (330), to which add D. B. Redford, *SSEA Newsletter* 3 (1973) 2f, fig. 1:1; blocks containing parts of a speech from Elephantine, W. Kaiser, and others, *MDAIK* 32 (1976) 32ff; cf. L. Habachi, *MDAIK* 31 (1975) 27ff; also a long text from Tod (author's hand copy translation, see below p. 260f); for Senwosret III's bombastic boundary inscription from the Second Cataract, see Lichtheim, *Literature* I, 118ff. For a speech by an 11th Dynasty king, see H. Fischer, *Inscriptions from the Coptite Nome* (Rome, 1964) pl. 37.

[96]Cf. Hazi, who tells us that he served under Dagy, Djef and Akhtoy (*Urk.* I, 151f; Clère, Vandier, *Textes*, 5, n. 8); Tchetchy who records his service to Wah-ankh Antef II, Nakhtnebtepnefer Antef III (A. M. Blackman, *JEA* 17 [1931] 55ff; Clère, Vandier, *Textes* 15, no. 19); Antef and Henen who tell how they functioned under three successive monarchs, Antef I and II, Se^{c}ankhibtowy Montuhotpe (Clère, Vandier, *Textes*, 19, no. 23; 20, no. 24); unnamed official who served 37 years under Antef II and III (I. E. S. Edwards, *JEA* 51 [1965] pl. 11:1). It was fashionable to convey the impression of one's reliability and competence by stressing the *number* of rulers one had served under: Nefru: "I reached the revered state in Thebes, having been secretary for seven nomarchs ..." (Clère, Vandier, *Textes*, 1, no. 1); Tchebu: "[Now I acted as steward] for six rulers, and never did a misdeed occur because of me" (*ibid.*, 3, no. 3); Merer: "I was pure (enough?) to slaughter and make offerings in two temples on behalf of the ruler; I made offering for 13 rulers ..." (J. Černý, *JEA* 47 [1961] pl. 1; Schenkel, *Memphis, Herakleopolis, Theben*, no. 42, p. 62ff).

[97]See above, p. 25.

[98]Building inscription at Elephantine: cf. R. Leprohon, in J. K. Hoffmeier, E. S. Meltzer (eds.), *Egyptological Miscellanies* (Chicago, 1983) 103ff.

[99]Cf. the Tod grouping (above, p. 27f); also the Shatt-er-Rigal relief (Winlock, *Rise and Fall*, 58ff, pl. 9-12; W. C. Hayes, in *CAH* I^2 [1961] ch. 20, 19); and the dedications in the chapels at Elephantine (L. Habachi, *Archaeology* 9 [1956] 8ff; *idem*, *ASAE* 55 [1958] 176f).

in a way favourable to himself;[100] and when he says "[how joyful(?)] are my fathers who are in the necropolis, at the place where the gods are, when they see what has happened to me," he seems to betray a consciousness that history is, as it were, looking over his shoulder.[101] In a fragment from his mortuary temple at Deir el-Bahari he is compared favourably by a god to "all your fathers," the word being significantly determined by a seated figure in the white crown.[102] This temple became a sort of dynastic shrine to which during the course of the 12th and 13th Dynasty, kings made votive offerings in honour of the author of Middle Kingdom prosperity.[103] With Montuhotpe's reign the cult of the offering to the ancestors at Abydos enjoys a rebirth,[104] and from Montuhotpe I to the beginning of the 13th Dynasty the kings' names are present without omission. It is not without significance that the last Montuhotpe of his line, *Nb-t³wy-rʿ*, declares in fulsome phrases the mutual affection which existed between himself and Min;[105] the ithyphallic god was the hypostasis of the progenitor, the founder of the royal house *par excellence*. In the form Kamutef he was the patron of the royal line since its inception in mythical times, and it was in his festival that the ancestral offering cult found its proper milieu in the South. In fact in

[100]Montuhotpe's pomposity is manifest in his sobriquet *ḫnty nsyw*, "foremost of kings," cf. *ASAE* 17 (1917) 234; L. Habachi, *MDAIK* 19 (1963) 20, fig. 5.

[101]Fischer, *Inscriptions*, pl. 37, line 5. That the text dates to this reign seems likely: *ibid.*, 105f.

[102]Clère, Vandier, *Textes*, 40. Montuhotpe's self-consciousness of his own importance seems attested by the liberties he takes with the time honoured motifs of the head-smiting scene: cf. Habachi, *MDAIK* 19, p. 38f, figs. 6, 16, 17: (cf. his elimination of the prisoner to be dispatched in fig. 6, the novel way the Libyan chief Hedj-wesh is depicted grovelling in fig. 16, and the insulting addition of the fish lying on the prisoner's leg!). I am indebted to my student, Lynda Green, for drawing my attention to this.

[103]J. von Beckerath, *Untersuchungen zur politischen Geschichte der zweiten Zwischenzeit in Aegypten* (Glückstadt, 1965) 42. For Montuhotpe I, already in the Middle Kingdom, incorporated into the *ḥtp-di-nsw* formula, see G. Steindorff, *Catalogue of the Egyptian Sculpture in the Walters Art Gallery* (Baltimore, 1946) no. 34A, pl. 6, 111; G. Legrain, *Statues et statuettes des rois et de particuliers* (*CCG*; Cairo, 1925) no. 887; Habachi, *MDAIK* 19, 50; W. Helck, *Historische-biographische Texte aus der 2. Zwischenzeit und neue Text der 18 Dynastie* (Wiesbaden, 1975) 36, no. 44; for Neferhotep's reverence for Montuhotpe, see L. Habachi, *SAK* 6 (1978) 89.

[104]For a statue of Montuhotpe at Abydos, as a participant in the offering cult of the ancestors there, see W. M. F. Petrie, *Abydos* II (London, 1903) 24; Habachi, *MDAIK* 19, 18.

[105]Cf. the language of the Hammamat texts (J. Couyat, P. Montet, *Les inscriptions du Wadi Hammamat* [Cairo, 1912-13] no. 110, 113, 191, 192; A. De Buck, *Egyptian Readingbook*, [Leiden, 1963] 74ff), where Min predominates. He is honoured in the formal building formula; it is he that vouchsafed the two miracles for the king, whereas he had not so favoured former kings; Nebtowyre was Min's son who occupied his throne, and so on.

the outgoing 11th Dynasty we are witnessing the birth and incipient growth of a Theban self-consciousness which, through the ancestral cult initially at Deir el-Bahari, but soon also at Karnak under the patronage of the ithyphallic god,[106] was to fare across two millennia and be translated into the "Diospolitan" tradition of kings.[107]

The Birth of the King-list Tradition

The resuscitation of the past and the recollection of the ancestors under the 12th Dynasty was also a trend set by the king. As the poet said, the king had "guarded antiquity."[108] At first it was a practical necessity. The civil strife at the end of the 11th Dynasty, and to a lesser extent the dislocation of the administration caused by generations of neglect during the First Intermediate Period, necessitated the collection of precedents and models. In particular the crying need was for a land survey to eliminate intestine feuds over boundaries, and the land cadaster which Amenemhet I produced was based as much on old texts as it was on surface survey.[109] The geographical information contained around the base of Senwosret I's

[106]For the relationship of Min to the kingship, see H. Jacobsohn, *Die dogmatische Stellung des Königs in der Theologie des alten Aegypten* (Glückstadt and New York, 1939) 29ff; *AEO* II, 28*; Kees, *Götterglaube*², 200f (Min and Isis); Frankfort, *Kingship and the Gods*, 189; cf. also E. J. Baumgartel, *Antiquity* 21 (1947) 145ff.

[107]Waddell, *Manetho*, 212ff (Pseudo-Eratosthenes); for Montuhotpe revered in the New Kingdom as a royal patriarch (largely due to the presence of his temple at Deir el-Bahari), see above p. 149f; also Fox, *Orientalia* 46, 400ff.

[108]E. Blumenthal, *Untersuchungen zum ägyptischen Königtum des mittleren Reiches* I (Berlin, 1970) 159.

[109]"... their waters identified in accordance with the contents of the writings, inventoried according to what was in ancient texts (*iswt*)," Beni Hasan (De Buck, *Egyptian Readingbook*, 68:11-12; "he was apprised of (the lie of) his boundary in accordance with the register (*ḫwdt*), inventoried in accordance with what was in ancient texts," (*ibid.*, 70:10-11). *Isw*, or *sš isw*, "ancient writings," are often alluded to as the written *Vorlage* of texts of great antiquity and importance: cf. the Hemerology, said to have been "found in ancient writings" (A. M. Bakir, *The Cairo Calendar No. 86637*, [Cairo, 1966] pl. 1, 1); genealogies could be based on "ancient writings from the time of the ancestors" (W. Spiegelberg, *PSBA* 24 [1902] 320ff; Wildung, *Imhotep und Amenhotep*, p. 281, pl. 66); medical prescriptions often had been "found in old writings" (Ebers xlvii, 15-16; P. Berlin 3038, xv, 1ff; Luft, *ZÄS* 99, 108ff); schoolboy admonitions (Anastasi v, 17, 6), tax lists (*Urk.* IV, 1120:5), the *sd*-festival liturgy (*Urk.* IV, 1867), mathematical papyri (Peet, *The Rhind Mathematical Papyrus*, pl. 1), data on geography (*Edfu* V, 126, 7) and cult prescriptions (*Edfu* VII, 27, 9) are all similarly derived from texts of great age, and therefore high authority. In one case (Kitchen, *RI* I, 293:12-13) the word *isw* takes on a meaning approaching our "precedent." Taking his cue from the tenor of the times, Sirenpowet I, a younger contemporary of Amenemhet I, boasts of having "established the laws of ancient times": *Urk.* VII, 2:12.

"White Chapel" at Thebes was in all probability a direct reflection of his father's survey.[110]

Another practical need was for scribes and literate bureaucrats. The results, a school at the capital,[111] and a teaching manual for scribes,[112] both fostered the resuscitation and preservation of traditions about the past.

Pharaoh also honoured his own forebears by refurbishing their cults. In Sinai the patron Sneferu was honoured with monuments.[113] In the Memphite region service in the mortuary temples of the Old Kingdom was restored,[114] and the Pyramid Texts recopied.[115] At the new temple, originally a family shrine, consecrated by Senwosret I to Amun at Karnak statues of Old Kingdom rulers were restored or dedicated anew.[116] Indeed at Thebes the offering tradition represented by these monuments and by the later "Chambre des ancêtres" of Thutmose III[117] probably dates from this dynasty, and stamps the cult in origin as a primarily royal one in which the worship of the ancestors played a dominant role. Under the aegis of the king,

[110] P. Lacau, H. Chevrier, *Une chapelle de Sésostris Ier à Karnak* (Cairo, 1969) pl. 42.
[111] W. K. Simpson (ed.), *The Literature of Ancient Egypt* (New Haven, 1973) 330.
[112] *Kmyt*: Sallier iv, 3; Chester Beatty IV, *vs.* vi, 11; H. Brunner, *Die Lehre des Cheti, Sohnes des Duauf* (Glückstadt, 1944) 57; A. H. Gardiner, *Hieratic Papyri in the British Museum* III Series *Chester Beatty Gift* I (London, 1935) 43, and n. 7; II, pl. 20; B. van de Walle, *CdE* 27 (1952) 380ff; Luft, *ZÄS* 99, 108; P. Kaplony, in *Akten des XIII. Internationalen Papyrologenkongresses*, 179ff; W. Barta, *ZÄS* 105 (1978) 6ff.
[113] Gardiner, Peet, Černý, *Sinai*[2] (1952) no. 67, p. 82ff; Wildung, *Die Rolle*, 128ff.
[114] For the kings of the 1st through 4th Dynasties, see Wildung, *Die Rolle*, *passim*; Sahure(?) (his temple was greatly admired in the New Kingdom, but may already have begun to fall to ruin: J. Baines, *GM* 4 [1973] 9ff; P-M III[3], 327; the graffiti of Ameny and Apopy [Borchardt, *Das Grabdenkmal*, 120] suggest that it was already abandoned in the late Middle Kingdom); Neferirkare (Cairo 72239: Zivie, *Giza*, 43ff); Newoserre (H. Schäfer, *Priestergräber und andere Grabfunde vom Ende der alten Reiches bis zur griechischen Zeit* [Leipzig, 1908] 15ff); Unas (J. Leclant, *Orientalia* 41 [1972] 255; 42 [1973] 401; H. Altenmüller, *SAK* 1 [1974] 1ff; A. Moussa, A. Altenmüller, *MDAIK* 31 [1975] 93ff, pl. 32); Tety (A. Barsanti, *ASAE* 13 [1913], 255f; C. Firth, B. Gunn, *Excavations at Saqqara* I *Teti Pyramid Cemeteries* [Cairo, 1926] 61ff; J. Yoyotte, *BIFAO* 57 [1958] 96, n. 4; Wildung, *Die Rolle*, 126f; H. Fischer, *Varia* [*Egyptian Studies* I; New York, 1976] pl. 17, p. 59ff; P-M III[2], 394; J. Berlandini-Grenier, *BIFAO* 76 [1976] 313f); Pepy I (J. Leclant, *Orientalia* 44 [1975] 207; *idem*, *Orientalia Lovaniensia Periodica* 6/7 [1976] 355ff); Pepy II (P. Vernus, *RdE* 28 [1976] pl. 14, p. 137, with notes 20, 21; P-M III[2], 429); Merikare (references in J. von Beckerath, *ZÄS* 93 [1966] 15, n. 21). It was mainly Saqqara that experienced the revival of Old Kingdom cults; Giza shows no signs of cultic restoration: Zivie, *Giza*, 26f.
[115] H. Altenmüller, in *Fragen an die altägyptischen Literatur*, 22ff.
[116] In general see D. Wildung, *MDIAK* 25 (1969) 212ff; Khufu: L. Borchardt, *Statuen und Statuetten von Königen und Privatleuten* I (*CCG*; Berlin, 1911) pl. 1; Sahure: *ibid.*, pl. 2; Newoserre: *Hieroglyphic Texts ... B.M.* IV, pl. 2, no. 48; B. V. Bothmer, *MDIAK* 30 (1974) 165ff; Blumenthal, *Untersuchungen*, 157; Djoser: Wildung, *Die Rolle*, 59.
[117] See above, p. 29ff.

and the patronage of the ithyphallic ancestor god, the royal ancestors attested from the region of Thebes by their monuments, were gathered into *Ipt-swwt*, and their statues there honoured in the offering cult.[118] Well might a Senwosret III be lauded by the poet with the ejaculatory observation "How euphoric are [thy] fa[thers] who were aforetime, now that thou hast enlarged their offering portions!"[119]

With perspicacious self-interest the 12th Dynasty kings saw themselves as true heirs linked to the legendary Old Kingdom line of monarchs by the intermediary of the 11th Dynasty. Far from anathematizing their immediate predecessors — the continued popularity of the Antefs and Montuhotpes would have made this unwise in any case — the family of Amenemhet took pains to honour them by erecting statues of them, or by refurbishing their monuments.[120] Everywhere under royal authorization delapidated ruins of byegone days were restored, and it almost was a watchword

[118]Whether the cult of Amun was present at Karnak during the early years of the 11th Dynasty, or before, is immaterial (on this question see Bothmer, *MDAIK* 30, 169f, with references); *Ipt-swwt* is a Middle Kingdom creation, *de novo*, and owes almost nothing to whatever cult (if any) preceeded it on the site. The members of the Chamber of Ancestors who belong to the Old and Middle Kingdoms and statues of Old Kingdom monarchs, are 12th Dynasty dedications: they owe nothing necessarily to the presence of Old Kingdom construction or statuary in some earlier *Ipt-swwt* at the site (cf. Wildung, *MDIAK* 25, 212ff and 219; P. Barguet, *Le Temple d'Amon-rê à Karnak* [Cairo, 1962] 2; W. Helck, *Ugaritische Forschungen* 8 [1976] 113, n. 113). This is not to deny that one statue of Newoserre is of Old Kingdom date (Bothmer, *MDAIK* 30, 169): there may well have been other, earlier shrines on the east bank, later supplanted by *Ipt-swwt*, which may have in part taken over their cults. That *Ipt-swwt* was in fact a "late arrival" in the area is graphically illustrated by the excavations in East Karnak (D. B. Redford, *JARCE* 14 [1977] 26f). All the building phases at the site which date from 18th Dynasty through 30th (viz. phases M to B inclusive) are oriented strictly in accordance with the orientation of the Amun temple, which was *ipso facto* the focus of all construction at the site. For the Middle Kingdom levels, however, which underlay the Akhenaten temple, the situation is wholly different: the houses are aligned to the points of the compass, as though the Amun temple was not in existence!

[119]Sethe, *Lesestücke*, 66:15-16.

[120]Dedication(?) by Amenemhet I to Montuhotpe IV (H. E. Winlock, *JEA* 26 [1940] pl. 21; W. J. Murnane, *Ancient Egyptian Coregencies* [Chicago, 1977] 23); statue of Antef-^{c}o born of Aku, set up by Senwosret I (Cairo, 42005/1) (Clère, Vandier, *Textes*, no. 7:11-13); group statue of Montuhotpe I and II, Amenemhet I and Senwosret I (W. M. F. Petrie, *Researches in Sinai* I [London, 1906] pl. 22 [no. 70]); statue dedicated to Montuhotpe I by Senwosret III and renewed by Sobekhotpe III (*ASAE* 7 [1907] 34); restoration of offering cult of Montuhotpe I by Senwosret III (E. Naville, *The Eleventh Dynasty Temple at Deir el-Bahari* I [London, 1907] 24, 5; 11, 12; cf. W. C. Hayes, *The Scepter of Egypt* [New York, 1959] fig. 111); refurbishing of the shrine of Heḳa-ib and Antef-^{c}o at Elephantine by Amenemhet III in his 34th year (above, n. 95); similar restoration of buildings of unknown predecessors by the same king (W. M. F. Petrie, *Hawara, Biahmu and Arsinoe* [London, 1889] pl. 27:1). It should also be noted that Amenemhet III's nebty-name, *W^{3}ḥ-^{c}nḫ*, recalls the high 11th Dynasty.

to say that "he refurbished what he had found in ruins ...."[121]

Under the influence of the royal example and the pietistic urgings of the new and popular wisdom literature, the private sector became aware of the past, and in an ancient Egyptian context, this could only mean the Necropolis. The celebration and commemoration of the ancestors had been, from the dawn of Egyptian history, naturally centred upon the tomb. The latter in its pristine form was solely functional: a place and table of offerings and libation, the magico-artistic representation of the funerary meal, the false door with its perpetuation of the name of the deceased — these were the features deemed necessary for the mortuary service to be carried out in perpetuity. But, from the late 4th Dynasty, when the cult place and the wall surface available for decoration was undergoing expansion,[122] the tomb gradually became transformed into a memorial of the owner's life and deeds.

Tomb owners are slow to tell us this, even though they or their relatives who sustained the cost of building[123] evidently took pride in recording their lives. To emblazon one's tomb walls with scenes of farming, viticulture, implement manufacture and feasting may well have been intended, at least in part, to transmute the activities depicted into an eternal realm to be of everlasting benefit to the departed soul.[124] But the activities presumed by the deceased to go on in his tomb after his death likewise display a functional, if not casual, approach to the Hereafter. The deceased knew his tomb would be frequented after his death, and so addressed proleptically his future visitors.[125] All and sundry are hailed, both professional (*ẖry-ḥb iw.ty.fy r is pn*), "a lector-priest who may come to this tomb"[126] and lay (*rmṯ nb*), "all people,"[127] both casual passersby (*swꜣty.sn*), and those more serious visitors (*ʿḳty.sn*). From this "address to the living" one may gain an accurate picture of the kind of activity expected to bring visitors to the tomb, and during the Old Kingdom

[121]Blumenthal, *Untersuchengen*, 118f; *idem*, in E. Endesfelder, and others (eds.), *Aegypten und Kusch* (Berlin, 1977) 68f. For the revived influence of the "Memphite" school of art in the Middle Kingdom, see J. Vandier, *Manuel d'archèologie ègyptienne* III (Paris, 1958) 176f, 262ff.
[122]W. S. Smith, *AJA* 45 (1941) 515; for the reign of Khufu as the point of greatest reduction of wall space, see A. Scharff, *JEA* 26 (1940) 45.
[123]J. A. Wilson, *JNES* 6 (1947) 240.
[124]G. Maspero, *Etudes de mythologie et d'archèologie ègyptienne* I (Paris, 1893) 393; cf. Firth, Gunn, *Teti Pyramid Cemeteries* I, 175, n. 1.
[125]Cf. J. Saint-Fare Garnot, *L'appel aux vivants* (Cairo, 1938), *passim*; E. Schott, in *Fragen an die altägyptischen Literatur*, 443ff.
[126]Garnot, *L'appel aux vivants*, 19.
[127]*Ibid.*, 11.

it is largely of a practical nature. There is the act of entombment on the day of burial, which brings the conclave of morticians and their helpers to close the coffin lid;[128] and of course the lector-priest is expected regularly to use the tomb chapel to perform "the rites in conformity with that text of the lector-priest's art."[129] Passersby might be expected to enter the tomb to gratify the owner's expressed desire to receive invocation offerings. But the atmosphere was not one of reverence for an ancestor, still less a dispassionate interest in the past; in fact the most common outcome of such visits the owner can envisage is violence and the defilement of his tomb![130]

In spite of the general lack of piety or veneration towards the past which Old Kingdom addresses to the living reflect, it is clear that by the end of the Old Kingdom the decorated tomb chapel had become the only repository of records about the past which ordinary people could see. It was expected that people would be sufficiently impressed when they "see my offices (bestowed) by the king" to offer an invocatory prayer spontaneously.[131] Visitors will warm to the owner's words because he is one of them: "[O] you priests and deacons of the pyramid 'Beautiful-are-the-Seats-of-Unas,' servants of the lord's house! I, Azy, am one of you ...."[132] People were expected to be attracted to the tomb to admire its contents and the list is broad: "any persons, any scribes, any wisemen, and private citizen or poor man who may enter this tomb and who may see what is in it and who protects its decoration (*sšw*) and honours its images ...."[133] The tomb is becoming a show-place for the deceased to record his deeds, a place where posterity may "see what I have done upon earth."[134] Men are becoming conscious of their tomb as virtually

[128] *Ibid.*, 34, 41.
[129] *Urk.* I, 186:14-17; 187:4-6; 202:15-203:3; cf. Garnot, *L'appel aux vivants*, 22, 32; Schott, *ZÄS* 90, 103ff.
[130] Defilement can involve the "impurity" of the visitor (Garnot, *L'appel aux vivants*, 48, 63, 78; *Urk.* I, 49), and destruction (*sšn*) of the tomb (Garnot, *L'appel aux vivants*, 50; *Urk.* I, 219), erasure of its texts (Garnot, *L'appel aux vivants*, 11; *Urk.* VII, 53:11), removal of its bricks (Garnot, *L'appel aux vivants*, 78; Junker, *Giza* VIII [Vienna, 1947] 134, abb. 62), damaging its images (reliefs? *Urk.* VII, 53:12). In Ankhtify's case it is the future nomarchs themselves that are suspected of harbouring designs to destroy the tomb! Cf. J. Vandier, *Moᶜalla* (Cairo, 1950) 206ff (inscr. 8).
[131] *Urk.* I, 119:11; Garnot, *L'appel aux vivants*, 66. On *i*^{3}*wt* or *i*^{3}*wt ẖrt-nṯr*, as a term for the "curriculum vitae" of an official, as expressed in his biographical statement, see Fischer, *Dendera*, 145, 180. Tomb owners were always concerned to portray themselves as responsible about their public duties; cf. in this regard the Beni Hasan tombs of the Intermediate Period: cf. Groenwegen-Frankfort, *Arrest and Movement*, 64.
[132] Helck, *ZÄS* 104, 89ff.
[133] Asyut, tomb 1, 226ff: *Kêmi* 4 (1935) 90ff; *Urk.* VII, 53-4.
[134] *Urk.* IV, 939.

their sole link with posterity: the tomb stela is "my image, my heir upon earth, my memorial in the necropolis,"[135] the *ku*-statue "my august and noble image which makes my name abide in the necropolis,"[136] or "a goodly reminder to [peo]ple of the future, in years yet to come" of the tomb owner.[137] And the owner might with confidence say "ho, all people who come after me, for millions of years! Let me speak to you and inform you how useful I was in His Majesty's opinion!"[138]

By the Middle Kingdom the necropolis was once again a place of rest, instead of a battle field or a quarry. Men looked to the preparation of their tombs, and in the process could not help but take note of the tombs of those long deceased. An upstanding citizen took to restoring those ancestral tombs. The fad had already begun in the 11th Dynasty,[139] and become widespread in the 12th. Nomarchs piously restored the tombs of their ancestors or predecessors[140] and took a pedantic interest in restoring the names of the forefathers on their tombs, properly written and correctly vocalized.[141] Numerous are the visitors to be expected at the tomb chapel. Scribes are expected to recite[142] for general interest the contents of the inscriptions.[143] A new element in the age-old address to the living which appears first in the 12th Dynasty conjures up the

[135] *Urk.* IV, 412:11, 1032:4-6.
[136] *Urk.* IV, 1036:12-13.
[137] *Urk.* IV, 408:16.
[138] A. Badawy, *ASAE* 44 (1944) 203.
[139] Cf. Antef's restoration of the tomb of Nakht-oker: Berlin 13272 (Clère, Vandier, *Textes*, 44, n. 31; see J. J. Clère, *ZÄS* 93 [1966] 39ff; J. Omlin, *Amenemhet I und Sesostris I* [Heidelberg, 1962] 7f.
[140] Cf. Blumenthal, *Untersuchungen*, 118f. The tombs of Uau, Meru and Imhotpe, restored by Iha: N. de G. Davies, *The Rock Tombs of Sheikh Said* (London, 1901) pl. 29E, 30; *LD* II, 113b; tomb no. 2 at Bersheh, restored by an official whose name is lost: *El-Bersheh* II (London, 1895) 11; the ancestral tombs in U.E. 16, restored by Khnumhotpe: *Beni Hasan* I (London, 1893) pl. 25-26, line 80ff; his son Nakht acted similarly in U.E. 17: *ibid.*, line 132f), Cf. H. Fischer, *JAOS* 76 (1956) 105.
[141] Cf. Khnumhotpe of Beni Hasan (De Buck, *Egyptian Readingbook*, 71:3-4): "I made the names of my fathers live on, after I had found (them) weathered away on the doors (of their tombs), the signs being identified and the readings correct, and without putting one in place of another" (i.e. mixing the order of names in the genealogy).
[142] *Šdi*: *Wb.* IV, 563-4; for its use in ritual contexts, see *AEO* I, 55*f (*šdi s³ḫw*), Goedicke, *Königliche Dokumente*, 80, text note 7; cf. also T. G. Allen, *JNES* 8 (1949) 351-2, n. *h*.
[143] Louvre C.50: "All prophets, priests, lectors and scribes of the House of Osiris who shall read this stela of the 'Lords of Eternity' ..."; W. M. F. Petrie, *Dendereh* (London, 1900) pl. 11A: "[O ye scribes] who read these offices (i.e. the biographical statement), and see [what is in the tomb(?)]"; cf. Fischer, *Dendera* 180; Cairo 20539, ii, c, 9; Florence 1551; Sethe, *Lesestücke*, 70:6 "(O ye living, etc.) who shall read this stela"; sim. G. Posener, *JEA* 54 [1968] pl. IX, line 6ff; *Urk.* IV, 1495:14-16, 1514:15-16, 1536, 1610 etc.

image of someone literate, a lector-priest or a scribe, reciting, perhaps at a festival, the texts in a tomb, while a crowd of bystanders listen. "As for any scribe who may read this offering stela (*ᶜbꜣ*) ... or any people who may hear this offering stone (read) ... they shall say 'it is true.'"[144]

In a time when a firmly established regime was casting about for "sons of gentlemen" to fill the growing bureaucracy, it was imperative to establish one's own pedigree. The classic example of the overwhelming importance of family descent in Middle Kingdom society is the long biographical statement of Khnumhotpe of Beni Hasan.[145] The contents and stucture of the text may be schematized as follow:

1. Name and titles (1-4).

2. Building formula (*ir.n.f m mnw.f*), with dedication to refurbish his city and the names of his people (5-13).

3. Statement (introduced by *rꜣ.f ḏd.f*).

His Matrilineal Descent

(a) Appointment and confirmation by Amenemhet II (*iw rdi.n wi* etc.: 14-24)

(b) Precedent set by his maternal grandfather under Amenemhet I (with family history: 25-63)

(c)*[146] His mother's marriage (*sᶜḥ.i tpy n mwt.i*: 63-72)

His Own Floruit

(d) His own appointment, and the good he did his city (72-96)

(i) increase in its wealth

(ii) the honouring of the ancestors

(iii) restoration of ancestral offering chapels

(e) Curse on defilers of the tomb (96-102)

(f) Unintroduced list of epithets, ending with name and titles (102-121)

His Sons' Floruits

(g)* His oldest son's appointment, ending with the king's name (*kt ḥswt iryt n.i*: 121-133)

(h) His oldest son's good deeds (*ir.n.f m mnw.f*, etc.: 133-150)

(i)* His second son's accomplishsments, ending in his name (*ky smsw*: 150-161)

[144]Sethe, *Lesestücke*, 80:1-4; cf. Cairo 20017: "... any scribe who may read, any people who may listen, or any priest who may look on ..."; *ASAE* 7 (1906) pl. 1: "any scribe who may read, any people who may listen, and who may enter this chapel ..."; J. J. Tylor, *Wall Drawings and Monuments of El Kab: The Tomb of Sebeknekht* (London, 1896) pl. 2-3, line 1: "O all ye living upon earth, all ye revered magistrates, or any scribe who may read and any people who may listen"; cf. also *Urk.* IV, 965-6.

[145]P. E. Newberry, *Beni Hasan* I (London, 1893) pl. 25-26; Sethe, *Urk.* VII, 25ff.

[146]* Nominalized heading, in tabulatory style.

His Own Memorialization of the Ancestors

(j) Unintroduced continuation of the speaker's biographical statement, ending in his name (161-169)

His Father's Accomplishment: a Tomb

(k)* Statement regarding his own tomb, which leads directly to a section about his father, his tomb and virtues, ending in his name (170-193)

His Own Accomplishment: a Tomb

(l)* Detailed description of his own tomb, ending in his name (*ḫprt* followed by his name: 193-221)

4. Signature of the one responsible for the tomb.

Far from being a haphazard creation based on a stream of consciousness, Khnumhotpe's biography is a carefully organized piece, the intent of which is to stress certain points. First, it is the matrilineal nature of his inheritance that he emphasizes above all else; in fact his father is mentioned at the end of the whole, and then only in connexion with the tomb he built! Second, he is at pains to show that his appointment, and those of his sons, were in no way untoward, but were in perfect keeping with what royal precedent had established. Third, both he and his sons were civic-minded, revered the ancestors and restored their monuments. Fourth, he emulated his forebears, not only in his life, but also in his death: like his father, he constructed a tomb of note. In striking contrast to the "competent commoner" (*nḏs iḳr*), so typical of the First Intermediate Period, who was responsible for his own life and status, the 12th Dynasty worthy boasted unabashedly of his conservatism.

The new interest in one's own family tree[147] gave rise to some bizarre examples of genealogical research. The nomarch of Meir, for example, solemnly records predecessors who held the post, all

[147]See Fischer, *JAOS* 76, 104f; *idem*, *Inscriptions*, 116, n. *m*; cf. Cairo 20543a, 8: Blumenthal, *Untersuchungen*, I, 149; *Urk.* VII, 8:2. Cf. the expression "of exalted seed, pre-eminent lineage, and son of the 'Womb' of antiquity": H. Brunner, *Die Texte aus den Gräbern der Herakleopolitanzeit von Siut* (Glückstadt, 1937) 63; J. P. Corteggiani, in *Hommages à Serge Sauneron* (Cairo, 1979) 129f; for the interest in genealogy as exemplifed in 4-generation pedigrees, cf. the graffiti from Buhen, H. S. Smith, *JEA* 58 (1972) 42ff, Senwosret-sonbu (BM 557: HT II, pl. 3); a 3-tiered genealogy is not uncommon: cf. Bersheh tomb 4 (F. Ll. Griffith, *El-Bersheh* II [London, 1895] pl. 11), Hatnub no. 10 (R. Anthes, *Die Felseninschriften von Hatnub* [Leipzig, 1928] pl. 13; cf. no. 16, pl. 16), stela of Ipu from Abydos (Cairo 20025); 3- and 4-tiered genealogies are known from the 13th Dynasty: cf. the pedigrees of Iy-meru (Cairo 20690: J. von Beckerath, *JNES* 17 [1958] 264; cf. also Cairo 20310), Sobeknakht of El-Kab (Tylor, *The Tomb of Sebeknakht*, pl. 3-5), Aya of El-Kab (El-Kab tomb no. 9: *LD* III, 62a; Helck, *Historisch-biographische Texte*, 76; statue from Elephantine: W. Kaiser, *MDAIK* 28 [1972] 188); for a 5-tiered genealogy, cf. Budapest 1939 (E. Mahler, *BIFAO* 27 (1927) 40ff, pl. 1, fig. 1).

represented by formal seated figures, and with their names duly recorded.[148] There is considerable doubt about the authenticity of the early portions of the list: but to its compiler it was probably the form alone which mattered. Thuthotpe of Hermopolis could boast of his accomplishment in erecting a colossus of himself;[149] but it was to the stelae[150] of his ancestors along the river, "the *ḥ^{3}tyw-^{c}* who held office in earlier times, and the *^{c}ḏw-mr* [who had jurisdiction] in this city" that he had recourse to prove that no one had ever thought of this before.[151] The forefathers and their deeds weighed heavily upon the minds of Egyptians during the Middle Kingdom.

It is clear also, that such preoccupation with the forefathers affected not only the upper echelons of society, but also that level wherein spontaneous folklore took shape. Aetiology is always the predilection of people with leisure, a modicum of security, and the resultant curiosity about the factors in the past which brought this about. People in the throes of a civil war rarely have the time or the interest. It is no accident, then, that the 12th Dynasty witnessed the inscripturation of oral narrative about the past, useful also for didactic purposes of the new "scribal school" of the Residence.[152] How had the line of three (sic) kings of the 4th Dynasty[153] suffered interruption? How had Woserkaf's family come to power, and how was it connected to the cult of Re? How came it that Pepy II had been discredited?[154] And how had Akhtoy the tyrant met his end?[155] These are the questions that underlay and gave rise to the extant *Märchen* from the 12th Dynasty.

The folklore of the day was, moreover, already conscious of an ideal, capitalized on and accentuated by the official didactic literature,

[148]A. M. Blackman, *The Rock Tombs of Meir* III (London, 1915) pls. 10, 11, 29; p. 16ff.

[149]P. E. Newberry, *El-Bersheh* I (London, 1892) pl. 14-15.

[150]*Mḫ^{3}wt*. *Wb.* II, 131:7 suggests a meaning "Zollstation," but this is wholly gratuitous: nomarchs do not memorialize themselves by erecting customs-sheds! It seems much more likely to me that we have here a cognate of *mḫ^{3}*, "shed(?)," or some similar light structure (R. A. Caminos, *Literary Fragments in the Hieratic Script* [Oxford, 1956] pl. 4, 1:4; p. 17). The nature of the object as a place where former nomarchs could be known by their names, suggests a *memorial*; and its location by the river (as at Silsileh) militates in favour of some sort of commemorative *chapel*, possibly of light construction, with stela.

[151]Newberry, *El-Bersheh* I, pl. 14; for texts in similar vein, see Blumenthal, *Untersuchungen*, 168f.

[152]See Posener, *Littérature et politique*, 7, 19.

[153]Westcar 9, 13f. The error originated in construing the number of Giza Pyramids as corresponding to the number of kings of the dynasty.

[154]Assuming that *Sisine and the General* (G. Posener, *RdE* 11 [1957] 119f) was told to his disadvantage.

[155]On the assumption that behind Manetho's story lies a folk-tale.

viz. that of the "good king," as well as the image of his opposite, the "bad king," or tyrant.[156] By the 12th Dynasty both roles were enshrined in the persons of Sneferu, prototype of the beneficent monarch, and his successor Khufu, the prototype of the despot.[157] While there may well have been a basis in historical fact for the vilification of Khufu, the classic "bad press" he was later to receive in Herodotus[158] owes as much to the contemporary example of the Persian king as it does to any accurate recollection of events. From the reign of the good Sneferu had come wisdom, prophecy, bonhommie and good government, which, *mutatis mutandis* also distinguished the regime of the 12th Dynasty.

It was in this atmosphere of reverence for the past and its precedents that the first true king-list was born. The euphoria which attended the settlement of Amenemhet I gave rise almost immediately to a self-awareness and a consciousness of the fact that with the new family had come a new beginning, a "repeating of creation."[159] In all probability the king-list was first simply another of the instruments forged by the House of Amenemhet to bolster its claims; but, while to strengthen Amenemhet's soteriological role the past had to be painted black, to lay claim to an unimpeachable pedigree where none existed, meant forging a link with the 11th Dynasty. The link was made early. Lists grouped Amenemhet I and Senwosret I with Nebhepetre and Se^{c}ankhkare,[160] and honoured the *pater familias*, Senwosret, by inserting his name before that of his son, Amenemhet I, even though he had never reigned.[161] Amenemhet's name was grouped with kings of the 11th Dynasty and the Old Kingdom at Elephantine.[162] The "Wady Hammamat" list[163] shows the succession of "4th Dynasty" kings in an order strongly reminiscent of TC; and the Koptos stela of Rahotpe mentions "the period of [your] fathers, the king[s who fol]lowed Horus," (the earliest such reference known) in a manner suggesting that the divine dynasties of the classical Egyptian king-list had already been

[156]On the "messianic" ideal in Egypt, see B. Lanczkowski, *Altägyptischer Prophetismus* (*Aeg. Abhandlung* 4; 1960), 97; additional material cited in Goedicke, *Protocol*, 3f.
[157]See Kákosy, *Selected Papers*, 94f.
[158]Herodotus, ii.125ff.
[159]Otto, *WO* III, 3, 164.
[160]Gardiner, Peet, Černý, *Sinai*^{2} (1952) pl. 22, no. 70.
[161]Karnak "list," above, p. 29ff. The names thus constituted more a "list of ancestors" than a king-list. By Manetho's time Senwosret was wrongly construed as a king, with disastrous results for the order of names in the 12th Dynasty; see further below, p. 239.
[162]See above, p. 25.
[163]Above, p. 25.

conceived.[164] From the same period comes the earliest reference to Osiris as king of the gods, with his name in a cartouche.[165] In short, the prototype of TC had begun to take shape, and its place of origin was undoubtedly the new capital, Itj-towy. The successors of Amenemhet I were already impressing themselves on the collective memory of the nation as a group, the embryonic 12th Dynasty.[166] From the reign of Amenemhet I on the scribes carefully noted the length of reign to the month and day, a practice which was carried on throughout the 13th Dynasty.[167] For the periods prior to the founding of the "House of Sehtepibre" the scribe often lacked precise data on lengths of reign; consequently months and days appear only sporadically.

The product of these labours was not an undifferentiated list of "ancestors" for the purpose of the offering cult, but a true king-list which recognized broader groupings of names into families. As the list had been created by and for Amenemhet and his successors, the 12th Dynasty was naturally a central pivot in the organization of the material. Thus we have "kings of Itj-towy," or "kings of the House of

[164]W. M. F. Petrie, *Koptos* (London, 1896) pl. 12:3; Helck, *Historisch-biographische Texte*, 60; cf. Blumenthal, *Untersuchungen*, 162 (for literature); *idem*, in *Aegypten und Kusch*, 73f; by the early 18th Dynasty the *Šmsw-Ḥr* had already been credited with annals: *Urk.* IV, 86. In general, see W. Kaiser, *ZÄS* 85 (1960) 132f; also Hornung, *Der Eine und die Vielen*, 147f; for the bifurcation of primeval times into "reigns of men and gods," see *Urk.* IV, 1326:8-12 (Amenophis II); cf. also D. Lorton, *JAOS* 99 (1979) 462.

[165]S. Hassan, *Hymnes du moyen empire* (Cairo, 1937) 106f; *Hieroglyphic Texts ... B.M.* III (London, 1920) pl. 28, no. 1367; cf. Wildung, *Die Rolle*, 30; Griffiths, *Osiris and His Cult*, 23; U. Luft, *Forschungen und Berichte* 14 (1972) 63f; *idem*, *Beiträge zur Historisierung der Götterwelt und der Mythenschreibung* (Budapest, 1978) 84, 88. By Ptolemaic times Osiris was the archetypal king *par excellence*: J. Yoyotte, *BIFAO* 77 (1977) 145ff. From the Middle Kingdom also dates the inception of the common response to the king, placed in the mouth of a god. "I grant thee the years of (god X)"; implicit here is the belief in a period of time, understandably of great length, in the remote past, which constituted the "reign" of the god in question (Luft, *Beiträge*, 167ff). Of course royal attributes had long been predicated of the gods; but, in PT for example, the "reign" of a god had been construed as a pale and contemporary reflection of the earthly reign. From the Middle Kingdom also dates the earliest unequivocal reference (excluding the Memphite Theology) to the kingship of Ptah: M. Sandman, *The God Ptah* (Lund and Copenhagen, 1946) 29f.

[166]Cf. the list of royal names from Amenemhet I to III: W. M. F. Petrie, *Historical Scarabs* (London, 1889) no. 272. The 13th Dynasty kings revered and emulated their 12th Dynasty predecessors: Helck, *Historisch-biographische Texte*, 36f, no. 44; 9, no. 13.

[167]The figure "213" which TC gives for the 12th Dynasty is remarkably accurate: see Murnane, *Ancient Egyptian Coregencies*, 28f; W. Barta, *SAK* 7 (1979) 1ff; M. Eaton-Krauss, *JSSEA* 12 (1982) 17ff. For the Old Kingdom, however, its figures and total have been questioned not infrequently by modern scholars. Again, this militates in favour of an historical vantage point for the composing scribe within the 12th Dynasty.

Sehtepibre" (the 12th Dynasty), and "kings who followed the House of Sehtepibre" (the 13th Dynasty). For the preceding period the scribes divided their source material into five sections: 1. the gods and followers of Horus; 2. the family of Menes; 3. the family of Tety; 4. the kings of Herakleopolis; 5. the kings of Thebes. The criterion seems to be, at least in part, the place of origin and/or rule: thus group 2 is linked to "White Fort" (*inbw ḥḏ*), no. 4 to Herakleopolis, no. 5 to Thebes, and the 12th and 13th Dynasties to Itj-towy. Just why Tety and his successors should have been singled out from the rest is not entirely clear; since his pyramid town, *Ḏdi-swwt*, was still flourishing, long after the Old Kingdom had come to an end, it may be that the founding of a new *ẖnw* prompted the scribes to create a new group.

As noted above, the sources employed by the Itj-towy scribes were uneven. In all probability behind the list from Menes to Djoser lay an edition of the early *gnwt*,[168] transmitted at a key stage (no later than the early 5th Dynasty, and probably earlier) in a hieratic form on papyrus. This edition of the *gnwt* ceased with Djoser (was it in fact drawn up under him?), and the subsequent section from Tety to Userkaf suffered from inferior source material. Not only were some names indistinctly preserved, but also the scribes at this point took folklore seriously: the quarter-century reigns of Huny, Sneferu and Khufu, resembling rough "generation" estimates, the tradition of the wise Imhotpe, and the false postulate of the reigns of Khufu's sons. The succession of names in what in Manetho would become the 5th and 6th Dynasties is reasonably accurate; and here we may suggest the existence of a Memphite-Abydene source, underpinned by a reliable offering tradition. The lengths of reign of these kings, however, pose a problem, as their reliability has recently been called into question.[169] But until we know something about the sources available to the Middle Kingdom scribes, and from what data the reign totals derive, it would be unwise to play "number games."[170] Are the figures ultimately totals of *gnwt*, or are they computed from other kinds of records, for example cattle-counts, or the like? We are equally benighted in our quest for sources for the Herakleopolitan

[168]See above, p. 135. Note the presence of year totals in months and days, certainly obtainable from *gnwt*.
[169]While back to the founding of the 11th Dynasty the figures for reigns may be confidently used in computing absolute dates, it seems to me quite unwise to use the earlier lengths of reign in TC uncritically to establish an absolute chronology: cf. W. Barta, *MDAIK* 35 (1979) 11ff; *idem*, *ZÄS* 108 (1981) 11ff (finding the total for the Old Kingdom appreciably inflated).
[170]As for example K. A. Kitchen, *Orientalia* 41 (1972) 124f.

period, since we know neither what records these kings kept, nor how they passed into the hands of the Itj-towy scribes.

The fate of the *gnwt*, indeed, as they evolved in the high Old Kingdom, is itself something of a problem. There is every reason to expect that, as the script developed more complex means of expression, and as methods of recording became more sophisticated, the old-fashioned *gnwt* would cease to be functional, or at least would have changed their form drastically. The 5th Dynasty entries on the Palermo stone are simply records of pious acts, and smack of artificiality. But perhaps, in fact, that is what the *gnwt* had become, viz. records of royal bequests and constructions for the gods, and nothing more! The increasingly frequent allusions to *gnwt* from the Middle Kingdom on suggests that the *form* survived, no matter what permutations it had undergone. But now the day-book had come into being, and was proving to be a much more efficient means of recording the detailed *res gestae* of the king; and significantly, when Zakar-baal has occasion to haul out his ancestral records, they are called "day-books"! Nevertheless, it seems likely, in view of the Egyptian reluctance to discard forms of proven worth, that an annalistic genre did survive under the label *gnwt*, approximating to some degree the format of ancient times.

The fate of the king-list tradition during the Second Intermediate Period is not attested. While Itj-towy remained the seat of government it cannot be doubted that the king-list continued, and it is highly probably that the tradition was transplanted to Thebes and Memphis. But did the violence of the Hyksos advent jeopardize its survival? *A fortiori*, since it reappears in Ramesside times, it did not. Whatever destruction attended the coming to power of this alien, West Semitic speaking dynasty in Egypt, it is clear that within half a century at the very least the "barbarians" had assumed a respect for Egyptian culture and mores. It is hard to imagine that Apophis, who prided himself on his literacy[171] and under whom literary and scientific works were copied,[172] would not have shown respect for a king-list tradition, no matter how foreign.

[171]On the palette of Atu he is called "scribe of Re, whom Thoth himself has instructed .... eminently successful (*ꜥšꜣ spw*) on the day when he recites with exactness every difficult passage in the writings, as (smoothly as?) flows(?) the Nile," Helck, *Historisch-biographische Texte*, 57.

[172]Rhind Papyrus (Peet, *The Rhind Mathematical Papyrus*, pl. 1); the Ramesseum Dramatic Papyrus (cf. the literature cited in A-P. Zivie, *Hermopolis et le nome de l'ibis* [Cairo, 1975] 45ff); probably Westcar (cf. Simpson, *The Literature of Ancient Egypt*, 15).

5

The King-list Tradition in the New Kingdom

The 18th Dynasty

Throughout the early 18th Dynasty there is some evidence, increasing as time progresses, of a re-awakened consciousness of the past. Several factors conditioned the Egyptians to look over their shoulders at their own earlier history. For one thing, the conquests of Thutmose I and III introduced a universalism into Egypt's relations with the outside world; and universalism inevitably awakens an interest in those who have gone before and their deeds, if only to accentuate the unique quality of the present imperial ideal. To judge from the extant texts Thutmose I is the first of the clan to realize the lack of precedent for his accomplishments. His father-in-law had, it is true, led armies at least as far as Tunip in Syria, and to the 3rd cataract on the Nile;[1] but Thutmose surpassed these razzias in distance and concept. For he attained the Euphrates in the north and Merwa in the south and beyond that no king of the dynasty would ever go. Moreover, his imagination grasped the possibilities inherent in the West Asian practice of oath-taking and treaty regulations. That he made little of the idea must be put down to his untimely death; but while still euphoric in the blush of his conquests he was able to say "the oath is taken by (me) in all lands."[2] The accounts of his conquests ring with the incredulity of one who against all odds has accomplished a "first": "the like has not happened to other (i.e.

[1]D. B. Redford, *JAOS* 99 (1979) 270ff.
[2]*Urk.* IV, 86:1.

earlier) kings[3] .... it has not been seen in the annals of former (kings) since the Followers of Horus,"[4] "I have surpassed what was done formerly[5] .... I have gone beyond what was done by other kings who ruled before me."[6]

The creation of an empire produced other results. The appearance in history of a bureaucracy on an imperial scale usually signals the advent in society of the polymath. A Cicero, Livy, Tacitus or a Suetonius can *mutatis mutandis* be found in the civil service of any growing empire, suddenly self-conscious of its past and present role. Egypt is no exception. The 18th Dynasty, certainly from Hatshepsut's reign, and perhaps before, yields a growing number of examples of the gifted man of letters, a "Renaissance Man" as it were, endowed with both a broad knowledge of the classical literature of the past, and creative ability. The aphorism recorded by Rekhmire sounds the keynote of the age: "every wiseman is one who can understand what the early ancestors said."[7] An education is a prerequisite and constitutes a mark of accomplishment: "I was educated in the God's-book and I looked on the 'Tools' (*ꜣḫw*) of Thoth (i.e. became conversant with the hieroglyphic script); I was prepared in their secrets, and I delved into (*pgꜣ*) all their difficult passages."[8] The product was a savant, "master of the secrets of the hieroglyphic script (*mdw-nṯr*),"[9] who could boast "there was no (hieroglyphic) sign at all of which I did not know the value; shapes which had no[t been drawn(?)], *ḫpšw*, old writings and worn, I [was knowledgable] about them."[10]

Even the king was a savant! Among the scions of the 18th Dynasty Thutmose III stands head and shoulders above the others as a literate intellectual. Of him Rekhmire sang: "lo, His Majesty knew history;[11] there was nothing at all which he did not know. He was Thoth in everything; there was not any subject of which he was not

[3] *Urk.* IV, 85:15.
[4] *Urk.* IV, 86:4-5.
[5] *Urk.* IV, 102:4.
[6] *Urk.* IV, 102:7-8; cf. 1260:10.
[7] *Urk.* IV, 1084:8.
[8] *Urk.* IV, 1820:12-14 (Amenophis, son of Hapu); cf. D. Wildung, *Imhotep und Amenhotep* (Munich and Berlin, 1977) 281.
[9] *Urk.* IV, 1897:12 (Amenemhet Surer).
[10] *Urk.* IV, 1082:2-5 (Rekhmire). There is in all this a subconscious looking ahead to what posterity will say: "as for one who exults in the acts of the ancestors, for him exultation will be made by them who come after": W. C. Hayes, *The Scepter of Egypt* II (New York, 1959) fig. 165, line 6.
[11] Literally "that which had happened" (*ḫprwt*), cf. H. Goedicke, *The Protocol of Neferyt* (Baltimore, 1977) 64; Coptic ϣⲡⲏⲣⲉ : J. Černý, *A Coptic Etymological Dictionary* (Cambridge, 1976) 250.

knowledgable [....] ... after the manner of the Majesty of Seshat. He could construe a sign according to its value, like the god who ordained it and created it."[12] The king delved into ancient writings: a decree regarding public health — of all things! — was promulgated after "His Majesty had seen a 'Protection-book' (*nht*) from the time of the forefathers."[13] An interest in copying, and presumably studying, the Pyramid Texts may be evidenced from his reign.[14] Similar consultation of ancient documents was indulged in by the king in the refurbishing of the Hathor temple at Dendera,[15] and perhaps also at Esna.[16] In all this Thutmose provides a parallel to his earlier contemporary Senenmut, who boasted that he was "educated in all the priestly writings; there was nothing that I did not know about what had happened since the dawn of creation (*sp tpy*) ...."[17] Elsewhere, in testimony of his antiquarian interests, he had rebus-signs of his own design carved on a cube statue of himself and Neferure, and glossed with the words "glyphs (*tiwt*) which I made after my own personal design (literally in the conception of my heart) .... and not found in the writing of the ancestors."[18] Thutmose III himself was "more conversant with the regulations than the scribes," and he admonished his officers "the writings are in your hands, preserved (*mn*) [as they were d]one by those who were aforetime."[19]

Secondly, the interest evinced by the Thutmosids in Memphis as a major capital had brought the royal family into direct contact (after a hiatus of over two centuries)[20] with a stretch of the Nile Valley which

[12] *Urk.* IV, 1074:2-9. Rekhmire is referring in the last passage to hieroglyphic signs (*tit*), not to "designs" in general: cf. Khnumhotpe, 164; *Urk.* IV, 406; P. Lacau, *ASAE* 26 (1926) 135; *tit r tit* "sign for sign," of the collation of a text: Naville, *Todtenbuch*, (Yuya), pl. 33; in bilinguals the term is rendered by ἐπίσμα, "sign": F. Daumas, *Les moyens d'expression du grec et de l'égyptien* (Cairo, 1952) 225. For Thutmose III's identification with Thoth, cf. T. Säve-Söderbergh, *Kush* 8 (1960) pl. 15 ("Thoth whom the gods adore in his name Menkheperre, the great god, who resides in *Tḥḫt*").

[13] Cf. P. Berlin 3049, *vs.* xix, 1: P. Vernus, *Orientalia* 48 (1979) 176ff.

[14] Cf. P. Berlin 3057, xxi, 15: G. Möller, *Uber die in einem späthieratischen Papyrus des Berliner Museums erhaltenen Pyramidensprüche* (Berlin, 1900) 2; U. Luft, *ZÄS* 99 (1973) 109.

[15] "The great plan, viz. (that of) Dendera, is a memorial-renewal effected by the King of Upper and Lower Egypt, the Lord of the Two Lands, Menkheperre, son of Re, Lord of Diadems, Thutmose, after it was found in ancient writings of the time of King Khufu": *Dendera* VI, 173; F. Daumas, *BIFAO* 52 (1953) 165ff; H. Fischer, *Dendera in the Third Millennium B.C.* (Locust Valley, N.Y., 1968) 45ff.

[16] M. Alliot, *Le culte d'Horus à Edfou* I (Cairo, 1949) 234; S. Sauneron, *ASAE* 52 (1952) 37f.

[17] *Urk.* IV, 415:14-16.

[18] *LD* III, pl. 25(i).

[19] *Urk.* IV, 1270f.

[20] Ever since the 13th Dynasty was obliged to quit Itj-towy in the face of the Hyksos incursion.

was redolent of antiquity. Thutmose I had chosen a site close to Memphis as his residence,[21] and his predilection had been shared by Thutmose III and his successors; and it had long been the king's practice to appoint the heir apparent to the priesthood of Ptah.[22] Amenophis II and especially Thutmose IV had taken a lively interest in the Giza plateau as a site for sporting diversions and relaxation. Thutmose IV's clearance of the debris from around the sphinx was something more than a pious act performed at the sun-god's behest: it was an attempt to commune with antiquity. As the king said to his companions, "... let us offer praise to those who were aforetime, [those who bore] the august [urae]us [...] Khafre."[23]

Third, the family solidarity and matriarchal tendency of the Thutmosid house prevented its scions from ignoring their predecessors, as so often happened in the course of Egyptian history.[24] In fact the family contretemps of Hatshepsut and her step-son nurtured an interest in *interpreting* the past for the benefit of contemporaries. The queen is famous for several "re-writings" of recent history: her birth narrative,[25] the text of her appointment by Thutmose I,[26] the story of her selection by the god.[27] with the miracle story of year 2 (Deir el-Bahari and the Red Chapel).[28] Some of this material is derived from earlier texts: the birth narrative, for example, is known (coronation pericope) from a 12th Dynasty exemplar, and is probably a Middle Kingdom creation;[29] the selection account is credited to Thutmose I in the final re-working of the inscription,[30] and would in fact be quite apposite of his situation at

[21]W. Helck, *Zur Verwaltung des mittleren und neuen Reichs* (Leiden, 1958) 7f.

[22]D. B. Redford, *JEA* 51 (1965) 111ff; B. Schmitz, *Untersuchungen zum Titel S^3-Njswt "Königssohn"* (Bonn, 1976) 301.

[23]*Urk.* IV, 1544:4-5; on the translation see C. M. Zivie, *Giza au deuxième millénaire* (Cairo, 1976) 145.

[24]On the veneration of the royal mother, current during the 18th Dynasty and its connexion with the renewed popularity of the birth legend, see H. Brunner, *Die Geburt des Gottkönigs* (Wiesbaden, 1964) 198; on the insistence of 18th Dynasty kings on divine birth and sanction, see E. Hornung, *MDAIK* 15 (1957) 130f; W. Helck, *Or. Ant.* 8 (1969) 312ff.

[25]*Urk.* IV, 215ff.

[26]*Urk.* IV, 241ff, 265ff.

[27]E. Naville, *The Temple of Deir el-Bahari* VI (London, 1908) pl. 166.

[28]Red Chapel block #287: S. Schott, *Altägyptische Festdaten* (Wiesbaden, 1950) 97; *idem*, *NGWG* (1955) 212; W. Helck, in *Studia Biblica et Orientalia* III (Rome, 1959) 116f; P. Lacau, H. Chevrier, *Une chapelle d'Hatshepsout à Karnak* (Cairo, 1977) 97ff.

[29]*Aegyptischen Inschriften aus den königlichen Museen zu Berlin* III (Berlin, 1924) 138 (dealt with by my student, Dr. R. Leprohon, *The Reign of Amenemhet III* (PhD dissertation, University of Toronto, 1980).

[30]D. B. Redford, *History and Chronology of the Eighteenth Dynasty of Egypt: Seven Studies* (Toronto, 1967) 75, n. 89.

the outset of his reign. The miracle story, in Hatshepsut's version is dated in year 2; but if as has been suggested,[31] Hatshepsut's intent was to have her readers believe the king was Thutmose I, she has given the game away. In year 2, vi, 29 Thutmose I was in Nubia, not Thebes![32] Again one wonders whether an original piece has not been "lifted" from its context, and transferred *en bloc* to the queen's reign. Nonetheless, Hatshepsut evinces a concern to convey a message which demands a special use of the past: she is at pains to show that her reign is unique, in her birth, her parentage, her selection, and her relationship with the deity. She was the first monarch since the Hyksos conquest, she claims, to rule with the sanction of the sun-god.[33]

For Thutmose III, as perhaps for the country, Hatshepsut's interregnum had posed an ideological crisis; and his remedial action effectually closed the *Thronwirren* chapter of his family's history. Essentially he appealed, as Hatshepsut had done, to his links, real or imagined, to the founder of the house, Thutmose I. Partly by emulating him,[34] partly by re-writing his biography,[35] and partly by making a point of revering his monuments,[36] Thutmose III healed the rupture in tradition and restored the *status quo ante*. Ironically, in the event, it was Thutmose III who was later revered as the great

[31]J. Yoyotte, *Kêmi* 18 (1968) 85ff.
[32]In ix of year 2 Thutmose I passed Tangur on his way south to engage the chief of Kush (H. Gauthier, *LdR* II, 214 [III]; F. Hintze, *Kush* 13 [1965] 13, n. 6; 14, n. 10); on 15, ii of year 2 Thutmose was in Tombos, authorizing the building of a fortress (*Urk.* IV, 82ff); on 21, vii year 3 began, and on 22, ix of year 3 the king returned to Aswan on his homeward journey (L. Habachi, *Kush* 5 [1957] pl. 5, inscr. 1; *Urk.* IV, 89f). Clearly the king could not have been in Luxor at the time of the alleged miracle, if the year-date is in fact his.
[33]*Urk.* IV, 390:9-11; D. B. Redford, *Orientalia* 39 (1970) 32f; in many ways she strove for "firsts": for example, she was the first ruler to have Amaunet's cult image appear in procession "for this image of the Majesty of this great goddess had never gone forth abroad"; Lacau, Chevrier, *Chapelle d'Hatshepsout*, pl. 14, p. 283.
[34]Cf., for example, the course and events of the 8th Campaign, which seem patterned on the exploits of Thutmose I: Redford, *Orientalia* 39, 41.
[35]Cf. the re-editing of the Deir el-Bahari inscription, originally set up by Hatshepsut for herself: Redford, *History and Chronology*, 74ff.
[36]Cf. *Urk.* IV, 847.

pater familias, "the father of the fathers,"[37] and Thutmose I receded into the background.[38]

In keeping with this Thutmosid awareness of being a member of an illustrious royal house, Thutmose IV paid careful attention to the monuments of his immediate predecessors. The Lateran Obelisk, which Thutmose III had left unfinished was completed and erected by his grandson.[39] who also erected a statue at Karnak to accompany a similar image left by his grandfather.[40] Similarly, statues of his father Amenophis II were refurbished,[41] and his mortuary temple kept equipped.[42] At Abydos Thutmose IV renewed the endowments of royal establishments of even remoter periods (*scil.* that of Ahmose).[43]

Fourth, and in keeping with the self-consciousness adumbrated above, the Thutmosids of the 15th Century fostered the worship of the royal ancestors, and re-awakened withal an interest in the king-list tradition. The kings of the late 16th Century found themselves rulers of a re-united state, but recently freed of foreign domination. Practical needs had to be met at once, and the solution to problems of city and temple construction, creation of a new civil service and restoration of the cult were uppermost in their minds. Such *ad hoc* solutions required models, and the models closest to hand to a family based in Thebes were those of the 12th Dynasty.[44] Here stood the great temple of Amun in essentially the same form as Senwosret I had left it, a medium-sized shrine to the divine patron of the house, conceived as a sort of family chapel to which it became customary for

[37] *Urk.* IV, 2135; cf. W. M. F. Petrie, *Historical Scarabs* (London, 1889) nos. 1443-52 (Sety I); nos. 1567-68 (Ramesses II); no. 1616 (Merneptah); no. 1652 (Ramesses III); Theban Tomb 31: P-M I^2, 47 (15: with Montuhotpe I); Theban Tomb 153: P-M I^2, 262 (with Amenophis I and Ahmes Nofretari); *Hieroglyphic Texts ... B.M.* VI (London, 1922) pl. 42 (offering with Amenophis I); *FIFAO* (année 1926), *Rapport préliminaire* IV, iii *Déir el-Médina* (Cairo, 1927) 7, fig. 1 (cartouches); *ibid.* 8, n. 3 (revered at Deir el-Medina in Ptolemaic times); J. Černý, *BIFAO* 27 (1927) 198(3) (Turo adoring his cartouches); A. R. Schulman, *Tel Aviv* 5 (1978) 149; offering table of Paneb: above, p. 44.

[38] Save when revered by one of his mortuary priests: cf. Userhat (P-M I^2, 97[9]); Wadj-mose (Turin 1457: P-M I^2, 735).

[39] *Urk.* IV, 1550.

[40] *Urk.* IV, 1554:4-5.

[41] L. Habachi, *ASAE* 38 (1938) 80; C. Aldred, *ZÄS* 94 (1967) 5.

[42] *Urk.* IV, 1563:17-18.

[43] Cf. Louvre C 53: P. Pierret, *Receuil d'inscriptions inédites du musée égyptien du Louvre* II (Paris, 1874-78) 14-15; cf. B. M. Bryan, *The Reign of Tuthmosis IV* (PhD dissertation, Yale University; 1980) 367f.

[44] Cf. Redford, *Orientalia* 39, 34, n. 6.

scions of the dynasty to dedicate monuments.[45] Under the aegis of Amun in his form of *K³-mwt.f*, closely related to Min, the offering cult of the royal ancestors flourished. To restore and further that cult became the overriding ambition of the 18th Dynasty, the heirs of the Middle Kingdom. In particular the founder, Senwosret I, was honoured by having his monuments refurbished or copied, an activity in which Amenophis I was especially active. Amenophis I set up several monuments in limestone: a gate on the south,[46] a barque-kiosk (in the same area?),[47] several small shrines, and a replica of the White Chapel,[48] all remarkably reminiscent of 12th Dynasty originals. It is in this context that we must view his inscripturation of the list of 11th and 12th Dynasty kings:[49] it is the earliest trace in the 18th Dynasty of the revived ancestor cult, and a fore-runner of the Chamber of Ancestors.

But it was not only practicality and convenience that prompted the early 18th Dynasty to copy the 12th: they in a very real sense viewed themselves as the legitimate *heirs*, both spiritually and politically, of the house of Sehtepibre.[50] No better index of this is the large number of scarabs on which 18th Dynasty kings group themselves with the illustrious pharaohs of the Middle Kingdom.[51] The more elaborate grouping, in art, of 18th Dynasty kings with their 12th Dynasty forebears, so common in the 19th Dynasty, also begins at this time.[52] Sometimes more formal veneration took the form of a cult centre, built specifically for a 12th Dynasty king.[53]

Hatshepsut too contributed to the revival of the ancestral offering traditions. One of the episodes of her adulterated[54] *sd*-festival of year

[45]An unpublished limestone block seen by the author in the Sheikh Labib storehouse at Karnak, dating from the early 18th Dynasty (cf. the reference to Ahmose, *ḥnwt* [*t³wy*(?)] *ẖnmt-nfr-ḥḏt*), speaks of "the kings who were [aforetime ... in] the temple of Amun."
[46]G. Legrain, *ASAE* 4 (1903) 14ff; P. Barguet, *Le temple d'Amon-rê à Karnak* (Cairo, 1962) 278; F-J. Schmitz, *Amenophis I* (Hildesheim, 1978) 241; Redford,*JAOS* 99, 270ff.
[47]G. Björkman, *Kings at Karnak* (Uppsala, 1971) 58.
[48]*Ibid.*, 58f; Schmitz, *Amenophis I*, 242f.
[49]See above, p. 29.
[50]Redford, *History and Chronology*, 78f; cf. U. Luft, *Forschungen und Berichte* 14 (1972) 62f; add the Karnak gate of Amenophis I (unpublished) on which the list of festivals is copied from a 12th Dynasty original without even shifting the *prt-Spdt* to its new position in the calendar!
[51]Cf. the list in W. J. Murnane, *Ancient Egyptian Coregencies* (Chicago, 1977) 222.
[52]Hayes, *The Scepter of Egypt* II, fig. 24 (Amenophis I with Senwosret I).
[53]Cf. Thutmose III's shrine to Senwosret III at Semnah: H. Frankfort, *Kingship and the Gods* (Chicago, 1948) 370, n. 3; D. Dunham, J. M. A. Janssen, *Second Cataract Forts* I *Semna, Kumma* (Boston, 1960) 8ff and *passim*.
[54]See below, p. 184.

16-17 involved "offering thanks for the Ennead and for the kings of Upper and Lower Egypt, and giving mighty adulation by all the plebeians."[55] The queen's *sd*-festival reliefs give prominence to the ithyphallic god, Amun, Lord of Heaven; and one recalls that the ancestors play a prominent role in ceremonies related to that more ancient ithyphallic god, Min.[56] Indeed, throughout Luxor and Karnak one is impressed by the predominance of this cras, but fascinating, form of ancestor-god in ritual and relief. Moreover, it was Hatshepsut, one will recall, that constructed the first great ancestral memorial in the New Kingdom, viz. the family temple at Deir el-Bahari,[57] which transformed the Theban necropolis from a provincial burial ground to an imperial cemetery. And it was also under her that the Feast of the Valley, a local celebration of Middle Kingdom origin,[58] was translated into the great annual commemoration of the ancestors, whether royal or private.[59] Indicative perhaps of the pretensions of the reign with respect to historical traditions was the linking of her name (and that of Thutmose III) with the legendary Menes, the great founder of the line.[60]

[55]Red Chapel block #140: Lacau, Chevrier, *Chapelle d'Hatshepsout*, § 563; the text is accompanied by the representations of gods'-fathers and three *ḥnwtyw*. In hour 6 of *Am-duat* Re addresses the "kings of Upper and Lower Egypt" (102, 4-5; 103:7): J. F. Borghouts, *JEA* 59 (1973) 117.

[56]Min and his festival, and presumably also the stress placed on the ancestor cult, were popular during the Second Intermediate Period (16th Dynasty) in the Thebaid: O. D. Berlev, *Orientalia Lovaniensia Periodica* 6/7 (1976).

[57]As a family temple, Deir el-Bahari involves every member of the Thutmosid clan, whether in the original decoration, or in the renovations effected by Thutmose III. Hatshepsut's design was to show herself proclaimed by her father Thutmose I as king (Naville, *Temple of Deir el-Bahari* III, pl. 61; VI, pl. 165), in his company (*ibid.*, I, pl. 9), or offering to him (*ibid.*, V, pl. 129). In her birth legend her mother Ahmose is honoured (*ibid.*, II, pl. 47-49). Thutmose II was also, if rarely, honoured (*ibid.*, I, pl. 2; IV, pl. 95; Hayes, *The Scepter of Egypt* II 82, fig. 44). In his unabashed re-write Thutmose III has ascribed Hatshepsut's coronation to Thutmose I (Naville, *Temple of Deir el-Bahari* VI, pl. 166-67; Redford, *History and Chronology*, 75f), and has even introduced Ahmes Nofretari (Naville, *Temple of Deir el-Bahari* II, 14).

[58]H. E. Winlock, *The Rise and Fall of the Middle Kingdom in Thebes* (New York, 1947) 84ff.

[59]S. Schott, *Das schöne Fest vom Wüstentale* (Wiesbaden, 1953) 5f, 123f.

[60]P. E. Newberry, *The Timins Collection of Ancient Egyptian Scarabs and Cylinder Seals* (London, 1907) pl. VI, p. 20 (no. 104); S. Ratié, *La reine Hatchepsout: Sources et problèmes* (Leiden, 1979) 301.

Finally we should note in her reign the first appearance in the Thutmosid clan of the hankering after authenticity, a sort of *Treulesen*, in the cult, which was to characterize Amenophis III's approach to the *sd*-festival.[61] Of Amun the queen states "I [caused] the Majesty of this god to [appear] in [his] festivals of [Ne]heb-kau and the Feast of Thoth, which I made over [a]new for him, since they had been (only perpetuated) by word of mouth, and none at its proper season."[62] In other words, she says that until her time the calendrical fixing of the dates of the festival had relied, not on accurate, written prescriptions, but oral tradition.[63]

If Hatshepsut was an agent in the revival of interest in the past, Thutmose III put that interest on a formal basis by devoting portions of the national shrine, that of Amun-re, to the worship of the royal ancestors.

His reverence for his grandfather — genuine or feigned, we shall never know — seems to have been a catalyst partly responsible for his overwhelming interest in the line of royal ancestors. On the pillars before pylon 6 a guiding principle of his Karnak building programme is enunciated:[64] "I swear, as Re loves me and my father Amun favours me! I have not made there ⌜great⌝ [works (?)] in order to conceal the monuments [of my father ᶜOkheperkare ...]";[65] and again "[No] new stonework has [ever] been laid in order to conceal the monuments of my majesty(?)], together with the monuments of my fathers, the kings of Upper and Lower Egypt."[66] The great monuments mentioned are probably those which were erected in the Amun temple proper, in a phase of the building programme to be dated from c. year 40 (or a trifle earlier) to year

[61]See below, p. 186.
[62]*Urk.* IV, 388:14-17.
[63]Like many of the queen's statements, this may be an exaggeration. The festival list of Amenophis I (above, n. 50) evinces some interest in fixing the dates of festivals, even though the list may be an unaltered copy of a 12th Dynasty original.
[64]P-M II^2, 87.
[65]*Urk.* IV, 846:17-847:4.
[66]*Urk.* IV, 847:12-16.

42.[67] These are the constructions of which Menkheperresoneb was put in charge, and which are mentioned specifically by him in his tomb:[68] "I was an eye witness when my lord, the King of Upper and Lower Egypt Menkhepperre set up [a .... in the temple of his father Amun, Lord of the Thrones of the Two Lands, the name of which is] 'Menkheperre-elevates-the-crowns-of-Amun', of hard granite on the way [of ...] ...; I was an eyewitness when His Majesty set up a great gate of electrum (called) 'Menkheperre-has-much-love-in-the-house-of-Amun'; I was an eyewitness when His Majesty made great pillars [overlaid(?)] with electrum ...; I was an eyewitness when His Majesty set up many obelisks and flag staves for his father Amun, I being his trusted man in supervising the work on his monuments."

The order in which the several stuctures are dealt with is from the barque-shrine out.[69] The first, as Barguet has shown,[70] is the enthronement kiosk southwest of the barque-shrine. The great gate listed next is the door of the vestibule to pylon 6[71] and significantly it is only by means of this door that one can proceed to the enthronement naos. Next comes what can only be the hypostyle between pylons 4 and 5, and finally the two sets of obelisks before pylons 4 and 7. Menkheperresoneb, whose floruit falls late in

[67]Thutmose III's building programme at Karnak is confined broadly speaking to 3 periods, viz. years 23-25 when the *Akh-menu* was under construction (planned year 23: Sir A. H. Gardiner, *JEA* 38 [1952] pl. 4, line 50; begun 10 months later in year 24: A. Mariette, *Karnak* [Leipzig, 1875] pl. 12, line 6-7; *Urk.* IV, 835:17-836:2; cf. also E. F. Wente, *JNES* 34 [1975] 265ff, and Bryan, *The Reign of Tuthmosis IV*, 15ff); the mid-4th decade of the reign, c. years 33-36, when the constructions along the north-south axis were put up (7th pylon: Barguet, *Temple*, 271, n. 3; peripteral kiosk between pylons 7 and 8 [second jubilee]: *Urk.* IV, 595:11 [possibly *Amn-mn-mnw*: E. Otto, *Topographie des thebanischen Gaues* (Berlin, 1952) 22; C. F. Nims, *JNES* 14 (1955) 113; L. Borchardt, *Aegyptische Tempel mit Umgang* (Cairo, 1938) 90ff]; the obelisks before pylon 7: Barguet, *Temple*, 270; L. Habachi, *The Obelisks of Egypt* [New York, 1977] 145ff); and years c. 39-42 when the work in the main temple along the east-west axis was effected and the main erasures of Hatshepsut's name carried out (obelisks before 4th pylon: P-M II^2, 74f; the 6th pylon: *Urk.* IV, 167:15ff; P. Barguet, *BIFAO* 52 [1953] 147; [*bḫnt špst nt ḫn*; there is no evidence, nor *a priori* likelihood that it was built as early as year 24, as Borchardt (*Zur Baugeschichte des Amonstempels von Karnak* [Hildesheim, 1905] 22) and Barguet (*Temple*, 116, n. 1) maintain], the north and south blocks of shrines for the ancestors [*Urk.* IV, 168:14ff], and the antechamber with the second installment of the annals).

[68]*Urk.* IV, 932:11ff.

[69]Exactly as in the fragmentary building inscription of Thutmose III before the 2nd pylon: C. F. Nims, in G. E. Kadish (ed.), *Studies in Honor of John A. Wilson* (Chicago, 1969) 69ff and fig. 7. Possibly the barque-shrine was mentioned in the lost section at the beginning; then follows pylon 6, the two courts north and south of the vestibule of the shrine, the granite doors in this part of the temple, the eastern temple, pylon 7, and the sacred lake.

[70]*BIFAO* 52, 148; *idem*, *Temple*, 115, 316f.

[71]*Urk.* IV, 845:13, 846:6, 14; P-M II^2, 86f(228).

Thutmose III's reign and overlapped into that of Amenophis II,[72] probably sprang to prominence about the time of the 8th — Mitanni — Campaign of Thutmose III,[73] and was thereafter put in charge of the Amun clergy and construction work in the temple (from c. year 34).

The circumstances under which the hypostyle between pylons 4 and 5 was rebuilt are given in detail on one of the columns of this hall;[74] they exemplify the aforementioned concern the king showed in not masking the work of former kings, and also his desire to refurbish the monuments of his forebears.[75] "Lo, His Majesty found the double hypostyle in ⸢a state of⸣ (?) [....] ... a ⸢cloud-burst⸣ upon its roof,[76] beginning at the time of noon and extending until midnight; and throughout the [entire] day it (i.e. the roof) was leaking[77] [...] its [...] which had been made in life, stability and prosperity to beautify this monument together with the ambulatory[78] which had been made[79] therein for the Majesty of [this god(?) ...] in this temple, creating a depression(?),[80] and not a single stone approached(?) its join(?);[81] although (*ẖr*) the ⸢rain⸣[82] had not reached the images along the wall.[83] [... I did not(?) ...] namely, the image of my father ʿOkheperkare, in order not to let the image of My Majesty conceal the images of ʿOkheperkare [...] My (sic) Majesty removed the (statues of) the other kings of Upper and Lower Egypt, so that ⸢they⸣ might be ⸢on view⸣ for millions of

[72]G. Lefebvre, *Histoire des grands prêtres d'Amon de Karnak* (Paris, 1929) 82ff, 233ff.
[73]The earliest event mentioned in the tomb: A. H. Gardiner, *The Tomb of Menkheperrasonb, Amenmose and Another* (London, 1933) pl. 7.
[74]*Urk.* IV, 839:10ff; C. Wallet-Lebrun, *BIFAO* 84 (1984) 317ff.
[75]Thutmose's inscriptions suggest that in his day the temple was in need of repair: cf. *Urk.* IV, 834:14-15, 848:9, 14.
[76]*Wrmt*: *Wb.* I, 333:3; read [*igp ḥr*].
[77]*Pnḳ*, literally "to empty, bale out," *Wb.* I, 510:12-15; Coptic ⲡⲱⲛ̄ⲕ : Černý, *Coptic Etymological Dictionary*, 126.
[78]*Tꜣ šmt*: *Wb.* IV, 466:14.
[79]*iry*; for the lack of agreement, see Gardiner, *Grammar*³, § 511:1-2.
[80]*ir* ⸢*m*⸣(?) *ṯꜣt* ⸢*ḥr*⸣ *iwtn*, literally "made into a taking from the ground"; another possibility, though less likely, might be to read *ir* ⸢*m*⸣ *ṯꜣt* ⸢*ib*⸣, "vexing/disagreeing with the ground," i.e. out of alignment? Cf. for the root *mṯꜣ* Ptahhotpe 19, 63; W. C. Hayes, *A Papyrus of the Late Middle Kingdom in the Brooklyn Museum* (Brooklyn, 1955) pl. VI, C, 5; p. 82f; R. O. Faulkner, *A Concise Dictionary of Middle Egyptian* (Oxford, 1962) 121. In either case a land-slip caused by rain is probably what is being alluded to.
[81]*Rwy.f*, literally "its (point of) cessation."
[82]*Mwy*: R. A. Caminos, *Literary Fragments in the Hieratic Script* (Oxford, 1956) 42.
[83]*Twwt n tꜣ sꜣt*: the Osiride colossoi are indoubtedly meant.

years."[84] And further on the matter is summed up: "My Majesty has made [for myself many] monument[s in my own name(?), while the name of my father abides] ⌜on his (own)⌝ [monuments] and the names of the kings of Upper and Lower Egypt abide on their monuments in the House of Amun-re, Lord of Karnak for ever and ever."

Although the inscription, a difficult text to begin with, has suffered since Piehl made his copy, enough remains to allow us to infer Thutmose III's purpose. The record implies that the motivation to renovate was supplied by a freak storm which did considerable damage to the hypostyle hall behind the 4th pylon and the axial ambulatory.[85] In this part of the temple there stood the colossal Osiride statues of Thutmose I, and as the text makes plain, the (statues of) former kings placed there on display.[86] Thutmose is quite explict: in the extensive renovations he contemplated, and later carried through, he in no way wished to mask or cover over the statues of Thutmose I or the earlier kings. Rather he wished them all to remain *on view*, their names and monuments remaining untampered with in the House of Amun-re. This is a far cry from the postulated clean-up of the statues and monuments of former kings, which resulted in compensation, as it were, of their royal owners, in the "check-list" of the Chamber of Ancestors.[87] Thutmose did *not* carry out such a clean-up and a different explanation will have to be found for the list in the Akh-menu.

The Chamber of Ancestors is really a cult room, in which the

[84]Sethe restores an *n* before *in.n*, which would have the effect of denying that the statues were removed. He further restores a m^3 before *.tw.sn*, although *smn* might do just as well. In either case Thutmose's intent was the same, viz. to preserve the images of the royal ancestors which had suffered from the freak storm, and were in danger of being concealed in the construction.

[85]The example of *šmt* in the ostracon MMA 23001.108 (W. C. Hayes, *JEA* 46 [1960] pl. 13, n. 21, *rt.* 2) suggests a central passage flanked by two columned rooms, exactly as in the Amun temple the passage along the central axis is flanked by the double hypostyle of Thutmose I. (Although by extension the central axis later became the nave of the hypostyle hall, the *šmt* was probably distinguished from the *ḫft-ḥr*, "nave," (Kitchen, *RT* II, 650:1-2), or later "dromos" (Daumas, *Moyens*, 171; J. D. Ray, *The Archive of Hor* [London, 1976] 147). It was precisely in such a passage, where they received a good deal of wear by passers-by, that private and royal statues were set: H. E. Winlock, *BMMA* 18 (October, 1923) II, 4; cf. such expressions as "may Amun greet it (the speaker's statue) whenever he comes out (of the temple) at a festival" (G. Lefebvre, *Inscriptions concernants les grands prêtres d'Amon Romê-Röy et Amenhotep* [Paris, 1929] 12f; "set garlands before me (i.e. the statue) when you enter (the temple)": *ibid.*, 33.

[86]It may well be that this is the w^3*ḏyt twwt*, "statue-hall," that Nespakashuty refers to, wherein Amun emerged: Cairo 42232, i, 2.

[87]See above, p. 29ff.

collective offering to the ancestors was carried on. The ancestors in question were probably those whose names and/or monuments were on display in the temple, and awareness of whom had just been sharpened through the king's restoration of the hypostyle. "My Majesty has commanded the perpetuation of the names of my fathers, the refurbishing of their offerings, the fashioning of their images ... and the offering to them of divine offerings anew, in excess of what had been formerly."[88]

The great conqueror separated his forebears roughly into three groups: the first two were the Old and Middle Kingdom monarchs, and the throng of short-lived kings who had followed the 12th Dynasty, both known from the temple offering lists. These two groups, placed on two opposing walls, were honoured in the "Chambre des Ancêtres"[89] in those parts of *ꜣḫ-mnw* devoted to Sokar, under whose sepulchral aegis the offerings to deceased ancestors had long since been placed at Memphis.[90] The chamber fulfils the function of cult seat for these offerings, and the 61 names, probably gleaned from the monuments in the *šmt*[91] behind pylon 4, have nothing to do with a temple clean-up. But the third group, Thutmose's immediate predecessors, the scions of the House of Seqenenre Taᶜo, were treated much more favourably, being granted special shrines closer to the Holy of Holies in the main temple. Here we have the beginnings of that special status accorded to the 18th Dynasty in Theban tradition, which emerges more fully attested in Ramesside times. It was born, not only of Thutmose's desire to legitimate his claim to the throne by linking himself to the bearers of legitimacy, but also of an appreciation of the unique contribution the 18th Dynasty was making. It might be added also that it was probably the Karnak "list," with its bipartite grouping, that nurtured the idea of a special group of "Theban" kings, which is misunderstood in Pseudo-Eratosthenes as kings ruling *at* Thebes.[92] Whatever the historical basis, the Karnak "list" treats the 13th Dynasty as a separate group, both in position and in iconography, and presages its

88 *Urk.* IV, 607. For other passages in which Thutmose III links himself with his ancestors, cf. Sir A. H. Gardiner, in *Studi in memoria Ippolito Rosellini* II (Pisa, 1955) pl. X, 3, "[the kings] who were aforetime, I am [their] son."

89 See above, p. 29f.

90 Above, p. 24; cf. above, p. 142 and p. 147. For "Sokar, residing in Karnak" see P. Bruyère, *ASAE* 54 (1956) 23; for "Ptah-Sokar residing in 'God's-Mound' which is in Thebes" see G. Steindorf, *Catalogue of the Egyptian Sculpture in the Walters Gallery* (Baltimore, 1946) pl. 29, 114; p. 56; cf. n. 162, pl. 30, 114, p. 54. In general on the Sokar cult at Karnak see H. Kees, *MIOF* 3 (1955) 342f.

91 See above, p. 29ff.

92 Waddell, *Manetho*, 212ff; and see below, p. 197.

treatment as a block, either by omission (as in the Abydos and Saqqara "lists") or by inclusion (as in TC).

With the accession of Amenophis III, one cannot help but detect a marked increase in interest in antiquity. The language is cliché-ridden, but the royal message is unmistakable. Amenophis III's avowed policy, the purpose in fact for which he was brought into being was "to make Egypt grow as (in) the Primordial Moment, in the condition of $m^{3c}t$,"[93] For him this meant constructing new monuments for the gods, and restoring those which had fallen into ruin. Of such overriding importance was this gigantic construction programme to the king that beside his sobriquet "Horus" (*par excellence*), he attracted to himself the nick-name *mnwy*, "the monument-man." One of the king's earliest recorded acts was the opening of new quarry chambers at Tura "after His Majesty found the temples which are in R^{3}*-wy* fallen into great delapidation since the time of those who lived long ago."[94] Amenophis was aware of what the ancestors had built, but he almost always mentions their work as something he has surpassed or can surpass.[95] He is "the maker of monuments in Karnak which surpass what they in the red-crown made,"[96] monuments which are "more distinguished than what the ancestors made";[97] of his construction it could be said that "the like has never been seen since the Primaeval Time of the earth; the kings who lived before His Majesty had not accomplished it."[98] "Lo, His Majesty's heart was pleased to make very great monuments (of which) the like had not been seen since the Primaeval Time of the Two Lands."[99] There was a conscious resistance to imitation of the ancestors, at least in architecture and art: Amenophis, son of Hapu says, "I published (*smn*) the king's name for eternity, I did not imitate what had been done before."[100]

The foregoing statements reflect only a desire to outdo past generations and in that respect the interest in the past of which they give evidence is negative. But there is good reason to think that Amenophis III took a more positive interest in the works and deeds of the ancients. The empire was now a fact, the wealth to make sophistication possible was now present. The fighting kings,

93 *Urk.* IV, 1725:5.
94 *LD* III, 71a; copied from the wording of his grandfather: *Urk.* IV, 1448.
95 On this theme in the 18th Dynasty, see Björkman, *Kings at Karnak*, 29ff.
96 *Urk.* IV, 1670:19.
97 *Urk.* IV, 1686:15.
98 *Urk.* IV, 1679:15-16.
99 *Urk.* IV, 1648:4-5; similarly 1683:6-7; 1687:3; 1690:4; 1751:10.
100 *Urk.* IV, 1822:11-12.

Thutmose III, Amenophis II, were gone and their ilk was no longer needed; the situation now called for the monarch with taste and self-indulgence who could set a standard of elegance. In fact the role of a paragon of pharaonic monarchy was waiting to be filled, and Amenophis III filled it admirably and in typical Egyptian fashion by the grandiose designs he conceived. But the "kingship of Horus," "the inheritance of Geb" entailed more than megalomaniac construction and sophistication: besides the mantle of deity he assumed which characterized him as a god absolute, outside of time and space, pharaoh had another cloak identifying him as an *heir* of the gods, a successor to a long line of earlier kings. If monuments enhanced Amenophis III's image as a god absolute, reverence for past precedence befitted his claim to the role of successor to the ancestors.

Amenophis III's reverence for the past is not evidenced in as many passages as those in which he boasts of having exceeded it. Aping Thutmose III[101] he once states the "the making for him (Montu) of a temple anew" was effected "without damaging former constructions."[102] The past was of practical use too, not only in providing a contrast to his own work but in offering precedents: "His Majesty caused that this temple (his Memphite mortuary temple) be a source of food income for the temple of Ptah, (authorized) in the various people, like the temples of the kings of Upper and Lower Egypt, which are beside his father Amun in the southern city."[103] Doubtless the rite of offering to the royal ancestors was kept up by Amenophis III, although what form it took is conjectural; and the statement of Kha^cemhat that he was one "that gave offerings to the gods, oblations to the kings of Upper and Lower Egypt and invocation offerings to the shades"[104] shows that the practice was already entering the private sphere, in anticipation of those multitudinous scenes in Ramesside private tombs.[105]

The best example of Amenophis's interest in, or perhaps better, use of, the past, (for the king was a practical man), is to be found in his celebration of the *sd*-festival. Of all Egyptian festivals this was the performance most imtimately connected with kingship, "Pharaoh's festival" in very truth. It constituted a glorious re-

[101] *Urk.* IV, 847.
[102] *Urk.* IV, 1667:17.
[103] *Urk.* IV, 1796:9-11.
[104] *Urk.* IV, 1853:2-4.
[105] See above, p. 45ff. It is interesting to note that the *serekh*-throne, with its symbolic reference to the divine forebears who had preceded the reigning sovereign, makes its appearance under Amenophis III: K. P. Kuhlmann, *GM* 50 (1981) 39ff.

affirmation of the right to rule Egypt, sanctioned by gods and people alike. The festival was, from the 12th Dynasty at least,[106] associated with the 30th year of the ruler *quā* king,[107] but for the ancient Egyptian this need not mean the beginning of a king's sole reign. The heir apparent could become king when his father or predecessor, still living, had him undergo a coronation, as happened to Hatshepsut, Amenophis II and Ramesses II, to name a few; or since mythologically pharaoh had been designated king while still "in the egg," the 30 years could conceivably be counted from the king's birth.[108] Only thus, it seems to me, can we explain the certain, though not numerous, cases in which a *sd*-festival is alluded to as having been celebrated before the 30th regnal year.[109]

From the beginning of the 13th Dynasty until the reign of Amenophis III, the evidence in art for the celebration of "real *sd*-festivals"[110] is scant and of a restricted sort. It consists of a limited number of generalized motifs, such as 1. statuary showing the king in *sd*-festival garment, 2. the scene of the king enthroned in the double kiosk amid sundry emblems, 3. motifs involving the *išd*-tree, 4. the ceremonial race.[111] These elements are fairly common in Egyptian iconography, and are, if taken alone, weak supports for the conclusion that a *sd*-festival was in fact celebrated.

In the field of inscriptional evidence, what might be called a "pillar benediction" appears on the base of square piers in kiosks and pillared halls from the 12th Dynasty on.[112] In the "White Chapel" of Sesostris I the text, in two lines, usually shows in the upper the formula (A) "beloved (said of Amun),[113] given life, stability, prosperity and health like Re for ever," and in the lower (B) "first occasion of the *sd*-festival, may he perform 'given life.'"[114] The second formula can, however, alternate *inter alia* with (C) "all life, stability, prosperity and

[106]W. K. Simpson, *JARCE* 2 (1963) 59ff.

[107]E. F. Wente, C. Van Siclen III, in J. Johnson, E. F. Wente (eds.), *Studies in Honor of George R. Hughes* (Chicago, 1976) 219f.

[108]See the discussion with references in E. Hornung, E. Staehelin, *Studien zum Sedfest* (*Aegyptiaca Helvetica* I; Basel, 1974) 11ff.

[109]Excluding those cases in which the wish is expressed that a jubilee be celebrated (in the future). Sometimes such examples have been construed as concrete evidence.

[110]Hornung, Staehelin, *Studien*, 13f; D. Kurth, *CdE* 51 (1976) 108. To judge by the biographical account of Nebi-pu-senwosret (A. M. Blackman, *JEA* 21 [1935] 1ff) Amenemhet III celebrated an "unabridged" jubilee; but he appears to have been the last Middle Kingdom monarch to do so.

[111]Hornung, Staehelin, *Studien*, 29ff.

[112]H. Ricke, *BABA* 6 (1969) 64, n. 106; for a more sanguine approach to the formulae than that presented here, see W. J. Murnane, *MDAIK* 37 (1981) 375f.

[113]The figure of the god in the scene above is to be construed in the text.

[114]Lacau, *Chapelle d'Hatshepsout*, *passim*.

happiness are at the feet of this good god," (D) "may he celebrate a myriad of *sd*-festivals, appearing upon the perch of Horus ...." In the relief decoration of the kiosk the *sd*-festival is not especially evident in emblems or inscription.[115] even though the kiosk is called the "place of appearance," and its construction coupled with "the first occurrence of the *sd*-festival."[116]

Similar pier texts appear in the New Kingdom under Thutmose III, Amenophis II, and Thutmose IV. The piers of the so-called "Festival Hall" of Thutmose III contain single line inscriptions at their base consisting of the formulae A or B, above (or variants thereof);[117] but the relief scenes on the pillars show the expected acceptance of the king by the god, and there are no special overtones of the jubilee. In fact the building, called in the dedication text simply a *ḥwt-nṯr*,[118] was begun in year 24[119] and completed sufficiently to have texts of the campaign of year 25 placed on its walls,[120] long before the date when a first *sd*-festival would have been celebrated. It's name, *Mn-ḫpr-rꜥ ꜣḫ mnw*, does not suggest a *sd*-festival, and is in fact modelled on the name of Senwosret I's temple at Heliopolis,[121] or the portico of Thutmose II(?) at Karnak.[122] In spite of the fact that some *sd*-reliefs are included in the decoration of this complex,[123] the presence of Sokarian, solar and ancestral elements suggest that the purpose of *ꜣḫ mnw* was to house a royal "Gedächtniskult."[124] On the piers of Amenophis II's shrine between pylons 9 and 10 formulae A and B similarly appear,[125] with B displaying the form "first occasion and repetition of the *sd* ...." This latter expression alludes both to the first and second occasions of a jubilee, and therefore must be prospective and optative, rather than commemorative.[126] The remainder of the decoration of the piers has scarcely any reference in

[115]On the "wish-formula," *ibid.*, pls. 24, 27, 33, 39.
[116]*Ibid.*, pl. 10.
[117]Cf. the variant *sp tpy wḥm sd*: *Urk.* IV, 596:1.
[118]Barguet, *Temple*, 161.
[119]*Urk.* IV, 836:7.
[120]Cf. the plant collection: *Urk.* IV, 777; W. Wreszinski, *Atlas zur altägyptischen Kulturgeschichte* II (Leipzig, 1923-54) pl. 26.
[121]G. Daressy, *ASAE* 9 (1909) 139.
[122]B. Letellier, in *Hommages à Serge Sauneron* (Cairo, 1979) 69.
[123]*LD* III, 36; Barguet, *Temple*, 160f.
[124]G. Haeny, *Basilikale Anlagen in der ägyptischen Baukunst des neuen Reiches* (Cairo, 1970) 14f.
[125]Along with the third formula (E): "all lands, the Fenkhu, and every foreign land (difficult of access) are at the feet of this god."
[126]Hornung, Staehelin, *Studien*, 63ff; cf. D. Müller, *Bib. Or.* 33 (1976) 172.

word or representation to the *sd*-festival.[127] The pillared hall of Thutmose IV, erected before the north wing of the 4th pylon, and later dismantled by Amenophis III, likewise displays the "pillar benediction" in variants of formulae A, B, and E upon numerous piers at present stored in the Musée en Pleine Air.[128] Again the relief decoration of the piers has little or nothing to do with the *sd*-festival. The walls of the building were decorated *inter alia* with scenes of 1. the foundation ceremony,[129] 2. driving cattle,[130] 3. standard scenes of the king before the god,[131] 4. the "Vasenlauf,"[132] and 5. procession of cattle, gazelles, and goats.[133] There is nothing here, beyond mere wish-formulae, that is unequivocally indicative of a jubilee! And the name helps not at all, for "great pillared structure," "great broad hall," or "forecourt of good sandstone, ringed with pillars"[134] in no way links the building to the *sd*-festival. By no stretch of the imagination can we call this pillared hall "a large jubilee monument ... built by Thutmose IV for his first jubilee."[135] As the discussion above will show, the writer is highly skeptical of a methodology and its results which relies heavily upon the chronological implications of *sd*-festival celebrations. The evidence cited by Wente and Van Siclen for their lengthening of the reigns of Amenophis II and Thutmose IV is particularly weak. The building of columned shrines has nothing especially to do with the *sd*; and the other references to the *sd*-festival occur in wish formulae. "The first occasion and repetition of the *sd*," on which the authors base their contention that Amenophis II had a 34 year reign,[136] is a meaningless conflation if taken as an historical record (on Thutmose IV's pillars the common variant contains only *sp tpy*) — the first and second jubilees were not celebrated at the same time! Rather it is a pious hope and expectation that the king will achieve a second, and more as the common addition of *ir.f ꜥšꜣ wrt* to the formula makes plain.[137] The

[127]In summary, the "evidence" for a jubilee during Amenophis II's reign is so sparse and so vague that it seems very unlikely that one was celebrated: see Hornung, Staehelin, *Studien*, 46, n. 29, answering Aldred, *ZÄS* 94, 4ff.
[128]Some blocks from this building now lie north of the temple of Osiris, Ruler of Eternity: see Letellier, in *Hommages à Serge Sauneron*, 51ff.
[129]H. Chevrier, *ASAE* 51 (1951) 568, fig. 1.
[130]*Ibid.*, 569, fig. 3.
[131]*Ibid.*, 570, fig. 5-6.
[132]*Ibid.*, 571, fig. 6.
[133]H. Chevrier, *ASAE* 52 (1952) pl. 8.
[134]Barguet, *Temple*, 95.
[135]Wente, Van Siclen, in *Studies in Honor of George R. Hughes*, 229.
[136]*Ibid.*, 227.
[137]Cf. Letellier, in *Hommages à Serge Sauneron*, 64.

other piece of evidence used to prove a lengthy reign for Amenophis II, viz. Thutmose IV's statement on the Lateran Obelisk,[138] is equally susceptible to another interpretation. Thutmose IV does not tell us when he completed and erected the obelisk, but *a fortiori* it was later rather than earlier in his reign. The dated inscriptions early in the reign come from the north: sphinx stela, year 1,[139] Sinai inscription, year 4,[140] year 7.[141] The campaign in Asia, though undated, must have taken place before year 6: Nebamun, still with the title of standard bearer, is shown in his tomb leading Syrian captives;[142] in year 6, however, he was appointed chief of the Medjay,[143] but since elsewhere in the tomb he rarely bears that title the tomb must have been all but completed when the promotion of year 6 took place. From year 6 on, however, there is good evidence that Thutmose IV devoted more time to Thebes,[144] undoubtedly in preparation for the southern campaign. It must have been at this time that the obelisk was completed and set up: note that the Syrian campaign was in the past, and wood taken as booty already made into Amun's barque when the text was engraved![145] The 35 years datum, therefore, can most probably be divided among the 3 kings as follows: 7 years under Thutmose IV, 25 years under Amenophis II and 3 years under Thutmose III. In other words, Thutmose III abandoned the work on the eve of the coregency with his son, when he was going into semi-retirement.

Wente and Van Siclen place confidence in Thutmose IV's being called *inpw* when he acceded; but the passage in *Urk.* IV, 1541:1, beginning *ist* has to be construed with what follows from 1541:8 on, and clearly describes him before he came to the throne, at the time of the sun-god's revelation to him. Moreover, if the protagonists of the long reign[146] are going to date the association of Thutmose IV with his mother Tiaa early in the reign,[147] they have done their cause a disservice by introducing the pillared shrine as evidence; for there,

[138]Wente, Van Siclen, in *Studies in Honor of George R. Hughes*, 227f.
[139]*Urk.* IV, 1540.
[140]Sir A. H. Gardiner, T. E. Peet, J. Černý *The Inscriptions of Sinai*[2] (London, 1952) pl. 20:58.
[141]R. Giveon, *Tel Aviv* 5 (1979) 170ff.
[142]*Urk.* IV, 1620.
[143]N. de G. Davies, *The Tombs of Two Officials of Tuthmosis IV* (London, 1923) pl. 26. See further Bryan, *The Reign of Tuthmosis IV* 367.
[144]Arrival in Thebes: cf. Davies, *Two Officials of Tuthmosis IV*, pl. 24; in the "town of Karnak" in year 8, cf. *Urk.* IV, 1545:7.
[145]*Urk.* IV, 1552:5-9; Bryan, *The Reign of Tuthmosis IV*, 234ff.
[146]By implication: I do not see a statement to that effect.
[147]Wente, Van Siclen, in *Studies in Honor of George R. Hughes*, 230.

in the decoration, watching Thutmose IV perform the ritual, is Tiaa herself.[148]

As if the pedestrian quality of these banal expressions were not enough to cast doubt on the veracity of early 18th Dynasty accounts of jubilees, the two monarchs who state unequivocally that they did in fact enjoy *sd*-festivals, are doubly suspect in their avowels! Hatshepsut implies that her *sd*-festival was celebrated in her 16th-17th year,[149] and, again by implication, Thutmose III alludes to three *sd*-festivals,[150] presumably in years 30, 33,[151] and 36(?). Yet in the text of the erection of the obelisks, upon which hangs the date of the festival, Hatshepsut does not even mention the jubilee, and the tomb biography of her nobles and the business texts[152] covering these years of her reign are silent on the subject.

As for Thutmose III, not only do his nobles avoid mentioning the jubilees, but there is reason to believe that Thutmose was not even in Egypt when his three recorded *sd*-festivals should have taken place! The dates for Thutmose III's 1st Campaign prove that it was his practice to leave Egypt in the spring, late in his regnal year,[153] so that the bulk of the campaigning season occupied the first months of the next regnal year. When in the course of an inscription a particular campaign has to be alluded to by regnal year only, without month and day, it is not the regnal year in which the army departed from Egypt that is used, but the year in which the bulk of the campaigning occurred. Thus "year 23" attaches itself to the 1st Campaign in texts of imprecise reference.[154] When, therefore, the Karnak extracts from the day-book of the king's house mention "year X" when His Majesty was in Djahy or Retenu on campaign so-and-so, one can be sure that the army had departed from Egypt at the close of the preceding regnal year. Thus the 6th Campaign, which is qualified in the Karnak extracts by the sentence "year 30, when His

[148]Chevrier, *ASAE* 51, 568, fig. 1; Bryan, *The Reign of Tuthmosis IV*, 127ff.

[149]*Urk.* IV, 359:1. There is no proof whatsoever that this was computed from Thutmose I's accession: Hornung, Staehelin, *Studien*, 52ff.

[150]*Urk.* IV, 590:15.

[151]El-Bersheh text: *Urk.* IV, 597.

[152]Yamu-nedjeh, whose first commission dates from year 15, does not refer to Hatshepsut's jubilee (*Urk.* IV, 946); nor do the account texts and memoranda from Deir el-Bahari: Hayes, *JEA* 46, *passim* (see pl. 11:13, year 16). Other dated texts from this period are the Sinai inscription of year 16 (Gardiner, Peet, Černý, *Sinai*[2] [1952] pl. 14:44), a graffito at Aswan, year ⌜16⌝ (L. Habachi, *Kêmi* 18 [1968] 55, fig. 5), dedicatory text on the wall of the block of Hatshepsut's rooms, north of the sanctuary, year 17 (*Urk.* IV, 376). None of these mention the jubliee.

[153]1st Campaign: year 22, viii, 25; *Urk.* IV, 647:6.

[154]Cf. *Urk.* IV, 734:14, 740:10, 743:6.

Majesty was in the country of Retenu on His Majesty's 6th victorious campaign,"[155] would have started from Egypt in year 29, sometime in the fourth month of *proyet*. In fact we do have a record of this event on the Armant Stela, where the last preserved hieroglyphs at the bottom read "regnal year 29, 4th month of *proyet*, day [ ]."[156] Since what immediately preceded (lines 12ff) was a description of the 1st Campaign, it is most probable that this date served to introduce the account of a later campaign; and on the basis of the evidence presented above, this can only be the 6th Campaign, of "year 30."[157] Now it has been convincingly demonstrated on the basis of the detailed records of Amenophis III that the first *sd*-festival was to be scheduled calendrically so that it straddled the 30th anniversary of the king's accession.[158] But the 30th anniversary of Thutmose III's accession would have found him in Asia on his 6th Campaign! There are then, only 2 possibilities: either Thutmose III's jubilee was not "performed" in ritual, or he celebrated it at some other time of year.

The conclusion to this rather lengthy digression is, I think, obvious. After the end of the 12th Dynasty the performance of the *sd*-festival, for some reason or another (economic?) fell into abeyance. Presumably it was ignored by the Hyksos kings. The evidence from texts and reliefs is so vague that it is doubtful to what extent the early kings of the 18th Dynasty felt the need to revive the celebration in all its detail. Most have to do with wishes and expectations that king so-and-so perform "myriads of *sd*-festivals," or "the first occasion and repetition of the *sd*-festival"; but this is nothing but a time-honoured stereotype, the expression of the thoroughly Egyptian hope that the king attain length of life. Such wishes came from the same stock as those involving such expressions as "the lifetime of Re in heaven," "many annals," etc. The "performance" of the *sd*-festival during this period of apostasy in Egypt probably consisted of little more than the erection of a monument (obelisks, shrine, peripteral temple or the like) and the carving of reliefs appropriate to the jubilee. In short, it was a jubilee "read by title" as it were. If any actual celebration was deemed necessary, it was abbreviated and adulterated: "Vasenlauf," hommage

155 *Urk*. IV, 689.
156 R. Mond, O. Myers, *The Temples of Armant* (London, 1940) pl. 88, 103; *Urk*. IV, 1247.
157 Not the 5th, as Wilson, in *ANET*², 238, n. 1, and A. Alt, *ZDPV* 70 (1953) 38f. Helck's notion (*Die Beziehungen Aegyptens zur Vorderasien im 3. und 2. Jahrtausend V. Chr.*² [Wiesbaden, 1971] 138), that the date refers to the *return* from the 5th Campaign, is quite gratuitous as far as I can see.
158 C. Van Siclen III, *JNES* 32 (1973) 290ff.

to the king, enthronement, — these are but the palest reflections of a true *sd*-festival, as celebrated according to the ancient prescriptions.[159]

The general desuetude the *sd*-festival suffered from c. 1750 to 1400 B.C. makes Amenophis III's elaborate performances that much more important as reflections of his sense of history. When he says, "It was His Majesty that did this in accordance with ancient writings; no earlier generation of mankind since the time of Re had performed the festival of *sd* (properly),"[160] he is not using hyperbole. In fact, in contrast to the immediate past, he was doing something which had no precedent: celebrating a jubilee as it should be celebrated, following the accepted, ancient and time-honoured order of service, which he had resurrected from the archives.[161]

It was a self-conscious monarchic idealism that informed royal policy at the turn of the 14th Century B.C. The royal family, when it first struggled for power in the 16th Century B.C., had perforce to cast itself in the role of a militant clan: Taᶜo I and his successors had been rebels and fighters, and *ergo* had lacked an aura of legitimacy.[162] No sooner had legitimacy been won by naked force in the expulsion of the Hyksos, than the "pure" stock had been "contaminated" by the infusion of different blood; and the reign of Thutmose I marked the beginning of a quarrel over succession. Once again the process of discrediting which such feuds among leaders inevitably entail, was arrested by the magnificent triumphs of Thutmose III on the field of

[159]If one cares to contrast the *sd*-festival scenes of Thutmose III from Karnak with those of Amenophis III from Soleb and Thebes (Hornung, Staehelin, *Studien*, 33ff for bibliography; also L. Habachi, G. Haeny, *Untersuchungen in Totentempel Amenophis' III* (Wiesbaden, 1981) and those of Akhenaten from East Karnak (R. W. Smith, D. B. Redford, *The Akhenaten Temple Project* I *Initial Discoveries* [Warminster, 1977], *passim*), striking differences will at once emerge. In the Sokar apartments of the *Akh-menu* Thutmose III is shown in the jubilee palanquin carried by the souls of Pe and adored by the gods (P-M II^2, 116[373]), running before the gods (P-M II^2, 113[353]), assisted in the cult by sundry deities (P-M II^2, 113[355]), and assisted in the arrow-shooting ceremomy by Horus and Seth (P-M II^2, 113[354])! In contrast, in the scenes from the reigns of Amenophis III and Akhenaten we are in the real world of men: the gods are represented only by their symbols and their priests. Real events are here being set on record: a vast array of priestly titles is presented and, in Amenophis III's case, the very celebrants themselves are named. Thutmose III's representations, on the other hand, are wholly fanciful, and cannot be used as proof that a real jubilee was celebrated.

[160]*Urk.* IV, 1867:15-16.

[161]Amenophis III's return to remote antiquity for archetypes is evidenced elsewhere. For indications that the foundation ceremony of the Luxor temple employed Old Kingdom prototypes, see P. Barguet, *RdE* 9 (1952) 3f; on the possible archaism of the rite of "Striking the Gates," dipicted at Soleb, see P. Munro, *ZÄS* 86 (1960) 70; on the possibiblity that the tememos wall at Soleb was inspired by the Djoser complex, see H. Kees, *ZÄS* 88 (1963) 111f.

[162]Redford, *History and Chronology*, 28ff.

battle: who could fault a winner? Thutmose III's successors, however, were born into an empire which could not be expanded. In place of fresh conquests nought was offered but the prospect of punitive campaigns which merely held the line, and denied the monarch the glory of novel success. Moreover, the monarchy was made to sustain new stresses, never experienced before. In place of absolute conquest of foreign states, treaties were now entered into, which even involved — save the mark! — marriages with non-Egyptian ladies! A crop of able officials had grown up, functioning more independently than their counterparts of earlier periods; and new institutions (the temples, the army), although still in incipient stages of development, rivalled the king's house in clout. What room was there for Pharaoh?[163]

Amenophis III fell heir to this problem of monarchy, and his activities constitute an attempted solution. In place of the novelty of unprecedented conquest he substituted an unprecedented building programme; in place of ever increasing feats of strength in the field of sport, he substituted a life of uncommon luxury. There is a touch of the authoritarian in him: kings by virtue of their position should do as they please. He breaks with tradition by marrying a commoner, and uniting with more foreign princesses than any king before him; he flouts accepted protocol in the matter of foreign emissaries by keeping them years on end at his court,[164] snubbing them in matters of etiquette,[165] and even cutting them off entirely.[166]

Although flouting tradition so cavalierly is a curious way to attempt a rehabilitation of the monarchy, Amenophis's restoration of the *sd*-festival in its pristine purity was a masterstroke. For here Egypt was communing with its most ancient past, and Amenophis III would inevitably appear, not as a maverick, but as a true successor to the ancestral kings. Of course the lavish preparations would entail thorough searches in the archives, and it is no surprise to find objects and texts from the remotest antiquity turning up with indications that they had passed through the court of Amenophis III.[167]

If Amenophis III at times shows himself to be a practical man, now

[163]See D. B. Redford, *Akhenaten: the Heretic King* (Princeton, 1984) *passim*.
[164]Cf. *EA* 2, 13-15.
[165]*EA* 1, 88-92; 2, 18-20.
[166]*EA* 1, 72-76.
[167]Cf. the slate palette of Protodynastic date, with the figure of Tiy carved on the reverse: B. V. Bothmer, *JARCE* 8 (1969-70) fig. 5-6. Cf. also the PT excerpt, said to have been (re)discovered under Amenophis III, in P. Berlin 3057, xxi, 15 (Luft, *ZÄS* 99, 109); cf. also xxii, 22 (*ibid.*, 110), from the library of the temple of Osiris, found on a roll of leather during the reign of <Neb>ma-re.

using the past as a foil, now as a model, there is some slight indication that for their own sake books and ancient lore may have appealed to him. The earliest activity that we have record of this king undertaking is the opening of the el-Bersheh quarry for construction work in the temple of Thoth in Hermopolis[168] and the work in question is probably reflected in the date in year 2 which is recorded on the base of the left colossal cynocephalus at Ashmunein. Now Thoth is master of writing, books and wisdom, and in a delightful hymn of *double entendre* Kheruef addresses him as follows:[169] "Praise on earth by the commons when they see Thoth as king; the gods and goddesses perform jubilation .... Hail to thee, O lord of divine words, master of mysteries in heaven and earth! Thou great god of the most remote(?) moment, thou primordial one who created speech and writing, who established dwellings and founded temples, who made the gods to know their possessions, all crafts their appurtenances, and the difficult countries and fields likewise ...." I dare say the veiled allusion herein is to Amenophis III himself, who was also king, who also received adulation, founded houses and temples, and instructed everyone in what they were to do.[170]

Whatever rising self-consciousness had directed attention to the past in the early and middle 18th Dynasty, the three decades of Amarna reaction resulted in an attempt to shut out the past and avoid its use in articulating statecraft. The shape of his beliefs in fact permitted Akhenaten no other course. He has only contempt for the traditional gods who, he avers, are failing and are already falling into desuetude (a situation, of course, which he welcomed and sought to bring about).[171] He has no need of, nor use for, the traditional practices of the cult.[172] His god is new,[173] and his revelation vouchsafed only to the king. The Sun-disc is not a god of time past, a god of primordial history, but an essentially "timeless" deity, whose

[168] *Urk.* IV, 1677: year 1, xi, 20(?), scarcely seven weeks after his accession at the beginning of the 10th month: D. B. Redford, *JNES* 25 (1966) 120f; Van Siclen, *JNES* 32, 290ff.

[169] P. Berlin 2293: *Urk.* IV, 1874f.

[170] For a cynocephalus Thoth on scarabs of Amenophis III (among others), see R. Hari, *Aegyptus* 57 (1977) 3ff, pl. III.

[171] Cf. D. B. Redford, *BES* 3 (1981) 87ff.

[172] D. B. Redford, *JARCE* 17 (1980) 21ff.

[173] While sometimes "sun-disc" is used as a metonym for the monarch in the earlier New Kingdom, and is a weak hypostasis connected with the solar cult from the end of the 3rd Millennium B.C. on, there is no evidence that the specific cult of the disc with which Akhenaten is so intimately connected predates his reign: cf. D. B. Redford, *JARCE* 13 (1976) 47ff.

very "lifetime" is time itself.[174] Akhenaten does not *need* the past. If the effect of his programme was to reinstate pharaoh as the king-pin of Egypt's system, he is by no means consciously emulating any earlier period in his country's history; if he followed ancient practice in celebrating the *sd*, it is simply a mechanical pursuance of his father's revised order of service. The new monarch blithely went his own way, consigning more and more tradition hallowed by history to the dust-bin. If he honoured his immediate predecessors at Amarna,[175] it was more a private matter of family affection.

Akhenaten's reign was an administrative disaster for Egypt, and his successors' initial attempts at restoration were of a practical rather than theoretical nature. At first they enlisted the past, if at all, in a purely traditional way, evoking the pale and ancient topos of "Chaos dompted by new king."[176] To re-affirm the continuum of divine kingship on earth the reign of Amenophis III became the focus for the desperate attempts to establish legitimacy. Tutakhamun called him "father," and restored his monuments;[177] Horemheb's accession was subsequently back-dated to the year of his death.[178] And sometimes in 19th Dynasty "lists" Amenophis III has the distinction of beginning or ending a sequence, or is singled out for honours.[179] His great cabinet minister and "wiseman" Amenophis, son of Hapu, came soon to be honoured as much as, and sometimes in company with, the kings of antiquity.[180]

[174]J. Assmann, *Zeit und Ewigkeit im alten Aegypten* (Heidelberg, 1975) 54ff.

[175]Cf. the sources in Murnane, *Ancient Egyptian Coregencies*, 129, n. 94, 214.

[176]Tutankhamun restoration stela: *Urk.* IV, 2027f; Horemheb decree: *Urk.* IV, 2155ff; J-M. Kruchten, *Le Décret d'Horemheb* (Brussels, 1982) 148ff; for the new mythological importance of Osiris in the post-Amarna period, see E. Otto, in W. Helck (ed.) *Festschrift für Siegfried Schott zu seinem 70. Geburtstag* (Wiesbaden, 1968) 104f.

[177]Gebel Barkal lion: *Urk.* IV, 1745f; for the significance of the term "father" in this connexion, see the author in *JSSEA* 9 (1979) 112ff; for Tutankhamun's honouring of Amenophis III at Luxor in the Opet festival scenes, see W. Wolf, *Das schöne Feste von Opet* (Leipzig, 1931) 31, 61f (no. 28), pl. 2; for a possibly similar attempt to unite himself with his illustrious forebear at Karnak, see Murnane, *Ancient Egyptian Coregencies* 167f; also *LD* III, 119a.

[178]Redford, *JNES* 25, 122f; G. A. Gaballa, *The Memphite Tomb-chapel of Mose* (Warminster, 1978) pl. LXIII. The renumbering of Horemheb's years from Amenophis III's death probably took place under Sety I, since during Horemheb's lifetime he seems to have numbered from his own accession. The actual length of Horemheb's reign is now fairly certainly estabished at between 25 and 30 years: J. von Beckerath, *SAK* 6 (1978) 43ff. (Helck's assertion [*CdE* 48 (1973) 258ff] that Josephus's figure of 12 years 3 months now by metathesis assigned to Ay [!] is correct for Horemheb, founders in my view on the clear dependence of that figure on the (false) datum for Akencheres, viz. 12, 1, see below, p. 252).

[179]Above, p. 37, where (Medinet Habu) Amenophis III is the earliest king in the row of nine; cf. p. 41 (Amenophis III at the front of a sequence).

[180]List of Anhur-khᶜu (above, p. 50); cf. Wildung, *Imhotep und Amenhotep*, 283ff.

Only under Horemheb do we sense a gradual re-awakening of a reverence for the past. Again, the king's acts and jargon are largely traditional: he restored the disturbed burial of Thutmose IV,[181] refurbished parts of Deir el-Bahari in deference to Thutmose III,[182] and took cognizance of the precedents set by this great king in matters of administration.[183] With Horemheb building operations at Thebes once again enter the mainstream of the history of construction of this national shrine: the jerry-built *Gm-p3-itn* of Akhenaten was totally demolished, the courts of Tutankhamun and Ay were torn down, and the two major axes of the Amun temple extended south and west.[184] At both Karnak and Luxor the tentative attempts of Tutankhamun to record his devotion to the gods were committed to oblivion by the simple expedient of replacing his name with that of Horemheb. The latter had thus successfully reached back over three decades, now devoid of four anathematized rulers, to link himself directly to the tradition of true kingship.

The re-establishment of the Memphite region as the favoured royal residence under Tutankhamun[185] had far-reaching effects. Once again the court was confronted by the Saqqara and Giza necropoleis, with their monuments of antiquity; once again the king resided, at it were, in the shadow of Ptah, the creator of the earth and founder of the state. A real consciousness of the past and a desire to savour it aesthetically is conveyed by the Memphite art of the period, which draws not only on the elegance of Amenophis III, the "naturalism" of Amarna, but also on the dignity of the Old Kingdom.[186]

The Ramesside Sense of History

From their earliest monuments as kings the scions of the Ramesside clan show a strong sense of family and ancestry.[187] In a

[181] *Urk.* IV, 2170f.
[182] *Urk.* IV, 2134f.
[183] *Urk.* IV, 2149f.
[184] That Horemheb was responsible for the dismantling of the *Gm-p3-itn* is proven, if any proof were still required, by the discovery in our 1978 campaign at East Karnak of a small stone appliqué with his prenomen, in a locus sealed by the destruction level of the temple. D. B. Redford, *ROM Archaeological Newsletter* 195 (1981) 3; *idem. JSSEA* 13 (1983) 214.
[185] Restoration stela, line 9, 27; W. Helck, *JESHO* 5 (1962) 241; L. Habachi, in J. Ruffle (ed.), *Glimpses of Ancient Egypt* (Warminster, 1979) 35.
[186] H. D. Schneider, *BSFE* 69 (1974) 24.
[187] On the family of the Ramessides, which can now be traced back to the Amarna Period, see L. Habachi, *RdE* 21 (1969) 27ff; E. Cruz-Uribe, *JNES* 37 (1978) 237ff; A. Radwan, *SAK* 6 (1978) 157ff; Kitchen, *RI* II, 664.

sense honouring the "father of the fathers"[188] by making their name to live[189] is a trait betraying plebeian ancestry; kings showed forth the same devotion in more formal ways: at the feast of *sd*, of Min, of coronation, in the offering cult, by restoring ancestral monuments etc. But the Ramessides had come to power after the preceding royal house had thoroughly discredited itself, and for two generations the hereditary principle had been superceded by right by appointment. The Ramessides, therefore, were even more conscious of the need to stress their family connexion than might have been the case under normal conditions. Numerous are the monuments in which the reigning king proudly announces his wish to memorialize his forebears. Typical is Sety I's monument to his father Ramesses I, later restored by Ramesses II. After the building formula Sety says: "His Majesty wished to cause his father's name to be perpetuated in the presence of this god, lasting, abiding for ever."[190] Sety was responsible for erecting his father's chapel at Abydos,[191] wherein the family was commemorated in relief.[192] To his father he says, in a discernibly loving tone, "I am thy true son, thy heart's (delight); I have had [thee reborn as] I am [obligated], inasmuch as thou didst beget me."[193] "Lo, my heart never tires of recalling him who be[gat me], his name is with me like the Eye!"[194] Ramesses II followed suit: he ordered the setting up of the 400-year stela "in order to set up the name of his progenitor King Menmare, son of Re, Sety-Merneptah, abiding, lasting for ever ...."[195]

It was Ramesses II that "beautified this monument of his father (the Popolo obelisk in Rome) in order to cause his name to endure

[188]For *it itw*, see W. Helck, *NGWG* (1965) 173ff; often applied to gods (cf. Amun): *Urk.* IV, 495:2, 1685:11; *Hieroglyphic Texts ... B.M.* IX (London, 1970) pl. 10B, line 1; M. Doresse, *RdE* 25 (1973) 130, 131, n. 3; Kitchen, *RI* VI, 13:12-13; for Ramesses II's use of the term on the 400-year stela, see Redford, *Orientalia* 39, 24, n. 2; the basic meaning *pater familias* comes through clearly in human contexts: L. Habachi, *Tavole d'offerta are e bacili da libagione* (Turin, 1980) no. 22030.

[189]On what is implied by the expression, see S. Schott, *NGWG* (1964) 67ff.

[190]Kitchen, *RI* I, 105ff.

[191]*Ibid.*, 109.

[192]H. E. Winlock, *The Bas-Reliefs from the Temple of Ramesses I at Abydos* (New York, 1973) pl. 6. For the commemoration of Ramesses I in Sety I's Qurneh temple, see Murnane, *Ancient Egyptian Coregencies*, 207.

[193]Kitchen, *RI* I, 110:1-2.

[194]*Ibid.*, 112:10-11.

[195]*Ibid.*, II, 288:5-6; Redford, *Orientalia* 39, 23, n. 3.

in the House of Re."[196] And his grandiose completion of Sety's temple at Abydos is heralded in the great Dedicatory Inscription as a remarkable act of piety and devotion towards his father:[197] "I have not neglected his establishment like those children who forgot [their] father[s ...] .... it is good to make monument upon monument, two useful deeds at one time, they being in my name and my father's name, the son like him who begat him."[198]

The solidarily and loyalty of the Ramesside clan produced a feeling of belonging to that broader "family" of all the kings of Egypt and a new consciousness of following in a long line of illustrious ancestors. "[As for tho]se ancient ones of primaeval time, see! He (Sety), as king of the Two Lands, is their heir for millions of years, for ever and ever!"[199] When Ramesses II arrived at Abydos his attention was arrested, not only by the incompleteness of his father's temple, but also by the delapidation of the cenotaphs of former kings. "He found the temples of the necropolis which belonged to former kings, and their cenotaphs which are in Abydos, fallen into a state of disrepair ...";[200] and he was wont to build "temples constructed of stone with the images (*šsmw*) of (former) kings, in order that their names might abide."[201] Not only was the offering tradition of his father's temple set on a firm basis, but Sety's name was duly entered in the on-going list of ancestor kings to receive offerings:[202] "He (Ramesses II) established rituals for him (Sety I), provided for with food-stuffs, for his titulary which is among (those of) the kings; (for) his heart was tender towards him who begat him, and his breast yearned for him who brought him up."[203]

In no other period was royally sponsored devotion to the ancestor cult as popular as in the Ramesside age. The reason for the

[196]Habachi, *The Obelisks of Egypt*, pl. 30.
[197]H. Gauthier, *La grande inscription dédicatoire d'Abydos* (Cairo, 1912), *passim*.
[198]*Ibid.*, lines 51-55.
[199]Kitchen, *RI* I, 108:8.
[200]Gauthier, *Inscription dédicatoire*, line 30.
[201]BM 1630; cf. K. A. Kitchen, G. A. Gaballa, *ZÄS* 96 (1969) pl. 5:7-8.
[202]Above, p. 20f.
[203]Gauthier, *Inscription dédicatoire*, lines 25-26; by the 20th Dynasty the tedium of having to acknowledge the royal ancestors can produce the counterblast. Note how Ramessses IV, not without subtle wit characteristic of this extraordinary man, turns the perfunctory piety towards the kingly line to his own advantage: "With the following words didst thou (Amun) proclaim me: 'He it is that shall receive the kingly office!' — even before these things were known, when they were as yet far from affecting me! Many are the kings since the dawn of time, even those of the gods' (own) promotion, who inscribed thy name in their cartouches — I, however, am actively useful for thine house! — from of old one knows this, but their names escape me ...": Sir A. H. Gardiner, *JEA* 41 (1955), pl. IX, 4-6.

popularity was the stress laid by the kings of the 19th Dynasty on the offering to the ancestors, the "Jubilant Summons,"[204] as an integral part of the offering ritual performed in any royal temple or shrine. Sety I left the best example of a royal offering text in his Abydos temple, the whole identified as a *nis ḥknw*, and displaying a chronological order in the list of kings allegedly honoured through the ages in the offering ritual at Abydos.[205] (Significantly the list is in the context of the Sokar rites[206]). Ramesses II followed suit in his own Abydos temple, adding his own name to the canonical list.[207] In a Theban context we have three examples of the offering to the royal ancestors incorporated in other rites, one in the daily liturgy of Amenophis I,[208] a second in the yearly festival of Min,[209] and a third in the yearly Feast of the Valley.[210]

While in Abydos, however, (and the north in general)[211] the offering to the ancestors was dominated by a name list reaching back over centuries, and attesting the continuity and universality of Abydene and Lower Egyptian tradition, at Thebes the rite took on a parochial aspect. The kings there honoured were those of the Theban house which had driven out the Hyksos, expanded by the names of one or two other rulers who had also contributed to Thebes' glory. To this illustrious and apocopated list – on the eve of the 19th Dynasty it must have terminated with Horemheb – the Ramessides added their own names. Neither Ramesses I, his son or grandson had been born in Thebes, yet such was the lingering renown of the 18th Dynasty that the new family felt constrained to

[204]*Nis ḥknw*: cf. above, p. 38, n. 135. For *nis* used of summoning the bai of deceased to the offering, see PT484c; *Hieroglyphic Texts ... B.M.* IX, pl. 10D, 19; for *ḥknw* used in the context of the royal acclamation, see J-C. Goyon, *Confirmation du pouvoir royal au nouvel an* (Cairo, 1972) 110, n. 242. The basically oral nature of the offering to the ancestors is aptly conveyed in the expression "invoked (i.e. the names of the kings) in one call (*ʿš wʿ*)": H. H. Nelson, *JNES* 8 (1949) 315, n. 92; that *nis ḥknw* involved a specific name (or names) is proven by the passage from a text in the Red Chapel of Hatshepsut: *nis ḥknw m rn wr n nb*, "The jubilant summons (was issued) in the Great Name of the lord": Lacau, *Chapelle d'Hatshepsout* I, 131.

[205]Above, p. 18ff.

[206]R. David, *Religious Ritual at Abydos*^{2} (Warminster, 1982) 197.

[207]Above, p. 20f.

[208]Above, p. 37f.

[209]Above, p. 34ff.

[210]Schott, *Das schöne Fest*, 8f.

[211]Cf. the list of Tjuloy, above, p. 21ff.

enhance rather than suppress the Theban tradition.[212] The Theban list of ancestors to be offered to thus became for the Ramessides a royal pedigree, a select group of potentates, membership in which conferred undying fame and unquestionable legitimacy. The Theban "list" thus extends through the Amenophises and the Thutmosids and includes the Ramessides without a break. There cannot be a break, and none could be envisaged; for Sety I and Ramesses II were legitimate "sons" of the Thutmosids in direct succession, their rightful heirs in very truth. Thus would the new kings stamp out for good and aye the claims of influence of that unfortunate twilight of the 18th Dynasty, the Amarna period.

The so-called "lists" we have passed in review in chapter 1 (above, p. 18f) are really assemblages of royal names or royal statues for cultic purposes. They comprise a group of royal ancestors who are present in three basic contexts: 1. at the offering ceremony in both state temples and royal mortuary temples,[213] 2. at processionals in festivals in which royal prerogatives are being re-affirmed,[214] and 3. at

[212]With one king they vied, viz. Amenophis III. Ramesses II aped this most magnificent of forebears by himself erecting a statue with the name "Ruler of Rulers," identical to that of both Memnon colossoi: A. Scharff, *ZÄS* 70 (1934), 47ff; L. Habachi, in *Festschrift Walter Till* (Munich, 1972), 67ff; cf. also G. Roeder, *Die Denkmäler des Pelizaeus Museums zu Hildesheim* III (Berlin, 1921) abb. 33. Ramesses also plagiarized, it seems, some of the topographical lists of Amenophis III: cf. R. Giveon, in J. Assmann, and others (eds.), *Fragen an die altägyptische Lituratur* (Wsiesbaden, 1977) 178ff.

[213]A very old ceremony: cf. the offering to the royal statues on the first day of the lunar month during the Old Kingdom, as attested in the Abusir papyri, P. Posener-Kriéger, J. de Cénival, *Hieratic Papyri in the British Museum* V Series *The Abusir Papyri* (London, 1968) pl. 4-5 (the determinatives, viz. three statues with white, red and *nms* crowns, may indicate that a variety of images were intended; but whether they included some ancestral kings is not clear). For other references to offerings to the royal statues, see W. M. F. Petrie, *Abydos* II (London, 1903) 24; E. Blumenthal, *Untersuchungen zum ägyptischen Königtums des mittleren Reiches* I (Berlin, 1970) 137 (=Neferhotpe 25-26). What is entailed is nicely summed up by Wepwawet-ᶜo (Sethe, *Lesestücke*, 74:21-23) whose statues were "in the temple in the following of the great god, with meat offerings established for them, and food offerings by written contract (*m sš*)." Cf. also *Urk.* IV, 408:12-13; Lefebvre, *Inscriptions concernant les grand-prêtres*, 12f, 19, 25; for the involvement of statues in the processional, see P. E. Newberry, *Beni Hasan* I (London, 1893) pl. 25, lines 83-84.

[214]For the Min-festival, see above, p. 34ff; for the presence of statues of the royal ancestors at the Feast of the Valley, see Schott, *Das schöne Fest*, 32ff; (the offering to the ancestors at the Feast of the Valley is the inspiration in the Late Period, for the flight of the winged god Amen(em)apet every 10 days across the river to Djeme "to make offerings to the Fathers": Doresse, *RdE* 25, 124; cf. *RdE* 35 [1984] pl. 9, line 4; Djeme was the place of interment of the primordial gods: F. R. Herbin, *ibid.*, 111, n. 12); for the close connexion between the "lists" and the cult of Sokar, see above, p. 24, and David, *Religious Ritual*^{2}, 310, n. 6 (for Sokar's association with kingship cf. M. Atzler, *RdE* 23 [1971] 7ff); for their role at the *sd* see Björkman, *Kings at Karnak*, 89f, and the literature there cited.

private mortuary rites where they are the recipients of offerings and pious veneration.[215] In none of these contexts is the primary interest in depicting former kings a purely historical one:[216] they are participants in the cultus on a par with the gods. The concrete ceremony lying behind these rites presupposes cult images. *Twt*, the common word for "statue," is used,[217] but also *ꜥẖm*, "image (of a god),"[218] *šsp*, "cult statue,"[219] and *sꜥḥ*, "holy form, eternal image."[220] Like divine cult images, the royal statues have their own shrines, and can partake of offerings or be carried in procession. For the king they constitute a body of royal ancestors through whom he derives his power and legitimacy.[221] He is part of a divinely sanctioned, uninterrupted line of rulers which goes back ultimately to Menes, and before him the demi-gods and the Great Enneads.[222] A ruler who stood outside this line was a usurper, contemptuously characterized as "one who made himself"[223]

An age-old wish piously expressed was that the god might "nourish thy statues .... while thine images abide in his temple";[224] this would result in "thy name remaining in *Ipt-swt*, while thy son remains in thy post — without interruption for ever."[225] Though sometimes denied, it is easy to demonstrate that the Amarna interlude had resulted in loosening the hold many great families had enjoyed over particular offices of state: Akhenaten certainly displayed a predilection for

[215]These private assemblages of royal ancestors are closely connected with the worship of the reigning king's *ku* (on the *ku*[s] of the king, see Frankfort, *Kingship and the Gods*, 74f), and probably have essentially the same purport as that type of scene in which the owner adores a vignette of his sovereign (sometimes accompanied by a high official) worshipping a god: James, *Hieroglyphic Text ... B.M.* IX, pl. 40(1), and p. 49 for other examples. They thus stress the owner's loyalty to the reigning house.

[216]Cf. H. H. Nelson, *JNES* 8 (1949) 317ff; David, *Religious Ritual*[2], 198.

[217]*Wb.* V, 256:1; W. Vycichl, *BSEG* 5 (1981) 51ff.

[218]*Urk.* IV, 607:10; *Wb.* I, 225:15f; Faulkner, *A Concise Dictionary of Middle Egyptian*, 48; Nelson, *JNES* 8, 314, n. 89; H. Altenmüller, *LdÄ* I (1972) 55f.

[219]D. Wildung, *MDIAK* 25 (1969) 214 and n. 8.

[220]H. Jacobsohn, *Die dogmatische Stellung des Königs in der Theologie der alten Aegypten* (Glückstadt and New York, 1939) 31, 34; *Wb.* IV, 52:13-15; A. E. Reymond, *ZÄS* 98 (1972) 132ff.

[221]The Min-reliefs are instructive in this respect: note how the statue of the reigning king is grouped with the ancestral images, and both ancestors and reigning king partake in the elevation of the offerings.

[222]In the Theban tradition this also meant Amun-re, that "lord of lords, king of the gods, and father of the fathers" (Kitchen, *RI* II, 637:10). Significantly, at the celebration of that ancestral feast, the Festival of the Valley, Amun-re is called "the first of the kings" (*ibid.*, 636:5, 637:5): he is the archetypal pattern and source of legitimacy for every subsequent king.

[223]Harris I, 75:4 (=W. Erichsen, *Papyrus Harris* I [Brussels, 1933] 91).

[224]Karnak J 37512: H. Kees, *ZÄS* 83 (1958) 130.

[225]H. Gauthier, *Cerceuils* (*CCG*; Cairo, 1914) no. 41068, 467f.

parvenus. On the morrow of the discrediting and eclipse of the 18th Dynasty, the need for princes of "sound speech and good character"[226] was uppermost in pharaoh's mind; and the best credential was to be a scion of a civic-minded family which had long functioned in an office of state. With the Ramesside age we occasionally find the consciousness of lineage translated into a formal genealogy of length.[227]

What is so characteristic of the Ramesside age is the popularity in *private* tombs of the motif of the offering to the "list" of royal ancestor.[228] The notion of the pedigree, and its bestowal of legitimacy upon the royal family, were very much "in the air" during the 19th Dynasty; and the fashionableness of the Min festival and the Feast of the Valley ensured that they remained in the collective consciousness of the nation.

Visually memorializing the past focused attention on the Giza and Saqqara necropoleis; and while Ramesses II moved to the new city of Pi-Ramesses, his son the *sm*-priest of Ptah, Khamwese, dominated the Memphite region with his presence.[229] Curiously, the true reverence for antiquity which this man displayed[230] did not prevent him from removing stone from old structures. Nevertheless, this activity was balanced by the wholesale restoration of royal cults, and the resuscitated practice of offering to the deceased kings which evidences itself in the Saqqara necropolis at this time.[231] In fact, this is a species of "civic religion," a public act of piety and veneration which takes as its object some aspect of the nation's past, in this case the "founders of the state"; as such, it betrays the presence of a loyalist spirit abroad, honouring and confirming the present dynasty and its historic roots. In addition, it was under Ramesses II that a new underground hypogaeum ("les petits souterrains") was hollowed out at Saqqara for the burials of the Apis bulls,[232] that manifestation of Ptah cult-service for whom was to become the supreme

[226] *Urk.* IV, 2155.

[227] Cf. Louvre C.50 (*temp.* Sety I): D. A. Lowle, *Or. Ant.* 15 (1976) 91ff (6-generation genealogy); Theban Tomb 359 (Ramesside): P-M I^2, 423 (4-generation genealogy); Kitchen, *RI* I 298 (Paser: 3-generation genealogy).

[228] Above, p. 45ff. Private reverence for the Ramesside family alone is, of course, widespread.

[229] F. Gomaà, *Chaemwese, Sohn Ramses' II und Hohenpriester von Memphis* (Wiesbaden, 1973) 34, and *passim*; Wildung, *Die Rolle* 170f.

[230] M. Gitton, *CdE* 51 (1976) 296.

[231] Above, p. 21ff; cf. J. Berlandini-Grenier, *BIFAO* 76 (1976) 313ff.

[232] M. Malinine, G. Posener, J. Vercoutter, *Catalogue des Stèles du sérapéum de Memphis* I (Paris, 1968) xi-xii.

legitimation of a monarch, and the index of his acceptance.[233]

Practical necessity often carries speculative interest in its wake. The needs of legitimization having been met, the Ramessides began to evince a genuine interest in antiquity. We find Ramesses II entering the library and consulting old manuscripts to learn about the origins and theological importance of Thebes;[234] Merneptah consults the *gnwt* with respect to the Libyans,[235] and Ramesses IV is proud to be able to read archaic texts about primaeval times.[236] Throughout the life and society of the 19th Dynasty one can trace the revival of reverence for antiquity. It became almost a fetish to cite, yea or only to allege, a *Vorlage* consisting of an "old manuscript" for the text one was presently copying.[237] Small wonder, then, that the one true king-list we possess, the Turin Canon, should have been a product of this period, when interest in antiquity ran high.[238]

The Ramesside version of the king-list, as exemplified in TC, owes its form and content to at least four sources. First of all, as we have attemped to demonstrate in the previous chapter, there existed by the 13th Century B.C. the formal king-list begun and transmitted by and under the aegis of the scribes of Itj-towy during the Middle Kingdom.[239] Second, there was the immediate family tree of Ramesses II about which no one had any doubt. Third, it was also in Thebes that, nurtured in the cult of the Amun temple, a list of "Theban rulers" was taking shape, already presented in embryonic form in Thutmose III's "Karnak list," later to appear after many transmutations in Eratosthenes. Finally, from some such Theban source, now lost, must have come the names in TC x, 22 through the remainder of column xi, i.e. the Theban kings later to be divided by Manetho into the 16th and 17th Dynasties. From Thebes alone,

[233]See below, p. 298.
[234]Above, p. 91.
[235]Above, p. 83.
[236]Above, p. 85.
[237]Luft, *Forschungen und Berichte* 14, 62.
[238]The Turin Canon is on the *recto* of a tax-quota list (*ḥtr*), possibly from the treasury of Amun. The list was characterized by Wilson as "baffling" (*JNES* 19 [1960] 299), but its importance to the study of the economy of the Ramesside age cannot be gainsaid (cf. the writer in J. W. Wevers, D. B. Redford (eds.), *Studies on the Ancient Palestinian World* [Toronto, 1972], 151; J. J. Janssen, *SAK* 3 [1975] 175). That the king-list was written on the *verso* does not in the least detract from its importance, and any suggestion that we should treat it with some suspicion as an "unofficial" document is simply a counsel of despair.
[239]The vicissitudes of the Itj-towy king-list tradition from the time of the Hyksos invasion down to the 19th Dynasty is a subject for speculation. But it is by no means unlikely that copies of the list were already in the archives at Thebes and Memphis during the 12th Dynasty, and survived into the New Kingdom.

therefore, the Ramesside scribe would have derived all the ingredients necessary to reconstruct a line of kings from Ramesses II back to the beginning of the "16th Dynasty"; and with the grafting of this line onto the Itj-towy list a line of Egyptian kings could have been established linking the contemporary monarch through seventeen centuries with the gods, and ultimately with Re himself.

To this point one major section of TC has remained unexplained, and that is the list of names from ix, 9 to x, 21, dealing with the Hyksos. In no Theban cultic list are Hyksos or any other Asiatic names mentioned, and it would be surprising if they were, in the light of the Theban role in the war of liberation, and the visceral feelings that must have engendered. But in the Delta the situation may well have been wholly different. One major clue is provided by the Ramesside devotion to Seth,[240] who was indigenous to the area of the northeast Delta during and even before the Hyksos period,[241] and had sprung to prominence through the syncretism of West Semitic cultural traits and those of the conquered.[242] Whatever may have been the hatred expressed by the Thebans towards the Hyksos, in the north the Ramessides could unabashedly espouse a god associated with their memory, and even go so far as to commemorate the period inaugurated by the Hyksos as *still continuing* under the guise of Seth's reign.[243] With their capital located very close to the

[240]See L. Habachi, *ZÄS* 100 (1974) 95ff. For the worship of Seth in the New Kingdom see J. Vandier, *MDAIK* 25 (1969) 188ff.

[241]Cf. *inter alia* the dedication of the king's son Nehesy to Seth: W. M. F. Petrie, *Tanis* I (London, 1885) pl. 2; J. von Beckerath, *Untersuchungen zur politische Geschichte der zweiten Zwischenzeit in Aegypten* (Glückstadt, 1965) 263; the dedication to Sopdu, under the guise of Seth, and labelled "Lord of the East" in Sinai: Gardiner, Peet, Černý, *Sinai*[2] (1952) pl. 42 (n. 119), *temp.* Amenemhet IV; the PNN Seth-re, possibly from the Delta: Cairo 20345; ᶜAkhem-Seth: G. T. Martin, *Egyptian Administrative and Private-name Seals* (Oxford, 1971) no. 363*; Sat-Seth: *ibid.*, no. 1366*; Seth: *ibid.*, no. 1663*-1665*; Seth-mose: *ibid.*, no. 1666*; Seth is popular in frontier regions during the Middle Kingdom: cf. the invocation to Seth and to the gods who are in Nubia at Kummeh: Dunham, *Second Cataract Forts* I, 141, pl. 96G.

[242]Cf. R. Stadelmann, *Syrisch-palästinische Gottheiten in Aegypten* (Leiden, 1967) 32ff; H. Te Velde, *Seth, God of Confusion* (Leiden, 1967) 118f, 121, n. 3. For Seth as a storm god see J. Zandee, *ZÄS* 90 (1963) 144ff; for his role as slayer of the monster, which brought him even closer to the West Semitic Baᶜal, see H. Te Velde, *JARCE* 7 (1968) 39f.

[243]Cf. the writer, *Orientalia* 39, 28ff.

ancient Avaris,[244] the Ramessides kept alive, unconsciously or intentionally, the memory of the Hyksos and the specific traditions relating to them which survived in the region. If it had been left to Thebes in all probability no reference to the Hyksos would have been included in the king-list; for the history of the Intermediate Period would most easily have been represented as a single line of kings, first at Itj-towy and later at Thebes. The Ramessides alone are responsible for the inclusion of the Hyksos, and the fourth source contributing to the configuration of the king-list as it appears in TC is thus the Hyksos tradition emanating from the eastern Delta.

But what of the 30 odd names which precede the six *ḥḳ³w ḫ³swt* in TC (viz. ix, 13 to x, 11)? The writer has maintained that behind these names lies a list of West Semitic names, distorted by oral tradition, and, if anything, the case is stronger now than he once averred.[245] Coming as they do immediately before the six "Great Hyksos," and being wholly divorced in form from the Egyptian names elsewhere in the papyrus, they cannot be explained by any hypothesis which does not take into account their intimate association with the 15th Dynasty. Now in the Amorite dominated world of the 18th through 16th Centuries B.C. it was the accepted practice of great royal houses to show forth their ancient lineage and undoubted legitimacy by prefixing a genealogy to the dynastic list. This genealogy constituted their pedigree, and carried their line back to a group of semi-nomadic chieftains of remote antiquity, whom all Amorite tribes had apparently revered as ancestors. The king-list tradition of the 1st Dynasty of Babylon incorporated such a pedigree

[244]Both now, beyond doubt, to be located in the environs of modern Khatana-Qantir: M. Bietak, *Tell el-Dabᶜa* II (Vienna, 1975) 179ff; cf. J. Yoyotte, P. Brissaud, *BIFAO* 78 (1978) 104. That Ramesside texts and statuary, presumably originally set up at Pi-Ramesses, should now be found at Tell el-Maskhuta (see most recently K. Mysliwiec, *BIFAO* 78 [1978] 171ff) must now be explained, as is the case with Tanis, by the purloining of materials by later builders when Pi-Ramesses was dismantled; apart from occupation in the MB period, it is known that Maskhuta was unoccupied before Saite times: J. Holladay, *ROM Archaeological Newsletter* 166 (1979); D. B. Redford, in *LdÄ* IV (1982) 1054f.

[245]*Orientalia* 39, 20, especially n. 4. To these considerations more may now be added. The group *ib* of x, 7 recalls the use of this group in the transliteration of *-abi-* in Byblian royal names of this period (see now W. Helck, *Historisch-biographische Texte aus der 2. Zwischenzeit und neue Texte der 18. Dynasty* [Wiesbaden, 1975] 20); the use of the group *ḥm* in x, 10, 11 possibly betrays the presence of the common *ḫamm* (*ᶜamm*) ("paternal uncle") of Amorite proper names (H. B. Huffmon, *Amorite Personal Names in the Mari Texts* [Baltimore, 1965] 196ff; for *ḫam-* rendered by *ḥ* in group writing, see M. Görg, *Untersuchungen zur hieroglyphischen Wiedergabe palästinischer Ortsnamen* [Bonn, 1974] 90ff), misconstrued as Egyptian *ḥmt*, "wife"; for the *šmš* of ix, 20, cf. the hypocoristicon *šmšt* in the list of slaves in the Brooklyn Museum papyrus: Hayes, *A Papyrus of the Late Middle Kingdom*, ix, 26 (cf. W. F. Albright, *JAOS* 74 [1954] 231).

carrying back the line of Hammurabi to "Aram";[246] and the "Ahnentafel" of the dynasty of Shamshi-adad I of Assyria traced his long descent through 26 predecessors to "Adamu" and "Tudiya."[247] A similar family tree, though with different names, is known for the Ammishtamru dynasty at Ugarit;[248] and it is likely that most of the city-states of the Levant, whether Amorite in origin or under Amorite influence, could boast such pedigrees for their dynasts.[249] Probably in all cases the family trees involved a simple linear descent from a group of legendary, "tent-dwelling" chiefs who incorporated an ancestral purity deemed sufficient to bestow legitimacy on direct descendents. It is important to note that, although the ancestral names are not those of kings whose reigns were on record, the practice nonetheless was to include them in the king-list as part of the ongoing succession.

What little we know of the names and culture of the Hyksos links them convincingly with the Amorite states of the MB II period; and Manetho's sources correctly recorded this fact by identifying them as "foreign kings from Phoenicia."[250] Contemporary names,, few though they be, suggest the Hyksos invaders were mostly, if not wholly, West Semitic speaking;[251] and in origin they thus belonged spiritually within the sphere of their cousins who had founded the dynasties of western Asia. It seems very likely that the enigmatic names from TC

[246]J. J. Finkelstein, *JCS* 20 (1966) 95ff.

[247]I. J. Gelb, *JNES* 13 (1954) 209ff.

[248]C. Virolleaud, *CRAIBL*, 1962, 95; C. F. A. Schaeffer, *AfO* 20 (1963) 214f; see W. T. Pitard, *BASOR* 232 (1978) 65ff; R. R. Wilson, *Genealogy and History in the Biblical World* (New Haven, 1977) 121f; M. Pope, in G. D. Young (ed.) *Ugarit in Retrospect* (Winonoa Lake, 1981) 175.

[249]Cf. P. Matthiae, *UF* 11 (1979) 563ff; see also A. Malamat, *JAOS* 88 (1968) 163ff; J. Van Seters, *Abraham in History and Tradition* (New Haven and London, 1975) 152f; on the whole topic, see R. R. Wilson, *BA* 42 (1979) 11ff.

[250]Manetho's Egyptian sources probably read *Ḫ*^{3}*rw* (for Φοίνικη as the equivalent of Demotic *p*^{3} *tš n Ḫ*^{3}*r*, see W. Spiegelberg, *Der demotische Text der Priesterdekret von Kanopus und Memphis (Rosettana)* [Berlin, 1922] glossary, no. 477), less likely *Fnḫw* (for Demotic *Ḫ*^{3}*rw* corresponding to hieroglyphic *Fnḫw*, see H. Gauthier, H. Sottas, *Un décret trilingue en l'honneur de Ptolemée IV* [Cairo, 1925] 25 and n. 28); see *AEO* I, 181*f; Gauthier, *Dictionnaire géographique*, IV, 151; for a discussion of Φοίνικες, see C. Vandersleyen, *Les guerres d'Amosis* (Brussels, 1971) 103ff; for the use of *Ḫ*^{3}*rw* in late hieroglyphic texts, see the writer in *A Study of the Biblical Joseph Story* (Leiden, 1970) 202, n. 3.

[251]Cf. M. Astour, *Hellenosemitica* (Leiden, 1965) 94, n. 4; J. Van Seters, *The Hyksos: a New Investigation* (New Haven, 1966) 181ff; Redford, *Orientalia* 39, 6f; the discredited view that a non-Semitic element, possibly Hurrian, was present among the Hyksos (cf. M. Noth, *ZDPV* 65 [1937] 27; *idem*, *Die Herkunft der Hyksos in neuer Sicht* [Berlin, 1961] 5, n. 3; Helck, *Beziehungen*^{2} [Wiesbaden, 1971] 100ff) is still supported by W. Ward: *UF* 8 (1976) 353ff. I have yet to see one name convincingly derived from Hurrian.

ix, 13 through x, 11 are in origin the "Ahnentafel" of the house of Salitis, translated into an Egyptian context when the family took over Egypt, and garbled through oral transmission almost beyond recognition.[252] Under the Hyksos in Egypt the list became the indispensible preamble to the recitation (or inscripturation) of the line of the reigning royal family, and entered the popular oral tradition of Avaris and its environs.[253] That the Ramesside scribe tried to interpret some of the names as Egyptian shows that it had ceased to be understood correctly.

Thus to the original Itj-towy king-list, which formed the trunk of the tradition in Ramesside times, were grafted three separate branches: the line of Theban kings of the Intermediate Period, the Ramesside line of descent, and the Hyksos line with its family tree.

[252]In fact, some of the names in TC ix and x are strikingly similar to names in the pedigree of Shamshi-adad. For example the *Ink*[... ?] (=* *ank/g* on the nasals involved, cf. C. Carter, *JAOS* 99 [1979] 93f) of ix, 14, may be compared to the *Ia-an-gi* of AKL i, 2 (no. 3 of the list); and the *n-ib* of x, 7 looks suspiciously like the *Nu-a-bu* of AKL i, 7. We should also remind ourselves that the Hyksos bearer of the name Khayan finds a namesake in the *Ḫa-ia-a-ni* of AKL i, 17. (Ward, *UF* 8, 355ff treats the ^{3} in the transcription of *Ḫy^{3}n* as a rendering of *r/l*; whereas the name has descended into later times as 'Iavvàs, which suggests that the *alif* was already otiose in the New Kingdom group writing.)

[253]Interestingly Matthiae (*UF* 11, 563ff) had adduced evidence for just such a cult of the royal ancestors at Avaris in the 17th and 16th Centuries B.C.!

6

The King-list Tradition in the Late Period

When one wishes to examine the king-list tradition in the years that follow the Ramesside Age in Egypt, one is thrown back on to Manetho; for we lack any reliable evidence on how the official king-list was faring from the end of the reign of Ramesses II to the 3rd Century B.C., a span of 1,000 years. The scattered cultic assemblages might suggest it was a chequered transmission: the Ramessses III Min-reliefs attest a gross re-writing of recent history,[1] and the doctored assemblage of Ramesses III's sons at Medinet Habu[2] and the partially preserved "Musée"-list evince the visceral atmosphere of anathematization. Yet the late private genealogies, such as the Memphite, Heliopolitan or "Copenhagen,"[3] when they are glossed with king's names, show an ability to reach back into recent and more remote history with few blunders (at least in the order and names of kings); and Manetho himself gives evidence of the use of source material which was laudably free of error. Consequently one must conclude that, despite the evidence of cultic assemblages, the tradition of a "running king-list," attested by TC, was not interrupted at the end of the New Kingdom, but continued unimpaired down to the Ptolemies.

In essaying the task of analysing Manetho, one is entering a "no-man's land" whose paths are uncharted though nonetheless discussed

[1] Above, p. 36f.
[2] Cf. K. C. Seele, in A. Firchow (ed.), *Aegyptologische Studien* (Berlin, 1955) 296ff; *idem*, *JNES* 19 (1960) 184ff; J. Černý, *JEA* 44 (1958) 31ff; J. Monnet, *BIFAO* 63 (1965) 209ff; W. J. Murnane, *JARCE* 9 (1971-72) 121ff; J. von Beckerath, *ZÄS* 97 (1971) 7ff; see also K. A. Kitchen, *SAK* 11 (1984) 127ff.
[3] Cf. the writer's *A Study of the Biblical Joseph Story* (Leiden, 1970) 6ff.

widely in current scholarly literature. When one considers that virtually everything told about the man, including his name,[4] is at present in the realm of the unverifiable, at least from the vantage point of external controls, one may better appreciate the absolute necessity of the inductive process of investigation.

At the outset, of course, it must be stated that there is every reason to believe that a man named Manetho, a priest of Sebennytos, did indeed live and accomplished pretty much what tradition said he did. Being a native of the seat of the last native regime, he may well have had access to materials of which others would have been ignorant. The reigns of Ptolemy I (in part) and Ptolemy II are characterized by a desire for conciliation with the autochthonous population, and a practical urge to know more about them, and copy their ways where necessary.[5] Especially in the early years of his regime, Ptolemy I deferred to Memphis as capital,[6] placated the priests by returning their lost property,[7] honoured the memory of native potentates,[8] and he and his son even appointed their kinsmen and officials to positions of responsibility in the new order.[9] More often than not the Ptolemies were crowned at Memphis,[10] and their visits to native temples and Nile trips have been likened to a sort of "Besitzergreifung" in imitation of pharaonic practice.[11] Far from setting themselves apart from the historical traditions of the land, the Ptolemies refurbished the monuments of antiquity, and wished to have their constructions commemorated in stelae on a par with the

[4]The suggestions have been conveniently listed by J. G. Griffiths, in his edition of *Plutarch's De Iside et Osiride* (Cambridge, 1970) 79f; cf. also D. B. Redford, in L. Lesko (ed.), *R. A. Parker Festschrift*, forthcoming.

[5]On the internal policy of Ptolemy I, see J. G. Milne, *JEA* 14 (1928) 226f; P. Jouguet, *BIFAO* 30 (1931) 513ff; H. Volkmann, *PWK* XXIII, 2 (1959) 1630ff. The early Greek rulers were undoubtedly chastened by the bad example of Kleomenes: Aristotle, *Econimica* ii.2.32-33.

[6]See below p. 301.

[7]Satrap Stela, 13-14: *Urk.* II, 14:9-11 (images of the gods, cult paraphernalia and sacred books).

[8]Thutmose III: *Urk.* II, 7:8, 10:8-9; Amenophis III: *Urk.* II, 8:4; Khababash: *Urk.* II, 16:8, 21:2; A. J. Spalinger, *ZAS* 105 (1978) 147f; 107 (1980) 87; R. K. Ritner, *ZÄS* 107 (1980) 135ff.

[9]For bibliography, see *ibid.* 153f. For Petosiris, adviser to Ptolemy I, see E. Otto, *Die biographischen Inschriften der ägyptischen Spätzeit* (Leiden, 1954) no. 46, p. 112f, 174f, 180ff. It has even been suggested that Ptolemy I married a princess of the 30th Dynasty: W. W. Tarn, *CQ* 23 (1929) 138ff; but cf. now K. P. Kuhlmann, *MDAIK* 37 (1981) 267ff.

[10]For Ptolemy V, see below. It may be that Ptolemy II was crowned at Memphis as well: L. Koenen, *Eine agonistische Inschrift aus Aegypten und frühptolemäische Königfeste* (Meisenheim an Glan, 1977) 32; J. Quaegebeur, *JNES* 30 (1971) 245, n. 41.

[11]H. Heinen, *Gnomon* 51 (1979) 399 (quoting his own *Rom und Aegypten* [PhD dissertation, Wurzburg, 1966] 148ff).

works of "ancient kings."[12] The creation of Serapis by Ptolemy I may even have something to do with his emulation of the age-old cults of the universal gods Amun or Ptah.[13] While the early Ptolemaic period is free from the great "Verschmeltzung" of the races and cultures which took place from Ptolemy IV on.[14] nonetheless the first two monarchs of the line evince an unmistakable interest in Egyptian kingship,[15] cult practices[16] and history.

It is precisely in the light of these well-attested interests that the work of Manetho makes the best sense. Thus, to view his output as constituting basically *two* works, viz. the *Aegyptiaca* fulfilling the demand for information on political history, and a treatise on cult and

[12]Τα κατεσκευασμένα μὲν ἐπι βασιλέων ἀρχαίων: G. Wagner, in *Akten des XII. Internationalen Papyrologenkongresses* (Munich, 1974) 441. Since this is probably a trilingual inscription, an Egyptian *Vorlage* must be postulated behind "ancient kings," but there are too many possible renderings for this to decide the matter.

[13]Cf. R. Pettazzoni, *Essays on the History of Religion* (Leiden, 1954) 167f; in general, W. Otto, *Priester und Tempel im hellenistischen Aegypten* I (Leipzig, 1908) 12ff; II, 267ff; H. I. Bell, *Egypt from Alexander the Great to the Arab Conquest* (Oxford, 1948) 38f; E. Kiessling, *CdE* 24 (1949) 117ff; P. Swinnen, in F. Dunand (ed.), *Les syncrétismes dans les religions grecque et romain* (Paris, 1973) 115ff; popular tradition even back-dated the founding of the Serapeum to Alexander himself: R. Merkelback, *AfPap* 17-18 (1960-66) 108f.

[14]Cf. *inter alia*, F. W. Walbank, in J. Ruffle (ed.), *Glimpses of Ancient Egypt* (Warminster, 1979) 181ff; on the increasing influence of Egyptian ideas of kingship on the Ptolemies, see C. Onasch, *AfPap* 24-25 (1976) 137ff; ancient Egyptian influence on Ptolemaic titles and rank still seems likely, in spite of L. Mooren: in *Proceedings of the XIV. International Congress of Papyrologists* (London, 1975) 233ff; on the ever increasing attraction of the native cults for the Greeks, see Sir H. I. Bell, *JEA* 34 (1948) 82ff; S. K. Eddy, *The King is Dead* (Lincoln, 1961) 277, n. 38; Griffiths, *De Iside et Osiride*, 40ff, and the literature there cited; on the essential Egyptian root, and continuing Egyptian content, of the Isis mysteries, as they spread abroad to the Greeks, see F. Junge, in W. Westendorf (ed.), *Aspekte der spätägyptischen Religion* (Wiesbaden, 1979) 93ff; on the growing cultic relationship between Egyptian queens and the goddess Isis, see F. le Corsu, *Isis, mythes et mysteres* (Paris, 1977) 84ff; on the honouring of Ptolemaic queens by making them "wives" of the god, see D. J. Crawford, in W. Peremans (ed.), *Studies on Ptolemaic Memphis* (Louvain, 1980) 8; on Egyptian literary influence on Greek, see J. W. B. Barns, *Egyptians and Greeks* (Oxford, 1966) 14; Egyptian influence on Ptolemaic ship designs, see A. B. Lloyd, *JEA* 64 (1978) 110ff; on Ptolemaic deference to the natives on the matter of coinage, see Milne, *JEA* 14, 228; for native influence on the Ptolemaic legal system, see E. Seidl, *Ptolemäische Rechtsgeschichte* (Glückstadt, Hamburg and New York) 104, 184f; in spite of H. J. Wolff (in *Essays in Honor of C. Bradford Welles* [New Haven, 1966] 73f), the boards of *dikasteria* and *laocritae* sound very Egyptian in inspiration.

[15]Cf. the work of Hecataeus of Abdera: W. Jaeger, *Diokles von Karystos* (Berlin, 1938) 132; O. Murray, *JEA* 56 (1970) 141ff; also C. Préaux, in J. Harris (ed.) *Legacy of Egypt* ^{2} (Oxford, 1971) 326f; R. Drews, *The Greek Accounts of Eastern History* (Cambridge, Mass., 1973) 123ff.

[16]Cf. the "calendar of Sais" (P. Hibeh i, 27) with its list of festivals (W. W. Tarn, *Hellenistic Civilization* [Cleveland and New York, 1952] 287), clearly an attempt to familiarize the new regime (c. 300 B.C.) with the native festal calendar; cf. Crawford, in *Studies on Ptolemaic Memphis*, 15ff.

related matters (whatever it was called)[17] directed towards introducing the foreigner to religion, would be in complete accord with what we might well imagine Philadelphus's commission for the new museum to have been.

One of the major problems, however, in using Manetho as a source is the fact that we do not have the original; and to make matters worse there is no consensus among scholars as to how we go about ascertaining what the original looked like. Was it a single king-list? Or was it a king-list embellished by narrative passages? Or, yet again, was it a narrative history in which any king-list source was completely interwoven and submerged? The fact that it was a work in three books militates emphatically against the first; but the choice between the remaining two is difficult.

Manetho's Sources

The theory of the history, transmission and modification of the *Aegyptiaca* which has achieved a sort of canonicity among scholars is that set forth by Laqueur.[18] This maintains, undoubtedly with justification, that Manetho's work did not long survive untampered with; and that, although what Josephus saw and quoted from was in large measure genuine Manetho, the work had long since spawned an extensive "Pseudo-Manethonian" literature. Possibly, already in Ptolemaic times, someone had made an epitome of Manetho's work by simply extracting a framework of kings to which clung, in the later versions of Africanus and Eusebius, the occasional historical statement, ostensibly distilled from the original. But at the same period the work was being employed for less honourable purposes. Those involved in the Judaeo-pagan polemic had recourse to Manetho to prove their point, and the upshot was, not only tendentious commentaries, but also new works masquerading under Manetho's name. Josephus knew both the genuine Manetho and the pseudepigraphical literature, but could not always clearly distinguish between them. Africanus knew and used the Epitome; Eusebius knew and used both Africanus and a version of the Epitome modified by Hellenistic Jewry.

Though by and large this picture must be accurately drawn, the

[17]Discussion in Waddell, *Manetho*, xivf; cf. J. Hani, *La religion égyptienne dans la pensée de Plutarque* (Paris, 1976) 19.
[18]R. Laqueur, *PWK* XXVII (1928) 1060ff.

postulate of a pseudepigraphical literature opens a Pandora's Box. We have come to use the term "Pseudo-Manetho" glibly.[19] But on what basis would one identify and separate out material *not* from Manetho's hand? Can we know beforehand what Manetho would and would not have written? Naturally anachronisms must come from a later editor or glossator;[20] but there is a tacit assumption underlying the customary critical approach to Manetho. That is that Manetho, being able to read the native scripts and thus having the historical contents of temple libraries and the monuments available to him, would surely have seen the error of such folklore as the Osarsiph or Lamb legends, and thus would not have incorporated them into his work. With a good king-list before him, moreover, he would certainly not have produced so garbled a version of the 3rd, 18th or 26th Dynasties as at present is found in the Epitome. No, these travesties must come from the hand of a "Pseudo-Manetho."

This is all very well, but such a judgement is *a priori* and therefore dangerous. We ought in fact to suspend judgement in this area until two questions have been answered: 1. what is the nature of the Epitome, and precisely what prosopographical, chronological and historical information does it contain, and 2. what source material, both in temple libraries and in the more public domain of the stela, would Manetho have had access to in the early 3rd Century B.C.?

The Epitome has preserved for us some precious snippets of the historical "meat" of the *Aegyptiaca* which was once woven around the king-list. An examination of this material may be expected to shed some light on the extent to which Manetho did in fact make use of his sources. The following material is provided in the form of glosses to the bare list of kings to which the epitomizer has reduced the *Aegyptiaca*:[21]

Dynasty 1

1) Menes: carried off by a hippopotamus (A); led a foreign expedition (E).
2) Atotis: built a palace at Memphis; wrote books on medicine.
3) Wenephes: built the pyramids at Kochome; sustained a famine.
4) Semempses: suffered a calamity.

Dynasty 2

5) Boethos: chasm opened at Bubastis.

[19]Cf. R. Weill, *JA* 1910, 313ff; D. B. Redford, *Orientalia* 39 (1970) 39ff; most recently R. Krauss, *Das Ende der Amarnazeit* (Hildesheim, 1978) 204ff.
[20]For example, all those glosses which evince an interest in linking Egyptian chronology with Biblical history betray the activity of Christian chronographers.
[21]A = Africanus; E = Eusebius; T = Theophilus.

6) Kaechos: Apis, Mnevis and the Mendesian goat worshipped.
7) Binothris: women were allowed to hold kingship.
8) Neferkeres: Nile flowed with honey for 11 days.
9) Sesochris: was 5 cubits, 3 palms in height.

Dynasty 3

10)Necherophes: Libyan revolt; waxing of moon.
11) Tosorthos: medical skill; building in stone; writing.

– – – – –

Dynasty 4

– – – – –

12) Suphis: Great pyramid built; contempt for gods; wrote Sacred Book.

Dynasty 5

– – – – –

Dynasty 6

13) Othoes: murdered by bodyguard.

– – – – –

14) Phiops: reigned till 100th year.

– – – – –

15) Nitocris: beautiful woman; built 3rd pyramid.

Dynasty 7

– – – – –

Dynasty 8

– – – – –

Dynasty 9

16) Akhtoy: a cruel man, went mad and was killed by a crocodile.

Dynasty 10

– – – – –

Dynasty 11

– – – – –

Dynasty 12

– – – – –

17) Ammanemes: murdered by his own eunuchs.
18) Sesostris: physical stature; conquest of Asia and the erection of stelae; honoured next to Osiris.
19) Lamares: built the Labyrinth.

Dynasty 13

– – – – –

Dynasty 14

– – – – –

Dynasty 15

20) Salitis: seized Memphis; Saite nome named after him.

Dynasty 16

– – – – –

Dynasty 17

— — — — —

Dynasty 18

21) Amosis: Moses departed under his reign (A).

22) Misphragmuthosis: Deucalion's flood occurred.

23) Amenophis: reference to the vocal Memnon.

24) Cencheres: Moses departed (E).

25) Sethos: reference to his fleet (T); Armais legend.

Dynasty 19

26) Thuoris: reference to Homer and Troy (A) (E).

Dynasty 20

— — — — —

Dynasty 21

— — — — —

Dynasty 22

— — — — —

Dynasty 23

27) Petubates: first olympiad (A).

28) Osorkon: called Heracles (A) (E).

Dynasty 24

29) Bocchoris: legend of lamb (A) (E).

Dynasty 25

30) Sabaco: caught Bocchoris and burned him (A) (E).

Dynasty 26

— — — — —

31) Necho: took Jerusalem (A) (E).

32) Wahibr[c]: remnant of Jews fled to him (A) (E).

Dynasty 27-30

— — — — —

First of all, it is quite clear that a large percentage of the material considered necessary to be included in the Epitome was designed to satisfy the appetites of two groups: 1. Hellenists interested in Egypto-Hellenic synchronisms, and 2. participants in controversies centring upon Biblical matters. Chronologically group no. 1 precedes group no. 2, the latter belonging in the main to the centuries subsequent to the late Ptolemaic period. Strikingly entries nos. 21 to 32, with the exceptions of nos. 28 to 30 viz. all entries from the 18th to 30th Dynasty belong to this category. The first group, in all probability is to be credited to Manetho himself whose interest in correctly informing the Greek audience is manifest in his diatribes against Herodotus. The second group comes from later Jewish or Christian writers who apparently felt free to gloss the Eptiome vouchsafed to them.

Behind a number of other entries lie documents which were well known in the corpus of Egyptian literature that had come down to Manetho's time. The connexion of the kings of the 1st and 2nd Dynasties with medicine and writing in that field had become a cliché long before Manetho. (cf. no. 2)[22] The reference to medicine, to construction and to writings which are appended to the name of Djoser (no. 11), but which undoubtedly derive from the legendary wisdom of Imhotpe, heark back to texts allegedly authored by or featuring Imhotpe, extant in Manetho's time.[23] The allusion to the Sacred Book, under Suphis (Khufu) no. 12, is a clear derivation from the apocryphal authorship attached to such anonymous works in the late period.[24] Behind entry no. 13, viz. Amenemhet's assassination, there clearly lies a reminiscence of the popular Instruction of Amenemhet for his son Senwosret.[25] Finally, the legend of the talking lamb of Bocchoris (no. 29), points directly to the genre of popular writings of the Late Period which deal with a foretold

[22]Cf. Ebers C, 111, 1ff; P. Berlin 3038, xv, 1ff; U. Luft, *ZÄS* 99 (1973) 110f (ascribed to Kenkenes); Ebers 46B (ascribed to Atotis, wrongly interpreted as Tety). But the tradition may well be genuine: it is interesting to note that, when a script was invented for the Bamum in the Cameroons, the first oral traditions committed to writing, besides the chronicles and the laws, were those relating to the pharmacopoeia: E. Mveng, *Histoire du Cameroun* (Paris, 1963) 235f; for a possible allusion to a work ascribed to Neferkasokar, see M. Smith, *JEA* 66 (1980) 173f.

[23]Cf. the Famine Text: P. Barguet, *La stèle de la famine à Séhel* (*IFAO*, Bibliothèque d'étude XXIV; Cairo, 1953); D. Wildung, *Imhotep und Amenhotep* (Munich and Berlin, 1977) 149ff; cf. the stories of Imhotpe and Djoser's campaign against the queen of Assyria and the king of Babylon: *ibid.*, 130ff; on Imhotpe's book on temple construction, see K. Sethe, *Imhotep* (Leipzig, 1902) 108ff; P. Barguet, *RdE* 9 (1952) 22; Wildung, *Impotep und Amenhotep*, 144ff; see also below, n. 67. The association of Djoser with innovation in building, undoubtedly through the continued survival of his great monument, has a long history: cf. above, p. 14, n. 54.

[24]It is probably to be explained by the tendancy, certainly in evidence from the New Kingdom on, of ascribing well known magical spells to the 4th Dynasty: cf. Naville, *Todtenbuch*, 137A, 23; II, 99; Sir E. A. W. Budge, *The Book of the Dead: The Chapters of Coming Forth by Day* (London, 1898) ch. 137, 37-39; *idem*, *Facsimilies of Egyptian Hieratic Papyri in the British Museum* (London, 1910) pl. 41, 9:11 (ch. 64); Luft, *ZÄS* 99, 111; Wildung, *Die Rolle* 219; C. J. Bleeker, in F. F. Bruce, E. G. Rupp (eds.), *Holy Book and Holy Tradition* (London, 1968) 28. For the prominence of Menkaure in the story of P. Oxyrhynchus 1381, see Wildung, *Die Rolle*, 93ff. It may well be that the "book" mentioned in this papyrus as that through which Menkaure won fame (B. P. Grenfell, A. S. Hunt, *The Oxyrhynchus Papyri* XI [London, 1915] p. 229, line 227), was in fact the Sacred Book here referred to, and nominally written by him (*ibid.*, 223, 234).

[25]Millingen i.11-ii.4; cf. G. Posener, *Littérature et politique dans l'Egypte de la XIIe dynastie* (Paris, 1956) 68f; *idem*, in S. Donadoni (ed.), *Le fonti indiretti della storia egiziana* (Rome, 1963) 14. The entry under Othoes is probably an erroneous doublet from the same source.

invasion of foreigners from the north.[26]

Two particular entries, those under Menes and Achthoes, may attest the attachment of a "floating" plot motif to royal names in the realm of folklore. The story of the unfortunate individual carried off, for whatever reason, by an aquatic monster, is known to us from the corpus of Egyptian folk-tales.[27] In Diodorus i.89, Menes' hippopotamus has become a crocodile,[28] which need not be a modification of the framework of the plot. On the other hand, it may owe something to the presence of annalistic material in the Late Period, which would have apprised Ur-Manetho of the pre-eminence of the hippo in the early cultus.[29]

One clearly defined group of entries must be construed as folkloristic "readings" of monuments still standing in the Late Period. The information appended to the name Wenephes of the 1st Dynasty derives from a confusion of Wadji (Wennefer)[30] with Wenes (Unas), and the consequent ascription to him of the pyramids and tombs south and southwest of the Djoser complex.[31] The reference to the famine is based on the famous "famine" relief from the Unas causeway,[32] which was still visible in late times. The descripion of

[26]E. Meyer, *ZÄS* 46 (1910) 135f; J. Janssen, in *Historische Kring: Varia Historica aangeboden ann A. W. Byvanck* (Leiden, 1954) 17ff; E. Lobel, C. H. Roberts, *The Oxyrrhunchus Papyri*, part 22 (*EES Greco-Roman Memoire* 31; London, 1954) 89ff, 162ff; Griffiths, *De Iside et Osiride*, 550; cf. the writer in *Orientalia* 39, 4, n. 1 and 3; also below, p. 285f.

[27]Cf. Uba-oner's rival in the Westcar Papyrus: 3, 1ff; the crocodile in the Doomed Prince: Harris 500, 8, 10ff.

[28]G. Posener, *JEA* 39 (1953) 107. I see little reason, however, to believe that Diodorus *copied* Manetho: so A. Burton, *Diodorus Siculus I: A Commentary* (Leiden, 1972) 13; see also M. Muszynski, *CdE* 48 (1973) 199.

[29]See above, p. 162. That classical authors should have made of Menes a Promothean figure who introduced civilization and sophistication to the Egyptians is understandable (cf. Griffiths, *De Iside et Osiride* 282), since he is the first "human" king of Egypt; but it smacks of an Hellenic approach to antiquity. In Egypt the arts of civilization were the creation of the gods; writing by Thoth (*Philebe*, 18B), language by Thoth (above, p. 66, n. 11) time-reckoning by Amun-re (Kitchen, *RI* VI, 22:4ff), clothing by Hedjhotpe (*Edfu* II, 163:14-15), and so forth. In Egyptian tradition Menes was associated with rites of foundation: Memphis, the kingship, etc. (P. Derchain, *RdE* 18 [1966] 31ff). He also enjoyed an association with Min, on which see S. Morenz, *ZÄS* 99 (1972), xvf.

[30]On the identification of Djer's tomb with that of Osiris, see W. Helck, *ZDMG* 27 (1952) 46, n. 1. By the early Ptolemaic period "Onnophris" had everywhere become "le dieu-pharaon" *par excellence*: W. Clarysse, *CdE* 106 (1978) 252f.

[31]G. Fecht's identification of Kochome with *T3-wr*, Abydos, is preposterous (*ZDMG* 35 [1960] 122); the word is undoubtedly to be derived from *(K3)-Ḳmt*, the serapeum at Memphis: Gauthier, *Dictionnaire géographique* V, 194f, 200f; J. Vercoutter, *Textes biographiques du Sérapéum de Memphis* (Paris, 1962) pls. 2, 7; 3, 5; 4, 5; 6, 7; cf. already J. Krall, *SAWWien* 95 (1879) 129 (who came close).

[32]E. Drioton, *BIE* 25 (1942-43) 45ff; S. Schott, *RdE* 17 (1965) 7ff.

Nitocris as a beautiful woman and builder of the third pyramid stems from the same folklore to which Herodotus was privy,[33] and which constituted in part an aetiology on the Giza group.[34] Although the entry under Sesostris owes its presence and format largely to an epitome of the Herodotan and Hecataean account,[35] the notation of Sesostris's size most likely is grounded in the observation of one of the statues (supposedly life-sized) before the Temple of Ptah.[36] Lamares (Amenemhet III) is thought worthy of a note only because of his connexion with the fabulous labyrinth, still standing in the Late Period;[37] while Amenophis is known as the king represented in the two colossoi at Thebes, named popularly after Memnon. It may be that the identification of Osorthon of the 23rd Dynasty with Herakles (Khonsu)[38] stems in part from construction work undertaken by him at the Temple of Khonsu at Karnak.[39]

Finally, a large number of entries, beginning with Menes and terminating with Necherophes (3rd Dynasty) can only be understood as garbled or misconstrued readings of the old annals.[40] The hippopotamus incident and foreign expedition under Menes are cases in point, "shooting the hippo" and hacking up such-and-such a country being known entries in 1st Dynasty annals.[41] The "Running

[33]Herodotus ii.30.

[34]Nitocris, possibly derived from Neith, Pepy II's queen: P. E. Newberry, *JEA* 29 (1943) 53; on her "Typhonian" attributes, see G. Wainwright, *The Sky Religion in Egypt* (Cambridge, 1938) 53; for her identification in the king-list, see J. von Beckerath, *JNES* 21 (1962) 140; in general, C. Coche-Zivie, *BIFAO* 72 (1972) 115ff.

[35]Cf. Murray, *JEA* 56, 162, n. 1. I have serious doubts, in the light of Manetho's consistent aversion to Herodotus, whether in fact this entry is from Manetho's hand.

[36]Cf. G. Maspero, *JdS* 1901, 599.

[37]K. Michalowski, *JEA* 54 (1968) 219ff; A. B. Lloyd, *JEA* 56 (1970) 81ff. Priests and stolists were still attached to the Labyrinth in the 1st Century B.C.: A. S. Hunt, C. C. Edgar, *Select Papyri* I (*LCL*; London and New York, 1932) 292ff.

[38]D. B. Redford, *JSSEA* 9 (1978) 33ff.

[39]Some imposing reliefs of Osorkon III and his successor Takelot (III — then only high-priest) have turned up in the *dallage* in front of the temple of Khonsu: cf. *Karnak* VI (1980) pl. XIII(b).

[40]That the annals of the early Old Kingdom were notoriously difficult to read was a commonplace by the New Kingdom: cf. the remarks of Ramesses IV, above, p. 92.

[41]On "shooting the hippo" (*sṯit ḫ^{3}b*), see H. Schaeffer, *Ein Bruchstück altägyptischer Annalen* (Berlin, 1902) 20; W. Barta, *Untersuchungen zur Göttlichkeit des regierenden Königs* (Munich and Berlin, 1975) 108ff; foreign campaigns are rather common: W. M. F. Petrie, *The Royal Tombs of the First Dynasty* I (London, 1900) pl. 17:30; *idem*, *The Royal Tombs of the Earliest Dynasties* II (London, 1901) pl. 7:11, 3:2, 11:1; L. Borchardt, *MVAG* 22 (1917) 342ff.

of the Apis" (*pḥrr Hp*),[42] a feast held at six year intervals in the Proto-dynastic Period,[43] was common enough in early annals to dispel surprise at the mention of Apis and Mnevis in Manetho under Kaechos of the 2nd Dynasty; and the reference to women holding the kingship under Binothris might have been a misunderstanding of the practice, attested from the Palermo Stone,[44] of occasionally appending the name of the queen mother to the name of the reigning king. The reference, under Neferkare and Sesochris of the 2nd Dynasty, to the Nile, honey, a calendrical datum and measurement rendered in cubits and palms, will be familiar to students of the Palermo stone. Each year-rectangle is provided with a record of the height of the Nile during inundation; and "king of Lower Egypt" is so common an element in names of festivals and the like that one cannot wonder that an occurrence of *bity* was misinterpreted as *bit* "honey." *Ṯḥnw*, "Libya," and the people who occupy that region, are ubiquitous in inscriptions of the 1st and 2nd Dynasties; and a final year-rectangle displaying a large number of month-signs[45] might have given rise to the notion of a moon waxing phenomenally.

It would thus appear that material drawn upon by Manetho as sources may be categorized under the following four heads: 1. material derived from Greek sources and from the Bible, (pandering to the appetites of Hellenists and Biblical polemicists), 2. folk traditions and folk-tales, 3. folkloristic "readings" of surviving monuments, and 4. "annalistic" writings.[46] If we examine the extended quotations of Josephus and the latter's own comments, we find some corroboration of this postulated list of sources. In 5 passages Josephus speaks of Manetho's sources:

1. *Contra Apionem* i, 14, 73. γέγραφεν γαρ Ἑλλάδι φωνῇ τὴν πάτριον ἱστοριαν ἐκ δέλτων ἱερῶν ὥς φησιν, "for he wrote the history of his country in the Greek language from sacred tablets, as he himself says."

[42]E. Otto, *Beiträge zur Geschichte der Stierkulte in Aegypten* (Leipzig, 1938) 11f. It is intriguing to reflect that "bull" and "goat" are the two sacred animals the tyranical Ochus is supposed to have slaughtered in the generation before Manetho: J. Schwartz, *BIFAO* 48 (1949) 68, 79. Is this the reflection of an attempt to pinpoint the inception of their worship to the earliest period, as a sort of counterblast with nationalistic overtones?

[43]S. Schott, *Altägyptische Festdaten* (Wiesbaden, 1950) 57.

[44]Cf. the name "Meret-[Neith]" the mother of Den, added in the third register of the *recto*: cf. Sir A. H. Gardiner, *Egypt of the Pharaohs* (Oxford, 1961) 63.

[45]Cf. Palermo stone, *rt.* ii, 2-3; v, 7; cf. A. H. Gardiner, *JEA* 31 (1945) 11ff.

[46]Cf. the close reliance which, it is now realized, Manetho's contemporary Berossos placed on the Babylonian chronicles in the writing of his history: R. Drews, *Iraq* 37 (1975) 39ff.

2. *Ibid.* i, 14, 83. The alternative interpretation of the "Hyksos" is said to derive from ἄλλῳ αὐτιγράφῳ "another copy"; but in 91 it is said to come from ἄλλῃ δέ τινι βίβλῳ τῶν 'Αιγυπτιακῶν "another book of the *Aegyptiaca*."[47]

3. *Ibid.* i, 16, 105. Narrative interpolations in Manetho's account are said to be drawn (for the 18th Dynasty at least) not from 'Αιγυπτίους γπαμματῶν ἀλλ' ὡς ἀυτος ὡμολογηκεν εκ τῶν ἀδεσπότους μυθολογουμένων προστέθεικεν, "Egyptian records, but, as he has confessed himself, from anonymous legendary tales."

4. *Ibid.*, i, 26, 228-29. Up to the expulsion of the Hyksos, according to Josephus, Manetho ἡκολούθησε ταῖς ἀναγραφαῖς, "followed the records"; but thereafter he recorded τὰ μυθενόμενα και λεγόμενα "the folk-tales and popular stories" about the Jews, with the result that he produced λόγους ἀποθάνους, "incredible stories."

5. *Ibid.*, i, 31, 287. When, in Josephus's opinion, Manetho followed ταῖς ἀρχαίαις ἀναγρυαθαῖς, "the old records," he was accurate; but where he used ἀδεσπότους μύθους, "anonymous tales" he strayed from the truth.

The first, third, fourth and fifth passages bear abundant witness to Manetho's claim to have used written records in the writing of his history; but they also attest the presence of folkloristic material. More important, the third passage makes it quite plain that *there was an admission by Manetho in the text to the effect that certain narrative portions were derived from such oral tradition.* Can we accept this? Is it indeed Manetho speaking?

In the discussion to this point we have isolated the following types of source material in the Epitome of the *Aegyptiaca*: 1. records or annalistic writings, 2. "sacred tablets," 3. classical and Biblical chronographies, and 4. aetiologies and folk-tales. Of these, no. 3 is clearly not wholly of Manethonian origin, being part of the glossography of the epitomizers. The remaining three, however, undoubtedly characterize, however broadly, the spectrum of Manetho's sources. Where did he go to avail himself of this material? Was it indeed gathered together in one place? If so, was it likely to be under civil or sacerdotal custodianship? Clearly it could not, in times when Greeks ruled Egypt, have been the former, since according to the reliable tradition it was the civil authority itself that "commissioned" Manetho to write his work. We must be dealing with priestly resources, and that can mean only one thing: a temple library.

[47]It is difficult to comprehend this passage. Any discussion of the word "Hyksos" could only have been appropriate in book ii, which begins with the 12th Dynasty and ends with the 19th.

In the light of hieroglyphic allusions, as well as the papyri themselves which have survived, a temple library in Egypt of the second half of the 1st Millennium B.C. is likely to have contained the following:[48]

1. History and Narration.
   (a) King-lists[49]
   (b) Annals (*gnwt*)[50]
   (c) Pseudo-Prophecies and Chronicles[51]

[48]Cf. most recently V. Wessetzky, *GM* 83 (1984) 85ff.

[49]Herodotus ii.100: "then the priests read to me from a written record the names of 330 monarchs, in the same number of generations ...." For Herodotus's reliance on priestly informants, see A. B. Lloyd, *Herodotus, Book II: Introduction* (Leiden, 1975) 89ff. The priests in question are presumably of the temple of Ptah in Memphis. The "330" is most likely in origin a misinterpretation of the plural of "hundred" and of "ten," in an expression equivalent to our "scores and scores" (literally "hundreds and tens"). For another allusion to a king-list, see Plutarch *De Iside et Osiride* 355c (Griffiths, *De Iside et Osiride*, 134); also Theophrastus *De lapidibus*, 24, 55. These "king-lists" accessible to later classical authors will have been Greek writings, similar to those of Hecataeus of Miletus and Herodotus; but undoubtedly the originals from which the priests read were in Demotic.

[50]See above, p. 65ff. An edition of the *gnwt* from the 1st Dynasty to Djoser seems to have survived (above, p. 94f), but the term had probably broadened to include mythological tales (above, p. 212f). Diodorus's description of "records which were regularly handed down ... giving the stature of each of the former kings, a description of his character, and what he had done during his reign" (i.44.4) sounds very much like a late edition of the *gnwt*, in which an innocent numerical datum had been regularly misinterpreted as the king's height (above, p. 213). The old papyrus which, according to P. Oxyrhynchus 1381 (Grenfell, Hunt, *The Oxyrhynchus Papyri* XI, 221ff; cf. J. B. Hurry, *Imhotep* [Oxford, 1926] 29ff) was found in the temple of Asklepios (Imhotpe) at Memphis under Nectanebo I, is characterized obliquely as "the mighty acts of the gods" (τὰς θεῶν δυνάμεις: 41-42). This sounds very much like a rendering of *gnwt nṯrw* (cf. above, p. 90ff); and although the contents sound like a novella (it is, in fact specifically and frequently termed ἱστορία: lines 17, 38 and *passim*!), this may simply attest the loose usage of the term *gnwt* in the Late Period.

[51]Pseudo-prophetic literature, with an historical basis and admonitory tone, is well known in ancient Egypt. The Admonitions of Ipuwer, the Teaching of Akhtoy (Merikare 109-10), the Prophecy of Neferty, the Lament of Khakheperrasonbu, possibly the Declamation of Si-Sobk (J. W. B. Barns, *Five Ramesseum Papyri* [Oxford, 1956] pl. 1ff) all belong in this category. Chronicles *per se* do not constitute a native genre, being derived from Babylonia. For the Late Period there is the so-called Demotic Chronicle (E. Drioton, J. Vandier, *L'Egypte*[4] [Paris, 1962] 616; J. Johnson, *Enchoria* 4 [1974] 1ff; *idem*, *JSSEA* 13 (1983) 61ff), of selected events of the past which, in form and inspiration, shows strong Asiatic influence.

2. Reference Compendia.

(a) Mythological compendia of each nome, or group of nomes[52]

[52]Such texts constitute "mythological catalogues" for a district, and well illustrate, in the cultic sphere the Egyptian scribal penchant for listing things *in toto*. The intent in the case of this genre was to list deities, cult centres, cult objects and measurements, and cult myths, all centring upon a particular township. The best example is P. Jumilhac (J. Vandier, *Le papyrus Jumilhac*, Paris, 1962) , which exhaustively lists all the above categories of information on the 18th nome of Upper Egypt. Similar compendia are the Brooklyn Museum papyrus acc. no. 47.218.84, of 22nd or 23rd Dynasty date (cf. S. Sauneron, *Brooklyn Museum Annual* 8 [1966-67] 99), giving information on several nomes of the Delta, and the Geographical Papyrus from Tanis (F. Ll. Griffith, *Two Hieroglyphic Papyri from Tanis* [London, 1889] pl. 9-15), which did the same for several nomes of the Delta and valley in tabular form. Without doubt it is just such a compendium which is the immediate source of the Edfu nome-list: *Edfu* I, 329ff. The 30th Dynasty naoi from Bubastis and Saft el-Henne have essentially the purpose of listing the divine denizens of a particular locality, and most probably are derived from the compendia we are discussing: cf. E. Naville, *The Shrine of Saft el-Henne and the Land of Goshen* (London, 1888) pl. 1-7 (papyri sources are indeed mentioned: cf. pl. 4, Ba, 6); *idem*, *Bubastis* (London, 1891) pl. 44-48; similar allusions to papyri sources come from the *Naos des decades*: cf. L. Habachi, *JNES* 11 (1952) pl. 28. The Osiris-naos of Amosis in Leiden, though it does not refer explicitly to a papyrus source, undoubtedly derives from the same type of document: P. A. A. Boeser, *Beschreibung der aegyptischen Sammlung ... Leiden. Die Denkmaeler der saitischen, griechisch-römischen und koptischen Zeit* (The Hague, 1915) pl. 1-5. The divine denizens in question are often the *B*^{3}*w* of the place, which Y. J-L. Gourlay has shown (in *Hommages à Serge Sauneron* [Cairo, 1979] 363ff) are the personifications of the punitive powers of the deities of the place; cf. also a block from the White Monastery at Akhmim (possibly from a Late Period naos) whereon mention is made of "the names of the gods and [their] images ..." (personal hand-copy). An oblique reference to a compendium such as these may be contained in the statue inscription of Senu (*temp.* Ptolemy II), BM 1668, line 9: "I built up what I found in ruins in thy (the god's) house, and I made an enclosure wall of fine, sturdy limestone, carved with the roster of gods and goddesses, more beautiful than anything to look at." The word rendered "roster" is *sipty*, and the reference is most likely to the rows of deities which in a Ptolemaic temple have cluttered up the enclosure wall. The use of *sipty* puts us in mind of the *sipty wr* (below, p. 221, n. 66), which may very well be related to the compendia here discussed. Another term might be the "Souls of Re of the Temples (*B*^{3}*w R*^{c} *n gs-prw*)" which seems, in one Edfu text (*Edfu* VII, 22:6) to be a high-flown designation for this kind of catalogue: cf. E. A. E. Reymond, *The Mythical Origin of the Egyptian Temple* (Manchester, 1969) 6. I suspect that the book called *s(i)p i*^{3}*t nb(t) rḫ imy.sn*, "reckoning every cult place and knowing what is in them" (*Edfu* III, 351, 5) is just such a catalogue, as is also the "scroll (*šfdw*) of the 'Directory (*šsr*) of Mounds (*i*^{3}*wt*) of the Early Primaeval Ones' as they call it," according to which the ground-breaking ceremonies were performed at Edfu (*Edfu* VI, 326:1-2; cf. Reymond, *The Mythical Origin*, 28; also *Edfu* VI, 181:11 ["in accordance with what Thoth wrote at the dictate *ḏ*^{3}*isw* ... 'Directory of the Mounds of the First Occasion' is what they call it"], Reymond, *The Mythical Origin*, 8f.). We are dealing in most of the above cases with subtitles or popular designations of a genre of works of a fairly extensive reference; the "*dicitur*-tag" (*ḫr.tw r.f*) of the two immediately preceding passages proves it. Finally, one wonders if it is possible that the 42 sacred books which, according to Clement, contained all Egyptian religious lore were in fact the compendia we are here describing: see Clement of Alexandria *Stromata* vi.4.36.1; J. Leipoldt, S. Morenz, *Heilige Schriften, Betrachtungen zur Religionsgeschichte der antiken Mittelwelt* (Berlin, 1953) 40f; E. A. E. Reymond, *From Ancient Egyptian Hermetic Writings* (Vienna, 1977) 40f.

(b) Medical Texts[53]
(c) Wisdom and Ethical Teachings[54]
(d) Hemerologies[55]
(e) Oneiromancies[56]

[53]In general, H. Grapow, *Untersuchungen über die altägyptischen medizinischen Papyri*, Leipzig, 1935. The presence of medical texts in temple libraries is proven by the long-standing traditions which claim specific texts to have been discovered in the temple of a particular god: Ebers C, 111, 1ff; P. Berlin 3038, xv, 1ff; Luft, *ZÄS* 99, 110f.

[54]*Sb^{3}yt*, the ubiquitous term for the moralizing precepts of the wisemen of old: R. J. Williams, *JAOS* 92 (1972) 214ff; *idem*, *JAOS* 101 (1981) 1ff; Chester Beatty IV, *vs.* 2, 8-9; Millingen I, 1 (Amenemhet: A. Volten, *Zwei altägyptischen politische Schriften* [Copenhagen, 1945], *ad loc.*; Luft, *ZÄS* 99, 113); Merikare, 109-110 (Akhtoy); Ptahhotpe, 1 (Z. Zaba, *Les maximes de Ptahhotep* [Prague, 1956], *ad loc.*; Luft, *ZÄS* 99, 113); Hordedef, 1 (G. Posener, *RdE* 9 [1952] 109f; Luft, *ZÄS* 99, 114); Satire of the Trades (H. W. Helck, *Lie Lehre des Dw^3-ḫtjj* [Wiesbaden, 1970] Ia); Amennakhte (G. Posener, *Catalogue des Ostraca hiératiques littéraires de Dier el-Médinah* [Cairo, 1938ff] 1248, 1-2; BM 41541: *idem*, *RdE* 10 [1953] pl. 4, 1; cf. *idem*, *RdE* 6 [1951] 42); Amenemhet (A. H. Gardiner, *ZÄS* 47 [1910] 87ff; Hory (Sir A. H. Gardiner, J. Černý, *Hieratic Ostraca* [Oxford, 1957] pl. 6: 1, 1); Piyay (J. Černý, *Ostraca hiératiques* [*CCG*; Cairo, 1930-35] no. 25771, *rt.*; Gardiner, Černý, *Hieratic Ostraca*, pl. 41: 1, 1-5); a man for his son (Posener, *Ostraca hiératiques littéraires*, 1266, 1); Anii (Luft, *ZÄS* 99, 114); Amenemope 1, 1-4; 27, 8-9 (*ibid.*, 115); this is what schoolboys learn: Chester Beatty IV, *vs.* 6, 3; cf. 3, 10; 4, 6; A. H. Gardiner, *Late Egyptian Miscellanies* (Brussels, 1937) 3, 13; cf. *sb^{3}yt n š^{c}t*: *ibid.*, 79, 5; R. A. Caminos, *Late Egyptian Miscellanies* (London, 1954) 125; H. Grapow, *Sprachliche und schriftliche Formung ägyptischen Texte* (Glückstadt and New York, 1936) 60, n. 30; the onomasticon of Amenemope is also called *sb^{3}yt*: *AEO* III, pl. VII. The library of the Sobek temple of Ptolemaic date in the Fayum proves that "Wisdom Texts" were still part of the collection in Greco-Roman times: E. A. E. Reymond, *From the Contents of the Libraries of the Suchos Temple in the Fayum* 1 *A Medical Book from Crocodilopolis* (Vienna, 1976) 22. The operative designation in Demotic seems to be *rḫw* or *mri-rḫw*: *idem*, *Hermetic Writings*, 20, 35, 40.

[55]The terms vary. The Cairo Calendar (A. M. Bakir, *The Cairo Calendar No. 86637* [Cairo, 1966] pl. I, 1) begins "here begins the epiphanies of every god and goddess, each day being written up, (as) found in writings of old." The second book (*ibid.*, *rt.* iii, 1-2) commences with "here begins the 'Beginning of Eternity, the Uttermost parts of Everlasting,' made by the shrine-gods and goddesses, and the assembly of the Ennead of the gods, compiled by the Majesty of Thoth in the *Pr-wr* before the Eternal Lord, and found in the House of Books." Book III begins (*ibid.*, *vs.* xxi, 1) "the Festival book of divine words; discerning propitious from inimical days." Hemerologies are referred to obliquely in the Libyan prophylactic texts for children (I. E. S. Edwards, *Hieratic Papyri in the British Museum* IV Series *Oracular Amuletic Decrees of the Late New Kingdom* [London, 1960] pl. VII, B, 9ff): "gods of the months of the years"; (*ibid.*, pl. VII, B, 14) "thd gods of 'The Year-book (*imy-rnpt*).'"

[56]The term probably involved *rswt*: cf. Chester Beatty III, *rt.* 11, 18; on dream interpretation see the literature and discussion in J. Vergote, *Joseph en Egypte* (Louvain, 1959) 50ff; Redford, *Biblical Joseph Story*, 204, n. 6; E. Bresciani, *Egitto e vicino Oriente* 1 (1978) 95ff.

(f) Astrological lore[57]
(g) Lexical texts (Onomastica, sign-lists, etc.)[58]
(h) Geographies (?)[59]

3. Ritual Literature.
(a) "Festival" books (*ḥbt*)[60]

[57]See O. Neugebauer, *TAPA* 32 (1942) 212ff; G. R. Hughes, *JNES* 10 (1951) 256ff; R. A. Parker, *A Vienna Demotic Papyrus on Eclipse and Lunar Omina*, Providence, 1958; Reymond, *Hermetic Writings*, 40, n. 111. Astrological and omen literature is a late genre in the roster of literary types in our hypothetical temple library. That it was inspired by Babylonian forms, knowledge of which was gained by the Egyptians during Saite and Persian times, seems fairly certain: cf. Parker, *A Vienna Demotic Papyrus*, 53f; cf. *ibid.* 20 (A, IV, 7), "knowing the eclipses of the moon [... ac]cording to the new writings" (note *ad loc.*).

[58]For onomastica, cf. the statement of authorship of the Onomasticon of Amenemope: On. Am. i, 4 (*AEO* III, pl. 7); "... authored by the scribe of the god's-book in the House of Life, etc." (which at once yields a temple context); cf. also the hieratic onomasticon with Demotic and Greek glosses in the Copenhagen collection: A. Volten, *Arch. Or.* 19 (1951) 71. For sign-lists, cf. the Sign-papyrus from Tanis: Griffith, *Two Hieroglyphic Papyri from Tanis*, pl. 1ff. Since it was incumbant on the sacred scribes to transcribe decrees (originally in Greek) into Demotic and hieroglyphic (cf. *Urk.* II, 154, 197, 213; cf. 149), they must have possessed the necessary lexical tools in their temple libraries.

[59]Cf. *Edfu* VI, 201:4. Information concerning Egypt, its arable land etc. are said to "all abide in the 'Great Plan' (*snty*) of the Two Lands." The term *snty-t³* also has overtones of "creation": cf. J-C. Goyon, *Confirmation du pouvoir royal au nouvel an* (Cairo, 1972) 92, n. 78; for the basic meaning see A. Badawy, *ASAE* 54 (1957) 57f; cf. also the hieroglyphic nome list in the Copenhagen collection: Volten, *Arch. Or.* 19, 71.

[60]*Ḥbt*: *Wb.* III, 61:1-4; *AEO* I, 55*. Traditionally this is the document carried by the lector-priest, and often referred to obliquely in the context of the moruary service: cf. J. Saint-Fare Garnot, *L'appel aux vivants* (Cairo, 1938) 22(V), "the lector that shall perform for me the excellent rituals of Thoth, in accordance with that secret writing of the lector's art" (cf. 32 [VIb]); sim. *Urk.* I, 186:14-15, 187:13-14, 189, 190:17; H. Junker, *Giza* VIII (Vienna, 1947) abb. 56 (fac. p. 116). In fact, it is a liturgy and order-of-service combined, the official "prayer-book" of any ritual, for temple service (F. de Cénival, P. Posener-Kriéger, *Hieratic Papyri in the British Museum* V Series *The Abusir Papyri* [London, 1968] pl. 19), and as such it was to be recited by the prophet (cf. Bremner-Rhind 20, 29; R. O. Faulkner, *Papyrus Bremner-Rhind* [Brussels, 1933] 41:2; *Belegstellen* to *Wb.* III, 61:2 [both Sokar Festival]), the scribe of the god's-book (*Edfu* I, 540), the chief lector-priest (*Edfu* I, 555 [processional]: *RT* 4 [1881] 24 58 [lector-priest reciting at the sowing of the "Field of Osiris"]), or even the deceased: A. Moret, *Sarcophages de l'époque Bubastite et l'époque Saïte* (*CCG*; Cairo, 1913) 15. Ritual is said to be preformed "in accordance with the *ḥbt*": cf. *Medinet Habu* III, pl. 138, line 30 (of the House of Ptah); Petosiris: G. Lefebvre, *ASAE* 22 (1922) 34; *Urk.* II, 48:15; A. H. Gardiner, *JEA* 24 (1938) 170; *Edfu* II, 61; Sauneron, *Esna* II, 11:1; Kitchen, *RI* V, 116:12-13; W. Spiegelberg, *ZÄS* 56 (1922), 21 (xiii, 20); for oblique references employing *sš*, *drf* etc. but undoubtedly alluding to the *ḥbt*, see *Urk.* II, 37:13, 38:14-16; Sauneron, *Esna* II, 123 (no. 55, 1); *Edfu* VI, 88:2; P. Louvre N.3176(S), v, 1; vi, 1; for the locution *mi nty r*, see F. Daumas, *Les moyens d'expression du grec et de l'égyptien* (Cairo, 1952) 216, n. 10. The lamentations of Isis and Nephthys in Bremner-Rhind are, in fact, introduced by the title "Here begins the stanzas of the *ḥbt* of the Two Kites, performed in the House of Osiris ... they sing the stanzas of this book in the presence of this god" (Bremner-Rhind 1, 1-2). Brooklyn Museum P. 47. 218.50 (Goyon, *Confirmation*) is undoubtedly a *ḥbt* or *sšm ḥb*. Often a particular *ḥbt*

footnote 60 continued ....

(b) Ritual books (*nt-^{c}*)[61]

footnote 60 continued ....
might be referred to simply by its title, as for example the *wpt-r^{3}*, "Opening of the Mouth" (S. Sauneron, *BIFAO* 69 [1971] pl. 57; E. Naville, *The Temple of Deir el-Bahari* IV [London, 1901] pl. 110; *JEA* 24 [1938] pl. 5; H. Grapow, *SBAW* 1915, 380; *idem*, *Sprachliche und schriftliche Formung*, 13), the *ihb* "Dance-rite" (H. Jacobsohn, *Die dogmatische Stellung des Königs in der Theologie der alten Aegypter* [Glückstadt and New York, 1939] 30f, 34; E. Brunner-Traut, *Aegyptologische Forschungen* VI [Glückstadt, 1938] 80); the *sẖ^{c} Skr*, "Presentation of Sokar" (P. Louvre N.3176[S], iv, 27); *sm^{3c} ẖrw Ḥr r šfdw.f*, "the Justification of Horus over His Enemies" (*Edfu* VI, 61:2, A. M. Blackman, H. W. Fairman, *JEA* 28 [1942] 37, n. 4). One late text (*Edfu* VI, 23; cf. K. Sethe, *ZAS* 56 [1920] 51) cites the *ḥbt* as source reference for the location of the oasis; but this does not necessarily introduce a new meaning of the word. An incidental qualification of a word or phrase in a genuine liturgy is all that, in all probability, is to be read into this passage. Ramesses II's use of the word in the *Inscription Dédicatoire* (72) is puzzling: "he wrote up (*smn*) his ritual book (*ḥbt*) with fields, serfs and cattle." This sounds distinctly like the *ipw* (see below), the function of which is to list god's-property.

[61]Possibly easily confounded with *ḥbt* (which would be a broader category: cf. in fact *Medinet Habu* III [Chicago, 1934] pl. 138, line 30; *Edfu* VII, 282), the *nt-^{c}*, literally "that which conforms to the regulation" and therefore "customary procedure," would have referred to the rites in their traditional *performance*, rather than the text which accompanied them; (possibly identical with "the document of correct procedure." [*drf n tp bi^{3}*]: A. Gutbub, *Kom Ombo* I [Cairo, 1973] 373, no. 497, cf. E. Graefe, in *Aspekte der spätägyptischen Religion*, 49f). Nevertheless, the term is consistently prefixed to the book of the specific ritual: A. W. Shorter, *JEA* 19 (1933) 60, line 8 (*nt-^{c} ḥb*); P. Bremner-Rhind, 18, 1; Goyon, *Confirmation*, pl. 4 (112, 1: the Sokar processional); *ibid.*, 18f (*nt-^{c} n st wrt*); P. Barguet, *Le papyrus N. 3176(S) du musée du Louvre* (Cairo, 1962) 52ff (v, 4; vi, 16 [*s^{c}ḳ Wsir*], v, 11-12 [*ẖnw n Wsir*], v, 12 [*wn nšmt*]; Spiegelberg, *ZÄS* 56, 20 (water-procession of the Apis); J-C. Goyon, *JEA* 57 (1971) 155, n. 5 (of magic ritual); *Edfu* III, 351 (5) (*sẖ^{c} ḥm.k r ḥwt.k*); *Dendera* VI, 158, 34-5 (rites for Hathor); *BIFAO* 73 (1973) pl. 29 (Tod: *nt-^{c} mḥ Wḏ^{3}t*); cf. H. Fischer, *Dendera in the Third Millenium B.C.* (Locust Valley, N.Y., 1968) 45 (h); Vercoutter, *Textes biographiques du Sérapéum*, 18 (rites of Apis burial); Sauneron, *Esna* II, 171:2 (rites for Neith); 207 (rites of [i.e. authorized by(?)] Geb); J-C. Goyon, *BIFAO* 65 (1967) 141 (P. Louvre I 3079: *nt-^{c} n s^{3}ẖ Wsir*), 109, n. 1. One wonders whether, under certain conditions, a large compendious order-of-service might not be alluded to under the general rubric of *tmt*, "the complete guide": cf. J. Vercoutter, *MDAIK* 16 (1958) pl. 31, line 3 (the Apis buried and the rites performed *mi nty r tmmt ḥn^{c} sš nb m mdw-nṯr*); cf. D. Meeks, *RdE* 28 (1976) 95f ("amulet-ritual"); *Reliefs and Inscriptions from Karnak* III *The Bubastite Portal* (Chicago, 1954) pl. 18, col. 32; *CCG* 42208, c, 23-4 (temple rites in general). This use seems to be early: cf. Sethe, *Lesestücke*, 71, 7; *Urk.* IV, 1264; Kitchen, *RI* V, 116, 12-13. The meaning of *nt-^{c}* under discussion here stems from the nuance of obligation, or ordained procedure, inherent in the term: cf. Amenemope i, 4 (parallel to *tp-rd* and *sb^{3}yt*), Kitchen, *RI* I, 49, 1. For its employment as a translation of Akkadian *rikiltu*, "treaty," see Redford, *Orientalia* 39, 43, n. 1; Occasionally *mḏ^{3}t* appears as a substitute for *nt-^{c}*: cf. *BIFAO* 73, pl. 29 (*mḏ^{3}t ^{c}ḳ Mnṯw r W^{3}st*). The "document of the ancestors" (i.e. an ancient and therefore authoritative "blue book") which the high-priest Osorkon called for when judging the Theban rebels, may have been simply a ritual book: their crime had been, in fact, the frustration of divine service in the temples: *Reliefs and Inscriptions from Karnak* III, pl. 18, col. 35; R. A. Caminos, *The Chronicle of Prince Osorkon* (Rome, 1958) 49, n. *c*.

(c) Magical texts (*mḏꜣt nt / sꜣw nw*)[62]
(d) (Festival) Instructions (*inw*)[63]
(e) Beatifications (*mḏꜣt nt sꜣḫw*)[64]

[62] These abounded in the temple libraries of Manetho's time: note how in book catalogues in Ptolemaic temples the vast majority of titles belong in this category: *Edfu* III, 347; Bleeker, in *Holy Book and Holy Tradition*, 34; *BIFAO* 73, pl. 28-29 (Tod); Spiegelberg, *ZÄS* 56, 20f (after the initial *nt-ꜥ* nearly every entry is of a magical nature!). They are referred to collectively, along with related genres, by the broad designation the "Souls of Re": J. Bergman, *Isis-Seele und Osiris-Ei* (Uppsala, 1970) 39, n. 3; E. A. E. Reymond, *CdE* 47 (1972) 124. *Isdn* (Thoth) is called "master (*nb*) of the 'Souls of Re'": H. Junker, E. Winter, *Das Geburtshaus des Tempels der Isis in Philä* (Vienna, 1965) 236; cf. the "library containing the 'Souls of Re'" (*Edfu* III, 355), which sound like a generic term for all sacred literature; also *Edfu* VII, 4:5. In fact, they are referred to collectively as the *šfdw nw pr-ꜥnḫ*, "the scrolls of the House of Life," and in Greek bilinguals as *ιερα βύβλα*: W. Spiegelberg, *Der demotische Texte der Priesterdekrete von Kanopus und Memphis (Rosettana)* (Berlin, 1922) no. 412. Blackman and Fairman (*JEA* 28, 34) render simply "material derived from old books." Certain wall surfaces at Edfu were decorated "with what is appropriate for it from the 'Souls of Re' of the Primordial Ones" (*Edfu* III, 14); at Dendera cult implements and prescriptive acts used in the offering are supposed to be "in accordance with what is in the 'Souls of Re'": *Dendera* II, 3:1. For *mḏꜣt* used of magical works, see *Wb.* II, 187:16; used of amulets, S. Sauneron, *Le rituel d'embaumement* (Cairo, 1952) 4, 11-12; U. Luft, in *Festschrift zum 150 jährigen Bestehen der Berliner ägyptischen Museum* (Berlin, 1974) 175, n. *a*; CT II, spell 94, *Urk.* IV, 1364:17 (mortuary contexts); T. G. Allen, *JNES* 8 (1949) 351; P. Bremner-Rhind, 22, 1; 23, 17-18, 24, 21; 26:11-12, 21 (all Apophis spells); Edwards, *Oracular Amuletic Decrees*, pl. V, 55, 56; p. 17, n. 54; for further examples with discussion, see D. Lorton, *GM* 23 (1977) 55ff; J-C. Goyon, *P. Louvre 3279* (Cairo, 1966) 85f; B. Stricker, *OMRO* 23 (1942) 46; on prophylactic magic, see *Wb.* III, 414:12 (*sꜣ*); *Edfu* III, 347 (*sꜣ niwt, sꜣ pr, sꜣ ḥḏt, sꜣ st sꜣrnpt*; Goyon, *Confirmation*, 114, n. 277; Spiegelberg, *ZÄS* 56, 20f (*sꜣ nšmt, sꜣ Dp*); *Wb.* IV, 220:15-16 (*sḥry*); for the "Protection of breathing" (*sꜣ n snsn*) see W. Erichsen, *Eine neue demotische Erzählung* (AWMainz, 1956) iii, 7-8, p. 72; Sauneron, *Embaumement*, v, 10-11; for the "Protection-book" (*nht/nhy*), see *Wb.* II, 282:3-4; P. Berlin 3049, *vs.* xix.1: K. P. Kuhlman, *MDAIK* 29 (1973) 210, n. 51; for the book "Protection of the body" (*mkt ḥꜥw*), and related literature, see F. A-M. Ghattas, *Das Buch Mk.t-ḥꜥw "Schutz des Leibes"* (PhD dissertation, Göttingen, 1968); cf. also H. Altenmüller, *GM* 33 (1979) 7ff; "Protection of the barque": Spiegelberg, *ZÄS* 56, 21. Because of the essentially oral nature of the use of magical literature, the basic component of all magic is the "spell" (*rꜣ*): cf. E. Schott, *GM* 25 (1977) 73ff; but they can also be called *ssw*, "writings": cf. "the [writings] of Bes with 7 faces": S. Sauneron, *Le papyrus magique illustré de Brooklyn* (New York, 1970) pl. IV, 1, p. 24. For a general and brief survey of the terms used in magical literature, see J. F. Borghouts, *Ancient Egyptian Magical Texts* (Leiden, 1978) 118.

[63] See F. M. H. Haikal, *Two Hieratic Funerary Papyri of Nesmin* I (Brussels, 1970) 1 (p. 25 [*inw n ḥb Int*]); II (1972) 22f; S. Schott, in *HO* I, 2 (Leiden, 1952) 228; Barguet, *Papyrus N.3176*, 22, n. 2, 51.

[64] In all probability these would have been classed under the broad heading of *nt-ꜥ* (above, n. 61), or *ḥbt*; nevertheless *mḏꜣt nt sꜣḫw* does occur: Sckowski Papyrus: A. Szczudlowska, *ZÄS* 98 (1970) 50f; *mḏꜣt nt sbb nḥḥ* J. Assmann, in *LdÄ* II (1976) 54f; cf. *Urk.* IV, 1364:17; Naville, *Todtenbuch*, 100, 1 (*mḏꜣt nt sikr ꜣḫ*); A. M. Blackman, *The Rock Tombs of Meir* II (London, 1915) pl. 8; *šdt sꜣḫw*, *ibid.*, II, pl. 10; *ibid.*, III, pl. 22, 23; P. E. Newberry, *Beni Hasan* I (London, 1893) pl. 17; N. de G. Davies, A. H. Gardiner, *The Tomb of Antefoker* (London, 1920) pl. 28; H. E. Winlock *Bas-Reliefs from the Temple of Ramesses I at Abydos* (New York, 1973) pl. 9; *LD* II, 71b (J. A. Wilson, *JNES* 3 [1944] 215); M. A. Murray; *Saqqara Mastabas* I (London, 1905) pl. 23; N. de G. Davies, A. H. Gardiner, *The Tomb of Amenemhet* (London, 1915) pl. 21; beatifications for Osiris: *Edfu* III, 347; Spiegelberg, *ZÄS* 56, 21.

(f) Hymns (*dw^{3}w*)[65]

4. Directories.

(a) Master Book of Cult Prescriptions ("The Great Inventory")[66]

(b) Construction manuals[67]

[65] *Dw^{3}w* appears to be the generic term for hymns of adoration: cf. *mḏ^{3}t nt dw^{3}w R^c m Imnt*, E. Hornung, *Das Buch der Anbetung des Re im Westen* (Geneva, 1975); W. Barta, *OLZ* 74 (1979) 112; A. Piankoff, *The Litany of Re* (New York, 1964) pl. 1, 3; Neferhotep, 22 (E. Blumenthal, *Untersuchungen zum ägyptischen Königtum des mittleren Reiches* I [Berlin, 1970] 127); Gardiner, *Late Egyptian Miscellanies*, 18, 12-13 (parallel to *sm^{3}w* and *snmḥ*); P. Ramesseum VI, 42 (of an *inḏ-ḥr* hymn); the testimonial statements illustrative of the personal piety of the working class are called *dw^{3}w*: A. Erman, *SBAW* 30 (1911) pl. 16, 11 (parallel to *rdit i^{3}w*) 17 and 23f; Chester Beatty VIII, *vs.* 10, 1, 8; H. Goedicke, E. F. Wente, *Ostraka Michaelides* (Wiesbaden, 1962) pl. 27, no. 74. For litanies accompanying the offering (*wdn*), see S. Schott, in O. Firchow (ed.), *Aegyptologische Studien* (Berlin, 1955) 289ff. The great hymn to Khnum of Esna is called *ky inḏ-ḥr*, "another hymn of adoration": Sauneron, *Esna* III, 130 (250, 6). "The Bequest of the Field" (*swḏ sḫt*) is called simply "the writing (*sš*)": *Esna* II, 171.

[66] *Sipty wr*, the standard prescriptive text for cult images, various cult paraphernalia, temple decoration etc. For complete discussion with references, see the present author in *BES* 3 (1981) 92ff. This work sounds rather like the list of emblems and other paraphernalia with which the scribe of the god's-book was supposed to be familiar, according to Clement *Stromateis* vi.4.

[67] Cf. the "god's-book about 'Stretching the Cord'": P. Berlin 3029 *vs.*, 15; PD 6319 (Reymond, *Hermetic Writings*, 52), *rt.* x + iii, 21: "temples conforming to what is prescribed in the books of the [chief] lector-[priest]"; *ibid.* x + v, 17 (Reymond, *Hermetic Writings*, 95): "written ground-plan," "architect's manual" (*p^3 ḳdy n sḫ*). One was reputed to be of celestial origin: "... the Great Plan of this book which fell from heaven on the north of Memphis" (*Edfu* VI, 6:3-4); another was allegedly written by Imhotpe: *Edfu* VI, 10:10 ("the scroll of designing a temple [*šfdw n sšm ḥwt-nṯr*] made by the chief lector-priest Imhotpe"): Sethe, *Imhotep*, 108ff; Blackman, Fairman, *JEA* 28, 36; Barguet, *RdE* 9, 22; Wildung, *Imhotep und Amenhotep*, 144ff. This seems to have had general application: cf. Imhotpe's epithet "he who gives instructions to the gods ... and lays down the blue-print for their temples," Naville, *The Temple of Deir el-Bahari* V, pl. 148-50; R. Weill, *REA* 2 (1929) 102. For the entry in the library list see *Edfu* III, 351, col. 3; cf. also the priestly admonition (*Edfu* III, 362): "look ye to the ancient writings and the temple inventory (*sšm ḥwt-nṯr*), and deliver it as teaching to your children." In fact, the compass of this document may be somewhat broader, embracing not only temple design, but also the general running of the entire cultic establishment together with its appurtenances: cf. E. Chassinat, *BIFAO* 28 (1929) 7. Geometrical information may also have been included, but this was often of a magical or esoteric nature: P. Barguet, *BSFE* 72 (1975) 28f. For the possibility that the redaction of such prescriptive texts on the building and furnishing of temples dates from Amasis' reign, see Reymond, *Hermetic Writings* 30f. The "Laying the Ground-plan" (*p^3 g^{3}y snty*) of PD 6319. x + ii, 20 (*ibid.*, 50) seems to be one of these. One wonders whether the *snṯt wrt* "the Great Plan," in certain priestly titles from Karnak is related to this document: H. Kees, *Das Priestertum im ägyptischen Staat* (Leiden, 1953) 209, n. 3.

(c) Manuals of painting and relief[68]
(d) Manuals of purification[69]
(e) Offering Manuals[70]
(f) Calendars of Feasts[71]
(g) Manuals of cultic receipts[72]

5. Inventories and Business documents.
(a) Inventories (*ipt*)[73]
(b) Property-list instructions (*ḫt-nṯr*)[74]

[68]Cf. *Edfu* III, 351, col. 3. The pylons at Edfu were decorated "according to all the instructions (*tp-rd*) of (the depiction of) the punishing of the foreign lands": *Edfu* VII, 19:3-4. Such instructions were avowed to be ancient: Horus's names and epitheta were "in accordance with what was in ancient writings and his temple likewise": *Edfu* VII, 27:9:10. If is doubtful whether the "Handbook for Painters" mentioned by Petronius as of Egyptian origin (*Satyricon*, 2) has anything to do with native temple decoration. More likely it is of Alexandrian origin.

[69]Cf. the statement of Montuemhet: "I purified the temples of all the gods throughout the entire southland in conformity with the contents of (the book entitled) 'The Purification of Temples'": J. Leclant, *Montouemhât, quatrième prophète d'Amon et prince de la ville* (Cairo, 1961) 197, 3; 205, n. *i*.

[70]"The specification of your divine offerings, in all its detail": *Edfu* III, 348:1-2.

[71]Cf. Sauneron, *Esna* II, 123, "the tally (*rḫt*) of the festivals of Esna ... which are on the roll of the gods (*ꜥr<t> n ntrw*)": cf. *Edfu* III, 351, col. 6.

[72]*Tp-rd*: cf. *Edfu* VI, 162ff.

[73]A list of the possessions of the temple estate, whether of personnel (BM 10052:9, 1; P. Abbott, docket A, 7: G. Lefebvre, *Histoire des grands prêtres d'Amon à Karnak* [Paris, 1929] 51), of land (Kitchen, *RI* I, 50; *Inscription Dédicatoire*, 84), or of quotas receivable (Sallier II, 8, 9). The passage in Sallier I, 9, 8, while not entirely clear, probably refers to an inventory of land: Gardiner, *Late Egyptian Miscellanies*, 87, 15-16; Caminos, *Late Egyptian Miscellanies*, 328 (with references); similarly, the use of the term on the boundary stela of Sety I (Kitchen, *RI* I, 45:5) probably derives from its primary application to the type of document we should call a "land cadaster"; cf. *Wb* I, 67:2; oblique references in *Urk.* IV, 1796:14; Kitchen, *RI* V, 117:10-11; also used of lists of cult objects stored in temple magazines: cf. the bronze tablet, Cairo 30619.

[74]Nauri, 20: various offerings "exacted (for?) offering on their prescribed dates, as per instruction of the god's property-book"; cf. also *Edfu* I, 557, and perhaps III, 351 (3); VII, 299; Sauneron, *Esna* II, 226 (*dbḥw n ḫt-ntr*). From these examples it would appear that this type of text is prescriptive for the disbursement of the god's property, especially in offerings, and therefore similar to 4 (e) (cf. above, n. 70). But the texts from the Kom Ombo mammisi (P-M VI, 198 [6-7]) prove that it also contained liturgical material: "here beginneth the spells of the *ḫt-ntr*, performed for the House of Harweris, Lord of Ombos, in the course of every day, by the chief *wꜥeb*-priest who is on duty ...." Edfu, too (cf. *Edfu* V, 343:15 and 392:7) refers to "reciting (*šdi*) thy *ḫt-ntr* at the (appropriate) seasons, reciting their months by those who are in thy temple." *Edfu* VIII, 111:10ff cites the *ḫt-ntr* as the source for certain items (lost in a lacuna) inscribed on the pylon; while *Edfu* VII, 16:6 refers to certain surfaces "carved on the front with the cult functions (*irw*) of the *ḫt-ntr*, and the instructions (*tp-rd*) of its lords"; cf. *Edfu* VIII, 85, "walls carved with spells from the *ḫt-ntr*"; also J. Champollion, *Notices descriptives* I (Geneva, 1973) 194; cf. H. Junker, *Das Götterdekret über das Abaton* (Vienna, 1913) 76. For the basic meaning "god's-property," see D. Meeks, *Annèe lexicographique* I (Paris, 1980) 43.

(c) Oracle Texts and petitions to the god[75]
(d) Priestly correspondence
(e) Temple Day-books[76]
(f) Account Texts[77]

As is plain from this list, the contents of a temple library meet a number of needs. The cultic and religious needs of such a sacerdotal institution are obviously met by categories 3 and 4; but by the 5th Century B.C. the temple considered itself to be, and in fact was, a repository of all the texts preserving Egyptian civilization. Hence none should be surprised to find categories 1 and 2 well represented here. One category of texts not present would have been government documents from pharaonic times, including reports, tax documents, day-books,[78] census lists etc. Temples would have had little use, if any, for all this "waste paper" from the civil service of a byegone era, although the new administration in Alexandria might

[75]For questions put to oracles (pharaonic period), see J. Černý, *BIFAO* 35 (1935) 41ff; 41 (1942) 13ff; 72 (1972) 49ff; for Demotic examples, see G. Botti, in *Studi in memoria Ippolito Rosellini* (Piza, 1955) 11ff; E. Bresciani, *L'archivo demotico del tempio di Soknopaiu Nesos* I (Milan, 1975) 2ff; *idem*, *Egitto e vicino Oriente* 2 (1979) 57ff; for a selection of Greek examples, see Hunt, Edgar, *Select Papyri* I, 436ff. On the formal term *ḫr.tw*, "oracular utterance (of a god)," see Edwards, *Oracular Amuletic Decrees*, 4, n. 27; cf. Kitchen, *RI* VI, 5:5; Great Harris 79, 10; on *bi³i*, "to give an oracle," see G. Posener, *ZÄS* 90 (1963) 192; J. Yoyotte, *Kêmi* 18 (1968) 87, n. 2; Meeks, *Année lexicographique* I, 114; on the title "oracle scribe" (*sš bi³wt*),, see R. A. Parker, *A Saite Demotic Oracle Papyrus from Thebes* (London, 1962) pl. 2, 7-8. Formal oracular decisions were doubtless kept on beautiful papyrus copies: *ibid.*, 35ff; cf. also G. Legrain, *ASAE* 16 (1916) 161ff; A. M. Blackman, *JEA* 11 (1925) 249ff; 12 (1926) 176; C. F. Nims, *JNES* 7 (1948) 157ff; E. Naville, *Inscription historique de Paynodgem III* (Vienna, n.d.); S. Allam, *JEA* 53 (1967) 59ff; J. J. Clère, in W. Helck (ed.), *Festschrift für Siegfried Schott zu seinem 70. Geburtstag* (Wiesbaden, 1968) 95ff. For petitions to the god, cf. G. R. Hughes, *JNES* 17 (1958) 1ff, especially 3f; for additional examples *idem*, in G. E. Kadish (ed.), *Studies in Honor of John A. Wilson* (Chicago, 1969) 43ff; also J. D. Ray, *JEA* 61 (1975) 181ff. By their very nature such texts were intended to be deposited and kept in the sanctuary, and curses could be invoked on those who removed them: *ibid.*, 187f. In general, see E. Seidl, in *Essays in Honor of C. Bradford Welles*, 59ff; *idem* in *LdÄ* IV, (1982) 600ff.

[76]See above, chap. 3.

[77]Cf. E. A. E. Reymond, *JEA* 60 (1974) 189ff.

[78]Temples, of course, kept their own day-books, but these would have been of an extent limited to the history of the temple in question.

have profited from it.[79] In any case, the first and second Persian invasions had not only terminated the 26th and 30th Dynasties, but had also wrought a destruction from which government archives would scarcely have emerged unscathed.[80] It is probably safe to say that to that genre of government documents represented by such papryi as the Wilbour, Great Harris, the Abbott or the Mayer, Manetho would have had no access.

But it is equally plain that Manetho did have access to sources which we would call historical, and those kept on perishable material like papyrus must have been found in temple archives, and largely written in Demotic. Certainly one such document (or documents) was a king-list, and others must have belonged to the genre known as *gnwt*. This latter category, as it emerged in the Old Kingdom, constituted a true set of annals, with the major events of each year noted, along with the height of the annual inundation. But by the New Kingdom the term had been given broader reference, and now was applied to stories about the gods of a quasi-annalistic nature. There may have been an attempt in the Late Period to make the stories approximate the form of early annals. The titles of such "scribes of holy writ"[81] as Amenwahsu and his son Kha^{c}emope,[82]

[79]Precisely what type of "sacred record" Diodorus refers to as a source for his statement on the number of towns and villages in ancient times (ὡς ἐν ταῖς ἱεραῖς ἀναγραφαῖς) is not known (Diodorus i.31.7; cf. C. Preaux, in *Akten des XIII. Internationalen Papyrologenkongresses* [Munich, 1974] 13); but I doubt that it was an administrative document on papyrus. Most likely Diodorus is thinking of hieroglyphic nome lists and the like, visible on temple walls.
The question as to the degree to which the Ptolemaic government modelled itself on the pharaonic is a moot one. Ptolemy I, during the early years of his regime, apparently pursued a policy of political and cultural fusion between Greek and Egyptian: cf. Murray, *JEA* 56, 141 and n. 1; but this was soon superceded by a period in which Greek models were sought after.

[80]On the dislocation of life attendant upon Cambyses' invasion cf. the statue inscription of Udja-Horessne (Vatican 158; G. Posener, *La première domination Perse en Egypte* [Cairo, 1936] 1ff, especially line 17ff for the occupation of the temple of Neith by the invading army, and line 33ff for the description of the "great trouble" in the land); for the dereliction of the Wady Tumilat canal, cf. Maskhuta stela of Darius, line 15ff (*ibid.*, pl. 4), Kabrit stela, x + 3ff; archaeological evidence from Thebes has been interpreted as evidence of the destruction of Cambyses (C. Robichon, A. Varille, *Karnak-Nord* III [Cairo, 1943] 51ff, 61; P. Barguet, *Le temple d'Amon-rê à Karnak* [Cairo, 1962] 6), but this is very uncertain. On the interruption of work at the temple of Thoth in Hermopolis because of Artaxerxes III's invasion, see Lefebvre, *ASAE* 22, 34; *idem*, *Le tombeau de Petosiris* I (Cairo, 1923) 3ff; on the havoc Artaxerxes III wrought in Egypt, see A. T. Olmstead, *A History of the Persian Empire* (Chicago, 1948) 440, n. 22. The inscriptions of Djed-Hor (*ASAE* 18 [1918] 145) and Samtowy-tefnakhte (*Urk.* II, 4:3ff) eloquently attest the disruption of the Egyptian community brought on by Alexander's invasion.

[81]*Sš mḏ^{3}t nṯr*.

[82]Above, p. 84.

show clearly that such works were written out, copied and (presumably) stored in the "House of Life," an institution connected, especially in the Late Period, with the temples.[83] And the pious care with which ancient documents are treated from the 25th Dynasty on, which we sense already in Shabaka's copying of the ancient cosmogony, the new edition of the Book of the Dead, the renewed interest in the Pyramid Texts, and the general resuscitation of ancient idiom in the inscriptions, is well mirrored in the cluster of titles with which the high-priests of Ptah honour themselves during Ptolemaic times: "prophet of the sacred library, scribe of the sacred library ... he who reckons all the contents of the sacred library, who restores what is decayed in the 'Souls of Re' (sacred literature in general)."[84] Manetho, who enjoyed a prestige only slightly less than that of the sacerdotal magnates of Memphis, must surely have prided himself on a like veneration of ancient documents, and an ability to edit them.[85]

That Manetho should have felt inclined to make use of earlier Greek writers on Egypt is most unlikely. Manetho had access to all the temple literature and to monuments as well, both of which the Greeks were unable to use. Why should he consult the garbled jottings of a foreign sight-seer? It has been claimed that Manetho shows a debt to Hecataeus in his treatment of the Sesostris legend, or in his division of the "prehistoric" section of his work into gods,

[83] Above, p. 91, n. 72.

[84] Wien 154, 5: W. Wreszinski, *Aegyptische Inschriften ... Wien* (Leipzig, 1906) 105; E. A. E. Reymond, *Orientalia* 46 (1977) 4; Wildung, *Imhotep und Amenhotep*, pl. 8, 2, p. 52f; similar sentiments in Louvre C 232 (Gardiner, *JEA* 24, 172f): scribes are to be conversant "with the collections of the House of Books, (able to) interpret the difficult passages in the 'Souls of Re.' skilled in the craft of the ancestors." Significantly, most of the great scribes of the period, especially those of Memphis, honour Imhotpe, the patron of literati: Wildung, *Imhotep und Amenhotep*, 65ff. The same interest in the careful collation and restoration of ancient manuscripts is expressed in the epithets attached to Amenophis, son of Hapu, on a colossal statue dedicated to him under Ptolemy II (Cairo, 37206, back pillar): "I restored everything that was decayed in hieroglyphic (texts), I illumined the difficult passages(?) of the 'Souls of Re'": Wildung, *Imhotep und Amenhotep*, 251ff; cf. also *sš gm wš*, "scribe of what is found lacuna-ridden": Cairo 1353. On the expression *mḥ gm wš*, see Leclant, *Montouemhât*, 70, n. *e*; *Wb.* I, 368:10, 12; V, 167: 26-7; *gm wš* itself comes to mean simply "missing," "in abeyance": BM 1668, line 20: "I caused Isis to appear in procession ... after the many years (when the ceremony) had been in abeyance." It can also be tantamount to "restore ruins": cf. P. Montet, *Kêmi* 7 (1938), 144, 150 (parallel to "making great monuments in his temple").

[85] Ability to handle Greek, such as Manetho must have enjoyed, was an accomplishment of distinguished priests: cf. A. F. Shore, in *Glimpses of Ancient Egypt*, 147, 150, n. *n*.

demigods and spirits.[86] But this is surely not the case. In the latter connexion Manetho simply renders into Greek the tradition of the old king-list, to which he had direct access, as it had been since the New Kingdom, a tradition, one might add, which Hecataeus had only on hearsay, and which he transmits in the predictably inferior manner of one not conversant with the primary sources. In the former both Manetho and Hecataeus (not to mention Herodotus)[87] are reflecting a popular tradition, which was largely oral.

One source of information available to Manetho which is apt to be ignored or played down in discussion, is the vast corpus of monuments standing in his day. Most of the major temples in Lower Egypt, especially those of Neith at Sais, Isis at Per-Heby, Re at Heliopolis, Bast at Bubastis and Ptah at Memphis, were still flourishing when Manetho wrote; and in Upper Egypt the temple of Amun had not yet suffered from its first revolt against the Ptolemies.[88] The "Karnak cachette" shows what type of material must have been "on display," as it were, in the Amun temple until quite late, turning the whole area into a sort of "Westminster Abbey" of memorials. That in the Late Period the cult consciously revered the memories of defunct kings, centred upon their statues on view in the temples, is adequately proven by the title "prophet of the kings of Upper and Lower Egypt and their statues, *wꜥeb*-priest of their shrines.[89] The Ramesseum, Medinet Habu and Deir el-Bahri, of course, never suffered total destruction, and the royal tombs were still tourist attractions in the 1st Century B.C.[90] Even provincial temples might still display the occasional stela from centuries before,

[86]Murray, *JEA* 56, 162, n. 1, 168. It is very doubtful whether Hecataeus's claim to have had direct access to priests and their archives, is to be believed; on the antipathy towards non-Egyptians which caused them to be excluded from certain sacred precincts, see *Dendera* V, pl. 361, p. 54, 60f; S. Sauneron, *BIFAO* 60 (1960) 111f; J. Vercoutter, *BIFAO* 48 (1949) 172; P. Derchain, *Le Papyrus Salt 825* (Brussels, 1965) 140 (vii, 5). If he did converse with the priests, their statements to him will have been intentionally vague, and couched in the slightly Hellenized form that would have been intelligible to him.

[87]It seems fairly certain that Herodotus had access to only the middle-ranking priests, and not the upper class: cf. P. Mertons, *CdE* 27 (1952) 386; but cf. Lloyd, *Herodotus, Book II: Introduction*, 89-112.

[88]Oct. 205 B.C.: P. W. Pestman, *CdE* 40 (1965) 157ff; T. C. Skeat, *JEA* 59 (1973) 169ff.

[89]E. Otto, *MDAIK* 15 (1957) 203, with references.

[90]Diodorus i.45-49; Strabo xvii.1.46.

revered and consulted as a valid record.[91]

The question arises whether Manetho, who was eminently able to read the stelae and correctly identify the statues and relief figures, felt inclined to do so; more important, whether he eschewed the wide-spread oral tradition which had grown up around such visible monuments.[92] This question we are now in a position to answer.

We have attempted in the foregoing pages to reconstruct the contents of a Ptolemaic temple library, on the basis of book lists of Ptolemaic date, isolated surviving papyri, earlier hieroglyphic evidence, and common sense. An excellent check on the results is provided by the haply surviving library of the temple of Sobek, Lord of "the *Pay*-land" in the Fayum dating from the 1st Century B.C. to the 4th A.D., brought to light over the last hundred years, and currently in process of publication.[93] Broadly speaking this material may be categorized under the following heads:[94] 1. historical romances, 2. prophecies, 3. ethical literature, 4. wisdom texts, 5. scientific works. 6. astrological texts, 7. animal stories, 8. mythological narratives, 9. temple ritual books, and 10. historical records of the priests. Strikingly, all the categories, the existence of which was postulated above (p. 215ff), are here represented, but in the present endeavour nos. 1 and 2 arrest our attention particularly. For these encompass such narratives as the Stories of Setna,[95] of Petubastis,[96] of Djoser and his Assyrian campaign.[97] the Amazon Romance,[98] and the Prophecy of the Lamb.[99] It ought to be evident now why Manetho encorporated such a piece of folklore as the Osarsiph Legend in his account of the 18th Dynasty: he found it in his temple library! The same is undoubtedly true of the Prophecy of the Lamb (s.v. Bocchoris), the legends of Nitocris and Akhtoy, or the Hormais legend: Manetho included them because they were *in*

[91]Edfu: stela of Thutmose III surviving into Roman times, M. Alliot, *Le culte d'Horus à Edfu* (Cairo, 1954) 234; Sauneron, *Esna* II, 126; *idem*, *ASAE* 52 (1952) 37. Esna, stela of Thutmose III: Sauneron, *Esna* III 287; Dendera, Thutmose III's "great plan" (*sntt wr*): *Dendera* VI, pl. DLXXXIII, DXCI; Luft, *ZÄS* 99, 112. Edfu, epic tradition of Ramesses III surviving into Ptolemaic times: J. Yoyotte, *RdE* 12 (1952) 92f.

[92]On the dependence of the Herodotan material on Sesostris on such folk interpretations of surviving memorials, see Maspero, *JdS* 1901, 599.

[93]Cf. Reymond, *A Medical Book from Crocodilopolis* 21ff for references.

[94]*Ibid.*, 22.

[95]Volten, *Arch. Or.* 19, 72.

[96]E. Bresciani, *Der Kampf um den Panzer des Inaros*, Vienna, 1964.

[97]Wildung, *Imhotep und Amenhotep*, 130ff.

[98]A. Volten, *Aegypter und Amazonen* Vienna, 1962: E. Otto, in *LdÄ* I (1972) 183.

[99]See below. p. 286.

writing in the temple library.[100] There is absolutely no justification in labelling them "Pseudo-Manetho" and construing them as interpolations. Nor is it correct to imagine Manetho garnering *oral* traditions and committing them to writing. He would have had no use for, and probably would have despised, material circulating orally and not found formally represented by a temple scroll. What he found *in the temple library* in the form of a duly authorized text he encorporated in his history; and conversely, we may with confidence postulate for the material in his history a written source found in the temple library, *and nothing more.* The fact of inscripturation in a library "entry" was all that was needed to lend a composition solemn authority.[101]

If the foregoing is true, then one of the questions posed earlier may be answered. We must not imagine Manetho consulting standing stelae, or ancient temple reliefs, in an effort to collect source material. On the spot collation is at once "too modern" and "too European." Of course, as will appear below, Manetho had access to the contents of ancient hieroglyphic inscriptions and the aetiological interpretations of extant monuments, but it was only through the contents of the temple library. Manetho was always *at least* one stage removed from the monuments themselves.[102]

There is therefore no need to react to the presence of outlandish tales in Manetho by seeking their *fons et origo* in the Judaeo-Hellenistic polemic of late Ptolemaic Egypt, and assigning them to a later hand than Manetho's. Through the library of the temple Manetho was privy to the folklore of his people and was not averse to using it.[103] Indeed, he treated it much more seriously than we should ever have imagined *a priori*, and the argument that Manetho, being able to read the native scripts would surely not have used such

[100]Note how, in the recently discovered Saqqara collection of texts, romances predominate: H. S. Smith, *A Visit to Ancient Egypt* (Warminster, 1974) 19.

[101]The question as to whether Manetho simply translated Demotic material in his *Aegyptiaca*, or paraphrased it, is probably to be decided somewhere between the two; although this need not preclude creative ability on his part. There were enough texts circulating in Ptolemaic times claiming, perhaps honestly, to be renderings of Egyptian originals, which were nonetheless pure Greek creations philologically speaking: see A. D. Nock, *Gnomen* 21 (1949) 221ff.

[102]Herein lies a major difference in the use of sources between Manetho and Greek authors such as Herodotus, Hecataeus and Diodorus: the "histories" of these latter are inevitably built around nothing more than aetiologies or descriptions of the physical, pharaonic ἔργα, still visible in the Nile Valley: cf. Drews, *The Greek Accounts of Eastern History*, 57ff, 123ff. Manetho, on the other hand, had access to much more material.

[103]Cf. J. von Beckerath, *OLZ* 54 (1959) 6.

fanciful legends, is simply — and surpisingly — not the case.[104]

The Format of the *Aegyptiaca*

As the original, three volume, *Aegyptiaca* is lost[105] and was probably already unavailable by the 2nd Century A.D., the task of trying to establish the format of the original is a difficult one indeed. Sometime during the Ptolemaic era an epitome was made of the original,[106] and this in its purist form was the document used and carefully transmitted by Africanus.[107] That the original could be so easily distilled into an epitome which so closely resembles a king-list, militates strongly in favour of the hypothesis that the *Aegyptiaca* ultimately derived from a king-list, fleshed out by narrative sections.[108]

What little evidence we have tends to support this hypothesis. The extended quotation preserved in Josephus on the advent and identity of the Hyksos[109] begins *τουτίμαιος ἐπὶ τούτου οὐκ οἰδ' ὅπως ὁ φεος ἀντέπνευσεν* etc. There follows the account of the conquest and the reign of Salitis told in *narrative* form, followed in turn by the names of Salitis's 5 successors, *listed* with lengths of reign. Although Josephus lapses at this point into a paraphrase of Manetho, it is clear that he followed the 5 names with (a) an explanation of the word "Hyksos," and (b) a *narrative* account of the expulsion of the invaders.[110] In his account of the 18th Dynasty, Josephus again

[104]In 1970 the writer was sufficiently impressed by the distortion in Manetho's account of the Hyksos to ascribe much of the material quoted by Josephus to a "Pseudo-Manetho": *Orientalia* 39, 40f. While details (especially numbers) may well have been modified or interpolated thanks to the Judaeo-Hellenistic polemic folkloristic material is so evenly strewn throughout the Epitome that a Manethonian authorship of the Hyksos passage must be seriously considered. That Apion's *Aegyptiaca* incorporated all that survived for later generations of Manetho's works, I seriously doubt (so I. Lévy, *RHR* 61 [1910] 186): Josephus would thus have been entirely beholden to his adversary for the substance of his rebuttal!

[105]On the variants for the name of the work, see Waddell, *Manetho* xv, n. 1.

[106]See Laqueur, *PWK* XXVII, 1060-1101.

[107]See H. Gelzer, *Sextus Julius Africanus* (Leipzig, 1888), 191ff. Eusebius praises the *Chronographiae* of Africanus as a "monument of labour and accuracy" (HE 6.31.2), and apparently relied upon it to the extent that it is unclear as to whether he preserves a truly independent witness to Manetho's *Epitome*: cf. R. Helm, *Eranos* 22 (1924) 39; also T. Barnes, "Eusebius's Chronicle" (unpublished paper delivered at the symposium on *Histories and Historians of the Ancient Near East*, at Toronto in 1975).

[108]So also Drews, *The Greek Accounts of Eastern History* 208.

[109]*Contra Apionem* i.14.75: Waddell, *Manetho*, 78.

[110]Confused with the Megiddo campaign of Thutmose III: cf. the author in *Orientalia* 39, 41ff.

purports to be quoting from Manetho.[111] This section comprises a *list* recounted narratively, slightly embellished with verbs for "reign," relationships and epithets, covering the kings from Amosis/Tethmosis to "Amenophis." To the end of this list are appended two *narratives*: 1. the Harmais legend and 2. the Osarsiph legend. Both were preceded by two kings' names which, unlike those of the preceding list, were not supplied with a figure for the total regnal years of the reign, an omission seized upon by Josephus as proof of the spurious nature of the story.[112] But a pattern seems to be emerging, viz. that of a king-list interspersed with narrative sections, each beginning with a personal name followed (probably) by ἐπὶ τουτού, or ἐφ' οὖ.[113]

The thesis that the *Aegyptiaca* is basically a king-list expanded by glosses and narratives finds some support in a comparison between TC and Manetho in their respective treatment of Imhotpe. Wildung's plausible reconstruction of TC, fragment 40,[114] would make of it a gloss on Huni of the 3rd Dynasty: "[under whom died(?)] the builder and leader [Imhotpe], the son of Ptah, born of [Khratonkh], who causes [mankind] to live." The similarity of the entry in the Manethonian Epitome under Tosorthos is striking: "<in his reign lived Imouthes> who because of his medical skill has the reputation of Asclepius among the Egyptians, and who was the inventor of the art of building in hewn stone. He also devoted attention to writing."[115] In its present form this comes from the hand of a Greek; but the easily discernible *Vorlage* has most of the elements of the TC gloss: medical skill (*sꜥnḫ* [*rmṯ*]), engineering skill (*pꜣḳd*), literary skill (*sšm* [ ](?). It can scarcely be doubted that the entry in the Epitome derived ultimately from the gloss in TC, or something remarkably like it. The latter typifies the early stages in the process of expanding a king-list; but that the epitomizer could so easily produce the same content as the TC gloss must mean that Manetho himself had not altered by much the entries he inherited from the king-list tradition.

[111]*Contra Apionem* i.15.93 (φὴσι δε οὔτως), and 103 (ταῦτα μὲν ὁ Μανεφώς).
[112]*Ibid.* i.26.230.
[113]For a similar conclusion with respect to the historical writings of Menander, see J. Van Seters, *Orientalia* 50 (1981) 177f. This is not to deny that the section in Josephus dealing with the 18th Dynasty is itself an epitome of a longer passage in Manetho, larded *passim* with narrative.
[114]See above, p. 14.
[115]Waddell, *Manetho*, 40-42.

7

Manetho on the Old to New Kindgoms

Manetho's Dynastic Divisions in *Aegyptiaca I*

As we noted above (p. 13), the king-list tradition as represented in the 19th Dynasty by TC, had already introduced the following groupings of kings:

1. The Gods and Followers of Horus.
2. The "Menes"-group, from Menes to Wenis.
3. The Tety Group, from Tety to the last member of the "6th" Dynasty.
4. The kings of [Herakleopolis].
5. The kings of [Thebes].
6. The kings of Itj-towy.
7. The kings who followed the "(House) of Sehtepibre."
8. The *Ḥḳ*^{3}*w ḫ*^{3}*swt.*

By the time of Manetho the process of groupings had been carried much farther.

The "prehistoric" section of the king-list tradition in ancient Egypt was organized on a tripartite pattern. Manetho, discernible in this earliest part of his work in the Armenian of Eusebius and Syncellus, and TC of one millennium earlier are in remarkable agreement at this point. Manetho spoke of θέοι, ἡμιθέοι and νεκῦες.[1] The first are the male members of the Great Ennead (with Ptah), while the

[1]Africanus, fr. 2, 1 τῶν λεγομὲνων ... θεῶν και ἡμεθέων και νεκύων; the 1st Dynasty was placed μετὰ νέκυας τοὺς ἡμιθέους; the Armenian of Eusebius speaks of "seriem ... deorum, heroum et manium."

second correspond, as the passage in Syncellus clearly showns, to the Lesser Ennead. The ἡμιθέοι are also the *Vorlage* of the *Heroes* of the Armenian version of Eusebius, but the latter gives only the first and last members of the Lesser Ennead, viz. Horus and Bata (Bydis).[2] Moreover, the Armenian has conjured up a 2nd Dynasty of *Heroes*, ruling for 1,255 years, out of what was most probably a line of summation appended to the names of the Lesser Ennead. If this rectification be accepted, Manetho, as represented in the Armenian of Eusebius, corresponds well to the tradition reflected in TC.[3] The "seriem ... deorum" signifies the members of the Great Ennead, the θέοι of Syncellus, and the 9 from [Ptah] to Horus in TC i[4] (called "kings of Upper and Lower Egypt," though whether either of the two concluding lines of summation used *nṯrw* is a moot point); the "seriem ... heroum" designates the Lesser Ennead beginning with Horus, the ἡμιθέοι of Syncellus, and the *Šmsw-Ḥr* of TC ii, 8-9. Finally, the "seriem ... manium" (i.e. those rulers called "reges" in the itemized list) are the νεκύες of Syncellus and the *ꜣḫw* of TC ii, 2, 3, 5, 6, 8.[5] The faithful transmission of the tradition at this point is arresting: thus Eusebius's "alia reges" correspond to TC ii, 1-4, the 30 kings of Memphis to TC ii, 5, and the 10 kings of This to TC ii, 6. Only the "7 ladies who [ ] for the Father" of TC ii, 7 seem to be absent from Manetho.[6]

[2]I.e. Bata: cf. E. Blumenthal, *ZÄS* 99 (1972) 5, n. 34.
[3]Cf. K. Sethe, *Beiträge zur alteste Geschichte Aegyptens* (Leipzig, 1905) 9f; E. Meyer, *Aegyptische Chronologie* (Berlin, 1904) 122; E. Hornung, *Der ägyptische Mythos von der Himmelskuh* (Göttingen, 1982) 88f.
[4]There is nothing inherent in the contents of this column nor on the *verso* (viii, pl. 8) that would militate in favour of placing the fragments of column 1 so low down. All the rest of the columns are fairly well preserved at the top. Fragment 12, is probably the sum total of the years of the Lesser Ennead, and is therefore rightly placed at the bottom of column 1, inspite of Gardiner (*The Royal Canon of Turin* [Oxford, 1959] note to i, 24). But the rest of the cluster of fragments should probably be elevated by some 5 or 6 lines. This would make Gardiner's present line 22 into line 16, and leave nine lines lost at the bottom of the column. Since line 22 (i.e. 16) records a King Horus, we are probably to reconstruct the rest of the column as recording the remaining eight members of the Lesser Ennead; (their presence in the *Vorlage* is assured by the Syncellus version). This would leave the last, 25th, line of the column for the total.
[5]On the *ꜣḫw* in the Late Period, see J. Leclant, *Enquêtes sur les sacerdoces et les sanctuaires égyptiens à l'époque dite 'éthiopienne'* (Cairo, 1954) 76; D. Meeks, *Année lexicographique* I (Paris, 1980) 8; J. von Beckerath, in *LdÄ* III (1980) 534.
[6]Number and sex suggest the 7 Hathors: although their activity on behalf of "the Father" i.e. Atum,, suggests a more likely connexion with the 7 uraei: cf. S. Schott, *Urk.* VI, 55:17 (=P. Louvre 3129 E, 13-14). Cf. also PT 511a, CT II, 52h, BD 83, 4. Why they do not appear in Manetho is not clear: perhaps their prominence in the cult and euhemerized role in primordial history was confined to the New Kingdom, when they seem to have been most popular.

It has been suggested that the *ꜣḫw* and the *Šmsw-Ḥr* are not separate groups but synonymous terms, and that the same is true of the ἡμιθέοι and νεκῦες in Manetho.[7] However the other versions of the Epitome may be construed, the Armenian of Eusebius clearly separates out three groups of non-human predecessors of Menes; and with equal clarity the close parallel between Eusebius and Syncellus pairs off "gods" with θέοι, "heroes" with ἡμιθέοι, and "spirits" with νεκῦες.[8] In the Turin tradition the collocation of *ꜣḫw* and *Šmsw-Ḥr* occurs only in the lines ii, 8-9: in that part of the canon devoted to what Eusebius calls *reges/manes*, only *ꜣḫw* is found (ii, 2, 3, 6).

Nevertheless, the lines in which *ꜣḫw* and *Šmsw-Ḥr* occur pose something of a problem. While ii, 9 is clearly part of a summation, it is not clear whether 8 is as well. It could be argued that the Turin scribe gives the total number of kings and years for the first of the three divisions of his prehistoric section, viz. the Great Ennead in i, 21-22 (Gardiner's numbering), while he gives the totals for the second and third (*Šmsw-Ḥr* and *ꜣḫw* respectively) combined in ii, 8. In favour of taking ii, 8 as a summation is the size of the numeral: 13, 420 in contrast to numerals in preceding lines (2, 341 in 6, 100 + [x] in 7, 11 in 5, 330 in 3). In addition to this, to judge from the position of the right edge of fragment 1 in relation to the contents of each line, there is more space at the beginning of line 8 than could be filled by the *ꜣḫw*-sign, enough in fact for the *dmḏ*-sign. A supplementary total of the first and second sections combined ("down to the *Šmsw-Ḥr*," i.e. the Greater and Lesser Enneads) would then be given in ii, 9, and finally the grand total "[down to] King Menes, L.P.H." in ii, 10. In TC *Šmsw-Ḥr*, "Followers of Horus," are thus to be understood in a literal sense: they are the members of the Lesser Ennead which was headed by Horus, and therefore they are Horus's immediate successors.[9]

The total "9" in i, 15 suggests that the ennead concept was basic to the organization of the list of gods; and Diodorus does in fact simply give the members of the Great Ennead, both male and female, as the

[7]W. Kaiser, *ZÄS* 86 (1961) 56f; I. E. S. Edwards, in *CAH* I^2 (1965) ch. 11, 3f.
[8]Syncellus, fr. 2, 1 (Waddell, *Manetho*, 10). Too much weight is placed on the introductory statement to the 1st Dynasty in Africanus: μετὰ νέκυας τοὺς ἡμιθέους .... This is not a line of summary, but simply a means of placing the 1st Dynasty chronologically, and certainly it cannot be construed as precise wording.
[9]The *Šmsw-Ḥr*, no later than the Middle Kingdom, had been translated into the primaeval kings who had reigned before Menes: see above, p. 160.

first rulers.[10] On this basis the "Diodoran" version has by some[11] been given priority over the Manethonian Epitome and even over TC, on the assumption that the latter has extracted the 5 male members of the Ennead to whom it has had to add 4 other names *ad hoc* to make up the 9. But this is not the case at all. The ennead *concept* was all that dominated the tradition TC reflects: the number *9* was required. It was a *king*-list tradition that was being transmitted, and this had no place for consorts who did not independently rule. There is no reason to doubt therefore that TC records the pristine tradition which from the first added the 4 "weak" members to the males of the Great Ennead, and transformed all 9 into primordial "kings."

Again the number and organization of the θέοι and ἡμιθέοι (cf. Syncellus) are governed by the concept of the ennead. In this case, however, it is the Theban tradition that had been translated into the official doctrine. Zeus who brings the list to an end is clearly Amun, and by insertions[12] the number from Hephaestus to Zeus has been inflated to 15.[13] Thus all indications are that the "prehistoric" section of the king-list tradition in Egypt owes its shape and content in its final form to Thebes of the late Middle Kingdom and the 18th Dynasty.

As it emerged from the New Kingdom the king-list tradition showed an unbroken block of names from Menes to Unas. By the time it emerged from the hands of Manetho this block of 39 names had been divided into 5 dynasties.[14] Two factors were at work here: the geographic distribution of the mortuary monuments of the kings in question, and the concept of the ennead as an archetypal

[10]Diodorus i.13. Herodotus gives five primordial god-kings, viz. Pan (=Amun-kamutef?), Herakles (=Khonsu), Dionysus (=Osiris), Typhon (=Seth), and Horus: ii.144-5; A. B. Lloyd, *Herodotus, Book II: Introduction* (Leiden, 1975) 186. This clearly shows a Theban source. See also L. Kákosy, *Selected Papers, 1956-73* (*Studia Aegyptiaca* VII; Budapest, 1981) 37.
[11]Helck, *Manetho*, 4.
[12]Agathodaimon, Ares, Herakles, Apollo, Titoes and Ammon.
[13]On the Theban Ennead of fifteen, see G. Maspero, *Etudes de mythologie* VIII (Paris, 1913) 165f; P. Barguet, *Le temple d'Amon-rê à Karnak* (Paris, 1962) 22f; E. Hornung, *Der Eine unde die Vielen* (Darmstadt, 1973) 218.
[14]For the locutions used in TC, viz. "House of ...," or *H̱nw*, "Residence," or simply the place-name, Manetho uses δυναστέια, "regime." Possibly the current *nsyw*, "kings of ..." in the king-list tradition had influenced his choice; but far more likely Manetho's immediate *Vorlage* in the native language had conjured up a nominal formation from either (a) *ir sẖr*, Coptic ⲣ̄ϣⲓϣⲓ (*Wb.* IV, 260; see Meeks, *Année lexicographique* I, 342), or (b) *ẖrp* (*tꜣwy?*) (*Wb.* III, 326ff; Meeks, *Année lexicographique* I, 285), both of which in bilinguals are rendered by (and render) forms of Greek δυναστεύω: F. Daumas, *Les moyens d'expression du grec et de l'égyptien* (Cairo, 1952) 223.

"Ahnendynastie."[15] Geographic distribution provided rudimentary divisions: there were the North Saqqara group, the South Saqqara group, the Giza group and the Abusir group. None of these correspond exactly to the dimensions of specific Manethonian dynasties; but the nuclei of dynasties had been clearly provided. Some refinement could be introduced by considering traditions of long-standing: already in the Old Kingdom Hotep-sekhemwy seems to have been regarded as marking a new beginning (above p. 60, n. 205), Djoser was known to have been the first to build a step-pyramid, Sneferu the first to have built a true pyramid, Userkaf descended from a cadet branch of the 4th Dynasty, and the first to have built a sun-temple.

But it was the concept of the cycle of 9 kings that dictated the divisions in the 39 names from Menes to Unas. From Menes to *Ḳbḥw* (Qa-ᶜa), the last king before Hotep-sekhemwy, there were only 8 names, and an additional one would have to be found. From early times Den had shown a tendency in the lists to be treated as two kings, probably through the proclivity of scribes to write both his Horus and his *nbty*-name together.[16] At some time subsequent to the 19th Dynasty this tendency was formalized by treating "Kenkenes," a popular misreading of *Ḥsp.ty* (Usaphais), as the name of a separate king.[17] This made *Ḳbḥw* the ninth king from Menes, and the first 18 names (down to *Bb.ty* in TC) were divided into two equal dynasties.[18]

[15]W. Barta, *Untersuchungen zum Götterkreise der Neunheit* (Berlin, 1973) 41f. This concept is hypostasized interestingly enough in the 9 "Divine Souls," sometimes called "the Ancestors," who were worshipped annually at Edfu in the harvest festival: cf. *Edfu* IV, 240:5-9; H. W. Fairman, in S. H. Hooke (ed.), *Myth, Ritual and Kingship* (Oxford, 1958) 88f. That the number "19" also functioned as an informing principle in the ordering of the king-list tradition (cf. P. O'Mara, *The Chronology of the Palermo and Turin Canons* [La Canada, Calif.; 1980] 16ff) I very much doubt. O'Mara must indulge in too much jockeying of figures to be entirely convincing.

[16]Cf. P. Kaplony, *MDAIK* 20 (1965) pl. 4, no. 22; *idem*, *Monumenta Aegyptiaca* I (Geneva, 1968) pl. 2, 11, 18; p. 20ff, no. 9.

[17]Edwards, in *CAH* I^2 (1965) ch. 11, 21 (with references). On *Ḥsp.ty* and the relationship of the name to an Osirian epithet, see Wildung, *Die Rolle*, 30; U. Luft, *Forschungen und Berichte* 14 (1972) 62f. Apart from the obvious motivation behind the fabrication of *Wennephes*, similar Osirian overtones may be heard in the misunderstanding of the name of the second last king as *Semempses*, "the eldest": G. Fecht, *SAK* 1 (1974) 186.

[18]At some point in the transmission, through a misguided desire to emend a dittography, one Atoty of the Turin-Abydos exemplars has been omitted. (On Atoty, see N. Dautzenberg, *GM* 69 [1983] 33ff.) That this has anything to do with Manetho (cf. Helck, *Manetho*, 18) I very much doubt. Manetho recognized the possibility of more than one king with the same name: cf. two kings Souphis in the 4th Dynasty, two kings Menthesouphis in the 6th, etc. What can be charged to Manetho, perhaps, is the addition of the name "Wennefer" to the second Atoty (Djer). With the excision of one of the Atotys an original 9 kings has been reduced to 8.

The creation of a 3rd and 4th Dynasty in Manetho was based on two considerations which were mutually exclusive: the need, as with the earlier part of the list, to model dynasties on cycles of 9 names, and the feeling that, with Sneferu, a new house had begun. Counting nine places from Nebka (Νεχερώφης) brought one, in the king-list tradition represented by TC, to Khafre, and this in fact is the name that lurks behind the last name in Manetho's 3rd Dynasty, viz. Κερφέρης. The derivation and identity of the other names is clear. Σώυφις is Khufu, Τοσέρτασις is Redjedef, modified to a form consonant with Τόσορθρος (Djoser), and Σήφουρις is Sneferu. In 'Αχης we probably have a garbled from of *Ḥwny*.[19] How the five achieved their present arrangement is unclear. The order Khufu-Redjedef is historical, and if 'Αχης is *Ḥwny*, the succession *Ḥwny*-Sneferu would have suggested itself readily from longstanding tradition.[20] What may have happened is a metathesis of the first two pairs of names, possibly under the influence of a tendency towards dissimilation, in the light of the clear reduplication in the following dynasty.

What is clear, however, is that names 5 through 9 in Manetho's 3rd Dynasty are simply derived from the 4th Dynasty, and the whole exercise has resulted in an unhistorical reduplication. There is thus no reason to postulate a dissolution of the state with many ephemeral kings not considered legitimate in some lists.[21] Nor is the expansion of the dynasty in Manetho to be explained on the basis of two alleged *Vorlagen* that Manetho is supposed to have used.[22] The need for 9 names is all that is at the root of the problem.

In the 4th Dynasty the Manethonian succession for the first four members and their identities stems from the popular tradition, as attested in Middle Kingdom literature and in Herodotus. The point of departure was the pyramid fields at Dahshur and Giza (i.e. those which contain the pyramids which visually were far larger than any others). The order Sneferu-Khufu was long fixed in oral tradition. The order and number of the "Giza" kings, Khufu, Khafre and Menkaure originated in the number and manifest order of construction of the three Giza pyramids. Thus Redjedef, whom all the formal *written* lists remember and place correctly, simply has no

[19]On the original meaning of the name, see G. E. Kadish, *JNES* 29 (1970) 99ff; E. S. Meltzer, *JEA* 57 (1971) 202f; W. Barta, *MDAIK* 29 (1973) 1ff; W. Helck, *SAK* 4 (1976) 125ff.

[20]Cf. the opening passage in Neferty.

[21]So Meyer, *Chronologie*, 152.

[22]Cf. Helck, *Manetho*, 22ff; cf. J. von Beckerath, *OLZ* 54 (1959) 9; G. Fecht, *ZDMG* 35 (1960) 117.

place in the *oral* tradition (which is clearly older than our king-list), because he had no pyramid at Giza.

The end of the dynasty from Menkaure on owes its shape to different factors, which are nonetheless bound up with popular folklore. The Middle Kingdom tradition attests to the fact that already at the outset of the 2nd Millennium B.C. "Khufu and His Sons" were becoming the object of popular interest and "literary" activity. Stories were told of them, and legends recounted about their exploits: each of them, we may venture to say, began to assume a definite personality, each of them became a "wise man." Part of this interest entailed the assumption, quite natural for those times, that each of the sons had been king and reigned in succession to Khufu. Three of them, in fact, had done so, and why not the rest? The Wady Hammamat graffito (above, p. 25) suggests that the tendency to make kings out of Hordjedef and Bauefre as well, had already begun by the 12th Dynasty; and the Abusir "list" (above, p. 25f). of the New Kingdom proves that by the 19th Dynasty this falsification of the 4th Dynasty succession had achieved canonicity. TC and the Saqqara "list"[23] undoubtedly embody this distortion, the former ending the dynasty with Shepseskaf, Hordjedef and Bauefre in that order, the latter perhaps adding a fourth at the end, the enigmatic *Vorlage* of Θαμφθις. The tradition to which Manetho fell heir is precisely this one. Following the two sons of Khufu (Khafre and Menkaure) he adds the two other sons, who by now have crystallized in order and position, viz. Hordjedef[24] and Bauefre. Then comes Shepseskaf and Thamphthis, bringing up the rear chiefly because they were remembered as the last members of the dynasty.

There is thus no need to involve the ingenuity of a postulated *Doppelkolumne* mistakenly read.[25] Africanus shows how the Epitome faithfully mirrors a tradition, popular in origin, which had become canonized both in the king-list and in the cult.[26]

The total for the dynasty as preserved in Africanus is 8; but the Saqqara list seems to have had 9, a number apparently reflected in Eusebius. The latter makes the builder of the Great Pyramid, i.e.

[23]For the length of the gap in the Saqqara list, see Meyer, *Chronologie* 104, 143.

[24]῾Ρατοίσης is *not* Redjedef; the falcon sign at the beginning of the name was probably suppressed in the transmission by the ubiquitous sun-disc which heads many cartouches.

[25]Cf. Helck, *Manetho*, 25f.

[26]As we have been at pains to show, all the "lists" save that of TC are in reality lists of offering recipients; and it is quite likely that the interpolation of Hordjedef, Bauefre and the original of Thamphthis entered the tradition in the first place by being included in the list of deceased royalty to whom offerings were made.

Khufu, the third king of the dynasty, not the second. Another name had been inserted either before or after Soris which would have had the effect, all things being equal, of increasing the total to 9. It is tempting to invoke the same tendency as reflected above, viz. the tendency to inflate by however many names were required to reach the number 9.[27]

Between the 19th Dynasty and the 3rd Century B.C. a break was construed to have existed after the reign of Nitokerty (TC iv, 8), and the family of Tety, or the 6th Dynasty, was terminated at that point with a total of six names. In the tradition transmitted by TC this left 5 names[28] unaccounted for before the summation (iv, 14), and a *wsf*-entry of six years. If, as seems likely, Iby of TC is identical with *Ḳ^{3}w-k^{3}-r^{c}*, no. 53 of Abydos,[29] then nos. 41-50 of the latter list are missing in the TC tradition, and would have had to be interpolated after Nitokerty. J. von Beckerath has argued persuasively[30] that the *wsf*-entry refers to this missing block of names, and was originally present in the line referring to Nitokerty. The tradition Manetho reflects construed the *wsf* of six years, the "kingless period,"[31] with the dimly-remembered rapid succession of 10 rulers, as a "7th Dynasty." and yielded to the enticements of folklore by conjuring up 70 kings for 70 days.[32] The five remaining names, viz. TC iv, 9-13, were then made into an "8th Dynasty," and interestingly Eusebius preserves the correct number of kings, viz. five.

The preoccupation with groups of nine rears its head once more in Manetho's *Aegyptiaca* Book I, in the section devoted to the aftermath of the Old Kingdom. The tradition of TC preserved the names of what undoubtedly are kings of Herakleopolis, with the line of summation which gave a total of "18." Interestingly and significantly, at this point in Manetho we encounter *two* dynasties of Herakleopolis, numbered 9 and 10. Dissimilation has produced an

[27]It is possible that Eusebius is mistakenly referring to the second Souphis who does, indeed, occupy third position in Africanus.

[28]Gardiner's placement of fragment 43 (*Canon*, pl. 2) is undoubtedly correct; *a fortiori* Iby, who of his immediate predecessors or successors was the only one to build a pyramid, modest though it was, should be credited with the longest of these short spans, viz. 4 years, 2 months.

[29]W. C. Hayes, *JEA* 32 (1946) 3ff.

[30]J. von Beckerath, *JNES* 21 (1962) 144f.

[31]We have given reasons above why *wsf* should be taken as "kingless period" rather than simply "missing (section)": p. 14ff. Why these 10 names should have been suppressed is impossible now to discover.

[32]Abetting the process may have been the aetiological understanding of [*w*]*sf*, "kingless period," as the numeral "70," Coptic ϣϥⲉ.

imbalance in the numbers of names, but the factor "9" is unmistakably present.[33]

Manetho's Dynastic Divisions in *Aegyptiaca II*

In his *Vorlage* Manetho encountered a fixed and received text in those columns dealing with the kings who were to comprise his 11th, 12th and 13th Dynasties. "The 6 kings [of Thebes(?)],"[34] "the total of kings of the residence [of Itj-towy], 8," (TC vi, 3), and "the kings [who fol]lowed [the House] of [King of Upper] and Lower Egypt [Sehte]pibre" (TC vi, 4) are unequivocal entries which permitted no tampering.

The state of the 12th Dynasty in the Epitome is, needless to say, not a pristine one; but the high quality of the original Manetho shows through at several points. Amenemhet I was mentioned at the end of Book I, in the catch-line which concluded the MS.[35] When his name occurs under the 12th Dynasty, however, it is preceded by that of a "Sosonchis," which can only be a garbling of "Senwosret" the father of Amenemhet I. Most likely Manetho included him, as the king-list of Amenophis I had done,[36] correctly noting him to be the progenitor of the family, but not suspecting that the epitomizer would misconstrue him as its first king. The number of kings of the dynasty is correctly noted as 7 (ignoring queen Sobek-nefrure), but their identity is confused and some have been omitted. Senwosret I, Amenemhet II and Senwosret II have been omitted (probably by homoioteleuton), Amenemhet III has been reduplicated,[37] and Sobek-nefrure added to fill out the required number.

For that section of his *Vorlage* extending from the end of the "Kings of the Residence [of Itj-towy]" (TC vi, 3) to the beginning of the Hyksos entry (TC x, 14) Manetho had something slightly in excess of 130 names to dispose of, a figure which corresponds well with the total 136 for the 13th and 14th Dynasties. The king-list tradition, as represented by TC, made a clear distinction between the block of names between vi, 3 and ix, 9, which are good Egyptian,

[33]As against J. von Beckerath, *ZÄS* 93 (1966) 13.
[34]Presumably an original * *W³st* stood at the head of TC v, 12-18, to account for Manetho's "Diospolis": Waddell, *Manetho*, 62f.
[35]There is no ambivalence in Amenemhet I's placement here: *pace* J. von Beckerath, *ZÄS* 92 (1965) 9-10.
[36]Above, p. 29.
[37]'Αμερής is a variant derived, like Λαμάρης from *Ny-m³ᶜt-rᶜ*. By Ptolemaic times Amenemhet III had long since achieved a celebrated deification in the Fayum: see E. Geraud, *ASAE* 40 (1940) 553ff; L. Habachi, *JEA* 41 (1955) 106ff.

and those between ix, 14 and x, 13, which make no sense as Egyptian names. This latter fact has prompted the counsel of despair by one scholar[38] that we are here dealing with "wholly fictitious beings." In fact, as I have pointed out elsewhere,[39] these names, fragmentary though they are, have all the earmarks of transliterated West Semitic names. They were remembered, correctly I think, to be intimately connected with the *ḥḳ³w ḫ³swt* which followed in the list, and it is probably they who, owing to a misinterpretation of *ḫ³swt*, gave rise to Manetho's 14th Dynasty of Xois (*Ḫ³sww*).

The subsequent period of invasion and foreign occupation is confused in the copies of the Epitome which have come down to us. Josephus's excerpt, as noted above,[40] treats the invasion in narrative form and ties it in to the name of Tutimaios of the 13th Dynasty. The Hyksos kings are then listed, but for the subsequent account of their expulsion the author reverts to narrative. Although it is clear that Josephus, or his immediate source, is at times abbreviating or paraphrasing, nonetheless, the broad outline of the account does not make clear how the numbered dynasties are distributed. Manetho must have indicated that from the Hyksos invasion to Ahmose, three dynasties intervened, but his treatment was sufficiently vague that the Epitome could throw up striking variants:

	Africanus	*Eusebius*	*Scholia*
Dyn. 15	"Hyksos"	Diospolis	---
Dyn. 16	"Shepherds"	Thebes	---
Dyn. 17	"Shepherds and Thebans"	"Hyksos"	"Hyksos"

Three salient facts must have shone through in Manetho's original: the Hyksos followed the "14th Dynasty"; their rule was contemporary with that of certain Theban kings; Manetho's "18th Dynasty" followed the expulsion immediately. The Epitome, used by Africanus, was influenced by the first two, the variant used in Eusebius by the last. Manetho's original must have been loose enough to allow such misinterpretation, and such vagueness could have inhered in a treatment which was almost wholly narrative to the

[38] Gardiner, *Canon*, 17.
[39] *Orientalia* 39 (1970) 21.
[40] Above, p. 229. On the identity of Tutimaios, see W. Helck, *AfO* 22 (1968-69) 94.

abandonment of the tabular form.[41]

That the Hyksos pericope Manetho quotes emanates from an Egyptian *Vorlage* is quite clear from the following considerations, though it is not always apparent to what extent Manetho departs from his original into paraphrase or summary.

1. The "East" (ἀνατολή). Manetho here uses the term as it is employed from the 5th Century B.C. on, as a reference to what in New Kingdom times would have been described as the "northern foreign countries."[42]

2. The "Assyrians." This blatant anachronism serves to explain why the tradition preserved a memory that the Hyksos had strongly fortified the eastern Delta. A *terminus a quo* for the formation of the present tradition thus emerges.[43]

3. "Phoenicia." The reference in Africanus[44] doubtless reflects the original Manetho. Behind it one can discern the Demotic *p³ tš n Ḫr*, "the land of Khor," which in Ptolemaic bilinguals is rendered into Greek as Φοινίκη.[45]

4. ὁ θέος ἀντέπνευσεν, literally "god blew against ..."; this sounds like an Egyptian locution. *Ḏꜥ*, "to storm," is used as a denominative verb in Ptolemaic times;[46] but more likely the key Egyptian word was *nšn*, "to rage," and the original phrase something like **wdi nṯr nšn.f ḥr.n*.[47]

[41]This is not to suggest that the 16th and 17th Dynasties are creations of the Epitome. TC already knows of two groups of kings following the Hyksos: cf. above, p. 13; and Manetho must somewhere have alluded to them. By no means, however, should one construe any of Manetho's numerical labels on "dynasties" as historically sacrosanct. (Cf. long ago the apt remarks of A. H. Gardiner, *JEA* 5 [1918] 48, n. 6) "14" was distinguished from "13" simply by a misunderstanding of *ḫ³swt*; "15" was distinguished from "14" because the former were "*ḥk³ ḫ³swt*" ruling from Avaris; "16" was distinguished from "15" because the former constituted the kings ruling in Thebes contemporary with 15 at Avaris; and "17" was distinguished from "16" simply because the former was a new family with Nubian connections and probably identified as from a town different from Thebes in TC (on the Nubian element, see D. B. Redford, *History and Chronology of the Eighteenth Dynasty of Egypt: Seven Studies* (Toronto, 1967) p. 28ff; The short-sightedness and ludicrous ramifications of accepting Manetho's numerical labels, totals of years and consecutive arrangement literally is well illustrated by the curiously naïve article of J. Mellaart, in *Antiquity* 53 (1979) 6ff (well answered by B. Kemp: *Antiquity* 54 [1980] 25ff).

[42]See below, p. 278, n. 77; on *i³btt* and its use here, see Gauthier, *Dictionnaire géographique* I, 17f; W. Helck, *Die altägyptische Gaue* (Wiesbaden, 1974) 198.

[43]Redford, *Orientalia* 39, 3ff.

[44]Waddell, *Manetho*, 90.

[45]Cf. H. Gauthier, H. Sottas, *Un décret trilingue en l'honneur de Ptolémée IV* (Cairo, 1925) 25 and n. 28; cf. J. J. Hess, *ZÄS* 30 (1892) 119, n. 1; C. Vandersleyen, *Les guèrres d'Amosis* (Brussels, 1971) 118; on *Fnḫw* see also K. Sethe, *Orientalistische Studien* (Leipzig, 1917) 305ff; J. Leclant *SAK* 11 (1984) 455ff.

[46] *Wb.* V, 534:8.

[47]Cf. *Wb.* II, 341:7.

5. ἀσήμοι, "undistinguished, worthless, picayune," is used of the invading people, corresponding very well to *ḫsi* in Egyptian.[48] *Ḫsi* means basically "weak," whether literally (of tired oarsmen,[49] a castrate,[50] rotten beams,[51] etc.), or figuratively "of low station."[52] A derived meaning is "vulgar" applied to speech or conduct,[53] and from there it is but a step to a nuance of contemptible worthlessness.[54]
6. The name of the foreigners. The etymology of *ḥ³swt* reflected in *-*sōs* (Coptic ϣⲱⲥ) indicates the phonetic shift *ḫ*>*s*, which must have taken place between c. 450 and 250 B.C.[55]
In all, therefore, it appears safe to say that the source of Manetho's account of the Hyksos was an Egyptian (Demotic) piece composed sometime late in the 5th Century B.C., or during the 28th through 30th Dynasties, and redolent of the patriotism of the times.

The Earlier 18th Dynasty

The state of the Egyptian king-list for the 18th and 19th Dynasties can be reasonably inferred from the New Kingdom offering list tradition (see above, p. 34ff), even though the final column of TC is now lost. Undoubtedly the correct order was preserved from Senakhtenre Taᶜo I[56] (c. 1600 B.C.) down to Merneptah, with the expected omission of Hatshepsut and the "Amarna" pharaohs. For the "Time of Troubles" which ushered out the 19th Dynasty, only

[48] *Wb.* III, 398; R. O. Faulkner, *A Concise Dictionary of Middle Egyptian* (Oxford, 1962) 204; W. Helck, *Die Lehre für König Merikare* (Wiesbaden, 1976) 54f.
[49] *Urk.* IV, 1280:2.
[50] D'Orbiney 8, 1: A. H. Gardiner, *Late Egyptian Stories* (Brussels, 1932) 17:4.
[51] G. Lefebvre, *Inscriptions concernant les grands prêtres d'Amon Romê-Roy et Amenhotep* (Paris, 1929) 33.
[52] Ptahhotep 175 (*ir ḫs.k šms s iḳr*, "if you are a 'weak' person, follow a competent man"); cf. 76, 489.
[53] Ptahhotep 209, 211.
[54] Peoples whom Egyptian texts term *ḫst* may very well have been (already), or were to be "defeated," but that in no way implies that the root *ever* meant "to be defeated": D. Lorton, *JARCE* 10 (1973) 65ff. Coptic ϩⲓⲥⲉ makes quite clear that the root always meant "to be troubled, wearied, suffering" (W. E. Crum, *A Coptic Dictionary* [Oxford, 1939] 710b; J. Černý, *A Coptic Etymological Dictionary* [Cambridge, 1976] 297). Significantly, in the Canopus decree the Persians are called *ḫsyw nw Prstt*, "the miserable Persians": K. Sethe, *Hieroglyphische Urkunden der Griechisch-Römischen Zeit* II (Leipzig, 1904) 128:11.
[55] K. Sethe, *ZDMG* 77 (1923) 159; J. Vergote, in *Textes et langages de l'Egypte pharaonique* (Cairo, 1972) 99; A. F. Shore, *ibid.*, 143.
[56] See now C. Vandersleyen *GM* 63 (1983) 67ff.

Sety II's name will have been recognized formally, at least to judge from the practice reflected in the Medinet Habu reliefs (above, p. 36f).

In however accurate a state the king-list emerged from the New Kingdom, however, Manetho's 18th Dynasty owes it only limited debt. The versions of the Epitome vary, probably indicating considerable distortion in the transmission and editing of the *Aegyptiaca* itself. Both Josephus and Theophilus give 18 names beginning with a Tethmosis who expelled the Hyksos, and ending with a "Sethos also called Ramesses." Africanus and Eusebius both give 16 names, commencing with an Amos(is) and ending with an Amenophath. Taken as a whole, all four share certain features in common: 1. they begin with the king who expelled the Hyksos, 2. they encorporate the first few kings of the 19th Dynasty, 3. they include rulers, like Hatshepsut and the "Amarna" pharaohs, who are never mentioned in official lists, and 4. they contain folkloristic material, not derived from official records.

The state of the 18th Dynasty in Manetho is the best example of this writer's willingness (if indeed he was conscious of what he was doing) of modifying a reliable king-list tradition in favour of aetiological *Märchen* in his temple library. In our view Manetho's 18th Dynasty knows well the pristine form of the king-list, but the latter has been re-worked in obedience to folkloristic and aetiological "readings" of the surviving monuments of the Thebaid, which were still standing in the 4th and early 3rd Centuries B.C. The thesis, that underlying the Manethonian version of the 18th Dynasty is the historical king-list of the New Kingdom, is supported both by the regnal year figures for positions 1, 6 and 7, and by the names in positions 1 and 6 through 9. The appended tables make this apparent:

The Early 18th Dynasty
(Hatshepsut excluded)

Position	*Name*	*Regnal years/months*
1	Amos(is)	25/4
2		
3		
4		
5		
6		25/10
7	Tuthmosis (IV)	9/8
8	Amenophis (III)	
9		
10		
11	(Tutankhamun)	9
12		

The Early 18th Dynasty
(Hatshepsut included)

Position — *Name*

1------------------------ Amos(is)
2
3
4
5
6-------------------- Thutmose (III)
7-------- Amenophis (II) [line from 7 crosses to Thutmose (IV)]
8-------- Thutmose (IV) [line from 8 crosses to Amenophis (II)]
9-------------------------- Orus
10
11
12------------------------ (Tutankhamun)

Clearly the surviving numbers for kings 1, 6 and 7 are based on a copy in which Hatshepsut is not present, i.e. the "official" version. The names, however, which appear in correct position can only be explained on the postulate of a name list in which she *was* present.

In both cases, however, names in positions 2 through 5/6, 7 and 8, and even that of position 1, have suffered an erroneous re-ordering. One hypothesis which has been tendered in explanation, viz. the misread columnar format, is too ingenious to command much respect.[57] If the error were as mechanical as this, would it not be soon detected and rectified? After all, there were enough *correct* lists extant in the Thebaid and elsewhere to provide ample opportunity for rectification. No, the erroneous ordering of certain names to have survived at all must have had a firm grounding in traditions, unquestioned at the time Manetho lived, which lent overriding weight to the new arrangement of names. In fact, these traditions are not at all difficult to discern.

Thutmose III is a pivotal figure in Manetho's 18th Dynasty. There is small wonder in this, as his memory lived on through Ramesside times and the Late Period.[58] and fostered a genuine interest in the works of this king in the Thebaid. The "Great Plan" of Dendera, which he found and refurbished, was commemorated in the 1st Century B.C.,[59] and his stela at Esna continued to be referred to in

[57]Helck, *Manetho* 40; cf. von Beckerath, *OLZ* 54, 9.
[58]Revered as *S³ Imn* by the king's-butler Ramesses-em-per-Amun (20th Dynasty): L. Speleers, *Recucil des Inscriptions égyptiens des Musées royaux du cinquantenaire à Bruxelles* (Brussels, 1923) 37, no. 133; as Osiris figure on 22nd Dynasty coffin, C. R. Williams, *JEA* 5 (1918) pl. 31.
[59]*Dendera* III, 78n, k; VI, pl. DLXXXIII, DXCI; U. Luft, *ZÄS* 99 (1973) 112.

Roman times.[60] In addition, he continued to be revered at Kom Ombo,[61] and Akhmim.[62] At Karnak Philip Arrhidaeus restored Thutmose III's shrine, thus inaugurating the reconstruction of the great king's monuments which continued into Ptolemaic times.[63]

A persistent tradition, which has affected the transmission of the Epitome, has it that the Hyksos were defeated by a "Misphragmouthosis," and finally expelled by his son, a "Thoumosis."[64] This tradition correctly maintains that the liberation of Egypt from Asiatic domination was the work of more than one king; but it has suppressed the names of the real participants in favour of better known kings. Long ago and convincingly was Misphragmouthosis identified as a melding together of the prenomen and nomen of Thutmose III;[65] Thoumosis is simply "Thutmose," pushed forward from 8th position to satisfy the historical fact that a king of that name had received the surrender of the *ḥḳ*^{3}*w ḫ*^{3}*swt* (at Megiddo).[66] The way the early 18th Dynasty was treated in the oral and king-list tradition also fostered confusion. Not only was Thutmose III considered by his successors to be an illustrious "father of the fathers," a term which would invite the false construction "founder (of the house),"[67] but also the earliest members of the family were often singled out and set apart in the public veneration of the Thebans. Assemblages of royal ancestors inspired by the Amenophis I - Ahmes Nofretari cult, such as those in the tombs of Khabakhent and Irdjanen,[68] concentrated on Amenophis I and his family to the *exclusion* of the Thutmosids. Small wonder, then, that the oral tradition which stemmed from a "reading" of such tomb scenes considered the name "Thutmose" as belonging to a group different from, and earlier than, Amenophis I and his clan. And in such an interpretation there is a grain of truth; nevertheless, conflation has introduced error.

[60]S. Sauneron, *ASAE* 52 (1952) 37; *idem*, *Esna* III, 287.
[61]*LD* III, 28, 1.
[62]H. Kees, *RT* 36 (1914) 51ff.
[63]Sethe, *Urk.* II, 7, 10; P-M II^{2}, 91 (206); 198 (12); J. Simons, *Handbook for the Study of Topographical Lists Relating to Western Asia* (Leiden, 1937) list V; Barguet, *Temple*, 110.
[64]Waddell, *Manetho*, 86.
[65]K. Sethe, *Die Thronwirren unter den Nachfolgern Thutmosis' I* (Leipzig, 1896) 71f; G. Maspero, *RT* 27 (1905) 15f; R. Weill, *JA* 1910, 325f; Helck, *Manetho*, 40; D. B. Redford, *JNES* 25 (1966) 119f; R. Krauss, *Das Ende der Amarnazeit* (Hildesheim, 1978) 25f.
[66]Cf. the writer in *Orientalia* 39, 41ff.
[67]Above, p. 52.
[68]Above, p. 45 and 48.

Primacy of place for a Thutmose (I), followed by a second (Chebron = *<ʿꜣ>-ḫpr-n-rʿ*)[69] is also suggested by the Ramesside groupings. At the Ramesseum Thutmose I appears as the leading figure in the second row, while the first row is brought to an end by Thutmose II;[70] in the orderly grouping in the tomb of Hormose[71] Thutmose I is the first king mentioned, and he is followed immediately by Thutmose II. At Deir el-Bahari, after the contemporary sovereigns Hatshepsut and Thutmose III have been excluded from consideration, the only ones remaining, who are commemorated both in original and modifed contexts, are Thutmose I and Thutmose II. In short, if any aberrational tendency forced the adoption of a "Thutmose" (who could be construed as the first) as the leading name in the list of 18th Dynasty kings, Thutmose II was bound to follow in his wake.

There is no need to conjure up a "Pseudo-Manetho" to explain away thc confusion here;[72] what we must realize is that Manetho in the original often displayed as "patchwork" a piece of writing as his motley sources! We have seen above that Manetho's organization of material at the 15th through 17th Dynasties was of a narrative sort sufficiently loose to invite confusion and variation in the versions of the Epitome. His account of the end of Hyksos rule was probably no different. Leaping ahead proleptically, he inserted the seige of Avaris (=Megiddo) and the treaty by which the Hyksos (=the coalition of Kadesh at Megiddo) were allowed to depart, under a Thutmosis (=Thutmose III), in his genuine and justifiable belief that "Thutmosis" had dompted the *Ḥḳꜣw ḫꜣswt*. Only then did he return to his king-list source and, by abruptly switching to a tabulary form, list the early kings of the 18th Dynasty. In short, Manetho's original presented an aspect basically the same as that which appears in Josephus!

That a queen should appear early in the list is not surprising, in the light of the historicity of Hatshepsut; but it also witnesses to the currency of a tradition independent of the written king-list. Whence and of what nature was this tradition? That it must somehow have been tied to the queen's sole surviving monument, Deir el-Bahari, seems obvious: very little of her work at Karnak was still on view in

[69]On the identity of Chebron, see Redford *JNES* 25, 117, n. 35; Krauss, *Das Ende der Amarnazeit*, 232.
[70]Above, p. 35.
[71]Above, p. 48.
[72]Krauss, *Das Ende der Amarnazeit*, 208.

the Late Period, thanks to the renovations of her successor.[73] But her temple at Deir el-Bahari was thriving in the Late Period; and from at least as early as the beginning of the 3rd Century B.C. was the centre of a healing cult of a divine ancestor named "Amenophis."[74] Small wonder, perhaps, that in the Manethonian tradition an "Amenophis" (scil. the first) should have found a place immediately before the name "Amesse." That the latter name belonged to a woman, a sister of an earlier entry in the list, would emerge from a simple perusal of the reliefs in the temple.

Another collocation of names which probably butressed the choice and sequence of "Amenophis, Amesse" was the ubiquitous combination, both in private and royal commemorative reliefs, of Amenophis I and his mother Ahmose (Nofretari).[75] This was the source whence emerged the name *Amesse* (<Ahmose),[76] which attached itself to the tradition of a female pharaoh. The sequence Amenophis, Ahmose, Thutmose (I) was historically sound, and it is this sequence that underlies the names in the third, fourth and fifth positions in Manetho. Thutmose I's name is here replaced by a reduplication of the prenomen of Thutmose III, but his 12 years and 9 months betray his erstwhile presence.[77]

In positions 6 through 8 of the Manethonian list two matatheses have taken place: one of names, the other of numbers.[78] Misphragmouthosis (position 6), one of the few "complete" names (nomen + prenomen) we have in Manetho, derives from *Mn-ḫpr-rꜥ Ḏḥwty-ms*, and the identity was so firmly fixed to the birth name "Thutmose," that it attracted to it the name "Tuthmosis" (originally position 8). This relegated "Amenophis" to eighth position, a change bolstered by the attraction of the adjacent "Hor" (Amenophis III). The interchange of numbers came about when Thutmose III gravitated to the sixth position, viz. 25/10, while "Amenophis" was compensated by 30/10, originally attached to the name Misphragmouthosis.

[73]On the date and motivation of Thutmose III's renovations, see C. F. Nims, *ZÄS* 93 (1966) 97ff.

[74]D. Wildung, *Imhotep und Amenhotep* (Munich and Berlin, 1977) 257ff.

[75]See above, p. 52f; M. Gitton, in *LdÄ* I (1972) 104ff.

[76]Cf. von Beckerath, *OLZ* 54, 10; E. Meyer, *Geschichte des Altertum* II (Stuttgart and Berlin, 1938) 1, p. 78. Certainly not a derivation from *Ḥꜣt-Špswt*, as Fecht, *ZDMG* 35, 120; cf. E. Hornung, *Untersuchungen zur Chronologie und Geschichte des neuen Reiches* (Wiesbaden, 1964) 33 and n. 22.

[77]Redford, *JNES* 25, 116f.

[78]Helck, *Manetho*, 40, 66; J. von Beckerath, *OLZ* 62 (1967) 10.

The Lost Tale of King Hor

Hor has been identified with Amenophis III,[79] Akhenaten,[80] Horemheb,[81] and even with Horus son of Isis.[82] The grounds for the identification with Akhenaten, viz. the postulated derivation of Ωρ from *Ḫurriya* (EA 41), has been found wanting;[83] and I can find no attested hypocoristicon "Hor" for Horemheb.

On the other hand, several considerations militate in favour of an identification with Amenophis III. The position, ninth, in the list of 18th Dynasty rulers, if Hatshepsut be included, is the same in both cases; and the length of reign given Hor corresponds very well (in a variant preserved in Eusebius) with Amenophis III's floruit.[84] Moreover, the name Ωρ is understandable, not on the basis of a supposed origin in a compound involving *ḫpr*, but as a straight rendering of *Ḥr*, "Horus." As a common noun denoting the monarch, *Ḥr* can be applied to any king in contexts not directly related to the myth;[85] but during Amenophis III's reign such uses abound to a striking degree. *Ḥr* in titles relating the king to his palace, a use known elsewhere, is predicated of Amenophis III in the epithets of his nobles.[86] A close personal relationship is indicated by the affixing of a third person suffix to *Ḥr* in some cases: Mutemweya, in a text dating from her son's reign, is called "one who soothes (*sḥtp*) her Horus with her voice,"[87] while Amenophis son of Hapu calls himself "one who does good things for his Horus."[88] In a

[79]Cf. Helck, *Manetho*, 40; Meyer, *Chronologie*, 90, n. 1.
[80]K. Sethe, *ZÄS* 41 (1904) 50; Maspero, *RT* 27, 18; R. Hari, *Horemheb et la reine Moutnodjmet* (Geneva, 1961) 228.
[81]Krauss, *Das Ende der Amarnazeit* 224f.
[82]J. Krall, *SAWWien* 96 (1880) 265.
[83]G. Fecht, *ZÄS* 85 (1960) 86, n. 1.
[84]Hornung, *Chronologie und Geschichte*, 36; von Beckerath's objections (*OLZ* 62, 11) are not compelling.
[85]Cf. the queen's titles *smrt-Ḥr*, *ḫt-Ḥr*, *tist-Ḥr*: H. Gauthier, *ASAE* 24 (1924) 206; L. K. Sabbhy, *The Development of the Titulary and Iconography of the Ancient Egyptian Queen* (PhD dissertation, Toronto, 1982); "Horus, that is (*imy*) Osiris N," PT 19a; "revered before his Horus (i.e. the king)," Cairo 1277; *Ḥr Wn-nfr* (in cartouche), Ranke, *PN* I, 246:17.
[86]*Imy-ib Ḥr nb ꜥḥ*: *ASAE* 42 (1942) 458, *Urk.* IV, 1908:9; *imy-ib n Ḥr m pr.f*: *Urk.* IV, 1811:18, cf. 1790:4; *swꜥš.n.f Ḥr nb ꜥḥ*: *Urk.* IV, 1846; *ẖn n Ḥr m-ẖnw ꜥḥ.f*: *MIOF* 4 (1956) 11ff; *ꜥḳyw ḥr Ḥr m ꜥḥ*: *Urk.* IV, 1927:8.
[87]*Urk.* IV, 1771:14; Tiy is *sm³yt Ḥr imyt-ib.f*: G. Jequier, *Les temples memphites et thébines* (Paris, 1920) pl. 77.
[88]*Urk.* IV, 1817:11.

sd-festival text from the Karnak talatat reliefs of Akhenaten,[89] but clearly derived from the *Vorlage* resuscitated by Amenophis III, the "king's-children" intone a hymn in which they call the king "our Horus." The tendancy to call Amenophis III "Horus" may have been inspired by the rhetoric surrounding the concept of the falcon on the *serekh* as an hypostasis of the king. "Horus *Ḫ*ᶜ*-m-ḥ*ᶜ*t*" is found as an appelative of Amenophis III,[90] and Nefersekheru is "one who enters the palace, an enforcer of the laws in exalting Him-Who-is-upon-His-Serekh."[91] The imagery of the falcon, suggesting the hybrid icon of the "falcon-king" known during this period.[92] insinuates itself into the royal epithets of Amenophis III: he is "a divine Horus, of variegated plummage, who enfolds the Two Lands with his wings."[93] "this Horus, strong-armed,"[94] "a good Horus, lord of Eternity,"[95] "a divine falcon (*bik*) who came forth from the body of god,"[96] "a champion of all the gods, Horus, variegated of plummage."[97]

There is no doubt, therefore, that "Horus" was, along with the "Dazzling Sun-disc,"[98] a known and long remembered sobriquet of Amenophis III, and there is no reason to reject the identification of the Manethonian "Hor" with this king.

The only tradition preserved in Manetho has to do with Hor's alleged "desire to see the gods"; and this is mentioned in a single aside appended in Josephus to the start of the Osarsiph legend.[99] The latter, through its setting in time in the reign of an "Amenophis" and the role of Amenophis son of "Paapis," clearly is to be placed in the reign of Amenophis III. In keeping with Manetho's practice of not interrupting his condensed tabulation of dynasties, but of reserving long narratives for the end of the table, keying them into the proper reign by prefixing them with the name of the king in question, the Osarsiph tale comes at the end of Manetho's list, but should be

[89]R. W. Smith, D. B. Redford, *The Akhenaten Temple Project* I *Initial Discoveries* (Warminster, 1977) pl. 77; at the raising of the *djed* in Memphis Amenophis III is likened to "the father Horus Tatenen": *Urk.* IV, 1860:12; cf. 1865:13.
[90]*Urk.* IV, 1795:1, 1745:2.
[91]*MIOF* 4, 15.
[92]D. B. Redford, *JARCE* 13 (1976) 51; B. M. Bryan, *The Reign of Tuthmosis IV* (PhD dissertation, Yale University, 1980) 239ff.
[93]*Urk.* IV, 1761:7.
[94]*Urk.* IV, 1694:12.
[95]*Urk.* IV, 1747:11.
[96]*Urk.* IV, 1701:5, 1743:15.
[97]*Urk.* IV, 1695:14.
[98]See the writer, *JARCE* 13, 51.
[99]Waddell, *Manetho* 120 (232).

construed as coming from the reign of Hor. In the post-Manethonian transmission of the text the two names "Hor" and "Amenophis" were falsely understood as two different kings, and with the passing from memory of Manetho's simple format, its position in the *Aegyptiaca* was construed as its correct historical placement. That is to say, it belonged to a king called "Amenophis" who had followed Ramesses the Great.[100] The topos of the "Impure Ones," represented here by the Osarsiph account, is one of those "floating" plot motifs, now attached to the memory of Bocchoris, now to Amenophis, possibly also to Nectanebo II; but the tradition of "seeing the gods" is peculiar to Hor/Amenophis III alone.[101]

Now "seeing the gods" and the desire to do so are themes well known in Egyptian literature. While it is true that in the Late Period and Ptolemaic times visibly conjuring the gods by occult means was a favourite motif,[102] it is also true that "seeing the gods" was a cultic act of long-standing,[103] and the expressed wish to "see the beauty of god X" a pious hope.[104] It might also signify to attend upon a god, to be in the congregation, as when Amenophis son of Hapu calls the Thebans "ye who desire to see Amun."[105] Seeing the sun-(god) was also a well-known theme in New Kingdom sun-hymns, which were especially popular in Amenophis III's reign, on the eve of the Amarna period.[106] Amenophis III states expressly that "seeing the gods of the West" was the specific purpose of the Feast of the Valley,

[100]The mistake probably lies in the connexion of the name "Amenophis." One version of the motif of the "Impure Ones" is set in the reign of an "Amenophis" (undoubtedly the third of that name), and another in the reign of Bocchoris: see below, p. 276f. The historical reality of invasion from the north under Merneptah, as well as the vague similarity of the names *Amenophis and *(M)enephthah (Ammenemphthis in Africanus) probably abetted the transfer to a third king. (For the transcription of the names see Maspero, *RT* 27, 19; Meyer, *Chronologie*, 29; W. Struve, *ZÄS* 63 [1929] 46ff; K. Sethe, *ZÄS* 66 [1931] 1f). The desire to *see* the gods should possibly also be compared with the tradition in Herodotus (ii.111) and Diodorus (i.59.3) that Pheron (i.e. Proteus, or Merneptah) had been struck *blind* for blasphemy.

[101]In the version of the "Impure" motif in Josephus it is extraneous to the main plot, simply providing, and that artificially, a motivation for the king's approach to the wise man.

[102]Cf. I Khamois, iii, 14 and *passim*; for personal names of the pattern *M³.n.i DN*, see Ranke, *PN* I, 143, no. 22; J. G. Griffiths, *Plutarch's De Iside et Osiride* (Cambridge, 1970) 80; for Herakles' desire to see his father Amun (Zeus), see Herodotus ii.42 (W. W. How, J. Wells, *A Commentary on Herodotus*² I [Oxford, 1928] 187; Lloyd, *Herodotus, Book II: Introduction*, 192ff) cf. also Clement *Exhort* vi.59.

[103]*M³³ nṯr*: *Edfu* III, 58, 245.

[104]*Wb.* II, 7:14-16. Mortuary wishes of this sort are no more common than in other reigns: cf. *Urk.* IV, 1819; 1830:2, 18; 1874:12; 1854:3; for a royal wish, see R. Mond, O. Myers, *The Temples of Armant* (London, 1940) pl. 104 (Ramesses II).

[105]G. Legrain, *ASAE* 14 (1914) 19.

[106]Literature in Redford *JARCE* 13, 50.

and his mortuary temple constituted to that end "a resting place" for Amun when he crossed the river.[107] In the vicinity of that temple, at a point opposite (*ḫft-ḥr*) Luxor, Amenophis III built a *m*^{3}*rw* for Amun, a garden where he might enjoy himself, and where foreign tribute might be received.[108] Now it is quite clear both from the monuments he has left behind, and from his unequivocal statements that Amenophis III's main policy throughout his reign was the restoration of temples and their cults. The repeated epithets "building the temples of all the gods and fashioning their cult images" adumbrates this policy succinctly.[109] He was the "Golden Horus, champion (*nḏ*) of the gods, who fashioned their bodies (*ḥmw*),"[110] and of him Amun said that he had "fashioned the Ennead, each one in his body, (as) I had made him."[111] In fact, the Ennead themselves in their address to Amun on Amenhotpe III's behalf on the stela in the mortuary temple, are made to say[112] "It is Nebmare, thy son, that has made this temple for thee. Praise thou him for it, for he has fashioned us in the knowledge that our lord would rejoice, that he[113] might see us existing upon earth."

It seems to the present writer that it is Amenophis III's oft-repeated goal of restoring temples and gods' images that they might be seen upon earth, that lies at the root of the later tradition of Hor's desire to see the gods. Both the name "Hor" and the folklore about him could easily have been derived, 1000 years later, from the monuments still standing at Thebes. By that time, too, the *magical* significance of "seeing the gods," an ability ascribed to the occult, would have lent an added dimension to the phrase.[114]

[107] *Urk.* IV, 1650:7-8; S. Schott, *Das schöne Feste vom Wüstentale* (Wiesbaden, 1953) 6; cf. also Kitchen, *RI* III, 163:6, 185:6.

[108] *Urk.* IV. 1651f. The rendering "viewing place" is that of B. Gunn (*City of Akhenaten* I [London, 1923] 156f) and A. Badawy (*JEA* 42 [1956] 58f). M. Görg may well be correct in relating *m*^{3}*rw* to Hebrew מְלוֹא (*GM* 20 [1976] 29f), but the customary determinative (Gardiner, *Grammar*^{3}, D6) still suggests a connexion with *m*^{33}, "to see." Note especially that in the Ptolemaic period the shrine on the west of Thebes devoted to Amenophis son of Hapu, who himself figures prominently in the Osarsiph legend, is called a *m*^{3}*rw*: Wildung, *Imhotep und Amenhotep*, 166f.

[109] Cf. *Urk.* IV, 1690:2, 1743:3.

[110] *Urk.* IV, 1751:13; 1668:13, "refurbishing [the temples of all the gods], fashioning their bodies (*ḥmw*) of gold."

[111] *Urk.* IV, 1754:8.

[112] *LD* III, pl. 72:21-22; *Urk.* IV, 1676:9-13.

[113] The antecedent is ambiguous: it could be the king, but more likely the god.

[114] Already J. Krall, *SAWWien* 105 (1883) 406ff; cf. also the Aramaic *ʾš ḥzh ʾlhn*, "the man who saw the gods," as an epithet of Balaam at Deir ᶜAllah: J. Hoftijzer, *BA* 39 (1976) 13; A. Cacquot, A. Lemaire, *Syria* 54 (1977) 194. Interestingly, Nectanebo II took "falcon" as one of his epithets (cf. H. De Meulenaere, *CdE* 35 [1960] 99f); and this may well have contributed to the Hor legend.

The Last 9 (7) Names of the 18th Dynasty

The four entries in the list from Akencherres to Harmais are among the most enigmatic in Manetho, despite the recent exhaustive treatment that has been accorded them.[115] One's initial impulse is to pose the question, in which sources did Manetho find these names? For the evidence of the state of the king-list in the New Kingdom, such as it is, suggests that the Amarna pharaohs had suffered the elimination of their names and the loss of their years to Horemheb.[116] Yet Manetho's account proves that later tradition correctly remembered that between Amenophis III and Horemheb four individuals, who had adopted the cartouche, had intervened. Several considerations may help in eliciting the sources.

1. *The names.* The names of the pharaohs in question were *not* remembered with exactness. Akhenaten's name was supressed in favour of the pejorative (*pꜣ*) *ḫrw* (<<A>χερρης);[117] otherwise the only names remembered were those of the two brothers, viz. the throne name of Smenkhkare, *ꜥnḫ-ḫprw-rꜥ* ('Ακενχερης) and a garbled form of the prenomen and nomen of Tutankhamun ('Ραθωτις).

2. *The lengths of reign.* Of these the figures given for the names in third and fourth position are fictitious, being derived from the 12/1 of Akencherres. Of the first two, the 9 years for Rathotis is a reasonably accurate reflection of the 9 years, x months of Tutankhamun,[118] while the 12/1 of Akencherres is based on a misunderstanding of a real date. The "durbar" held at Amarna under Akhenaten is dated to year 12, vi, 8.[119] This is twelve years and one month after the accession.[120] The total was undoubtedly the result of a misunderstanding of the date recorded in the two Amarna tombs in which the scene appears, misconstrued as the terminal date of the reign.

115 Krauss, *Das Ende der Amarnazeit*, *passim*.

116 Above, chap. 1, *passim*; Redford, *JNES* 25, 122ff.

117 *Wb.* III, 325; cf. the pejorative use in the 19th Dynasty, when Akhenaten is alluded to: A. H. Gardiner, *The Inscription of Mes* (Leipzig, 1905) 23, n. 82; G. A. Gaballa, *The Memphite Tomb Chapel of Mose* (Warminster, 1978) pl. LXIII; A. H. Gardiner *JEA* 24 (1938) 124. Helck's understanding of the name as an "auswählende Lesung" of parts of the cartouches of Akhenaten (*Manetho* 41) seems a trifle forced; cf. Krauss, *Das Ende der Amarnazeit*, 16.

118 Redford, *JNES* 25, 122.

119 N. de G. Davies, *The Rock Tombs of el-Amarna* II (London, 1905) pl. 37; III, pl. 13.

120 Redford, *JNES* 25, 121f; W. J. Murnane, in J. H. Johnson, E. F. Wente (eds.) *Studies in Honor of George R. Hughes* (Chicago, 1976) 163ff.

3. *The mode of transmission.* The offering list tradition as reflected at Abydos and in the Theban exemplars of the 19th Dynasty knows nothing of the four Amarna pharaohs. Horemheb follows Amenophis III immediately, and has even, in the tradition reflected in the Mes inscription, taken over the years of his four predecessors. But this is not the total picture. The Manethonian data must stem from another source, and that must be, at least in part, oral tradition.[121] Possibly before the close of the New Kingdom the oral transmission of names had coalesced with the folkloristic "readings" of extant monuments to produce in the king-list a *written* treatment of the "Amarna" kings.

It has long been recognized that, both in Josephus and the Epitome, the kings at the beginning of the 19th Dynasty have been reduplicated at the end of the 18th Dynasty.[122] Some writers have cried out in despair, calling Manetho "incredibly garbled," and speaking of "much obvious confusion,"[123] or branding his data "confused and corrupted almost beyond the point of repair in their present state ... and at our present level of knowledge."[124] Such remarks are in themselves somewhat confused and certainly despairing, but they are understandable and excusable as reactions to the fanciful solutions offered by some.[125] In fact, while unhistorical in its present condition, Manetho's list is certainly no mystery. Manetho has faithfully followed one source for the king-list tradition down to the Ramesside period; at this point there is a clean break, and with the 19th Dynasty a new source begins.[126] Above we have traced the origin of the king-list, of which TC is our surviving exemplar, from its beginnings in the 12th Dynasty, through the Second Imtermediate Period when it was passed on by the Itj-towy scribes, and into the New Kingdom when it came into the possession of, and was influenced by the Thebans. We have further taken note

[121]Cf. von Beckerath, *OLZ* 54, 10; but cf. Krauss, *Das Ende der Amarnazeit*, 250, notes 1 and 2 with the literature cited and discussion.

[122]Already observed by Lepsius and Bunsen: cf. A. Wiedemann, *Aegyptische Geschichte* I (Gottha, 1884) 305; Meyer, *Chronologie*, 90; Struve, *ZÄS* 63, 49f; Maspero, *RT* 27, 18; E. Drioton, J. Vandier, *L'Egypte*[4] (Paris, 1962) 352.

[123]Sir A. H. Gardiner, *Egypt of the Pharaohs* (Oxford, 1961) 241f.

[124]Kitchen, *Third Intermediate Period*, § 416.

[125]E.g. that the calculation of classical dates with relation to Egyptian chronology resulted in the reduplication of the person of Sety (Maspero, *RT* 27, 25f; *idem*, *JdS* 1901, 666f); or that the names Amenophis-Armais, standing in an original format before Sethos-Ramesses, migrated to their present position thanks to the insinuation of the Aegyptos-Danaos legend: Krauss, *Das Ende er Amarnazeit*, 228f.

[126]There is no real contamination: both sources were ancient and deemed authoritative, but were mutually exclusive: cf. Hornung, *Chronologie und Geschichte*, 115.

of the interest exhibited in the royal descent by the Ramesside kings and their subjects, which issued in the unparalleled display of reverential worship of the king's ancestors, both in the cult, and graphically on temple walls and in private tombs. In none of these "lists" is there any break indicated in the vicinity of Horemheb or Ramesses I,[127] but the line which ends with Ramesses II runs on without interruption from the beginning of the Theban house which drove out the Hyksos. Undoubtedly the same unbroken line was once present on the last page of TC (now lost), and probably listed *"Fourteen kings of Wese" beginning with Seqenenre and concluding with Ramesses II. The point which this presentation of the pedigree sought to make, as we have demonstrated above was that Sety I and Ramesses II were the legitimate descendents of the great kings who had come out of Thebes a century and a half earlier, and the list of these royal names constituted their august family tree.

This concept of the pedigree was a powerful one in the thinking of the Ramessides, and while it may have been lost on subsequent generations, the solid block of names ending with Sety I or Ramesses II, to which it gave rise in the king-list, remained the *only accepted* way of regarding the kings who had preceded Ramesses the Great. Whether the edition of the king-list produced under the Ramessides (i.e. the version represented by TC) survived intact and without additional names, a closed corpus, with a prestige sufficient to warrant its recopying down to Manetho's time, is a moot point. But that the predecessors of Ramesses II had made up a single, unbroken line was by Manetho's time an unquestioned truth which could be demonstrated, if need be, by recourse to the standing monuments of the Thebaid, viz. the walls of the Ramesseum (above, p. 34ff), or the Theban tombs (above, p. 45ff), or by surviving cult objects (above, p. 37ff).

The second source used by Manetho, viz. that for his "19th" Dynasty, is the living, on-going king-list which experienced a fresh start with the advent of a new family. While the "pedigree" concept which informed the "18th" Dynasty of Manetho shows marked southern influence, or at least pandered to Theban sensibilities, the list which underlies the 19th through 30th Dynasties shows all the earmarks of a northern origin.[128] It takes its rise from the strong feeling of family identity which was borne in on the consciousness of Ramesses II, and which we have seen reflected in the memorials he

[127]Soberly to ponder whether Horemheb is, or is not, to head *our* 19th Dynasty (as A. K. Philips, *Orientalia* 46 [1977] 116ff) is an exercise for schoolmen.
[128]Below, p. 297ff.

left behind honouring his father (and grandfather).[129] Born first perhaps in the new city of Per-Ramesses and later transferred to Memphis, the 19th Dynasty king-list tradition flourished with little influence from the Thebaid, and went back no further than the immediate family of Ramesses the Great. It was the mechanical and unhistorical tacking together of both sources, sometime in the millennium which intervened between the 19th Dynasty and Manetho's day, that produced the unhistorical conflation.

The specific configuration of the 18th Dynasty remained a trifle fluid thanks to the tension between two conflicting desiderata, viz. the urge to incorporate the *traditional number* of the members of the Ramesside pedigree, and the resolve not to ignore the seeming importance of folk history in shaping the account. The traditional number was 14 names,[130] or 15 if Ramesses II was set apart.[131] But the "folk-readings" of monuments in the Thebaid sought to interpolate names that had never enjoyed official recognition in the list, e.g. the queen and the Amarna pharaohs. Eusebius has preserved the number 14 by excisions at precisely the points where these expendable names occur.[132] Africanus gives 16 names, but he reveals vestigial evidence that the number "15" weighed heavily in his source: only 15 of his names are coupled with lengths of reign. Josephus, or his source, on the other hand, has inflated the number to 18 by (a) misunderstanding the mechanism of organization Manetho employed, and (b) using a glossed and slightly doctored version of the *Aegyptiaca*. As we pointed out above, and will have occasion to mention again, Manetho was wont to leave a bald list of kings intact, and reserve his narrative pericopes on any of the members of the list until a convenient stopping point,[134] Then, by repeating the name as a catch-line, he would key the narrative into the pertinent spot in the preceding list. In the copy used by Josephus, which originally, as in Africanus, ended with Sety I,[135] two narrative sections were appended to the list of 16 names, one on King Amenophis (position 8), and the other on Sety I (Amenophath, position 16), each introduced by the key name. These in the course of time were misconstrued as *additional* royal names and provided with lengths of reign, were duly tacked on to the end of the list to produce some such sequence as the following:

[129]Above, p. 191.
[130]Ramesseum and other private memorials: above, p. 34, 38, 40, 44.
[131]Cf. the Daily Liturgy: above, p. 37f.
[132]Waddell, *Manetho*, 116f: Amensis, Athoris and Cencheres are missing.
[133]Above, p. 229.
[134]On the identification, see Sethe, *ZÄS* 66, 1f; L. Borchardt, *Die Mittel zur Zeitlichen Festlegung von Punkten der ägyptischen Geschichte* (Cairo, 1935) 17.

....
Harmais
Ramesses
Amenophath
Amenophis
Sethos-Ramesses

Subsequently, partly by a process of dissimilation and partly through the attraction of the two preceding names, "Amenophath" was replaced by the slightly distorted nomen of Ramesses the Great; and the two narratives were reversed in order, because of the association of Sethos-Ramesses in the story with Harmais.

8

The Narratives at the End of *Aegyptiaca* II

As noted at the conclusion of chapter six, Manetho's 18th Dynasty ended with two narratives, one about Harmais, the other about Amenophis (III) and Osarsiph. Both, as will shortly appear, are of Upper Egyptian origin, and smack of the oral transmission the Egyptians would have denoted as "the *sd̲d* of the people."[1] In order the better to appreciate the Osarsiph tale the topos which we might dub "the dissolution and restoration of society" will be examined briefly.

The Harmais Story

The Harmais tale is appended by Manetho to the name which now stands last in the 18th Dynasty table, viz. Σεθος ὁ και Ῥαμεσσαμς.[2] In Herodotus it is part of the Sesostris story,[3] and in

[1] *Sd̲d* (*Wb.* IV, 394f) is the word which comes closest to our "oral tradition," or "orally transmitted folklore": cf. R. O. Faulkner, *A Concise Dictionary of Middle Egyptian* (Oxford, 1962) 260; also the semantic range of its descendent, Coptic ϣⲁϫⲉ : Sir W. E. Crum, *A Coptic Dictionary* (Oxford, 1939) 612b; J. Černý, *A Coptic Etymological Dictionary* (Cambridge, 1976) 263. This is not to say, of course, that *sd̲d* is a technical term for a particular *Gattung*: see H. Grapow, *Sprachliche und schriftliche Formung ägyptischer Texte* (Glückstadt and New York, 1936) 59, n. 24.

[2] Waddell, *Manetho*, 100ff; J. Krall, *SAWWien* 105 (1883) 403ff; for the unhistorical linking of the story with the Danaus legend, see A. Wiedemann, *Herodots Zweites Buch* (Leipzig, 1890) 417; and most recently R. Krauss, *Das Ende der Amarnazeit* (Hildesheim, 1978) 222ff; see also M. Astour, *Hellenosemitica* (Leiden, 1965) 95f.

[3] Herodotus ii.105-109.

Diodorus part of the related narrative of Sesoösis.[4] Its components may be listed as follows: 1. the armed forces Sethos disposed of were of surpassing magnitude, and comprised both an army and a fleet: 2. with them he led sea-borne and land attacks on Cyprus, Phoenicia, and later Assyria and Media: 3. Sethos's brother, whom he had left to govern Egypt, rebelled against him took the throne and violated the queen: 4. on his return Sethos was met by his brother and the priests at Pelusium and invited to the treacherous banquet from which he barely escaped; 5. Sethos re-took the kingdom and punished Harmais with expulsion.

The narrative knows that Harmais/Horemheb, the brother, was an *appointee*, and not one born to the purple; and also that he had married a queen with the right of inheritence.[5] Beyond that, however, the legend owes more to the aetiological "reading" of standing monuments than it does to historical record. Two misunderstandings are basic to the evolution of the Harmais story: 1. the identification of Sety I with Ramesses II, surviving vestigially in the *Beinamen* appended to "Sethos," and 2. the conflation of the reliefs at Medinet Habu with those at Karnak. Sethos's distinction of having amassed large forces of cavalry and a fleet surely arises out of the scenes of the sea-battle and the fight on land at Medinet Habu, where ships and chariots figure prominently.[6] The campaigns against Cyprus and Phoenicia are an interpretation of the reliefs of the wars against the Sea Peoples; for the former in fact one must read "northerners," or "the peoples of the sea,"[7] for the latter simply "Djahy" which also figures prominently in the Medinet Habu record. The second pair of names, introduced by και παλιν (which separates them from the first), removes us to Karnak and specifically Sety I's reliefs on the north wall of the hypostyle. Here we must discern behind "the Assyrians" and "the Medes" of the legend the original Amurru and Khatti respectively. For the making free with the queen with which the tale charges Harmais one need look no further than the High Gate at Medinet Habu, and the scenes of familiarity between naked harim-girls and a royal figure in *diadem*.[8] The triumphal return to Pelusium (for which read "Sile") is also a

[4]Diodorus i.57.

[5]For the discussion to date on Mut-beneret, see Krauss, *Das Ende der Amarnazeit*, 17, n. 2-4, where the relevant literature is cited.

[6]On the influence of the Medinet Habu reliefs on the Sesostris legend, see R. Hari, *BSEG* 5 (1981) 18ff.

[7]Tradition correctly remembered the Sea People's assocation with the island: cf. A. Strobel, *Der spätbronzezeitliche Seevölkerstrum* (Berlin and New York, 1976) 43ff.

[8]P-M II^2, 486f.

folkloristic interpretation of the relief on the north wall of the Karnak hypostyle, showing Sety, his army and their captives crossing the bridge over the frontier canal, to the cheers of the assembled throng.[9] Finally, the escape from the banquet is, as Spiegelberg has showed,[10] a dragoman's interpretation of the oft-recurring scene of pharaoh standing upon the prostrate forms of two enemies, transformed for purposes of the topos, into the unfortunate offspring of the king.

The Harmais legend is thus entirely Theban in origin. It purports to provide a consistent and unified interpretation, by and for those who could not read the sacred script, of the largest imperial monuments of the southern capital, still standing at a certain point in time. It is impossible now to specify a date for the story. Certainly we are well within the First Millennium B.C., and possibly even in a post-Saite milieu.

The" Dissolution and Restoration" Theme in the New Kingdom and Later

The theme of the break-down of society and the destruction of its physical creations is found among literary commonplaces beginning as far back as the First Intermediate Period.[11] In form, it first appears as a "Lament,"[12] placed in the mouth of a fabled wiseman and committed to a literary tradition; but it shows all the signs (metric structure, mnemonic devices etc.) of an origin and early transmission in the oral tradition. The troubles are set forth in terms of the anarchic and reversed social conditions of a revolution in human society.[13] The blame is variously assigned: now to human error and moral

[9]P-M II[2], 55(3).

[10]W. Spiegelberg, *Die Glaubwürdigkeit von Herodots Bericht über Aegypten im Lichte der ägyptischen Denkmäler* (*Orient und Antike* 3; Heidelberg, 1926) 25.

[11]Above, p. 114f.

[12]Possibly *nḫwt*: *Wb*. II, 305:17; cf. Grapow, *Sprachliche und Schriftliche Formung*, 60, n. 29. But it is difficult to discern in this word a technical, literary term: see H. Goedicke, *Report about the Dispute of a Man with His Ba* (Baltimore, 1970) 183, 210, n. 307; cf. also F. Junge, in J. Assmann, and others (eds.), *Fragen an die altägyptische Literatur* (Wiesbaden, 1977) 277f.

[13]H. Frankfort, *Ancient Egyptian Religion* (New York, 1948) 84ff; J. Spiegel, *Soziale und weltanschauliche Reformbewegungen im alten Aegypten* (Heidelberg, 1950), *passim*; J. Wilson, *The Culture of Ancient Egypt* (Chicago, 1957) 106ff; A. Klasens, *Etudes et travaux* 2 (1968) 5ff.

deficiency, now to incoming Asiatics and Nubians.[14] Occasionally the fault is laid at the door of the gods themselves.[15] Inevitably the treatment is poetic; the viewpoint (though not necessarily the time of composition) is within the "Time of Troubles."

From the Middle Kingdom a new, and royally sponsored, topos appears: that of the Time of Troubles, now set right, and viewed with the benefit of hindsight. The form is either that of a royal speech, or a preamble explaining government action, and as such does not share in the "epic" proportions of the older "Lament."

1. Tod-inscription of Senwosret I

From the First Intermediate Period come descriptions of anarchic conditions set right by the 11th Dynasty kings,[16] but they do not set out to expatiate upon the period when the lawlessness in question came about. The 12th Dynasty, however, does seem a little more interested in speculating upon what brought in the Time of Troubles. At Tod there is a long historical text of Senwosret I, now almost wholly concealed by reliefs of the Ptolemaic period,[17] which, in part, describes the conditions of the temples as he found them. The preserved portion begins couched in the laconic "day-book" style, then slips into a *verbatim* speech of the king.

x + 1) "... the King of Upper and Lower Egypt, Senwosret giv[en life(?) ...] ... for ever. Mooring (by) His Majesty at ⌜*Ḏrty*(?)⌝; making offering and burning incense on the fire; resting within (it); offering up oblation [... c. 80 cm. lost ...]

x + 2) consisting of various gems and things finer and more numerous than anything se[en] formerly in this land, consisting of

[14]From the dawn of Egyptian history the beduin willy-nilly had come to represent lawless disorder and chaos the quelling of which was the triumphant message in art of the head-smiting scene: cf. G. Posener, *Littérature et politique dans l'Egypte de la XIIe dynastie* (Paris, 1956) 104; H. Kees, *Ancient Egypt: a Cultural Topography* (London, 1961) 40; see also above, chap. 4, p. 133; on the head-smiting motif, see H. Schäfer, *WZKM* 54 (1957) 168ff; S. Moscati, *Historical Art in the Ancient Near East* (Rome, 1963) 78ff. Seth too, the god of the beduin wastes, suffered an uneasy and ambivalent relationship with the Chaos which was to be defeated: E. Hornung, *Der Eine und die Vielen* (Darmstadt, 1973) 151.

[15]G. Fecht, *Der Vorwurf an Gott in den "Manworten des Ipuwer"* (Heidelberg, 1972); W. Barta, *SAK* 1 (1974) 19ff; R. Grieshammer, *OLZ* 73 (1978) 445f.

[16]E.g. Cairo 20512; J. J. Clère, J. Vandier, *Textes de la première période intermédiare et de la XIe dynastie* (Brussels, 1948) no. 16, p. 10f; H. Fischer, *Inscriptions from the Coptite Nome* (Rome, 1964) pl. 37; D. Arnold, *Gräber des alten und mittleren Reiches in el-Tarif* I (Cairo, 1976) taf. 42, 52.

[17]Located behind the hypostyle hall, on the west face of the eastern-most wall still surviving. Only the chance placement of a later partition wall has preserved parts of some 14 columns of finely carved text.

the labour of the foreign peoples who had coursed through (*ẖns*) the lands during the time of (*ẖr*) My Majesty. For I indeed have been looking at the plac[es ... c. 75 cm. lost ... and the temples]
x + 3) of the gods which had deteriorated to the point of being watery cattle-fens(?),[18] each of its chambers being filled with mud(?), and alluvium[19] (having even encroached) upon its sanctum, through the destructiveness of what had been wrought therein. The food-provisions for [... c. 80 cm. lost ...]
x + 4) the paths; its (ruin) mound[20] reached the bank(?), detritus(?) being in[21] [3 groups; the ... was over]grown(?) with weeds[22] and the holy-place (*st ḏsrt*) was completely forgotten. That is absolutely true,[23] that is what I saw therein: its enclosure wall was [overgrown] and a conflagration had [... c. 80 cm. lost ...]
x + 5) ⸢a place for catching fish(?)⸣. The heartless one[s] had fallen into the practice of [... 4 groups lost ...] to it ... [... 5 groups lost ...] tramping through this land, rejoicing in civil strife (*ḥ³ʿyt*), (while) those poor ones who were not [... c. 90 cm. lost ...]
x + 6) fell on(?) the temple, and those who had trespassed upon th[is] house made [... c. 14 groups lost ...] both men and women. The valleys (were filled?) with fish, the hills (bore) sheaves of corn, and the enemy were in [... c. 95 cm. lost ...]
x + 7) [... 2 groups lost ...] they burned in the [... 17 groups lost ...] It was [...]. Then it happened that he commanded (me) to act, and I did not (do) what had formerly been done ...."

The prevailing conditions which produced this lamentable scene can be distilled from the king's description as follows: 1. willful destruction by fire of the holy places and their subsequent abandonment; 2. civil strife brought on by an unspecified enemy, who might possibly be identified as a foreigner. The text is too fragmentary to say how these ills were cured; but it is not too difficult to imagine these columns as a preface to the description of a royal building programme, such as the same king has described in texts from Elephantine, Thebes and Heliopolis.

[18] *Ṯwnw* [ ] *m mw*: cf. *Wb.* V, 359:13ff, 360:4.
[19] *Ḳ³w nw t³*: Sir A. H. Gardiner, *The Wilbour Papyrus* II (Oxford, 1948) 27f; cf. D. Meeks, *Annèe lexicographique* I (Paris, 1980) 383 (cultivable land in general).
[20] *I³t*: cf. Sir A. H. Gardiner, *JEA* 39 (1953) 21; Kamose II, 17; Gebel Barkal stela, 9.
[21] Or "the footpaths had reached its mound (on) (its) two banks ...."
[22] *Š³bwt*: *Wb.* IV, 410:7-8.
[23] Meeks, *Annèe lexicographique* III, 323.

2. Hatshepsut's Speos Artemidos Inscription

The earliest comprise several pericopes in Hatshepsut's "speech from the throne" at Speos Artemidos,[24] a text which summarized the queen's policies:
"(14) the roads which used to be completely blocked are now travelled; (15) my army, which was (formerly) unequipped, is now well provided for, since I appeared as king. The temple of the Mistress of Kos was one (16) that was fallen into ruin: debris had engulfed its sanctuary, and children played on its (17) roof; the shrine-serpent no longer caused fear ...., and the (18) festival dates of appearance were not celebrated. I hallowed it and built it a-new; I fashioned her image of gold (19) in order to protect her city in the cult-barque of the land-journey ...." Regarding the temple of Thoth prior to Hatshepsut's time, "(26) there was none knowledgable in his house, and the (institution of) the god's-fathers had been inoperative ... but action was taken through the agency of my father (27) along with My Majesty, and he made the god's-bearers step lively. I (re)built his great temple in Tura limestone .... I (29) [made] the Majesty of this god [appear] in [his] festivals ... (30) though they were (at the time) only by (word of) mouth and not (celebrated) at the (proper) seasons." And finally: "(35) Listen ye, all patricians and plebeians, as many as may be! (36) I have done these things through my personal design. I ⌜never⌝ slumbered in what I did, negligently, (but) I strengthened what had been decayed. I raised up what had formerly been in ruins (37) since the Asiatics were in Avaris, in the midst of the Delta, with nomads among them (38) destroying what had been accomplished. They ruled without Re, nor did he act by divine sanction down to (the reign of) My Majesty."

The Time of Troubles is here described in the following terms: 1. poor transportation and communication, 2. neglect of the army and professional priesthood, 3. ruin of temples and unauthorized use by the lower classes, 4. neglect of written, in favour of oral, prescriptions, 5. vandalism of Asiatic rulers, and 6. refusal by Re to sanction Asiatic rule. The evils summarised in points 1 through 4 were set right by Hatshepsut's programme of rebuilding and restoration (although in keeping with Hatshepsut's character there is a nod in her father's direction); the problems of divine disfavour were set right by the god himself.

[24] *Urk.* IV, 383ff; A. H. Gardiner, *JEA* 32 (1946) 43ff.

3. Amun's Injunction to Hatshepsut, Red Chapel

In his command to the queen (amounting really to a thumb-nail sketch of her policy on cult restoration), Amun has occasion to contrast his hopes for the queen with the ineffectual accomplishments of former kings.[25]

"Fill the ergastulum, provision the altars, guide the ordinary priests with respect to their duties! Establish laws, lay down regulations! Make larger offering table(s), increase the supply that you may exceed what was in time past. Enlarge the departments of my treasury with the riches of the 'Two Banks' .... my temple, give it a rebirth in fine, new white limestone, do something permanent for the future with your construction work! In accord with My Majesty's predilection (former) kings suffered(?) in doing what I commanded to be done in former times.[26] Shall I indeed frustrate your laws (which came) from me? Shall I indeed have the text (*scil.* of said laws) expunged for posterity? Shall I indeed interfere with the regulations you have set? Shall I indeed expel you from my abode? Order monuments in the temples! Set down a god according to his regulations, each one registered with repect to his possessions, and publish for him his bread portions. A god whose laws are published is a happy (god)."

If the above translation be accepted, Amun is in effect saying that former kings "botched the jobs" which the god commanded them to carry through, and that, strangely, this was his will. Hatshepsut, however, will not make this mistake, and Amun by a series of rhetorical questions makes it plain that he will ensure the permanence of her works. If the alternate translation (cf. n. 26) be accepted, Amun is enjoining the queen to complete and improve what former kings left incomplete and in poor order. Though the translations may differ, the meaning is broadly the same:

[25]P. Lacau, H. Chevrier, *Une chapelle d'Hatshepsout à Karnak* I (Cairo, 1977) 124ff.

[26]This is a difficult sentence, and Lacau to my mind rightly rejects E. Otto's contention the *šni n bityw* is an allusion to the Hyksos (*ZÄS* 85 [1960] 151f). But Lacau's own rendering, "surpasser(?) pour moi les rois anciens de Basse Egypte" (*Chapelle d'Hatshepsout*, 127) is itself objectionable. In the first place, the *n* which follows the verbal form, both in this and in the preceding line, is not dative plus 1. s. suffix: *n m-ẖt* is simply "for the future" (*Wb.* III, 346), and therefore the *n* following *šni* need not be understood as "for me." In the second place *šni* does not mean "exceed." The translation we have given above is based on two assumptions: 1. that the "rainfall" determinative (Gardiner, *Grammar*^{3}, N 4) is a playful transposition for an original "evil-bird," obliging us to understand the verb as *šni*, "to suffer" used intrasitively; 2. that any discomfiture of former Egyptian kings could be construed by the ancients as god's will. An alternate translation might be "put things to rights (literally, make a quelling [intrasitive]) on behalf of (former) kings, as is My Majesty's will, in performing what I ordered done for me long ago." This would have the advantage of finding a parallel in Hatshepsut's own texts for *šni* plus N 4: *šni ḥ*^{3c}*yt*, "put an end to civil strife!" (*Urk.* IV, 269:14, parallel to *dn ḏ*^{3}*ḏ*^{3}*w*).

Hatshepsut's reign will be a culmination in the history of cult restoration which was begun but not finished in the recent past.

4. The Thutmose III Retrospective[27]

"...(6) regnal year 22, 4th month of *proyet*, day 25: [His Majesty's departure from the fortress] (7) of Sile, on his first victorious campaign [to repulse those that had transgressed] (8) the frontiers of Egypt, in valour, [in victory, in might, in justification].[28] (9) Now for a long period of years Ret[jenu had fallen into] (10) a state of anarchy, each man ⌜violating⌝(?) his neighbour [....] ⌜the temples⌝(?). (11) Then it transpired that, in a later period, the garrison which had been there, was (now) (12) in the town of Sharuhen; and from Yurza as far away as (13) the Marshes of the Earth People were rebelling against His Majesty."

The retrospective envisages two periods: one, more remote, pictures social anarchy in Retjenu, while the second, immediately preceding the crossing of the frontier, pictures the Egyptian garrison repelled to Sharuhen, and all of Asia rebellious. Two key words in the understanding of the Egyptian reaction are *ḥꜥdꜣ* and *bšt*; the words rendered "later period," viz. *hꜣw kyw*, literally, the "times of others" may sustain the rendering "later reigns."[29]

5. The Tutankhamun Restoration Stela[30]

"Now His Majesty appeared as king[31] at a time when the temples of the gods and goddesses from Elephantine as far as the Delta Marshes ... ⌜had fallen⌝ into ruin, and their shrines become delapidated. They had turned into mounds overgrown with ⌜weeds⌝, and it seemed that their sanctuaries had never existed; their enceintes were (criss-crossed) with foot-paths. This land had been struck by catastrophe: the gods had turned their backs upon it. If (ever) the army was despatched to the Levant (Djahy) to extend the borders of Egypt, they would have no success; if (ever) one prayed to a god to ask something of him, he never would come at all; if (ever) one supplicated any goddess likewise, she never would come at all. Their hearts were weakened in their bodies, (for) they had destroyed what had been made."

[27] *Urk.* IV, 647-8; D. B. Redford, in M. Görg, E. Pusch (eds.), *Festschrift Elmar Edel* (Bamberg, 1979) 338ff.
[28] Sethe, *Lesestücke*, 70:18; D. B. Redford, *JAOS* 99 (1979) 280, n. 8.
[29] On *hꜣw*, "reign," see above, p. 139, n. 55.
[30] J. Bennett, *JEA* 25 (1939) 8ff; *Urk.* IV, 2027.
[31] Cf. D. B. Redford, *History and Chronology of the Eighteenth Dynasty of Egypt: Seven Studies* (Toronto, 1967) 3ff.

The period here described (undoubtedly the reign of Akhenaten) is characterized by 1. abandoned temples, 2. ineffective military activity, and 3. inactive gods. Interestingly, social anarchy is not listed. Unlike the preceding pericopes, the present passage hints at divine responsibility for the Time of Troubles, and in fact uses the same locution as had been used of the vandal Hyksos. This, however, is not at all like the wild abandon with which Ipuwer castigates the All-lord. The king's measures of reform consist almost wholly in restoring the cults in the temples.

6. The Former State of the Karnak Hypostyle[32]

A scene from the north half of the west wall of the Karnak hypostyle, which shows Sety I introduced to the Theban triad, was later glossed by a text of Ramesses II. In this Amun addresses the king as follows:

"Welcome, welcome! O perfect god! Lord of the Two Lands (Ramesses II)! My heart is happy, I am satisfied [....] and exultant at seeing thy beauty! I have given thee my office as king of Upper and Lower Egypt, my kingship and my lifetime as king, inasmuch as thou hast made a great monument for me in front of my temple, which had been left an undecorated court from the reigns ($h^{3}w$) of the kings of Lower Egypt. I never put in their hearts to undertake to embellish my monument; only (to thee) my son, effective for him that begat him ... (have I authorized it [or the like])."

Former kings are not especially castigated for their negligence in this text. Rather, it was the will of the god that was involved: Amun had not made them aware of the need to perform such a work, preferring that it be done by Ramesses II. Nonetheless, temples left undecorated — the text uses the adjective "empty" (*sw*)[33] — are incomplete, and do not exemplify the quality of "effectiveness" which characterizes a good ruler.

7. Ramesses II's Description of the Abydene Necropolis[34]

"He found the temples of the necropolis which belonged to former kings, and their cenotaphs which are in Abydos, fallen into a state of

[32]H. H. Nelson, W. Murnane, *The Great Hypostyle Hall at Karnak* I *The Wall Reliefs* (Chicago, 1981) pl. 137; cf. the similar sentiments in Kitchen, *RI* I, 201:12.

[33]This passage may throw some light on the *kry šw* of Chester Beatty I, iii, 10. For other interpretations, see E. Brunner-Traut, *Altägyptische Märchen*[2] (Düsseldorf and Köln, 1965) 271ff; M. Lichtheim, *Ancient Egyptian Literature* II (Berkeley, 1976) 223, n. 7; for *šw* used of a blank papyrus, see *Wb.* IV, 428:5-12.

[34]H. Gauthier, *La grande inscription dédicatoire d'Abydos* (Cairo, 1912) lines 30ff (p. 5ff).

disrepair, their sides being (still) in process of construction [....] in the ground. Construction of their walls had been discontinued, and no two bricks were together. What there had been in the sanctum was (now) turned into earth; and there was no-one who could have their plans completed since their owners flew to heaven. No son was there who would refurbish the monument of his father in the necropolis." Later Ramesses convened the court and said to them:[35] "Look, I have had you called concerning a matter which is before me. I have seen the temples of the necropolis and the cenotaphs of those who are in Abydos, and the work on them was (abandoned while) in progress from the reigns[36] of their owners until today. If ever a son succeeded to the seat of his father, there was no restoration of the monument of him that begat him."

The description of an old, delapidated temple the renovation of which is assigned to a particular official, appears as a common topos in inscriptions of all periods; but Ramesses II expands on this theme by characterizing the history of the Abydene necropolis as one of wholesale negligence. Here the Time of Troubles spans all past time until the present: no tomb or cenotaph was ever completed, and the fault lies with faithless sons. The result is, or so Ramesses would have us believe, a prospect of abondoned cenotaphs, half-built and falling to ruin.[37]

8. Merneptah on the Libyans[38]

The invasion of the Libyan tribes in the early years of Merneptah proved to be a traumatic event in Egyptian history, as it brought invaders from a quarter wholly unsuspected heretofore. An incursion of foreigners from the east had long since become a routine event, and a cliché and literary topos; but violation of the western frontiers was unheard of.

"[....] (8) uncared for, it had been abandoned as cattle-pasture because of the Nine Bows, laid waste in the reigns (*h³w*) of the ancestors, when each king dwelt in his ... [....] (9) the [...] of the kings of Lower Egypt, confronting their city, they being restricted in

[35] *Ibid.*, lines 40ff (p. 7f).
[36] *H³w*: see above, p. 139, n. 55.
[37] On the memorial chapels in question here, see W. K. Simpson, *The Terrace of the Great God at Abydos* (New Haven, 1974) 3; *idem*, in *LdÄ* II (1976) 390; for a similar text, exuding pride at having restored his father's unfinished work, cf. the dedication of the Qurneh temple: Kitchen, *RI* II, 636.
[38] *Ibid.*, IV, 3:6-9.

their governance of the Two Lands through lack of an army: they had no batallions for their protection ...." (The text continues with Merneptah's accession). "(19) .... they penetrated onto the soil of Egypt and it was (only) the Great River that stopped them; they spent days and months dwelling [....] (20) they reached the mountains of the oasis and cut off the land of Farafra. Investigation was made, since (former) kings, in the annals of previous reigns, but they were unable to [....]."[39]

Merneptah, in his encapsulated description of the Time of Troubles, lists its woes as economic, demographic and political. Certain territories, (certainly in the western Delta) had long been abandoned by agriculturalist in the face of the enemy, and were wasteland. The Libyans had invaded both the western Delta and the oases; and former kings, through lack of an effective military, had been powerless to stop them. This situation had prevailed for a considerable length of time: as a source for his information, the king cites the annals of earlier kings.

9. Ramesses III's Historical Retrospective[40]

The Great Harris papyrus is a species of *Apologia* incorporating as proof of his piety a long list of Ramesses III's donations to the gods. Of more limited extent, but of equal importance, are the sections dubbed "the laudations, adorations and the many, mighty and earnest supplications"[41] which are placed in the mouth of the king, and constitute his addresses to the deity. Pages 75 to 79 of the document comprise a speech made by the king to "the magistrates, the princes of the land, the army, chariotry, Sherden, numerous bowmen, and to every citizen of the Land of Egypt."[42] There is no telling whether this is a *real* address Ramesses made to the court, at a specific time and place, or whether the text simply recalls such a format and venue. The delivery, it is true, reflects the milieu of the "royal sitting (*ḥmst nsw*)," or "royal appearance (*ḫꜥt-nsw*)"; but the pericope concludes with a statement from the grave (79, 4ff), so that it may be a fictionalized speech. In any event, the content is wholly and plausibly historical, with no propogandistic overtones in favour of another ruler

[39] *Ibid.*, 4:9-12; above p. 83.
[40] Great Harris Papyrus, 75:1ff (W. Erichsen, *Papyrus Harris* I [Brussels, 1933] 91); J. von Beckerath, *Tanis und Theben* (Glückstadt, 1951) 76f; Sir A. H. Gardiner, *Egypt of the Pharaohs* (Oxford, 1961) 281; R. O. Faulkner, in *CAH* II^2 (1966) ch. 23, 26f; R. Drenkahn, *Die Elephantine-Stele des Seth-nakht* (Wiesbaden, 1980); A. J. Spalinger, *Bib. Or.* 39 (1982) 272ff.
[41] Harris 1, 3 and *passim*.
[42] Harris, 75, 1-2.

(save 75, 6ff), and quite likely derives from verbatim material of Ramesses III himself.

The pericope begins with an historical retrospective:
"The Land of Egypt used to be in a state of dislocation, and every man was a law unto himself. At the beginning they had no chief for many years, until a time came when the Land of Egypt had magistrates and town-rulers; (but still) one would slay his fellow, the greater the lesser. After came another span[43] of empty years[44] when a Syrian who was with them had turned himself into a magistrate;[45] for he had made the entire land subservient to him. One used to slay his companion, and their goods would be taken off, for they had treated the gods like men: no offerings were offered up within the temples.

Now when the gods relented in forgiveness in order to put the land right in its proper condition, they appointed their son, the issue of their (own) flesh, as ruler L.P.H. of every land upon the Great Throne, viz. ... (Sethnakht) .... He made ready the entire land which had formerly languished, he slew the refractory who had been in Egypt, and purified the Great Throne of Egypt, as lord of the Two Lands on the seat of Atum. He gladdened faces that had formerly been downcast so that each man accepted (literally 'knew') his fellow, (though) formerly kept apart(?). He made the temples secure with offerings to present to the gods, according to their customary rites ...."

Ramesses' description of the Time of Troubles is more specific than those which we have examined up to this point. While refraining from mentioning any names, he divides the period preceding his father's assumption of power into three periods: 1. a state of anarchy without ruler, 2. parochial rule by principalities, still anarchous and 3. tyranny of a foreign ruler, anarchy and godlessness prevailing. The specific evils include robbery, murder, heavy taxation, illegitimate rule, and the neglect of the temples. Things are set right by an act of will on the part of the gods, and their appointment of "their son" Sethnakht to the throne of Egypt; *ipso facto* he enjoys legitimacy, and becomes the divine agent of reform.

Though the passage has sometimes been used as a source in the

[43]It is entirely possible that h^3w here has the force of "reigns(s)"; see above p. 264f.
[44]J. Vandier, *La famine dans l'Egypte ancienne* (Cairo, 1936) 67.
[45]Circumstantialized second tense, *m sr* being the stressed adverbial element; for similar examples, cf. P. Salt 124, *rt.* 1, 7; Bologna 1094, 3, 8; Harris 75, 5-6. Goedicke's attempt to translate the passage (*WZKM* 71 [1979] 6ff), which treats *sw* as a personal name, in unconvincing.

reconstruction of the history of the outgoing 19th Dynasty, one is inevitably embarrassed in such an exercise by the vagueness and formulaic cast of the wording.[46] At what point in the recent past (if indeed he is not casting his net on a broader circuit) is Ramesses III beginning his exposition? Does the period leading up to Sethnakht's seizure of power, to call a spade a spade, really lend itself to a tripartite treatment? If period 3 truly reflects the "Shogunate" of Bay,[47] periods 1 and 2, "kingless" to be sure to judge from the text, cannot in any way truly describe the reigns of Merneptah, or Sety II or even Siptah. We are confronted rather with a stereotyped interpretation of history, which is a correct reflection of the New Kingdom "mind-set." If the family of Ramesses the Great had discredited itself in anarchy, which it had, that anarchy must be set forth in the prescribed way, no matter whether or not the resultant description corresponded to reality. Ramesses elaborates on the stereotype to the point of singling out three periods — perhaps he was thinking of Amenmesses, Siptah and Bay, but that is for our purpose irrelevant — each characterized by a different sort of political evil: 1. kingless period: anarchy through disregard of the laws, 2. parochial rule: anarchy through social oppression and 3. foreign tyranny: anarchy through taxation, robbery and cult neglect. The evils are here graded on an evolutionary scale: no government is equated with lawlessness, local autonomy yields oppression, and central rule by a foreigner brings tax-gouging and apostasy. No matter what political structure exists the social ills continue without diminution, and the reason is obvious: the gods have been "treated like men," and there is no *divinely authorized ruler*.

10. Ramesses III on the Libyan Invasion[48]

Strangely, the retrospective pericope we have just examined omits mention of the Libyans; but this theme is shortly taken up by Ramesses in his account of his foreign wars.

"See, I shall inform you of other events which took place in Egypt under (former) kings. The Labu and Meshwesh settled in Egypt after having seized the towns along the western edge (of the Delta) from Memphis to Qarbana. They reached the Great River on both its banks, and it was they that disrupted (*fẖ*) the towns of the Xoite

[46]Goedicke's attempt (*ibid.* 9ff) to read specific history into the piece founders on points of translation which appear to me highly suspect.
[47]Cf. J. Černý, *ZÄS* 93 (1966) 35ff; J. Vandier, *RdE* 23 (1971) 186 and n. 4.
[48]Harris 76:11-77:2.

nome during the very many years they were in Egypt."[49]

The content and reference recalls Merneptah's description of the Libyan invasion (above, no. 8) and may in part allude to the same events. As before, the woes are ascribed to the ingression and continued presence of non-Egyptian elements. The deliterious effects of their occupation are described by the verb *fḫ*, "to loosen," i.e. to render unfit for use or any further function by dislocating the parts. This passage and no. 8 share a geographical specificness that the other examples have lacked: both localize the events in the western Delta and set the central arm of the Nile, the Great River,[50] as the furthest limit of the incursion. It is doubtful whether Ramesses wished us to imagine, as Merneptah seems to have done, an analistic source lurking in the background: the information was common knowledge at the time, and had passed into the realm of oral tradition.

11. Ramesses IV on the Neglect of Osiris[51]

The king reports having found a "[book][52] of hieroglyphic text [*mdw-nṯr*], consisting of great and important hymns which Horus made" for Osiris; he then excerpts a portion, apparently breaking abruptly into the middle of a passage in which the lost antecedent appears to be kings of a byegone age: "they (viz. those) who feared thee not, were ignorant of thy name; and the Inundation (which flows) in the days of every (appropriate) [seas]on, was di[minish]ed(?)[53] during their years. The earlier (kings)[54] [....] themselves [....] in exalting their [...]. Then I mused in the divinity of my heart, and pondered things in an effort to exalt my kingship for a long period of years, with the lands in peace, and there being no civil strife. I have done all good things for thy house — the kings who were afore[time in] *my* place did not do them!"

The theme here is singular in condemning former kings, not only for their neglect of Osiris, but also for their ignorance of him and his name.

[49]The delapidation of cultic installations at Memphis ought perhaps to be seen in the same light: cf. Harris 49, 12 "I have repaired thy (Ptah's) temple and the *ḥb-sd* chapels which had formerly fallen into ruin since the (time of former) kings."
[50]*AEO* II, 157*f; W. Helck, *Die altägyptische Gaue* (Wiesbaden, 1974) 138ff; M. Bietak, *Tell el-Dabᶜa* II (Vienna, 1975) 118ff.
[51]M. Korostovtsev, *BIFAO* 45 (1947) 160; Kitchen *RI* VI, 21.
[52]Probably restore [*mḏ³t*] *nt mdw-nṯr m dw³w*: cf. H. Goedicke, E. F. Wente, *Ostraca Michaelides* (Wiesbaden, 1962) pl. 27, no. 74; A. Piankoff, *The Litany of Re* (New York, 1964) pl. 1, 3.
[53]Probably restore *s*[*ᶜnd*]*w*.
[54]*Kywy* with seated king determinative; cf. above, nos. 4 and 9, where *kywy* (or *kt-ẖt*) may also have the nuance of "other (kings)" apart from the living pharaoh.

12. Namlot's Report on the Temple of Arsaphes[55]

"(2) [Lo], His Majesty L.P.H. (i.e. Sheshonk I) was searching for every useful idea, in order to carry them out for his father Arsaphes, King of the Two Lands, Lord of Herakleopolis, who was in his heart now that he was king. (3) Then came the king's-son and army commander Namlot into His Majesty's presence, and said: 'the temple of Arsaphes, King of the Two Lands, has discontinued (4) the daily ox-offering, and I found it falling into delapidation from what it had formerly been in the reigns of (5) former (kings). It would be good to restore it (*di pr.f*)' ... (7) .... A decree was issued in the Privy Chamber L.P.H. (*stp-s³*) to refurbish the temple of Arsaphes, King of the Two Lands, Lord of Herakleopolis, and to (8) re-institute this daily ox-offering in it, as was done in the reigns of former (kings)."

This passage shares with nos. 1, 5 and 7 the topos of the ruined and abandoned shrine. In keeping with 5 and 7, but unlike 1, it generalizes about the *terminus a quo* for the desuetude of the cult. If specificness had been an interest of Namlot, he would probably have said *ḏr h³w Wsr-m³ʿt-rʿ Stp.n-rʿ*,[56] instead of *ḏr h³w ḏrtyw*.

13. Osorkons I's Retrospective[57]

In this sadly battered stela someone, possibly the courtiers, have occasion to praise the king, and in so doing a contrast is made between the present and the past.
"(frag. D) [...] in the time of (former) kings ... (frag. G2, line 1) [the gods], their bodies did [not] reside in their (cult)-seats, and none of their hearts belonged to them during (*ḫft*)[58] the years of civil strife in the time of former kings. (But) there is none like thee in this land! Every god abides on his seat, and happily cleaves unto his shrine! ...."

The word translated "civil strife" (*ḥ³ʿyt*) is the same word Sinuhe uses (B 7) of the impending trouble which he expects to follow the death of Amenemhet I, or which Hatshepsut uses in an obscure passage apparently with reference to conditions preceding her own

[55]P. Tresson in *Mélanges Maspero* I (Cairo, 1934) 817ff, lines 2-8; D. B. Redford, in J. W. Wevers, D. B. Redford (eds.), *Studies on the Ancient Palestinian World* (Toronto, 1972) 153f.
[56]The last king to undertake major constuction at the site: P-M IV, 118f.
[57]E. Naville, *Bubastis* (London, 1891) pl. 51.
[58]For a recent discussion of this preposition, used temporally, see R. D. Delia, *BES* 1 (1979) 15ff.

reign.[59] It is hard to say whether Osorkon's scribe is simply adhering to the time-honoured cliché, or whether he is honestly describing a period of stasis in the recent past. His third year, in which this text was inscribed, is less than 25 years from the coming to power of his father's house: could he be alluding to the 21st Dynasty? When viewed on the basis of their physical accomplishments all over Egypt, the kings of the 21st Dynasty have a woeful record: apart from some construction at Tanis and a little at Memphis, they built virtually nothing! It would be understandable for the new house to characterize their rule as a lamentable experience for the gods.[60]

14. The Report of Osorkon on the Theban Rebellions[61]

The nature of the uproar which attended the rebellion of the Thebaid against Takelot II is described in the address of welcome placed in the mouth of the delegation of priests and laity which came out to meet the high-priest Osorkon (Year 11). Unlike the examples of this theme reviewed up to this point, the present passage is in a *private* text, and may refer more to contemporary conditions than to those of a more remote past.

"(31) We have been beseeching you, (since) we have heard of your fondness for him (Amun); and look! he has brought you [to us(?)] to end our misery and still the storm menacing us. For this land has been flooded out and its laws destroyed through the activity (32) [of those who had re]belled against their lord, who had in fact been his magistrates. For every palette had been seized[62] in his temples in

[59]Lacau, Chevrier, *Chapelle d'Hatshepsout*, 97; it can also be used of foreign disturbances.

[60]On the other hand, a passage of a vaguely comparable nature turns up in the statue inscription of Nakhtef-mut, 4th prophet of Amun, a contemporary of Osorkon II (Cairo 42208 [c], 23): "I served (several) kings, and was unscathed by their strife (*nšni*); I achieved a doddering old age (*i*^{3}*wt m kḥkḥ*) in thy noble house (i.e. the temple of Amun)." Similarly Montuemhet calls himself "one who quels uproar (*nšni*) in the king's house" (Cairo 42236 [b], 2: J. Leclant, *Montuemhât, quatrième prophète d'Amon et prince de la ville* [Cairo, 1961] 7f, n. *b*). It is unclear here whether *nšni* refers to political turmoil, in implied contrast to the peace and safety of the temple, or simply to royal anger (cf. E. Otto, *Die biographischen Inschriften der ägyptischen Spätzeit* [Leiden, 1954] 142; cf. Cairo 42210 [d], 6; 42211 [e], 13). Possibly the prevalence of stasis in the royal administration had become a cliché during Libyan times.

[61]*Reliefs and Inscriptions at Karnak* III *The Bubastite Portal* (Chicago, 1954) pl. 18, cols. 31-32; R. A. Caminos, *The Chronicle of Prince Osorkon* (Rome, 1958) 42ff.

[62]On *šsp gsty*, see Caminos, *ibid.*, 44, n. *k*. It seems to me that in the following section the clear presence of complementary infinitives *r ḥḏ* and *r s*^{3}*ḳ*, demands a verb here, and so I have rendered *šsp* as a passive *sḏm.f*. For *šsp* with the meaning "seize" (almost "confiscate"?) cf. Lebensmüde, 89 (of catching fish). But perhaps the context can sustain the normal meaning "take up (in order to use)," and the rendering would then be "every palette was (mis)used ... in order to frustrate etc."

order to frustrate his proper procedure, which the Lord of the *hdn*-plant (Thoth) had authorized on papyrus, and to wreck the sacred rites. The temples of the gods had fallen into intestine strife (*ḥꜣꜥyt*), – and this without the ⌜knowledge⌝ [of] ⌜the king⌝!"

The second rebellion in year 15 is described *passim* in the following terms:[63]

"(7) ... an uproar happened in this land, as the children of rebellion fomented civil strife (*ḥꜣꜥyt*) in South and North .... Years passed when people preyed on each other unchecked ..... (16) ... cities were in disorder, nomes [were in conflict(?), turmoil(?)] was in each one of them (while) everyone was saying, 'I it is that shall seize this land!'"

The first rebellion is described almost entirely in terms of cultic apostasy. Official documents(?) had in some way been tampered with, and the result was that the sacred procedure had been changed or suspended. In consequence the temples had been the scene of strife. The second rebellion, in contrast, has all the trappings of a full-blown civil war, described in much the same way that Thutmose III (no. 4) and Ramesses III (no. 9) used in reporting on the periods of stasis which had preceded their reigns. Two novel features are the implication of royal negligence in the first passage, and the divine negligence pointedly referred to in the second.

The examples of the motif are as revealing in what they omit as in what they include. No criticism is ever made of the speaker's administration; and comments on a debilitated military crop up only during the period when the "empire" was still in existence (nos. 2, 4, 5). Civil anarchy proves to be a more frequent element in the description. Often a phrase will occur referring to one man's preying on his neighbour (nos. 4, 9, 14). *Ḥꜣꜥyt*, "internal strife," is commonly used, but *ḥꜥḏꜣ*, "anarchy," *bšṯ*, "rebellion," *nšny*, "uproar," are also found. It is a bad outcome for the state when tracts of land are cut off and removed from agriculture (nos. 8, 10).

By far the most common element in the description of the Time of Troubles is the suffering of the temples and their personnel. Shrines are physically abandoned and fall into ruin (nos. 1-3, 5-7) because of no revenue (no. 9); temple construction is suspended or neglected altogether (nos. 3, 6, 7). Offerings cease (no. 12), priests are disbanded (no. 2), and temple operations stop (no. 14). What is not given here, of course, is the translation into sociological reality. Closed temples mean a cessation of food production (in view of their

[63] *Bubastite Portal*, pl. 21.

No.	Century	Description of Troubles: Civil	Description of Troubles: Cultic	Description of Troubles: Military	Causes: Foreign	Causes: Divine	Causes: Other	Time Progression	Historical Period
1	20th	civil strife	temples destroyed		X(?)			unit	Middle Kingdom
2	15th	poor transport	temples abondoned		X	X		unit	Hyksos
3	15th		temple construction unfinished			X(?)		unit	Second Intermediate Period(?)
4	15th	anarchy in Syria		army on defensive	X			2 periods	Reign of Hatshepsut
5	14th		abondoned shrines	army ineffective		X		unit	Amarna Period
6	13th		temples left incomplete			X		unit	Amarna Period(?)
7	13th		temples etc. neglected				Selfishness of later generations	unit	
8	13th	areas cut off, fields neglected			X		lack of army	unit	Lybian invasion
9	12th	anarchy	cult neglected		X	X		3 periods	end 19th Dyn.
10	12th	dislocation of town life			X			unit	same
11	12th	diminished Niles	cult neglect				former kings at fault	unit	?
12	10th		cult neglect					unit	21st Dyn.?
13	10th		cult neglect			X	years of war under earlier kings	unit	21st Dyn.?
14	9th	anarchy	cult apostacy and laws destroyed			X	magistrates and children of rebellion	unit	Theban Rebellion

landed estates), suspension of food distribution and therefore unemployment. As a result the community starves.

The causes assigned reveal a similar pre-occupation with the divine. Foreigners (Syrians, Libyans) come in for their share of the blame, but only in cases where historically we know their presence to have been a decisive factor. Occasionally the writer hints at abnegation of responsibility on the part of older generations (nos. 7, 8, 11), but this is more often represented as a concomitant. A reaction on the part of the gods is the most frequently postulated cause. Sometimes it is an act of the divine will: Re withdraws his authorization of a dynasty (no. 2) or Amun ordains that former kings should not succeed (no. 3; cf. nos. 11, 14). The cessation of offerings and the dereliction of temples can cause the gods' "hearts" and "bodies" to be weakened (no. 5), with the result that they leave their abodes (no. 13);[64] they are treated "like men" (i.e. with no special respect: no. 9). They may even turn and destroy what they have created (no. 5), or turn their backs on it (no. 9), or at least acquiesce in its destruction (no. 14).[65]

"Dissolution and Restoration" is a theme heard on the lips of a chief of state responsible for the welfare of his community. It is always and of necessity *post eventum*, but never so far removed that the troubles are unfamiliar to the audience. As an official declaration, the piece is either a statement of policy and self-justification, or a report of *res gestae*. Though made up in large measure of recurring motifs, the theme is sufficiently elastic to allow it to be used in a variety of situations. In the light of the constant struggle in the mind of the Egyptian between historical reality and *Geschichtsbild*,[66] it is interesting to note that the fourteen examples noted above all follow and refer to periods of political and social distress the severity of which can be verified on other evidence. The pattern is not, then, as loosely used, and as divorced from reality, as is the theme of Horus Avenger of his Father, whose imagery informs much royal ritual and royal literature. Most certainly it may be classed as a species of historiography and, *mutatis mutandis*, its use as historical evidence justified.

[64]This, it seems to me, points the way to the correct understanding of Baba's taunt that Re-Harakhty's shrine is empty (Chester Beatty I, 3, 10 [=A. H. Gardiner, *Late Egyptian Stories* (Brussels, 1932) 40]). Re-Harakhte's cult establishment has suffered the worst fate: it has been abandoned. It is not a case of Re's shrine not existing (so J. Spiegel, *Die Erzählung vom Streite des Horus und Seth* [Glückstadt, 1937] 92, n. 1; cf. P. Derchain, *RdE* 9 [1952] 41f), nor of Re's not having a cult-image (Brunner-Traut, *Altägyptische Märchen*[2], 271f); much less is it an allologue for "go home!" Lichtheim, *Literature* II, 216, 223, n. 7.

[65]Cf. Hornung, *Der Eine und die Vielen*, 159.

[66]E. Otto, *WO* III, 3 (1966) 161ff.

The Theme of the "Impure Ones" and Related Motifs

In marked contrast to the *res gestae* of an "Autokrator" the 1st Millennium B.C. throws up a number of examples of a *popular story* about a Time of Troubles in the *remote* past. In place of the smug, self-justification of a "speech from the throne" is found the naïve aetiology of things officially unexplained; in place of the government's assurance that all is well is the prophetic assurance that they who find themselves in straits similar to those of the victims in the story, will likewise enjoy deliverance. The classic, and fullest, example is the story Manetho tells at the end of his 18th Dynasty about Osarsiph and the "impure people," which is tied to the name of a King Amenophis *alias* Hor.[67] The basic plot is found in other authors, however, and at times sufficiently distorted to cast doubt on whether they are directly related to the Osarsiph story. Any investigation of the theme must centre upon an attempt to answer three fundamental questions: 1. is the story a unit, or a composite of several unrelated "strands?" 2. is there any historical reality behind it? and 3. in what period in the past did the theme originate?

One prominent, though not central, element in the theme of the "Impure Ones" is invasion from the north. While infiltration from that quarter was a constant irritant to the Egyptian state, large-scale, destructive invasions were rare before the 7th Century B.C. Thereafter four were attempted by the Assyrians (three successfully) in the 7th Century,[68] at least two by the Neo-Babylonians (neither successfully) in the 6th,[69] before the two major incursions of the Persians. Though disastrous at the time and of profound effect on Egypt's immediate politics, the Assyrian invasions left little trace in the folklore of the land. *Išwr* (*Iḫwr*) in Demotic literature lingers on as a vague designation of the western half of the old Assyrian empire.[70] and when the Assyrians turn up in stories they are clearly

[67]See above, p. 284ff.

[68]See now A. J. Spalinger, *Orientalia* 43 (1974) 295ff; *idem*, *JAOS* 94 (1974) 316ff, where the relevant literature is cited.

[69]On the invasion of 601-600 B.C. see the writer, in *LdÄ* IV (1982) 369ff; on that of 568-67, see D. J. Wiseman, *Chronicles of Chaldaean Kings* (London, 1956) 94f; *idem*, *Iraq* 28 (1966) 154f; A. J. Spalinger, *SAK* 5 (1977) 237f; E. Edel, *GM* 29 (1978) 13ff.

[70]G. R. Hughes, *JNES* 10 (1951) 259f and n. 12 (references); R. A. Parker, *A Vienna Demotic Papyrus on Eclipse and Lunar Omina* (Providence, 1958) 6; D. B. Redford, *A Study of the Biblical Joseph Story* (Leiden, 1970) 201, n. 5.

anachronistic players in an innocuous yarn.[71] One obvious reason why the Assyrians do not appear in a well-defined role as villains of a threatening nature stems from the ambivalent stance which they adopted historically against Egypt. Conquerors they were, they could not deny, but in the event it was against the Sudanese kings that they warred, and thus could be, and were, construed by the Delta dynasts whence emerged the 26th Dynasty as saviours and allies.[72] Tales in which *they* were the enemy were not likely to flower in Saite times, and by the Persian invasion Assyria was virtually forgotten.[73]

The Persian invasions, however, left a more discernible mark on the Egyptian psyche.[74] In the 4th Century the success of the Egyptian resistance to Persian attempts to retake the country sparked in the literature two themes in tension, which run on into Ptolemaic times: 1. the patriotic fervour of a people willing to be free, and 2. the potential destructiveness of invasion from the north. These themes first colour and inform a traditional *mythological* setting. The three pertinent examples of this, ranging in date from the mid-4th to the mid-3rd Century B.C., may best be appreciated in the following conspectus.

1. The Northern Invasions under the Primordial Gods

(a) Source: Wady el-Arish naos (Ismailia 2248): G. Goyon, *Kêmi* 6 (1936) 1ff; U. Luft, *Beiträge zur Historisierung der Götterwelt und der Mythenschreibung* (Budapest, 1978) 219ff.

[71]E.g. the Book of Judith: W. S. McCullough, *The History and Literature of the Palestinian Jews from Cyrus to Herod* (Toronto, 1975) 180f; the Coptic story of Cambyses' invasion: I. Hofmann, *SAK* 9 (1981) 179ff; parts of the Petubastis cycle: A. Volten, *Arch. Or.* 19 (1951) 72; the story of Djoser's campaign against the queen of Assyria: D. Wildung, *Imhotep und Amenhotep* (Munich and Berlin, 1977) 130f; the Hyksos account of Manetho: Waddell, *Manetho* 80 (needless to say), mention here of Assyrians is no grounds at all for dating Manetho's source to the 8th-7th Century B.C.: *pace* J. Yoyotte, *RHR* 163, 1963); cf. also Herodotus ii.141.

[72]A. J. Spalinger, *Orientalia* 47 (1978) 16; *idem*, *JAOS* 94, 323f; *idem*, *JAOS* 98 (1978) 402.

[73]That the story of the Northern Invasion under Horus (see below, p. 279) refers in any way to the Assyrian invasion (so J. G. Griffiths, *JEA* 44 [1958] 83) is most doubtful: Assyrians are not even mentioned in the document.

[74]On the "Cambyses Tradition" in Egypt, see J. V. Prašek, *Der Alte Orient* XIV, 2 (1913); R. W. Rogers, *A History of Ancient Persia* (London, 1915) 198; J. Schwartz, *BIFAO* 48 (1949) 65ff; R. Merkelbach, *Numen* 6 (1959) 154ff; A. T. Olmstead, *A History of the Persian Empire* (Chicago, 1948) 89ff; S. K. Eddy, *The King is Dead* (Lincoln, 1961) 261f; J. G. Griffiths, *Plutarch's De Iside et Osiride* (Cambridge, 1970) 468.

(b) Date: mid-4th Century B.C.?[75]
(c) Period: the "reign" of Shu.
(d) Resumée:

- the children of Apophis, "desert brigands" originating in the east, attack Egypt on "all the roads of Yat-nebes" (i.e. through the Wady Tumilat).
- Shu created *Pr-Spdw* (Saft el-Henne) and its component installations as a defence at the western end of the Wady, and posted the gods there to meet the attack.
- Shu defeats the rebels by affixing the fire-breathing uraeus to his brow.[76]

What we have here is the topos of invasion from the "north"[77] fused with the Apophis myth[78] and the motif of Re's creation through the slaying of a noisome beast.[79] The deliverance comes through the agency of the supernatural. The description of the onslaught of the children of Apophis is clearly inspired by, and perhaps considered the archetype of, historical invasions of recent date which had entered by the same route.[80] Saft el-Henne and its cultic lore must be the source of much of the specific detail. The

[75]The el-Arish naos, though undated, undoubtedly belongs to the reign of Nectanebo I, whose construction of naoi and whose proclivity to decorate them with material from the *sipty wr* (above, p. 221) is well known: L. Habachi, *JNES* 11 (1952) 261 and n. 41.

[76]The text claims that Re had earlier defeated the "rebels" (*sbiw*) from the east by transforming himself into "a crocodile with the face of a falcon and the horns of a bull" in *Pr-Spdw*.

[77]The "east," or "Arabia" in late and classical texts seems always to be used where one might have expected "the northern foreign lands" in earlier, hieroglyphic inscriptions: cf. Sesostris's Arabian expedition, on which, like 18th Dynasty kings, he hunted wild game: Diodorus i.53.5; cf. Herodotus ii.102.2; the canals on the east of the Delta, located "in Arabia": Strabo xvii.1.24; Sethos's campaigns into "the lands of the east": Manetho fr. 50, 100; Tefnakhte's campaign "in Arabia": Diodorus i.45; the origin of the Hyksos in "the regions of the east": Manetho, fr. 42, 75; Sennacherib's "Arabian" army: Herodotus ii.141.3.

[78]Note Apophis's epithet "decrepit old man of Syria": R. O. Faulkner, *Papyrus Bremner-Rhind* (Brussels, 1933) 32:34.

[79]A plot pattern well known in West Asian creation myths, but confined in Egypt to contexts other than creation accounts (usually Apophis *versus* the sun, or the solar feline *versus* the snake): on the snake-fighter god of Letopolis see PT 1211; P. Kaplony, *MIOF* 11 (1965-66) 158, n. 83; on Neheb-kau, see PT 229; A. W. Shorter, *JEA* 21 (1935) 43, 47; on the sun-god and the snake, see *Dendera* V, pl. 374; T. Gaster, *Thespis: Ritual, Myth and Drama in the Ancient Near East* (New York, 1961) 141, 152; K. Sethe, *ZÄS* 57 (1922) 11ff; *idem*, *ZÄS* 63 (1928) 50ff; G. Daressy, *ASAE* 11 (1911) 188; 18 (1918) 116; H. Kees, *Totenglauben und Jenseitsvorstellungen der alten Aegypter*^{2} (Berlin, 1956) 140.

[80]Cf. the passage in the Amasis stela (1, 14f): "they came to tell His Majesty, 'the Asiatics have come in their self-confidence, they have moved along the Way of Horus; thousands are there, invading the land. They clog every road, and those in ships fare with good despatch. They think to lay waste our land!'" Edel, *GM* 29, 13ff.

horned falcon-crocodile is clearly Sopdu, and the whole is probably derived from one of those compendia, so common in the Late Period, which set forth the cult, ritual, paraphernalia, and mythology of a given nome.

2. The Northern Invasions under Horus

(a) Source: P. Louvre 3129, B39-E42; BM 10252, 13:1-18-27; S. Schott, *Urk.* VI, 1ff; E. Drioton, *Pages égyptologiques* (Cairo, 1957) 307ff; J. G. Griffiths, *JEA* 44 (1958) 82.
(b) Date: year 17 of Nectanebo I (361 B.C.).
(c) Period: the "reign" of Horus.
(d) Resumée:
- the Contest of Horus and Seth terminates with Horus's assumption of power, his legitimation and coronation. Seth is cast into Asia amid general rejoicing.
- Seth returns and breaks into Egypt and wreaks havoc, "overthrowing cult-seats (*st*), destroying their shrines (*ḫm*), and emitting the battle cry in the temples."
- Isis cries to Re, and there follows the long and formal execration of the invader by all the gods.

The book's title is "The Ritual for the Overthrow of Seth and his Confederates," and as such it was destined for daily performance in the Osiris temple at Abydos. It is thus in a long-standing tradition of cursing the disjunctive elements of nature, but here we are dealing with a recent recasting of the plot. The topos of "invasion from the north" is here fused with a slightly re-worked Horus-Seth myth. The date of the papyri and the nationalistic undertone of the whole[81] recalls a specific historical situation, viz. the Perso-Egyptian war of the 30th Dynasty.

3. The Triumph of Horus of Edfu

(a) Source: *Edfu* VI, 109ff; H. W. Fairman, A. M. Blackman, *JEA* 21 (1935) 26ff; 28 (1942) 32ff; 29 (1943) 2ff; 30 (1944) 5ff; A. H. Gardiner, *JEA* 30 (1944) 23ff; E. Drioton, *Le texte dramatique d'Edfou*, Cairo, 1948; Griffiths, *JEA* 44, 75ff (for a review of the literature to that date); G. E. Mendenhall, *The Tenth Generation* (Baltimore, 1973) 33ff; W. Schenkel, B. Sledzianowski, *GM* 3 (1972) 25ff; H. W. Fairman, *The Triumph of Horus* (London, 1974); W. Schenkel, *Kultmythos und*

[81]Cf. 3129 C, 11-12, various gods "cast thee (Seth) out in thine iniquity into the land of the Asiatics! Egypt is loyal to Horus!"

Märtyrerlegende (Wiesbaden, 1977); J. G. Griffiths, in J. Ruffle (ed.) *Glimpses of Ancient Egypt* (Warminster, 1979) 174ff; Luft, *Beiträge* 231ff.

(b) Date: 3rd Century B.C.

(c) Period: 363rd year of the "reign" of Re.

(d) Resumée:

- in the 363rd regnal year of Re, Horus of Behdet returns with his army from a successful campaign in Nubia.
- Re commissions him to drive Seth and his accomplices out of Egypt.
- beginning with a battle in the vicinity of Edfu, Horus engages the enemy 11 times, driving them farther and farther north, until they are pushed over the eastern frontier at Sile.

A century of investigation into the origins of this myth has produced two views, broadly speaking, neither of which rules out the other entirely. One would like to see the tale as a composite of aetiology and cult conflict; the other would discern the reflection of an historical event, most likely the expulsion of the Hyksos. In fact, those who champion the historical interpretation must admit that there is no direct or implied reference to the Hyksos or anybody else throughout the entire tale. The story simply purports to relate how Seth and his gang were expelled from Egypt, and how in the process certain cult places, names and practices came into being. On this has been superimposed a simple plot-frame: campaign in Nubia - running fight from south to north - expulsion through Sile. Now a northward thrust after a Nubian campaign is one of the most common patterns of military activity from Ahmose to Psammetichus II; and it is no surprise at all that it is taken over into the realm of mythology. And that Sile is the point of expulsion is likewise of little significance: where else would one exit on the eastern side of the Delta?[82] Sile is introduced in the 10th episode with aetiological intent only: it was the cult-seat of "Horus, Lord of Mesen, the noble winged scarab, who protects the two lands, the great god, pre-eminent one of Sile."[83] Even the "date" of the event is based on a shallow aetiology: 363 days from the beginning of the year is the birthday of Seth![84]

There remains one significant fact: a foreign enemy (=Seth) is driven across the eastern frontier into Asia. From the point in time

[82]On the supposed significance of Sile here, see Griffiths, *JEA* 44, 80f.

[83]G. Daressy, *BIFAO* 11 (1914) 29ff; P. Montet, *Géographie de l'Egypte ancienne* I (Paris, 1957) 189ff; J. Vandier, *RdE* 17 (1965) 169ff.

[84]See J. Krall, *SAWWien* 98 (1881) 839; most recently P. Derchain, *CdE* 105 (1978) 48ff.

of the Edfu priests this had happened most recently when the Persians were expelled. In spite of the fact that there is no direct reference to them it would seem that, as in the case of the two previous versions of old myths we have examined, the writer is subconsciously influenced by the most recent occupation of his land.

The full-blown motif of the "Impure Ones" is not the recasting of a known myth, but a *Märchen* set in historic times and tied in to the doings of real individuals. The examples at present extant range in date from the late 4th Century B.C. to Roman times, but it would seem that in some cases we are dealing with simple paraphrases. Differences between the accounts, however, are marked, and suggest that the constant use of a plot pattern in an oral tradition was keeping the theme in a fluid state. Once again a conspectus provides a good means of close examination.

4. Hecataeus

(a) Source: Diodorus xl.3.1-3; M. Stern, *Greek and Latin Authors on Jews and Judaism* I (Jerusalem, 1974) 26; F. R. Walton, *Diodorus of Sicily* (*LCL*; London and Cambridge, Mass., 1967) 281; R. Henry, *Photius. Bibliothèque* (Budé, ed.; Paris, 1971) 134f; A. Burton, *Diodorus Siculus I: A Commentary* (Leiden, 1972), *ad loc.*

(b) Date: last quarter of the 4th Century B.C.[85]

(c) Period: not given, although references to Danaus and Cadmus might suggest the time of "King Amenophis."

(d) Resumée:

- a plague ravages Egypt.
- the "common people" ascribe this to the presence of aliens and alien rites in their midst.
- the aliens are duly expelled, by implication, to the north.
- their ultimate dispersal brings Danaus and Cadmus to Greece and Moses and the Israelites to Palestine.

The basic component here is the "plague/expulsion" motif, used to explain events in classical and biblical history. The ultimate source is undoubtedly Egyptian, but Hecataeus is clearly at several removes from an Egyptian text, and is probably making use of a paraphrase which was transmitted to him orally. That reference to specific names and places is almost wholly absent may be explained by the fact that neither Hecataeus nor his audience were sufficiently interested in the details of native Egyptian traditions.

[85]See M. Stern, O. Murray, *JEA* 59 (1973) 159ff.

5. Manetho[86]

(a) Source: Josephus *Contra apionem* i.26-31; Stern, *Jews and Judaism* I, 78ff; R. Weill, *JA*, 1910, 507ff; E. Meyer, *Geschichte des Altertums* II, 1^2 (Stuttgart and Berlin, 1928) 421ff; Waddell, *Manetho*, 118ff; Helck, *Manetho* 42ff; J. Yoyotte, *RHR* 163 (1963) 133ff; D. B. Redford, *Orientalia* 39 (1970) 44ff; D. Wildung, *Imhotep und Amenhotep* (Munich and Berlin, 1977) 274ff; R. Krauss, *Das Ende der Amarnazeit* (Hildesheim, 1978) *passim*.
(b) Date: second quarter of 3rd Century B.C.
(c) Period: reign of a "King Amenophis" (*alias* Hor), and his son Rampses.
(d) Resumée:
- (i) Amenophis desires to see the gods, and Amenophis son of Hapu advises that this may be effected by removing the plague-ridden people and despatching them to the quarries.
- (ii) Amenophis son of Hapu prophesies that the plague-ridden and the shepherds will conquer Egypt and hold it for 13 years; then he commits suicide.
- (iii) the king sends the plague-ridden people to the quarries, where the rebel priest Osarsiph organizes them.
- (iv) the plague-ridden retire to Avaris, blockade themselves there, and invite the shepherds back from Jerusalem.
- (v) the outcasts and the shepherds defeat the king in battle, and hold Egypt for 13 years of havoc and destruction.
- (vi) the king and court flee and take refuge in Ethiopia.
- (vii) the king and his son Rampses return at the end of the prophesied period and drive out the foreigners.

The central topos of this piece is the "impure ones/expulsion" theme, although "expulsion into the desert" here translates into "banishment to the quarries." The latter, conveniently, are on the east of the Nile. The motivation for the banishment is given in (i), but as the theme works itself out the inclusion of (i) is not really consonant with the contents of (ii): the "Oracle of the Potter" (see below) encorporates the prophecy as an introductory motif, and no royal whim is required to set the story in motion. It is likely that (i) preserves a variant of the entire legend, tied in with "Hor." Appended to the central theme is the motif of "invasion from the north," with the corollary of "deliverance from the south" added on.

[86]Of the voluminous bibliography only the major and most recent references are given.

The introduction of the shepherds in (v) is extraneous to the plot, and presumably came about simply to provide the requisite foreign element to be expelled at the conclusion of the tale.

6. Poseidonius of Apamea

(a)Source: Th. Reinach, *Textes d'auteurs grecs et romains...* (Paris, 1895) 57; K. Reinhardt, *PWK* XXII, 1 (1953) 558ff and 639).
(b) Date: early 1st Century B.C.
(c) Period: not given.
(d) Resumée:
- in order to purify Egypt, the ancestral Jews who were leprous were gathered together and expelled from the country.
- they migrated from the Nile to the territory of Jerusalem and there founded a state.

Poseidonius, who is clearly several removes from an Egyptian source transmits the "plague-ridden-aliens" motif combined with the theme of the Egyptian origins of the Jews.

7. Lysimachus

(a) Source: Josephus *Contra Apionem* i.304-311; text and bibliography in Stern, *Jews and Judaism* I, 382f.
(b) Date: probably early 2nd Century B.C.[87]
(c) Period: reign of Bocchoris (717-711 B.C.).
(d) Resumée:
- the leprous Jews begged at the doors of Egyptian temples, causing a scarcity in the land.
- an oracle of Amun stated that, to solve the problem the lepers would have to be drowned and the rest (sic) expelled.
- forthwith the Jews were expelled into the desert, and thence made their way, under the guidance of Moses, to Jerusalem.

The account of Lysimachus is essentially the "leprous aliens" motif, here dated, coupled with the theme of the Egyptian origin of the Jews.

8. Polemo

(a) Source: "First book of the *Greek Histories*": Euesebius, *Praep. Evang.* x.10.15; Stern, *Jews and Judaism* I, 103.
(b) Date: probably early 2nd Century B.C.
(c) Period: the reign of Apis son of Phoroneus.

[87]A. Gudemann, *PWK* XIV (1928) 32ff.

(d) Resumée:

- (situation and decision not given).
- a part of the Egyptian army was expelled from Egypt and established itself in Palestine.

The account appears to be a variant of the "expelled lepers" motif of nos. 6 and 7, coloured by the historical defection of part of the Egyptian army in Saite times, which Herodotus popularized in ii.30.1-3. It is probable that behind "Apis" lurks the historical Apries, and that the vague similarity between the historical event and the theme of the expulsion of the plague-ridden has caused Polemo to err.[88]

9. Strabo

(a) Source: *Geographica* xvi.35.
(b) Date: late 1st Century B.C.
(c) Period: not given.
(d) Resumée:

- Moses, an Egyptian priest who held part of Lower Egypt, was dissatisfied with the "state of affairs there," and with Egyptian religion in general.
- he preached monotheism and persuaded thoughtful men to follow him.
- subsequently he organized his followers and led them to Jerusalem.

This seems to be a version derived ultimately from the theme of the expelled "plague-ridden" people, but here favourably re-worked in the light of the biblical tradition, with a slight nod in the direction of other polemics which make Moses a renegade priest.

10. The Oracle of the Potter

(a) Source: U. Wilcken, *Aegyptiaca* (Ebers Festschrift; 1897) 142ff; K. Wesselly, *Denkschriften, AWWien* 42 (1893) 3ff; cf. G. Maspero, *RT* 27 (1905) 22; C. C. McCown, *HTR* 18 (1925) 397ff, and n. 78; H. Gerstinger, *Wiener Studien* 44 (1925) 218ff; C. H. Roberts, *Oxyrhynchus Papyri* 22 (1954) 89ff; L. Kákosy,

[88]On the alleged defection of the Elephantine garrison *temp.* Psammetichus I, see Diodorus i.67.3-7; Strabo xvi.4.8; xvii.1.2, as well as the Herodotan passage cited above. On the remarkably similar event mentioned by Nesu-Hor in Louvre A 90, but there dated to the reign of Apries. see H. Shäfer, *Klio* 4 (1904) 152ff; W. Spiegelberg, *ZÄS* 43 (1906) 95f; T. Säve-Söderbergh, *Eranos* 44 (1946) 68ff; J. Vercoutter, *BIFAO* 48 (1949) 175; J. G. Griffiths, *ASAE* 53 (1955) 144ff; A. B. Lloyd, *Herodotus, Book II: A Commentary* (Leiden, 1976) 128ff; Spalinger, *Orientalia* 47, 25.

Acta Or. 19 (1966) 345; L. Koenen, *ZPE* 2 (1968) 178ff; J. W. B. Barns, *Orientalia* 46 (1977) 31ff; Wildung, *Imhotep und Amenhotep* 275.

(b) Date: possibly 2nd half of 2nd Century B.C.; (extant papyri: 2nd-3rd Century A.D.[89]

(c) Period: the reign of King Amenophis.

(d) Resumée:

- on a visit to Hermopolis King Amenophis encounters a potter whose kiln has been destroyed and its vessels confiscated because of the impropriety of firing them on the island of Helios.
- the potter construes this persecution as a prophetic sign and predicts that alien "girdle-wearers" (=Greeks)[90] worshippers of Typhon, will conquer Egypt, defiling the temples and introducing their own gods.
- the aliens will fall to intestine strife, and the king of Syria will come down.
- the king and court will consequently flee to Nubia and take refuge there for 7 years, after which a legitimate king will arise, expel the foreigners and purify the land.

The theme is clearly that of "invasion from the north," coupled with the related motif of "deliverance from the south," mixed with Osirian overtones. The "plague/expulsion" motif is not present *per se*, although the victorious aliens are described in pejorative terms, and it is they that are eventually expelled. Over against general plot pattern one must set the specific elements linking the piece historically to the events of 130 to 116 B.C.[91] It is not entirely clear why Hermopolis is singled out as the setting, unless this is simply the "Hermopolitan" version of this particular story. One can, however, be virtually certain that it is the Greek translation of a Demotic

[89]L. Koenen, *ZPE* 2 (1968) 186ff; Eddy, *The King is Dead*, 292ff; for the possibility of substantial influence by events of Roman times, see J. W. B. Barns, *Egyptians and Greeks* (Oxford, 1966) 16. On the use of the same motif in an anti-semitic piece, probably of the 2nd Century A.D., see V. A. Tcherikower, and others, *Corpus Papyrorum Judaicarum* 2 (Cambridge, Mass., 1960) 520, PSP 982; L. Koenen, *Gnomon* 40 (1968) 257f. On the further development of the theme in later times, see *idem*, in *Eleventh International Congress of Papyrology* (Toronto, 1970) 252ff.

[90]ζωνοφόροι: cf. U. Wilcken, *Hermes* 40 (1905) 550.

[91]Koenen, *ZPE* 2, 190ff; J. W. B. Barns, *Orientalia* 46 (1977) 31ff; nevertheless, the description of the good times which shall return with the advent of the saviour-king are quite in keeping with the cosmic and climatic regularity attendant upon one who adheres to *maʿat*: the Nile shall flood, seasons shall be regular, winds shall be well-ordered and mild, the sun shall shine forth etc.: R. Merkelbach, *AfPap* 16 (1956) 124.

original, possibly somehow tied in with Imouthes.[92]

11. The Oracle of the Lamb

(a) Source: Vienna Nationalbibliotek no. D.10000: J. Krall, *Festgaben zu Ehren Max Büdingers* (Innsbruck, 1898) 3ff; E. Meyer, *ZÄS* 46 (1909) 135f; H. Ranke, in H. Gressmann (ed.), *Altorientalische Texte und Bilder zum Alten Testament* (Leipzig, 1926) 204ff; McCown, *HTR* 18, 392ff; J. M. A. Janssen, in *Historische Kring. Varia Historica aangeboden aan ... A. W. Byvanck* (Leiden, 1954) 17ff; Kákosy, *Acta Or.* 19, 344f; Waddell, *Manetho* 164; Aelian, *De nat. animal.* xii.3.

(b) Date: 33rd year of Augustus.[93]

(c) Period: reign of Bocchoris (late 8th Century B.C.).

(d) Resumée:

- a lamb (or ram)[94] prophesies that Egypt will be desecrated by invaders at the end of 900 years, and that the shrines of the gods will be taken to Nineveh and Amor.
- subsequently a deliverer(?) will arise, the shrines of the gods will be brought back to Egypt, and the land will prosper.[95]
- the prophecy, taken down in writing, is laid before the king who decrees that the animal be embalmed and buried as a god.

Nos. 10 and 11 share the common plot framework of king, oracle and prophecy, long known in Egyptian literature from such works as Neferty. Again like no. 10 the core motifs are "invasion from the north" and "salvation from the south." Unlike no. 10, however the Oracle of the Lamb does not appear to be closely tied to political

[92]W. Struve (in *Raccolta di scriti in onore di G. Lumbroso* [Milan, 1925] 373ff) derives the epithet "potter" from *p*^{3} *ḳd*, used of Khnum; but Wildung (*Imhotep und Amenhotep*, 275) wonders whether κεραμεύς derves from *p*^{3}*ḳd*, the epithet of Imouthes.

[93]J. M. A. Janssen, in *Historiche Kring. Varia Historica aangeboden aan ... A. W. Byvanck* (Leiden, 1954) 29.

[94]For the appropriateness of the lamb (*sr*) prophesying (*sr*), see L. Kákosy, *Acta Or.* 19 (1966) 353. For the suggestion that this lamb is alluded to in the name Νεχεψω (=*p*^{3} *sr*), see J. Ray, *JEA* 60 (1974) 255f and our remarks below p. 326.

[95]The theme of the return to Egypt of the gods' images and other paraphernalia, taken into Asia by the enemy, is a common one: cf. the inscriptions of the early Ptolemies: H-J. Thissen, *Studien zum Raphiadekret* (Meisenheim an Glan, 1966) 59f; C. Onasch, *AfPap* 24-25 (1976) 141f, n. 35.

events. The entry in Manetho[96] shows the story of a prophesying lamb to have been current as early as the 3rd Century B.C. The ultimate source is probably a *post eventum* rationale on the Assyrian invasion, concocted sometime during Saite or Persian times.[97]

12. Chaeremon

(a) Source: Josephus *Contra Apionem* i.32; Stern, *Jews and Judaism* I, 417f.
(b) Date: 1st Century B.C.
(c) Period: the reigns of King Amenophis and his son Ramesses.
(d) Resumée:

- Isis reproaches the king in a dream with respect to her destroyed temple, and Phritiphantes,[98] the sacred scribe, advises the king to rid himself of such dreams by rounding up all the lepers and expelling them from Egypt.
- thereupon the king rounded up 250,000 diseased persons.
- Moses and Joseph met 380,000 at Pelusium, whom the king had not carried into Egypt (sic), and from there attacked and subdued the country.
- the king then fled to Ethiopia, and the queen hid in a cave where she gave birth to Messene.
- the latter in time drove out the invader, and the king could return from Ethiopia.

There are numerous indications that Chaeremon's account depends upon the "classical" Osarsiph tale: the instrumentality of a wiseman in advising the king on a course of action, the "leprous ones/expulsion" motif, the "invasion from the north" and "deliverance from the south" themes. But there are marked differences too, and these suggest a contaminated descendent, not a free and equal variant. For example, the function of the Isis dream-motif is weak in the context, and

[96]Waddell, *Manetho* 164. Generally the lamb oracle has been assumed to be of late origin, and not in the original Manetho (C. C. McCown, *HTR* 18 (1925) 394f); and certainly the reference in Aelian (*De nat. animal.* xii.3) may derive only from Apion (cf. E. Meyer, *ZÄS* 46 [1909] 135). But as Kákosy observes (*Acta Or.* 19, 343f) oracles by ram-gods are attested and are quite important from the late 22nd Dynasty on; and there is nothing inherently improbable about the present lamb oracle having taken its rise in late Saite times.

[97]See Koenen, in *Eleventh International Congress of Papyrology*, 252ff, for the intriguing suggestion that the 900 years teminates in relation to the Sothic era.

[98]*P*^{3} *ḥṛy-tp ḥwt-nṯr*: cf. the title of Montuemhet, *ḥry-tp* ^{c3} *n ḥwt-nṯr*: Leclant, *Montouemhât*, 68; possibly this is a form in which *ẖry-ḥb* has been elided: cf. *AEO* I, 56*; for φρι- as the vocalization of *p*^{3} *ḥry*, see J. Černý, in O. Firchow (ed.), *Aegyptologische Studien* (Berlin, 1955) 31f.

might even be construed as producing a non-sequitur.[99] Again, an alleged *title* of the wiseman has been misunderstood as his *name*. The introduction of Moses and Joseph clearly indicates a shaping of the present piece in the context of the Judaeo-pagan polemic to a greater extent than do the circumstanital elements of the Osarsiph tale. And the motif of the "birth in hiding," though endowed with excellent credentials in the theme of the "birth of the hero," is quite unknown in the earlier story.[100] Again, the figure 250,000 sounds suspiciouly like a rounding-off of the figure Manetho gives for the number of the Hyksos who were expelled under Thummosis.[101]

In sum, then it would appear that Chaeremon gives a late and inferior version of the story, partly dependent on Manetho.

13. Apion

(a) Source: from the third book of his *Aegyptiaca*;[102] Josephus, *Contra Apionem* ii.1-11; Stern, *Jews and Judaism* I, 389ff.
(b) Date: early 1st Century A.D.
(c) Period: first year of 7th Olympiad (725 B.C.)
(d) Resumée:
- (the exact circumstances are not given in Josephus: but apparently the account was similar to that of Lysimachus).
- Moses, a priest of Heliopolis, who had championed new cult installations, organized 100,000 lepers, blind and maimed who were to be expelled from Egypt.
- these he led across the desert into Palestine.

The account, which is presumably identical with that of Lysimachus, and was based on the same sort of material (albeit viewed negatively) that Strabo used (see above, no. 9), is a species of the "plague-ridden/expulsion" motif.

[99]The motif of the dream in which Isis appears, though this time as the recipient of the complaint about a ruined temple, is used again in the *Dream of Nectanebo*: U. Wilcken, *Urkunden der Ptolemäerzeit* I (Berlin, 1927) 369ff; A. Herrmann, *Die ägyptische Königsnovelle* (Glückstadt, 1938) 39ff; additional references in Spalinger, *ZÄS* 105, 144f, nn. 18 and 22. The story, however, seems not to belong to the present topos, being concerned with the theme of the jolly wine-lover, and the pursuit of carnal delights. If B. E. Perry is correct in his interpretation (*TAPA* 97 [1966] 327ff), the story will eventually have issued in the flight of Nectanebo, and perhaps the siring of Alexander, thus constituting a prototypical cast of the material of the Alexander Romance. Note also the observation of R. Giveon that temples dedicated to Isis are almost always of late date: *The Impact of Egypt on Canaan* (Göttingen, 1978) 26f.

[100]On the birth of the hero in an Egyptian context, cf. the tradition of Isis in Khemmis; see also the present writer, *Numen* 14 (1967) 209ff.

[101]Waddell, *Manetho*, 98.

[102]Or possibly the 4th: see M. Stern, *Greek and Latin Authors on Jews and Judaism* I (Jerusalem, 1974) 395.

14. Tacitus

(a) Source: *Histories* v. 2; cf. A. M. A. Hospers-Jansen, *Tacitus over de Joden* (Groningen, 1949) 119.
(b) Date: early 2nd Century A.D.
(c) Period: reign of Bocchoris.
(d) Resumée:
- when Egypt was plagued by disease, Bocchoris received from the oracle of Amun a directive to expel all the diseased victims into the desert, and thus purify the land.
- the order was obeyed, and the suffering multitude was organized and led by Moses to Palestine, where they founded Jerusalem.

Once again, we are in the tradition of the "plague-ridden/expulsion" theme.

Without exception, the stories summarized above display a vivacity and immediacy that is lacking in much of Egyptian mythology. They smack of the cut and thrust of heated discourse, in which the discussants paraphrase and deliver their arguments orally, without necessarily having recourse to written material. In short, we are from the outset in a polemic atmosphere.

The Oracle of the Lamb (no. 11) stands somewhat apart from the rest. It is specifically dated to the reign of Bocchoris, predicts the invasion of the Assyrians and its consequences, and prophesies eventual deliverance and prosperity. Within its own terms of reference it is consistent, plausible and introduces no major anachronisms. True, in the Ptolemaic and early Roman period it may have been treated as an "example" by those "upon whom the end of the world had come"; but in origin it has all the circumstantial (though not specific) earmarks of a "prophecy" concocted to the political advantage of Sais and its house. It is undoubtedly the dating of the oracle to the reign of Bocchoris that has been instrumental in colouring the "plague/explusion" motif in Poseidonius, Lysimachus, Apion and Tacitus. Here too we have an oracle, the presence of an undesirable alien element, and an expulsion. Now of the four, only one, Apion, was a native Egyptian; the others were unable to read a Demotic or hieroglyphic text. Tacitus and Poseidonius clearly depended on written sources, and probably among the authorities they used they counted Lysimachus. But Lysimachus also must have drawn on a written source in Greek, so that the *Vorlage* of the piece must be put back to a Greek text (translation of a Demotic original?) no later than the 3rd Century B.C.[103]

[103]That Manetho himself should have encorporated this tale *sub* Bocchoris seems doubtful to the present writer, in the light of his knowledge of the lamb oracle.

That the lost original in Greek dates to the century aforesaid finds some support from Hecataeus. The theme from Lysimachus to Tacitus is essentially the same[104] and depends, as contended above, on a single written original. But Hecataeus's version is markedly different. Those who suffer expulsion in Hecataeus's account are aliens who had previously been living among the Egyptians, not victims of leprosy.[105] There is a plague, but it apparently afflicts Egypt as a whole. There is, moreover, no oracle of Amun: the people decide on the course of action themselves. In sum, Hecataeus's account is rather close to the Exodus story of the Hebrews. In both the supernatural inflicts Egypt with plague(s); in both the cause of the misery is the presence of aliens/Hebrews within the country; in both the course of events issues in the departure of the aliens from the Delta northward; in both those who made the Exodus were led by Moses to Canaan. Hecataeus was undoubtedly familiar with the Jewish community in Judaea and their religious practices;[106] but, as he himself states, he used several other (Greek) sources which attempted to use the tale to explain the arrival of Danaus and Cadmus in Greece.[107] He also must have been privy to an account more directly derived from a native Egyptian source. What he has done, it would seem, is to produce a composite version of his sources, suppressing the anti-Judaic tone of his Egyptian informants and avoiding the patriotic jingoism of the Exodus.

Thus far we have spoken of a literary *Vorlage* for the "plague/expulsion" theme; but it was certainly a plot-motif alive in the mouths of the people. Apion, indeed, who as an Egyptian could have had access to Demotic literature, alludes to discourse by the older generation in his recounting of the tale![108] As so often was the case in the history of ancient Egyptian literature, the presence of literary versions, even a standard version, of a piece did not prevent the rise and development of a parallel *oral* tradition, which could at times return to warp the literary.

We have been able to trace back the "plague/expulsion" theme to the 4th Century B.C. Lysimachus and the others who transmitted it from Ptolemaic to Roman times lived within the period of the Jewish

[104]One variable element is the identity of those expelled: now they are leprous native Egyptians, now a discernible foreign group.

[105]Diodorus does, however, know of the other theme of the expulsion of the plague-ridden: cf. xxxiv.5.1.

[106]Stern, Murray, *JEA* 59, 167f.

[107]Diodorus xl.3.2: *ὥς τινές φασιν*.

[108]Cf. Josephus *Contra Apionem* ii.10 *ὡς ἤκουσα παρὰ των πρεσβυτέρων τῶν Αἰγυπτίων*.

controversy, and their accounts show that they were quite conscious of the bearing their work would have on the polemic. Whether *in origin* the "plague/expulsion" theme is simply a counter-blast to the Exodus tradition is a moot point; but it would seem that the basic ingredients go a little further back in time than the formulation of the Exodus material.

As would seem to be borne in upon the investigator by examining the mythological accounts (nos. 1-3 above), the motif of "invasion from the north" and its sometime corollary of "deliverance from the south," was brought to birth as a plot pattern thanks to the repeated invasions of Egypt from the north in the 7th through 5th Century B.C. Perhaps already by the end of the 26th Dynasty one such story, in this case a prophecy of invasion and deliverance, had attached itself to the reign of Bocchoris, the tragic ancestor of the Saite kings.[109] As the Oracle of the Potter suggests, the theme was used again in Ptolemaic times to expound present vicissitudes and offer hope in time of trouble.

The one account adumbrated above which combines the two themes of "invasion" and "plague/explusion" is that of Manetho.[110] There are differences in detail between Manetho's plague/expulsion story and that of the others we have just passed in review. In the Hor variant e.g. the motivation for the round up of diseased people is the king's expressed desire for a restoration of a good relationship between himself and the gods. Again, as in the Apion story those lepers who are rounded up are *native* Egyptians; only later do aliens enter the narrative. As in the versions of Hecataeus and Lysimachus the unwanted horde is expelled into the desert, east of Egypt; but this turn translates into a formal despatch of personnel to the quarries (which are all east of the Nile). There follow the organization of the lepers by Moses, and their conversion to new religious practices; but at this point the expected progression of the plot is suspended. Instead of leaving Egypt for Palestine, the lepers call in the "shepherds" from Jerusalem, and devastate Egypt for a period of 13 years after which they are thrown out by force. The bridge from the original theme to the "invasion" theme is poor and artificial.

In reading Manetho one has the gnawing suspicion that the turns of the plot, though familiar are not pristine in the motivation positted. The desire to see the gods, e.g., is decidedly less pleasing or plausible as the mainspring of the action than the simple desire to

[109]On the figure and role of Bocchoris in Saite tradition, see below, p. 327.
[110]On the dependence of Chaeremon on Manetho, see above, p. 288.

rid the land of a grievous plague (Hecataeus, Lysimachus, and others). Banishment to the quarries is a curious way to win the divine favour. Why not expel these undesirables from Egypt entirely? Moreover, it was common knowledge that quarry work was neither punishment nor quarantine, but rather part of everyone's corvée duty and for the administrators, a noble occupation. And why then frustrate the original purpose by bringing them back from the quarries and assigning them an Egyptian city to live in? These curious contortions of the plot-pattern produce puzzlement and rob the motif of its simple purity. Similarly in the appended invasion story an originally straightforward event has been twisted to create a "second-coming" of the Hyksos. For this reason the leperous quarry workers have to be got to Avaris, and a call must go out to the "shepherds" now at home in Jerusalem. To introduce the prophecy which the plot-motif demanded (cf. the Lamb, the Potter), Amenophis son of Hapu had to be turned into a clairvoyant; and to provide some thread of unity his prophecy had to be thrust back to an awkward point in the story, just after the round-up of the lepers.

It is not difficult to see that the Osarsiph story can lay little claim to being a *de novo* composition. Of the two themes he uses the Osarsiph author knows simpler and more aesthetically-pleasing exemplars, but he has chosen to distort them. Who was he, and why did he do it?

In the first place, I do not think this secondary hodge-podge derives from Manetho himself. In all likelihood he is here, as elsewhere simply paraphrasing, if not translating, a Demotic original which he found among his library sources. This view gathers weight when it is appreciated that the specific distortions of the plot which we have noted above, derive from a viewing and interpretation of monuments still extant in Upper Egypt in the Late Period. In the discussion of the Hor story[111] it was noted that the name of the king and the theme of seeing the gods emerged through a half-educated attempt to interpret Amenophis III's surviving inscriptions. The introduction of Amenophis son of Hapu, if he did not enter the story on the coat-tails of his illustrious sovereign, suggests the influence of the Amenophis cult at Deir el-Bahari.[112] Quarry work would have suggested itself as a substitute for expulsion because of the incidence

[111] Above, p. 248ff.
[112] Wildung, *Imhotep und Amenhotep*, 257ff.

of such activity under Amenophis III and Akhenaten.[113] The latter's stela at Silsileh is the largest surviving memorial from that quarry, and numerous traces of Amenophis III's work are also to be found there. The area was still extensively worked in the Late Period and Ptolemaic times, so that the remains of earlier times there would have had every opportunity to come under observation.[114] Manetho's statement that there were "learned priests" among the lepers in the quarries would find a ready explanation in awareness of the Wady Hammamat inscriptions of Akhenaten's year 4, which states that May, the high-priest of Amun, had been sent there to procure stone.[115] The plague motif itself has precedent in earlier hieroglyphic sources and quite likely reflects a reminiscence of the historic plague of Amarna times.[116] The plague also is connected with Kush in the tradition Eusebius transmits,[117] and its tied in with the 5th year of Amenophis III, possibly due to a false interpretation of his Aswan and Nubian stelae recording his victorious campaign of that year.[118]

The occupation of a deserted area, set apart, (though in the modified form of the story replaced by Avaris) sounds like the hejira to Amarna; and the 13 years of woe wrought by lepers and shepherds can only be the term of Akhenaten's stay in his new city. The figure of Osarsiph-Moses is clearly modelled on the historic memory of Akhenaten. He is credited with interdicting the worship of all the gods and, in Apion, of championing a form of worship which used open-air temples oriented east.

In short the combined themes of "plague/expulsion" and "invasion from the north," as they appeared in Manetho's source, have been modified to meet the requirements of an aetiology of Amarna period monuments in Upper Egypt. The date of this source is difficult to ascertain, though I doubt that it is much earlier than Manetho

[113]Amenophis III: year 1 stela, Bersheh quarries, stelae of years 1 and 2, Tura, P-M IV, 185; *Urk.* IV, 1677; J. H. Breasted, *Ancient Records of Egypt* II (Chicago, 1906) § 875, p. 351, n. *e*; Gauthier, *LdR* II, 306 (1, 2); *LD* III, 71a; *Urk.* IV, 1681; Akhenaten: Silsileh quarry inscription, *Urk.* IV, 1962. The name of the renegade priest, Osarsiph, i.e. *Wsir-Sp³* (cf. H. Kees, *ZÄS* 58 [1921] 89 and n. 3). points to the region of Tura-Heliopolis where Sepa was prominent: cf. J-P. Corteggiani, in *Hommages à Serge Sauneron* (Cairo, 1979) 136f. The extension of his worship to the east Delta meant mythological involvement in Asiatic incursions: cf. J. Cledat, *RT* 36 (1914) 107f, fig. 4.

[114]D. and R. Klemm, *SAK* 7 (1979) 132ff and abb. 2.

[115]G. Goyon, *Nouvelles inscriptions rupèstres du Wadi Hammamat* (Paris, 1957) pl. 25 and 31; D. B. Redford, *JAOS* 83 (1963) 240f.

[116]*Idem*, *Orientalia* 39 (1970) 44ff.

[117]*Ibid.*, 48.

[118]Inscription at Sai: J. Vercoutter, *Kush* 4 (1956) 81; Aswan stela: *Urk.* IV, 1665f; Konosso inscription: *Urk.* IV, 1662; Buhen stela: *Urk.* IV, 1758.

himself. What the tale does prove is that the Amarna debacle, with all its characters and events, had not been lost to the collective memory of Egypt, but had survived in some form.

Summation

When dealing with a subject as elusive as the origin and evolution of popular tales in antiquity, whether written or oral, one may find that one has essayed an impossible, nay even foolhardy task. The averral or denial of chronological *termini* for a piece may be met on the morrow by the discovery of a new papyrus, ostracon or stela; an elaborate *schema* confidently displaying the descent of a narrative may conceal the serious short-coming that the whole is based on a mere handful of textually inferior schoolboy copies! The thesis that piece A in one culture gave rise to piece B in a neighbouring culture may appear to solvc all outstanding problems, until an exemplar of piece B is found two centuries older than A. What has survived of the folkloric "output" of ancient Egypt is so small, spotty and haphazardly distributed in time and space that no one is yet in a position to claim a firm grasp of the range and nature of the material Egypt produced. Nonetheless, in the present investigation of the two themes that make up the "Osarsiph" tale in Manetho it would seem that some clarity can be achieved by way of ascertaining what is, and what is not, probable in the origin and transmission of the narratives; and with that sanguine observation the author will permit himself to outline a broad "overview."

The New Kingdom was conscious of its own achievement, and duly produced a literature about itself. The Hyksos expulsion prompted a folk literature of pure entertainment, neither prophetic, didactic nor admonitory in tone; and so did the military accomplishments of Thutmose III and probably many more of the warrior pharaohs. Before the demise of Theban power at the close of the 20th Dynasty the Amarna period had also become a subject for the story-maker, but the nature of the tale is wholly unknown save for the virtual certainty that it preserved the names of the four rulers of the period, and a number of the events in which they participated. If the late combination of the two themes in the Osarsiph narrative is any guide, this early treatment of the Amarna period may have telescoped events and pictured Ramesses II as restoring order to the realm.. The problems attendant upon the presence in Egypt of a large and dominant community of Asiatics never arose in the New Kingdom nor in the "Tanite" period which followed (21st-22nd

Dynasties); and xenophobia as a core around which narratives take shape therefore did not make its appearance until Saite times. Then, and after the turn of the 6th-5th Centuries, several folkloric pieces emerged which betray an underlying self-conscious apprehension of the dirty northerner and what he can do to Egypt. The earliest may be the Oracle of the Lamb with its prediction of the Assyrian invasion and the restoration (under the Saites). The theme in folklore of a northern invasion suddenly became, on the morrow of the Persian subjugation, a vehicle for expressing the earnest concerns of Egypt as never before.

The policy of Psammetichus I and his successors of welcoming foreigners as mercenaries and merchants to reside in Egypt put native Egyptians at a real (or imagined) disadvantage. It is no accident that Herodotus's informants (and he himself) are sensitive to racial origins and related squabbles.[119] As a reaction therefore against the growing foreign community in Egypt there grew up the coarse yarn about the ancient plague — the Hyksos were also so afflicted in New Kingdom literature — the isolation of the cause as the presence of foreigners and/or lepers, and their eventual exodus/explusion to the north where they turn up as contemporary peoples. The Hyksos expulsion to the north hovers persistently in the background as a great archetype of this Egyptian origin of certain nations. The Saite period witnessed a good deal of "textual activity": in the process of the extensive rebuilding of temples, which is one of the outstanding facts of Saite history, there must have been considerable rummaging in old temple libraries. Quite likely the old interpretation of the Amarna period whose existence we have above postulated, enjoyed "re-discovery" and re-editing sometime during the 6th Century B.C. Nor were the themes of Egypto-Asiatic relations dominated by Egyptian story-tellers and interpreted to their advantage alone: the peoples whose foreign communities resided in Egypt fashioned stories favourable to themselves. It had been the Greek Herakles who had punished and killed the wicked Busiris of Egypt;[120] it was the Hebrew Joseph by whose wise administration Egypt had been saved from famine and destitution.[121]

The Persian conquest threw up a self-conscious interpretation of contemporary and past history which emanated in large part from the

[119]Colchis: Herodotus ii.104-05; Athens, Babylon: Diodorus i.28.1-29.3; Egyptian influence on the inhabitants of Palestine: Herodotus ii.104.3.
[120]T. A. Brady, *OCD*, 185.
[121]On the probable Saite origin of the Joseph Story, see the present writer's *Biblical Joseph Story*.

priesthood.[122] Foreign communities were now no longer allies but enemies and occupiers;[123] and native kings and rebels were closely judged on their relations with god and temple.[124] In the 4th Century patriotism, jingoism and fear issued in the crystallization, first in mythology, of the plot-pattern "invasion from the north" and (later) "deliverance from the south." At the same time the "plague/explusion" motif enjoyed a wider currency to the derision of many foreigners Egypt now had to tolerate. In Egypt the events of the period 334 to 300 B.C. found ready parallels in traumatic turns of fortune over the previous two millennia of history. Two major themes had already risen to the consciousness of the nation: the expulsion of the Hyksos and the Amarna period. These now became great archetypes for the apocalyptic tales which began to appear. Probably in the last quarter of the 4th Century these two motifs were combined and melded into a (written?) aetiology of Upper Egyptian monuments to produce the Osarsiph tale. The flight of Nectanebo to Nubia and the coincidence of the 13 year period which elapsed between Artaxerxes III's reconquest and the coming of Alexander, influenced the writer into inverting the order: the Hyksos now experience a "second-coming" and after the 13 years up comes the great Ramesses to drive them out.[125] Alexander's feat is thus not unique: it enjoys a parallel in an event of long ago, and Ramesses becomes a "type" of Alexander.

In the subsequent century (the 3rd) and especially after the battle of Raphia, apocalyptic prophecies and related propaganda based on the plague and invasion themes began to circulate widely.[126] Now they took on, not only an anti-Semitic but also an anti-Hellenic colouring. Even though written down, oral tradition continued to dominate their evolution. Even Chaeremon, who must have known Manetho's work and most closely parallels the Osarsiph tale, had produced a widely differing tale, which owes as much to paraphrase and oral narrative as it does to the *Aegyptiaca*. For in the heat of the polemic it is the *memory* or *paraphrase* of the text which counts, not the ability to produce the written word.

[122]One thinks naturally of the Demotic Chronicle (W. Spiegelberg, *Die sogenannte demotische Chronik*, Leipzig, 1914; McCown, *HTR* 18, 388; J. Johnson, *Enchoria* 4 [1974] 1ff) with its curious prophecies and tedious moralizing. But the priesthood in the Late Period probably considered such history writing quite appropriate to their calling: they were the only ones dedicated to the true worship and service of the Egyptian gods, and their high-toned oath of moral rectitude fostered a tendancy to publish judgement on past and present society: cf. R. Merkelbach, in *Religions en Egypte hellénistique et romaine* (Paris, 1969) 69ff.

[123]Cf. the animosity towards the Jewish mercenaries at Elephantine: E. G. Kraeling, *The Brooklyn Museum Aramaic Papyri* (New Haven, 1953) 111ff.

[124]Eddy, *The King is Dead*, 264f.

[125]M. Braun, *History and Romance in Greco-Oriental Literature* (Oxford, 1938) 19ff.

[126]Eddy, *The King is Dead*, 278f.

9

Manetho's *Aegyptiaca* Book III

As we have attempted to demonstrate in the preceding discussion, by the time of Ramesses II the king-list had achieved a central position in the Egyptians' use of, and interest in, the past. The reign of the great king produced a sense of culmination; the literary and spiritual accomplishments of his time were shortly to become classic. The edition of the king-list which dates from the mid-13th Century B.C. also won classicality and was perpetuated for its own sake, despite the fact that offering lists in the temples and the official list of kings in the archives continued to add subsequent kings.

The Dominance of Memphis in Post-Ramesside Times

When one examines the nature of Manetho's list of kings in the section dealing with the 19th Dynasty and in the whole of Book III of the *Aegyptiaca* one can discern the unmistakable stamp of Memphis in the choice of kings and the transmission of their names. The Theban tradition may, because of the impression made by its surviving monuments in the minds of man, have driven out all trace of Memphite influence in Manetho's 18th Dynasty tradition; but its slow and inevitable decline as a centre important enough to exert any influence in politics left the field open to the ancient capital. The king might reside at Per-Ramesses or Tanis: still it was Memphis that preserved the right to crown him.

In the period beginning with Ramesses II the dominance of Memphis in the life and thinking of the Egyptian state can be amply demonstrated. If in the preceding period it had been Itj-towy and Thebes that dominated in the transmission of the historical tradition, now that honour gravitated north to the city in the shadow of the Saqqara pyramids. It might almost be enunciated as an historical rule-of-thumb that whoever among claimants to the regal office won acceptance by the Memphite "Establishment" duly found a place in the king-list. Much of the awakened consciousness of the link between Memphis and Egypt's past can be credited to the interests of Ramesses II and especially of his illustrious son and high-priest of Ptah, Khamwese.[1] Ramesses' own preoccupation with Memphis is evident in his choice of personal names[2] and his celebration of *sd*-festivals;[3] but his son's restoration of monuments and cults is more *a propos* of our present theme. Khamwese refurbished a large number of pyramids and their cult installations,[4] restored ancient statues of illustrious Old Kingdom princes,[5] and may even have been responsible, like Hordedef before him, for the redaction (if not composition) of (ancient?) religious texts.[6]

The great hold Memphis had over the monarch, apart from the coronation rites, lay in the festivals and obsequies of the Apis bulls.[7] Again, a great revival in the cult of Apis is to be credited to the policies of Khamwese, who rebuilt the temple of Apis. In keeping with his erudition, he had his deeds inscribed in the hypostyle, and exudes pride at his accomplishments, as well as contempt for the modest constructions of the ancestors which he had surpassed. "The things which I have done (are) engraved on the stone wall, viz. great and unique accomplishments (*ꜣḫw*) (whose) like had never happened, published in writing in the great festival-hall before this shrine.... (These) will indeed be useful acts for you (posterity), when you look at what the ancestors (*typw-ꜥ*) made, which is a puny and immemorable construction — why there is not (even) a place

[1]F. Gomaà, *Chaemwese, Sohn Ramses' II und Hohenpriester von Memphis*, Wiesbaden, 1973; K. Kitchen, *Pharaoh Triumphant* (Warminster, 1982) 103ff.
[2]J. von Beckerath, *Tanis und Theben* (Glückstadt, 1951) 64.
[3]A. Badawy, *Memphis als zweite Landeshauptstadt in Neuen Reich* (Cairo, 1948) 127f; L. Habachi, *ZÄS* 97 (1971) 64ff.
[4]Gomaà, *Chaemwese*, 61ff; Kitchen, *RI* II, 873ff. Numerous Old Kingdom royal cults attest revival of interest about this time: for the Giza cults, see C. M. Zivie, *Giza au deuxième millénaire* (Cairo, 1976) 185ff; for Sahure, see G. T. Martin, *The Tomb of Hetepka* (London, 1979) pl. 55 (238); for Tety, see J. Yoyotte, *BIFAO* 57 (1958) 96, n. 4.
[5]Gomaà, *Chaemwese*, 84, no. 51, pl. IV; Kitchen, *RI* II, 872 (no. 332).
[6]Gomaà, *Chaemwese*, 71; J. Yoyotte, *RdE* 29 (1977) 197.
[7]On the Apis cult in the Late Period, see J. G. Griffiths, *Plutarch's De Iside et Osiride* (Cambridge, 1970) 273, 425 and *passim*; J. Vercoutter, *Kush* 8 (1960) 62ff; in the First Millennium B.C. added prestige accrued to the Apis cult through the animal's being identified as Osiris: E. Otto, *Beiträge zur Geschichte des Stierkulte in Aegypten* (Leipzig, 1938) 27f.

prepared (*irt*) for another burial!"[8]

The coronation at Memphis might be omitted; the royal obligation to Apis could not. The king's duty was graphically figured in the common vignette which showed pharaoh offering or libating to the bull.[9] Probably during most reigns the king's place at the funeral ceremonies was taken by his appointee;[10] but in times of strong central control, e.g. the 26th Dynasty, it is clear that no one was allowed to participate or even put his name on a stela at the Serapeum without the king's authorization.[11] And by that time pharaoh's active participation in the rites of passage were *de rigueur*.[12]

Memphis in the First Millennium, although no longer the seat of a king, retained most strongly the right to maintain standards and bestow kingship.[13] The priestly governance of the city was hereditary, and itself employed the Pharaonic title *iry-pꜥt* "heir apparent."[14] The line of high-priests of Ptah constituted an unbroken chain, it was maintained, from the Old Kingdom on:[15] these were the "great princes of Egypt" who guarded the holy sepulchres of dead pharaohs, the sacred libraries of the gods, and the traditions of a once mighty

[8]Gomaà, *Chaemwese*, 43f, no. 31, abb. 10-11; Kitchen, *RI* II, 878:9-10, 878:16-879:1. In the last statement Khamwese is alluding to the former burial ground of the bulls, where space was now exhausted.

[9]Numerous examples: pertinent are those on Serapeum stelae: M. Malinine, G. Posener, J. Vercoutter, *Catalogue des stèles du Sérapéum de Memphis* I (Paris, 1968) no. 4 (pl. 1); nos. 25, 26 (pl. 9); nos. 36, 37 etc. (pl. 12); no. 125 (pl. 35).

[10]Chief lector-priest: *ibid.*, nos. 4, 5 (pl. 1); high-priest of Ptah nos. 19, 21 (pl. 7); nos. 22, 23 (pl. 8).

[11]Cf. J. Vercoutter, *Text biographiques du Sérapéum de Memphis* (Paris, 1962) B, line x + 5-6, "now it was His Majesty that authorized for me the inscribing (*rdi wn*) of my name in the Divine-chamber of the god, inasmuch as the Majesty of my lord loved me."

[12]*Ibid.*, E, pl. V, p. 37ff (crown-prince Psammetichus III); the worthy of the preceding note records favours done him "when he (the king?) proceeded from *Ḳmyt* to assume his regal seat in Memphis": line x + 7, p. 20.

[13]See E. A. E. Reymond, J. W. B. Barns, *Orientalia* 46 (1977) 1ff.

[14]See below, n. 114.

[15]Cf. the Memphite priestly genealogy: L. Borchardt, *Die Mittel zur zeitlichen Festlegung von Punkten der ägyptischen Geschichte* (Cairo, 1935) pl. 2, p. 96ff. The last 15 generations down to Sheshonk (V?) under whom the monument was set up, seem to be genuine (*ibid.*, 101ff); but the earlier names are uneven in their trustworthiness. For example, between the contemporary of Amenemope (21st Dynasty) and the generation of Ramesses II only one name is recorded (cf. the writer, *A Study of the Biblical Joseph Story* [Leiden, 1970], 7; H. Kees, *Das Priestertum im ägyptischen Staat* [Leiden, 1953] 175); but Tiy seems secure (Borchardt, *Mittel*, 104; C. Maystre, *RdE* 27 [1975] 175ff; J. Malek, *GM* 22 [1976] 43ff), and the eleventh through thirteenth generation from Senwosret III, contemporary respectively with kings Sharek, Apophis and Ahmose, must be based on reasonably accurate data (cf. L. Borchardt, *SBAW* 1932, 620f). The Middle Kingdom section also seems sound (cf. H. Fischer, *Varia* [*Egyptian Studies* I; New York, 1976] 63ff).

civilization. They set the standards of weights and measures.[16] The treasury of Ptah, over which they exercised control, became under the Persians the central repository of gold payments to the state.[17] Much of the prescriptive and regulatory literature which set the standards for cults in general was Memphite in origin;[18] and through the Memphite priests passed the right to confer kingship and the right to crown the king, from the 25th Dynasty[19] to Ptolemaic times. Indeed, in the latter period the high-priest of Ptah appears as a shadow king, an incarnation of the true "Horus," an *alter rex* of the Ptolemaic ruler in Alexandria.[20] Those whom Memphis and her priests accepted were kings indeed!

Ptah was very much the hypostasis of pharaonic kingship, more closely tied to the *earthly* institution than the king of the gods, Amun. Already in the Memphite theology[21] he is the one that is "proclaimed (i.e. as king) by the Great Name,"[22] and from the New Kingdom was called "king of Upper and Lower Egypt" and "king of the Two Lands."[23] Of him is predicated an eternal kingship, and, like an earthly king, his reign is recorded in annals.[24]

Alexander the Great realized the pre-eminence of Memphis as the royal city of Egypt, arbiter of who had the right to rule. According to Pseudo-Callisthenes Alexander made straight for Memphis and the Temple of Ptah to undergo a coronation according to Egyptian rites,[25]

[16]M. Malinine, *Choix de textes juridiques* (Paris, 1953) 25f.

[17]E. Bresciani, *Studi classici e orientali Pisa* 7 (1958) 132.

[18]E. A. E. Reymond, *From Ancient Egyptian Hermetic Writings* (Vienna, 1977) 30.

[19]Most of the kings of the 25th Dynasty enjoyed a coronation of sorts at Memphis: cf. Piankhi (stela, 98 [N-C. Grimal, *La stèle triomphale de Pi(ᶜankh)y au musée de Caire* (Cairo, 1981), pl. X]); Taharqa (M. F. L. MacAdam, *The Temple of Kawa* I [Oxford, 1949] pl. 9 [inscr. V, 15] p. 28; for Taharqa's close connexion with Memphis, see A. J. Spalinger, *CdE* 53 [1978] 23ff, and n. 2); Sabaco clearly favoured Memphis (H. von Zeissl, *Aethiopien und Assyrer in Aegypten* [Glückstadt, 1944] 14); for 25th Dynasty interest in Memphis cults, see J. Leclant, in *Mélanges Mariette* (Cairo, 1961) 279ff.

[20]Reymond, Barns, *Orientalia* 46, 15, 22; D. J. Crawford, in W. Peremans (ed.), *Studies on Ptolemaic Memphis* (Louvain, 1980) 18ff; J. Quaegebeur, *ibid.*, 47ff; the high-priest even underwent a coronation rite "according to the custom of his forefathers": Wien 82, 11.

[21]Col. 3: H. Junker, *Die götterlehre von Memphis* (Berlin, 1939) 20ff.

[22]The royal titulary: *Wb.* II, 427:19-23; cf. *Urk.* IV, 261.

[23]H. Frankfort, *Kingship and the Gods* (Chicago, 1948) 23; M. Sandman, *The God Ptah* (Copenhagen and Lund, 1946) 83ff.

[24]Above, chap. 2.

[25]Pseudo-Callisthenes i.34.2; Arrian iii.1.4; cf. H. I. Bell, *Egypt from Alexander the Great to the Arab Conquest* (Oxford, 1948) 29f; R. Merkelbach, *Die Quellen des griechischen Alexander-romans* (Munich, 1954) 24; J. Bergman, *Ich Bin Isis* (Uppsala, 1968) 92ff; L. Koenen, *Eine agonistische Inschrift aus Aegypten und frühprolemäische Königfest* (Meisenheim an Glan, 1977) 29, 53.

and pay honour to Apis.[26] Ptolemy I brought Alexander's body to Memphis initially, and only later removed it to Alexandria.[27] He too honoured the Apis cult by donating no less than 50 talents of silver to the interment of one animal.[28] The historical and political importance of the city evoked a special patronage from the new dynasty,[29] which in the 2nd Century B.C. regularly held court there,[30] and some of its members (e.g. Ptolemy V) deemed it expedient also to be crowned in Memphis,[31] as did Ptolemy VIII. Even the usurper Antiochus IV considered it prudent to undergo a Memphite coronation (169),[32] as indeed did native rebels.[33] In addition the performance of the Apis rites remained throughout the period very much a royal obligation,[34] and, certainly from Ptolemy IV on, the Memphite priests enjoyed a privileged position (to the chagrin of their Theban counterparts).[35] Though Alexandria soon dominated the cult of Serapis, the new god and his cult enjoyed a Memphite origin,[36] and this fact too undoubtedly increased the city's prestige in the eyes of the Ptolemies.

Even on the morrow of the Ptolemaic period Memphis retained its status as "the royal residence of the Egyptians."[37] The Ptolemies had lavished monuments upon it.[38] Heads of state were expected to visit it and honour the Apis bull as a sign of their legitimacy as successors

[26]J. P. Mahaffy, *A History of Egypt* (London, 1899) 4; E. Kornemann, *Die Alexandergeschichte des Königs Ptolemaios I von Aegypten* (Leipzig and Berlin, 1935) 124; G. Grimm, in H. Machler, V. M. Strocka (eds.), *Das ptolemäische Aegypten* (Mainz, 1978) 103ff and n. 2.

[27]Pausanius i.6.3; 7.1; J. Seibert, *Untersuchungen zur Geschichte Ptolemaios' I* (Munich, 1969) 67 and n. 3; O. Murray, *JEA* 56 (1970) 142.

[28]Diodorus i.84.8.

[29]J. Quaegebeur, *JNES* 30 (1971) 244f.

[30]W. Clarysse, in *Studies on Ptolemaic Memphis*, 86.

[31] *Urk.* II, 192; R. Merkelbach, *Isisfeste in griechischerrömischer Zeit* (Meisenheim an Glan, 1963) 67; Koenen, *Eine agonistische Inschrift aus Aegypten*, 73ff; C. Onasch, *AfPap.* 24-25 (1976) 148, 151.

[32]M. Cary, *A History of the Greek World from 323 to 146 B.C.* (London, 1951) 218.

[33]L. Koenen, in *Eleventh International Congress of Papyrology* (Toronto, 1970) 251f.

[34]K. Sethe, *NGWG* 1916, 284; cf. Ptolemy VI's epithet "twin of the living Apis upon the birth-brick," Gauthier, *LdR* IV, 288, n. 2; J. D. Ray, *JEA* 64 (1978) 117ff; Crawford, in *Studies on Ptolemaic Memphis*, 10ff.

[35]W. Clarysse, *CdE* 106 (1978) 251 and n. 2.

[36]Bell, *Egypt from Alexander*, 39; P. M. Fraser, *Opuscula atheniensia* 3 (1960) 1ff; 7 (1967) 23ff; L. Castiglione, in M. B. de Boer, T. A. Edridge (eds.), *Hommages à M. J. Vermaseren* I (Brill, 1978) 208ff; cf. J. E. Stambaugh, *Sarapis under the Early Ptolemies* (Leiden, 1972) 61ff; on Serapis in general, see J. Hani, *La religion égyptienne dans la pensée, de Plutarque* (Paris, 1976) 191 and n. 1.

[37]Strabo xvii.1.31.(τὸ βασίλεον τῶν Ἀιγυπτίων).

[38]H. S. Smith, in J. Ruffle (ed.), *Glimpses of Ancient Egypt* (Warminster, 1979) 164ff.

to the pharaohs;[39] and Augustus's refusal to do so was construed as an insult.[40] Even Hadrian was forced to pay attention to the problems caused by the installation of a new bull.[41]

While the king-list in the Late Period descends to us through Memphis, the Thebans suffered at best a secondary position in the transmission of the history of their country. As in the past the size and state of preservation of Theban monuments gave rise to aetiologies which insinuated themselves in folklore; but acceptance by Theban priests counted for little in the shaping of the list of kings which Manetho used.[42]

The Manethonian King-list for Dynasties 19-22

The 19th Dynasty in Manetho derives from the king-list maintained at Memphis. It probably once began correctly, with a "Ramesses" (now misplaced in Africanus and inserted after Ammenephthes, probably under the influence of the sequence in the Osarsiph tale), and wrongly credited with a reign similar in length to that of Ramesses II. Again correctly, it must have terminated with *Tꜣ-wsrt*, here worn down to Thuoris,[43] and mistakenly identified with

[39]Cf. Suetonius *Titus*, 5.
[40]Suetonius *Augustus*, 93.
[41]*Historia Augusta*, Hadrian. 12.1.
[42]Herihor and Harsiese both bear cartouches in Thebes (Gauthier, *LdR* III, 234ff; D. B. Redford, in *LdÄ* III (1980) 1131; Gauthier, *LdR* III, 348ff; Kitchen, *Third Intermediate Period* § 87, 274); the bricks of the high-priest Menkheperre from all over Egypt prove that his name and title also could be rendered in cartouches, possibly in imitation of Herihor (D. B. Redford, *JARCE* 14 [1977] 16ff); Kashta could erect stelae at Elephantine (P-M V, 227; J. Leclant, *ZÄS* 90 [1963] 74ff), and Piankhy in the oasis (J. M. A. Janssen, *JEA* [1968] pl. 25), and the latter could lend his name and regnal years to business documents in Upper Egypt (R. A. Parker, *ZÄS* 93 [1966] 111ff). Clearly all these kings were accepted by Thebes and her priests, but none appears in Manetho. Dating by a king's reign in everyday business documents is a practical expedient; nevertheless it denotes a degree of acceptance on the part of the community. Thus we may aver that Yewepet (Karnak quai graffito no. 26: J. von Beckerath, *JARCE* 5 [1966] 52), Piankhy (see above), and Tanwetamun (G. Legrain, *ASAE* 7 [1907] 226f; J. Leclant, *Recherches sur les monuments Thébains de la XXVe dynastie dite 'éthiopienne'* [Cairo, 1965] sec. 49, b, c) were all at one time accepted by the community at large in the Thebaid; yet Manetho knows them not.
[43]J. Quaegebeur, *BIFAO* 69 (1971) 205 and n. 3.

Homer's Polybus.[44] The other names have undergone some garbling and/or replacement. "Rapsaces," for example, is probably to be derived from *R^{c}-ms-sw* (*p^{3}*) *k^{3}* ...[45] while Ammenephthes is *Mr.n-ptḥ* with the first syllable misconstrued as part of another divine name. Amenemnes, as it now stands, must be *Imn-m-nsw*, the name of a king of the 21st Dynasty. Why the name turns up here is hard to say; possibly there is a confusion with Amenmesse.[46]

The numbers preserved in Africanus for the lengths of reign yield ample material for "number games" should one wish to play. To judge by the total Africanus gives, viz. 209 years for the dynasty, Rapsaces must have been once credited with 66 years,[47] which is the expected rounding-off of his historic 67; but what can one do with a 51 for Sety I or 20 for Merneptah, or 60 for Ramesses (I)? It would be all too easy to assume mistakes, whether *Hörfehlers* or purposeful chronography: ν´ for ι to yield an original 10 for Merneptah,[48] ν´ for ι to produce the expected 11 for Sety I,[49] or κ´ for ι for the original 1 for Ramesses I. And something like this may well have happened. It is, however, gratuitous to speculate, especially since we can otherwise ascertain the correct figures. Of slightly more interest are the figures for positions 5 and 6, viz. 5 and 7 years respectively, as these are very close to historical reality. Sety II probably reigned slightly less than 6 years,[50] and Tawosret very likely extending the floruit of Siptah as her own achieved a ninth year.[51]

Although the 20th Dynasty has been reduced to a figure total in

[44]This is nothing but an attempt to pinpoint in the king-list the approximate point at which the seige of Troy must have occurred, using the accepted chronology of Greek historians, the intent being to pander to the Greek reader's interests: there is little Egyptian in the Homeric Polydamna, Alcander and company: W. Burkert, *Wiener Studien* 89 (1976) 11. That Manetho should have made of Tawosret a king is not surprising, in the light of the lady's aspirations: see W. M. F. Petrie, *Six Temples at Thebes* (London, 1897) pl. 16; H. S. K. Bakry, *RSO* 46 (1971) 17ff; R. Drenkhahn, *GM* 43 (1981) 19ff.

[45]Either *k^{3}* (cf. A. H. Gardiner, *Late Egyptian Miscellanies* [Brussels, 1937] 13, 4; 41, 9 etc.) or *k^{3} ^{c3}* (cf. *ibid.*, 42, 5; 98, 12 etc.) in the epithet which informed the official name of Pi-Ramesses: Gauthier, *LdR* III, 63.

[46]On the current controversy over this king, see above.

[47]Waddell, *Manetho*, 148, n. 2.

[48]Year 10 is his latest known date: Sall. I, 3:4; cf. R. A. Caminos, *Late Egyptian Miscellanies* (London, 1954) 303; M. B. Rowton, *JEA* 34 (1948) 73.

[49]D. B. Redford, *History and Chronology of the Eighteenth Dynasty of Egypt: Seven Studies* (Toronto, 1967) 210; M. L. Bierbrier, *JEA* 58 (1972), 303.

[50]G. Daressy, *RT* 34 (1912) 39ff; A. H. Gardiner, *JEA* 5 (1918) 190; E. Hornung, *Untersuchungen zur Chronologie und Geschichte des neuen Reiches* (Wiesbaden, 1964) 96.

[51]Years 7 and 8 are attested: cf. Sir A. H. Gardiner, *JEA* 40 (1954) 43 and n. 3; graffiti dated in year 9 are found near her tomb: W. Spiegelberg, *Aegyptische und andere Graffiti aus den thebanischen Nekropolis* (Heidelberg, 1921) nos. 555, 579.

Manetho, the entry attests the survival of a lively tradition. The total of 12 kings is 2 too many, as Černý has pointed out;[52] but the number has considerable currency in Egyptian folklore. Twelve is the total of amphyctions of whom Psammetichus I was a member;[53] and twelve is the number of kings represented in the tomb of Imiseba, himself a contemporary of the 20th Dynasty.[54] Moreover, 12 is a total that could easily have been arrived at by grouping Sethnakht and Ramesses III with the 10 Medinet Habu "princes," these being misconstrued as the remaining kings of the dynasty.[55] That a tradition should depend upon the impressive mortuary monument of Ramesses III is not surprising in the light of the fact that the temple continued to be used down to very late times.[56]

From the end of the Ramesside House, when the last remaining formal tie between the ruling family and Thebes was severed, down to the middle of the 8th Century B.C. little survived in the collective memory of the people, as the accounts of Herodotus and Diodorus show;[57] but Manetho proves that a precise king-list continued to be maintained. Inspite of earlier scepticism by scholars towards Manetho's 21st Dynasty, archaeological discoveries have proven the number and sequence of names to be surprisingly accurate.[58] The same is true of the 22nd Dynasty, mutilated in Eusebius to only

[52]J. Černý, in S. Donadoni (ed.), *Le fonti indiretti della storia egiziana* (Rome, 1963) 40ff.
[53]Herodotus ii.147.2.
[54]See above, p. 51.
[55]Cf. *Medinet Habu* V *The Temple Proper* I (Chicago, 1957) pl. 250, 299-302; K. C. Seele, *JNES* 19 (1960) pl. 3-4. For recent chronological studies, see W. Helck, *GM* 70 (1984) 31f; R. Krauss, *ibid.*, 37ff.
[56]Throughout the 20th Dynasty Medinet Habu continued to be decorated by various kings, *inter alia* Ramesses IV, VI, and IX: P-M II^2, 481ff and *passim*. Reverence for its founder continued throughout the dynasty and into the 21st: cf. the renewal text of Paynodgem on the door of the pylon (P-M II^2, 490 [54g-h]): "the name of the King of Upper and Lower Egypt, the Lord of the Two Lands Usermare Maiamun son of Re, possessed of diadems, Ramesses, shall abide in his manson for ever and ever." In the Late Period the temple flourished as the centre of one of Thebes' major settlements, viz. $I^{3}t$ $\underline{T}^{3}mwt$: Gauthier, *Dictionnaire géographique* I, 35 (cf. VI, 66); E. Otto, *Topographie des thebanischen Gaues* (Berlin, 1952) index, p. 120 (s.v. $D^{3}mt$); J. Leclant, *Montouemhât, quatrième prophète d'Amon et prince de la ville* (Cairo, 1961) 226 n. *bh*; *idem*, *Recherches*, 266, 280, 285; F-R. Herbin, *RdE* 35 (1984) 105ff.
[57]In both Herodotus (ii.124-36) and Diodorus (i.63.2ff) the 4th Dynasty is made to fill the vacuum created by the omission of the 21st-23rd Dynasties: cf. A. B. Lloyd, *Herodotus, Book II: Introduction* (Leiden, 1975) 187ff. Erbse's solution of this puzzle, which Lloyd follows, is much too ingenious. It seems to me that the faulty location of the 4th Dynasty chronologically has to do with the prominence of 21st Dynasty construction and memorials at Giza: cf. P-M III^2, 17ff.
[58]Cf. Rowton, *JEA* 34, 57; Kitchen, *Third Intermediate Period*, § 417; W. Barta, *MDAIK* 37 (1981) 35ff.

three kings, under the mistaken impression that the three major names used by the dynasty, viz. Sheshonk, Osorkon and Takelot, were individual and specific kings. Africanus reflects what must be the Manethonian total "9," and this figure now appears to be accurate.[59]

The Geographical Qualification of Manetho's Dynasties

TC identified "dynastic" groupings partly by reference to the first king (cf. ii, 10; iii, 26), partly by the residence (*ẖnw*) from which they ruled (v, 19; vi, 3), partly by mere placement in the list (vi, 4) and partly by ethnic origin (x, 21). A millennium later Manetho, or his epitomizer, uses numerical sequence and a toponym as *nomen rectum* to identify separate dynasties. Curiously the toponymic data is often at variance with what we know of a dynasty's seat of rule, or their town of origin, as the accompanying table will demonstrate.

Dynasty	*Manethonian Toponym*	*Known Residence*	*Town of Origin*
1	Thinis	Memphis[60]	Hierakonpolis[61]
2	Thinis	Memphis	?
3	Memphis	Memphis	?
4	Memphis	Memphis	?
5	Elephantine	Memphis	Heliopolis?
6	Memphis	Memphis	?
7-8	Memphis	Memphis	?
9-10	Herakleopolis	Herakleopolis	Herakeolpolis
11	Thebes	Thebes	Ermant
12	Thebes	Itj-towy	Thebes
13	Thebes	Itj-towy	(various places)
14	Xois	?	?
15	(Thebes)[62]	Avaris	(*Ḫ³rw*)
16	Thebes	Thebes	?

[59]With the addition of Hekakheperre Sheshonk (II): P. Montet, *Les constructions et le tombeau d'Osorkon II à Tanis* (Paris, 1947) 11; *idem*, *Les constructions et le tombeau de Psousennès à Tanis* (Paris, 1951) 37ff; cf. Kitchen, *Third Intermediate Period*, § 418.
[60]Or the region of Memphis.
[61]E. Drioton, J. Vandier, *L'Egypte*[4] (Paris, 1962) 129; W. K. Simpson, in H. W. Hallo, W. K. Simpson (eds.), *The Ancient Near East: A History* (New Haven, 1973) 206.
[62]Eusebius.

17	Thebes	Thebes	Nubia?[63]
18	Thebes	Thebes/Memphis	Thebes
19	Thebes	Pi-Ramesses	eastern Delta
20	Thebes	Pi-Ramesses	eastern Delta
21	Tanis	Tanis	Mendes?[64]

The only hypothesis which adequately explains these discrepancies is that, while the *historical* seat of government or place of origin may, or may not, have been remembered, what impressed itself upon the collective historical memory of the *Volk* was the site where the major proportion of the monuments of a dynasty survived. Thus, the Early Dynastic kings are inseparably linked with the cenoptaphs at Abydos, and the Old Kingdom pharaohs with the environs of Memphis, through their association with the great pyramid fields, The 12th and 13th Dynasties were scarcely remembered as having had anything to do with Itj-towy;[65] the town which everywhere preserved their monuments was Thebes. Similarly no one recalled, in connexion with the 19th and 20th Dynasties, their association with Per-Ramesses (which no longer exsisted in the Late Period), or the east Delta: their massive monuments and structures survived in the 5th-4th Centuries B.C. only in Thebes.

While from the 25th Dynasty Manetho changes his criterion for dynasty identification to ethnic or municipal affiliation, the Libyan period remains problematical. The 22nd Dynasty is linked with Bubastis and the 23rd with Tanis; but what does this information mean? In the last two decades, it has become fashionable to exhibit scepticism towards the old belief that Herakleopolis constituted the ancestral seat of Sheshonk I.[66] The only text which yields any evidence at all on this thorny problem is the stela of Psenhor from the Serapeum.[67] The inscription states simply that the members of the family, from Psenhor back through a cadet branch of the royal house and the first four kings of the 22nd Dynasty to the remote

[63]Redford, *History and Chronology*, 66f; E. J. Harris, K. R. Weeks, *X-raying the Pharaohs* (New York, 1973) 123, 135.

[64]Cf. the locution used in Wenamun concerning Smendes and Tantamun: "The officers whom Amun has placed in the north of the lands," (2, 35), suggesting that they were transferred to Tanis, and not native there. (In any case Smendes' name points to Mendes as his place of origin.) At Tanis nothing *in situ* dates prior to the inception of the dynasty Smendes founded; cf. J. Van Seters, *The Hyksos, a New Investigation* (New Haven, 1966) 128ff; M. Bietak, *Tell el-Dabᶜa* II (Vienna, 1975) 213ff.

[65]In the Late Period, *Iṯ-tȝwy* had become virtually a common noun meaning "capital," or "residence": *Urk.* II, 39:3.

[66]J. Yoyotte, in *Mélanges Maspero* IV (1961) 135, 138 (who places it at Bubastis).

[67]Louvre 278: Malinine, Posener, Vercoutter, *Catalogue des stèles du Sérapéum*, pl. X (31).

ancestor Buyuwawa, remained firmly ensconced "in the temple of Arsaphes ... in Herakleopolis," each man the son of his predecessor. This is, therefore, the reflexion of a traditional offering list, which was at home in the temple of Arsaphes at Herakleopolis, belonging to a private family; and the likelihood is very strong that the family itself had enjoyed a long residence in the town that thus commemorated them by ancestral offerings! In the light of Sheshonk I's association, prior to his accesson, with the army, the fact that in his reign a well-entrenched military establishment is attested in the Herakleopolite nome, centred upon the extended household of the commander of the army,[68] should occasion no surprise: this was the ancestral headquarters of the clan which had but lately risen to the kingship.

If the evidence in no way disproves a prior residence in Herakleopolis by the ancestors of Sheshonk I, it is more difficult to identify his residence when he became king. To be noted in this connexion is the name given to the new dynastic seat in Gebel es-Silsileh 100, viz. "the Residence Pi-ese, the Great *ku* of Re-Harakhty."[69] One perhaps naturally thinks of *Pr-ḥbyt* in L.E. 12 in respect of the location of this otherwise unattested place;[70] and, under the designation *Nṯrw*, the locality could boast a cult of Isis already in the Old Kingdom.[71] In support of the identification one might cite the evidence of an early enclave of the Meshwesh in the environs of the town;[72] but, while in their mass incursion into the Delta, it is quite likely that *some* Meshwesh came to rest in L.E. 12, the

[68]Cf. P. Tresson, in *Mélanges Maspero* I (1934) 817ff. The estate is large, and bristles with military personnel: commanders of *Thr*-troops (line 13); naval detatchments (line 17); a military secretariate (line 18); *Sṯrps*-troops and retainers (line 19); various support staff, including scribes and chariot-makers (lines 26-27). Clearly, Herakleopolis is an armed camp which could not have sprung up over night!

[69]Col. 39-40: R. A. Caminos, *JEA* 38 (1952) pl. XIII. On temples of Isis and "Iseions" in Egypt, see Griffiths, *De Iside et Osiride*, 262, F. Dunand, *Le culte d'Isis dans le bassin orientale de la Mediterranéan* I (Leiden, 1973) 117ff; F. Le Corsu, *Isis, mythes et mystères* (Paris, 1977) 25ff; R. Giveon, *The Impact of Egypt on Canaan* (Göttingen, 1978) 26f; J. Bergman, in *LdÄ* III (1980) 195.

[70]Gauthier, *Dictionnaire géographique* II, 110f; Dunand, *Le culte d'Isis* I, 116f; P. Montet, *Géograhie de l'Egypte ancienne* (Paris, 1957) I, 107f; attested from the 18th Dynasty: see W. C. Hayes, *JNES* 10 (1951) 165ff; R. W. Smith, D. B. Redford, *The Akhenaten Temple Project* I *Initial Discoveries* (Warminster, 1977) 119f.

[71]Cf. PT 1140b; 2188. For the existence of *Nṯrw* in the Old Kingdom, cf. H. Jacquet-Gordon, *Les noms des domaines funéraires sous l'ancien empire égyptien* (Cairo, 1962) 115; W. Helck, *Die altägyptische Gaue* (Wiesbaden, 1974) 179ff.

[72]Yoyotte, in *Mélanges Maspero* IV, 159; J. Černý, in *CAH* II (Cambridge, 1965) ch. 35, 16; F. Gomaà, *Die libyschen Fürstentümer des Deltas* (Wiesbaden, 1974) 68ff.

evidence in question has, it would seem, been misinterpreted.[73] On the other hand, the epithet links Pi-ese unmistakably with the old Ramesside residence in the north, the Pi-Ramesses,[74] now identified with Khatᶜana-Qantir.[75] The broader environs of the locality on the upper Pelusiac branch had long associated Isis and Bast[76] as tutelary goddesses; and the dominance of the feline type of deity in the eastern Delta (scil. Bast, Hathor, Edjo, Isis)[77] makes one wonder whether Sheshonk's toponym is not an allogram of *Pr-Ḥtḥr*, itself attested for the region of Pi-Ramesses.[78] Certainly the cult of "Isis of Ramesses-beloved-of-Amun"[79] points to an origin in Pi-Ramesses.[80] What appears indisputable from all this is that a cult centre of Isis[81] survived in the region of Khaᶜtana-Qantir into the 10th Century, and

[73]In the passage in P. Louvre 3169:2-7 (G. Maspero, *Memoires sur quelques papyrus du Louvre* [Paris, 1875] 110f and plate) the vizier addresses the chief of the Medjay as follows: "come quickly ... with all the people of the chiefs of the Medjay who are in Per-ḥebyet ... not leaving out one of them — by their names which are with me in writing I name them! — having proceeded to reconnoitre the movements of the Meshwesh." There is not a particle of evidence herein that the Meshwesh in question are in Per-ḥebyet or its environs; in fact, they are on the move elsewhere, and therefore the police can leave the town for the duty the vizier calls them for. In Musée Guimet C.48 (A. Moret, *Catalogue du musée Guimet* [Paris, 1909] pl. 43) the toponym *M³* is of too doubtful meaning to be of any use, although it is associated, apparently, with Per-ḥebyet (cf. the epithet of Isis in the vignette).

[74]Gardiner, *JEA* 5, 179ff.

[75]L. Habachi, *ASAE* 52 (1954) 443ff; Bietak, *Tell el-Dabᶜa* II, 179ff.

[76]Cf. P. Lacau, H. Chevrier, *Une chapelle de Sésostris Ier à Karnak* (Cairo, 1969) pl. 42; for Bast and Bubastis in the titulary of officials at Per-Ramesses, see Habachi, *ASAE* 52, 495. Otherwise Isis is not well attested at Bubastis itself: Dunand, *Le culte d'Isis* I, 118f.

[77]For the identification of Isis and Edjo, see *Edfu* I, 335; J. Vandier, *Le papyrus Jumilhac* (Paris, 1962) 151 (94), 155 (130).

[78]Anastasi iii.3.3; Gauthier, *Dictionnaire géographique* II, 117f; Gardiner, *JEA* 5 (1918) 186, n. 3; Caminos, *Late Egyptian Miscellanies*, 80; also the Adoption Stela, 25 (see R. A. Caminos, *JEA* 50 [1964] 93). In the 18th Dynasty fragmentary papyrus in the Puskhin Museum the name is played upon thus (and reduplicated): *ḥwt-ḥrt* and *ḥwt-ẖrt*, and mentioned in the same context as Avaris, [*sẖt*(?)]*ḏᶜ*, and the Ways of Horus: R. A. Caminos. *Literary Fragments in the Hieratic Script* (Oxford, 1956) pl. 6, 3.14.

[79]Cf. A. H. Gardiner, *The Wilbour Papyrus* (Oxford, 1941-52) pl. 18, 33 (§ 34), though the particular shrine mentioned here is probably to be sought in northern Middle Egypt or the Fayum. *Ist n niwt n iḥ* (A. Varille, *ASAE* 50 [1950] 252) is most likely a form of the goddess of Atfih.

[80]For the pattern "God X of Ramesses (or Sety, or Merenptah)," as a cultic designation of deities associated with a royal temple in the Delta residence, see P. Montet, *Griffiths Studies* (London, 1932) 406ff; B. Couroyer, *RB* 54 (1946) 87ff; 61 (1954) 108ff; also the present author in a forthcoming article on the Exodus.

[81]Note that Osorkon II is also called "beloved of Isis" on the statue from Byblos: M. Dunand, *Fouilles de Byblos* (Paris, 1939) 116, no. 1741, pl. 43.

was used by the founder of the 22nd Dynasty as a residence.[82]

That the members of Sheshonk I's house built extensively at Bubastis, and were therefore closely associated in popular memory with that city, seems beyond dispute.[83] But Osorkon II was buried at Tanis,[84] as was Sheshonk III,[85] and Takelot II was in residence where Shu and Edjo were revered (i.e. along the lower Pelusiac branch), quite likely in the same city.[86] For the remainder of the dynasty the evidence suggests that Tanis had definitely become the main seat of the king. Isaiah associates it with the political power of the realm (cf. Isa. 19:10-13; 30:4), and Pemou is well attested there.[87] Sheshonk IV built so extensively at Tanis that it can scarcely be doubted that it

[82]Other statements regarding the whereabouts of the residence under Sheshonk I are lacking. If the Herakleopolitan decree (see Tresson, in *Mélanges Maspero*, 817ff) once had a reference to the location, it is now lost. At Tanis Sheshonk I is conspicuous by his absence, the granite sphinxes now bearing his name from the site undoubtedly having come from Pi-Ramesses: P-M IV, 15. The fragment from Tell el-Maskhuta (E. Naville, *The Store City of Pithom and the Route of the Exodus* [London, 1903] pl. 3B) was brought later to the site: cf. D. B. Redford, in *LdÄ* IV (1982), 1055; (as it apparently pictured Isis, its provenience may have been the present *pr-Ist*); and that from Bubastis (E. Naville, *Bubastis* [London, 1891] 46) is too slight to be used as evidence. In Karnak room VI (P. Vernus, *BIFAO* 75 [1975] fig. 10, pl. J, 1, col. 5-6) there is reference to "the Mansion [of Million of Years of the King of Upper and Lower Egypt] ... Sheshonk (I) ... which is in Memphis," which attests a mortuary temple in the Memphite region; but to what extent this entailed the king's residence in that city is difficult to determine. A similar mortuary temple appears to have at least been planned for Thebes: W. Helck, *Materialien zur Wirtschaftsgeschichte des neuen Reich* (Wiesbaden, 1960) 115.

[83]Osorkon I: Naville, *Bubastis*, pl. 39ff; Berlin 10834; (The principal seat of Osorkon I is difficult to determine; on the foundation that bears his name near the Fayum, see H. Kees, *Die Hohenpriester des Amun von Karnak* [Leiden, 1964] 89). Takelot I(?): S. Bosticco, *Museo archeologico di Firenze. Le stele egiziane* III (Rome, 1972) no. 7207 (pl. 3); Osorkon II: Naville, *The Festival Hall of Osorkon II at Bubastis* (London, 1892), *passim*.

[84]Montet, *Tombeau d'Osorkon II*, *passim*. Unfortunately, the inscription in room VI at Karnak recording the decree in favour of Thebes (Vernus, *BIFAO* 75, pl. II) is ridden with lacunae, and in its present condition does not indicate the whereabouts of the court. Certainly grandees of Osorkon II's court were interred at Tanis also: H. Jacquet-Gordon, *JEA* 53 (1967) 66f.

[85]P. Montet, *Les constructions et le tombeau de Chéchanq III à Tanis* (Paris, 1960). On a donation stela of year 18 (Moret, *Catalogue du musée Guimet*, C 73 [pl. 64] 2-3) Sheshonk III fails to notify us as to the location of his "residence in his great and august house." "The town (called) 'Fort of Sheshonk'" (mentioned on a donation stela from Heliopolis: G. Daressy, *ASAE* 16 [1916] 61f) is otherwise unattested, and may have been merely a strong point along the defensive line of the eastern Delta.

[86]Cf. *Reliefs and Inscriptions at Karnak* III *The Bubastite Portal* (Chicago, 1954) pl. 21, col. 1-2; R. A. Caminos, *The Chronicle of Prince Osorkon* (Rome, 1958) 79. Sadly a lacuna intervenes were a locative phrase would occur. For the uraeus designated as "Great of Magic, Mistress of Buto," probably under Osorkon II, see I. E. S. Edwards, *Hieratic Papyri in the British Museum* IV Series, II (London, 1960) pl. 16: 34ff. For Edjo at home in Tanis, see Kees, *Priestertum*, 92.

[87]P. Montet, *Le lac sacré de Tanis* (Paris, 1966) pl. 5-6.

was his principal residence.[88]

We are faced, then, in the case of the 22nd Dynasty, with discrepancies between the dynasty's historical capital and the place name assigned it in the Manethonian tradition. Once again, it would seem, the folk memory is at work.

Manetho's Version of the 23rd Dynasty

Few sections of the ancient king-list are as little known or as difficult to explain as the 23rd Dynasty. Even the epitomes differ one from another in a way that is hard to explain:

Africanus (4 kings)		*Eusebius* (3 kings)		*Sothis Book* (6 kings)	
Petaubates	40 yrs.	Petabastis	25 yrs.	Petoubastes	44 yrs.
Osorcho	8 yrs.	Osorthon	9 yrs.	Osorthon	9 yrs.
Psammous	10 yrs.	Psammous	10 yrs.	Psammos	10 yrs.
Zet	31 yrs.	-		-	
				Concharis	21 yrs.
				Osorthon	15 yrs.
				Takalophis	13 yrs.
Total:	31 yrs.		44 yrs.		112 yrs.

Only the first two names can, without fear of contradiction, be identified with known rulers, Petabastis with *Pꜣ-di-bꜣst* principally known from the Karnak quay graffiti,[89] construction abutting on the 10th pylon,[90] and from sundry monuments in the Delta,[91] and Osorthon with Osorkon (III) principally known from sundry Karnak statues,[92] the temple of Osiris Heqa-Djet,[93] the Karnak quai graffiti,[94] and a structure once standing near the Khonsu temple.[95] Psammous is difficult to interpret. It could be taken as false back-formation from a Psamouthis which name does occur in Manetho's 26th and 29th Dynasties[96] (in the former in place of the expected

[88] *Ibid.*, pl. 7, 10-14.
[89] Nos. 24, 26-29: von Beckerath, *JARCE* 5, 52.
[90] G. Legrain, *ASAE* 14 (1914) 14.
[91] Gauthier, *LdR* III, 380 (9); P-M IV, 119, 121 (possible; but perhaps another individual); cf. also A. R. Schulman, *JARCE* 5 (1966) 33ff; L. Habachi, *ZÄS* 93 (1966) 69ff; J. Yoyotte, *RdE* 24 (1972) 216ff (for the problem of like-named kings).
[92] Gauthier, *LdR* III, 385-6 (VIII-XIII).
[93] G. Legrain, *RT* 22 (1900) 125ff, 146ff; P-M II^2, 204ff; D. B. Redford, *JEA* 59 (1973) 16ff.
[94] Nos. 5, 13: von Beckerath, *JARCE* 5, 49f.
[95] Orthostats found in the *dallage* in 1977:cf. the present writer in *JSSEA* 9 (1978) 36; J. Lauffray, *Karnak d'Egypte, domaine du divin* (Paris, 1979) 217, fig. 186.
[96] Cf. Gauthier, *LdR* III, 394f.

"Psammethichos"). The closest identifiable Greek transcription would then be Ψεμουθης , for *Pꜣ-Šri-n-Mwt*.[97] On the other hand, "*Psan*" sounds remarkably like the vocalization of *Pꜣ sn*.[98] Either way we are no closer to historical reality.[99] Zet is well nigh impossible to find an explanation for. Petrie took it as a contraction of ζμτεῖται, and explained it as the mark of a scribal "query" about 31 years;[100] Helck thinks, similarly, that scribal doubt attached itself to the royal name which once stood there, and compares the earlier use of *wsf*.[101] For Kitchen, Zet is a possible garbling or substitute for Amun-rud, but if so "34 would be for 4."[102] To confuse the list still further, the Sothis Book gives 3 more names, 2 of which are clearly "Osorkon" and "Takelot," a combination which would have been well known from Osiris Heqa-Djet. The first, "Koncharis," contains the element *-kꜣ-rꜥ*, but *Kon* is not readily explicable. Plausibly it could be a misreading of a Demotic *nfr* (ɟ⊢) as *Kn* (≗), in which case the *Vorlage* would have been *Nfr-kꜣ-rꜥ*. More likely, however, *Konch'* is for *ḥḳn* (cf. the pronunciation of *knḥ* in Coptic ⲕⲛϩⲉ)[103] metathesized, with PIΣ a mistaken writing of ME.[104]

What is abundantly clear, in spite of all this uncertainty, is that beyond the first 2 names the Egyptians themselves knew little about the Dynasty. Even the informatory glosses are secondary. On the three comments our classical sources have preserved, two are clearly the result of *Greek* computation, and have nothing to do with Egyptian records. Eusebius's gloss on Psammous, to the effect that in his 8th year, Egypt "took over the (rule of the) sea after the Phoenicians,"[105] derives from the Thalassocracy list, and, at least for Egypt, has no independent value.[106] Similarly the dating of the first Olympiad to the reign of Petubastis, is based solely on Hellenistic

[97]Ranke, *PN* I, 118:19; but *Mwt* might descend to Greek -γους : cf. φεντενμους (*Pꜣ ḥm-ntr n Mwt*), W. Spiegelberg, *Die demotischen Papyrus der Strassburger Bibliothek* (Strasbourg, 1902) 23f.

[98]Ranke, *PN* I, 117:9, ⲡⲥⲁⲛⲕⲟⲩⲓ (*Pꜣ-sn-ky*); cf. II, 315:21, *Pisanhuru*.

[99]A *Pꜣ-Šry-n-Mwt* is known as a prophet of Amun and son of Montuemhet: Berlin 8739; Leclant, *Montouemhât*, 265; R. A. Parker, *A Saite Demotic Oracle Papyrus from Thebes* (London, 1962) pl. 14:18, p. 27, no. 47a.

[100]W. M. F. Petrie, *Ancient Egypt* 1 (1914) 32.

[101]Helck, *Manetho*, 48.

[102]Kitchen, *Third Intermediate Period*, § 451.

[103]J. Černý, *A Coptic Etymological Dictionary* (Cambridge, 1976) 60.

[104]*Ibid.*, 78.

[105]Eusebius, *Hieron. Chron.* (R. Helm, *Eusebius Werke* VII, 1, *Hieronymous* [Berlin, 1913] 85).

[106]On the thalassocracy lists, see R. Helm, *Hermes* 60 (1926) 241ff; A. Strobel, *Der spätbronzezeitliche Seevölkersturm* (Berlin and New York, 1976) 117ff.

computation, and nothing more.[107] The third gloss, that which identifies Osorkon with Herakles is, as the writer has attempted to show, a Theban tradition linking Osorkon with Khonsu, partly through misreading of Osiris Heqa-Djet reliefs and partly through the interpretation of his infix *s*^{3} *Ist*.[108] In fact, it is this erroneous linking of Osorkon with Khonsu that provides, to my mind, the best explanation for the presence of Psammous. The "child of Mut" is Khonsu himself, and the entry must originally have been a comment on Osorkon which in turn was glossed by "Herakles" for the benefit of the Hellenes.

Evidence, therefore, for the rentention of the 23rd Dynasty in the king-list, points to a strong Theban factor. Even the garbled Sothis Book knows the succession; Osorkon, Takelot, so well known from their association in Osiris Heqa-Djet,[109] and prefixes this sequence with a *Ḥkn-(m)-m*^{3c}*t* (Κόγχαρις) surely the enigmatic *nebty*-name seen on the lintel of the third door of their temple.[110] Shepenwepet, Osorkon's daughter, was appointed Divine Worshipper at Thebes[111]

[107]Eusebius's computation hit upon the reign of Bocchoris: Helm, *Die Chronik des Hieronymous*, 86! In fact, this vacillation in the identity of the contemporary in Egypt has probably produced the curious "Zet"-entry. Some commentators, fully aware that the Manethonian text gave 25, 9 and 10 years respectively to the three entries of the dynasty (see below), were puzzled that Petubastis was still signalled as the king in whose reign the games had been inaugurated. For the 44 years, when added to the 6 of the 24th Dynasty, the 40 of the 25th, and the 150 1/2 of the 26th, would have brought them to 765, necessitating the the dating of Petubastis's death to 741, thus *34* years after the first Olympiad.

[108]Redford, *JSSEA* 9, 33f.

[109]*Ibid.*

[110]P-M II^2, 206 (17); Gauthier, *LdR* III, 394. This block is rather more weathered than its neighbours; but as the inscription on it spills over on to the adjacent masonry, there is no question that the text properly belongs to this temple, and not to an earlier, prior, use of the stone. The royal names "Horus: Lord of Justification, the Good God, Usermare (in cartouche), Lord of the Two Lands, the Two Ladies: *Ḥkn-m-m*^{3c}*t*" is the titulary of neither Osorkon III nor Takelot III; and from the block's position it is quite likely that it belongs to a precursor of these two kings, undoubtedly Petubastis. The latter, then would have erected the shrine, but passed away almost as soon as its decoration began; alternatively, the inscribing of his name could have been merely an act of pious veneration by his son. Needless to say, it is *not* "highly probable" that the royal names on its lintel are to be ascribed to Amun-rud (Kitchen, *Third Intermediate Period*, § 101): would Osorkon III and his coregent have decorated the jambs and the lateral walls as high as the roof, in fact *all* the wall space of the original shrine — and left the lintel of door III blank?

[111]Kees, *Priestertum*, 203; *idem Hohenpriester*, 147ff; Kitchen, *Third Intermediate Period*, §§ 317-318. The main evidence is, in fact, the west inner room of the temple of Osiris Ruler of Eternity: P-M II^2, 206f. Here pretension to wide political power is evidenced by the curious, and unique, double *pschent* which Shepenwepet wears in the suckling scene: Redford, *JEA* 59, 23; on the almost regal nature of the office of Divine Worshipper, see J. Leclant, *MDAIK* 15 (1957) 166ff; *idem*, *Recherches*, 372f, 379f.

and Osorkon III may even have been buried there.[112] But, regardless of how firmly entrenched their memory was at Thebes, Memphis honoured the scions of this dynasty not at all:[113] neither they nor their representatives are present in an official capacity at the burial of the Apises, none of their members was crowned at Memphis, and they never succeeded in wresting control of the city from the 22nd Dynasty nor from the chiefs of the Labu.[114] How, then, can their names appear in the Memphite king-list tradition Manetho used, if Memphis never countenanced their rule? Would they not, like Piankhy of Napata, Namlot of Hermopolis, or Peftjauabast of Herakleopolis, drift into oblivion as far as the official record was concerned?

One important fact must be remembered and examined closely at this juncture, and that has to do with the way in which the 23rd Dynasty was regarded by the 25th. While the latter felt no qualms

[112]P. Louvre E 7128: Malinine, *Textes*, no. XI, p. 86, line 2 ("the tomb of King Userton" on the west of Thebes); similarly F. Ll. Griffith, *Catalogue of the Demotic Papyri in the Rylands Library in Manchester* III (London, 1909) 19, n. 2. Dates of these texts are Saite and Persian.

[113]The two stelae of Petubastis found at Mitrahineh (Cairo JE 45530: Schluman, *JARCE* 5, 33ff, pl. 13:2; and AIN 917; 0. Koefoed-Petersen, *Publications de la Glyptothèque Ny Carlsberg* 1 *les stèles égyptiennes* [Copenhagen, 1948], pl. 54, p. 40f) were certainly brought to Memphis at a later date from sites further south (the former mentions the chief of Per-Sekhemkheperre, between Meidum and Herakleopolis, and the latter certain fields [?] located near Tjaru and donated by the high-priest of Arsaphes). Of the other kings named Petubastis whose monuments were either found at, or betoken acceptance by, Memphis, Sehtepibre Petubastis is no earlier than 7th Century B.C. in date (cf. Habachi, *ZÄS* 93, 69ff – could he be the *Putubisti* of Assyrian sources?), and Seheribre Petubastis is certainly late Saite or early Persian (cf. Yoyotte, *RdE* 24, 216ff). The bronze of Osorkon III found at Mitrahineh (Gauthier, *LdR* III, 386 [XV]) is certainly no proof that Memphis accepted him: it may have been, to judge from the objects found with it, part of a cache deposited later: P-M III, 217.

[114]From the mid-9th Century to at least the first decade of the reign of ᶜOkheperre Sheshonk (IV), Memphis was controlled by a cadet branch of the Tanite Libyan dynasty (Manetho's 22nd), descended from Sheshonk son of Osorkon II: Yoyotte, in *Mélanges Maspero* IV, 130; Kitchen, *Third Intermediate Period*, § 81; Gomaà, *Die libyschen Fürstentümer des Deltas*, 5ff. These honour their 22nd Dynasty cousins almost exclusively. By the end of Sheshonk IV's reign control of Memphis had passed into the hands of the chief of the Labu (Yoyotte, in *Mélanges Maspero* IV, 130f, 153f; Gomaà, *Die libyschen Fürstentümer ds Delta*, 13ff), and remained in the hands of the Saite rulers until the coming of Sabaco.

about removing the monuments of the 22nd Dynasty,[115] they revered those of the 23rd.[116] When Piankhy exerted his control over Thebes and appointed his sister Amenirdis to be the Divine Worshipper, he did not supplant Shepenwepet of the 23rd Dynasty, as he easily might have done but rather had her adopt Amenirdis.[117] Her father, Osorkon III, does not drift into the same oblivion as was reserved for the other Libyan kings, but is not infrequently thereafter involved in the offering formula in one particular context, viz. the filiation of the Divine Worshippers! Here he appears, with equal prominence as the Sudanese kings, as the father of Shepenwepet I.[118] His son, the erstwhile solar high-priest at Karnak[119] who was elevated to the kingship as Takelot III, turns up in the genealogies of a number of prominent people of 25th or 26th Dynasty date, as to a lesser extent does Amun-rud.[120] Such a survival in a prominent social position of

[115]Cf. Karnak, north court (VI), where Taharqa's large relief scene and supplication to Amun on the south wall is superimposed over an original text of Osorkon II (P-M II^2, 92 [264]). The cornice blocks of Osorkon I, now in the *musée en pleine air* (G. Daressy, *ASAE* 22 [1922], 64) come from the original forecourt of the temple (the construction of which is referred to in Gebel Silsileh, no. 100: Caminos, *JEA* 38, 46ff), largely demolished by Taharqa. The small shrine of the high-priest Takelot, grandson of Osorkon II, west of the temple of Osiris, Ruler of Eternity at Karnak (J. Leclant, *Orientalia* 20 [1951] 462f; P. Barguet, *Le temple d'Amon-rê à Karnak* [Cairo, 1962] 15) was allowed to fall into delapidation.

[116]The best example is the temple of Osiris Ruler of Eternity (P-M II^2, 204ff), which remained virtually intact: the addition of Shebitku aimed solely at replacing an original mud-brick anteroom with a stone structure, now the first room of the shrine (*pace* Leclant, *Recherches*, 50): cf. the writer's archaeological report in *Annual Report of the SSEA* (Toronto, 1972) 19. Moreover, Taharqa's edifice by the sacred lake reproduces in part the scene on the east wall of room III (P-M II^2, 206 [22]): R. A. Parker, J. Leclant, J-C. Goyon, *The Edifice of Taharqa by the Sacred Lake of Karnak* (Providence, 1979) pl. 22, p. 48ff.

[117]On the adoption of Amenirdis see Kees, *Priestertum*, 266, *idem*, *Hohenpriester*, 158ff; Leclant, *Recherches*, 357f; Drioton Vandier, *L'Egypte*^{4}, 547, 563; M. Gitton, J. Leclant, in *LdÄ* I (1972) 196ff; II (1976) 805, no. 26.

[118]Cf. Gauthier, *LdR* III, 388 (IIB); G. Legrain, *ASAE* 7 (1907) 44; Leclant, *Montouemhât*, doc. 29, p. 140f ("the Divine Worshipper Amenirdis, king's-daughter of Kashta" balanced by "her mother, the god's wife Shepenwepet, king's-daughter of Osorkon"); cf. also the examples of filiation in the temple of Osiris Ruler of Eternity: Leclant, *Recherches*, 54.

[119]So called on the reliefs from the *dallage* in front of the Khonsu temple: see above, p. 310, n. 95.

[120]Cf. the god's-father of Amun and priest of Osiris of Koptos Ankhefenmut: E. P. Uphill, *JEA* 43 (1957) 1ff, pl. 1 (great-grandson through his mother of King Takelot); prophet of Amun Efc?ow, contemporary of Taharqa: A. Fakhry, *ASAE* 43 (1943) 411 and pl. 26 (grandson through his mother of King Takelot); Meresamun, singer of Amun: Cairo 41035 (granddaughter through her father of "the king's-son ... Takelot"); singer of Amun Esteru: P-M I^2, 773 (21) (daughter of Amun-rud); priest of ...(?) [Padiamun]-nebnesut-towy: *Aegyptische Inschriftenaus den Staatlichen Museen zu Berlin* II (Berlin, 1924) 540; P-M I^2, 678 (Berlin 2100: grandson through his mother of Amun-rud).

various branches of the family was not the fate of the 22nd Dynasty, and indicates a measure of favour accorded by later generations to the descendents of Petubastis. Finally, when Piankhy came north to engage the hostile coalition of Tefnakhte, – the references are brief but explicit – King Osorkon "who is in Bubastis and the District of Ra-nofer" was alone of the northern rulers, allowed to come "to see the beauty of His Majesty" (i.e. Piankhy),[121] even though Osorkon had been listed among the enemies! Even so, when first mentioned[122] Osorkon's name is kept apart from the main roster of rebels; but later he heads the list of those whom Piankhy re-instated.[123]

If, now, the question be posed as to why such an otherwise ephemeral group of rulers as the 23rd Dynasty should have enjoyed such undeserved commemoration in the memory of the nation, the answer appears to be clear: it is because of the deference shown to it by the conquering Sudanese kings. When the latter appear upon the scene in Egypt there are really only two centres claiming legitimacy: Sais and Bubastis. By its military strength and posture the former had made itself the enemy of Kashta and Piankhy; by its weakness and its acceptance in Thebes, the bailiwick of Amun, the latter proved to be the natural friend to court. By having his sister adopted by Shepenwepet, Piankhy had implicitly recognized this "queen" and through her the family to which she belonged as having a legal right to Thebes, if not to all Egypt. Scholars have from time to time claimed to be mystified as to why the conquering Piankhy should have retired from the scene so quickly, leaving Egypt leaderless. But this puzzlement would disappear if we only reflect on Piankhy's character. With this humorless traditionalist custom and law weighed heavily, and to him Egypt *already had* legitimate leaders in the scions of the house of Petubastis! What right had he to overthrow them?

[121]Piankhy stela, line 106: *Urk.* III, 42.

[122]Piankhy stela, line 19: *Urk.* III 11. The reference is actually *inserted* into the generalizing statement which concludes the list: "every chief who bears the feather who is in Lower Egypt ... and every mayor and the village headmen etc."

[123]Piankhy stela, line 114; cf. A. J. Spalinger, *SAK* 7 (1979) 287. That this Osorkon IV belongs to the 22nd Dynasty (Kitchen, *Third Intermediate Period* § 92) has now unfortunately become part of the chronography of the Late Period. The question shall be addressed by the author elsewhere.

He was related to them![124]

The 23rd Dynasty, then, entered the king-list through the dominant position ultimately enjoyed by the 25th Dynasty in Memphis. The family of Shepenwepet I had been grafted on to the family tree of the Sudanese kings and, thanks to the strength of the institution of the Divine Worshipper, the memory of this connexion was never suppressed. In keeping with this fact, it is only the first two scions of the 23rd Dynasty that were clearly remembered and recorded, viz. Petubastis and Osorkon III, as the immediate progenitors of the Divine Worshipper.[125] The descendants of

[124]The writer has maintained for some time in lectures that it was not only the Ashdod affair in 713-12 (cf. A. J. Spalinger, *JARCE* 10 [1973] 95ff) that prompted Sabaco's invasion of 711, but the demise of the 23rd Dynasty line in Bubastis. Osorkon IV is still alive in 716, as the tribute of *Šilḫanni* to Assyria in that year attests: cf. H. Tadmor, *JCS* 12 (1958) 78; *idem*, *BA* 29 (1966) 92f; M. Elat, *JAOS* 98 (1978) 23; on the identification, see W. Fr. von Bissing, *AfO* 14 (1941) 44; W. F. Albright, *BASOR* 141 (1956) 24 (the first syllable of the name, viz. *U*-, can sometimes be elided, as is shown by the compound name *T*ꜣ*-nt-Srkn*, Ranke, *PN* I, 363:3). The tribute may be reflected in documents from Assyria: cf. R. F. Harper, *Assyrian and Babylonian Letters* (Chicago, 1914) no. 1427; H. W. F. Saggs, *Iraq* 17 (1955) pl. 33, p. 134; 21 (1959) 168f; J. N. Postgate, *Taxation and Conscription in the Assyrian Empire* (Rome, 1974) 117f. This, however, is the latest reference to him.

[125]The 23rd Dynasty has suffered at the hands of modern scholars who have felt free to treat it as a sort of "catch-all" into which they can throw any name they cannot otherwise place, a tactic that smacks more of chronography than historiography: cf. in particular, K. Baer, *JNES* 32 (1973) 11ff; Kitchen, *Third Intermediate Period*, § 419 (table) and *passim*; J. von Beckerath, *OLZ* 74 (1979) 8. Yuput I(?), solely on the basis of Karnak quai inscription no. 26 (von Beckerath, *JARCE* 5, 52) is made a coregent and successor of Petubastis, while a new Sheshonk is created, admittedly on empirical grounds, from the replacement of *stp-n* + DN by *mry-Imn* (Kitchen, *Third Intermediate Period*, § 68), and thrust between Yuput and Osorkon III. But no. 26 says nothing more than that Yuput is a later contemporary of Petubastis, not that he belongs to the same house, or was a son of Petubastis. In view of the importance the Libyans placed on kinship such a relationship would have been indicated, as it is in fact in quai inscription no. 13! (cf. also Gauthier, *LdR* III, 373 [II]; Malinine, Posener, Vercoutter, *Catalogue des stèles du Sérapéum*, pl. 9, no. 26: Sheshonk IV son of Pamy). That the Sheshonk in question was a scion of the dynasty is wholly unproven, as there is no other text linking him with any known member of the house. The atmosphere prevailing in Thebes during and immediately following the reign of Petubastis is one of confusion and uncertainty at the welter of petty dynasts springing up in the Delta as the power of the 22nd Dynasty declined: generally the descendents of Petubastis were acknowledged, but the community also accepted the "reigns" of certain *Nebenkönige*, possibly through commercial relations Thebes enjoyed with them, or because of their apparent political power or because one of their daughters had been dedicated to the service of Amun (cf. Yoyotte, in *Mélanges Maspero* IV, 147). That no Yuput or Sheshonk intervened between Petubastis and Osorkon III is strongly suggested by the important scene on the west wall of the second room of the temple of Osiris, Ruler of Eternity (P-M II^2, 206 [15], incompletely described). Here Shepenwepet is shown twice in the presence of four other persons who seem to be collectively referred to as "her fathers and her mothers." One of the four, the goddess Hathor, suckles the princess in her curious double *pschent* (Redford, *JEA* 59, 23), a rare cultic act when women are involved, but occasionally found during this period (cf. W. F. Smith, *Egypt as Represented in the Museum of Fine Arts, Boston* [Boston, 1942] 150; I. Hofmann, *Studien zum meroitischen Königtum* [Brussels, 1971] 37: I owe these references to the kindness of Dr. R. Fazzini). The three remaining figures are human royalty: a king facing Shepenwepet across an offering table, and a king and queen on the left. To judge by the prominence given Shepenwepet's mother elsewhere in this chapel the

footnote 125 continued ....

Osorkon, other than Shepenwepet were not distinctly recorded, although Manetho's sources may have imparted a vague feeling that there were others.[126]

Manetho's Epitome gives Tanis as the locative element attached to the 23rd Dynasty, as it had to the 21st Dynasty. That the house of Petubastis is connected with this city is ostensibly a puzzle, as no monuments of its kings have been found at the site. But I would suggest that Osorkon IV's connexion with *R*ᶜ*-nfr* latterly brought about this connexion,[127] at a time when the dominance of the Sudanese kings was being extended over Egypt.

footnote 125 continued ....
couple can only be Osorkon III and Karatjet. The single, male royal figure most probably is Petubastis, and he is thrown into prominence in the scene, not only by his central position, but also by the blue colour of his figure: cf. Legrain, *RT* 22, 131; P. Reuterswärd, *Studien zur Polychromie der Plastik* I *Aegypten* (Uppsala, 1958) 45. On this, the most likely identification of the figures, Yuput and Sheshonk are nowhere to be seen.

[126]Takelot III and Amun-rud should be added as sons, and in all probability also the Osorkon (IV) who turns up in the Piankhy stela (line 19: *Urk.* III, 11; line 114: *Urk.* III, 38), and probably in Sargon's annals. (above, n. 91). He is assigned, quite gratuitously by Kitchen to the close of the 22nd Dynasty (*Third Intermediate Period* § 84) but there are good reasons for rejecting this placement. First, the roster of the 22nd Dynasty in the Epitome lists three kings following *Takelothis*, (i.e. Takelot II) who would thus be Sheshonk III, Pamay, and ᶜOkheperre Sheshonk (IV); here there is clearly no place for another Osorkon. Second, the Memphite authorities acknowledged the kingship of the 22nd Dynasty right down to the end of the reign of the nonentity ᶜOkheperre Sheshonk. Why, if Osorkon (IV) followed immediately in the same line, does Memphis suddenly and completely ignore him? Third, Osorkon on the Piankhy stela is not said to be "in Tanis," but to have jurisdiction over a region of indeterminate location (see below n. 127), and to reside in Bubastis. ᶜOkheperre Sheshonk certainly resided in Tanis (cf. the numerous blocks, depicting his *sd*-festival: Montet, *Le lac sacré de Tanis*, pl. 8ff). The picture that emerges is this: Memphis was consistent in its honouring the 22nd Dynasty while it remained in power, but ceased to do so on the demise of Sheshonk (IV), the last of the line. At that time the bailiwick over which he had ruled, viz. Tanis and its environs, passed under the jurisdiction of the contemporary 23rd Dynasty ruler at Bubastis. (It might be added that any theory which proposes a release from the difficulties of this period by claiming that the "Petubastids" attested at Thebes were a local dynasty, not to be confused with the 23rd [cf. K-H. Priese, *ZÄS* 98 (1970) 20, n. 23] is a counsel of despair and ought to be rejected.)

[127]On *R*ᶜ*-nfr*, see Gauthier, *Dictionnaire géographique* I, 190; III, 130; Montet, *Géographie de l'Egypte ancienne* I, 201; Helck, *Die altägyptischen Gaue*, 190; Grimal, *La stèle triomphale*, 152, n. 464. (On *R-nfr*, probably no relation in origin with the toponym under discussion, see A-P. Zivie, *Hermopolis et le nome de l'ibis* [Cairo, 1975] 165). Because of its occurrence with Bubastis on the Piankhy stela, some have been inclined to locate it close to Tell Basta (Gauthier, Helck), but the connexion with Sile (cf. *inter alia* P. Montet, *Kêmi* 8 [1946] 64, pl. 15) has prompted others to place it in the northeast Delta (Montet): cf. G. Daressy, *BIFAO* 11 (1914) 35ff. Vandier pointed out that *sḫt ḏ*ᶜ is mentioned in the same breath as Sile (*RdE* 17 [1965] 170ff), and located it west of the latter; Yoyotte equated it with the nome of Tanis itself (*Mélanges Maspero* IV, 129, n. 2; cf. von Beckerath, *OLZ* 74, 10). The name itself, if understood as "Re(?) of the Extremity(?)," would invite comparison with *p*ꜣ *rwḏ n p*ꜣ *R*ᶜ, applied to the eastern desert tract along the side of the Delta: Gauthier, *Dictionnaire géographique* III, 184 (cf. however Gomaà, *Die libyschen Fürstentümer*, 132ff [between Bubastis and Tanis]). Could it be that both names are in fact designations of the tract contained within the angle of the "eastern canal" running from the coast at Pelusium to Qantara (cf. W. H. Shea, *BASOR* 226 [1977] 31ff)?

The Interest in Antiquity in the Late Period

While few may have mourned the passing of Ramesses XI, with his death a great change overcame Egyptian society. For five centuries the Egyptian monarchy, regardless of where the kings resided, had displayed a decidedly "Theban" face to the world. Pharaoh must needs secure the approval of Amun at the outset of his reign, would repair south from time to time for the key Theban festivals, and, upon his death, would occupy an official tomb on the west bank. Theban society, though provincial by Memphite or Lower Egyptian standards, could always boast a connexion with royalty or the royal administration. With the passing of Ramesses XI, however, the monarchic tradition was ruptured. No longer did Amun figure prominently in the sanctioning of a king, nor did his festivals attract a royal party. Burials in the Valley of the Kings ceased, and royal mortuary service was discontinued at Thebes. With the withdrawl of the kingship to the north, the Theban priesthood found the framework which had provided them with an identity, a thing of the past. Now increasingly they tended to resort to the glories of an illustrious ancestry, and would advertise these in a lengthy genealogy in the dedicatory inscriptions on their statues.[128]

Especially in the Thebaid, but also elsewhere throughout the kingdom, there was an awareness of being in a long succession of dignitaries and office holders, uninterrupted through centuries: "one son following another in this house (i.e. the temple of Amun), the fathers of the fathers, since the time of former kings."[129] One wished one's membership in this long and prestigious line to be openly displayed for posterity by having one's statue included among the "praised ones" (statues) in the temple,[130] and to be honoured with the rites "as they do for the forebears."[131] One "exalted the names of the fathers and made their monuments to endure" in the hope that one would enjoy like treatment from posterity.[132] And further, one "was not forgetful about [those who were aforetime], like a child of the ancestors."[133] Restoring ancient stelae and strolling about in

[128]Redford, *Biblical Joseph Story*, 6ff: cf. also A. Kadry, *JSSEA* 13 (1983) 35ff.
[129]Cairo 42211, k. 8. An oft-repeated statement is that the deceased is the progenitor of "great prophets": Cairo 42215, d, 3; 42206, e, 2; 42210, e, 3-4; 42225, c, 6.
[130] *Wb* III, 157:1; Cairo 42229, c, 7-8.
[131]Cairo 42207, f, 6; 42210, d, 2-3; 42222, c; 42224, q, 7-8; 42230, d, 9.
[132]Cairo 42241 C(a), 8 (=Leclant, *Montouemhât*, 83); cf. the epithet of ᶜOnkh-sheshonk: *ḳm^3 ẖnty n it itw.f*: P. Vernus, *BIFAO* 76 (1976) pl. VI, 2.
[133]C. Robichon, A. Varille, *Karnak-nord* IV (Cairo, 1951) fig. 141, col. 7.

necropoleis were acts of piety for the ancestors.[134]

The temple was now the custodian of very ancient documents. A priest could draw up a genealogy "from ancient writings of the time of the ancestors."[135] The temple libraries also contained the accumulated "legislation" of past reigns, and it was becoming a cliché to identify political wisdom with familiarity with this body of records. "Regular decisions in the privy chamber were taken through his (Osorkon's) awareness of all the policies brought into being through the generations of former kings."[136] Ancestral documents had the weight of statutory law: Osorkon "brought everyone that would transgress the charter of the ancestors" and punished them.[137] Hory also, the mentor of King Petubastis, claims to have been "skilled in the laws of the palace, the instruction of those who were aforetime."[138] By Graeco-Roman times a temple could not even be founded without provision being made in the ritual to "praise the ancestors."[139]

Though people may boast of their ability to summon up accurate records of the past in written form, the reality of such a link with the remote past depends entirely on the peaceful continuum a community has enjoyed over the years. Only if my library escapes fire and vandalism do I have any chance of laying my hands on the original text of McCauley! A priceless example of the effect on the community's collective memory of antiquity wrought by a chequered history, is provided by the ancient states of the Levant. Time and time again, in the archaeology of both the coastal and the inland cities of Palestine and Syria, destruction levels of awful proportions attest to the interruption of all aspects of civilized living which periodically overtook the communities of this region. With homes burned and razed, and a population put to the sword, what chance would a survivor have of rescuing a precious "historical" document, or questioning an aged inhabitant? And so, when we examine the written record of Hebrews or Phoenicians, we find exactly what archaeology implies. The coastal cities in classical times recall the invasion of the Sea Peoples one thousand years before in a startlingly garbled form; and Hebrews of the 7th Century B.C. could reach back in their collective memories scarcely to the Iron I period! A Jew of the post-Exilic period has few reliable documents dating even from

[134]*JEA* 53 (1967) pl. XI.
[135]W. Spiegelberg, *PSBA* 24 (1902) 320ff.
[136]*Reliefs and Inscriptions at Karnak* III *The Bubastite Portal*, pl. 21, col. 4.
[137]*Ibid.*, pl. 18, col. 35; Caminos, *The Chronicle of Prince Osorkon*, 49, n. *c*.
[138]Cairo 42226, h. 5.
[139]PD 6319, *rt.* x + ii, 22: Reymond, *Hermetic Writings*, 73; *Edfu* VII, 27:9.

the Divided Monarchy; and for earlier periods he must rely on folk tradition. Sanchuniaton in Phoenicia can, in the 6th Century B.C., reproduce Canaanite mythology fairly accurately, but it is euhemerized and misunderstood.[140]

If we examine the state of the Egyptians' knowledge of their past, even our initial impression will be markedly different. On the whole the preservation of Egyptian archives over centuries and millennia is a remarkable fact which is born out, not only by the circumstantial evidence of contemporary ability to reconstruct antiquity accurately,[141] but also by the history of the archives themselves. Memphis is a good example. Between the reign of Piankhy in the second half of the 8th Century B.C. and Artaxerxes III's invasion in 343 B.C. Memphis underwent five known cases of seige and reduction by military means. Piankhy himself captured and destroyed the harbour with its ships, and later "seized (the city) ... like a rainstorm," slaughtering a large number of people;[142] but while the attack undoubtedly involved destruction, the temples remained inviolate. "When day dawned and the morrow had come, H.M. despatched people into it (the city) to protect the temples of the gods ... and Memphis was purified with incense and natron."[143] In 671 Esarhaddon assaulted and captured the city. But while in the Sinjirli stela he speaks of destruction and burning,[144] in the Nahr el-Kelb stela he refers to entering the city amid general rejoicing, and occupying the palace peacefully.[145] Again, it seems unlikely that the temples suffered significantly. Cambyses' seige of Memphis ended in surrender with minimal destruction, although indignities were heaped

[140]On the Sea Peoples, see Strobel, *Der spätbronzezeitlichen Seevölkersturm*, 31ff, 48ff, 210ff and *passim*; W. Helck, *Beziehungen Aegyptens und Vorderasien zum ägäis* (Darmstadt, 1977) 132ff (and the writer's review in *JAOS* 103 [1983] 481ff). It is now becoming clear, with respect to Hebrew literature, that the Pentateuch and the historical books reflect the 7th Century B.C., the Exile and the early post-Exilic period: cf. in particular the works of J. Van Seters, *Abraham in History and Tradition* (New Haven, 1975); *idem*, *The Journal for the Study of the Old Testament* 1 (1976) 22ff; Redford, *Biblical Joseph Story*; the Exodus and the Conquest themes derive from the dimly-remembered expulsion of the Hyksos and the Shasu-movement respectively: A. H. Gardiner, in *Receuil Champollion* (Paris, 1922) 204; D. B. Redford, *JSSEA* 12 (1982) 74, n. 155. On Sanchuniaton, see W. F. Albright, *Yahweh and the Gods of Canaan* (New York, 1969) 223ff.

[141]Of course, this is not to deny that a lively folk tradition lived at all periods side by side with the scribal tradition, but the former was not generally held in esteem.

[142]Line 96: Grimal, *La stèle triomphale*, pl. IX.

[143]Line 97: Grimal, *La stèle triomphale*, pl. X. Cf. the similar protection afforded the temples in Per-sekhemkheperre, Meidum and Itj-towy: lines 77ff.

[144]R. Borger, *Die Inschriften Asarhaddons, Königs von Assyrien* (Graz, 1956) 99.

[145]*Ibid.*, 101.

on the inhabitants.[146] Similarly, in the revolt of Inaros, while the city was taken by the rebels, and the keep of White Walls invested, the militants were forced to withdraw without doing any damage.[147] The capture of Memphis by Artaxerxes III did, indeed, result in devastation. But it is significant that the contents of the sacred libraries were deemed so valuable by the Persians that they were saved and sold back to the priests at a high price.[148]

If the fate of Memphis is a reliable indicator, then we may confidently conclude that temple archives in Egypt suffered remarkably little over time. Priests such as the aforementioned Osorkon and Hory are not mouthing meaningless clichés when they refer to the availability of the documents of the ancestors. On the other hand, it goes without saying that other factors, such as the periodic cleaning out of old manuscripts, or the presence in a collection of written folk-tales with a prestige equal to that of a more reliable document, imposed on the priestly user of a library the need for a critical judgement he might not have possessed!

The Kings of Sais

The expansion of the "Kingdom of the West" under the chief of the Labu Tefnakhte in the 3rd quarter of the 8th Century B.C. for the first time brought the city of Sais into a direct and dominant position vis-à-vis Memphis.[149] While Tefnakhte is absent from the Memphite or Saqqara monuments,[150] Bocchoris his successor was certainly contenanced by the Memphite clergy, who dated the burial of an Apis to his reign[151] Yet the texts from this burial are singular for two reasons: 1. none is an *official* record, all being from private

[146]Herodotus iii.13.2 (cf. iii.14.1ff).
[147]Thycidydes i.104.2; Diodorus xi.71.3-6, 74.1-4; Lloyd, *Herodotus, Book II: Introduction*, 45.
[148]A. T. Olmstead, *A History of the Persian Empire* (Chicago, 1948) 440: Diodorus xvi.51.1-2.
[149]On Tefnakhte's take-over of Memphis, see Piankhy stela, line 3: *Urk.* III, 5; Gomaà, *Die Libyschen Fürstentümer des Deltas*, 15f; Yoyotte, in *Mélanges Maspero* IV, 153ff; the fact that Memphis offered some resistence to Piankhy must indicate some sort of favourable attitude towards Sais: cf. Spalinger, *SAK* 7, 285ff.
[150]It would be gratuitous to assign Serapeum stela 123 (Malinine, Posener, Vercoutter, *Catalogue des stèles du Sérapéum*, pl. 34) dated in the 14th Year, 4th month of an unspecified king's reign, to Tefnakhte.
[151]Cf. P-M III, 209f(G); Gauthier, *LdR* III, 410 (I); see also the following notes.

individuals incidentally of low rank,[152] and 2. only two stelae bear the cartouche of Bocchoris, not prominently displayed, while most squeeze "year 6" in as though it were an afterthought![153] What is the reason for this rather cavalier treatment of a king who, during his lifetime, was known abroad.[154] and who posthumously became one of the great lawgivers of Egypt?[155]

Thanks to the work of Tadmor, Spalinger and Kitchen, the year 712 B.C. had emerged as an anchor-date in the study of the Late Period in Egypt.[156] It was in that year that Yamani of Ashdod, after an unsuccessful attempt to organize resistence to Assyria, fled south into Egypt.[157] By the time the Display Inscriptions and the Annals had been composed for publication at Dur-Sharrukin[158] Yamani had been extradited to Assyria and Egypt was in Kushite hands.[159] It has been suggested that this case of extradition was in conformity with a treaty which must have been drawn up between Sabaco and Sargon, since clauses covering such eventualities are always prominent in ancient Near Eastern pacts.[160] The time required for the negotiations for such a treaty, and the deporting of Yamani pursuant thereto, suggests that Sabaco's invasion had occurred at some distance in time prior to 707 B.C.

Now Isaiah (20:1-4) signals the year 712 B.C. by the following incident: "in the year that (the) Tartan came up against Ashdod when Sargon the king of Assyria sent him, and fought against Ashdod and took it, at that time Yahweh spoke to Isaiah the son of Amos as

[152]Malinine, Posener, Vercoutter, *Catalogue des stèles du Sérapéum*, no. 92 (goldsmith); no. 93 (god's-father); no. 94 (junior priest?); no. 97 (craftsman); no. 101 (doorman).
[153]Malinine, Posener, Vercoutter, *Catalogue des stèles du Sérapéum*, no. 91 (pl. 26), "year 6 of the king of Upper and Lower Egypt, *W*^{3}*ḥ-k*^{3}*-rʿ* son of Re, *B*^{3}*<k-n>-rn.f*, living for ever" in lines x + 2-3; no. 92 (pl. 26), text at bottom begins with "year 6"; nos. 93-95 (pl. 27), "year 6" is crudely squeezed in at the bottom; no. 97 (pl. 28), "year 6" is squeezed into the text between the names of the wife and the second son; no. 101 (pl. 29), "*B*^{3}*k-n-rn.f*" (in cartouche) and "year 6" are squeezed into the protruding flange at the top of the stela; no. 102 (pl. 29), "year 6, first month of *akhet*, day 5" added at the bottom of the text.
[154]Cf. Gauthier, *LdR* III, 412 (VIII); J. Leclant, *Orientalia* 30 (1961) 404; M. Schmidt, *ZÄS* 97 (1971) 118ff; J. Leclant, in W. A. Ward (ed.), *The Role of the Phoenicians in the Interaction of Mediterranean Civilizations* (Beirut, 1968) 26, n. 50.
[155]Cf. the tradition in Diodorus i.65.1; 79; 94.5; see A. Moret, *De Bocchori rege* (Paris, 1903).
[156]Tadmor, *JCS* 12, 92f, 95; Spalinger, *JARCE* 10, 95ff; Kitchen, *Third Intermediate Period* § 115; general remarks, H. von Zeissl, *Aethiopen und Assyrer in Aegypten* (Glückstadt, 1944) 12f; C. Schedl, *VT* 12 (1962) 112ff.
[157]Tadmor, *JCS* 12, 92f, 95; Spalinger, *JARCE* 10, 95ff; for the Assyrian strategy in reducing Ashdod, see now N. Na'aman, *Tel Aviv* 6 (1979) 71, n. 7.
[158]Cf. Tadmor, *JCS* 12, 97 (707 B.C.).
[159]*ANET*^{2}, 285f.
[160]So Tadmor, *BA* 29, 94 and n. 34.

follows: 'take the sackcloth off your buttocks, and remove your shoes from your feet'; and so he did and went around naked and barefoot. And Yahweh said, 'As my servant Isaiah has gone about naked and barefoot for three years as an object lesson of Egypt and Kush, so shall the king of Assyria lead away the captivity of Egypt and the exiles of Kush etc.'"[161] Thus, according to this text, for three years following Ashdod's defeat (i.e. 712-709 B.C.) Isaiah made a fool of himself in an attempt to impress upon his fellow countrymen the folly of relying on Nilotic powers. The reference to Egypt might be explained on the basis of the help she had been expected to give to the Ashdodites which as it turned out, did not materialize. But the significant entry in the chapter is Kush, which seems to take precedence over Egypt.[162] That is to say, within three years of 712 B.C. Kush had come into a position of being an object of trust to southern Palestine, such as it had never been prior to that time. In the Assyrian texts relating to events of 722, 716 or 713 there is no mention of Kush. It is to Sais (to Tefnakhte) that Hoshea goes for aid in 722,[163] and Delta kinglets that present Sargon with tribute, and are approached by the Philistine conspirators. In the sources for the fall of Samaria (2 Kings 17:4) and the defeat of Gaza[164] and in Isaiah's tirade against Egypt (Isa. 19) Kush is conspicuously absent.[165] In spite, then, of how affairs looked from inside Egypt, from Asia it seemed as though Middle Egypt and the Delta were free and independent down to the coming of Sabaco.

If we put stock in the reference to "3 years," therefore, Isa. 20 ensures 709 B.C. as the *terminus ad quem* for Sabaco's conquest. But the chapter insists markedly on the year of the taking of Ashdod (i.e. 712 B.C. [Spring] to 711 B.C. [spring]) as the date for what follows. It is most likely, therefore, that the 3 years is a projection into the future, and that the description of the object lesson and the postulated explanation of it by Yahweh, must be understood in relation to the date in the superscription to the chapter, and the composition of the chapter would then date to 712-711 B.C. Thus,

[161]On Isaiah's general attitude towards Sargon, see H. L. Ginsberg, *JAOS* 88 (1968) 47ff; H. Donner, *Israel unter den Völkern* (Leiden, 1964) 113ff.
[162]In vs. 5 the order is Kush-Egypt; the former is מַבָּטָם the latter only תִּפְאַרְתָּם
[163]D. B. Redford, *JSSEA* 11 (1981) 75f.
[164]*ANET*[2], 284f.
[165]Isa. 20 is probably the earliest allusion to Kush of the 25th Dynasty in the Old Testament. All other passages are demonstrably later. Isa. 11:11 has a clear eschatological tone, and presupposes a Diaspora, while 18:1 is fairly clearly an illusion to Hezekiah's intrigues after 705 B.C. (cf. Donner, *Israel unter des völkern*, 124). Gen. 10:6-7 belongs in a context which can be dated no earlier than the close of the Judaean monarchy.

when Isaiah made his enunciation sometime during that year, Kush was already in control of the Delta.[166]

If the datum given by Africanus for Bocchoris's reign is correct, and all indications are that it is,[167] then part at least of his last year must have fallen in 712-711 B.C.. Now the Apis was buried according to stela no. 102[168] on the 5th day of the first month of *akhet* in Bocchoris's 6th year, a calendrical date which would, in the last quarter of the 8th Century B.C., correspond to February 23.[169] At that time, therefore, in the mid-winter of 712-711 B.C., Bocchoris's reign was still acknowledged at Memphis, but in such a curiously cautious manner that one can only conclude his claim to suzerainty was in doubt. The only event that *could* have created uncertainty in the minds of the Egyptians was the war with Sabaco; and we must therefore conclude that when the Apis was laid to rest that war was impending, if not already in progress.[170] That Sabaco was in control of all Egypt and Bocchoris dead by the early summer of 711 at the latest becomes a virtual certainty.

Saite hegemony over Memphis was interrupted by the 25th Dynasty invasion. The Kushite kings honoured Memphis, as we

[166]E. Meyer (*Geschichte des Altertums* III (Stuttgart and Berlin, 1938) 41) set 715 and 711 as termini for Sabaco's invasion; cf. J. Leclant, J. Yoyotte, *BIFAO* 51 (1952) 27; Yoyotte, in *Mélanges Maspero* IV, 172, n. 5; for the recent acrimonious debate on the chronology, see W. Barta, *GM* 70 (1984) 7ff, n. 1-2.

[167]"Six years" is clearly a rounding-off, probably to the next highest number, but it is questionable how many months and days into his 6th he lived. The 26th Dynasty was later to adopt the earlier practice of antedating the first year to the preceding New Year's day of the civil calendar: R. A. Parker, *AJSL* 58 (1941) 298; A. H. Gardiner, *JEA* 31 (1945) 16ff. It is a moot point as to whether their Saite forbear had followed the practice also. The antiquity of antedating in the Late Period is a problem. Piankhy's stela begins (*Urk.* III, 4) with year 21, first month of *akhet*, which, though it lacks the day, may be a reference to the beginning of the civil year; but there is no implication that this was the anniversary of the accession. Osorkon I's record of donations from Bubastis (Naville, *Bubastis*, pl. 51) lists [donations to the temples (?)] made from "⸢year 1⸣, first month of ⸢*akhet*⸣, day 7 to year 4, fourth month of *shomu*, day 25; making 3 years, 3 months (sic! but emend to 11), 16 days" (fr. G1), parameters which, in spite of the faulty arithmetic, show a pre-occupation with the civil calendar. But above (fr. B) the phrase *ḥ^{3}t-nḥḥ šsp-ḏt*, which may be an allusion to the inception of the reign — for the application of this phrase to the New Year see J. Assmann, *Zeit und Ewigkeit im alten Aegypten* (Heidelberg, 1975) 34f — are preceded by a date (now lost) which ended in a month of *proyet*.

[168]Malinine, Posener, Vercoutter, *Catalogue des stèles du Sérapéum*, pl. 29.

[169]Cf. R. A. Parker, *MDAIK* 15 (1957) 212 (in 664 i *akhet*, 1 fell on February 5.

[170]Spalinger curiously seems to date Sabaco's conquest to 713 B.C. (*CdE* 53, 33), but the Ashdod incident followed quickly, probably within months, upon a period when the potentate on the Nile from whom Yamani sought help could be meaningfully called "Pir'u king of Egypt," surely a reference to either Bocchoris or Osorkon IV: cf. the same author in *JARCE* 10, 97.

have seen,[171] and in return were accepted by its priests and duly entered in the king-list. The number "3" and the total 44 years as given by Eusebius,[172] are remarkably accurate, and constitute the dynastic "record," as it were, in 669-668 B.C. when Ashurbanipal's first invasion effectually deprived Taharqa of control of Memphis.[173] At the time, however, Memphis continued to honour Taharqa, even though he had been driven out of Egypt never to return, by dating monuments to his regnal years down to his death in his 27th year.[174] From Sabaco's conquest in 711 B.C. to this event amounted to a span of 44 years, divided somewhat artificially,[175] between the three historic kings of the house.

With the advent of Psammetichus I Sais won universal acceptance in the Nile valley north of the First Cataract, but the king-list does not in Manetho's version begin with his name. Instead, it relegated him to fourth position (fifth in the adulterated version of Eusebius) by introducing three names at the beginning:

	Africanus		*Eusebius*	
1.	-----		Ammeris	12
2.	Stephinates	7	Stephinathis	7
3.	Nechepsos	6	Nechepsos	6
4.	Nechao	8	Nechao	8
5.	Psammetichos	54	Psammetichos	45
6.	Nechao	6	Nechao	6
7.	Psammouthis	6	Psammouthis	17
8.	Ouaphris	19	Ouaphris	25
9.	Amosis	44	Amosis	42
10.	Psammecherites	6 mos.	-----	

The tendancy has been to dissociate the names in positions 2 through 4 from any known rulers of Sais in the 8th Century. Thus Wiedemann supposed Manetho to have found these three names in a

[171]Cf. above, p. 300, n. 19.
[172]Waddell, *Manetho*, 166-8.
[173]Cf. A. J. Spalinger, *JAOS* 94 (1974) 317, 320.
[174]Louvre stela 121 (year 24): P-M III, 210; Malinine, Posener, Vercoutter, *Catalogue des stèles du Sérapéum*, no. 125 (pl. 35); cf. J. H. Breasted, *Ancient Records of Egypt* IV (Chicago, 1906) §§917-18; year 26 is referred to in Louvre no. 190: P-M III, 210 (H); for discussion of the latest year of Taharqa, see G. Schmidt, *Kush* 6 (1958) 121ff, answered by R. A. Parker, *Kush* 8 (1960) 267ff.
[175]Taharqa's "20" is reckoned from his accession down to the Assyrian invasion of Esarhaddon in 671, and the remaining 24 years are then divided equally between his two predecessors. No reliance, therefore, can be placed on "12 years," either for Sabaco or Shebitku. The 50-year period in Herodotus (ii.137) for Kushite domination is likewise a poor foundation for chronology (*pace* Leclant, Yoyotte, *BIFAO* 51, 27), as it is simply the above 44 augmented by the 6 of Bocchoris.

Memphite document as local rulers, and to have misconstrued them as rulers of all Egypt.[176] Petrie tried to conjure up a Tefnakhte II, different from the adversary of Piankhy, and out of the Strogonoff *contrepoid*[177] a king *Ny-k^{3}w-b^{3}*, or Nechep(sos).[178] Von Zeissl doubted the identification of Stephinates with a "Tefnakhte," but concurred with the majority of early scholars in equating Nechepsos with *Ny-k^{3}w-b^{3}*.[179] Priese,[180] apparently followed by Spalinger,[181] would now identify Stephinates, not with the father of Bocchoris, but with a Tefnakhte II whom he identifies with the king of the Athens stela. John Ray agrees with Petrie in deriving Nechepsos from *Ny-k^{3}w-b^{3}* but believes the *b^{3}* has been misinterpreted as *sr*, "lamb," resulting in a connexion with the prophesying animal of the Bocchoris legend.[182] In Kitchen's *magnum opus* Ammeris becomes "perhaps a Nubian commander," Stephinates "perhaps a 'Tefnakht II'" and Nechepsos *Nyk^{3}w-b^{3}*. As Manetho's 6 years for the latter seems too short (to Kitchen), it "may be for 16 years."[183] Helck, almost alone among moderns, believes the name in no. 2 position to be Tefnakhte the father of Bocchoris, and thinks he was placed at the head of the 26th Dynasty since the official king-list traced its claim to the rule of this king.[184]

The tendancy has thus been to connect Necho I and his descendents with the earlier 24th Dynasty,[185] but not all agree on how many generations Necho is removed from Tefnakhte. The trend has been — Helck is the exception — to make Stephinates and Nechepsos into ephemeral and otherwise unattested local potentates who governed Sais during the 25th Dynasty. They who resort to this expedient freely admit that on the basis of this hypothesis nothing is certain: identifications in hieroglyphic texts are wanting, and lengths of floruit are conjectural.

In fact, an important point in the transmission of the king-list has been overlooked, viz. the dominance of the number "9." From Africanus to Eusebius a name has been omitted, but one has had to be added, in order to preserve the total of 9 names. To the post-

[176]A. Wiedemann, *Aegyptische Geschichte* (Gottha, 1884) 600.
[177]Gauthier, *LdR* III, 414.
[178]W. M. F. Petrie, *A History of Egypt* III (London, 1924) 317ff.
[179]Von Zeissl, *Aethiopen und Assyrer in Aegypten*, 55f.
[180]Priese, *ZÄS* 98, 18f.
[181]Spalinger, *JARCE* 10, 96, n. 8; *JAOS* 94, 322, n. 44.
[182]J. D. Ray, *JEA* 60 (1974) 255f.
[183]Kitchen, *Third Intermediate Period*, §§116-17.
[184]Helck, *Manetho*, 48.
[185]J. H. Breasted, *A History of Egypt* (New York, 1964) 471; Sir A. H. Gardiner, *Egypt of the Pharaohs* (Oxford, 1961) 352.

Psammetichan transmitters of the tradition the 26th Dynasty had constituted an "ennead," just like the 3rd or the 5th or the 9th and 10th. This is an important concept in the shaping of the tradition, for once it is appreciated how the Egyptians employed it, the historicity of the early names goes by the board. Necho I *must* be preceded by two names, and who better than the founders of Saite power, Tefnakhte[186] and his son. The latter, however, who was historically *W*^{3}*ḥ-k*^{3}*-r*ʿ *B*^{3}*k-n-rn.f*, here appears under the guise of "Nechepso." Ray, who has seen that we are confronted here by another form of the name "Necho" followed by an epithet *-pso*, has ingeniously connected the latter element with *p*^{3} *sr*, "the lamb," and thereby linked the name with the prophetic creature of legend who lived under Bocchoris.[187] In fact, while Nechepso may simply be a reduplication of the following entry, viz. "Necho" plus added epithet "the Saite" (*p*^{3} *S*^{3}*w*),[188] the *position* is influenced by the person of Bocchoris. Both the latter and Nechepso have identical lengths of reign, both are wisemen, Bocchoris is a lawgiver[189] Nechepso an astrologer;[190] both are vouchsafed glimpses of the future, Bocchoris through a prophetic lamb, Nechepso by the stars. They are really the same, and the 26th Dynasty as it descended to Manetho is nothing more than the official pedigree established by the Psammetichid family while it yet reigned.

It is interesting to trace the continued influence of Sais beyond the demise of the 26th Dynasty. Inspite of the later Cambyses tradition,[191] it is clear that the conquering Persian kings won a degree of

[186]The variants in the transmission of the name (Στεφινάτες: Manetho, Fr. 68; Τνεφάχθον: Diodorus i.45; Plutarch *De Iside et Osiride*, 8; Στεφινάθης: Sothis Book, Waddell, *Manetho*, 248) should occasion no surprise, much less lead us to postulate several kings! Dissimilation is here at work, abetted by the absence of a fixed form of the name which might have been bolstered by an official entry, *sub* the 24th Dynasty.

[187]A Theban papyrus of Antonine date does, in fact refer to Nechepso as Νεχέυς, i.e. Necho: cf. R. Reitzenstein, *Poimandres* (Leipzig, 1904) 119. A difficulty in postulating a *p*^{3} *sr* behind -ψω might be the vocalization of *sr*, "lamb," elsewhere in Greek and Coptic, which seems to show a retained *r* in the singular: Σρω (<*srt*): *Wb.* III, 462; ⲥⲣⲟ, Černý, *Coptic Etymological Dictionary*, 161. The writer has elsewhere argued (*JSSEA* 11, 75f) that *-pso* is actually derived from *p*^{3} *S*^{3}*w*, "the Saite."

[188]*Ibid.*

[189]Above, n. 155.

[190]Literature: A. A. Barb, in J. R. Harris (ed.), *The Legacy of Egypt*^{2} (Oxford, 1971) 165f; A. J. Spalinger, *Orientalia* 43 (1974) 298, n. 17.

[191]Above, p. 277, n. 74.

acceptance in Egypt that resulted in their legitimation,[192] Their garrison was at Memphis, and the Persian reigns were used to date transactions in the business communiy. A Petubastis might have arisen at Tanis,[193] or the Libyan Inaros in the western Delta,[194] but the Memphite establishment refused recognition. As soon, however, as Amyrtaeus mounted a successful rebellion in *Sais*, Memphis accepted him, and his name entered the king-list.[195] The two families from Sebennytos and Mendes who made up the 29th and 30th Dynasties favoured Sais and undoubtedly resided there, as well, perhaps, as in Memphis.[196] Saite influence remained strong throughout the period, and it may be that the list Manetho used owes far more to its Saite "edition" than we can ever guess with the meagre evidence at our disposal.

As scholars never tire of admonishing us, the archaizing tendencies seen full blown in the 7th-6th Centuries B.C. are neither to be described by the term "Renaissance"[197] nor is their inception to be dated to the 26th Dynasty. The first evidence of a turn to the past for models even antedates the 25th Dynasty:[198] The Kushites did not begin it, but merely adopted a fad already current.[199] The earliest examples, in art, orthography and ancestor cult come from the Delta,

[192]See G. Posener, *La première domination Perse en Egypte* (Cairo, 1936) *passim*. The evidence of burning found in the French excavations between the west wall of the Montu enclosure and the north wall of Karnak has been taken as evidence of Cambyses' invasion: Robichon, Varille, *Karnak-nord* III, 51ff, 61; Barquet, *Temple*, 6; but this is far from certain. Our excavations in East Karnak have revealed a continuum from the 6th into the 5th Centuries B.C. (phase C), although early in the preceding phase (D: 7th-6th Centuries) there is some evidence of burning: *JARCE* 14, 12ff; *ROM Archaeological Newsletter* 154, 1978. Nothing certain can be said about the excavations in north Karnak until section drawings and pottery are published.

[193]Above, n. 113.

[194]Cf. Lloyd, *Herodotus, Book II: Introduction*, 38ff, and the literature cited there.

[195]Waddell, *Manetho*, 173.

[196]H. S. Smith, *A Visit to Ancient Egypt* (Warminster, 1974) 86, n. 20; on the 29th and 30th Dynasties, see G. Daressy, *ASAE* 18 (1918) 37ff; Drioton, Vandier, *L'Egypte*[4], 622ff, 679f; Smith, *A Visit to Ancient Egypt*, 3ff.

[197]Cf. H. Brunner, in *LdÄ* I (1972) 386f; A. J. Spalinger, *Orientalia* 47 (1978) 12f.

[198]H. Brunner, *Saeculum* 21 (1970) 156; J. Yoyotte, in *Histoire de l'Art* I (Paris, 1961) 238.

[199]The Kushites in the early stages simply borrowed the materials at hand in the south as models, and this meant the relics of the 12th, 19th and 20th Dynasties: Senwosret III's buildings at Semna (Leclant, *Recherches*, 332f); the Soleb sphinxes of Amenophis III (E. R. Russmann, *The Representation of the King in the 25th Dynasty* [Brussels and Brooklyn, 1974], 18); the ram-icon of Amun at Napata (*idem*, *Brooklyn Museum Annual* 10 [1968-69], 91); the numerous Ramesside remains which fostered a Sudanese "Ramesside" style (W. S. Smith, *The Art and Architecture of Ancient Egypt* [Harmondsworth, 1959], 245).

in particular the western side,[200] and point to the Sais-Memphis axis as the place where we should look for the origins of the movement. But there is another consideration which prompts a closer look at the northeastern Delta as a source of inspiration towards cultic renewal; and that is the prominence of the motif of the young Isis and the divine child in the Libyan period. Already from the 21st Dynasty the title "god's-mother" is born by the queen in her role as mother vis-à-vis the royal Horus child, whether it be Horus himself, or Khonsu-pa-khered, or Wepwawet.[201] And one can scarcely divorce from this new accentuation on one aspect of the myth of Divine Kingship the tendency from c. 800 B.C. on of infixing the epithet *s³ Ist* in the royal name.[202] Noteworthy are the "Horian" overtones heard in the bombastic self-adulation of magnates of the later Libyan period;[203] and we are reminded of the sudden spread of shrines devoted to the Osirian cycle in northeast Karnak from 800 B.C. on.[204] Earliest among these is the "House of Isis of the Great Mound of the God's-land of Wese," (temple J), built by Hory the son of Neseramun, mentor of Pedibast of Dynasty 23.[205] Before the end of the century it was followed by the "Temple of Osiris Ruler of Eternity"; and "other Osirian" installations in the same area.[206]

All things considered, the revival signalled by the renewed interest

[200]The plaque of Maiamun si-Bast Yuput: R. A. Fazzini, *Miscellanea Wilbouriana* (Brooklyn, 1972), 64f, fig. 36; Serapeum stela no. 117, with its reference to Djoser: Brunner, *Saeculum* 21, 154 n. 12; bronze of Bocchoris: J. M. A. Janssen, in *Historische Kring. Varia Historica aangeboden aan... A. W. Byvanck* (Leiden, 1954) 22, fig. 2; faience vessel of Bocchoris: Smith, *Art and Architecture*, 242, fig. 76; *idem*, *Interconnections in the Ancient Near East* (New Haven and London, 1965) fig. 74; already in late Libyan times some archaizing is evident in royal titularies: Leclant, in *Mélanges Maspero* IV, 255 and n. 6; Kitchen, *Third Intermediate Period*, § 317; J. Berlandini, in *Hommages à Serge Sauneron* (Cairo, 1979) 93f.

[201]*Ibid.*, 102ff.

[202]Takelot II: Gauthier, *LdR* III, 351ff; Petubastis: Von Beckerath, *JARCE* 5, 46f and 51 (no. 24); Osorkon III: Gauthier, *LdR* III, 383ff; Takelot III: *ibid.*, 389ff; Pharaoh "Iny": H. Jacquet-Gordon, in *Hommages à Serge Sauneron*, pl. 27B, 28, fig. 3, p. 174; Piankhy: BM 24429, line 6 (J. Leclant, *Enquêtes sur les sacerdoces et les sanctuaires égyptiens à l'époque dite 'éthiopienne'* [Cairo, 1954] 23, n. *n*) on *S³-Ist* applied to Montu, see C. Traunecker, *Karnak* 6 (1980) 191, n. 2.

[203]Caminos, *The Chronicle of Prince Osorkon*, § 114; Yoyotte, in *Mélanges Maspero* IV, 140f.

[204]Barguet, *Temple*, 14ff.

[205]Cairo 42226, k; cf. the present writer's forthcoming article "New Light on Temple J at Karnak," in *Orientalia* (1986).

[206]P-M II², 204ff; G. E. Kadish, and others, *The Temple of Osiris Ḥḳ³ Ḏt* (Toronto, forthcoming). Perhaps pertinent to the present discussion is the observation that the contemporary rites of Djeme, with which the lower part of the east wall of the third room in this temple is concerned, centres upon Horus on the lotus, of Butic origin: P-M II², 206 (22 II); J. Leipoldt, S. Morenz, *Der Gott auf der Blume* (*Artibus Asiae Supplement* XII; 1956) 64ff.

in the cultural and cultic impedimenta of the northwest Delta, would seem to correspond to the appearance toward the end of the 9th Century of the powerful chiefs of the Labu in the western sector of Lower Egypt.[207] Their bailiwick, be it recalled, included Buto, the Horite cult centre whence many of the new influences emerged.[208] The fad of calling up old models, sparked by the old cult and its practices, spread like wild-fire to Tanis and Memphis and thence to the Said and its Sudanese sphere. It was the fate of this "archaizing" movement to be linked falsely with the 25th Dynasty (which in fact lacked the imagination to initiate it: it was only after craftsmen were imported from the north that the new forms flourished under Sudanese sponsorship). Nevertheless Sais provided the continuum. The chiefs of the Labu of the 8th Century spawned cultural, if not blood, heirs in Sais and Buto, and 200 years later the 26th Dynasty carried to its logical conclusion the trend established by its spiritual forebears.

But art, which is the best attested and most obvious reflection of fascination with ancient models, is perhaps but a peripheral manifestation of the more central, and cerebral, interest in ancient cultus as a canon for present reform. That it should have been deemed necessary to promulgate such a pedigree should not be surprising in the light of the 26th Dynasty's view of kingship.[209] The official commemoration of the Saite royal house while it still held sway is reflected in the mortuary cults of deceased rulers of the line which flourished at Sais. With the royal necropolis of Sais within the very precincts of the great temple of Neith, close to the residence, it is not surprising to find courtiers fulfilling the functions of priests of the mortuary service of various kings.[210] So little has survived from the Saite kings that would yield an insight into their approach to the past that speculation might seem idle; nonetheless one wonders whether the slant Manetho gives his material in fact is the effect in large measure of the use of the past as a model by the Kushite — Saite period. In particular one thinks of the use of the Ennead as an organizing mechanism in long, undifferentiated blocks of royal names in the king-list, which we have found operative in Manetho. Its use

[207]Cf. most recently Berlandini, in *Hommages à Serge Sauneron*, 162f.
[208]*Ibid.*, 163, n. 2; cf. D. B. Redford, *BES* 5 (1983) 82f.
[209]Spalinger, *Orientalia* 47, 12ff.
[210]Wahibre Psammetichus I: E. Otto, *MDAIK* 15 (1957) 196ff; Wahibre: E. A. E. Reymond, *ASAE* 55 (1958) 121, no. 68; Neferibre Psammetichus II: *ibid.*, 125 no. 101; Menkheperre Necho: H. De Meulenaere, *BIFAO* 60 (1960) 117ff; Khnumibre: R. Saad, *Documents relatifs à Sais et ses divinités* (Cairo, 1975) pl. 19, p. 133; additional bibliography, *ibid.*, 135 n. *i*; Zivie, *Hermopolis*, 143 n. *g*.

in the Saite period, which has just been demonstrated above, may well have been the initial application of the device from which the others followed (e.g. 1st-5th, 9th, 10th Dynasties etc.).

Spotty as it is, the surviving evidence seems to point to Amasis as a major agent in the revival of elements of antiquity in the cultus.[211] We have had occasion to remark (above, p. 221, n. 67) that the revival of the mortuary cults of 3rd Dynasty kings may owe something to this king; and a resurgence of interest in the cult of Imhotpe dates from the same reign.[212] Cultic interest in the Giza kings is attested by celebrants of their mortuary service from Apries on.[213] In a sort of "Mishnaic" tractate on temple building of the 2nd Century A.D., whose *Vorlage* may be ascribed to the reign of Amasis,[214] special provision is made for the cults of deceased pharaohs.[215]

The Conclusion of Book III

Manetho terminates his work with the last king of the 30th Dynasty, Nectanebo II, who was shortly to become the subject of popular legend.[216] It would be interesting to know whether any of the material later to turn up in the Nectanebo tales and the Alexander romances was found already in Manetho, but there is no evidence that it was; Manetho, living in time so close to these events probably conveyed a sober record of the period.

Manetho's omission of Artaxerxes III and the last Persian kings, as well as Khababash,[217] must mean that he had chosen to end his work with the great Persian invasion of 343 B.C., which provided a great

[211]On the reign of Amasis in general, see E. A. E. Reymond, *ASAE* 52 (1954) 251ff; W. Helck, *Geschichte des alten Aegypten* (Leiden, 1968) 256f; H. De Meulenaere, in *LdÄ* I (1972) 181f.

[212]R. Reitzenstein, *Poimandres* (Leipzig, 1904) 120; D. Wildung, *Imhotep und Amenhotep* (Munich and Berlin, 1977) 33ff.

[213]Wildung, *Die Rolle*, 177ff.

[214]On the possibility that under Amasis a major redaction was undertaken of those sacred prescriptive books dealing with the building and function of temples, see P.D. 6319, *rt.* x + iii, 2ff: Reymond, *Hermetic Writings*, 30f; B. E. Klakowicz, *Orientalia* 50 (1981) 200.

[215]P.D. 6319 *rt.* x + iv, 29: "[along] the entire temple, on right and left (sides) [are shrines(?)] with pictures of the kings on them, their faces (turned) towards the temple." This word picture conjures up the Karnak Chamber of Ancestors.

[216]On the Nectanebo literature, see the good survey of A. J. Spalinger, *ZÄS* 105 (1978) 144ff.

[217]Cf. Waddell, *Manetho*, 184, n. 1; Spalinger, *ZÄS* 105, 142ff; E. Cruz-Uribe, *Serapis* 4 (1977-78) 3ff; A. J. Spalinger, *ZÄS* 107 (1980) 87; R. K. Ritner, *ibid.*, 135ff.

and natural watershed in his work. To go beyond it would involve him in a period when his royal patron's forebear and fellow countrymen had fulfilled a significant role in his country's destiny, and about which discretion would have counselled complete reticence. There is the further possibility that the major king-list he was following simply came to an end with the flight of Nectanebo II; but it is not likely that this would have deterred him from going on, had he wished to do so. No, failure to involve himself in the events which resulted in the liberation of Egypt from the Persian yoke can only be interpreted to mean that discretion and self-interest had shut his mouth.

10

Conclusions

The archaic period, in the process of founding a centralized state, developed two mechanisms for chronicling the past: the annals, *gnwt*, and the ancestral offering cult. The former, originally a practical record of Nile heights linked to year names, rapidly developed into a means of committing to record the salient cultic, military or constructional events of each year. This record early adopted a rectangular format for each year, conforming most likely to the dictates of the papyrus medium adopted by the royal chancery; but the form was secondarily employed for wood or ivory labels used for purposes of identification.

The cult of the ancestors probably could trace its roots to the prehistoric past; but in historic times it enjoyed royal patronage. The private cult could clearly trace sequences of ancestors, but preferred not to do so graphically; the royal cult of ancestors honoured all kings of the past and the invocation, if written, would have constituted a king-list in embryo. Such lists used in invocations were undoubtedly kept in the archives of all royal mortuary shrines and sun-temples where they came under the protection of Sokar, but the cult which was principally responsible for keeping such a list was that of Ptah at Memphis.

The finalization of the unification of the realm which is evidenced by the mortuary and cultic remains from the time of Djoser carried in its wake a heightened interest in the past. Sometime, possibly during the 3rd or less likely early 4th Dynasty, the *gnwt* from Menes to Djoser were assembled and achieved a final sort of publication in a hieroglyphic form which forever canonized the mistaken readings of the original cursive script in which the early kings' names were written.

Gnwt as a genre continues throughout the Old Kingdom but during the 4th Dynasty a change of emphasis is in evidence. Military exploits are now almost wholly absent, and the field is dominated by events concerned with the cult and benefactions for the gods. That the genre had lost some of its earlier functional nature is apparent, though it is doubtful whether we should postulate the disappearance of the form as originally devised. Neferirkare's "publication" of the *gnwt* to his own reign constitutes an exhibition of personal piety, but may also betray an interest in antiquity for its own sake.

The continued success of the pharaonic system over eight centuries prevented the crystalization of any sophisticated view of history. Records were not lacking. A 'golden age' of the god was asserted. The individuality of past reigns could be demonstrated; but all conformed to what was expected of Horus.

The collapse of the Old Kingdom forced on the Egyptians a closer look at their past. An ambivalence appears in the literature, one attitude being characterized by contempt, another by reverence and mimesis. The inverted snobbery of the *nḏsw*, manifest in pride of accomplishment and pride of ancestry, makes its appearance in the provincialism of the Theban kings. The intensely personal texts of the time display a greater appreciation of the individuality of the reigns of the 11th Dynasty rulers. For the first time the king makes use of forms of composition formerly reserved for commoners: the biographical statement, the speech, the address to posterity.

The Middle Kingdom confronts us with a genuine and well-attested resuscitation of the past, albeit one which was consciously designed to serve the ends of the 12th Dynasty regime in power. Some aspects of this antiquarianism were pragmatic: a cadaster had to be drawn-up from old sources, the new family had to be seen as legitimate. But the movement soon turned into a spontaneous groundswell. Old tombs were refurbished in acts of piety which became fashionably desirable in and of themselves; popular stories about the remote past were written down and fostered, while backdated prophecies and corpora of wisdom were disseminated. Old Kingdom cults of kings and commoners enjoyed a revival, and any "gentlemen" who could prove or pass off a link with these worthies of the past was avidly sought by the regime. Old recording forms were maintained: the *gnwt* are mentioned, but no surviving exemplar suggests what format they had adopted, or function fulfilled. On the other hand, new genres, like the day-book of various institutions, both governmental and private, make their first appearance.

It was in the 12th Dynasty that the first true king-list of which we have direct evidence was brought to birth. All the ingredients later to appear in one form or another in Manetho are already present: an euhemeristic translation of the gods into Gargantuan *Ur-könige*, recording of "exact" lengths of reign, rudimentary divisions into "houses," special attention to what later would become the 12th Dynasty. Clearly the new genre served the ends of the Itj-towy monarchy.

The fate of all these forms during the 15th-17th Dynasties, *gnwt*, day-books and king-lists, must be inferred from meager evidence; but all emerge strong and vibrant in the 18th Dynasty. The preference for Memphis as a residence put the new ruling house in contact with the remote past of Egyptian history. The new empire contributed to the creation of the polymath, whether royal or private. Hatshepsut's writings may show her to have been egotistical, and willing to interpret recent history to her own ends, albeit in a manner in touch with the past; but Thutmose III had true breadth of vision. The reconstruction of the ancestral shrine of the Karnak temple, which Thutmose undertook, resulted in the revival of the cult of the ancestors, and the inscripturation of a cultic list of ancestors that was to descend through 1 1/2 millennia into Eratosthenes' list of "Diospolitan" kings.

By the reign of Amenophis III the interest in the past evinced, for practical reasons, by the Thutmosids, had issued in a genuine *Treulesen* of ancient documents for their own sake. It is this interest in the letter of the law that informs much of Amenophis III's approach to the past as well as, in a bizarre though discernible way, his son's revolutionary movement.

By the time the Ramesside family was promoted to the rule of Egypt, the achievements of the Thutmosids had long since established standards (a) in providing "cultically" for ancestral kings and (b) in display of reverential pride in the contemporary ruling house. Two policies were pursued in tension throughout the 13th Century B.C. One, perhaps strongest in the Delta, accentuated the family love and loyalty which (genuinely) characterized the Ramessides; the other, occasioned by the position of Thebes in the recent passed, was at pains to link the family directly to the preceding Thutmosid house. Interest in the past and its memorials increased. Sometimes it was genuine, if not academic, interest in the past for its own sake; mostly it involved the piety attendent upon refurbishing ancestral monuments. The ancestral offering cults thrived as never before. It now became popular in the private sphere to memorialize the continuum of kingship the monarch stressed by depicting the ancestral offering to the statues of kings from Ahmose to the ruling king lined up in a single line, without interruption.

The king-list achieved under Ramesses II a form which was accepted as a sort of standard and was re-copied without additions by later generations. Four strands are visible in its make-up; 1. the old Middle Kingdom king-list of the scribes of Itj-towy, devised by and for the kings of the 12th Dynasty, 2. the "Theban" kings of the Intermediate Period and the later 18th Dynasty, 3. the Hyksos kings and garbled names of the kings who formed their family-tree and 4. the Ramesside house.

The outgoing New Kingdom leaves the strong impression that historical record keeping was a flourishing enterprise. The king-list continued, during the millennium which separated Ramesses II from Manetho, to be maintained at the city of Memphis which exerts a strong influence over the official acceptance of kings. *Gnwt* are frequently mentioned as available in libraries, and are freely consulted, but what form they now took is quite unknown; there is some evidence that the term had been extended to include mythological writings. Day-books also continue, and are sometimes used as witnesses to past events.

The cataclysmic events of Egyptian history from c. 712 to 663 B.C. left their stamp on how Egyptians looked at their past. 1. The piety and conservatism of the Kushites sparked a favourable vision of the past and its modes of cultural expression which invited close imitation. 2. The repeated foreign invasions gradually made Egyptians aware of a constant configuration of foreign powers which was shortly to find expression in the common plot-motif of "invasion from the north / deliverance from the south." 3. The revival, beginning with the Saites, of the cults of ancient kings spawned an apocryphal literature attached to their names. 4. The prospect of threatening foreign powers whose monuments rivalled those of Egypt, turned the eyes of all Egyptians towards their own visible past and prompted the proliferation of aetiological stories about ancient monuments, especially those of the Thebaid.

The *Aegyptiaca* of Manetho is the response to the second Ptolemy's policies of political conciliation and scholarly patronage. Manetho was chosen from the priesthood of the city which had given the land its last native dynasty, rather than the more important temple community of Memphis. In the main he worked from Demotic sources in temple libraries, not from the monuments themselves; but since the point of his work was to make the history of his land available to Greeks, he did incorporate some material of interest to Hellenists. Since they were found in the temple libraries and were therefore *ipso facto* acceptable, folk-tales and related genres found their way into Manetho's work.

The form taken by Manetho's history was that of the Memphite king-list interspersed with narrative sections. Divisions into houses, already evidenced by the New Kingdom tradition reflected in the Turin Canon, is taken a good deal farther. One dominant principal in the division is the concept of the Ennead as the prototype of the ancestral family unit. Thus the block of Old Kingdom names from Menes to Unas are divided into 5 groups, 2 are made out of 18 Herakleopolitan names, while the 6 Saites are augmented by the names of the ancestors back to Tefnakhte. The Hyksos pedigree was misunderstood as a 14th, Xoite, Dynasty. His 18th Dynasty is dominated by aetiological interpretations and mistaken translations of standing Theban monuments; not least is this in evidence in its point of termination. Most likely Manetho owes much of the form and content of the 18th Dynasty section to a separate work, probably in Demotic, dating from the 5th or 4th Century B.C. For the post-Thutmosid history Manetho relied on the Memphite tradition almost entirely. The narrative content is almost wholly unknown, but Manetho may well have been circumspect in his description of the times immediately preceding Alexander's invasion.

PLATE I

Stela of Pahy and Neferkha^cu from Thebes (reproduced by courtesy of the Brooklyn Museum.

PLATE II

Stela of Siptah, Qurneh.

PLATE III

Assemblage of Ramesside royal statues, Karnak.

PLATE IV

Thoth, inscribing cartouches and annals (Ramesseum).

Selected Bibliography

Assmann, J., *Zeit und Ewigkeit im alten Aegypten*, Heidelberg, 1975.

Barta, W., "Bemerkungen zu den Summenangaben des Turiner Königspapyrus für die Frühzeit und das Alte Reich," *MDAIK* 35 (1979) 11ff.

------, *Untersuchungen zum Götterkreise der Neunheit*, Berlin, 1973.

------, *Untersuchungen zur Göttlichkeit des regierenden Königs*, Munich and Berlin, 1975.

Beckerath, J. von, "Die Dynastie der Herakleopoliten (9/10 Dynastie)," *ZÄS* 93 (1966) 13-20.

------, "Königslisten," in *LdÄ* III, Wiesbaden, 1980.

------, *Untersuchungen zur politische Geschichte der zweiten Zwischenzeit in Aegypten*, Glückstadt, 1965.

------, "Zur Begründung der 12. Dynastie durch Ammenemes I," *ZÄS* 92 (1965) 4-10.

Bell, H.I., *Egypt from Alexander the Great to the Arab Conquest*, Oxford, 1948.

Björkman, G., *Kings at Karnak*, Uppsala, 1971.

Bleeker, C.J., "Religious Tradition and Sacred Books in Ancient Egypt," in F.F. Bruce, E.G. Rupp (eds.), *Holy Book and Holy Tradition*, London, 1968.

Blumenthal, E., *Untersuchungen zum ägyptischen Königtums des mittleren Reiches* I, Berlin, 1970.

Braun, M., *History and Romance in Greco-Oriental Literature*, Oxford, 1938.

Bresciani, E., *L'archivo demotico del tempio di Soknopaiu Nesos*, Milan, 1975

Brunner, H., "Zum Verständnis der archaisierenden Tendenzen in der ägyptischen Spätzeit," *Saeculum* 21 (1970) 151ff.

Bryan, B.M., *The Reign of Thuthmosis IV* (PhD dissertation) Yale University, 1980.

Caminos, R.A., *The Chronicle of Prince Osorkon*, Rome, 1958.

Černý, J., *A Community of Workmen at Thebes in the Ramesside Period*, Cairo, 1973.

------, "The Contribution of the Study of Unofficial and Private Documents to the History of Pharaonic Egypt," in S. Donadoni (ed.), *Le fonti indirette della Storia egizianna* (Rome, 1963) 31-58.

Culley, R.C., "An Approach to the Problem of Oral Tradition," *VT* 13 (1963) 113-125.

------, *Oral Formulaic Language in the Biblical Psalms*, Toronto, 1968.

Denton, R.C. (ed.), *The Idea of History in the Ancient Near East*, New Haven, 1955.

Derchain, P., "Ménès, le roi 'Qelqu'on'," *RdE* 18 (1966) 31-36.

------, "Le papyrus Salt 825 (BM 10051) et la cosmologie égyptienne," *BIFAO* 58 (1959) 73-80.

Drews, R., *The Greek Accounts of Eastern History*, Cambridge, Mass., 1973.

Fairman, H.W., "The Myth of Horus at Edfu — I," *JEA* 21 (1935) 26-36.

------, and A.M. Blackman, "The Myth of Horus at Edfu — II," *JEA* 28 (1942) 32-38.

------, "The Myth of Horus at Edfu — II," *JEA* 29 (1943) 2-38.

------, "The Myth of Horus at Edfu — II," *JEA* 30 (1944) 5-22.

Faulkner, R.O., *An Ancient Egyptian Book of Hours*, Oxford, 1958.

------, *Papyrus Bremner-Rhind*, Brussels, 1933.

Frankfort, H., *Kingship and the Gods*, Chicago, 1948.

Gardiner, A.H., "The House of Life," *JEA* 24 (1938) 157-179.

------, "Regnal Years and Civil Calendar in Pharaonic Egypt," *JEA* 31 (1945) 11-28.

------, *The Royal Canon of Turin*, Oxford, 1959.

Goedicke, H., *Königliche Dokumente aus dem alten Reich*, Wiesbaden, 1967.

------, *Die Stellung des Königs im alten Reich*, Wiesbaden, 1960.

Griffiths, J.G., *The Origins of Osiris and His Cult*, Leiden, 1980.

------, *Plutarch's, De Iside et Osride*, Cambridge, 1970.

Habachi, L., "King Nebhepetre Mentuhotep: His Monuments, Place in History, Deification and Unusual Representations in the Form of Gods," *MDAIK* 19 (1963) 16-52.

Hallo, W. and W.K. Simpson, *The Ancient Near East: A History*, New York, 1971.

Helck, H.W., *Altägyptische Aktenkunde des 3. und 2. Jahrtausends v. Chr.*, Munich and Berlin, 1974.

------, *Geschichte des alten Aegypten*, Leiden, 1968.

------, *Untersuchungen zu den Beamtentiteln des ägyptischen alten Reiches*, Glückstadt, 1954.

------, *Untersuchungen zu Manetho und den ägyptischen Königslisten*, Berlin, 1956.

Hornung, E., "Chaotische Beriche in der geordneten Welt," *ZÄS* 81 (1956) 28-32.

------, *Der Eine und die Vielen*, Darmstadt, 1973.

------, *Untersuchungen zur Chronologie und Geschichte des neuen Reiches*, Wiesbaden, 1964.

------, "Zur geschichtlichen Rolle des Königs in der 18. Dynastie," *MDAIK* 15 (1957) 120-133.

Jacobsohn, H., *Die dogmatische Stellung des Königs in der Theologie der alten Aegypten*, Glückstadt and New York, 1939.

Janssen, J.J., "Prolegomena to the Study of Egypt's Economic History during the New Kingdom," *SAK* 3 (1975) 127-186.

Johnson, J., "The Demotic Chronicle as an Historical Source," *Enchoria* 4 (1974) 1-18.

Junge, F., "Die Welt der Klagen," in J. Assmann, and others (eds.), *Fragen an die altägyptischen Literatur* (Wiesbaden, 1977) 275-284.

Junker, H., *Die götterlehre von Memphis*, Berlin, 1939.

Kaiser, W., "Einige Bemerkungen zur ägyptischen Frühzeit," *ZÄS* 85 (1960) 118-137.

------, "Einige Bemerkungen zur ägyptischen Frühzeit, II," *ZÄS* 86 (1961) 39-61.

Kákosy, L., "Schöfung und Weltuntergang in der ägyptischen Religion," *Acta Antiqua Acad. Scient. Hungarica* 11 (1963) 17-30.

Kitchen, K.A., *The Third Intermediate Period in Egypt*, Warminster, 1973.

Krauss, R., *Das Ende der Amarnazeit*, Hildesheim, 1978.

Lloyd, A.B., *Herodotus, Book II: Introduction*, Leiden, 1975.

Malamat, A., "King Lists of the Old Babylonian Period and Biblical Genealogies," *JAOS* 88 (1968) 163-173.

Malek, J., "The Original Version of the Royal Canon of Turin," *JEA* 68 (1982) 93ff.

------, "The Special Features of the Saqqara King List," *JSSEA* 12 (1982) 21-28.

Morenz, S., "Tradition um Menes," *ZÄS* 99 (1972) x-xvi.

Murnane, W.J., *Ancient Egyptian Coregencies*, Chicago, 1977.

------, "The Sed-festival: A Problem in Historical Method," *MDAIK* 37 (1981) 369ff.

Murray, O., "Hecataeus of Abdera and Pharaonic Kingship," *JEA* 56 (1970) 141-171.

Otto, E., "Ein Beitrag zur Deutung ägyptischen Vor- und Frühgeschichte," *WO* I, 6 (1952) 431-453.

------, "Geschichtsbild und Geschichtsschreibung in Aegypten," *WO* III, 3 (1966) 161-176.

------, *Handbuch der Orientalistik* Abt. I *Der Nahe und der Mittlere Osten* Bd. 1 *Aegyptologie, Abschnit Aegyptische Schrift und Sprache*, Leiden, 1959.

Phillips, A.K., "Horemheb, Founder of the XIXth Dynasty?" *Orientalia* 46 (1977) 116-121.

Posener, G., *Littérature et politique dans l'Egypte de la XIIe dynastie*, Paris, 1956.

------, "Les richesses inconnues de la littérature égyptienne," *RdE* 6 (1951) 27-48.

Posener-Kriéger, P., *Les archives du Temple funéraire de Néferirkarê-Kakaï*, Cairo, 1976.

Preaux, C., "La place des papyrus dans les sources de l'histoire héllenistique," *Akten des XIII Internationalen Papyrologenkongresses*, (Munich, 1974) 1ff.

Ranke, H., "Vom Geschichtsbilde der alten Aegypter," *CdE* 6 (1931) 277-286.

Redford, D.B., "The Hyksos Invasion in History and Tradition," *Orientalia* 39 (1970) 1-51.

Reymond, E.A.E., *From Ancient Egyptian Hermetic Writings (From the Contents of the Libraries of the Suchos Temples in the Fayum, II)*, Vienna, 1977.

------, and J.W.B. Barns, "Alexandria and Memphis: Some Historical Observations," *Orientalia* 46 (1977) 1-33.

Ridley, R.T., "The World's Earliest Annals: A Modern Journey in Comprehension," *Acta Antiqua* 27 (1979) 39ff.

Rowton, M., "Manetho's Date for Ramesses II," *JEA* 34 (1948) 57-74.

Schäfer, H., "Das Niederschlagen der Feinde: zur Geschichte einer ägyptischen Sinnbildes," *WZKM* 54 (1957) 168ff.

Schaeffer, H. *Ein Bruchstück altägyptischer Annalen*, Berlin, 1902.

Schenkel, W., *Kultmythos und Martyrerlengende*, Wiesbaden, 1977.

------, *Memphis, Herakleopolis, Theben*, Wiesbaden, 1965.

Schott, E., "Bücher und Bibliotheken im alten Aegypten," *GM* 25 (1977) 73-80.
------, *Mythe und Mythenbildung in alten Aegypten*, Berlin, 1945.
Sethe, K., *Beiträge zur älteste Geschichte Aegyptens*, Leipzig, 1905.
Smith, H.S., *A Visit to Ancient Egypt*, Warminster, 1974.
Spalinger, A.J., *Aspects of the Military Documents of the Ancient Egyptians*, New Haven, 1982.
------, "The Concept of the Monarchy during the Saite Epoch — An Essay of Synthesis," *Orientalia* 47 (1978) 12-36.
Spiegel, J. "Die religionsgeschichtliche Stellung der Pyramidentexte," *Orientalia* 22 (1953) 129ff.
------, *Soziale und weltanschauliche Reformbewegungen im alten Aegypten*, Heidelberg, 1950.
Spiegelberg, W., *Die Glaubwürdigkeit von Herodots Bericht über Aegypten im Lichte der Aegyptischen Denkmäler.* (*Orient und Antkike* 3), Heidelberg, 1926.
Van Seters, J., *The Hyksos: A New Investigation*, New Haven, 1966.
------, *In Search of History*, New Haven and New York, 1983.
------, "Israelite Historiography," *Orientalia* 50 (1981) 137ff.
Wente, E.F., and C. van Siclen III, "A Chronology of the New Kingdom," in J. Johnson, E.F. Wente (eds.), *Studies in Honor of George R. Hughes* (Chicago, 1976) 217-262.
Wildung, D., "Aufbau und Zweckbestimmung der Königsliste von Karnak," *GM* 9 (1974) 41-48.
------, *Der Rolle ägyptischer Könige im Bewusstsein ihrer Nachwelt* I, Berlin, 1969.
------, *Imhotep und Amenhotep*, Munich and Berlin, 1977.
Wilson, J.A., "Buto and Hierakonpolis in the Geography of Egypt," *JNES* 14 (1955) 209-236.
Wilson, R.R., *Genealogy and History in the Biblical World*, New Haven, 1977.
Yoyotte, J., "Les principautés du Delta au temps de l'anarchie libyenne," in *Mélanges Maspero* IV (*MIFAO* 66; Paris, 1961) 121-182.

Indices

Subject

A

Abu Roash, 143
Abusir, 25, 27, 141, 235, 237
Abydos, 18-20, 22f, 24 n. 83, 29, 31, 37, 39f, 51, 72, 91, 142f, 150 and n. 104, 158 n. 147, 170, 178, 191ff, 265f, 279, 306
Achthoes, 211
Adamu, 200
Adj-ib, 87 n. 51
Aegyptiaca, 205-207, 214, 228 n. 101 (Demotic material in), 229 (format of), 230f, 238, 243, 250, 255, 296f, 336
aetiology, 93f, 129, 138, 147 n. 86, 159, 214, 228, 238 n. 32, 243, 258, 276, 280, 293, 296, 336f
Africanus, 206, 229 and n. 107, 237, 240f, 243, 250 n. 100, 255, 302f, 305, 324
Aha, 86, 133
Ahhotpe, 43, 48, 50, 62
Ahmes, 48, 60, 62
Ahmes Nofretari, 18 n. 72, 42ff, 47, 49f, 52 n. 165, 53, 57, 60f, 172 n. 57, 245, 247
Ahmose (Amosis), chapter 1 *passim*, 19, 22, 35, 39f, 43, 51f, 55, 60, 170, 172 n. 57, 230, 240, 280, 335
Ahmose Panekhbet, 60
Aken, 107
Akencheres, 189 n. 178, 252
Akhem-seth, 198 n. 241
Akhenaten, 153 n. 118, 186 n. 159, 188-90, 195, 248f, 252, 265, 293
Akh-menu, 32, 174 n. 67, 176f, 181
Akhmim, 245
Akhtoy I, 143, 159, 215 n. 51
Akhtoy III, 127
Aleander, 303 n. 44
Alexander, 205 n. 13, 224 n. 80, 296, 300f, 331, 337
Alexandria, 223, 300f
altar, 58
Amasis, 62 n. 225, 221 n. 67, 331
Amarna, 189f, 252, 293
Amarna period, 134, 145 n. 72, 188, 190 n. 187, 195, 250, 294ff
Amarna Pharaohs, 19, 22, 35, 44, 242f, 252f, 255
Amaunet, 38, 70f, 169 n. 33
Amazon (romance), 227
ambulatory, 34, 64, 175f
Amenemapet, 194 n. 214
Amenemhat I, 7 n. 24, 10, 15f, 25f, 28, 29, 33f, 56 n. 191, 144 n. 69, 151 and n. 109, 153 n. 120, 157, 210, 239, 271
Amenemhet II, 34, 157, 160f, 239
Amenemhet III, 18 n. 72, 28, 153 n. 120, 180 n. 110, 239
Amenemhet IV, 9, 19, 34, 198 n. 241
Amenemhet Sobekhotpe, 68f
Amenemhet Surer, 166 n. 9
Amenemirdis, 72, 314 and n. 117
Amenemone, 50, 61
Amenemope, 16, 49, 63 n. 232
Amenmen, 49
Amenmesse, 37, 57, 269, 303
Amenmose, 46, 52 n. 166, 53 n. 175, 54
Amenophath, 255f
Amenophis I, chapter 1 *passim*, 18 n. 72, 29, 37ff, 42, 44, 46, 49, 50, 52ff, 60f, 171, 173 n. 63, 193, 239, 245, 247; cult-forms of, 46, 52 n. 166, 53
Amenophis II, 41, 46, 48, 51, 54 n. 180, 80, 111ff, 123, 161 n. 164, 168, 170, 175, 179ff, 182 and n. 127, 183
Amenemnes, 303
Amenophis III, chapter 1 *passim*, 29, 37, 41, 48, 61, 75, 77, 80, 145 n. 72, 173, 178ff, 182, 185ff, 188 and n. 170, 189 and nn. 178-179, 190, 194, 204 n. 8, 212, 247-253, 257, 292f, 335; mansion of, 50
Amemophis son of Hapu, 50, 52, 61 n. 214, 166 n. 8, 178, 189, 225 n. 84, 248ff, 282, 292
Amenwahsu, 84, 224
Ameny, 152 n. 114
Amesse, 247
Ammenephthes, 303
Ammeris, 326
Ammishtamry, 200
Amorite, 199f
amulet, 28
Amun, 33 n. 115, 38, 42, 50, 52 n. 165, 53, 66 n. 11, 68 n. 24, 69f, 75ff, 123, 152, 153 n. 118, 171-174, 179f, 192 n. 203, 205, 234, 250f, 263, 265, 275, 283, 289f, 315, 318
-----, barque of, 81, 183
-----, bouquet of, 39
-----, estate of, 45
-----, high-priest of, 50, 293
-----, priesthood of, 32, 56 n. 193, 100, 175
-----, temple of, 3, 29, 33f, 39, 51, 95, 96 n. 98, 99f, 103, 122, 170, 171 n. 45, 173f, 176 and n. 85, 190, 197, 226, 318
Amunrasonther, 52, n. 166, 57
Amunre, 80, 91, 195 n. 222, 211 n. 29
Amunre of *Ṯḥn-nfr*, 44
Amunre-Kamutef, 38, 71, 171
Amunrud, 311, 312 n. 110, 314, 317 n. 126
Amurru, 258, 286
Amyrtaeus, 328
ancestors, 22ff, 26, 29, 32 and n. 109, 33-36, 38ff, 42, 45f, 52, 56 n. 188, 57, 64, 84, 90, 96 n. 99, 101, 123 n. 76, 134, 137-140, 142, 143 n. 65, 145-148, 150ff, 154, 157, 161, 166, 170ff, 176ff, 179, 181, 192-196, 219 n. 61, 235 n. 15, 245, 254, 266, 298, 318f, 321, 328, 333, 335
ancient texts, 146 n. 81, 319
Anedjib, 9 n. 35
Anhur-kha^{c}u, 50
Ankhtify, 141, 155 n. 130
annals, 63 n. 229, 65, 67ff; chapter 2 *passim*, 123f, 134ff, 142, 161 n. 164, 185, 212ff, 215, 224, 300, 333f
-----, of the priests, 100
-----, of Karnak, 103
-----, chamber of, 80
Antef, 25, 33, 128, 145 n. 72, 156 n. 139
Antef (Sehertowi), 28
Antef (Wahankh), 10, 28
Antef-^{c}o, 153 n. 120
Antiochus III, 301
Anubis, 39
Apion, 229 n. 104, 287 n. 96, 288-291, 293
Apis 89, 100, 196, 213, 298 and n. 7, 299, 301, 313, 321, 324
Apophis, 163, 278
Apopy, 152 n. 114
Apris, 331
Arabia, 278 n. 77
Aram, Aramaic, 121 n. 65, 200
Archaic Period, 67, 89, 130
archaizing, 328-331
archivists, 63, 86, 89, 94
Armant, 38
Arsaphes, 63, 271, 307, 313 n. 113
Artaxerxes III, 224 n. 80, 296, 320f, 331
Aruna, 125
Ashdod, 316 n. 124, 322ff
Ashurbanipal, 325
Asia, 114 n. 48, 117, 126, 260, 264, 279f, 323
Asklepios, 215 n. 50, 230
Asosi, 136
Assyria, 200, 210 n. 23, 227, 241, 258, 276, 277 nn. 71 73, 287, 289, 295, 316, 322f
astrology, 218, 227, 327
Aswan, 169 n. 32
atef, 40, 53, 55

Atet, 62 n. 225
Atothis, 26, 210 n. 22, 235 n. 18
Atu, 163 n. 171
Atum, 27, 69, 71-74, 76, 82, 137 n. 42, 232 n. 6, 268
Augustus, 302
Avaris, 199 and n. 244, 201 and n. 253, 246, 262, 282, 292f, 305
Awetibre, 14
Ay, 189 n. 178, 190
Aya, 158 n. 147
Azy, 138 n. 53, 155

B

Ba^{c}al, 198 n. 242
Baba, 275 n. 64
Babylon, 199, 210 n. 23, 215 n. 51
Bah, 79
bakery, 110
Balaam, 251 n. 114
Bauefre, 25 and n. 87, 26
barque, sacred, 77, 112
barque, processional, 32
barque-shrine, 174 and n. 69
Bast, 226, 308 and n. 76
Bata, 232
Bauefre, 237
Bawerded, 139
Bay, 269
Beatifications, 220
Bedjau, 24, 136 n. 36
beduin, 133, 260 n. 14
benediction, 180, 182
Beni Hasan, 155 n. 131, 156 n. 141, 157
Berossos, 213 n. 46
Bersheh, 156 n. 140, 188
Bible, 213
Binepu, 55
Binothris, 213
biographical inscriptions, 59f, 62, 128, 134, 135 n. 33, 136, 148f, 155 n. 131, 156 n. 143, 157f, 180 n. 110, 184, 334
birth narrative, 168 and n. 24, 172 n. 57
"birth of the hero," 288 and n. 100
blue crown, 36, 48f, 51, 53f, 54 n. 180, 55, 57
Bocchoris, 210, 227, 250 and n. 40, 283, 286, 289, 291, 312 n. 107, 321f, 324, 325 n. 175, 326f
"Book of Horus," 64
"Book of the Cow of Heaven," 94
Book of the Dead, 225
"Book of Thoth," 66 n. 11, 92 n. 76
booty, 89, 103, 124
bouquet, 48, 51
branch, 67, 69ff, 74f, 79, 81, 86 n. 49, 90
Bubastis, 226, 306, 308 and n. 76, 315
bull-headed deities, 64
bull's tail, 31
bureaucracy, 138
Buhen, 158 n. 147
Busiris, 295
Buto, 330
Buyuwawa, 307
Byblos, 126 n. 87

C

Cadmus, 218, 290
calendar, 121
Cameroons, 210 n. 22
Cambyses, 277 n. 74, 320, 327
Canaan, 290
canonical order, 146 n. 82
cartouche, 5, 7, 14, 16
cat, 93
cat, solar, 82 n. 37
cenotaph, 192
censor, 46, 51
census, 134
Chaeremon, 287f
chamber of writings, 91
chancery, 106, 142
chancery document, 2
Chebron, 246
chief lector, 21 35f, 38 n. 135
chronicles, xv n. 10, 65, 94f, 213 n. 46, 215
chronography, 65, 67, 207 n. 20, 214
Cicero, 166
"civic religion," xix, 196
Clement, 216 n. 52
Coffin Texts, 93, 154, 335,
Coke, Sir Edward, 102 n. 20
community, sense of, 137
compendia, mythological, 216
Conquest, 320
Coptos, 110 n. 30, 129 n. 6, 160
coronation, 7, 33, 77, 81, 85, 89, 142, 168, 180, 191, 298, 300 and n. 19, 301
court of law, 101
creation, 66 n. 11, 131, 160, 278 and n. 79
crocodile, 211 and n. 27
"(cult)-seat," 131f, 132 n. 17
"cutting the sheaf," 36f
Cyprus, 258

D

Dagy, 149 n. 96
Dahshur, 236
Danaus, 281, 290
dating, double, 121 n. 65
day-book, 63 n. 229, chapter 3 *passim*, 184, 223, 260, 334ff
"Dazzling Sun-disk," 249
deben, 100
Dedia, 60
deeds, 102
Deir el-Bahri, 60, 150f, 151 n. 107, 168, 169 n. 35, 172 and n. 57, 184 n. 152, 190, 226, 246f, 292
Deir el-Medina, 42, 44, 47, 49f, 56
Delta, 117, 130 n. 10, 198f, 241, 262, 264, 267, 269f, 276, 280, 290, 310, 323f, 329f
demigods, 11 n. 42
Demotic, 66 n. 11, 289f, 336
Demotic Chronicle, 296 n. 122
Den, 86, 87 n. 51, 133, 213 n. 44, 235
Dendera, 64, 167, 244
department of the Deep South, 107ff
deputy priest, 49
Diodorus, 127, 224 n. 79, 233, 258, 304
Diospolis, 66 n. 8, 151
Divine spirits, 13
Divine Worshipper, 72, 110 n. 30, 312, 316
divinity of pharaoh, 130f
Djahy, 184, 258, 264
Djedefre, 24, 60 n. 205, 89
Djef, 149 n. 96
Djeme, 4 n. 17, 194 n. 214, 304 n. 56, 329 n. 206
Djer, 86, 211 n. 30
Djeser-nub(?), 27
Djoser, 8, 10, 14 n. 54, 17, 26, 62 n. 225, 90, 92, 132 and n. 32, 135, 162, 186 n. 161, 210 and n. 23, 211, 235f, 333
Djoser-atet, 62 n. 225
Djoser-Tety, 27
double crown, 46, 55 n. 184, 139 n. 55
dream, 288 n. 99
Drovetti, 4
Dur-Sharrukin, 322
dynasties, artificiality of, 241 n. 41
dynasty, divine, 160
dynastic forefather, 44
Dynasty 0, 133

E

East, 133, 198 n. 241, 241, 278 n. 77
Edfu, 62, 71f, 279ff
Edjo, 74, 86, 308f
Eighth Dynasty, 23, 90, 143, 147, 238
Eighteenth Dynasty, 22f, 33 n. 115, 35, 39, 43, 45f, 53, 81, 153 n. 118, 161 n. 164, chapter 5 *passim*, 207, 209, 227, 229, 234, 240, 242f, 245, 257, 297, 335ff
el-Arish, 94f
Elephantine, 2, 25, 56, 92, 105, 107, 139 n. 55, 149 and n. 95, 98, 153 n. 120, 158 n. 147, 160, 261, 265, 284 n. 88
elevation of offering, 37f
Eleventh Dynasty, 10, 12, 17, 19, 20 n. 76, 22, 27, 29, 33ff, 56, 128, 148f, 151, 153 and n. 120, 156, 160, 171, 239, 260, 334
El Kab, 158 n. 147
empire, 166
Ennead, 11 and n. 41, 13, 16, 38, 41, 52, 72, 75, 82, 92, 94f, 137, 172, 195, 231f, 251, 326f, 330, 336
Epitome, 206f, 209, 214, 230, 233f, 237, 239f, 243, 245f, 253, 317
Eratosthenes, 66, 197, 335

Ermant, 305
Esarhaddon, 320, 325 n. 175
Esna, 110 n. 30, 167, 244
Ethiopia, 282, 287
euhemerisation, 82
Euphrates, 126, 165
Eusebius, 11 n. 42, 206, 231ff, 237f, 240, 243, 248, 255, 293, 304, 311, 312 n. 107, 325
Exodus, 290f, 320 n. 140
Expulsion motif, 282

F

falcon, 249
false door, 154
famine, 129 n. 8, 141, 211, 295
Farafra, 83, 267
"father of the fathers," 52, 170, 191, 245, 318
Fayum, 227
Feast of the Valley, 52 and n. 166, 193, 194 n. 214, 196, 250
Fenkhu, 181 n. 125, 200 n. 250
festivals, 89, 173, 180, 222 (calendar of), 262, 318
"Festival" books, 218
(Festival) Instructions, 220
Fifteenth Dynasty, 199, 246
Fifth Dynasty, 5, 12, 24, 33, 88ff, 136, 162f
First Dynasty, 9, 12, 17, 23, 35, 88 n. 59, 92, 127, 130 n. 10 (royal names of), 133ff, 210
foundation ceremony, 182, 186 n. 161
four-fold repetition, 24 n. 85
four-hundred-year stela, 191
Fourteenth Dynasty, 12, 34, 239f, 337
Fourth Dynasty, 17, 25f, 33, 89, 132 n. 17, 134f, 154, 159f, 210 n. 24, 235f, 237, 304 n. 57
funerary meal, 154

G

Gallery of the Lists, 37f
garrisons, 98, 115, 122, 264, 328
gates, 79, 81
Gaza, 125, 323
Geb, 94, 137, 179
genealogies, 56 n. 188, 62f, 141, 151 n. 109, 156 n. 141, 158 n. 147, 196, 203, 318f
genealogy of Memphite priests, 299 n. 15
genres, xvi
Genut, 78
geography, 151 n. 109, 218
Germanicus, 65
Giza, 24, 27, 90 n. 71, 135, 136 n. 36, 141f, 152 n. 114, 159 n. 153, 167, 190, 196, 212, 235f, 237, 331
God's-book, 84, 91 n. 72, 96 n. 99, 166
God's Mound, 177 n. 90
"Gods, Seeing the," 250, 282, 291
graffiti, Theban, 42
Great Black, 78
Great Harris Papyrus, 16 n. 64, 267
"Great Names," 7
Greeks, 214, 225, 285, 290, 336

H

Hadrian, 302
"Hall of Kings," 22
Hammurabi, 200
harim, 107
Harmais, 227, 230, 252, 256ff
Harpare, 73
Harper Song, 145 n. 72
Harpokrates, 55
harpoon, 93
"Harpoon Lake," 133
Harsiese, 302 n. 42
harvest-rite, 36
Hathor, 28, 52 n. 165, 71, 74, 148, 167, 232 n. 6 (7 Hathors), 308
Hatshepsut, 16 n. 64, 19, 22, 35, 45, 60, 70, 75f, 81ff, 166, 168f, 169 n. 35, 171ff, 174 n. 67, 180, 184, 242ff, 246, 248, 255, 262f, 271, 335
Hazi, 149 n. 96
head-smiting, 129 nn. 7-8, 133, 150 n. 102, 260 n. 14
"Hearing," 80
heart pendant, 27
Hebrews, 290, 319
Hecataeus, 65, 205 n. 15, 212, 215 n. 49, 225f, 226 n. 86, 281, 290ff
Hedj-hotpe, 211 n. 29
Hedj-wesh, 150 n. 102
Heka-ib, 149, 153 n. 120
Hekau, 75
Heliopolis, 78, 82 and n. 37, 91, 110, 115ff, 136, 142 n. 62, 149 n. 96, 181, 226, 261, 288, 305
Helios, 285
Hemerology, 151 n. 109, 217
Henen, 149 n. 96
Hephaestus, 234
Herakleopolis, 8 n. 25, 10, 13, 17, 19, 20 n. 76, 28, 63, 128 n. 4, 147 and n. 86, 162, 231, 238, 271, 305, 307, 337
Herakles, 212, 295, 312
Heribre, 16
Herihor, 302 n. 42
Hermopolis, 69f, 71, 79, 159, 188, 285
Herodotus, 56 n. 193, 65, 127, 129, 148 n. 94, 160, 209, 212, 215 n. 49, 226 and n. 87, 234 n. 10, 236, 257, 295, 304
Hesret, 79
Hierakonpolis, 134, 305
hippopotamus, 211f
historicization, 92
historiography, xivff
history, xiiif
Holy Places, 66 n. 11, 261
honey, 213
Hor, 247ff, 250f, 276, 282, 292
Hory, 319, 321, 329
Hordjedef, 25 and n. 87, 145, 146 n. 82, 237, 298
Horemheb, chapter 1 *passim*, 40f, 47f, 55, 59, 61 and n. 217, 99, 102, 189 and n. 178, 190, 193, 248, 252ff, 254 n. 127, 258
Hormose, 48, 246
horned disc, 28
Horus, xix, 11 and n. 42, 19, 35 (sons of), 36 (coronation of), 39, 41 (children of), 48, 69, 72f, 76, 78, 81f, 95, 132f, 136, 138, 142, 143 n. 65, 160, 162, 178, 179, 181, 232, 248f, 270, 275, 279f, 300, 329, 334
Horus-name, 5, 7, 28, 70
Horus-throne, 74f, 77, 79ff
Horus, followers of, 11, 83, 90f, 166, 231
Horus, following of, 88f
Hoshea, 323
Hotep-sekhemwy, 60 n. 205, 88, 235
House of Books, 74, 83, 91, 225 n. 84
House of God's-book, 66 n. 11, 74
House of Life, 81 n. 36, 84f, 91 and n. 72, 92, 225
Huny, 14, 16, 17 n. 68, 162, 230, 236
Hurrian, 200 n. 251
"hydraulic" society, 87
Hyksos, 12f, 17, 22, 52, 163, 167 n. 20, 169, 185f, 193, z97 n. 239, 198, 199, 199 n. 245 (PPN), 200f, 214, 229, 239, 241ff, 245f, 254, 263 n. 26, 265, 280, 288, 292, 294ff, 336f
hymn, 221
hypostyle, 174ff, 176 n. 85, 177, 258f, 265, 298

I

Iby, 238 and n. 28
Idu, 60 n. 205
Imhotpe, 14, 62 n. 225, 92, 145, 156 n. 140, 162, 210 and n. 23, 221 n. 67, 225 n. 34, 230, 286, 331
Imiseba, 51, 304
"Impure Ones," 250 and n. 100, 276-296 (*passim*)
Inaros, 321, 328
Ineny, xv
infinitive, absolute use of, 122f
inundation, 84f, 87, 224, 270
inventory, 94, 221f
Iomitru, 110 n. 30
Ipu, 158 n. 147
Ipuwer, 144 n. 69, 215 n. 51, 265
Irdjanen, 45, 245
Isaiah, 322ff
Isesy, 60 n. 205, 139
Isis, 50, 71f, 75, 82, 110, 205 n. 14, 226, 248, 279, 287, 307 and n. 69, 308 and nn. 76-77, 329
-----, Temple of, 329

Israel(ites), 281
Itj-towy, 12f, 141, 161ff, 167 n. 20, 197 and n. 239, 198f, 201, 231, 239, 253, 297, 305f, 306 n. 65, 335
Ius-aas, 74f
Iy-kaw, 141
Iy-meru, 158 n. 147

J

Jerusalem, 282ff, 289, 291f
Jewry, Hellenistic, 206
Jews, 283
Joseph, 287f, 295
Josephus, 66, 206, 213f, 229f, 240, 243, 246, 249, 253, 255, 288
journals, 63, 96 n. 98, 97, 100, 102
jubilee, 69, 71, 74, 78f, 80, 82, 91, 146 n. 79, 180 n. 109, 181f, 184f
"Jubilant Summons," 18, 193
Judaea, 290

K

Kadesh, 122, 125, 246
Kaechos, 213
Kagemni, 146 n. 82
Kahun, 97 n. 4, 103
Kakai, 8, 139
Kamose, 19, 39, 45, 48, 51, 60
Kamutef, 150
Karnak, 29, 31ff, 33 n. 115, 39, 42, 56f, 65, 70, 72, 100, 123f, 152, 153 n. 118, 170, 172, 174 n. 67, 176, 177 n. 90, 181, 184, 212, 245f, 258f, 265, 310, 335
Kasa, 48
Kashta, 302 n. 42, 315
Kenkenes, 235
Kha^{c}bakhent, 48, 245
Kha^{c}emhat, 179
Kha^{c}em-ope, 84, 224
Kha^{c}kheperreseneb, 144 n. 69
Khababash, 204 n. 8, 331
Khafre, 24ff, 56, 60 n. 205, 62 n. 225, 168, 236f
Khakaure, 106
Khamwese, 77, 196, 298
Khaneferre, 56 n. 191
Khasekhenwy, 130, 136 n. 36
Khatana, 199 n. 244, 308
khato-land, 120
Khatte, 258
Khayan, 201 n. 252
Kheperkare, 44
Kheruef, 188
Khonsu, 48, 61, 73f, 81, 212, 310, 312, 329
Khopry, 68
Khor, 241
Khnum, 69, 71, 286 n. 92
Khnumhotpe, xv, 156 n. 140, 157f
Khnum-Ptah, 79
Khufu, 17, 25f, 60 n. 205, 62 n. 225, 89f, 129, 154 n. 122, 160, 162, 167 n. 15, 210, 235ff
Khutowyre, 8
"kingless" period, 15
kiosk, 70, 180f
Kleomenes, 204 n. 5
Klio, 81 n. 36
Kochome, 211 n. 31
Kom Ombo, 245
Koncharis, 311f
Kos, 262
"Kriegstagebuch," 122f
ku, 35, 52, 64, 137, 140f, 156 (statue), 195 n. 215
Kush, 3, 169 n. 32, 293, 323f
-----, viceroy of, 120

L

labels, wood/ivory, 67, 85, 87f, 88 n. 59
Labu, 269, 313, 321
labyrinth, 212
Lake-land, 78
Lamares, 212
Lamb, legend of the, 207, 210, 227, 286, 287 n. 96, 289, 295
lament, 259 and n. 12, 260
land cadaster, 151, 222 and n. 73
languages, Thoth creator of, 66 n. 11
Lateran obelisk, 170, 183
laudatory invocation, 38
laws, 66 n.11, 102
lawgiver, 322, 327
lector-priest, 7, 18, 24 n. 83, 36, 38, 64, 147 n. 84, 154f, 157
ledger, 142
leopard-skin, 51
Levant, 126, 264
library, 197, 207, 230, 299, 319, 336
-----, temple, 214ff, 295, 321
Libya/Libyans, 83, 129 n. 8, 197, 213, 266f, 269f, 275, 306
Lifebook, 84
Litany, 39, 66 n. 11
Litany of Re, 16
"literary" figures, 26
Livy, 166
log, ship's, 115ff
"Lords of Eternity," 52
Luxor, 33 n. 115, 55, 74, 91, 169 n. 32, 172, 186 n. 161, 190, 251
Lysimachus, 283, 288ff, 291f

M

ma^{c}at, xvii, 41, 80, 132, 178, 285 n.91
macehead, 134 n. 28
Madu, 109
magic, 93, 95, 210 n. 24, 220
Mahu, 27
Makare, 69f, 76
Makhrure, 8
Manetho, 7, 9, 11 n. 41, 12f, 17, 20 n. 76, 23, 25, 29, 33ff, 53, 59, 65f, 90 n. 71, 95 and n. 94, 127, 135, 143, 159 n. 155, 162, 200, chapter 6 *passim*, chapter 7 *passim*, 257, 276, 282, 287f, 291-294, 297, 302-306, 310, 317, 325, 327, 330f, 334, 336f
Mansion of Writing, 81 n. 36
mathematical papyri, 151 n. 109
matrilineal descent, 157f
May, 243
Medamud, 107
Media, 258
medicine, 210, 217
Medjay, 3, 105ff, 108f, 183, 308 n. 73
Medinet Habu, 36f, 52 n. 167, 95, 203, 226, 243, 258, 304 and n. 56
Megiddo, 99, 103, 122f, 125, 229 n. 110, 245f
Meidum, 143
Meir, 141, 158
Memnon, 194 n. 212, 212
Memphis, 3f, 20, 24, 27, 56, 58, 63, 77, 111 n. 34, 113f, 117f, 121, 128 n. 4, 130, 134, 142f, 147f, 152, 163, 167f, 177, 190, 198 n. 239, 204, 211 n. 29, 225 and n. 84, 226, 232, 255, 269f, 272, 297-302, 305f, 313 and n. 114, 316, 320f, 324f, 328ff, 333, 335ff
Memphite Theology, 161 n. 165, 300
Menander, 230 n. 113
Mendes, 328
Menes, 8, 10f, 11 n. 42, 12f, 16, 20, 23, 35, 39, 62 n. 225, 90, 127, 130 n. 10, 148, 162, 172, 195, 211 and n. 29, 212, 231, 233-235, 333, 337
Menkauhor, 56, 60 n. 205
Menkaure, 56, 60 n. 205, 138 n. 53, 210 n. 24, 236f
Menkheperre, 71, 167 n. 12, 174, 302 n. 42
Menkheperreseneb, 174
Menkheprure, 61
Menmare, 18f, 191
Menthesouphis, 235 n. 18
Merbiapa, 23
Merenre, 33, 60 n. 205
Merer, 149 n. 96
Meret-[neith], 213 n. 44
Meret-seger, 44, 49, 52 n. 165
Merikare, 90, 128 n. 4, 141, 145, 147, 152 n. 114
Mermesha, 56 n. 188
Merneferre, 8
Merneptah, 2, 36, 42, 83, 139 n. 55, 197, 242, 250 n. 100, 266f, 269f, 303
Mer-su-iotef, 51
Mertityotes, 59
Meru, 156 n. 140
Merwa, 165
Mes, 253
Meshwesh, 269, 307f
Mesopotamia, 126
Messene, 287
messianic ideal, 160 n. 156
military camps, 89, 94
Min, 34, 35 n. 123, 36f, 44, 52 n. 167, 129 n. 6, 150, 151 n. 106, 171f, 172 n. 56, 191, 193, 194 n. 213, 195 n. 221, 196

Min-Amun, 66 n. 11
Misphragmouthosis, 245, 247
Mitanni, 175
Mnevis, 213
Moeris, 127 n. 2
monarchy, problem of the, 187f
monotheism, 284
Montu, 28, 38, 52 n. 165, 68 n. 24, 108f, 148 n. 90, 179
Montuemhat, 222 n. 69, 262 n. 60, 311 n. 99
Montuhotpe the elder, 28 n. 95
Montuhotpe I, 22, 28, 35, 40, 44, 48, 50, 63, 148 n. 90, 149f, 150 n. 100, 102-104, 153 n. 120
Montuhotpe II, 153 n. 120
mortuary cult, 60, 62, 131
mortuary priesthood, 139
mortuary records, 141
mortuary temple, 129, 152, 179, 194, 330f
Mose, 60
Moses, 281, 283f, 287-291, 293
mother, royal, 168 n. 24, 213
museum, 206
"musical" stela, 148
Mut, 50, 70, 312
Mut-beneret, 258 n. 5
Mutemweya, 248
myth, 92ff, 136

N

Nakht, 22 n. 81, 156 n. 140
Nakhtefmut, 272 n. 60
Nakht-nebtepnefer, 28, 149 and n. 96
Nakht-oker, 156 n. 139
Namlot, 63, 271, 313
Narmer, 86, 130 n. 10, 133
narrative (in art), 133
Nebamun, 183
Nebereraw, 55
Nebethotpet, 74
Nebhepetre, 23, 27, 29, 33, 45-48, 60, 143, 160
Nebipusenwosret, 180 n. 110
Nebka, 23, 236
Nebkaure, 98
Nebmare, 80, 251
Nebsenre, 14
Nebsumenu, 91 n. 72
Nebtowy, 45
Nebtowyre, 15
Nebty-name, 7
Nechepsos, 326f, 327 and n. 187
Necherophes, 212
Necho, 326f
necropolis, 102, 118f, 121, 145, 150, 154, 156, 172, 192, 265f, 319, 330
Nectanebo, 62 n. 225, 215 n. 50, 250, 278 n. 75, 279, 288 n. 99, 296, 331f
Nefer^{c}abet, 42
Neferbauptah, 60 n. 205
Neferhat, 62
Neferhotep, 91, 150 n. 103
Neferirkare, 9, 24, 32 n. 109, 60 n. 205, 90, 134f, 135 n. 33, 136 n. 36, 141 n. 59, 148, 152 n. 114, 334
Neferka, 14
Neferkare, 33, 55, 129 n. 6, 213
Neferkasokar, 210 n. 22
Neferkhau, 51
Neferronpet, 102 n. 19
Nefersekheru, 249
Nefertum, 94, 137
Neferty, 127, 146 and n. 79, 215 n. 51, 286
Neferure, 167
Neferys, 50
Nefru, 149 n. 96
Nefrusy, 110 n. 30
Negeb, 125
Neheb-kau, 173, 278 n. 79
Nehesy, 198 n. 241
Neith, 137 n. 45, 212 n. 34, 226
Nekhbit, 74
Nekhen, 106
-----, Souls of, 93 n. 82
Neo-Babylonians, 276
Nephthys, 80, 81 n. 36
Nespakashuty, 176 n. 86
Netjery-khet, 62 n. 225
Netjery-pu-nysu, 60 n. 205
Neuserre, 56, 60 n. 205, 152 n. 114, 153 n. 118
Nile, 87f, 130, 133, 213, 270, 325
-----, levels, 134
-----, trips on the, 204
Nine Bows, 266
Nineveh, 286
Ninteenth Dynasty, 16, 22, 34, 40, 43, 45, 54, 56, 101, 189, 196f, 231, 235, 237f, 242f, 253ff, 269, 297, 302, 306
Ninth Dynasty, 12, 20, 144
Nitocris, 127, 212, 227
Nitokerty, 238
nomarch, 128, 140f, 149 n. 96, 155 n. 130, 156, 158f
nome, 216
North, invasion from the, 211, 277-295
Nubia/Nubians, 105f, 114 n. 48, 129 n. 7, 169, 198 n. 241, 260, 280, 285, 296, 305
Nun, xvii, 83
nursery, 107f
Nut, 92
Ny-neter, 60 n. 205, 88f

O

oases, 3, 83, 267
oath, 165
obelisks, 174, 183-185, 191
Ochus, 213 n. 42
offering cult, 139, 141ff, 147, 150, 153, 161, 171, 177, 179, 191, 194, 333, 335
----- list tradition, 20, 22, 24 n. 83, 55, 57, 128, 137 n. 45, 142f, 148, 152, 162, 177, 192, 196, 242, 307
----- manual, 222
----- table, 43-46, 49, 51, 144, 263
^{c}Okheperkare, 113, 173, 175
Olympiad, 311, 312 n. 107
omissions (in king-list), 20
oneiromancy, 217
onomastica, 218
^{c}Opehty, 44
Opet festival, 189 n. 177
oracles, 223 n. 75, 289
Oracle of the Potter, 282, 284f, 291
oral tradition, 66, 122, 129, 140f, 144 n. 69, 146 n. 82, 159, 173, 199, 201, 210 n. 22, 226ff, 236f, 245, 253, 257f, 270, 283, 290, 295
Orus, 11 n. 42
Osarsiph, 207, 227, 230, 249f, 257, 276, 287f, 292ff, 296f, 302
Osiris, xix, 19, 21f, 22 n. 81, 39ff, 50, 52 n. 165, 61, 66 n. 11, 72, 75, 79, 82 and n. 37, 95 and n. 94, 130 n. 10, 138, 142 and n. 62, 143, 161 and n. 165, 187 n. 167, 189 n. 176, 211 n. 30, 244 n. 58, 270, 279, 329
-----, book of hours of, 64
-----, emblem of, 55 n. 184
-----, house of, 118
-----, myth of 94, 131 n. 14
-----, Neb-onkh, 57
-----, Souls of, 93
-----, Heka-Djet, 310ff, 314 n. 116, 329 and n. 206
Osiride figures, 55 n. 184, 175 n. 83, 176
Osorkon I, 271, 309 and n. 83
Osorkon II, 63, 272 n. 60, 309 and n. 84
Osorkon III, 212 n. 39, 310, 312ff, 316
Osorkon IV, 315 n. 123, 317 and n. 126, 324 n. 170
Osorkon, high-priest of Amun, xv, 219 n. 61, 272f, 319, 321
Osorthon, 212, 310, 313 n. 112
ostracon, 40
Othoes, 210 n. 25
ox-offering, 271

P

Pahemneter, 49, 54
Pahu, 51
Pakhet, 95
Palermo stone, 32 n. 109, 85, 87ff, 90, 135f, 163, 213
Palestine, 126, 281, 291, 319
palette, 24, 133f, 134 n. 28, 187 n. 167
Pamuha, 110 n. 30
Paneb, 44f, 52f
papyrus, 18f
participle, 122
parvenus, 196
Paser, 21 n. 78
Paynehsi, 120
pavillions, 71, 76, 80, 82, 91

Petjauabast, 313
Pelusium, 258, 287
Pemou, 309
pen, 71, 81
Penhuy, 47
Pepy I, 25, 33, 60 n. 205, 68, 129, 136, 138 n. 53, 147 n. 87, 152 n. 114
Pepy II, xvii, 16, 19, 23, 25, 33, 60 n. 205, 68, 142, 144, 147 n. 87, 152 n. 114, 159
Pepy-hotpe, 98
Per-Heby, 226
Persen, 140
Persians, 120, 224 (invasions), 276, 281, 300, 327f
personified estates, 60 n. 205
Peru-nefer, 111f
Petosiris, 204 n. 9
Petronius, 222 n. 68
Petubastis, 227
Petubastis I, 310f, 313 n. 113, 315f, 319, 328f
Pheson, 250 n. 100
Philae, 71f
Philip Arrhidaeus, 245
Phoenicia, 200, 241, 258, 311, 319f
Phritiphantes, 287
Piankhy, 302 n. 42, 313ff, 320, 325
Pi-Ramesses, 115f, 196, 199 n. 244, 255, 297, 303 n. 45, 305f, 308
Place of Truth, 42ff, 47f, 50, 53, 61
plague, 83, 281, 283f, 285, 289ff, 293, 295f
plant-collection, 181 n. 120
Plato, 66 n. 11
Plutarch, 95 n. 94
Polemic, Judaeo-pagan, 206, 228, 229 n. 104, 288
Polemo, 283f
Polybus, 303
Polydamna, 303 n. 44
polymath, 166, 335
Poseidonius, 283, 289
prenomen, 7
primordial kings, 94
progresses, 87, 114
prophecy, 145, 227, 334
propoganda, 146
"Protection-book," 167
Psammetichus I, 85, 284 n. 88, 295, 304, 325
Psammetichus II, 280
Psammetichus III, 299 n. 12
Psammous, 310, 311f
Psenhor, 62, 306
Pseudo-Callisthenes, 300
Pseudo-Eratosthenes, 151 n. 107, 177
Pseudo-Manetho, 207, 228, 229 n. 104, 246
Pseudo-Prophecies, 215
Ptah, 9, 11, 26, 52 n. 165, 74, 76ff, 80ff, 139 n. 55, 140, 143, 161 n. 165, 168, 177 n. 90, 190, 196, 205, 226, 230ff, 300, 333
-----, priests of, 225, 298ff
-----, teachings of, 179, 212, 215 n. 49
Ptah-Sokar-Osiris, 19, 142 n. 61
Ptahshepses, 59
Ptolemies, Egyptian influence on, 205 n. 14
Ptolemy I, 204 and n. 5, 205, 224 n. 79, 301
Ptolemy II, 204 and n. 10, 336
Ptolemy III, 72f
Ptolemy IV, 205, 301
Ptolemy V, 204 n. 10, 301
Ptolemy VII, 76
Ptolemy VIII, 301
Ptolemy of Mendes, 65
Pwenet, 139
pyramid age, 131
pyramid temples, 59, 132 n. 17, 136, 141, 143
pyramid texts, 94, 132, 136, 142, 152, 161 n. 165, 167, 187 n. 167, 225
pyramids, 144, 148, 236, 297f, 306
purification, manual of, 222

Q

Qa-a, 87, 235
Qar, 141
Qarbana, 269
Qebehu, 142 and n. 62
Queen, titles of, 248 n. 85, 329
Qenhirkhopshef, 43, 53 n. 169
quai graffiti, 310
quarries, 282, 291ff
Qurneh, 57, 191 n. 192, 266 n. 37
Qus, 110 n. 30

R

Ra^{c}et, 62 n. 165
race, ceremonial, 180
Rahotpe, 160
Ramesses I, 47f, 50, 57, 191, 193, 254, 303
Ramesses II, 2, 28, 20f, 32 n. 109, 34, 36f, 39f, 42ff, 47f, 55 n. 184, 57f, 61, 63 n. 232, 70, 76f, 83, 91, 127, 139 n. 55, 143 n. 65, 180, 191ff, 194 n. 212, 196ff, 203, 250, 254f, 258, 265, 267, 294, 297f 302, 335f
Ramesses III, xv, xx, 36f, 51, 58, 203, 227 n. 91, 268ff, 304
Ramesses IV, 50f, 56, 58, 78, 84f, 91f, 192 n. 203, 197, 270
Ramesses V, 58, 99
Ramesses VI, 51, 58
Ramesses VIII, 58
Ramesses IX, 51f, 58
Ramesses XI, 120, 318
Ramesseum, 34ff, 37, 39, 226, 246, 254
Ramose, 47, 56, 61, 77
Rampses, 282
Ra-neb, 60 n. 205
ranking system, 136
Ranofer, 315, 317 n. 127
Raphia, 296
Rapsaces, 303
Rawer, 135 n. 33
Re, 26, 70f, 73ff, 77ff, 82, 93f, 136, 138, 159, 198, 226, 262, 278ff
-----, Eye of, 91
-----, house of, 192
-----, Souls of, 92, 216 n. 52, 225
"readings," folkloristic, 211, 213, 243, 255
rebellion, Theban, 272f
red chapel, 168, 263
red crown, 19, 22, 33 n. 115, 54, 55 n. 184, 64, 74, 141 n. 59, 178, 194 n. 213
Redjedef, 25, 62 n. 225, 236, 237 n. 24
regnal years, 85, 103, 113 n. 46, 324 n. 167
Re-harakhty, 22, 27, 52 n. 165, 75f, 275 n. 64, 307
Re-harmakhis, 50
reign, 139 n. 55
Rekhmire, 166, 167 n. 12
Renenut, 72
Rensonb, 8
residence, 13, 305f, 308f
Retenu, 184f, 264
revolution, 132
Rom-Roy, 50
romances, 227
rubrics, 10ff
"Ruler of Rulers," 194 n. 212

S

Sabaco, 316 n. 124, 322-325
Sabu, 59 n. 204
Sacred Book, 210
Saft el-Henne, 278
Sahure, 24, 60 n. 205, 139f, 152 n. 114
Sais, 205 n. 16, 226, 289, 315, 321, 323, 325f, 329
Salitis, 201, 229
Samaria, 323
Sanchuniaton, 320
Sapair, 46, 48ff
Saqqara, 21, 26f, 134, 141, 152 n. 114, 190, 196, 228 n. 102, 235, 237, 297, 321
Sargon, 322
Sat-Amun, 49
Sat-Kamose, 49
school, scribal, 152, 159
scribe of offerings, 49
sculpting, 87
sd-costume, 46, 180
sd-chapels, 270 n. 49
sd-festival, 68-81, 85, 171f, 179-182, 184-187, 189, 191, 298
sd-liturgy, 151 n. 109
Se^{c}ankhibtowi, 149 n. 96
Seankhkare, 15, 29, 160
Sea Peoples, 258, 319
Sebennytos, 204, 328
Second Cataract, 149 n. 95

Second Dynasty, 17, 88f, 130 n. 10, 135, 210, 213
"Seeing," 80
Sefkhet-ᶜabwy, 74, 77, 81
Sehebre, 8
Sehtepibre, 7 n. 24, 8, 12f, 29, 161f, 231, 239
seige, 319f
Sekhemkare, 60 n. 205
Sekhemkare Amenemhet Sonbef, 14
Sekhentenre, 48
Semempses, 23, 86, 235 n. 17
Semna, 105ff, 171 n. 53
Senakhtenre, 43, 55, 242
Senenmut, 167
Sen-nefer, 46, 60
Sentsonbu, 45
Senwosret I, 33f, 39, 44, 56 n. 191, 68, 82 n. 37, 148 n. 94, 149 and n. 95, 151f, 153 n. 120, 160, 170, 180f, 239, 260
Senwosret II, 56 n. 191, 239
Senwosret III, 32 n. 109, 68f, 149 and n. 95, 153 and n. 120, 171 n. 53
Senwosret, god's-father, 29, 160
Senwosret-sonbu, 158 n. 147
Sepa, 293 n. 113
Seqenenre, 43, 45, 48, 50f, 177, 254
Serapis, 205, 301
Serapeum, 205 n. 13, 211 n. 31, 299, 306
serekh, 78, 86, 88 n. 59, 179 n. 105, 249
Seshat, 70f, 74f, 78-81, 95, 142, 167
Sesochris, 213
Sesonchosis, 239
Sesoösis, 258
Sesostris, 148 n. 94, 212, 225, 227, 257
Seuserenre, 14
Seth, 95, 110, 112, 142, 186 n. 159, 198 and nn. 240 242, 279f
Seth-mose, 198 n. 241
Sethnakht, 36, 51, 268f, 304
Seth-re, 198 n. 241
Setna, 227
Sety I, 18f, 21f, 36, 37 n. 131, 42, 46, 48, 55, 57, 60f, 72, 75, 77, 113f, 120, 142, 143 n. 65, 189 n. 178, 191-194, 254f, 257f, 265, 303
Sety II, 2, 36, 42, 44, 50f, 57, 243, 269, 303
Seventeenth Dynasty, 20, 33, 39, 43, 197, 246
Seventh Dynasty, 238
Shabaka, 225
Shamshi-adad, 201 n. 252
Sharuhen, 264
Shayet, 72
Shebitku, 325 n. 175
Shechem, 126 n. 87
Shemsu, 8
Shepenwepet, 312, 314ff
Shepseskaf, 60 n. 205, 89, 138 n. 53, 237
Shepsesptah, 138 n. 53, 140
Sherden, 267
Sheshonk I, 63, 271, 306f, 309 and n. 82
Sheshonk III, 139 n. 55, 309 and n. 85
Sheshonk IV, 63, 309, 317 n. 126
ship-building, 89
shipyard, 111, 121
Shu, 76, 94, 278, 309
Si-Amun, 50
sidelock, 64, 93
Si-ese, 60
Sile, 125, 258, 264, 280
Silsileh, 159 n. 150
Sinai, 18 n. 72, 129 n. 7, 152, 198 n. 241
Siptah, 37, 57, 139 n. 55, 269
Sirenpowet, 151 n. 109
Sisine, 127
Si-Sobek, 215 n. 51
Sixteenth Dynasty, 13 n. 51, 172 n. 56, 197f
Sixth Dynasty, 10, 12, 23, 33f, 67, 90, 127, 142, 162, 238
sm-priest, 116
Smendes, 306 n. 64
Smenkhkare, 252
Smentowi, 49
Sneferu, 17 n. 68, 18 n. 72, 49, 89, 135f, 146 n. 79, 152, 160, 162, 235f
Sobekemsaf, 62
Sobekhotpe, 7, 25
Sobekhotpe III, 107, 153 n. 120
Sobeknakht, 158 n. 147
Sobeknefrure, 19, 23, 34
Sokar, 22, 24, 142, 147 and n. 86, 177 and n. 90, 181, 186 n. 159, 193, 194 n. 214, 333
solar high-priest, 314
Soleb, 186 nn. 159 161
Sopdu, 198 n. 241, 279
Sothis-book, 311f
Souls (of Pe, Nekhen etc.), 11 n. 42, 186 n. 159
Souris, 238
speech, royal, 148f
Speos Artemidos, xv, 16, 76, 95f, 262
sphinx, 168
sport, 187
statues, 29, 31f, 34, 36, 53, 56-58, 63, 89, 112, 141 and n. 59, 152f, 175f, 180, 194 and n. 213, 195, 226, 298, 335
stelae, 66f, 128f, 136f, 159 n. 150, 227, 299, 318
Stephinates, 326
Step-pyramid, 88, 235
stolist-priest, 35f
Strabo, 284, 288
Sudan, 124, 277
Suetonius, 166
sun-disc, 58, 73, 79, 188 and n. 173
sun-god, 34 n. 119, 35, 169, 183, 250
sun-temple, 136, 235
Suphis, 210, 235 n. 18
Syncellus, 11 n. 41, 65f, 231-234
symbols, royal, 130 n. 10
Syria/Syrians, 98, 103, 122, 126, 129 n. 8, 165, 268, 275, 285, 319

T

tablets, 66, 69, 71, 86, 214
Tacitus, 65, 166, 289f
Taharqa, 74, 84, 325
Takayet, 110 n. 30
Takelot II, 100, 272, 309
Takelot III, 76, 212 n. 39, 312, 314 and nn. 120 126
talatat, 249
Tangur, 169 n. 32
Tanis, 56, 272, 297, 306, 309, 317, 328, 330
Tanodjmehemsi, 102 n. 19
Tanwetaman, 302 n. 42
Tatenen, 74, 82, 142, 249 n. 89
Tatian, 65
Tawosret, 37
tax list, 2
taxation, 87, 120
Tchebu, 149 n. 96
Techetchy, 149 n. 96
Tefnakhte, 315, 321 and n. 149, 323, 326, 327 and n. 186, 337
Tefnut, 80, 94
Tenth Dynasty, 12, 20, 144, 147 n. 87
Tety, 24, 27, 33, 136, 138 n. 53, 152 n. 114, 162, 231, 238
Teye, 51
thalassocracy, 311
Thamphthis, 237
Thebes, 13, 31, 33, 38, 55f, 91, 109, 117, 120, 148, 149 n. 96, 152f, 162f, 169f, 177, 183, 186 n. 159, 190, 193, 197, 199, 231, 235, 239, 261, 304ff, 313ff, 318, 335
Theban necropolis, 4, 35 n. 126, 40, 46
theocracy, 130f, 134
Theophilus, 243
Theophrastus, 65
Thinis, 110 n. 30, 140, 232
Third Dynasty, 5, 17, 27, 33 n. 115, 62 n. 225, 89, 130, 134f, 207, 212, 230, 236, 331
Thirteenth Dynasty, 7, 9, 12, 20, 25, 34, 144 n. 69, 150, 158 n. 147, 161 and n. 166, 162, 167 n. 20, 177, 180, 239f, 306
Thirtieth Dynasty, 153 n. 118, 204 n. 9, 209, 224, 242, 279, 328
Thoth, 16, 41, 66 and n. 11, 69-72, 74-81, 85, 92, 96 n. 99, 166, 167 n. 12, 173, 188 and n. 170, 211 n. 29, 224 n. 80, 262
Thuoris, 302
Thuthotpe, 159
Thutmose I, 48, 50f, 54, 60ff, 83, 165, 167, 169f, 172 n. 57, 176 and n. 85, 184 n 149, 186, 246f

Thutmose II, 48, 54, 60, 181, 246
Thutmose III, xx, 29, 31ff, 40f, 44, 48, 50ff, 54, 60f, 71, 77, 96, 98, 103, 110, 122-127, 152, 165-170, 172f, 174 n. 67, 175f, 177 n. 88, 179, 181, 183ff, 186 and n. 159, 187, 190, 197, 227 n. 91, 244 and n. 58, 246f, 264, 294, 335
Thutmose IV, 41f, 47f, 54f, 60f, 168, 170, 181-184, 190
Thutmose, 120
Tiaa, 183f
titulary, 66 n. 11, 81, 135 n. 33
Tiy, 50, 61, 187 n. 167
Tjaneny, 123
Tjaru, 110
Tjauty, 10 n. 205
Tjed-^{c}o, 116
Tjuloy, 21f, 23, 24 n. 83, 27
Tjuna, 62
Tod, 27, 149 n. 95, 260
Tombos, 169 n. 32
toponyms, 125f
treasury, 48, 50, 96 n. 98, 98, 101, 103, 109, 122, 197 n. 288, 263, 300
treaty, 165, 187, 322
Trimalchio, 122 n. 66, 148
Troy, 303
Tunip, 165
Tura, 178, 262
Turin Canon, xx, chapter 1 *passim*, 23, 25, 28, 35 n. 126, 127, 134f, 147, 160f, 197f, 200, 203, 230-234, 236ff, 242, 253f, 336
Tutankhamun, 189f, 252
Tutimaios, 240
Twelfth Dynasty, 7, 8 n. 25, 9, 12, 16f, 23, 25, 28f, 33f, 69, 136, 144 n. 69, 148, 150f, 153, 156, 158ff, 161 and n. 167, 162, 168, 170f, 173 n. 63, 177, 180, 185, 237, 239, 253, 260, 306, 334ff
Twentieth Dynasty, 3, 22, 37, 52, 54, 62 n. 226, 192 n. 203, 303f
Twenty-fifth Dynasty, 135 n. 35, 225, 300 and n. 19, 306, 313f, 316, 323 n. 165, 324f, 328
Twenty-first Dynasty, 63 n. 232, 272, 303f, 317, 329
Twenty-fourth Dynasty, 326
Twenty-ninth Dynasty, 310, 328
Twenty-second Dynasty, 53 n. 175, 62 and n. 227, 63, 304, 306, 309f, 313, 314 and n. 115, 315, 316 n. 126
Twenty-sixth Dynasty, 207, 224, 277, 291, 299, 310, 314, 326ff, 330
Twenty-third Dynasty, 212, 306, 310-315, 316 n. 125, 317, 329
Typhon, 285

U

Uau, 156 n. 140
Uba-oner, 211 n. 27
Ugarit, 200
Unas, 21 n. 78, 25, 136, 138 n. 53, 139, 152 n. 114, 155, 211, 234, 337
universalism, 165
uraeus, 58, 232 n. 6
Usaphais, 235
Userkare, 23
Usermare Setepenre, 22, 38, 43
Userhat, 48, 61, 85, 96
Userkaf, 8 n. 28, 27, 60 n. 205, 159, 162, 235
usurper, 195

V

Valley, Feast of the, 172

W

Wadj-kheperre, 43
Wadji, 211
Wady Hammamat, 25f, 150 n. 105, 160, 237, 293
Wady Tumilat, 278
Wah-ankh, 128 n. 5, 148f, 149 n. 96
"war-diary," 123
Wash-ptah, 135 n. 33
Wen-Anum, 306 n. 64
Wenephes, 211, 235 n. 17
Wenes, 211, 231
Wennofer, 61, 211
Wepwawet, 329
Wepwawet-^{c}o, 194 n. 213
Westcar, 127
white bull, 36
white chapel, 152, 171, 180
white crown, 19, 22, 33 n. 115, 46, 54, 55 n. 184, 64, 74, 133, 141 n. 59, 150, 194 n. 213
White Fort (Walls), 64, 162, 321
wills, 102
Wisdom, 90, 146, 154, 217, 227, 334
wish-formula, 181
work-house, 110 n. 30

X

xenophobia, 295
Xois, 240, 269, 305, 337

Y

Yahweh, 322f
Yamani, 322
Yamu-nedjeh, 184 n. 152
Yat-nebes, 278
Yewepet, 302 n. 42
Yuf, 62
Yurza, 264

Z

Zakar-baal, 163
Zet, 311, 312 n. 107
Zeus, 11 n. 42, 234

Egyptian

ꜣms, 135 n. 33
ꜣḫw, 166, 232 and n. 5, 233
iꜣwt, 59, 155 n. 131
iꜣbtt, 251 n. 42
’I-wr, 2
iwn-mwt.f, 21, 51, 75, 82
ibs, 53 and n. 171, 54
ipt, 222
’Ipt-swwt, 33, 44, 153 and n. 118, 195
’Imy-whm.f, 93 and n. 84
imyw-ḥꜣt, xviii, 138
imy-r h(?), 100
imy-r gnwty, 67
imyt-pr, 66 n. 11, 142
inw, 107, 124 and n. 79
inpw, 183
int Nb-ḥpt-rꜥ, 35 n. 126
iri m hps.f, 148 n. 94
iry-ꜥt, 108
iry-pꜥt, 61, 229
iri-ḫt, 132 n. 17
ir.n.f m mnw.f, 89f, 157
ir.n.f m nsyt, 8ff, 10, 11 n. 42
irt snṯr, 51
’Ihrꜥ, 2
iswr, 276
iswt, 151 n. 109
’Isdn, 142
išd, 66 n. 11, 70, 74, 76ff, 82 and n. 37, 84, 91, 93, 180
it.i Imn, 58
itnw, 85 n. 42
ꜥ, 129, 142 and n. 62
ꜥ-mḥty, 114 n. 48
ꜥ-rsy, 114 n. 48
ꜥwty, 102 n. 19, 110 n. 29, 113 n. 47
ꜥbꜣ, 157
ꜥnw, 67, 128 n. 3
ꜥnḫ wḏꜣ snb, 16
ꜥrt nt hrw, 97
ꜥḥꜥ, 67, 128 n. 3, 142
ꜥḫm, 195
ꜥtḫ.ti, 141 n. 57
ꜥḏw-mr, 159
wꜣḥ-ḫt, 21 n. 80
wꜣs, 25, 28
wpwt, 140
wpt-r, 89, 219 n. 60
wrmt, 175 n. 76
Wrt-ḥkꜣw, 70
wsf, 14ff, 238, 311
Wsr-ḫprw, 44
wsḫt, 100
wdn, 47ff, 51
wḏ, 67, 96 n. 98, 102 n. 20, 128 n. 3
wḏyt, 103 n. 21
bꜣ, 38 n. 135, 87 n. 57, 216 n. 52
bꜣw Rꜥ, 92 n. 78
bꜣkw, 3
biꜣi, 222 n. 75
bity, 213
bḫnt, 174 n. 67
pnḳ, 175 n. 77
pr-ꜥnḫ, 66 n. 11, 91 n. 72
pr-mḏꜣt, 143
Pr-hbyt, 307
Pr-ḥtḥr, 308
prt Spdt, 171 n. 50
pgꜣ, 166
pt, 25, 28
fꜣt-ḫt, 37 n. 130
fḫ, 270
fkꜣw, 108
mꜥꜣt, 73
mꜣrw, 251 and n. 108
min, 138
mit, 106
mnwy, 178
mnw, 32, 128 n. 4
mnyw, 104
Mn-ḫpr-rꜥ ꜣḫ-mnw, 29
Mn-st, 53 n. 173
Mn-kꜣw-rꜥ, 26
mhwt, 4 n. 17
mḫꜣwt, 159 n. 150
ms 87 n. 55
mks, 142
mtr, 4 n. 17
mṯꜣ, 175 n. 80
mdw-nṯr, 66 n. 11, 166, 270
mḏꜣt, 139, 219 n. 61, 220 n. 62
nis ḥknw, 23, 37 n. 131, 38 n. 135, 39, 193 and n. 204
nꜥt, 103 n. 21
nbw nḥḥ, 4 n. 17
Nb-pḥtt-rꜥ, 54 n. 183
Nb-mꜣꜥt-rꜥ, 58
Nb-tꜣwy-rꜥ, 150
nb.ty, 86, 235
nms, 28, 31, 35f, 40, 49, 51, 54, 55 n. 184, 57, 141 n. 59, 194 n. 213
nhwt, 67 n. 16, 259 n. 12
nht, 167
nḫb, 80
nsyw / nsw, 4 n. 17, 22, 25
nsyt, 11 n. 42
nsyw-bityw, 4 n. 17, 7, 21, 33, 86
nšn, 241, 272 n. 60
nt-ꜥ, 219 n. 61
nṯrw, 232
nṯr nfr nb tꜣwy, 33
nḏsw, 148, 158, 334
Rꜣ-wy, 178
rnw, 4 n. 17
rnpt-sign, 86, 88f
rnpt.sn m ꜥnḫ, 8 n. 26
rswt, 216 n. 56
rk, 138
rdit-iꜣw 41, 49
hꜣw, 100, 139 n. 55, 264f
hꜣyt, 113
hpw, 102 and n. 20
hrw, 97
hrwyt, 97, 99, 102 and n. 20, 103, 110, 112, 120ff
----- nt pr-nsw, 122 n. 66, 124 n. 78
ḥꜣ, 89
ḥꜣꜥyt, 271ff
Ḥꜣrw, 200 n. 250
ḥꜣst, 252
ḥꜣty, 53 n. 172
ḥꜣtyw-ꜥ, 159
ḥꜣt-ꜥ m sbꜣyt, 4 n. 17
ḥwt-Nit, 87 n. 56
ḥwt-nbw, 82 n. 37
ḥwt-nṯr, 181
ḥbt, 218 n. 60
ḥmst-nsw, 149 n. 95
ḥry-tp, 287 n. 98
ḥst, 128 n. 3
Ḥkꜣ-mꜣꜥt-rꜥ, 58
ḥkꜣw-ḫꜣswt, 199, 231, 240, 245
ḥknw, 18
ḥtp-di-nsw, 19, 21, 29, 43f, 48, 51, 150 n. 103
ḥtr, 3, 197 n. 238
ḫꜥ-nsw-bity, 87 n. 52, 88f
ḫwdt, 151 n. 109
ḫprt, xiii, 93, 158, 166 n. 11
ḫpsw, 166
ḫft, 271
ḫft-ḥr, 176 n. 85
ḫti, 81
ḫt-nṯr, 222 and n. 74
ḫnw, 162, 305
ḫnmt, 3 n. 13
ḫnty, 54, 55 n. 184
ḫry-ḥb, 154, 287 n. 98
ḫsi, 242 and n. 54
Sꜣ-’Ist, 329
Sꜣw, 327
sipty wr, 221 n. 66
sꜥḥw, 195, 143 n. 65
sbꜣyt, 216 n. 54
sp tpy, xix, 167
spḫr, 81
spr, 117
sm, 22 n. 81
smn, 80, 123, 178
smnḫ, 80
smdt, 119
snwt, 93
snty-(tꜣ), 218 n. 59
sr, 146 n. 79
sr (lamb), 327 and n. 187
sḥwy 4 n. 17
sḫꜣ, 110 n. 29
sš, 81 n. 33, 99 n. 7, 106, 123, 155
sšmw, 192
sšn, 155 n. 130
st-ir, 132 and n. 17
stp-sꜣ, 271
sdꜣwty-bity, 140
sḏfꜣ-tryt, 100 n. 11
sḏm.ḫr.f, 83 n. 40
sḏd, 257 and n. 1
šꜣyt, 3
šꜥt, 106
šw, 265 and n. 33
šmmwt, 111
šms-Ḥr, 87 n. 53, 88 n. 61, 161 n.

164, 232f
šmt, 176 n. 85, 177
šny n bityw, 263 n. 26
šndyt, 18, 28, 31, 36
šsp, 110 n. 29, 120, 195
šdi, 156 n. 142
šdyt, 111f
ḳnbt, 101, 102 n. 19
kꜣi, 146 n. 79
(Kꜣ)-Kmt, 211 n. 31
Kmyt, 152 n. 112
kry, 34 n. 119
gm wš, 225 n. 84
Gm-pꜣ-itn, 190 and n. 184
gn, 67
gnw, 67
gnwt, 66 n. 11, 67, 69, chapter 2
passim, 123, 129, 134ff, 142, 162f, 197, 215 n. 30, 224, 335f
gnwty, 67
gnn, 67
tꜣ, 25
twt, 54f, 55 n. 184, 176 n. 86, 195
tp-rd, 102 n. 20
tpy, 52 n. 166
tpyw-ꜥ, xviii, 138
tmt, 219 n. 61
Tẖht, 167 n. 12
tkꜣ, 38
ṯnwt, 88f
ṯst, 117
dwꜣw, 221 n. 65
dmḏ, 11 n. 42, 14
drf n Ḏḥwty, 66 n. 11
ḏꜥ, 241
ḏfꜣ, 15f
ḏrtyw, xviii, 138
Ḏdi-swwt, 13, 148, 162
Ḏd.f-rꜥ, 26

Demotic

Iḫwr, 276
ir sḫr, 234 n. 14
md, 101
mḏꜣt n ḏmꜥ, 84
rḫw, 217 n. 54
sꜣw n snsn, 85
sẖ, 101
knyt n sẖ, 85

Greek

ἀβασιλευτα ἐτη, 15 n. 60
Ακενχερης, 252
ἀναγράφαι, 65
'Αιγυπτιακοῖς υπομνήμασι και ὀνόμασι, 65-66
'ασημοι, 242
δελτων ιερων, 66
δυναστευω / δυναστεια, 234 n. 14
ἐφημέριδες, 120n. 63
ἐπισμα, 167 n. 12
ζμτειται, 311
ἡμιθεοι, 231ff, 234
θεοι, 231ff, 234
ἱερα βυβλα, 220 n. 62
ἱερων γραμματων, 66 n. 9
κεραμευς, 268 n. 92
νεκυες, 231ff
Νεχεψω, 286 n. 94
ꜥΡαθωτις, 252
Φοινικη, 200 n. 250, 241
Ψεμουθις, 311
ꜥΩρ, 248

Akkadian

Ḫurriya, 248
rikiltu, 219 n. 61
Šilḫanni, 316 n. 124